GHOST RIDERS
THE MINERS' LAST GENERATION

Ghost Dancers
The Miners' Last Generation

Part 3 of
Stardust and Coaldust

A Coalminer's Mahabharata

by
David John Douglass

Ghost Dancers
The Miners' Last Generation
(Part 3 of Stardust and Coaldust)
First published in Great Britain in 2010
by Read 'n' Noir
an imprint of ChristieBooks
PO Box 35, Hastings, East Sussex, TN34 1ZS

Distributed in the UK by Central Books Ltd
99 Wallis Road, London E9 5LN
orders@centralbooks.com

ISBN-10 1-873976-40-2
ISBN-13 978-1-873976-40-1

British Library Cataloguing in Publication Data.
A catalogue record for this book is available from the British Library

Ghost Dancers

PITRACIDE

Who am I to ask them why?
This pit may live that pit must die?
They say but Sir its economics.
That's juggling by financial comics.
What maxim has the NCB?
The miner's lot or LSD
And further Sir it can be said
A pit must die if in the red
Be this so I must resent
This anti-social precedent
So until the happy day
When every pit can pay its way
You cannot Sir rebuke the tide
Or get away with Pitracide!

— JOCK PURDON

Pitracide was the decimation of the coal industry, a culture, a people, in continuation of class warfare waged by the rich and powerful against the working population. It was committed to wipe out the forces of resistance located among the coal communities.

Nothing more or less than ethnic cleansing is evidenced in the abandoned and forgotten coalfield communities the length and breadth of Britain. It is something like the fate of the Native Americans, or the Palestinians – without of course the mass murder, but with the same social and political design.

Killed with the mines are the miners as an ancient, specific, fixed, skill-and vocation-based populace dwelling in highly concentrated geographical locations, ethnicities and nationalities. The miners' roots under the land run as deep as those of the hill farmers or shepherds who worked above it, or the fisherfolk who sailed the coasts. Many mining families in mining regions stretched back to pre-Norman times, and the language of those regions was the ancient dialect of Angle and Saxon, often shot through with Norse, or the Britannic tongue which had predated the arrival of the English. These were the last surviving direct ancestors of the island's ancient inhabitants, who took their ancient twang below ground where it continued for hundreds of years as in some philological lost world.

Pitracide was waged against the miners, who were in many ways almost an ethnic minority, not simply the practitioners of a trade or a skill — an ancient tradition, a way of life, of speech, of outlook, of community and solidarity. We have witnessed the massacre of a people's whole way of life.

This book has been written as part of the continuing last stand of that people who – as at the annual festival of a far-flung ancient tribe – dance on, defiant in the face of their exterminators, refusing to disappear or conform to the social design of our masters.

Acknowledgements and Dedication

Thanks are due to many. First, Stuart Christie for keeping faith with this book and investing his time and energy in the previous two. Mark Hendy, my editor, who has tried to prompt me to get the more obscure of my illiterate sentences and wild visions into some form of readable English. Phil Wharton, my fellow Tyneside 'Wob', who has proofread the book, together with an 'all hands to the pumps' IWW team of Louise van der Hoevan, Alan Telford, Lewis and Peter Mates, John Charlton, a founder member of the SWP and veteran of the Tyneside IS – all of whom I pulled together at the last moment as the deadlines came and went. Comrades who have read through various chapters checking dates and events. Chris Skidmore, the president of the Yorkshire miners. Davie Hopper and Davie Guy, the president and general secretary of the Durham Miners. Keith Stanley, national vice chair of the NUM and chair of the Nottingham Area for adding insights on Nottingham. Ian Lavery, the National president of the NUM, for his checking, debating and agreeing to differ on one or two of the more vexed interpretations of Union history. For all that, any mistakes in chronology or sense or spelling remain my own.

The book is dedicated to the heroes of this last generation from the beginning of the 1980s to the end of the first decade of the new millennium. A million men, women and children of the British coalfields whose lives were touched by the huge events of 1984/85, also those of the forgotten struggle of the decade after that, who made such an honest and noble stand throughout. To the Poll Tax resisters who proved we can win if we have enough courage, unity and the right cause. To the Palestinian people, whose heroism and tragedy marks every bloody page of every generation since the imposition of the Zionist state at the end of World War Two. To the communities of republican Ulster and their bold and selfless volunteers who brought the British state to a score draw, but were left short of their goals.

The Author

Restarting back down the Doncaster mines after my sabbatical at Strathclyde University, I kick over any number of apple carts with the launch of a scandalously satirical and biting journal *Hot Gossip*. Management throughout the coalfield, at pit level and within the Area offices, fume as it lands on their desks, a must-have read, if only to know what I'm saying about them this time.

July 1979. Meeting of all Doncaster Branches with the NCB Area director. This homes in on Hatfield and *Hot Gossip*'s 'William Claxtan Publishing Company', which he misquotes in a furious attack, and I respond to in kind. *Hot Gossip*, probably the most successful paper I ever produced, was within a short period acclaimed by the Hatfield miners and the wider community at large. *Hot Gossip* was also the raunchy team of girl dancers who on TV had succeeded Pan's People in terms of highly sexual dance routines. There was none of that in the paper, but the title grabbed your attention. People could be seen chuckling at pub tables, columns would be being read in shops by groups of people looking over each other's shoulders. The local music scene, the festivals, the parties, the 'scene' and the characters round town all vied with local news and stories from neighbouring areas as the paper crossed village borders and into other pits. The serious articles were used in arguments, were nicked as part of delegates' speeches, or stuck up on local council and management notice boards as acts of defiance. The whole community became our reporters; they knocked each over to tell me the latest gossip, who had dropped themselves in it, who had said what, what ballsups the management and the officials had made. It was 'hot' all right and there was no end to the stories and humour. It was funded entirely by donations. The Broadway would buy a clump and leave them on the bar, but not before, I was mobbed by lads looking for the first editions to come off the press, sticking fivers into my hand to 'keep up the good work'. Many of the clubs took them or else I went round the tables and people chucked coins and notes across. I had regular subscribers and regular distributors on each shift. The canteen would fall silent as the entire shift of miners read their papers, then it would erupt in raucous laughter. Management was pitilessly pilloried, as were the local bigwigs on the Council and in Parliament. Internal union issues were also thrashed out and point-by-point arguments behind pay and conditions claims or ongoing disputes were spelt out. It addressed, almost as they were raised, doubts, fears and rumours, and countered management's propaganda quicker and more often than they could ever hope to do.

Meantime the efforts to get the pit established in the mighty Barnsley seam were floundering amid heroic efforts by the men working in the strange environment. Hatfield had ever since its inception largely left the big Barnsley seam alone and worked on the much smaller though higher-quality High Hazel. The Barnsley, 18 to 20 feet thick, was prone to 'sponcom' (heatings and fires) and massive weight movements. B30's[1] was being equipped with huge chock supports 2 to 5 yards in height with masses of power per square inch. But a massive hade dogged the efforts to get the chocks under solid ground, and rocks and minerals flooded down in great cascades and landslides of debris. In short time we had two young lads with their backs broken as rocks loosed themselves from the blackness of the unsupported ground and dropped silently onto their bodies. In the initial falls sandstone tops conspired with fractured soft coal to hade well in advance of the face panzer and roof supports, leaving a chasm of unsupported ground in advance of the machines and the supports.

As panzers worked night and day to clear the mineral away and the belts ran in white and red crushed rock, the holes spread. By the third week, the chocks were standing supporting nothing in a cavern 18 yards high above the chock roof and rising with the minute; above the crushed soft coal was feet of silty mudstone and ironstone and above that crushed and fractured sandstone for 50 feet above the seam.

Hatfield needed this seam, Hatfield needed this Barnsley; in 1979 pits did not walk away from prospects like this, this was mining, this was what we did. The workers came up with the most bizarre and ingenious idea. They decided to build themselves a roof. They shuttered the holes in advance of the AFC (the armoured face conveyor, a scraper chain moving over a set of steel plates the full length of the face, which carries the cut coal away to the belts in the main gate (roadway)); they shuttered the areas to some feet above the chock canopies, then yard by yard they filled it with gallons upon gallons of packbind, a sort of soft concrete. A new 'face' was constructed of solid concrete that filled all the holes. When it was set, forepolling and bars were positioned on top and a further layer of packbind applied until a new wall was constructed maybe 20 feet above the top of the chocks. Then the machines cut forward, inching the chocks forward, their massive pressure was reduced to stop them crushing the fragile top, yard by yard until they sat under a roof, an artificial roof, but a complete roof down the length of the face. It was nursed forward, every new cavity filled and barred at once and not allowed to 'weather' or extend. We battled forward, splattered and drenched in packbind, stone and iron dust and coal dust, we were cut to ribbons from the die hard fractures of rocks which continued to try and rain down on us, but we moved forward relentlessly until we were into the solid ground of more secure coal and strata.

To achieve this a whole new technology had to be developed. The concrete was specially selected so it could be pumped from a remote outstation outbye through pipes. It had to be strong enough to form a supporting seal and form a new roof and face, but soft enough to be cut out again by the machines. Ninety-seven tonnes of material was pumped over the course of that weekend. Apart from saving this face and any more broken backs, it set in motion a new system of support, which would develop into the 'pump pack' system and eventually save us hours of crippling work hand-filling packs with rocks from our shovels, often kneeling in water up to our thighs. (It would also however increase the incidence of dermatitis.) The pit would remain the pit. The miners' pit sense often triumphed over the earth and left the clever mining engineers wide-eyed with respect.[2]

THE DONNIE SCENE

The scene back in Donnie had been developing while I was away. Apart from the growing political movements of the left and the clear militancy of the union orientations, there was a growth in the numbers and quality of our type of milieu. Parts of the town were now cool in their own right, frequented by hippie-type lads and lasses, with lang hair and all the trappings of the earlier 'beat' generation. The bikers were now no longer Teds but had made the graduation to hippies on bikes, all right, fucking hard hippies on bikes, not so much into peace and love but of that species. Our political attitude of social revolution and union militancy were already fairly common among the young folk of our generation, and the sexual revolution had taken off quite on its own. Free relations both official and covert were very common and nobody in these days talked of abstinence or restraint among those unattached. Heavy rock was as much a driver as the impulses of the world revolution; in part heavy rock was part of that revolution – many of the bands and their music were certainly addressed to us and it. The drug culture was pot-based; loads of ordinary youngsters were engaging in smoking joints and getting high. Beetham's was a pub straight out of the Sixties or you'd think it was – Sixties Newcastle that is, not Sixties Doncaster. It reminded me of the Doonbeat.[3] Bikes filled the little road outside the pub, gleaming in defiance, bikers in leathers squeezed past lang-haired blokes in kaftans and the air was filled with smells of patchouli oil, almost a membership badge among both groups, roll-your-own tobacco, the occasional whiff of dope. The air was filled with heavy metal. There wasn't room to dance here anymore. Downstairs used to be a place alive with writhing bodies and flouncing hair in the dark of the cellar bar, but now it was too full for that and folk stood round or sat on the big central pool table which was covered over with a large stage-like board at weekends. The Silver Link was another of our centres and sources of our kind of folks; we gathered there politically but also socially any time we were out. If you wanted a partner, a joint, an in-depth discussion on revolutionary politics or Rainbow,[4] or the latest festival, you couldn't really fail at the Link or Beetham's despite the constant attention by the cops, who all the time tried to close them down. After I came back the Abbey at Dunscroft was practically our social club and most folk would make the trek there if they wanted to find us and the left political scene. Beetham's and the Link were 'our pubs' too, though bit by bit we started to infect the whole market place, with the IS staking out their mark in the Masons, while the CP could always be found down by the Railway, the Horse and Jockey or at the Trades Club. They tended to be older workers and not much involved with the youth scene unless there was a meeting or rally. What wasn't at once obvious was that the bulk of this leather-clad, hippie-on-bike throng were in fact coal miners. Not the stereotypical, flat-capped type at all, but coal miners none the less. They smoked dope, freaked out to heavy metal, went en-masse to festivals, but come Monday

3

day shift were back down t'pit. At Hatfield, I was seen as one of their own – it was a sort of social confirmation that they too had a union rep who was like them.

It's too long a hall of fame to glide along the list of Beetham's characters in turn, but Spot sticks out. He was the archetypal Hell's Angel in full beard and flowing main, almost 6 foot and built like an overweight scrumhalf. Down pit, he was, as one would expect, a main gate ripper, a man-mountain lifting steel arches like wooden planks. He was also bliddy hilarious sober and twice as funny when drunk. One of his early tragedies was to write off a big-fork bike he was paying for in instalments. There was something wrong with the insurance and he ended up having to continue to pay for the damn bike without actually having a bike. His first day getting on the bus in all his biker gear, he stepped aboard and warned the occupants of the bus: 'Nobody laugh!'

The week of the Reading Festival, the Beetham's crowd hired a furniture wagon, and following an extended drinking session at Beetham's poured, almost literally, into the back of the wagon for the drive down south. It was a bit hefty and unmanoeuvrable for the volunteer driver, who if truth was known had smoked more than an odd toke of grass and had more than a pint before setting off. The corner was a little tight and the driver of the big saloon car cut in too soon, causing the wagon to veer to the left and begin to topple over, staggering along on two sets of wheels before glancing a lamppost and banging down straight again but up the bank and into a hedge.

The car pulls up and the driver, apologetic and concerned, runs up to see if everyone is OK. They open the back gates and hippies and heavies fall out in all directions and lie in the road, or on the verge, some head in hands, some out flat. The car driver looks horrified. OK says our driver, they were like that when they left Donnie. Actually, the cloud of dope smoke and petrol fumes gliding their way skyward from the back of the lorry was the chief cause.

Apart from the lorry full of latter-day working-class hippies, we had a phalanx of a dozen motorbike outriders. Spot was dressed up in a full German army uniform with a Nazi helmet on. On the bike, he cut a dash. Later that week as we staggered the deserted streets of Reading, Spot in his uniform with strictly non-regulation axe stuck in his belt together with a giant bowie knife, we were stopped by a solitary fool of a policeman. He squared up to Spot and shone his torch on the axe and dagger.

'What's all this?' he asks in a slightly camp voice.

'I'm camping, ain't I?' Spot replied, very drunk and very swaying, 'It's for skinnin' fires and choppin' rabbits', he explained, and then swayed backwards right through a shop window where he collapsed flat backward, in among all the dummies. Spot rolls his head sideways, and seeing the naked model starts to stroke its plastic tits. Just then, along comes Sergeant Boothead on his bike, jumps off and shines his torch into the shop, sees the flat form of Spot on the window floor.

'Oy, what's fackin' going on?'

Spot still laying flat salutes and clicks his heels: 'Corporal Shultz, and I know nutting.'

Well, the Sarge looks at the size of Spot, looks at the puny constable, thinks, 'Shite! I'm on me way home!' 'Well, get his arse out of there and get off', he suggests very obligingly. But this was easier said than done. Pulling Spot up from a flat collapse defies science, not helped by his attempts to snog and grope the models. At last we stagger off as two cops are seen rapidly exiting left.

Actually Spot was a man of above average intelligence and for all his rock-hard exterior, he could be deeply sympathetic and concerned. He was at length to join the Hatfield Main NUM Branch Anti Nuclear Campaign, together with Catweasel, another of the pit's hippie bikers. Catweasel was so called because his hair and beard was of the style of a medieval Saxon character of that name, in a comic kid's version about Arthur (that's King and not Scargill).

Beetham's. Big John, former Edlo miner, is the bloke in charge; he is serving in a crowded downstairs cellar bar, packed with novo-freaks, as heavy metal fills the room. A big gorilla (not the armed urban type, the swing-through-the-trees type) comes up to the bar with a bloke. John points at the gorilla without any laughter, says 'I'm not serving him!' The gorilla puts its head on one side in a questioning manner. 'Get him out now!' John shouts with that tone which suggests imminent violence. The gorilla drops his arms dejectedly and turns round slowly, slouching to the door. I am creased up laughing. John doesn't laugh. 'I know who it was,' he says and just carries on serving.

The Labour Party Rejects Democracy – Again

The 1981 conference of the Labour Party saw the left in the ascendancy. We had never been so strong in the constituencies; the leadership was in a no-holds-barred contest to stop the politics expressed in conference and resolutions becoming manifest in Parliament or the leadership. The selection for deputy leader was to be a battle royal, on the left Tony Benn and on the right Denis Healey. The run-up to the vote on the Sunday night had been electric, with meetings all over Brighton and fur really flying, the right crying hell-fire if Benn was elected. When it came to the vote their shenanigans and last-minute wheeling and dealing had worked. Healey was elected by a less than 1 per cent majority. The rank and file of the party had voted massively for Benn; while the last-minute arm-twisting of mass union votes had still left a 50–50 split. It all came down to the MPs, for whom the choice of their political careers and an easy life versus following their constituency mandates would be no choice at all really. Seventeen of Tribune's MPs abstained! And swung the vote to Healey. Seventy MPs voted *contrary* to their constituency decisions[5] to support Benn. Something of the mark of difference between the two men showed when I was wandering lost around the magnificent hotel and blundered past the Healey reception, full of glittering tiaras, evening suits, flowing silk dresses and silverware; a little later I saw Tony and his wife, eating fish and chips at a crowded fish shop on the waterfront.

This rigged 'election' was either very long-sighted or anyway useful for the British state, as events were to show. Had it faithfully reflected the democratic wishes of the party as a whole, then Tony Benn was odds-on to have been leader of the Labour Party during the greatest industrial conflict in British history in at least half a century and maybe ever. In a very finely balanced contest of class forces, Benn's leadership and enthusiastic support for the NUM could well have tipped the balance in our favour and washed the vacillating union bureaucracies off the fence and into a common solidarity front. The Labour establishment however could be relied upon to uphold the established order by any means, fair and foul. Was there a conspiracy to make sure he wasn't in the leadership as the biggest industrial battle of the century loomed? I'm not great on conspiracies but a coincidence of that sort is barely credible.

24 NOVEMBER 1981. TEN YEARS OF THE IRISH WAR – FIVE YEARS OF THE PREVENTION OF TERRORISM ACT

Demonstration and march to Brixton Prison supported and sponsored by Sinn Féin, IRSP, trade unions and left groups. Groups we approached who refused to sponsor: the IMG, the Sparts, the WRP; also Ernie Roberts MP.

We are working in a united front with the (American) Revolutionary Communist League (Internationalist) in the International Committee for a United Front International Labour Defence. Trying to defend all class war prisoners, publicise their cases, support their efforts in prison and raise the issues we adopt as questions for the working class and labour movement. We are an 'International Committee' first, because although we are functioning, in the meantime we are trying to build the committee, trying to draw in other sectors of the left and progressive movement and individuals with the solidarity work. At the same time we are developing close links with the RCL(I) as a political tendency, so we approach almost every issue which produces conflict and struggle (particularly armed struggle) and prisoners on two levels. On the United Front level we fight to defend and assist the prison struggles and support them as class war prisoners, but on the political level in relation to their own political organisations and their programmes we come up against this 'support versus defend' argument. On the repellent request to work with the Sparts, they respond to us (17 November 1979):

> On their refusal to support the IRA … either wing, we point out that the RCL(I) does not politically support. By 'support' we mean endorse politically, implying a high degree of political agreement which we don't have with either wing. But we *unconditionally defend* them against Capital and on the question of armed struggle defend the Provos against the Officials lecturing … Formally we (RCL(I)) have a similar view of the Catholic and Protestant working class in Ireland, i.e. that they are both following the bourgeoisie. At every turn, at every opportunity, we proletarian revolutionists emphasize to the exploited and oppressed masses: NO CONFIDENCE in the bourgeoisie, be it the imperialist, or, especially, our own liberal bourgeoisie. We show in all history since 1848 the liberal bourgeoisie has betrayed the masses, made rotten compromises, disorganised struggles, rather than permit proletarian revolution. ALL confidence in the revolutionary potential of the proletariat!

This was the same beef the Revolutionary Workers Party (RWP) had had with our proximity to the republican movement, and the apparent nit-picking differences of expression: we could call for 'Victory To The IRA', we could defend the IRA (which was laughable) but we couldn't support the IRA or Sinn Féin. The same terminology would see us defend the USSR against imperialism, when we couldn't scrape together a solitary tank between the entire British and American Trotskyist left put together. For us this was just playing around with words. We supported the struggles our comrades in Ireland were engaging in, and as far as possible got down to join in that struggle with them. We tended to support the organisations, which the struggle was taking place in, too – not to do so was a sheer abstraction unless we had developed or were developing something stronger and more effective and principled.

That didn't mean we didn't continue the fight within the organisation, oh no. But we would attempt to do this from within the fight, not outside in pristine purity.

February 1980. I am invited to give a paper at the Science and Society History Workshop, on mine safety and mine legislation, which is something of an honour. I get to take a load of miners from the branch down with me and we all stay at Raph Samuels's place in Spitalfields. Accompanying us is big Brian Roberts, an enthusiastic member of the Branch Committee. This is a great adventure for Brian; it is the first time he has ever been on a train, and the first time he has ever travelled outside Yorkshire. As soon as we hit Kings Cross he comments on how 'big London is'. Later he is introduced to a female French academic of about his age who was having dinner at Raph's. We all go out for a pint, and Brian is thrilled to sit and talk to this lady. For him she is from another social class as well as another country; she is a completely new experience. He can't get over the fact that he is able to converse with her, about life in general and the village and families in particular.

I am talking amongst the scientists and tutors. The awkward bastards I have brought with me from the Branch ask more difficult questions than anyone else does, about such things as the ability of water sprays to suppress dust from coal cutters once it is airborne. It leads to heated discussions among the science graduates and many formulae on the blackboard. Billy Matthews the communist coal-cutter tells them all flatly: once the dust is flying you cannot knock it down; if you try then it just flies lower then dries out and takes off again. Billy has had a lifetime observing the dust as an ornithologist would flights of birds.

BAZO

Maureen is at the head of a British Anti-Zionist Organization–Palestine Solidarity[6] conference on the growing tensions in the Gulf, hosted in Baghdad. We the members of the SUI could clearly see that a struggle for ideology and direction was developing among the basic component strands of the Middle-Eastern countries. The Iranian revolution had in our view been defeated; it had been usurped by the mullahs. The communists, the socialists, the secularists and the democrats had all been disarmed, their movements smashed and their leaders murdered. Notwithstanding this, the revolutionary left in Britain led by the former IMG still called for a 'victory' and 'defence' of the Iranian revolution. In effect, it meant victory and defence of the priests and the sky pilots who were preaching medievalism. Islamic law would rule all questions of life and death; 'women's liberation' was evil and ungodly, but middle-class well-heeled women here still shouted in defence of the hujab.

Iraq was not a workers' state, even by old Posadas's view. There was no workers' democracy in Iraq, though it was by and large secular; there was no religious compulsion and no repression of religion, both Catholic churches and a Jewish Synagogue survived happily in Baghdad. Women wore western clothes, or the religious garb; women were in high-role occupations in politics, the army and civil service. Socialistic Pan-Arab[7] rhetoric flowed from Saddam's lips and ostensible trade unions were able to put forward demands on pay and conditions, and health and safety. Sixty per cent of the economy was nationalised, including the massive oil wealth, which helped to fuel advanced education and health schemes. On a world scale, Iraq stood with the anti-imperialist camp; on a Middle-Eastern scale, it was a loyal supporter of the Palestinian cause. For me, when push came to shove, as the Yanks say, and a head-on clash loomed between the Iranian 'Magicians' as Saddam called them and the distorted Ba'athist 'socialist' regime in Iraq, I would have cheered on Saddam, if for no other reason than to halt fundamentalist Islam and reaction which was fighting for hegemony across the Muslim world. However, after exhaustive reading of all sides of the dispute and the nature of both states, we decided this was indeed an inter-imperialist type conflict, a row between two sets of despots, one perhaps more despotic than the other, certainly potentially so in terms of the growth of reactionary ideas, but a pox on both their houses. We had concluded 'no war but the class war', and that workers across the Middle East should united against Zionism, the mullahs, the shahs and the dictators. The conference had been called as 'a peace conference' by the International Arab Students Assembly; however they would be too late to generate enough outside and internal forces to halt the war and bring about negotiations. For Maureen, these times were to be among the most exciting and revealing of her life; with the comrades from across the progressive movement, the armed groups, the anti-imperialist groups, the women's organisations. She assimilated the Arab socialist cause, and I believe would have died for the cause of Palestine had she been called upon to. Meanwhile, back home in Britain *Socialist Challenge*, the new paper of what would soon be the former IMG, called for 'Victory to the Iranian Revolution', but declined to show us a mullah in beard and robes; it was a long, long way from 'Victory to the IRA'.

JOHN LENNON ASSASSINATED

8 December 1980. It is almost impossible to comprehend; John Lennon is murdered, shot dead, the voice, the music, the reason, an echo of the beat of my heart and my being, is no more. Taken from us. Shot, we think, for John's far-left affiliations, his refusal to bow to the powers of the most powerful state in the world. Scathing in his music and words, supportive of more and more workers'

actions, like Martin Luther King before him, cut down in gunfire. The assassin walking up straight to him and John with his beaming smile probably thinks it's an autograph-hunter and is shot at point blank range. Oh yes, the old 'lone mad gunman with an obsession' is reeled out once more, but it doesn't wash. Even America hasn't got such a queue of lone gunmen waiting in line their turn to kill off whoever is in the state's politically awkward category this week. Within hours, Posterman has his big wall posters out across the city of New York announcing JOHN LENNON'S MURDER WAS A POLITICAL ASSASSINATION. Next time I am there I take a bundle of these posters home with me, but not enough; soon they are adorning the walls of Hell's Angels and hippie pitmen across Doncaster and in cities up and down the country. I ought to have had them reproduced and posted around Liverpool.

John's death leaves a real vacuum. He is missed heart and soul. We needed him, we needed his wisdom and his humour and the power of his music. I can think of no one to fill his very unique boots.

PRELUDES TO A CLASS WAR

In preparation for the task of smashing the so-called 'power of the unions' and taming the militants, direct measures were drawn up. The Employment Act 1980 declared secondary (that is, solidarity) strike action illegal. (The cornerstone of both miners' victories in the 1970s, and at least the potential of success in earlier conflicts, was solidarity action by other workers 'blacking' coal and alternative fuels.) The act also outlawed the mass picket. Following on from this, the Employment Act 1982 opened up trade unions to unlimited fines for illegal industrial actions. Government programmes favouring the expansion of nuclear energy at the expense of coal-fired stations, regardless of cost, were also political and not financially motivated actions – as revealed in government reports:

> A nuclear programme would have the advantage of removing a substantial portion of electricity generation from the dangers of disruption by industrial action by miners or transport workers.[8]

Preludes to what would become the most monumental clash in the history of the coal industry could be seen when the NUM published its *The Miners and the Battle for Britain* in 1979. It forewarned that: 'The future of the coal industry is being placed in jeopardy. The Government has reneged on an expansion plan that has been pursued since 1974.' This was the famous *Plan For Coal*, which would become a Holy Grail despite its shortcomings in the most monumental battle we ever fought.

The NUM reflected that between 1956 and 1974 no less than two-thirds of the mining manpower and three-quarters of its coalmines had already been lost. That decline had been halted only with the advent of the Plan, which safeguarded the mines, future investment, and a secure place in the fuel economy. With the election to power of Mrs. Thatcher, and the end of the agreement, it was becoming clear that all the gains for the industry in terms of security and expansion were now in jeopardy:

The policy of the NUM, which was reaffirmed at the Union's Special

Conference in March and at the Annual Conference in July [1979] is to oppose any attempt at closing collieries where there are workable reserves of coal remaining. But in an economic climate of mass unemployment, industrial recession and falling demand, it is natural that many people will be attracted by arguments which focus solely on short-term problems at the expense of long-term objectives. To do so however is to ignore the lessons of the past.[9]

Facts that would become central to the great arguments about the future of the coal industry were never presented by the media, and were basically never understood by the public at large. The fact was the Britain was producing the cheapest deep-mined coal in Europe and among the cheapest in the world. This it did while engaging in the safest coal production anywhere in the world.

As the following EEC figures show, the NCB has the lowest coal production cost in Europe:

1979 Coal Production Costs
£ per tonne

Belgium	58
France	45
West Germany	41
UK (1979/80)	29

On top of this subsidies per tonne from other EEC countries show how great is the unfair relationship between costs and prices:

Direct aid to Production in ECSC Coal Industries 1979

	£m	£ per tonne
Belgium	207.7	34.05
France	334.1	17.96
West Germany	1,385.7	41
UK	195.4	1.62

Sources: EEC documents quoted in *The Miners and the Battle for Britain*.

In other EEC countries indirect government subsidies are larger than the direct aid to production. While the UK Government is cutting its aid to coal and launching other financial and economic attacks upon the industry, Governments elsewhere are recognising the political, social and economic importance of maintaining coal production capacity even at a time of recession by increasing their level of support. Thus in the case of coking coal alone, the German coal industry received £418.3 million in Government aid last year compared to £8.4m in the UK.[10]

The 1974 *Plan For Coal* was, even with its shortcomings (lack of security of markets) the first real attempt at trying to plan the industry. It was anathema to the incoming Tory government in 1979 and in spite of assurances from Margaret

Thatcher that she would honour the *Plan For Coal*, by the beginning of 1981 schemes were afoot to destroy it. In 1981 coal still supplied over 80% of electricity generation.[11] But let's not be coy here – all the arguments in the world around costing and markets and fuel requirements were shadows of the real naked class forces on both sides. We were fighting for our ability to fight, our place in the more important struggle to change society. They were determined to clip our wings to rob us of any such power, in order that we couldn't challenge their power and the status quo. The arguments are important, as they are the means by which both sides defended their ground, but they are not the motive, and anyone who thinks that the emerging battle was just about keeping open some hole in the ground or a pithead gear in some field in far-off Barnsley or Durham is severely missing the point, and will surely never understand the fire and flame, the venom and hate which was to be generated around the clash. At something like £3 or less a tonne subsidy, the British coal industry received by far and away the lowest subsidy in Europe. David Howell, the Labour energy minister, started the war on the miners, by cutting the subsidy; this forced the NCB to draw up a programme of closures.[12]

8 August 1980. The Coal Industry Act becomes law. It starts to set out the parameters of government cutbacks on what little aid the NCB receives, and hence cutbacks in production. Inevitably, it is a signpost for a new phase of ruthless and possibly relentless pit closures. We set our stall out early with a brilliantly argued *The Miners and The Battle for Britain*, launched jointly by the NUM and the TUC. It seeks to draw a line in the sand, behind which the entire trade union movement will stand with the miners. In September, we launch a joint campaign with the steel and rail unions. The NUM, the NUR and the ISTC start to warn of thorough-going attacks upon all traditional industries, workforces, communities, regions and countries, which rest upon them. To read the material, to see the hopes which the miners place in their allies, to look into the eyes of this old union as it surveys the pledges from the TUC of solidarity and loyalty and support from brother industrial unions, distant echoes of so many similar pledges from the 1920s, is to be at once struck by a deep sense of impending doom and foreboding. We seem to be retracing the steps of our fathers and forefathers as they stepped up to the line, alone. But we had the right to demand joint action; it is in reality their fight as well as ours. That is not simply a slogan but a fact. We have no other allies other than our fellow workers; if we can't trust the leaders at least we can expect a joint fight from our fellow workers, can't we?[13]

12 December 1980. Hatfield Main pit is out on strike. It is a vexatious dispute, which goes back decades. Essentially the management had decided to pull the jackboots on again and start imposing their arbitrary prerogative. They decreed that if you didn't have your check out by 15 minutes before the start of your shift you would be sent home. This was an outrage to us, one and all. We actually only began to get paid from the start of our shift, but you had already to be down the pit by then, getting your token out to identify you. Getting changed, getting your lamp out and travelling down the pit you actually didn't get paid for – you did

that in your own time. If you were down the pit by shift start time, we reasoned, then the rest of the time was ours, not theirs. The question of riding times went back to the defeat of 1926 when we had an extra hour and a quarter *plus one winding time* imposed on us. Now this *one riding time* to us plainly meant the time it takes to get one draw into the pit, or if you believed it applied individually, it meant we worked 7¼ hours *plus one* riding time. Management however seemed to think the winding times at the beginning and at the end of the shift were theirs too. They allowed all the overmen and deputies to ride up the pit before the miners. We now insisted that one riding time meant we had to be out of the pit by the conclusion of that 7¼ hours, in other words the time they were riding their officials out of the mine was *our time*. We weren't after all being paid for it. The branch instructed its onsetters to ensure that deputies and overmen stood in the queue and were not ridden out of the pit before everyone else. We would still not be being paid for getting out of the pit but at least nobody was now making us wait any longer. The management responded by sending our onsetters out of the pit, and the pit walked out with them.

We were on strike, the first since I came back from college and to be honest on an issue I had raised. Our Area was now wringing its hands as to what could we do – this was a national issue really; it couldn't be fought to a conclusion at Hatfield. At length they came back with the offer of payment for the shifts we had lost, but a return to status quo. We insisted the instruction of closing the time office before the shift start be withdrawn, which it was, although the men a little foolishly perhaps told them to stuff the money up their arses as the principle of the dispute hadn't really been resolved. We agreed to return to work and raise the question through the formal conciliation machinery. It took till April 1982 to successfully get the issue before the NEC for them to thrash out with the NCB. It had already become a unanimous Conference resolution in 1981, but like many another resolution was just to gather dust in some office. In fact, it still hasn't been resolved to this day and miners still do not get paid for the time it takes to wait to get out of the pit – 30 minutes or often more in a big pit.

The first of the 'big' redundancy offers was made to Boldon Colliery miners to get the pit closed. It's tragic but even though by later standards it was small sums of money, it was more money than a miner could ever expect to accumulate without starving to death and living in a field. Forty years down a 2-foot seam, with water and danger and away from the joys of daylight, is a poor choice when set against a stack of £5 notes. Both me and me Da hope the Boldon men will fight the closure, but it's a tough thing to ask anyone. The wee fiery chairman of the lodge Davison Brennan is 'a dam ant' in the phrase of the aud Wardley pit men; he damns to hell any suggestion that Boldon should close or the men should ever think about letting it happen. I think Davie would have worked the mine on his own if that was the only way of keeping it open.

APRIL 1981. MINING SUPPLIES/LAWRENCE SCOTTS DISPUTE

This was a particularly vicious industrial relations struggle. The firm Mining Supplies was based in the Doncaster coalfield and supplied and repaired mining equipment, mainly cutting machines. They should have found allies in us; what they got was lacklustre support. Despite picketing from the Manchester plant, the Doncaster works carried on working, and carried on supplying the Doncaster coalfield with cutting machines and repaired equipment. Over in Manchester at the Lawrence Scott end of the operation the workers had occupied the factory. The struggle waged for months with the pickets dead on their feet, and despite secondary picketing, particularly of the Doncaster mines, the strike was going nowhere. In Manchester the occupation was stormed by 50 armed bailiffs who smashed their way in with raw violence using pickaxe handles. Two vivid images remain in mind of this dispute. One is the furious argument on the floor of the council chamber of the NUM as Hatfield and other Doncaster branches sought countywide blacking of all MS products, at which Arthur Scargill spoke against support. I will never forget his argument: the miners would not be used as the muscle to win everyone else's battles. 'It wouldn't surprise me if we seen miners picketed by bakers because we sell sandwiches in the pit canteen' – or words to that effect – was his final coup de grâce. As if miners were constantly on strike in support of other workers – actually we were rarely if ever called into other workers' disputes, although we always thought every other worker in the country should be called into ours. The other was the scene on the gates at the Doncaster plant, in the thick of a blizzard and belting hail, as the freezing, exhausted pickets clustered round a brazier of coal, which the miners had supplied. Snipe, the owner, creeps up the road in his Rolls toward the plant, and the men shout through the windows, 'We've got you on your knees yi bastard', as they dripped frozen rain from their faces and he sat wearing his fur-trimmed overcoat and leather gloves in the warmth of his luxury. Mining Supplies was in my view a shameful page of our history, despite the stand made by Hatfield and other Doncaster mines in blacking Snipe's equipment and severely cutting down on coal production at those pits.

A BRANCH OFFICIAL OF THE NATIONAL UNION OF MINEWORKERS[14]

I am elected the NUM branch delegate in the June elections. I am ecstatic. It is by a clear and decisive margin. My Mam and Dad are over the moon and so proud:

> We couldn't be more pleased if we had won the treble chance. To receive the number of votes you did was a wonderful result. You have a large number of men behind you, always bear that in mind when you go to represent them, wherever you may go, or in what ever company you may be in, stick in David, make a success of this, you may make a lot more progress in union work, once you get real experience in this kind of thing. Your Mam and I are right behind you and this is what I have always wanted for you, we are very proud of you …You will find enclosed £10 which your Mam sends for you to celebrate your victory. Take it David, your Mam wants you to have it and wishes you all the best. She's a good woman David isn't she?

This is perhaps the proudest moment of my life. I will represent these men through thick and thin from now almost until the last mine closes. I will face election challenges from Stalinists and social democrats and at one time a close-the-pit candidate, but I will always secure a clear victory despite never compromising my political stance one iota. The Hatfield miners are the salt of the earth by my reckoning and we shall stand or fall together from this day on.

SINN FÉIN

June 1981. Leo McLaughlin, a recently arrived Irish recruit to Sinn Féin Tyneside, had made his way quietly through the ranks of the Cumann until by June he had become *runai* (secretary). He was in regular contact with Dublin, both physically and by post. It was some shock when that very month I receive a letter from Leo, saying, inter alia:

3rd June 1981

James Connolly Cumann Tyneside

David a Chara

As you know the constitution and rules of Sinn Féin state 'No person who is a member of a secret society shall be eligible for membership and no person known to be a member of any secret society shall be admitted to membership' (rule 1C).

At a General meeting of Sinn Féin (Britain) May 31st a ruling was given by the Ard-Chomhairle rep that your membership of Sinn Féin was invalid, as laid out in the constitution and rules of Sinn Féin.

As the James Connolly Runai I am mandated to write to you pointing out your position, and to encourage you to rejoin Sinn Féin by submitting a written resignation of membership of your present organisation, which I shall forward to the Ard-Chomhairle rep – Kevin Colfer. It is the wish of the Ard-Chomhairle Rep that you contact him as soon as possible ...

I hope you treat this letter in friendly terms as it is intended. I urge you to rejoin Sinn Féin as your support is needed for the struggle of a democratic Socialist Republic and supporting our P.O.W.s in Ireland and Britain ...'

Is Mise, Leo McLaughlin

A little later he writes:

The next James Connolly Cumann meeting will be at the above address on Sunday June 14th at 4.00 p.m. At that meeting there is to be a full discussion concerning members of this Cumann belonging to other political organisations re: Constitution and Rules: rule 16 and 1C. With reference to yourself and your membership or not of the SUI. I hope you can attend.

Whoa – I had been here before, but little expected it in this organisation, my organisation. The rules quoted had been drafted for Ireland, and ruled out joint membership in most cases; they hadn't been drafted for the situation of Cumainn operating outside of Ireland where other political forces, events and issues were taken place alongside Cumann business. Aside from which, as a political tendency we had enjoyed the closest relations with the An Ard Comhairle both in Britain, and as far as we knew with the clear approval of Dublin. I had never heard of this Kevin Colfer, the new Ard Chomhairle. The 'secret society' stuff was baffling, unless it was a reference to our Embryonic Military Caucus (EMC) work and the prospect of some other armed team on the block – who, us? More probably there was no rule, which outlawed a political tendency such as ours – this was the only thing they could find to bash us with. But why us, and why now, and who had gone running off to discuss all this? Leo seemed the obvious suspect but why and on whose behalf?

Leo was adamant; the meeting, at the Bridge as I recall, actually 'exposed' one of our other members who was a member of the SWP, it seemed. It shocked me that he had never said anything about his membership with them. He saw the Irish struggle as unique and a separate entity from his SWP membership. Sinn Féin was the party of the Irish working class in his view and he had seen no contradiction. Neither did we. In the case of the SUI our approach and proximity to Sinn Féin had not been that of a hostile organisation like the SWP, though, and the case for our defrocking was even weaker. Sean too, by association with us, and occasional work with IRSP, was to be voided, along with all other SUI members. There was no discussion, no vote; this was the rules, direct from Dublin. We were out.

The Cumann, much depleted and now wracked by internal dissent (especially about Leo's credentials and role), staggered on a little longer before the big blow came a little later. ALL British-based, indeed, all non-Irish-based Cumainn and organisations of Sinn Féin outside Ireland would be closed down and cease to exist. So, Leo and the other 'pure' members of the Cumann soon joined us outside the organisation. It was an undoubtable purge, and part of a plan, conscious or coincidental, which marked the start of a long road of retreat from revolutionary socialism, and at length from republicanism too. Those forces moving within the leadership of the movement had long-term aims, to seize control of the direction of the movement, and take it onto an entirely new trajectory. This would be done incrementally, and for many in the movement almost imperceptibly.

6 JULY 1981. NUM ANNUAL CONFERENCE

It is Joe Gormley's last Conference. B. Davaney, a sympathetic reporter with the *Daily Express*, had christened him 'The Battered Cherub', and there was much of a Jimmy Clithero character in him, just a working-class, no-bullshit lad from Lancashire. I can't allow myself the indulgence of inserting a biographical note on Joe, but in his own way, Joe was a giant of the miners' union too, albeit on the right, and with some very unsavoury state connections – as we were to discover later. He was, they said, pugnacious, straight from the shoulder, didn't spare anyone's blushes. He carried the common-sense pit wit in his bones and battered the at times weak-kneed intellectual concerns and phraseology of the left. Arthur, serious and straight-laced, a bit pompous, was Joe's favourite sparring partner, who he met with 'common sense' practicality. He managed to create an impression of being the true working-class spokesperson and Arthur some popinjay with his head in the clouds. I recall a Conference where Peter Heathfield, an upcoming leader of the left, leapt to his feet to come into the debate uninvited and Joe slapped him down. 'I was provoked,' announced Peter, and Joe, as if he was talking to his little lad, replied, 'Provoked, av told thee to stay away from them.' I can't describe his humour; it was often hysterically funny, frequently using the entire Conference as his straight man as he bounced responses and repertoire off them. There is a hilarious sequence where Sid Vincent, his Lancashire soulmate, is trying to move a vote of thanks to him, and Joe keeps bouncing comments back, not least because he is describing a time when they slept in the same bed, 'I had me pants on,' Joe interjects. I think there is no finer example than this last Conference, which readers can perhaps track down to the Annual Conference Report and its verbatim record. Joe had picked the venue, and he came up not for the first time with Jersey in the Channel Islands. The venue caused outrage among the rank and file and it was soon resolved that Conferences would no longer be held outside of coalfield areas. Joe, already an OBE in 1981, went on to enter the Lords as Lord Gormley of Wigan, many said for services rendered.[15]

Arthur Scargill is elected National president of the NUM with 70.3% of the vote.

BACK TO THE STATES

September 1981. I had arranged to go over to America on holiday with Emma but include a couple of serious academic lectures at Wellesley and Cambridge, which would pay me enough for the flights and the holiday. We would be staying with Joel. Joel and Emma had been great mates since her early childhood. Emma christened him the 'great Hulk' and he in response called her 'the wee Hulk'. Joel, apart from being our main American organiser, was also head of the English Department at Wellesley, THE top women's college in the US. We were more or less set to fly when PACTO, the US air traffic controllers, struck. The strike originally was about breaks, time off work, rosters and safety margins of their intensely disciplined and concentrated work. The state acted with fury, first off arresting the leaders of the union, then prohibiting the strike and finally outlawing the union itself. This was the time for the American unions, fractured and weakened though they were, to launch solidarity action and shut down the country in support of the basic *human right*, never mind the civil or worker's right, to strike without legal penalties. It was a good time to go to the States, but the worst time to get there. The scene of American workers, skilled and dedicated men, garbed in prison fatigues and literally chained to a metal ball, with iron manacles on their wrists and feet, dragged before the courts, shuffling and stumbling off to prison for the crime of going on strike, is an image I shall never forget. Yet the politicians beat their chests and insisted it was because they were defending 'democracy' that they did this.

I think the highlight of my speaking tour was the lecture at the Political Economy Group of Wellesley and Cambridge, speaking to a packed room of senior academics and students, Joel's colleagues and also his bosses. I was speaking on the theme 'Conflict and Ireland'. The local campus paper *Wellesley News* give me star billing on its front page, standing relaxed at the lectern, shirt wide open, hand in pocket, well into my theme. The headline was 'Ex IRA Member Views Ireland'. Benay Lazo, the headline line author, drew no distinction between the military and political wings of the Provisional movement, so there I am down in US posterity as a member of the distinguished armed team. The talk was immensely popular, though Joel slid under the seat when in response to a head of department I proclaimed it was 'time for Britain to shit or get off the pan' – not very academic, I suppose, but was an American expression I had heard and it just came to mind.

ON HOME GROUND

I hadn't long been elected branch delegate when we got raided for growing hash plants in the garden, and we anticipated the press publicity and a backlash from 'normal' public opinion. Maureen agreed to take the bulk of the rap, although my being the tenant of the house meant I would still be charged for allowing the premises to be used for growing an illegal drug. I decided to meet the charge in the open. During one of my first delegate reports to a mass Branch meeting, I announced that I had been visited by the gardening section of the police force who didn't think my leeks were up to scratch. I also decided to pen an informative article on what exactly pot was, what it did exactly and combat some of the myths and hysteria around the substance. I had by way of explanation of the effects said it was like being drunk, but you could still get a hard on.

A few days later an old wizened pitman in a cap came into the union office and announced 'Wor lass says I've to get some of that marijuana coz you can get an 'ard on wi' it.' The event was such non-news that by the time we went to trial most of the sting had been drawn. Our solicitor Mr Cunliffe was better than most and made a splendid defence of pot and how in comparison with drink it was positively benign. He argued that our conduct was naive, growing the plants in the front window knowing that a serving police officer lived in the street. We got off with a fine, and a drugs record; the latter was to prove much more of a problem than the former as years went by.

October 1981. *The Link*, a paper greatly inspired by our *Hot Gossip*, makes its appearance at Edlington. Theirs is a professional job, but is formally produced by the lodge, which has its drawbacks in legality, but they more than make up for that with wit and humour, not least their excellent cartoonist Brennan.

10 November 1981. The Socialist Union (Internationalist) agrees to call it a day and wind up, issuing a powerful 'Ultimate Statement':

> The tasks of the revolution are still before us, but we in the SUI have no longer the means to meet them. Our manifesto and political publications are today as relevant fresh and dynamic as on the day we first published them. The members who remain hold no substantial disagreement with them. None of our past members left via political disagreement with our programme, but rather via physical social and mental exhaustion in attempting to carry them out. It is true to say some took fright as our

group steered from time to time close to the wind of illegality.

28 November. I am addressing a mass protest in Trafalgar Square to mark Palestine Day. It had been organised by the General Union of Arab Students and marked 34 years since the forcible expulsion of the Palestinian people from their homeland. I am on the platform with the PLO, and Mike Banda from the Workers Revolutionary Party, who had become a frequent visitor to my house for a cup of tea and argument. We liked the same music, enjoyed the same causes, but could agree on hardly anything. Still, he was highly personable, which was odd for that group. There was David Kadouri from the Sephardic Jews and myself from the NUM. The rally was well reported in the Arab press and I was proud to be mentioned there.[16]

January 1982. We lose the first of two ballots staged this year. The first was in relation to wages, reduction in hours, protection of earnings, early retirement, improvements to the incentive scheme, no pit closures … or else! The Board and the press had lobbied hard against the miners taking industrial action, and at the end of the day we didn't lose by a million miles; 55% accepted the NCB's offer. Owen Briscoe, the Yorkshire Area general secretary, swears the majority difference was swung against the union's case by Joe Gormley who had in fact canvassed against the NEC and Conference recommendation for action, even launching a major appeal in the *Daily Express* urging the miners to accept the offer.[17] Joe was regarded by many of the older miners in particular as being a common-sense leader with his head screwed on right as against the looney wild-eyed militants. Owen believed the wily Gormley was even more pragmatic than that, for two reasons:

One, the fat fee we are led to believe he received for writing the article and
two, to obtain the peerage I know he was hell-bent on obtaining, and that
as we know he accepted from a Tory Prime Minister.[18]

In the second vote in November, the NEC had recommended industrial action against the Board's wages offer. We lost it by 61% to 39% in a ballot of 206,825.[19]

The report put this result down to miners being fearful of industrial action speeding pit closures, together with high unemployment, anti- union legislation and 'blackmail'.[20]

TEMPEST IN A TEAPOT

Friday 2 April 1982. The Falklands War started, with the Argentine invasion and occupation of the Falkland Islands and South Georgia. It ended with the Argentine surrender on 14 June 1982. The war lasted 74 days, with 255 British and 649 Argentine soldiers, sailors and airmen, and three civilian Falklanders killed. Had it not been for the Falklands War, and had Thatcher not won it, she would have been very unlikely to have been re-elected. Thatcher needed that war like nothing else in her career. It is telling that sources suggest the Foreign Office, through the good offices of third parties, had drawn up a peace formula, which conceded everything to both sides, and all but signed it. Thatcher hit the roof and sent the fleet. She had to win and win magnificently against 'the Argies' and stoke up patriotic passions around the flag and getting tough with the unions. It was a calculated gamble, all about getting her re-elected on the barrel of Royal Navy guns and Royal Marine bayonets, in a flag-waving patriotic bloodletting. It had little to do with the issues of 'sovereignty' and defending the impoverished Falkland islanders. The solution worked out by Peru[21] would in its subsequent drafts have conceded national sovereignty to the people of the islands, and geographical sovereignty to Argentina. Fishing and mining rights would stay British. The people on the island could wave whatever flag they wanted; but as a statement of fact the island would be Argentinean, but under the control and sphere of influence of Britain. The foreign secretary thought he and his team had done a grand job and almost signed the document before Thatcher got wind. Not for the last time did she snatch away an agreement ready for signing; she was to do it at least twice during her next major war – the one with the miners.

24 June. We unveil our new Lodge banner. I was pleased to have helped design it, although the back scene didn't work out as I had intended. Instead of a miner standing in front of a huge IWW-type globe, it is a smallie globe, which seems to be sitting Atlas-style on his shoulder. Mind, I managed to add A. J. Cook to Keir Hardie for the front scene. The previous banner had come into this world in 1950 and had been designed by Dick Kelly, the old radical Branch secretary and now left-wing MP for Doncaster. He was given pride of place and a few words at the ceremony. Jack Taylor, the Yorkshire president, speaking at the launch, said: 'There were two crucial strikes in 1969 and 1970 which were led by the Doncaster Panel and in which Armthorpe and Hatfield played a leading role.'

In Arthur's Yorkshire Area presidential address of 1982, he is able to proudly mention 'the fact that only seven pits have been closed in the Yorkshire coalfield – all on the grounds of exhaustion – whilst eleven new pits have been opened …' We didn't know at this time that the coal industry, mining, our jobs and our union had anything but a secure future; we were actually living in the lee of a most tremendous storm which would ultimately change the face of industrial Britain for ever, and have its epicentre in the coalfields.[22]

June 1982. I stand for election to the Area Executive Committee. It is a highly prized position. Branch officials with a lifetime of service often fail to be elected despite numerous attempts. I have only been an official for 12 months; remarkably, I am elected. This is due undoubtedly to the loyal support I am being offered by some of the coalfield's most militant collieries: Frickley, Goldthorpe, Highgate, Hickleton, Yorkshire Main and Askern – these are the block of branches who cast their votes of preference for me in a multiple-choice selection. I think it's true to say none of these branches ever lets me down. However, following closures I lose the bulk of my supporting branches and am forced to rely upon more transient comrades, who trade votes as the will takes the delegate in order to gain the best reciprocal deals for their own elections. Time will prove 'you scratch my back' is not a good motto in what can be a backstabbing contest.

The Annual Conference this year sees a resolution from Kent calling for the NUM National Office to be situated in a coalfield area. It is passed. The love–hate relationship with London has become just hate–hate. The miners have deeply resented our offices and more so our National officials being in London and away from the coalfields. We have watched good men become distant and then resentful of the grubby colliers in their far-off coalfields. It was the start of a march that would take the NUM HQ, with much fanfare, from Euston Road to a gleaming reclaimed office in the centre of Sheffield. We were optimistic for the union and our relocation back into the heart of the coalfields. We little knew that the world was about to start being blown from under our feet, and that we would see our fine office stillborn.

At that same Conference, Cumberland had called for the winding-up of all area incentive schemes and the negotiation of a new single national incentive scheme. Had this latter been passed and pursued with vigour the former may not have come to pass, but the divisive and cancerous nature of the area schemes ensured that self-interest would defend its existence, and a little while later this ticking bomb in the solid ranks of unity would detonate, just as it had been designed to do, at the time when we needed unity most. True to form also, the resolution from Derbyshire calling for all full-time officials of the union to come up for re-election not less than every 5 years is ruled out of order. It wasn't worded correctly, but everyone knew exactly what it meant, too bliddy right! The NEC weren't having any of that whatever way it was worded. Most of them hoped to sit in a big chair for life too.[23]

Saturday 19 June 1982. The Yorkshire Miners' Gala is again at Doncaster. This time the march is preceded by 19 children's jazz bands from all over Yorkshire, our youth militia. The Chairman was Arthur and the guest speaker was Michael Foot, Leader of the Labour Party. My Dad always loved Michael Foot, an honest politician and a great friend of the miners he had always said. We didn't have enough time to get a proper social organised, because ironically this being in Donnie we all wanted to stay to the end, and have a good day. I am now an Executive member and couldn't be prouder if I tried. I am greeted by enthusiastic members from the branches who voted for me and assured the branch rooms rang with arguments over my nomination. There were more than sour looks from those branches who regard me as the devil incarnate – that's politics. We had two special guests with the Branch in the shape of Davison Brennan and his wife Frances. Davison was the former Boldon lodge president, and quite a character. He wore a big brimmer of a hat, and a gold watch chain spread across his chest in the manner of the aud miners' officials. A little miner's oil lamp hung from his lapel. Davison was still deeply embroiled with all things mining. He had me up as a guest of the Boldon miners on a number of occasions and frequently at the Tommy Hepburn memorial prior to the Durham Miners' Gala. I had had the privilege of marching round Boldon Colliery with the lodge and the band in the last days of the pit. At 10 p. m. we meet up at the Broadway that evening anyway, and then go on to a folky party at Jim Shipley's house on Parks Road, Dunscroft,.

There is some disquiet on the top table of the Area officials over my selection to the EC. The first meeting saw the customary 'nomination' by the officials of Executive Committee members onto the various Area committees of the union. Basically, the officials recommend those who they think fit to serve the respective committees. I am not expecting to be given any influential cabinet position. I wasn't wrong; they appointed me to the Gala Committee, to help plan and organise the annual gala with the Administration Officer. I couldn't do any harm there – it was non-controversial. Or so they thought. The gala of 1983 was well under way and in full flight when some of the old branch stalwarts started to ask, 'Hey up, where's Coal Queen Competition this year? It in't in programme.' 'Bloody Douglass has abolished it, an't 'e?' Yep, to my credit I thought, it had long stuck in my craw. Apart from the stupefying sexist pageant that it was, this was the NCB's Coal Queen! Bonny though many of the pitmen's daughters were, the queen was a propaganda piece, a symbol of joint collaboration between industry and union at a time when they were about to turn all their guns on us. Bollocks to that. Oh, there were some wailings and gnashings of teeth, but it never came back. I didn't like the 'Miss Miner's Lamp' either. Emma had summed it up: 'Won't all those little girls who didn't get picked think they aren't pretty any more and be sad?' She was seven or eight when she made this observation and was of course dead right. No, I didn't mind the baby show or the fancy-dress competition, or surprisingly the fashion show – it was aimed at the women attending the gala and was drawn from local designers and dress shops in the coalfields, although it attracted the odd group of leering tipsy pit lads with no intention of buying anything.

July 1982. We are taking strike action at pits all over Yorkshire, in support of the struggle of the NHS workers. It is more than a 'nurses' dispute'. Hatfield as the result of my coaxing has been in the fore of the struggle.

As we agenda'd yet another strike day, some rumblings of discontent were heard throughout the mine. Hatfield had struck more than any other mine, with the possible exception of Markham Main, who had struck on the same days as us. The meeting at the welfare was packed to capacity. My old marra Jimmy Wood tells me two-thirds of the men have come to the meeting to vote against any further days of action. But I had a cunning plan, as Baldric would have said. I had let it be known that I was proposing 3 consecutive days of strike action, and let the rumour rip. When I took to the platform I gave it some welly for almost an hour, but I pulled the punch at the end, and said that the call for 3 days of action was too much considering how many days we had already fought, and received a standing ovation and near unanimous vote for one-day strike action instead. We also went down to picket at the DRI.[24] Groups of health workers and nurses stood around at the gates a little confused. We took charge of the situation at once, with the nurses in front and the miners as backup. Only essential materials and emergency cases would get through. The first ambulance to come sailing up through the picket line I stopped, much to everyone's dismay.

'What you got on?' I asked, as if it was a fuel tanker.

'I'm delivering mail,' the driver replied.

'Do you know why?' I asked.

'Well, not really,' the frightened driver replied.

'Because the postal workers are out on strike in support of your union and your job,' I bellowed.

'Well nobody told me what to do.'

'Here's what you do,' I replied. 'Go and park your ambulance over there, outside this line, and come and join us standing here because you're on strike.'

Which he did, and became an enthusiastic picket. We stopped a whole convoy of builders' wagons and trucks going into the back onto the new extension work. Emma sat by the Hatfield NUM Branch banner, which we had erected on the gates of the DRI, with a sign saying, 'I was born in this hospital, I support the Health Workers.' There was no nastiness this time; last time we had gone along to Bootham Lane bus depot to picket out the bus drivers from their first shift. The TGWU had said the strike was up to individuals. Some of the drivers not only crossed the picket lines, they crossed them two or three times doing the shifts of those drivers who had taken the day off. At one point after a bus swept round a corner and almost gave me the treatment poor Freddie Matthews got in the '72 strike, with me nearly pinned against an iron gate and the bus brushing past me, tempers got really frayed. Jimmy Wood yelled out, 'I've got three full lemonade bottles here. The next bus through this line gets one through the front window, till you cool down a bit!' The first of the drivers to join us, a young girl, got out of her cab and ragged up, followed by a number of others. Some, though, scabbed and scabbed until their hearts and wallets were content. Next time, we resolved, we would fix the buses before the start of their shifts. As it turned out, they joined us, operating an emergency service only. Mind, the bloody bin men were going their rounds, and we had quite a run-in with them.

'Aah, you'd soon complain if your bin wasn't emptied,' one of them opined.

You what?' we yelled. 'We're losing a day's wages and week's bonus, in support of your flaming union, and you think we're bothered about the bins not getting emptied?'

The nurses in general at the DRI kept a special place for the miners of Markham and Hatfield, and for years afterwards thanked us for our stand.

Well, someone thought I had some literary judgement and merit as they allowed me to start writing shorter book reviews for the *New Statesman*. This may seem small beer to some, but to me it was an amazing achievement: I was actually being paid for my writing. Plus I got a regular book hot off the press, which ensured I had to read and think about it, and someone thought my views sensible enough to print. Ironically, I suppose, one of the first I got to review was *Jarrow March*, by my fellow Geordie Jarra Lad Tom Pickard. Tom had been a terrific influence on my thinking and writing. He was part of that beat scene, the northern edge of the Ginsberg revolution, a working-class poet and speaker. His *Guttersnipe* actually inspired me to write this whole autobiography in the part dialect style I have done. I managed here and there to collect all his works. This *Jarrow March* was a terrific piece of art and history in fusion. There was to have been more. Alan Price at first came up with the idea of doing a TV drama/documentary using Tom's format of poetry and voices from the past and pictures with captions and poems, with Pricey's music of course. Alan was like me and Tom a Jarrow lad, although not in that order as I think they two were older than me, a little. Tom was doing some work for the BBC and Alan was down in London for the programme, in fact had been installed in a smart London flat. As luck would have it, the street on which Tom and Alan Price were living turned out to be Balcombe Street.

Anybody who knows Alan knows him to be a chronic paranoiac. For some reason known only to himself he thinks people are out to do him serious harm. Something like the way cats will always seek out and sit on people who have a cat allergy, events tended to feed Alan's paranoia.

Now here he was on Balcombe Street, a quiet, upper middle-class street in central London. Tom was happily installed along the same street in a flat loaned while he worked on the *Jarrow March* film/TV project.

As luck would have it, a crack unit of the Provisional IRA got holed up in the Balcombe Street flat of Mr and Mrs Matthews. They weren't invited, and it wasn't supposed to be an extended stay. They were fleeing a gun battle in Mayfair. The arrival of the armed police and special shoot-to-kill units of the British army ensured they were now in a hostage situation.

It is late evening and Tom is standing on his balcony watching the cops running up and down shouting to each other (which I am certain they do when they can't actually think of anything useful to do), getting searchlights in place, diving about, pointing guns up and down the street. The phone rings. It's Alan.

'There's loads of blokes with guns and black suits! I'm for the off, me, tha gaana shoot 'is, man, what'l' Ah dey?'

'Look Al, tha not here for ye man, there's an exercise or something gaan on man.'

'Nor man, divind be stupid. This just happens to be the street that Alan Price lives on, huw the hell tha knaa that man, someone's gunnin for is.'

'Tha not, man, its a film or someit.'

'Ower real for that, ya, bullshittin' is, what'll Ah dey?'

'Look Al, put the leets oot, shut the door, gaan an sit in the wardrobe, be still, have a kip, Ah'l come for ye when its all ower.'

Which Alan actually does, a bit like drawing the covers up ower ya heed, when ya a kiddha and somethings gone 'bump' in the neet. Tom, meantime, gets a chair and goes out on the balcony with a six-pack, to watch and observe the drama. He is a great collector of emotions and events, which he stores away for future imagery in his poetry, and he wishes he had a movie camera – he could incorporate some of this in the film. He's deep in thought, watching like an owl on some lofty roost, when suddenly a searchlight beam picks him out, feet up on the balcony, chair leaned back, can of broon in one hand, notebook in the other. The cops are down below, crouching and laying, guns at the ready, handguns and Sten guns, rifles with telescopic sights,

'You! You up there!' the chief inspector with the gold braid round the cap and the loudhailer in hand is shouting: 'You, sir!'

Tom: 'What's up, like?'

'Get back inside your building!'

'Ah'm watching!'

'Get back inside the building!'

Tom moves back into the shadow of the doorway and puts the light out, repositions his chair, opens another can. It was some time later, just as Tom decided to gaan a bed, and tek a break, he remembered Alan. Coming down the stairs in his jamas and sandals and out the front door to slooter towards Pricey's flat, half asleep, he quite forgot that lying in every doorway was a spread-eagled cop with a rifle. Little red dots focused on his back as he walked down the deathly quiet street, and into Al's. He was asleep leaning in the wardrobe as Tom let himself in and put him to bed, assuring him it was all over.

Five days later, one of the IRA team comes on the siege balcony and says they will talk. A telephone is lowered down. The hostages are exchanged for hot sausages, Brussels sprouts, peaches and cream. Well, we've all been there I suppose; I don't feel so bad about the embassy occupation in Havana now. A day later, they surrender, intact and still alive along with the poor couple who happened to live in the street. I can't help think that today the whole incident would have been handled differently with everyone in the flat, 'hostages' and guerrillas blown to kingdom come by some SAS unit, determined to demonstrate that you don't take up armed struggle in London, rather than actually save anyone's life. Eeh but what if they'd actually picked Alan's pad? It might have cured his paranoia.

Martin O'Connell, Edward Butler, Harry Duggan and Hugh Doherty were nicked. They had in their whirlwind assignment assassinated Ross McWhirter and carried out 20 bombings, 10 of them in 5 days. Why McWhirter? The world couldn't understand why the super-intelligent Ross, co-compiler of the *Guinness Book of Records* should be targeted, and nobody ever explained. In fact, Ross McWhirter was up to his armpits in extreme right-wing, anti-union, anti-working-class, anti-communist, anti-republican organisations and causes, many of which he funded. Not a nice man from our position. In fact when I was over in the States and round a few Irish Bars in New York, I knocked together in my head a little ditty which I performed then and there, to the tune of 'The Girl I Left Behind Me':

McWhirter died some days ago, he left me all his riches:
A wooden head and a poisoned tongue and country full of leeches.
A band of bold determined men,
Of fascist-thugs and Mafia.
Oh, you might cry but you might just find
I've pissed meself with laughter
Oh we give him the lead in the back of the head and said
'Good-bye ye bastard!'

The team was charged with 10 murders and 20 bombings and jailed for life. They were eventually freed under the terms of the Good Friday Agreement in April 1999, after 24 years apiece. Tom told me the story while I was attending his *The Writer In The City* stage production in London in 1983. I was a guest, as a singer, in amang the Geordie poets Barry MacSweeney, Tom, and the showing of the film *Quayside*. I went with Rachael,[25] who found the whole experience unique. I had stayed at Raph's place with her, and we shared a bed and some heavy petting but we were not yet having full-on sex and Rachael was still a virgin. She wasn't going to jump into anything she wasn't quite sure of. Both Tom and Raph were quite taken with Rachael and how young and beautiful she was.

December 1982. We lose the second industrial ballot this year. This time it wasn't Gormley, the press or the NCB – though the latter two had pulled out all the stops to defeat the ballot – but the stupid decision to link wages and pit closures on the same ballot paper, with a single answer for both. 'Are you in favour of taking industrial action to stop closure of pits except on grounds of exhaustion or safety, and in order to secure a substantial wage increase – Yes or No?' It was words to the effect of, but what it meant was the men who were prepared to fight on closures felt on pain of agreeing to job losses had to vote in favour of strike action on wages, which they didn't want to take on. They felt they were being conned, and the TV satirists had a field day. The Union's tacticians for their part said they weren't trying to con anyone; the Board had told them if we were prepared to accept pit closures there would be more money in the pot for pay rises for them that were left, thus linking the two questions together. Fair enough, but that doesn't explain the one answer for the two questions, and the members didn't think it did either.

19 December 1982. Joint anti-nuclear Red Star Folk night at the Broadway. Jock Purdon and his son Gavin were the guests. Jock is a legend of the North East coalfield, a lifelong miner and singer-songwriter in the tradition of the aud pit poeties and sangsters. Like the Elliott family of Birtley, he had worked at Scotia Pit, so called because of the number of Scottish miners who worked there. About 100 people packed the upstairs room to hear Jock sing, a historic evening for many. Jock and Gavin stayed at my house; we had much in common, although Jock had found his way back to anarchism before I had. His songs expressed his deep felt frustration with the misleaders of our movement and our class. Gavin had become a great collector of pit stories and history and was the author of some fine pictorials.

July 1983. One of those rare privileges, which stand the test of time. I get to take part in a BBC documentary about the Durham Miners' Gala, an excellent presentation of history, pageant and politics. I am chuffed to wee bits to have been not just chosen by John Mapplebeck the producer but also suggested by the Durham Miners Association as a spokesman. I talk of the banners, the culture and the history but also the sex. Sex at the Durham Miners' Gala? It is little reflected on but of course for teenagers from the pit villages in the Sixties and Seventies the wave of sexual freedom swept through the ancient streets of Durham too; or more particularly its riverbanks and woods. The big fair, which accompanies the gala, is second only to the Hoppins on Newcastle Toon Moor, and what with the relaxation on drinking laws and all other laws on the point of the miners' banners, tens of thousands of mining folk young 'uns flocked there.

As we marched through the streets of Durham on that July day, a couple of old ladies in the crowd spotted me off the telly from the night before.

'Ee, ye dorty bugger!' was their comment on my revelation of 'splendour in the grass'.

'Whey, it's true to life,' I responded.

'It wes on wor day anarl,' they shouted back, 'but wi divind ta'alk aboot it!'

The Cause Of Ireland, produced by Platform Films, wins the Tyne Award at Newcastle Film Festival. No, I'm not in it; but I have watched it hatch, watched it grow, seen it groan as it is cut and left on the cutting room floor, heard it scream through the night as it fasts forward and back. Seen its grainy images so many times as the team worked on it in the Cinema Action studios at Swiss Cottage. This was Chris Reeves's work; Chris was a student of the Cinema Action team and their best graduate. Schlacke thinks it the best film to come out of their studio, a fine film. I'm not struck; it's 104 minutes, its very long, very talky, but it is grappling with complex ideas and a complex cause for a very mixed level of audience. It is more than documentary and qualitatively higher than agit-prop. The musical background is by Christie Moore. *Moving Hearts* and *People Of No Property* is a major part of the film's impact. The other major highlight is the voices and thoughts of the people of Ulster from both communities, raw and direct. The best quote comes from Harry Murray of the Ulster Loyalist Association of Workers: 'We're prepared to go to any lengths to remain British, and we'll fight anybody to remain British, even the British – that's going to the extreme. That's the way the Protestant feels in Northern Ireland.'[26] Chris was later to work tirelessly at the CA Studio to produce *The Miners' Campaign Tapes*[27] in an effort to challenge the wall of lies coming from the media about the most important dispute of the century and to offer an alternative view of what was really happening in the coalfields.

October 1983. The Workers Revolutionary Party launch an amazing attack upon Arthur Scargill, in particular his views on the Solidarnosc (Solidarity) union in Poland. Arthur, like many on the left believe this 'union' to be a 'scab' union insofar as its aim is the downfall of the 'Polish workers' state', and its allies are Reagan, Thatcher and every enemy of the workers' movement worldwide. WRP, along with many Trot and 'third camp' organisations support Solidarity as a genuine attempt by workers to form an independent fightback organisation free of the party and state. I issue a four-sided 'Open Letter' in response. The WRP daily paper *News Line* had launched daily attacks on Arthur, the leadership of the NUM and in many ways the union itself. Arthur was set up for a public kicking, as they requested his view on Solidarity knowing damn well he would condemn it and they would leap to its defence and 'expose' him. They held onto this coup for 6 weeks until the TUC Conference, when they let it burst on the scene just at a time when the bourgeois press was raving about Arthur's attempt to guarantee support for the impending action with the NCB and the government. It was seized upon as a rope to trip us at the first hurdle. For my efforts, the *News Line* ruthlessly condemns me in a massive article by Mike Banda, the national secretary of WRP and up until this point a regular visitor to my home.[28]

Two years later the WRP implodes, and throws up three factions, all distorted and spitting fire. Banda regroups his team, abandons Trotskyism, which he now describes as the biggest disaster ever to hit the labour movement, and re-embraces his Stalinist roots. Healy and Redgrave go on to form the Marxist Party, and this then further splits and one wing becomes the 'A World To Win' tendency. Ee whey, what goes around … My enemy's enemy is my friend? On the back of the scandalous WRP attack against Arthur, the *Yorkshire Miner* and me – and in reality the NUM as such – the Spartacist League launch a series of rallies in support of Arthur's position, declaring that Solidarnosc is counter-revolutionary! I am invited to speak from their platform in Sheffield and then at a mass meeting at the Broadway, which I enthusiastically agree to and decide that the war between us is now over and we can conduct things on a more rational political level. I am a moth circling a lightbulb.

2

FIELDS OF DESTRUCTION, BAPTISMS OF FIRE:
THE GREAT COAL STRIKE OF 1984/85

Thatcher came to power with vision and a mission. Along with Reagan in America, she clung to a kind of fundamentalist fire-and-brimstone creed: the free market, control of the money supply, while abolishing controls on currency exchange, dismantling the welfare state, creation of mass pools of unemployed (it rose to 3.25 million in 1981)[29] to drive down wages and conditions, smashing the power of the unions. The vision was one of individualism, stand on your own two feet, 'end of society', promotion of individual ownership and private debt in order to achieve it. The whole concept of 'society' was suspect; municipalisation was mini-socialism, and local government must be increasingly stripped of its powers. Profit was the sole criterion of worth.

The unions, of course, had a vision and a mission, which was diametrically opposed to hers. A clash was inevitable. To this extent – the reality of Thatcher and her programme, and the existence of the trade union movement – conflict was preordained. The presence or non-presence of Arthur Scargill could in no way affect this fact. Had Arthur not been born, the clash would still have occurred, although obviously it may not have occurred in exactly the same way. I say this because virtually all the histories of the strike written by outside commentators and media academics have floundered and come to grief because of their focus on Arthur as central to there being a strike. This history will dispute that and hopefully fit Arthur into the correct context of events.

Thatcher knew that 'the storm troops of the TUC', or rather of the union movement, were the National Union of Mineworkers. She had two stated tasks on that front – defeat the NUM as a social force to implement her assault on the unions per se; and withdraw state support for the massive mining industry, cut it down to levels of unit profitability and privatise it. Meantime, break the hold of the unions over energy and transport of energy. This would involve building up private road transport, from union-controlled rail to non-union private hauliers. It would involve dual fuel sources into conventional power stations, and the development of long-term nuclear energy to ensure that coal, its miners, transporters and power users could never challenge government and big employers in those strategic fields again. This much is surely agreed. That being the case, how could one possibly draw the conclusion that Arthur Scargill was responsible for the clash? The miners were in the cross-hairs; we truly could fight with a chance we might win, or we could surrender without a fight and lose. The industrial history of Britain, and Thatcher's elaborate and long-term planning strategies, demonstrate that she knew that the miners – with or without Scargill – would fight and fight like there was going to be no tomorrow. Every page of the miners' history will point to that conclusion.

The Myron Plan I have discussed earlier, but that bold vision drafted in 1973 clearly had become the base foundation, the basic scenario of almost everything that was to follow. Thatcher was well known for her class war credentials. To use a quote from the 1920s, she was to the employers what anarcho-syndicalism was to the labour movement. She and Keith Joseph had bitterly opposed Edward Heath's strategy in attempting to defeat the miners in 1974; they believed the challenge should have been made head-on using all the might of the state. I have outlined the possible consequences such a policy would have evoked; certainly, there were many determined forces on our side ready and willing to take it on.

It was a strategy she was to return to in the future, only this time we were to be less prepared in every conceivable way. The years between Heath's going and the Tories' re-election were spent elaborating Thatcher's plan; defeat of the unions in general and the miners in particular were absolutely essential to their entire programme. Nicholas Ridley drew up the blueprint; it included systematic stockpiling of coal at power stations, provision for the long-term mass importation of foreign coal via the ports, withdrawal of state benefits from strikers and their children and dependants, and the creation of specially trained police squads, nationally coordinated to prevent the success of miners' flying pickets. It called for the creation of an army of non-union private lorry drivers to block solidarity by railworkers, and the transferring of increasing amounts of fuel from rail to road. Long term, it would aim at an energy policy based on an expanding nuclear industry at the expense of coal.

Within weeks of the Thatcher government's election came the start of a stream of legislative assaults on union 'rights'. There were tighter and tighter constraints on ways of launching industrial action, and secondary action so called would be open to legal sanction. Additionally, a number of secret state bodies were set up to take on what were perceived as the 'enemies of democracy': militant trade unionism, communists of all descriptions. Arthur Scargill loomed high among the personal targets of these bodies.

One of these covert organisations called itself 'Shield'. The chief figure in this shadowy organisation was Brian Crozier, a man with MI6 and CIA credentials. One of his more public works was *The Reds Are Back,* a consultative document examining political activists in the unions. Arthur and the NUM were subject to his special attentions. Ten years on from that time, and retired, Mr Crozier made no secret of his close liaison with Mrs Thatcher in relation to the NUM and its leadership. In an excellent revisitation of the period, I teamed up with Nick Wood, the BBC's industrial correspondent, in the making of Look North's excellent exposure documentary *The Big Picture.* Crozier was frank in his interview with Nick:

> I had made a study of subversion and particularly subversion in Trade
> Unions, and the committee [Shield] as a whole had a lot of expertise to
> bring to the matter, so I think she was very pleased to have this advice.[30]

Margaret Thatcher had said that she would honour the *Plan For Coal,* guaranteeing the British coal industry and power generation; but by the beginning of 1981, plans were afoot to destroy it. The NCB at the government's behest were operating policies which were already producing colliery closures. But the real sign of the intention to disregard the *Plan For Coal* came in an announcement in February 1981 when the Coal Board said that they had to bring the 'supply of coal into line with demand' and said that this could only be done be reducing output – in other words through the closure of pits.

Ian MacGregor had been appointed chairman of the NCB amid great controversy; he came with a track record. In 1979 he had been approached (probably by Sir Keith Joseph) to head up British Steel which he did in 1980, with a transfer fee of £875,000 to his Lazards Company.[31] Remarkably, he had been introduced into British industrial relations by a desperate Jim Callaghan as a part-time director of the nationalised motor industry giant British Leyland. His brief clearly was to take on the car workers – and their rank-and-file leader, Red Robbo (Derek Robinson), was the first scalp he claimed, along with shop floor power and the general standing of the formal union. He went through the government-owned British Steel like a dose of salts. He remorselessly closed down steel plants and shed steel jobs wholesale. Under his direction the workforce fell from 166,000 in 1979 to 71,000 in 1983. The steelworkers had lost their belly for a fight after an unsuccessful 13 weeks on strike just prior to Mac's appointment. Mac went over the heads of the unions and balloted the workforce directly on his redundancy and closure programme; like turkeys voting for Christmas they agreed. It was for us a sign of things to come.

Arthur Scargill had in 1980 revealed NCB plans for the closure of 50 pits and the elimination of roughly 50,000 jobs. The NCB condemned and denied the figures. But a year later (10 February 1981) the NCB chairman Sir Derek Ezra announced a plan to close up to 50 pits and cut 30,000 jobs. This revelation led to the first serious shot in what was to become all-out war: strike action by South Wales was soon followed by Kent, Scotland, Durham and Yorkshire. By 23 February 1981 the NCB withdrew the list and the government announced it was reviewing its financial policy for the coal industry, pledging to continue its support for the *Plan For Coal*.[32]

The NCB under Thatcher's direction moved quickly to savage the unsuspecting ranks of the miners, launching a new and thoroughgoing pit closure programme, while Joe the aud moderate is still asleep at his desk. They declare unconditionally 25 pit closures and the loss of 25,000 jobs. At precisely the same time, they nakedly announce to the 'surviving' pits that they must take up the slack in lost production, meeting the same tonnage targets with 25 less pits and 25,000 less men. The blows would fall in South Wales, Scotland, Durham, Yorkshire and elsewhere. Despite the inaction of the National leadership, the new leadership-elect was already in the wings; the militants were still in the ascendancy. The Yorkshire Area had been hammering home the impending challenge for 12 months and more. There was immediate strike action. No ballot – flying pickets called out pit after pit, or else they just struck using their own initiative when the news filtered through.

As soon as the new Thatcher offensive was launched, a wildcat leapt from coalfield to coalfield bringing out South Wales, Kent, Scotland, Yorkshire and Durham. The rest of the coalfields called for action from 23 February until the closures were withdrawn. By 18 February almost all the coalfields were at a standstill, pits jumping the deadline date and joining those already out in other areas. It led to a radical rethink by the government. We now know Thatcher was taken totally aback and was informed that nothing was ready from their side for a prolonged and united strike by the miners. They decide to buy time and back off. It was Arthur's view that we should press on now while the metal was hot, but that is not the prevailing view nationwide. Gormley was still ostensibly National president though Arthur was president-elect. Gormley and some hand-picked members of the NEC, though not all, meet the NCB chiefs and David Howell, who withdraws the plan. He promises that any future pit closure will go through the normal lengthy consultation machinery. Thatcher declares she wants no fight with the miners.[33] Howell, though, was doubled-dyed. It was he who had proposed the secret Cabinet committee convened to lay a plan to take on and defeat the miners, and had made long-term nuclear power the ace in his pack.[34] The NCB and government issued statements that they had met the miners' demands; the closure threats were withdrawn. The small print said nothing whatever about how long this would be the case or gave any guarantee that pits would not close except on grounds of proven exhaustion or safety. Arthur believed then, and even more so later in hindsight of subsequent events, that we had them by the balls and we were in the winner's seat, that we were fools to let go and let them regroup and come back for us once we had shown our hands. History would prove he was right. We thought the blow was a body blow and a knockout; but we just winded them and warned them how to dodge our punch when it came next time. We warned them that area wildcats were the likely response, so they would know to work on weakening the areas one from the other. They gave themselves 2 years and a bit more to prepare their battle forces. Did we do enough to secure our own forces and those of the allies we most assuredly would need? It was our 'Red Friday'.[35] In the intervening 3 years another 9 million tonnes of coal was put into stocks. Total stocks by the start of the 1984 strike would stand at 48.7 million tonnes.[36] But the point is, here was another semi-official/unofficial strike, like the one that broke in 1969, driving the bosses and government into a corner, and no ballot. Nobody is crying 'Ballot, Ballot, Ballot' because it's the other side that've launched the attack on us, and we're simply responding to it. Stopping the assault is seen as the task, not sticking to the terms of rules drawn up for premeditated and long-considered action. Nobody cried 'ballot' in 1969, mainly I guess because it was called against the concerted opposition of the NUM National leadership, perhaps also because it was essentially successful.

In his autobiography, NCB chairman Sir Ian MacGregor put it like this:

> She [Mrs. Thatcher] looked calmly around the battlefield, examined her forces, recognised that she was outmanoeuvred by the enemy – and wisely withdrew in relatively good order, if somewhat bloodied in the process.

His more detailed assessment reveals:

> There was very little coal in stock ... the TGWU's grip on haulage was still too tight.

It was, in the words of Mick McGahey, National vice-president of the NUM and the leader of the Scottish mineworkers, 'a body swerve'. Few thought the government's commitment to the *Plan For Coal* was genuine or long lasting. There was something of Red Friday 1926 in it, when the Conservative government of Stanley Baldwin declared they would provide a subsidy to maintain the miners' wages, which appeared as a victory forced by working-class solidarity; in fact the plan all along was to buy time for the mine owners, and for the government to prepare for the coming struggle. The parallel with 1926 was not lost on Arthur Scargill.

Arthur had been passed secret documents by leading NCB officials in the autumn of 1982, which highlighted the government's long-term closure plans. The Government denied the existence of such a plan. Arthur observed:

> The government's £230 million subsidy to our industry for one year represents an insult when compared with the aid given in all Common Market coal producing countries. In West Germany, the subsidy is £35 per tonne, whilst in Belgium it is a massive £105. Even in Eastern Europe there are huge subsidies of over £30 per tonne, whilst we receive less than £2 per tonne plus the additional aid for one year only.[37]

But there was a case anyway that a narrow definition of 'profit' and 'loss' was never the yardstick by which the *Plan For Coal* had been drafted and agreed. Coal was a national asset, it was something the island had in great volumes. We should mine it, and use it. It was a generator not simply of power, but of everything made and built of steel, plus a million and one by-products. It was also the motivator for advanced mining technologies and the manufacture of mining equipment with a high export value. The employment of large numbers of workers in a high-income industry acted as a classic 'multiplier', the purchasing power of the coal communities repaying many times the value of the investment in the industry. In terms of health and safety and working conditions, although the pit was still the pit, this was the safest, most advanced mining industry in the world; that it tended to be more expensive in cash terms was a saving in terms of blood, bones and bodies. The idea that, say, farming would have to meet the criteria of profitability and price against the world agricultural market, and those farms that couldn't produce as cheaply as anywhere in the world would be closed, with farm workers dispersed or dumped, and farms demolished, would have sounded stupid. It would have decimated the countryside, produced millions of rural poor and made the whole island dependent solely on imports to feed itself. Besides, the rural areas of this fair and pleasant land had traditions of Tory voting, conservative patriotic values, a sense of knowing one's place, which ensured agriculture and coal would be given two entirely different market criteria and treatments.

If there was any doubt about which way events were turning, Peter Walker, the new secretary of state for energy, made things perfectly clear when he reaffirmed the government's determination to deregulate public sector control, arguing that British Coal should operate within a context set by market forces, and receive no subsidies.[38]

Against this backdrop of government deception and the looming peril of pit closures, between 1980 and the start of the strike proper in March 1984, industrial action against the impending closures began in earnest. There were false starts in Scotland, Durham and more importantly in South Wales. As mentioned in the previous chapter, in 1982 had come the disastrous attempt to link a whole shopping list of wage and condition demands to a stand against pit closures. But there was only room for one 'yes' or 'no' to the whole diverse question. The idea was to use the opposition to pit closures to spark action on wages, but it backfired: the men voted against action, making it look like they had lost their resolve to fight closures.

In fact, Conference demands were routinely loosing track of tactical reality. Nobody ever would oppose demands for higher wages, earlier pensions, less hours, more holidays etc. and they all sailed through, but they were now *all* linked to demands to 'consult the members on strike action' if the NCB turned down the demands. The rank and file knew, better than their delegates dared to say, that the powder had to be kept dry for the looming big fight on closures. In fact the wage offer from the NCB was 8% on top of incomes, which were high by comparison to any comparable workers; 8% was enough to keep wages from becoming a strike issue. But 'going back to the well' of proposed industrial action too many times was testing our credibility. We had cried wolf a little too often perhaps, when in March 1983 the NUM held a national ballot in support of strike action to back the South Wales Area's strike against pit closures. A sign of things to come was my village witnessing the first mobilisation of women with homemade banners and their kids demanding support for South Wales and Merthyr Lewis. Diane Richardson came from a Welsh mining family and her brother and husband worked at Hatfield; she was out with her kids in defence of her old coalfield and the implicit threat to this new one. We quickly staged a mass Branch Meeting and the Branch voted to strike with Merthyr and Wales. On Monday 28 February the Yorkshire Area as a whole voted to stand with the Lewis men and strike alongside them. 65,000 men would be called through their branches to stand from Sunday 6 March. The similarities to later events in both content and dates are striking. (No pun intended.) Tragically, though, and I do not pretend to understand through what process or on whose advice, the unofficial strike action that had stopped the NCB in its tracks 2 years earlier was not given its head. The South Wales Area could reasonably have sought national endorsement for strike action under rule 41. The action would have been no more than an unofficial area wildcat, but what if it had been? So had the successful action in 1981. The Branch and the South Wales Area instead called for and launched a national ballot vote of the members. We lost the national ballot. The press had for months been constantly vilifying Scargill, with some sections of the 'left' joining in.

The tactical blunder of the 1982 wages/closure ballot was still fresh in members' heads, and perhaps the threat of piecemeal area closures wasn't being taken seriously enough, wasn't seen as an overall common issue. Everyone it seemed could quote some pit closure issue nobody had taken up. Most recent was the case of Kinneil in Scotland, where the rank and file took up the issue with little enthusiasm from their area leadership. Many regarded the failure to mobilise on Kinneil a 'sell-out', which then impacted on the ballot for Lewis. It had certainly impacted on the decision of the Snowdown men in Kent not to take up the fight or utilise the ballot vote of their area backing the action. Demoralisation and high redundancy terms did the rest. In retrospect, we would have been better off if we had just let the Welsh pickets have their heads and picket throughout the country as we had done 2 years earlier.

There is much bitterness in Wales that the ballot went against them, but we try to regain the momentum. We go ahead and implement a nationwide overtime ban to reduce coal stocks, to stop redundancies, and to halt closures. For the rank and file the argument couldn't be clearer. We were being told there was too much coal, produced by too many miners. If we only turn coal on five shifts and do not produce coal in overtime maybe they will find that there actually are only enough men and pits to meet demand. That's quite aside from any strategic consideration of the coal stocks and the power supply.

Yorkshire miners had made a commitment to all-out action in support of the Welsh coalfield, but many thought the support given by area leaderships in the run-up to the ballot was half-hearted if not hostile. We aren't doing well with ballots. This is to rebound later when Yorkshire miners call in turn for support from Welsh miners. On 1 November 1983 we begin industrial action in the form of the overtime ban against the intended wave of pit closures. Of course, this is not an end in itself. Like all of our serious engagements in the past we are squaring up to the foe, we are trying to shift the ground on which we fight to our advantage. We must lower production, cut stocks at pitheads and power stations and, at the same time, ensure that our men are still earning a living wage. Tactically we have to try resisting all urges and provocations to get us to engage in all-out strike action until we 'see the whites of their eyes' as it were. During this time the NCB will let loose a host of provocations. The lefty paper-sellers on the gates will chastise us for not taking up this or that local dispute and for not bringing the troops out at every turn. They do not understand that workers – even miners – only have a limited capacity for all-out action. We are saving our shot for the big fight. The problem for us is: how far we allow the enemy to advance into our territory before we are forced to engage with them? The longer this overtime ban continues, the weaker they grow, and the stronger we become.

The impact of this ban, was, without too much cost to our own side, shifting the balance of strategic power back in the direction of the miners. Doubtless this was a factor in the NCB trying to jump start the all-out action early before the stocks dropped too low to sustain a drawn-out conflict.

Six months before the start of the strike, MacGregor met with Thatcher to plan how to provoke it and take it on. This was revealed 25 years ago but nobody picked it up and the latest books on the issue still don't recognise it. Mac had talked of a short Falklands-style engagement of about 6 months duration. He told Thatcher his 'three golden rules' in getting the strike started. One was don't engage in a struggle of wages – 'it will always end in a settlement'; never have a strike unless it is about a crucial issue, like 'the right to manage'; and finally don't take it on if you aren't going to see it through. MacGregor, in *Business Magazine*, an influential business executive publication, tells of how he 'persuaded the Prime

Minister to force Arthur Scargill into beginning the strike in the first week of March 1984'. This revelation at the time had the government in a flat spin of denial, and Peter Walker, the energy secretary, put extreme pressure on Mac to retract the story. With £1½ million still owed by the government to him for his 'services', he quickly issued a statement saying the mag had misquoted him. The magazine, a highly prestigious journal of top business and finance writers, was adamant they quoted him word for word, as well they might since it was part owned by MacGregor himself.[39]

6 March 1984. The NCB announces its plans for 20,000 job losses and the closure of 20 pits over the coming year. They have already moved to close Polmaise in Scotland, Snowdown in Kent, Bullcliffe Wood and Cortonwood in Yorkshire, and Herrington in Durham. If those closures steam through without resistance and we make no stand at this point, it will become clear to them that the whole programme could be introduced piecemeal, picking off collieries within areas in apparently uncoordinated sets of selective closures, while sticking firmly to the national closure plan. Worse still, they have reasons to be optimistic, as earlier efforts to generate national action, particularly the ballot for action in support of Merthyr Lewis in Wales, had failed.

Someone once said, 'If your opponent is sitting holding all the aces, the only answer is to kick the table over.' A recent book, *Marching to the Fault Line*, reveals that actually it was the NCB who had kicked the table over and prematurely started the strike, which is confusing because *they* thought they were sitting with a winning hand. On 1 March 1984[40] the strike proper started when George Hayes, the South Yorkshire NCB director, announced that Cortonwood would close in 5 weeks time. This was a challenge we couldn't ignore. The authors now say *it was a mistake* – Hayes had misunderstood his brief. He had jumped the gun and lit the blue touch paper on the NUM's cannon. The authors have made an astounding amount of this interesting but very marginal aside. *So what?* The authors go on to say *MacGregor* was supposed to announce plans to cut *20,000* jobs 6 days after Hayes had jumped the gun. Which he in fact went on to do, confirming the suspicions that Cortonwood was the tip of very big iceberg. 20,000 jobs equates to roughly 20 or more mines.[41] The authors claim that Hayes spoiled Mac's national strategy. He had predicted he would make the announcement to the union as a whole. The union NEC would call a Conference and a national ballot, we'd lose the strike vote, and the closures would sail through. But by the time of the announcement the troops were in the field, the pickets were already flying and Yorkshire was stood. The strike had started by other direct means.

But who says Yorkshire, or Scotland, or Wales, or Kent, or Durham and Northumberland, or any of the areas now gearing up for strike action to defend their own mines and those of other areas, would have waited for a Conference and national ballot? We had already had a ballot in Yorkshire anyway, giving authority to the officials to call industrial action if a pit was threatened in Yorkshire. You wouldn't have to be a strategic genius to work out that among the twenty there would be pits in Yorkshire. Even without that Yorkshire Area ballot, branches would have held mass meetings and taken decisions to strike off their own bat. So I believe Beckett and Hencke are making far too much of a small and slightly amusing feature that was to make no long-term difference to the outcome of events. Indeed, had things went the way Mac expected and had there been a national ballot without the pickets flooding over the border from Yorkshire then it's possible Nottingham might have voted to strike. It is doubtful – among the 20 MacGregor named not one Notts pit was included, and Notts had struck in 1981 against closures too.

7 March. MacGregor meets the NUM NEC. And formally announces 20,000 job losses and over 20 pit closures.

The Yorkshire Area (NUM) Council[42] proposed we would strike from 9 March, effectively from Saturday the 10th. There had been no time for an Area Executive meeting; that wasn't held until 26 March, by which time the strike was up and running. I make this point because most of the 'histories' of the strike by academics and journalists have no idea how the strike started and through what process.

The Yorkshire miners voted unanimously at their Area Council meeting to strike in support of Cortonwood Colliery, from the last shift on Friday 9 March 1984; that this would be the recommendation to mass pithead and welfare hall meetings, held that weekend, and that we seek the endorsement and approval of the members for this course of action. Cortonwood had been guaranteed 5 years employment following the completion of extensive development work; men had been transferred there from the closed Elsecar Colliery just 3 weeks previously on that basis. Votes were taken at mass meetings at every pit.

Arthur now tells us it was *he* who drew up a resolution, to put to the Council meeting, which called upon Yorkshire to strike; he gave it to Jack Taylor, he says. As if Jack Taylor, the Area president, needed to be told how to draft such a resolution. In fact, the decision of Council came directly in support of Cortonwood's own resolution, whatever Arthur may have written on the back of a brass band programme (at the Band Festival in Sheffield that Sunday evening). Both the press and Arthur himself often think he is of far more importance than he actually is to many situations.

My own pit met on 10 March. 1,800 men turned up to it, as well they might, with the TV screens announcing a showdown, and with all the clubs interrupting the turns to announce the meeting, and with loudspeaker cars touring the villages. We voted as did all the other pits in Yorkshire to strike with Cortonwood and until the total closure programme was withdrawn (3 against).[43] From 12 March every pit in Yorkshire was standing, with the mass enthusiastic support and votes of the members.

These are the facts. The Cortonwood Branch (Arthur Scargill wasn't in the Cortonwood Branch) tabled the motion for Yorkshire to strike. It was presented to the Yorkshire Area for debate on Monday 5 March and the Cortonwood men lobbied the meeting. Arthur didn't make any recommendations or speak at the crucial meeting because he wasn't 'in' Yorkshire; he was National president and didn't attend Yorkshire Area meetings. The decision to strike was made at pitheads, by the members, over the weekend of 10–11 March; Scargill wasn't present at any of them. So whatever Arthur may or may not have said to the media it *was not* Arthur Scargill who called the strike. Arthur had no means of 'calling the miners out on strike'. Miners do not get called out on strike except by their mates. The NEC met on 8 March and ruled that it would endorse as official the strikes against closures in Scotland and Yorkshire that they presumed (it must be said – because at this stage only Cortonwood (in Yorkshire) was on strike at that time on this issue) would result from the branch meetings over the following 2 days.

Incidentally, 'the Yorkshire Area' did not sanction pickets going over the border in Nottingham prior to the Notts ballot. This was a totally unofficial Doncaster action, which I, as elected picket planner for the Doncaster NUM Panel, did not plan or approve of. It was a spontaneous flush of enthusiasm with probably more than a hint of involvement by the SWP 'hole in the wall gang' from Armthorpe pit, tearing off to kick-start the picket. Actually, we had elaborate plans for picketing and didn't need the wildcat, which at this time was unhelpful in my view, but it wasn't planned by any formal structure of the NUM at any level, unless one calls the miners welfare clubs part of the 'Yorkshire Area'.[44] A left myth has since been constructed from this that 'the union' or 'the officials at Barnsley' tried to suppress picketing. We didn't: the whole plan *was* to picket out the coalfields with rolling area actions; we had simply yielded to a request from Nottingham not to picket the coalfield until they had had a chance to address pithead meetings and try and get a ballot decision in favour of area strike action alongside Yorkshire, Scotland and Kent.

Let us be clear: the union's overall perspective had been to keep in place an overtime ban, which had been operating for 18 weeks. The object was to reduce coal stocks and bring about conditions that are more favourable for a strike that many thought inevitable. The NCB, under the probable direction of the government, sought to provoke a strike in unfavourable conditions, as winter was passing and the coal stocks were still high. The gauntlet thrown down in Yorkshire, the strongest of the NUM's regions, was one the NUM could not ignore.

One thing that can be nailed to the floor at once is the absurd notion that the government had no involvement in the strike. Using documents now released under the 25-year rule together with the Freedom of Information Act, in *Marching to the Fault Line* Beckett and Hencke reveal that the government ran little else during that 12 months and the whole of society was left on hold in terms of expenditure, policing and much else while they fought the miners:

> Sir Robert's memo records that Peter Walker chaired a daily meeting to co-ordinate action during the strike with senior officials from the Home Office, Employment, Transport, the NCB and the Central Electricity Generating Board (CEGB). Twice weekly, on Mondays and Wednesdays, Thatcher herself chaired MISC101, the ministerial group on coal. Its purpose was to exchange information, give a ministerial steer to the line with the media and work out policy.[45]

Also dismissed can be the paper-thin legend that the police were not under the political direction of the government, or that they weren't deployed and used as an adjunct in the anti-strike government offensive. The BBC's *Inside Out North* programme, using the Freedom of Information Act, and also the expiry of the 25 years secrecy period which coincided with the twenty-fifth anniversary of the strike, found some interesting documents. One of these was a Home Office document to ACPO, and in particular to David Hall, chief superintendent of Yorkshire and Humberside Police Force. It discusses ways and means of arresting Arthur Scargill, and urges the direction of a chief constable to watch and discover the best means of doing it.[46] Just to restate that: here we have the government directing the heads of the police as to whom they should arrest for entirely *political reasons.*

It was in the early hours of 15 March when news came in of a death on the picket line at Ollerton in Nottinghamshire. The Brodsworth (Doncaster) Strike HQ log records:

1-40 a.m. Report from Hatfield, South Elmsall/Kirkby lad been hit in throat by brick. Killed. Request 'flood Ollerton'.
Informed Area, Area to inform Area Officials.

From then on the book is full of entries of branch pickets heading for Ollerton. Hatfield pickets were leaving Clipstone and Thoresby and converging on Ollerton. As was Brodsworth. As news spread, pickets started to head en masse for Ollerton. It was clear with fury and revenge in their hearts.

3-10 a.m. Jack Taylor states officials going to Ollerton. Instructs 'Do not deploy any men to Ollerton. Send to stated pits.'
4-33 a.m. Confirmation Coal Board shut Ollerton. Men deployed to other pits, all pickets to disperse. Scargill involved. 2 minutes silence observed.
4-55 a.m. F Cave requests we try to get all pickets 'to cool it'.[47]

Before David Jones collapsed and died, there had been a number of clashes between the police and the pickets. David had been in action at a number of pits in Nottingham before arriving with a flying squad at Ollerton, deployed by South Yorkshire Area. There were crowds of jeering scabs on the streets; our pickets say there were bricks flying, and one hit David in the throat before he went down. This is the version most miners accept as the reason for the cause of death.[48] What is certain is that there was no media and parliamentary outrage of the kind that greeted the later death of the taxi-driver taking a scab to work in South Wales. There was no police inquiry of any substance and no public inquiry into how David died and who killed him.

It should also be noted perhaps that many of us wished to flood Ollerton and burn the place down – the pickets wanted to vent their anger on the village and the blacklegs. While this was understandable, we were in fact in Nottingham to try and either persuade or else stop the Notts miners going to work; we were unlikely to achieve the long-term objective of stopping the whole of the coalfield if we rampaged through Ollerton and made everyone who lived there a victim of our anger. The whole situation was a powder keg. Arthur decided to call for calm, called for and got a 2-minute silence, in which time the cops withdrew and removed their helmets. In that 2 minutes, scabs ran through the lines and went to work. Even the NCB closed the colliery as a mark of respect, while the blacklegs to their eternal shame were prepared to step over the body of a dead fellow-miner in order to go to work as if nothing else in the world mattered. That has always convinced me a ballot of such gutless, selfish individuals would never have convinced them to vote for or take strike action. I have to admit that when I received the call at 2 a.m. that one of our pickets had been killed; I fell silent and dumbstruck, believing at first he was a Doncaster miner killed following one of my own deployments. The guilt made me physically sick. It was an hour later I discovered he was a South Yorkshire picket answering a deployment from their strike centre. This made no real difference, I know, but those were my feelings at the time, that I had perhaps sent this lad to his death. It was no relief whatever to his family to know who sent him. Of course, Dave was a volunteer, going willingly not to his death but to fight for his community, socialist values and the NUM. None of us expected we would start dying in that cause or that the media and political system would be utterly indifferent to it.

DECENTRALISM AND THE MINERS

One thing that has dumbfounded most of the subsequent writers and contemporary observers of this great movement is the actual structure of the miners' union. Without an understanding of this, it's hard for anyone to gauge how things happened.

The NUM is not as its title suggests a 'national union' in the ordinary meaning of the phrase. Despite its formation in 1944 as a national union, it retained its federal identity. It was a federation of separate areas and constituent bodies, each self-governing and individually registered as independent unions in their own right. Areas and constituent bodies had various numbers of full-time officials and an elected executive committee. Within the areas and constituent bodies, branches and sections enjoyed a great deal of independence and autonomy, indeed quite a few branches were also individually registered as independent unions in their own right. Any of these bodies could take action and frequently did, quite independently of each other; although the national rules suggest areas and branches seek permission to do so, they rarely if ever did. Within the branch, four officials were elected, bi-annually, two in each year, subject to recall at any time. The branch had an elected branch committee, its size depending on the size of the branch; usually there were 12, with 6 elected each year, again subject to recall.

The Yorkshire Area for example had a standing monthly 'Council' of all NUM branches in the county. It featured a delegate from every branch, the members of the Yorkshire Area Executive Committee, and the Area NUM Officials. Branches vote initially on a show of hands unless a card vote is called for, in which case branches will be allocated numbers of votes in accordance with the number of members they have. There is an Area Executive Committee drawn from the four districts of the area, in the case of Yorkshire these being North Yorkshire, Barnsley,

South Yorkshire and Doncaster. However, underlying this are the panels, semi-official bodies set up to hear reports from the Executive Committee members representing the respective districts. These panels sit as a check on the power of the Area officials and sit without them. They host all the branch officials and often numerous members of the branch committee, and sometimes rank-and-file activists. The panels often decide their own fate and take action quite outside the control and sanction of the EC or the Area. So too did they vet and debate the decisions of the EC prior to the Council meetings, and coordinated their responses to the NEC and the EC as well as preparing district support for specific branch resolutions. There was a tendency, especially during strike action, for panels to become the real source of power and direction of the strike. Within days of the start of the strike, panels had elected a picket organiser and strike planner to deploy their own district pickets and draw up plans for picket targets and strategies. In the first 6 months of the strike, the panels deployed the bulk of the pickets, and welfare and legal representation was coordinated through them. Because of fear of losing control and direction of the picket operation, the Area officials set up an Area Coordinating Committee comprising elected members from the panels. Underneath all of this, and despite the existence of already constitutional branch committees, the rank and file from the floor form a strike committee. Its logic is that the branch official or committee member elected to serve in time of industrial peace, and adequate to that moment, may not be up to the measure of the demands and tempo of the strike. The officials of the strike committee, elected en masse from the floor from mass meetings, are not necessarily the branch officials; the members of the strike committee are men of different talents and not necessarily the members of the branch committee. Formal branch committee meetings and branch meetings are still held and continue with the normal function of the branch, and so too and quite separately do the strike committee and strike meetings. Outside the whole structure, formal, informal and semi-official, are the actions of independent groups of strikers and their families, the hit squads, sometimes operating on a nod and a wink from the branch or the strike committee, sometimes totally independent, in the tradition of Rebecca and the Scotch cattle of earlier decades and centuries; they nonetheless reflect the temper and mood of the community.

When one stands back and looks at the informal and decentralised character of the miners' structures, their inherently democratic culture, the mass control and the activist input, one is confronted at once with the utterly contrasting theories of having been 'brought out on strike' or 'called out on strike' by dictatorial leaders. People who assume strict national rules and formal structures and procedures that have not existed and still do not exist offer such theories. It is a failure to understand the power of the rank and file in mining which has so damned most histories hitherto.

From the opposite pole, but just as mistaken, Workers Power, one of the tiny Trotskyist groups, prescribes for the Nottingham miners:

> They must be ordered to strike by a fixed date and addressed at mass union
> meetings by Executive members and strikers before that date. If they refuse

to obey this order they must be suspended from the union and lose all protection that it gives them. This situation will make the waverers think again ...any moves toward either a breakaway union or court action can be fought by determined action.[49]

Like going on all-out unlimited strike, one supposes?

WHO PICKED MARCH?

Why did MacGregor decide to kick-start the strike in March by confirming the closure programme? As it turned out, it matters not for the purpose of answering this question whether or not Hayes jumped the gun and started the strike around Cortonwood. He himself intended to start a reaction and start a strike ballot, which he thought would say no, but why now? Our subsequent critics on the left who thought the overtime ban was an excuse for 'no action' can't answer this question. Alternatively, there are those in the academic field or on the right who say the overtime ban was a blind ally and we were being misled into a fruitless endeavour.

In fact, it is because the overtime ban was being thoroughly effective and draining away the stocks they were so carefully stacking that it had to be ended by kick-starting the strike before the time our strategy had planned. Thatcher was warned (by Sir Walter Marshall from the CEGB) that if the overtime ban continued through the summer months, a short strike the following winter would rapidly shut the power stations and end power generation. As already mentioned in Chapter 1, coal stocks were revealed by Beckett and Hencke[50] as 48.7 million tonnes at the start of the strike. That's about a year's production for roughly a third of the industry, or 4 months' production for the entire industry. Do the maths: an overtime ban staying in place, causes the stocks to decline and not be replaced over the period of 7 or 8 months, followed by a total shutdown or even a major shutdown of weeks not months, takes away the strategic reserve then turns off the tap. Power consumption massively outstrips supply, resulting in shutdown. Gameshot. The writing on the wall and doubtless on quite a few blackboards suggested the stocks would be exhausted and they couldn't get enough from any source to replace them and keep the lights on. *That* is why the strike had to be kick-started – to displace the overtime ban we had in place, to neutralise our strategy, to start the strike prematurely, or according to Mac's calculations, lead us to have an unsuccessful ballot. We didn't pick the date to start the action, they did. With good reason.

So could we have ignored the challenge, let the 20 mines close and keep the overtime ban in place until more favourable times to launch the all-out strike action?

Hardly, with a closure programme continuing through the 7 or 8 months as we got strategically stronger, we'd have lost twenty and more mines in the process. Or as Dennis Murphy[51] used to say, 'While the grass is growing the cow is dying.' We'd have arrived at the optimum period for action but without any logic or rationale, having allowed more than 20 mines to already close without an all-out fight. The members would ask why pit closures should now be fought when

20,000 men had just walked out of the industry without a struggle. Beckett and Hencke, who aspired to write the definitive history of the strike (failing miserably in my estimation, with a book shot through with errors), claim, despite the facts, that 'Unfortunately for the union, it [the overtime ban] was too late to dent significantly the stockpile which had been built up since November 1981.'[52]

Joining the public debate which followed the twenty-fifth anniversary of the start of the strike, Maurice Jones resurfaces. Maurice was the one-time communist editor of *The Miner*, one-time comrade of Arthur Scargill, now an obsessive critic.

Jones calls the 'timing of the miners' strike a monumental misjudgement'. He of course knows we *responded* to an attack and didn't in fact pick the time or the issue. But no, he suggests, 'left wing members of the NUM's National Executive' agreed to 'allow and/or encourage "spontaneous" industrial action, creating an unstoppable momentum'.[53] He was listening at the door apparently! But this makes nonsense of the crucial strategy of the overtime ban, which ensured the opposite; he didn't listen hard enough, clearly. The point is, anyway, that *in fact* it wasn't the Union that started the action; *it was the NCB*. So given that, how should we have reacted? 'With mass community campaigns,' offers Jones – not strike action. We had to let the pits close, let the men be thrown on the scrapheap, but, just to show we were really concerned, have mass protests and street campaigns around the issue. Just how you would sit on the clamour for industrial action, or prevent it just happening anyway, we aren't told. But this, we are urged, should have been undertaken until the odds turned to us, in autumn. Comrade Jones can only make such a silly suggestion from the safety of 25 years on. The movement of the rank-and-file miners would have swept aside such a 'strategy' in favour of action. How differently he wrote 25 years previously:

> It is as though a dam has burst, bathing and enriching the land in the waters of human creativity … In the years to come historians and analysts will give their endless judgements on the strike of '84 trying to grasp the essence of the people who took part and supported this most titanic of labour struggles …
>
> Our greatest tribute however goes to all the 150,000 striking miners and their families without whose immeasurable courage, dedication compassion and loyalty the inspiration for these poems would not exist.
>
> Against all odds – the media and mounted policemen, Government, courts and Coal board – you have shifted the very centre of social gravity.[54]

As we have seen, Frank Ledger, Central Electricity Generating Board (CEGB) director of operations, had warned Thatcher that should the overtime ban continue into August (1984) then it was likely that a relatively short strike, 'say 12 weeks would be enough to put the lights out'.[55] For the government, it becomes quite clear that the start of the strike is crucial to their whole counter-strategy. The strike had to be kick-started before the overtime ban seriously weakened their stocks and supplies. Were the ban to continue as Frank had feared into August, and perhaps the strike proper had started in the November of '84, the power supply would have failed within weeks, possibly days.[56]

This point is of such vital importance to understanding events that it is worth just making it again, this time as illustrated in my book researched for the National Coal Mining Museum For England: *Strike Not the End of the Story*.

By October 1984, 6 months into the strike, the future of the government hung in the balance. There were less than 6 weeks' coal stocks left. Frank Ledger, Central Electricity Generating Board (CEGB) Director of Operations, revealed that they had only planned for the strike to last 6 months: power supply by this time was 'catastrophic'. Former chairman of the CEGB Sir Walter Marshall (who Thatcher made Lord Marshall in 1985 for 'keeping the lights on during the strike') spelt out what this meant: 'Our predictions showed on paper that Scargill would certainly win by Christmas.'[57]

Beckett and Hencke state:

Many people, including most trade union leaders, thought Scargill had been outmanoeuvred into calling a strike in March, and he would have to struggle to sustain the strike all through the summer before it started to bite in the cold days of winter when a lot of fuel would be needed.[58]

They write this ignoring their own evidence; that MacGregor had planned the announced closure of 20 pits – Mac had chosen the time to kick-start the strike. At the risk of repetition, that wasn't our strategy; our strategy, as demonstrated, was winning. Despite them choosing the optimum time to start the strike, they were far from sure of victory and all their advisers told them so. Peter Gregson, head of the Economic Secretariat at the Cabinet Office, and chair of MISC57 (the state's special secret cabinet committee established in 1981 to take on and defeat the miners), prepared a brief to Thatcher, MacGregor and Brigadier Budd, of the Civil Contingencies Secretariat of the Cabinet Office. He told them all that the stocks could last months and weeks, not a year.

Steel had 6 weeks, the cement industry 14 to 18 weeks. Domestic stocks 6 weeks. The logistics of keeping the power stations going for 6 months would necessitate using an additional 300,000 tonnes of oil *per week*, a sixfold increase in oil deliveries; an additional cost of £20 million per week. The committee went on to discuss containing pickets and widespread use of employment laws and centralised police operations.[59]

14 May 1984. Peter Gregson at the Department of Energy sent a blunt memo to Thatcher. The NCB could deliver only 1.85 million tonnes of coal to power stations. There would be huge costs to the taxpayer if the power stations were to be kept going. Gregson's memo revealed that even if the strike was called off at the end of May, the oil – 350,000 tonnes of it per week – would have to be continued to be delivered until mid September to keep the power stations open. If it ended in June, huge oil deliveries would be needed until December, while if it continued to July, oil deliveries could not be reduced until March 1985.

Say Beckett and Hencke:

The memo concluded: 'This has serious implications for costs, bearing in mind that the net extra cost of burning oil rather than coal is £20 million per week and that during the recovery period, the CEGB would be buying oil in addition (underlined) to buying coal, so that relevant figure would be the gross cost of £50m per week.[60]

Beckett and Hencke present this in the same breath as saying that Scargill was 'outmanoeuvred' and it 'was the wrong time'. We knew it was the wrong time – we didn't pick this time, but since it had been chosen for us, we would fight now; as demonstrated, that was far from foredoomed and their concerns and panics show this quite clearly.

So how did the NCB and the government react to the warnings? Beckett and Hencke write:

> Like Gregson, MacGregor saw grounds for hope that the strike might be quite short. He told Peter Walker, the Energy Secretary, that the strike would be certain to be over by May, when deductions of benefits hit miners and their families.[61]

Peter Walker, without any sort of shame apparently, tells this to Beckett and Hencke. They intended and planned to punish the miners' wives and children in order to break the strike, and they planned this as cold, calculated action: the £15 deduction from the social support payments for strikers' wives and children (a deduction by the way not made from the social support for wives and children of mass murderers, armed robbers or any other criminal), plus withdrawal of a whole range of poverty line benefits to striker's families, such as Family Income Supplement or Unemployment Benefit in the case of miners who had taken redundancy and got out in large numbers in the run-up to the strike. Government circles knew the redundancy money among these older, now early-retired miners would help bolster the communities, so they moved to stop all their benefits too. Along with the financial pressure on wives and children, all this was designed to create hardship and social community pressure on the strikers.

By the start of the strike, MacGregor was expressing his faith in a new saviour – not the starving miners' families, but a breakaway movement in Nottingham. 'If we could keep this vast and prosperous coalfield going then I was convinced however long it took, we could succeed.'[62] With this in mind would come unlimited police resources, no-holds-barred tactics, prevention of picketing, roadblocks, mass arrests, violence, intimidation and second fronts. Ultimately would come the creation of an anti-union, yellow-dog organisation – built, funded and directed by Thatcher and MacGregor and the state counter-insurgency forces. Strangely, while the NUM's lack of national ballot remains the cause of much complaint for its lack of constitutionality and unlawfulness, none of the government's clearly unconstitutional and unlawful action has ever attracted anything like the same moral indignation and clamour.

ASLEF, the rail drivers' union, met with the other rail unions on 27 March to confirm their support for the NUM, and to help convene a meeting of ASLEF, NUM, NUR, NUS, ISTC, TGWU and TSSA. This was convened on Thursday 29 March. At the start of this meeting, the National Union of Seamen (NUS) announced that it had instructed its members to take all action to prevent the movement of coal around the UK coast and to block the importation of coal from abroad. As a result, the coastal collier trade was brought to a complete standstill. 'Ships were lying idle in the Tyne, Tees, Thames, and Medway, with vessels tied up at power stations and other points.'[63] We are told that the leaders of all these unions, and one supposes at that stage that this included the ISTC, reaffirmed their support for the miners, agreeing 'To extend this support by referring a recommendation to the unions' respective Executive Committees to block all movement of coal in Britain and instruct all members of the unions concerned not to cross picket lines.'

To that effect, they agreed to establish a Central Co-ordinating Committee based at the TGWU Head Office in London. Local committees should also be established and based in each region with representatives of the International Transport Workers Federation being asked to attend the meetings.[64]

All the unions pledged support for the course of action. With such a speedy and comprehensive organisation and resolution, the NUM had every right to feel confident; such a course of action if faithfully carried through couldn't fail but to deliver up a victory, by shutting the country down 'tight as box' as we say in the pits. The situation on the ground was another matter; in the way that the Notts blacklegs clung on to the failure to hold a national ballot as justification for scabbing, so unionised lorry drivers now hung onto the fact that Notts miners were scabbing – so why shouldn't they? When Ken Adams, a TGWU regional officer charged with co-ordinating solidarity, was contacted and asked why oil delivery drivers had failed to respect our picket lines, he responded:

The oil workers had decided to carry oil as normal, they would not increase the loads. As for crossing picket lines, he has asked his men not to, but what could we expect when 'our own men' are doing so.[65]

We were to hear this response time and again. It demonstrated to us the importance of keeping pressure on the working coalfields, to minimise their impact on coal supplies and anti-solidarity propaganda. By 11 May, the Yorkshire Area NUM Strike Coordinating Committee was complaining that they 'were a bit disappointed with the TGWU in their dealings with problems at Glasson Dock and Horbury Bridge'.[66]

29 March. Rail, sea and transport unions agree to instruct their members to halt the movement of coal and coke. Jim Slater, the charismatic Geordie leader of the National Union of Seamen, tells the men aboard the Tyne and Wear coal ships not to move their vessels 'even if I tell you', suspecting that the union might be sequestrated and ordered by the court to call off the blacking action. Three weeks *after* the strike was over, he had to come up in person and plead with the crews: 'No, this time I mean it, you can lift the blacking, honest.'[67]

Beckett and Hencke, using 'meticulous records' kept by the North Notts Mining Board, demonstrate the saturation deployment of police with the sole aim not of preventing 'trouble' but of preventing picketing as such. Picketing was not of course a crime, and neither was travelling to Nottingham to picket. Evidence had shown that before the policy of saturation policing, the Notts coalfield had only been able to deliver a paltry 46,000 tonnes of coal a week by rail, and only slightly less than double that overall.[68] However, after MacGregor had demanded from Thatcher action from the police, at Thoresby Colliery on 19 March 300 pickets were faced by 800 police. The following day, 435 pickets faced 1,300 police. By Thursday, 1,350 pickets had succeeded in getting into Nottingham but faced 1,880 police. By Friday, only 727 pickets had got through, facing 1,135 police.[69]

Despite this, coal production was minimised, and records reveal that standing orders for fuel were being lost to other coal-producing countries. The saturation policing, intensified as the strike goes on, causes some to question where all these surplus policemen came from, and whether the armed forces weren't being deployed in police tunics.

I have explored this question in other publications and found no absolute proof. We get hints, though, like the fact that the police are unable to take up any accommodation in any of the army's many bases and barracks throughout the coalfields, because they are all in use owing to 'exercises'. Strange that all their premises were full; even more strange when requests to the NHS for the use of closed hospitals to house police officers bring the reply that they also were already being used by the army on 'a major training programme'.[70] I have spoken to White Caps (RAF police) who told me they were transferred to civil police duties to free normal cops for the picket lines. I have spoken to SAS men who say they trained intensely for forthcoming physical and possible armed combat with us, but weren't used. I have also investigated stories from soldiers themselves who volunteered that they were actually dressed up in police uniforms and served on picket lines, but then in the eleventh hour wouldn't take the stand and give evidence to that effect, usually for reasons of extreme pressure and fear of reprisals. Men have sworn to seeing their army brothers, members of their own family, in action on picket lines. Our photograph of the army sergeant driving the police transit, which appeared under the title 'Gotcha', in a strike edition of *The Miner*, turned out to be a bomb disposal team member, given (they said) to driving police vehicles. What is more important is not so much that the army were used as police, as that the police became militarised and overtly politically partisan.

150,000 TALES OF HEROISM

There are 150,000 individual stories of the strike. That year, how it impacted on individual families in all of its tragic, proud, gut-wrenching, comic, exhilarating, fearful, desperate, heroic and indescribable emotional variants is another story. That story, told well and in the necessary detail, would fill volumes and every page would resist the gross stereotyping of the strikers which the media, sympathetic as well as hostile, have made out for us *since* the strike ended. Very few strikers or their families ever went near a picket line. For those that did, few pickets were ever violent, and most were humdrum and boring, at least until the government decided to open up a second front by seeking to put a scab into every pit. Then an occupation army arrived and all the paraphernalia of flying pickets and confrontation landed on the doorstep every day. Then the ordinary men and women and their kids in the coalfield experienced something they never thought they would in their lives: an alien armed force on their streets, patrolling their towns and villages, threatening, arrogant, often insulting and provocative.

Most strikers' daily battle was with the cold, and efforts to scrabble enough bits of coal and slack from the abandoned spoil tips to make a fire at home to keep the kids warm. Armies of lumberjacks felled trees or hustled old timbers and railway sleepers. Old shoes, which for some reason kindly folks across the country thought we desperately needed, became a welcome source of fuel for many coal-starved families. The strike was marked by quiet stoicism and a determination not to buckle, not to let the side down, reflected in the resolve of hundreds of thousands of individuals, standing together firstly as families, and without great back-slapping and public displays, as conscious members of a living community in continuity with mining union tradition. Such families, who are never portrayed in sensational TV and press documentaries about hand-to-hand combat with the cops, violence, sabotage and riot, were nonetheless the very bedrock of the strike. Their stories, far too banal for the dramatic requirements of the current media, are probably destined to remain unsung. The Home Front could be seen as the communal kitchen, the endeavours to feed the families, the socials, the day trips, and the unspoken resolve of those who never appeared on platforms but who had committed themselves to stick to the cause of defending their work, and community, through thick and thin.

Not only is the standard outsider's line that this strike was all about Arthur Scargill, and that the miners somehow just danced to his tune, deeply degrading, but also those who push it have totally missed the real point and substance of what this momentous struggle was all about.

From a personal point of view, as an activist and leader of the strike, I rarely if ever found time to go scrabbling for coal, or logging; my own family home was cold throughout the strike. It breaks my heart still when I think how Emma my daughter would come in from school cold and often wet, sometimes in snow, and all I had was enough old shoes to light a fire in the grate, to heat enough water for a bath and light a bit cheer before she went to bed. We had to be more careful than most that none of our logging teams working for our pensioners dropped any fuel for me, as they sometimes did for families going cold; nor could I buy coal from the merchants working the docking system. As the family of a leader of the strike we had to never bend from the strict embargo on fuel or any charge of privilege. My only source of 'fuel' was gathering up the hundreds of old abandoned shoes well meaning folk around the country (and, I suspect, charity shops looking for room) sent up to us.

South Wales, Scotland, Derbyshire, Kent, Durham and Northumberland followed the Yorkshire lead in endorsing joint strikes in their areas, although some of them had actually lost area ballots to take strike action. The mood and temper of the spreading strike was that seen earlier in 1969 and 1970, and in February 1981. These were semi-official reactions to events, area by area, rolling strikes building a momentum. Nottingham Area would greatly question the lack of a national ballot, but the feeling among the bulk of members was that this was a 'hot' strike, taken in response to a provocative plan. It was rolling forward on impulse, area by area as allowed under rule 41 with the endorsement of the National Executive Committee. The Yorkshire Area had previously held an Area ballot to sanction strike action in the event of non-agreed pit closures (which produced in 1981 a 86% majority 'yes' vote). Other areas such as South Wales and Lancashire failed to secure a 'yes' vote in a ballot, but later agreed 'in the interests of unity' to join the national action, as individual pits in their own areas picketed them out and explained the case face-to-face. In fact, South Wales became one of the strongest supporters of the strike, the only area to have mines with no strikebreakers throughout the entire 12 months.

By April 3 the situation in Lancashire was as follows:

Agecroft working normally.

Parkside partially working.

Bold on strike.

Sutton Manor on strike.

Bickershaw almost totally on strike.

Goldborne almost totally on strike.

Parsonage almost totally on strike. [71]

By 16 April it was reported that 2,000 men were working out of a total of 6,000. [72]

By 15 March, only 21 of 174 British pits were 'working normally'.[73] MacGregor claimed it was only 11, and complained that the police were either incapable of doing their jobs or unwilling to halt the success of the pickets. He called for, and got, a 'get-tough, gloves-off' confrontation by police. Along with David Hart, hardline adviser to MacGregor, and conduit between the NCB and Thatcher during the strike (a man in contact and consultation with Rimington of MI5), he set up the 'back-to-work movement' and spearheaded a multi-million pound media campaign, which he called 'saturation coverage'. They engaged an army of lawyers to tie down and break the union with costs; but he reports in his autobiography that by January 1985, 9 months into his counter-campaign, 104 pits were still totally idle with only 47 working.

The Strike Coordinating Committee, compiling its reports from our pickets and Nottingham miners, had reported the numbers of Nottingham miners on strike as of 8 May as follows:

Harworth	150.
Cresswell	450.
Bevercotes	500.
Ollerton	500.
Silverhill	76.
Welbeck	600.
Thorseby	650.
Sutton	100.
Mansfield	300.
Clipstone	500.
Sherwood	500.
Blidworth	650.
Rufford	650.
Pye Hill	40.
Bentinck	30.

Calverton	working normally.
Hucknall	no available information.
Linby	450.
Annesle	100.
Babbington	working normally.
Newstead	50% on strike.
Cotgrave	no available information.
Gedling	150.[74]

Such results gave us every hope that with persistence and 'our witness', as the Christians might call it, we were holding the bulk of the Notts coalfield out. Certainly, we were seriously damaging their efforts to turn coal and keep power stations supplied. The strike logs report a considerable success for picketing operations in Nottingham, together with the Notts pickets themselves. In April, the entire branch committee and all branch officials at Bevercotes resigned in protest at men crossing the picket lines.[75]

At the end of March, in response to demands from Yorkshire Area NUM Financial Secretary Ken Homer, the number of pickets we put out is limited. He claims this is due to the rate of expenditure on picketing operations and the 'problems' of unrestricted picket numbers. We have a godalmighty clash and nearly come to blows, with Ken threatening to hit me with an ashtray. We are restricted to seven cars per branch maximum. It is a bucket of cold water that is not what we need at this time. Although the restriction is gradually lifted, the number of lads volunteering declines as they turn up for duty but don't get one of the seven cars, and so find other ways to fill their time. It is a major tactical blunder from where I stand.[76] It takes me and Frank Cave and not a few protests from the pickets themselves to get this restriction lifted on 21 April 1984, and allows up to 14 cars per branch per 24 hours; this gives me usually 168 cars and over 1,600 pickets per day.[77] Any branch unable to supply the 14 cars has its unmet capacity offered to the bigger branches to fill. I never fail to put a full compliment out from the coalfield as a whole. We should remember too that this is solely 'flying pickets'; it doesn't include pickets at pits, rail depots and local power stations which are within walking or public transport distance, and so require no petrol expenses.

On 11 May, I am given a commission to discover the best form of helmet and its cost with a view to issuing them to all pickets to minimize head injuries and fear of death from clubbing. After exhaustive studies and presentation of the report, Briscoe[78] knocks the plan into touch. He fears this is a manoeuvre by me to create a paramilitary squad. The very idea.

The story of the strike is often cast as class warfare write large; as Thatcher, Hart and their minions of rabidly right-wing businessmen versus Scargill and his working-class warriors. But the real story of the strike is shown best in the more complex emotions and motivations revealed in the less visible individual lived experiences of the strike. Here is one such story in the very large canvass. In the first weeks of the strike, Spot is an enthusiastic picket. He heads off down on the first unofficial picket at Harworth on his big-forked bike and arrives long before the rest of the raggy lads from Hatfield and Armthorpe. As trickles of early starters arrive, he has little choice but to man this picket line himself. He strides into the middle of the road. He is wearing a big poncho, like Clint Eastwood in *A Fistful of Dollars*, in his hand a 2-litre earthenware jug of whisky. He is wearing pit boots and stands there with his hair now flowing out behind him in the morning breeze. He holds up his other hand, as a couple of cars slowly come to a stop, and a few walkers start to gather round. Not a great or particular loud spokesman for the impending revolt, he says in what he thinks is a Nottingham type pit greeting:

'Ow doo, lads – tha's all having an early ride today, so ger on back to your lasses' bones, cos the pit's on strike!'

'I'm not!' cries one of the Nottingham dissidents.

'No and neither am I', comes another and tries to push by.

I think it was the pushing-by that caused Spot to smack a hefty nut into the side of the man's face as he went by. He fell in a crump with his towel splayed out on the road, just as a couple of big bikes were heard coming down the lane. 'Now we'll see if we're working,' one of the slowly growing crowd at the gate announces.

These bikers work here at Harworth. They drift though the crowd, booling their bikes forward with their feet, their headlights illuminating the huge Spot in a floodlight presentation centre stage. They pull their bikes onto the stands and dismount. 'Fuckin' always late!' announces Spot as the bikers embrace in a fusion of hair and leather. These lads work at Harworth right enough, geographically a Donnie pit, and the bikers are part of Beetham's biking miners. They will be among the last two strikers at the pit on pain of their girlfriends leaving them and being ostracised from all that is cool in Donnie. The bikers are not there long before the confusion of pickets and workers in cars and buses descend on the pit. The gates are alive with pushing and shoving and some sporadic fighting, before the bulk of the Harworth men turn back home and the pit is stood. Only Harworth pickets on the gates, and Spot and his two motorcycle comrades suppin the whisky at 6 a.m. in the early morning light remain.

Over the first couple of months the bikers became a sort of flying column, initially joining pickets, but then as Orgreave unfolded, Spot and the others declined 'all that medieval shite' as Spot put it. I used them as spotters, riding behind the lines, checking out roadblocks, probing routes, checking picket line strengths. Catweasel[79] fixed up a sidecar combination and I cruised the roads and strike-torn villages undisturbed by the cops and their preoccupation with picket cars.

As the crunch came down on picketing finances and I was forced to justify more elaborately the escalating sums, the Finance Office suddenly decided they weren't paying for motorbikes. I was outraged, and later got it restored, but by that time, my flying column was confined to barracks, suppin broon ale, beating up the odd scab who crossed their path, but from then on out of the front line. When I came to start up the Beetham's Miners Support Group, with financial sponsorship from Class War, and militant anarchist and gays and lesbian group Wolverine down in London, Spot and the lads were all too glad to meet visiting delegations and accept donations. Most of it went on beer rather than food, but that was their choice. Those lads held the line mostly for the single town lads, not village miners. Not the more common view of who the miners were, they were not going to break any strike even though the Coal Board perceived them to be a weak link and tried to start a back-to-work movement among them, but 99% of them stuck it out. Some of them were in the process of buying houses or flats, while a group of them were building their own house on farm land. They lost it as loans and mortgages went unpaid; two lads lost their flat, two others their house, with nowt to show for all the years they had been paying for them.

But they didn't flinch ... As the strike continued and picketing became more vexed, Class War and the London Anarchists also dropped us special orders as we requested them, a consignment of Black Widow catapults and boxes of steel ball bearings. A prize group of volunteers in a flying hit squad made full use of these. One in particular I shall mention operated from a fast Triumph Stag sports car. They laid low in Sherwood Forest and swept out into the convoys of coal lorries shipping fuel from the scab pits. While the driver skipped in and out of the huge vehicles, his 'rear gunner' walloped ball bearings through the wire mesh, shattering windshields and causing chaos among the fortune-hunters. On occasion, squad cars chased them off, but always declined to follow them into the woods lest some modern-day gang of outlaws ambush them. I myself was never quite sure about the fearful things; for a start I never knew which hand you gripped it in and which hand you pulled back with. (It required quite some strength with either arrangement.) I was also never certain that once pulled back to full extremity there was any certainty the ball bearing would actually travel through that little space formed by the Y and not into my thumb or knuckles. So I suppose I was afraid of it, rather than of using it. Mind, the windows of police transits and NCB offices demonstrated that our catapult teams had none of my reservations.[80] Our consignment of chainsaws from SOGAT, the print union, arrived at the kitchen to assist with logging operations and keeping the families warm. They could be borrowed on rotation for private use. One lad knew of just the spot with a small wood of dead and dying old trees; some walk, mind – he howked the chain saw over field and valley over the moors. Finally, he came to the trees and unhitched the saw. Total confusion, no plug! They had sent us electric chainsaws. Ee whey, they came in handy in the wood yard and for domestic use but it wasn't until they were supplemented by the petrol variety that we got into the lumberjack business with any gusto.

Into this situation came MacGregor, hectoring and daily complaining. Thatcher agreed to give the Association of Chief Police Officers their head. They moved into this dispute in a totally partisan manner. They are after all supposed to be a neutral agency in trades disputes. On average 500 miners per week were arrested in that 12-month strike. 'Secondary picketing' was only an offence under the Employment Act 1980 if you were not picketing 'your own place of work'. We were employed by the NCB. It was a single employer. We weren't employed by 'a pit', so we regarded all the premises of the NCB as our place of work, potentially anyway. In any case, the police never did have any responsibility for cordoning off pickets because they thought a civil tort was about to happen. But who was to stop them? They didn't have the right to stop us demonstrating, or rallying or protesting; these were supposed to be our civil rights. But try to stop us they did.

Our plan was to achieve a de facto national strike of area strikes. This had not been planned as such; it was simply the way the struggle evolved. Some on the NEC thought the rolling strike would be an initial phase to be endorsed by national individual ballot later as the strike gained momentum. (Indeed a hurried Rule Revision Conference had met to agree a rule change, which allowed sanction for national strike action to be reduced from 55% to 51% majority in anticipation of a future national ballot.) However, when branches were polled at mass pithead meetings, as to approval for such a ballot or not, the overwhelming majority of branches, and through them areas, voted to reject such a national ballot as unnecessary.[81]

We had called mass branch meetings to discuss the proposition. At Hatfield, the Welfare Hall was mobbed to capacity and overflowing out into the street. As I took the stage, there were discontented murmurs and rumblings.

Someone shouted: 'Don't you come here an' ask us to start having any ballots at this stage!'

And another less aggressively: 'They think the Executive is trying to ballot its way off the hook, Danny.'

It was clear the members thought the EC and the Area Leadership didn't have the belly for the fight. They thought this ballot was a kind of Pontius Pilate washing bowl: we would wash our hands of the question, maintain our class purity, but be able to blame the members for not backing our lead. None of these things was true, but the members thought we were trying to constitutionalise the threatened pits out of existence and walk away.

I had no intention of calling for a ballot and the committee said we should leave it to the men to decide and allow the committee a free vote and voice from the floor, lest anyone say in the future we had twisted any arms. They voted amid great cheers, unanimously as I recall, *not* to have a ballot. The Yorkshire Area Council meeting of 13 April witnessed the streets round the offices heaving with bodies of striking miners singing 'Stick Your Ballot Up Your Arse!' to the unlikely tune of 'Bread of Heaven'. As my wee form pushed through the crowd of laughing and shouting men, I was recognised, and they opened up the lines a little to let me through, shouting, 'Stick to your guns, Davie boy!' They needn't have worried; the resolution on the floor said simply: 'We oppose taking a national ballot.' Twelve branches voted against, the rest of the Council voted in favour, the die was cast and our cards were marked.

That there was such antipathy to a ballot is related to the earlier period when the NCB (with government approval) had tried to encourage the miners to accept an area-based incentive scheme. Although this idea enjoyed the support of more moderate areas in the Union such as Nottingham and the Midlands, it was heartily rejected by National Conference on two separate occasions. A ballot was then sought, and when this was returned the miners had voted overwhelmingly to reject the incentive scheme. The NEC then went ahead and sanctioned areas, despite the national ballot result to negotiate area incentive schemes. The rest of the miners' areas next sought a court judgement, which remarkably decided that national ballots were not binding upon the NEC and areas were free to decide their own fate outwith the national view.

When the same areas, markedly Nottingham and the Midlands, started demanding a ballot during the strike, there was a strong backlash as a result. Most commentators and pollsters of the period, even by the winter of 1984, predicted that such a national ballot would easily have secured the 51% required. It has become the subject of much retrospection since the end of the strike, but in the heat of the strike the ballot was regarded by most as at best a distraction and at worst a tactic to deflate the action. From the beginning, defying the strike or it making it a point of principle – 'no ballot no strike' – was always an excuse for cowardice. The issue and the fact of the strike was far more important than how it was achieved. The fact was: we were on strike. How we got on strike wasn't as important as the reason we were on strike. The strikebreakers ignored the reasons and justification for the strike and the fact that it was actually happening, and concentrated their attention on how the strike was achieved, which to everyone else was a minor detail.

One historic fact, which must be made clear, is that the NEC and the National leadership under the chairmanship of Arthur Scargill made no recommendation to reject a national ballot. A Special Conference had been convened in anticipation that such a ballot would be approved. At that Conference, Mr Scargill in the chair expressed no view on the matter either way, did not speak on the subject and did not cast a vote on the matter. Whatever the rights and the wrongs of that Conference decision, Mr Scargill was not responsible for it. Although the press and some historians have always suggested it was he who 'refused to have a ballot,' this was in fact never the case.[82]

The ballot in South Wales, Durham and Northumberland, Lancashire and Nottingham had gone against taking strike action. But as the unofficial strikes in these areas and the official area strikes of Scotland, Yorkshire and Kent rolled forward, those areas' executive committees called upon the miners to join the action 'in the spirit of unity'. This call was also made by the area officials and Area Executive Committee of the NUM in Nottingham; only the Notts Area ignored the call by their own elected leaders. That tends to suggest something different was at large in that coalfield.[83] This is not to try and suggest scabbing stopped in Lancashire or Northumberland, for example, but it continued only as an unofficial minority. The area unions stood with the strike.

The impact of the 'incentive' scheme was to drill perforations across the thinly concealed fault lines left by Spencerism, opening up regional identities against national ones, embedding a false sense of security that some regions – the big-bonus earners – had futures while those of the thin seams and hard-got coal had not.[84] The reluctance of areas like Nottingham and the Midlands to join any strike movement was based quite simply on their belief that they were all right, Jack, and didn't need to join any movement against pit closures. They focused on the lack of a national individual ballot as an excuse for not joining the movement.

But it is quite clear that an external hand had already been at play spreading divisions. My earlier work *Pit Sense Versus the State*[85] clearly demonstrates that although the bulk of the Nottingham miners didn't want to strike, the bulk of them had no wish to be scabs either. In forceful though not unduly violent pickets in the early days, 80% of the Nottingham miners respected the picket lines, and collieries stood idle. It was to break this reluctant solidarity that another state agent was introduced. With almost sole responsibility for creating and funding the so-called 'back-to-work movement', David Hart ran his counter-strike operations along military lines from Claridges Hotel in London. Officially, he was a playboy and a wealthy property developer with a large country estate; despite a Rolls Royce and a BMW, he commuted by helicopter. *The Sunday Times* described him as 'Mrs Thatcher's adviser'. He was a regular visitor at No. 10 throughout the dispute. He planned the 'back-to-work' movement and established the Working Miners Committee, the forerunner of the UDM. MacGregor got used to having him as a frequent companion at Hobart House, the NCB HQ, advising on strategies to defeat the NUM and hold their overall operation together. His role was entirely political, as he himself said: 'It wasn't anything to do with the coal industry. It was about Scargill's idea of Britain, versus Mrs Thatcher's idea of Britain.'[86]

Ian MacGregor readily acknowledged that Hart was his agent:

His job was to find intelligence on which we could base our campaign, it's just like in war time, the army finds it absolutely essential to know exactly what is going on, what the enemy is doing.

It is clear from this that surveillance was another of Hart's briefs, other than building his fifth column among the Notts miners.

It must be said that traditional members, more so senior members, of the NCB management in Hobart House bitterly resented the intrusion of the creepy and at times utterly eccentrically-garbed Hart, because of his upstart intrusiveness as well as his manipulation of events and subterranean activities. It is hard to discover who at core Hart was truly working for – neither Thatcher nor MacGregor seem to have brought him in, but found him a welcome attachment during the course of the strike.

He was determined that Thatcher should not yield to the NUM no matter what the cost. It was his prompting which swung the government and the NCB away from surrender on a number of occasions when everything had seemed 'in the bag'. Ned Smith was a man schooled in the old pit school and the human relations tradition of compromise; he was utterly incompatible with Hart – and MacGregor, whose ear Hart now held:

The fact that government agents were used in that way was improper. In the society of this country, in any industry in my judgment, it's improper; it's dishonest, it's politicians being dishonest.

If you talk about all the families, and all the people, in involvement, you are talking about a million people, directly involved in all this. To have been deliberately driven into the ground, so to speak, when it wasn't necessary – that has got to be wrong. We took a slice off the pattern of our behaviour in this country, and it can never be put back, sadly.[87]

Smith was a man of principle among a new crude mob. He resigned from the NCB in the middle of the whole controversy as the only way he could signal up to anyone who was still listening how unsavory and manipulated events had become. MacGregor deemed him too soft: 'The heat of the battle was something beyond his capabilities.'[88]

By 27 April 1984, 60% of Nottingham miners were on strike.[89] On 21 May, North Notts NCB Area Office reported only 54.3% of the Nottingham Area's miners were actually going in to work. Although this increased sharply via the efforts of the 'National Working Miners Committee', and the police operation, perhaps a quarter of all Nottingham miners stuck with the strike for most of the period.

TO BALLOT OR NOT TO BALLOT

That question faced us at the recalled National Conference on that historic day, 19 April 1984, at Sheffield City Hall. But it wasn't the only question. First we had a proposed rule change, from the currently required 55% to that of a simple majority. It stood in the name of NEC. It was to most of us simple justice: a majority of one in any proceedings in the union was sufficient to swing a decision, or get anyone elected. However, the necessary condition for a strike ballot was a 55% majority. With the impending decision on whether to hold a national ballot on strike action, the discrepancy needed ironing out. Arthur argued that the current rule meant that a 'yes' vote would have to overcome 18,000 'no' votes before we got to an even playing field.[90]

The rule change was opposed by Nottingham, the area that had been most vociferous in demanding a national ballot. Roy Lynk said a majority of one was not enough on a decision like this. He said the Nottingham Area was in fact against pit closures and committed to fighting them; that it had stuck 100% to the overtime ban; that Notts had been 100% on strike in 1972 and 1974. 'But I can tell you this, whatever happens, whatever the decision is, the Notts Area will stand by you.' When put to the vote (a card vote of course), those in favour numbered 187, with 59 against and two abstentions.[91] The two abstentions were from the same area and since we don't know, because it's not in the Conference report who the various votes came from, I guess they were Cumberland. In addition, one must likewise conclude that Nottingham had a card vote of 59 and appears to be the only area to have voted against.

This was a Conference unlike any other in the history of the NUM or its predecessor the MFGB. It met while 80% of the coalfields were on strike. Six of those areas had balloted against strike action but had been picketed out and then resolved in the interests of unity to formally declare the areas officially on strike; these were Lancashire, Durham, Northumberland, Durham Mechanics, South Wales and Derbyshire. Four areas had balloted not to strike and were either working or trying to work: South Derbyshire, Nottingham, North Wales and Leicester. Three areas were officially on strike: Yorkshire, Scotland and Kent. Other areas stood or part worked, depending on the force of pickets and arguments: Midlands, Derbyshire, Cumberland, COSA, North Western, Power Groups, and Cokemen. COSA declared that 10,000 of their members were on strike, which meant less than half were working.

However, the consensus was that 80% of British miners were on strike, to general and enthusiastic acclaim, while in the working coalfields battles raged between police and pickets, and scabs and pickets. The argument had come to be centred on the question of a national ballot. Those already on strike and behind the strike thought there was no need, either practically or in principle, to hold one when the task was actually stopping pit closures by taking action; we already *were* stopping pit closures by taking action, so why ballot? Some argued that we couldn't unify the national coalfields in a disciplined way without a national ballot. Some who were scabbing said they would strike if there was a national ballot whatever its outcome. Others thought: 'If you can't strike now, in the middle of the greatest industrial conflict since 1926, a ballot ain't going to convince you.' Amid all this, the recalled National Conference met.

There were five resolutions – four broadly in favour of a national ballot, and one against a national ballot and calling for the national action to be endorsed by this Conference and call out all areas in support. Durham Mechanics had tried to be all things to all men: yes, they said, we should have a national ballot, but the results of that ballot didn't nullify the official support for the area action currently being undertaken or the national overtime ban.

Mr Ellis representing North Wales spoke in favour of a national ballot. He told us they had two pits in their area. They had stuck to the national overtime ban and one of them had been working 3 or 4 days in the week only, and had been out on strike solidly for the last 5½ weeks; the other pit was 30% out 70% working. He said that the 70% had demanded the national ballot, and that he believed they would join the action if they had one.

My good mate Dennis Murphy followed him from Northumberland. Mandated to call for a national ballot, they had had a mass meeting with nearly 2,000 men there, and 52% had voted to support the national strike if they called too for a national ballot. He feared they would have lost a straight vote to support the strike with no mention of a ballot.

Scotland's George Bolton spoke against the need for a ballot with 80% already on strike. Working when others were on strike was stabbing them in the back, strikebreaking.

I spoke (of course) for action now; just cross the line Mac and this government had drawn in the dirt and come back to our side – that was all we needed.

Cairns for the Midland Area said his area was on strike; their pickets were facing every sort of abuse and hostility but they too came here to vote for a national ballot.

The chair (Arthur Scargill) announced that the resolutions would be voted on by show of hands, not a card vote unless that was called for. (Surprisingly, no one on either side called for a card vote.)

Leicester's resolution is to call for a national strike ballot with a campaign to win over the membership to backing the vote for strike action. South Derbyshire seconds it. It is supported by Nottingham and others and gains 51 votes against 69.

One presumes then that the areas in favour of a national ballot now vote again on the next resolution closest to their own.

The next resolution stands in the name of the North Western Area. Mr Donaghy for the area instructs the Conference that strikers and non-strikers in the area unanimously supported this resolution. 40% of the area was already on strike. The resolution is little different from Leicester's and one wonders why they weren't in fact composited. When put to the vote this time the national ballot proposal achieved 55 votes in favour, 69 against.

The third resolution comes from Power Group; it is seconded by Mr Morgan of Cokemen's Area. He said they had decided not to call their area out and officially join the strike, but at the same time instructed their members not to cross picket lines, which they had honoured, but as of a few days ago, the area had voted to join the action, and they were now officially on strike. However, they were in support of a national ballot to seal the unity of the union and coalfields.

Fourth came Durham Mechanics and the highly amusing and colourful Billy Etherington. Their resolution stands in the name of Group 1, an alliance of small constituent bodies. It aimed at having the national ballot so craved by those working, but defending the position of the areas already officially on strike under the endorsement of rule 41. Billy said they had had an area ballot and only achieved 36% in favour of strike action. He said the branches voted overwhelmingly to fight against the closure of their collieries, but then voted against area strike action. Only four mechanics branches were officially on strike out of 19 in their area. North Western, who had lost their own resolution and were now free to support the nearest next one down the line, formally seconded it. However, when put to the vote, the resolution achieved only 8, which must have been Group No. 1 and North Western with 4 delegates each.

Finally comes the Kent motion, seconded by Yorkshire, supported by Durham, Scotland and South Wales. It simply endorses the action now being undertaken and calls upon all areas in the coalfields to join the action. Jack Collins, who I nickname 'the gunslinger' for his style of shooting down left, right and centre across the Conference floor and areas, forcibly argues it. Jack Taylor from the Yorkshire Area seconds it with great skill and passion. Then Tommy Callan from Durham, and Terry Thomas from South Wales. When put to the vote, it achieves 69 in favour and 54 against. The decision *NOT* to have a national ballot is carried. It is carried by an exhausting debate and exploration of opinions by *all* areas, all constituent parts and all branches. It is a democratic decision. Mr Scargill is in the chair; he makes determined rulings throughout the debate for order and stops all interruptions and heckling. He calls for respect for all viewpoints and all opinions. He makes one call only, that when discussing the rulebook, one rule is sovereign and that is that you don't cross picket lines. He did not speak in support of any of the resolutions and did not speak against any of the resolutions. As chair, of course he didn't vote for or against any of them either. In later years, the whole description and morality of this massive movement will be judged around this one tactical consideration. For us it was a distraction then, and it is even more of a distraction now, taking a long view backwards. However, one thing is certain: whatever its merits or demerits the decision was *ours* and was certainly not imposed upon us by anyone, least of all Arthur Scargill.[92]

There is another point of historic conjecture, which is also worth putting to rest. It was alleged that had we conducted the ballot, the Notts 'working miners' would have followed that mandate for strike action and struck. Leave aside that you can't make a stand with your mates when miners are being killed on picket lines and an army of police is taking you to work; and leave aside the disregard for the national ballot result on the incentive scheme expressed by the Notts miners. But what of subsequent ballots? In 1994, British Coal came up with its 'Flexible Working Package.' It basically scrapped all agreements on working hours, shift lengths, the 5-day week, etc. The yellow-dog UDM conducted a ballot of its members, mostly based in Nottingham. 93% of them voted to reject outright the 'package' with its 'flexible working' arrangement, yet within 2 weeks 97% of its members were scabbing on their own 'union' and ballot decision and working the new 'package'.[93] This would indicate to me that all things considered, if we had had a national ballot it might well have taken away any excuse to bash the NUM with; it would not however have taken away the scabs.

In retrospect, we now know that the other side – the government and the NCB and all their allies – were terrified we *would* hold a ballot, because we *would* have won it and derailed all the elaborate scab-herding, strikebreaking operation they were putting into place. The proof is in the fact that Mac and the NCB commissioned an opinion poll among the miners on the likely outcome of a nationwide strike ballot (National Opinion Poll (NOP), 31 March) and discovered that a yes vote would win, by some margin in many areas.[94] Gregson warned MacGregor of the forthcoming Conference on the issue of the ballot: 'There is just the possibility that Scargill will seek agreement at the conference for a snap ballot.' MacGregor thought that Scargill would strengthen his central control and 'stifle dissent' and that the government must be ready to counter him. 'It will be necessary to exploit this fully in the media in the hope of alienating Scargill from the rank and file miners and from public sympathy generally.'[95] Remember, if we had voted to actually *have* the ballot, then the media would be unleashed in a monumental campaign to influence the miners and their families to vote against the strike. We of course would have no mass media or propaganda machine such as the one they had full use of. Despite this, it is clear *they all knew* there was strong evidence we would have won a national ballot. On reflection, one wonders if we should indeed have called that snap ballot they so feared, perhaps at the end of July when clearly the vast majority of miners had been won to the cause. ORC (a government-commissioned opinion poll) in July recorded that 8 out of 10 miners 'were certain' they would not go back to work in the next weeks, and that the NCB would lose.[96]

The fact is, though, that this was truly the rank and file's call. Talk of a ballot, especially from their own leaders, was seen as a sign of weakness and impending treachery.

What is clear is that one of Mac's responses to a successful strike ballot would be to plough on with the manufacture of the blackleg organisation and the division. To permanently entrench the split and consolidate the scabs outside the NUM organisation, regardless of any ballot result, within what became the UDM. Walker, Thatcher and Lord Falconer agreed on this course and set about legal procedures with top lawyers to bring it about. Although they saw this as a marginal strategy, at this time (July) the thinking was clear. What is not drawn out from this, though, is that the scab operation would continue, regardless of any national ballot, or its result. Thatcher's team debated bringing forward a redundancy scheme while the strike was in operation, to defeat any strike ballot. They realised that the people accepting the package would be the ones to vote against the strike and thus they would be assisting the numerical opposition to the closures.[97]

Meantime, the demands of the strikers were:

- Withdrawal of 20 pit closure plans.
- Withdrawal of 20,000 job losses plan.
- Reprieve of the first five pits in the closure plan.
- Review of all 'economic grounds' closure plans.
- Defence of the *Plan For Coal* agreement.[98] The plan, formally agreed in the 1970s, had been ratified by all successive governments (including Mrs Thatcher's in 1979 and 1981). It specified a minimum of 135 million tonnes of coal production or a maximum of 150 million tonnes per annum.

FLYING PICKETS

As our pickets sweep into the neighbouring coalfields, serious fighting erupts at Ollerton and Thoresby. At Ollerton, the pickets had arrived quietly the night before in dribs and drabs, hid their cars and slept in the woods. Only a skeleton force of cops was in place as the pickets emerged from the woods and threw back the day shift. But once the Nottingham miners had gone home the police, now with reinforcements arriving, prevented our pickets leaving until there were four policemen to every one picket. The police then attacked the pickets with truncheons.

A legal injunction was served against the Yorkshire Area preventing us picketing (except at each respective pit). We ignored it.

By the end of March, the strike touched every corner of the pit communities. The kids wanted to make a stand too, and school strikes were starting to spread and on occasion turned to 'riot.' At Mexborough, 150 school students charged through the town calling out their fellow students. According to one report, 'Desks were smashed, windows broken and bottles and abuse hurled at staff during the day as students aged between 14 and 16 protested about rules and regulations at their school and showed their support for the miners' strike.'[99] The major fight took place at the Maple Road end of the school, where 30 pupils had blockaded the main road outside the school. A school spokesman said 'This was ostensibly against alleged treatment of pupils wearing spiked hair styles and in support of the miners.'[100]

The press is full of 'mastermind' stories and covert picket organisers. At the end of March, the *Daily Express* gives my unsung covert operations national publicity, reporting:

> Jack Taylor, leader of Yorkshire's 55,000 miners, admits the official committee of the union is not in complete control. Many of the real decisions in attempts to spread industrial strife are taken at the militant-operated picket centre at Brodsworth near Doncaster. A key figure there is David Douglass, a 38 year old graduate of law and industrial relations who is a member of the union's Yorkshire Area Executive ...

Meanwhile, Tory MP Geoffrey Dickins commented: 'I seriously wonder if the money being used to push this dispute is coming from the Kremlin.' (*Daily Express*)

For the moment I was deeply in me element. I was immensely proud that the Doncaster branches had elected me to co-ordinate and plan the picketing operations for the Area. Doncaster was producing the highest number and quality of pickets, up for anything and brave to a fault. It was clear to me we were up against the concerted effort of the national police operation, directed through the state's special forces and with more than a hint of military involvement. We were in a situation where we were fighting a better-equipped and normally more numerous enemy. So, of course, we used classic guerrilla tactics: secrecy, hit and run, mass pickets switching from one site to another, one county to another, or spreading out to hit all the pits of one region, then regrouping to take all the pickets to one target. Secrecy was the absolute key to the operation, and a disciplined response to the sealed orders opened each morning at an agreed time and not before. To counter this, cops tried phone taps, and plants in village pubs, informers and helicopters, spotters in unmarked vehicles to track us or predict our targets. When they got fed up of this, they simply stopped us picketing, threw up roadblocks and illegally stopped cars. They smashed windscreens, dragged drivers through windows, took crowbars to car boots and wrecked the vehicles.

At remote colliery sites where we parked out of sight in woods, we returned to find cars wrecked and the little PR sticker from the Met 'You Have Just Met The Met' stuck on doors and windows. The motorway was being used to curtail our movements, our right to picket, our right to demonstrate. Clearly, this wasn't simply an industrial relations protest. Our protests could now be anywhere against any target in protest at our loss of freedom and civil liberties. It opened the map up to mass actions, which the cops were not predicting. I launched the country's first motorway blockade, to demonstrate that we too could use the motorway as a weapon in this war. When I first announced this to the crowd of 200 pickets with their cars crowding round the Brodsworth HQ, there was pandemonium.

'I want us to drive down the motorway, group together until we fill all three lanes, at least four deep without trapping any non-picket vehicle in the first four ranks, when we've done that, cars from the rear will move up to fill the emergency lane, then we successively slow down and stop.'

'Then what?' comes a shout.

'Then you get out of the vehicles and throw your car keys up the bank and stay put till hell freezes over.'

There is silence for a minute, then big Harry, the six-foot-tall colliery electrician from Hatfield, takes me by my elbow and turns me to look toward the cars. 'Now that there, Dave, might not look much to you,' he said pointing to his car. 'But its took me years to get and is my pride and joy.'

I made the point to them that their cars were being wrecked by the cops anyway; what would they be like by the time we had driven the equivalent to round the equator three times in trying to get to targets? If we lose this battle and we're out on the cobbles?

'They'll be the ones throwing the keys away,' shouted another voice from the crowd.

'No they won't,' I replied. 'If it's illegal at all, it's a minor offence, its just obstruction of the motorway, it doesn't carry a jail sentence.'

'So how do we do it, just stop anywhere?'

'No,' I tell them, 'I have worked out a spot equidistant between the entry junction and the exit junction so they can't get down to split us up from behind or in the middle.'

There is silence again, then suddenly a mixture of cheering and belly laughing.

'That is one fucking great bastard plan,' shouts Steve Clarkson,[101] a big fitter from Brodsworth—and this is generally acclaimed, as the drivers crowd round to inspect the maps and work out the m.p.h. and synchronise their watches.

This was one of my 'big plans'. I assembled a mass picket at Coal House, and didn't make a secret of it. Masses of women from the women's support groups round Doncaster hated these snooty, white-collar staff who it was considered lived off the sweat of the miners, receiving an added incentive bonus payment every time the men underground increased production. Worse, never in any of our strikes had they ever stood with us; we had always had to fight tooth-and-nail to close down the massive office block.

Since the start of the strike, a handful of loyal COSA reps had picketed outside and watched an army of clerks walk past them. They regularly held office collections and bought flowers and chocolates for the police sent to get them to work. I had planned a mass picket which wouldn't play by the rules. We invaded the spaces they assembled at, we waited at the bus stops where they got off public transport, we occupied the pavements they walked along to get to their assembly points. The cops weren't ready for this, though they had assembled their whole anti-picket force outside the offices. In the process of the picket, the log records 21 arrests, 8 police in hospital, 'considerable violence; some of the miners' wives and daughters were kicked and kneed by the police.' Despite this, we actually succeed in dispersing the staff, few make it through the lines and most of these, distressed and shaken, rush back home. But Coal House wasn't the main target. At the magic stroke of 9 a.m. all the pickets melted away, leaving the cops thinking, 'Ha! We won that one!' We were heading en masse via Warmsworth roundabout en route to Ollerton. The cars, as per plan, took over all three lanes, they slowed to 2 miles an hour, gradually closing the motorway.[102] In addition, the effect of my Coal House operation meant the staff who input the wages for the Nottingham coalfield couldn't get through and the strikebreaking coalfield now wouldn't get paid, not this week anyway.

So it was that on Tuesday 27 April 1984, 160 cars flanked by transit vans and minibuses full of back-up support pickets blockaded the A1 (M) and closed the motorway. I was listening into the police radio reports and heard the chief constable on the line. 'They've done what?!' I then hear him say 'You get a JCB down the sliproad, and you push the bastards off the road.' But there was no sliproad and anyway I hear the beleaguered sergeant tell him, 'They have placed themselves in among "civilian" drivers so we can't get to them.'

Actually, that had just happened by accident, but it was to our advantage. The pickets were at first ecstatic, little Joey Brooks sitting on the front of the bonnet of a car with the sheer empty mass of motorway lanes in front on him, and behind him disappearing over the horizon a huge glinting, stationary file of vehicles of all descriptions as far as the eye could see, 20 miles, 30 miles, or more. The reaction of the lorry drivers flying up the motorway on the opposite carriageway we hadn't predicted. Speeding along in the outside lane they were flinging bolts, spanners, lumps of wood and bricks at the lines of stationary cars on the opposite lanes, impervious to the fact that many of the windows they were smashing and cars they were hitting didn't belong to miners. I had to intervene quickly to stop hundreds of pickets returning the compliment and raining bricks onto lorries in the opposite lanes, mainly because they were hard to hit accurately and overshoots would hit innocent drivers and maybe cause serious injury or death.

We sent lines of miners down the stationary lines of vehicles, giving out copies of *The Miner* and leaflets and explaining why we were doing what we were doing. Most people expressed their support for our stand; many got out and stood with us, though at times we had to shelter at the far side of the lines to prevent being hit by missiles from the scab drivers and their comrades. With helicopters circling above, and streams of police vehicles pouring down from the nearest exit lane and heading toward us, they also closed the lanes going in the opposite direction in order to get to us down that side. Did we cause chaos? No! The illegal infringement of our civil liberties and the attacks upon our vehicles, not to mention ourselves, caused the chaos – chaos was the symptom. As the big man said on TV, 'I love it when a plan comes together.' So did Derek Francis from the South Yorkshire NUM Panel, as he, inspired by the action, dispatched cars to blockade the M18. The cops struggled to clear the roads, confused because at first they arrested all the drivers and left the passenger pickets free to continue to block the road, then unable to move the cars because either none of them could drive or they had no keys, some of which very faithfully had been thrown away – Harry's, for a start. Then they corralled all the cars onto the hard shoulder, then decided hours later they couldn't do that. Drivers, pretend drivers, wrong drivers, were freed and arrested all day and most of the evening.

Bribed and threatened, in the end they let most go on condition they collected their damn cars and took them off the road. The ones that were charged were charged only with 'obstruction' and fined a few pounds. The tactic caught the imagination, but not that of the leadership at Barnsley. Ken Homer in particular, the financial secretary, had me back in front of Jack Taylor and they hit the roof. 'The money is for picketing pits, tell me what stopping the motorway has to do with that?' The accusations came fast and furious. 'We are wide open to prosecution and writs now, we cannot allege we are in furtherance of a trades dispute, we are stopping bloody motorways and smashing lorries going in the opposite direction.' The air was blue while I taught Ken the facts of life such as I had seen them. Sammy Thompson, the dynamic revolutionary socialist vice president of the Area, who had clearly been told to stay out of it until I had been duly bollocked, strode in and, red-faced and pointing right into Ken's ribs, told him we were at war.

'These lads', he said, waving at me with his enormous sweeping hand-gesture, 'are taking our side forward, we've got nowt wi'out these lads.'

This dispute – between me for unbridled, unrestrained picketing and Ken watching the dwindling funds of the union's money, fearful of more and more writs taking the union to bankruptcy – became more ferocious and bitter as the strike went on.

The Executive Committee of 13 April records the death of Dick Kelly, our MP, former Branch secretary at Hatfield, fellow Geordie.[103]

Meanwhile, right from the word go, or even before that, the Hatfield Main Women's Support Group had become a flying column of their own. Maureen, Carol Greathead, Maggie Bennet and Lynne Clegg all lived in the same street; with Elaine Robe and the others they were the backbone of that movement, demonstrating and picketing down in Derbyshire, in Leicester, down with the Kent women, linking up with the Kersley Wives and the Stoke Women. They were like demons once they got started – raw, passion-filled and totally committed like never in their lives before. Miners' wives and daughters moved into the dispute on a scale never seen in the history of miners' struggles. Women had been militant and often violent supporters of strike actions in the nineteenth century on a village-by-village level – they had supported both kitchens and fundraising events in the 1920s as well as pickets in the 1970s – but the scale of women's involvement in 1984 was unprecedented. A huge and complex operation touched every village in the mining communities right across the country.

On 12 May in Barnsley, 10,000 women, miners' wives, daughters, granddaughters, sisters and mothers rallied in an unprecedented demonstration of solidarity and support. 'Wor Maureen' was speaking for Hatfield Main Women's Support Group at the mass women's rally, now quite unfazed by masses upon masses of people. One of the principal speakers, Maureen made the most important speech of her life, and one which captured exactly the views of those women who had taken the lead from the bottom up to first of all create this body, and then fight to give it political and social dimensions far beyond those who had first tried to suppress it, and then ultimately tried to control it. She spoke from this platform straight into the ranks of our wild and unruly pickets who hadn't yet thought through what sort of commitment they owed in return to the women. 'Most of us have had a really good response from the men whatever we've done. Their [the miners] attitude toward us, whether picketing, demonstrating or whatever would seem to indicate that we are indeed regarded individually as equals in this struggle. However I would make this appeal. Please don't insult us by shouting crude remarks at other women who pass by our demonstrations,' she insisted. 'All women must be regarded as equals, not just those of us who are involved. It is really a very intimidating experience to be the subject of abuse in that way and it certainly doesn't encourage any sympathy those women may have for our cause.'

Having demonstrated that the women would come into this struggle on their own terms, she spoke to the women directly, who hung on her every word. 'What we are doing as women in this 1984, maybe 1985, miners' strike, is making history. We are setting a pattern for the future, for the involvement of women in political struggle, which will show what a formidable force we can be.

'Without our organised support this strike can't win; but we also want the active support of the whole of the trade union and labour movement, and all of us can work to win this support ... None of us here will be daunted by hardship, no matter what difficulties we face, for certain we will win.'[104]

This was part of the struggle within the struggle, to fight for a better understanding of the cause of women's liberation; and to improve the consciousness of the miners and see other people's struggles as related. It coincided with the struggle against racialist attitudes, which some miners perhaps were unaware they possessed. Likewise, when it came to sexual orientation, it took this bitter strike and the wholehearted support of all oppressed sections of society coming out and supporting the miners to change attitudes towards gays for example. Something that would have been inconceivable within closed pit communities before the strike experience, a new kind of solidarity, had emerged in the heat of battle.[105]

In April, international solidarity started to take effect. Australian dockers refused to load hundreds of thousands of tonnes of coal aboard ships bound for Britain. The Soviet Union and Vietnam cancelled all coal contracts with Britain and suffered massive financial penalties as a result, something Vietnam in particular found painful given their level of development.[106] Despite pickets of the Polish Embassy, and meetings with the Polish Embassy staff, the official state unions and Solidarity, coal from Poland continued to flow in; at first they said they would limit the supply to no more than 700,000 tonnes for the year, but they knew (and we didn't at the time) that they had already shipped 900,000 tonnes to Britain.[107]

THE STRIKE IN DONCASTER

It is truly remarkable to read again the daily accounts of the 1926 strike in Doncaster. Flashpoints: Hatfield, Edlington, Rossington and Armthorpe – cavalry charges, barrages of bricks, barricades, vehicles overturned and set ablaze, hand-to-hand fighting. The same places, the same battle scenes, the same police raids and the same responses to the police occupation forces and efforts to install a few scabs. It could be '84/85 – it is almost impossible to tell them apart. It should be added that in the case of aud 'Bant' Hardy from Dunscroft it was actually the same bloke! A young pit lad in 1921 up in Durham, he came to the Doncaster coalfield and was in the thick of the 1926 strike. Was with the nationwide wildcat in 1969, struck and picketed in '72 and '74. By the time of '84, he was retired but still militant, and still picketing as the bricks flew, though being a man of small stature everyone commented how he didn't have to 'dook'. In '26 Doncaster had 30,000 miners, in '84 12,500.

I have mentioned a little of the Doncaster picket operation and my projection as its central planner in the battered old office at Brodsworth Home Coal Depot in Woodlands. At one point, I got Buckton to agree his drivers would turn a blind eye as we filled empty freight wagons with pickets, and flooded from the train as it passed the back of Ollerton, dumfounding the roadblocks. Later I planned a canal-borne invasion, hiring huge barges filled with pickets to sail down the backwaters and discharge like Vikings up the canal banks and up the backs of the Nottingham collieries. I had volunteers to jump from small monoplanes with parachutes and come screaming down behind enemy lines. Few of my 'crazy' ideas were given sanction from Barnsley, ever fearful of writs and being sued for not carrying out 'proper picketing'. Few of these actions were actually put into practice, but they remained in our bottom drawer of untried tactics.

I stopped telling them in the end. Picket plans, numbers and unlawful actions were to become a flashpoint with many of the Area officials, in particular poor Ken Homer, the man charged with guarding the Union's funds. He was, as most treasurers are, a man most miserly with the miners' precious money; and here was I spending it like a drunken sailor in wild adventures, letting loose the Doncaster lads like some crack shock troops.[108]

Almost as soon as the strike started, a wild enthusiasm gripped the Doncaster coalfield. Over the course of the opening months, new attitudes, a new set of principles and new imperative took over. As our pickets pushed forward in huge numbers, they became 'the red guards' of our operation, and also to some extent a law unto themselves. Old laws and modes did not apply in this current situation: it was war and few holds would be barred. I visited Alan 'Gaddafi's'[109] house and answered a call of nature in his toilet. As I sat on the lavi bowl, I peered into the bath and was horrified to find a butchered sheep, the blood from its cut throat running down the plughole. 'Alan,' I shouted. 'There's a sheep in ya bath!' 'Aye, Ah knaa, we usually get spiders, but wor lass isn't scared of sheep,' he replied nonchalantly. He then explained that the picket vans had been returning from an operation in Notts, when they came upon a field of sleeping sheep. Leaping from the vans, they at once set upon the flock and killed at least three of them. 'We have to eat, this is survival man,' Alan explained. We were three weeks into the strike, money was still in the back pocket, never mind the bank, and the larders were full of war chests of tinned food, which the women had been stocking up on for months. Something of the spirit and abandon of 'the mob' sometimes took over at these times.

The strike was all-consuming. A kind of fundamentalism developed among groups within the community. Scabs of course would be hounded and killed if necessary; but if there were no scabs, there were dissenters, or critics, or people not on strike like us.

The tide of fundamentalism swept in all and any directions, and for a time it raged against my door too: 'Where is Douglass? Why isn't Douglass with the pickets?' Discordant voices started to piss up my back while I poured over plans and schemes coordinating the Doncaster pickets. I was outraged when I discovered what was being said, and called a noisy mass meeting crammed to the gunnels with strikers and pickets and not a few wives. I was livid and give everyone both barrels. I talked about where we had been as mates, as comrades, the job they had elected me to do, the job the Area had elected me to do – did we only trust people we could actually see? I was elected to be the strike coordinator for Doncaster not just by all Doncaster branches but also by this one. 'What have I been doing? Working 15 hours a day! I have about 2,000 pickets, 500 cars, 12 branches to deploy over three shifts, in firstly an Area employing 15,000 men in 13 collieries, taking action in another area a 200 mile round trip away with eight branches and something like 12,000 men. I've had to put that lot together to try and adapt and meet a situation changing by the hour. In addition it is my job to keep the whole show on the road ... cash! I have to get it, and that's far from easy; I'll never have friends in those Barnsley offices again, if I ever had any before. I have to get cash to pay out a bit of snap money and keep 500 cars rolling further and further south. I've administered £27,000 in notes and coins, not cheques, and all of this in 4 days. That's what I've been doing.'

But that wasn't all, as I explained. 'In 4 days I've had four EC meetings; every one of those meetings could have voted to end our action altogether and sell this strike out. If I had followed my heart alone Dave Douglass would have been down on the picket line with Hatfield and Armthorpe, in the thick of it. Suppose we stopped a colliery, great, I'd be one of the heroes. Then we'd come back to find the Yorkshire Area Executive Committee by one vote had voted to call off the strike and the picketing; because the Hatfield delegate had not been in Barnsley to cast his vote in the correct fashion the whole action had collapsed – and all the efforts of our heroic pickets had been for nowt, because I was with you physically, and not putting my body in the place where the decisions are being made. There are only 12 people on that Executive, so my vote and my presence at those meetings is crucial. You lads have been at the sharp end, but if I am not where I have to be there won't be a sharp end to be at. Those are the facts lads ... Trying to run a national strike with an Area organisation, and basically trying to take on three counties from Brodie Home Coal Depot with whatever bits of ingenuity and intelligence we have.'

There was silence, then we moved on to reports on meetings, and the internal battles raging behind the closed doors at Barnsley and Sheffield.

Jim Shipley was a local lad and a mate of mine. He had a past in so far as he went to school with most of the lads at the pit and within the community. But old school rivalries and long-gone battles and resentments were still under the surface, despite the passage of years. Jim had also struggled free of the pit, and was operating a 'home coal' company, delivering house coal. Mostly this was private cartage, although when the Union Home Coal system was under pressure, we would take him on as a contractor to catch up with backlogs.[110] Of course, when the strike started, all the home coal to working miners stopped, at least that provided by the Union. In theory, the retired miners and widows were still entitled to receive it. The private operators, however, kept going. It is a fair question to ask how that was possible in strikebound coalfields like Yorkshire. As in the major strikes of the '70s, we operated an exemption system. First of all, we allowed enough coal from stock to be washed to send to our own pensioners. Second, it necessitated us allowing supplies of coal to coke works, Manvers, Orgreave etc. so that concessionaires burning coal might get their fuel. We allowed authorised coke to hospitals and schools and to people issued with dockets from us via the social services, OAPs, and families with little kids. The coke was from authorised coke stocks, the coal either from stocks or that produced at opencast workings, or pits where the roof and roadways demanded the odd cut of coal to prevent the faces caving in and roadways collapsing. We regarded this as 'safety work'; the men were paid only the £1 per day that the pickets got; the remainder of the wages went either to the Old Folks' Treat or the food kitchen. Private operators were allowed to apply to our strike HQs, and if they weren't on our blacklist they got an authorisation from the NUM to pick up coal or coke and deliver it to exempted needy cases. In Yorkshire, because of the way the metropolitan councils were bending over backwards and stretching every rule in the book to support us and more particularly our kids, we allowed them enough coal to heat swimming pools. It is true to say Arthur didn't agree with any of these exemptions; on the other hand, we saw it as a measure of our control of the entire process. Lorries and firms, that scabbed, couldn't carry our authorised loads, couldn't drive through villages with the 'Official NUM Sanctioned Delivery' notice on their front window which kept them from being bricked. The system, though, could be 'worked' to a degree. A private haulier might have a docket to deliver (and sell) coal to a young family or an OAP, maybe five or six bags per month. If the pensioner couldn't afford the six bags, it meant the operator had buckshee bags to sell. In Jim's case he always sold these to striking miners, who maybe also had kids, but not young enough to come under the exemption. All hauliers did this.

The problem for Jim was, he had a big coal yard with a little conveyor system; all the one-off owner-operators came to pick up their loads from Jim's yard. Jim didn't deliver the coal to his own yard; a big lorry brought this from coal and coke depots. He had no control whatever over the credentials of one-man operators (OMOs) or the big delivery company. Both of these were given sanctions by the NUM itself and not by Jim. However, our keen-eyed pickets soon spotted 'scab' firms running into Jim's yard, and scab delivery services (those who were trading in foreign fuel brought into the wharves) picking up loads. They charged Jim with being a scab driver and scab agent. This was a crucifying charge. Jim stuck firmly to his guns; he came to the picket meetings, brought his books, demonstrated where his coal came from and every single person he delivered to. The National Fuel Office had determined his yard would be the pickup point and the NUM who should pick it up. The fur was flying. I was in danger of being charged with collaboration and sticking up for him, and someone brought up at a meeting that Maureen was doing his books for him, which she had done some years before but not since the strike – but if she had, so what?

Was I in the firing line because my mate was a coal merchant? Yes. Jim appealed his case to the Area EC, and in order to remain strictly impartial I declined to judge the case. They found him innocent of anything and everything he had been charged with, and issued a long statement to the Branch to this effect (which was read out to derision), plus the accusation that I hadn't defended the Branch by not seeking to prosecute Jim. I explained that a charge which takes a man's livelihood and reputation away from him had to be proved, and this had to be an impartial trial; I wouldn't have been judged impartial whichever way I went, so that is why I stood down from the case. This was normal procedure. The matter was barely laid to rest when Jim was 'spotted' on the M18 'driving his coal from Nottingham'. Jim again presented himself to the Strike Committee, which was baying for his blood. Because of the scab lorries, which had been dropping his fuel off, despite being sanctioned by the NUM HQs, Jim had stopped all deliveries to his yard. Instead, he would go to Manvers (the coal distribution centre being run by the NUM) with his dockets and collect his own sanctioned coal. Jim was not coming from Nottingham but Manvers main fuel depot, and he had the dockets and receipts signed and sealed. They had no case against him. But his name was shot, his business went bust. He left the village, dejected and disillusioned.[111]

10 May. Nottingham Working Miners Committee makes its first public announcement, claiming (and listing) its representatives at every colliery and at Area level and operating as the real voice of the Nottingham miners in opposition to the Notts NUM. It quotes bodies not at work in Nottingham to be 4,300, and claimed only 3,100 of those were 'on strike'. Meaning only a quarter of the workforce was not working. How many in reality we don't actually know; depending on the strength of the picket and the ability to picket, it swung from the quarter of the total workforce actively on strike to 50% on strike and picketed out. At the very least, it meant we were restricting coal production by at least a third, and up to 50%; and considerably more than that in actual distribution and consumption terms. Bill Ronksley, the communist leader of ASLEF in the Yorkshire and Humberside Region, had reported of Shirebrook Rail Depot, which handled all of the Nottingham coalfield's rail freight, that they were moving only 10,000 tonnes as against 50,000 as normal. Pressure was ongoing to black it altogether.[112] In the middle of June, the Nottingham strikers listed their own pickets as 1,661, and broke this down pit by pit.[113] This is a far more reliable set of statistics; and given the usual ratio of pickets to non-active strikers elsewhere, would suggest a non-working force of in excess of 12,000. For both sides the situation in Notts was the seesaw between power cuts and continued

supply.[114] For a complete list of all NUM officials, at area and branch level, including branch officials and committees, at every Nottingham pit in the strike period, see my file in the Doncaster Library Service Archive at Balby.[115]

More testing were the 'dispensations' made to coke works and steelworks; the coke ovens we could justify as being beneficial to our own families and communities, but battles raged around the steelworks. The deal was we supplied them with enough coal and coke and keep the furnaces running, and in the process enough 'throughput' to 'tick over'. A steelworker explained: 'The coke is used in the iron-making process. You then make steel from the iron, so you can run the iron-making but don't have to take it to the steel plant, but you still need coke in the furnace to keep it going.'

As said, Arthur never agreed with any of these dispensations, but we considered it allowed us a major measure of control, which we wouldn't otherwise operate. This was true of those big transport firms, who we allowed to deliver exempted fuels. They had no idea as to the possible outcome of the strike. If they defied us now and broke picket lines, they were blacked, couldn't do any of the work for BSC, or coke works, or NCB right now and throughout the strike; but more particularly, if we won they were finished and would never be allowed back on colliery sites, and probably dock sites either, again.

Real problems emerged on the committee when at the Grimethorpe plant of Coalite (a smokeless-fuel manufacturer) the workers voted unanimously to accept coal from anywhere, including scab fuel, to keep the plant running at full capacity. Ken Homer the Area financial secretary was of the opinion we should release coal to them, because otherwise if we blacked them the plant would shut; and what would be the knock-on effect at Askern Coalite, which Askern Colliery largely depended on for its survival?[116] The Doncaster reps – myself and Frank Cave the Area Agent – had told the committee if Grimethorpe Coalite didn't change its viewpoint then coal to Askern would stop. This view was taken by the South Yorkshire reps, in particular Alan Gosling, saying we should block the coal being brought by rail from Bowers (opencast) into Grimethorpe. Homer then threatened to stop picket money to any Doncaster or South Yorkshire pickets doing any such thing. The South Yorkshire Area Agent Mr Clark told him we would lose the support of the branches if any attempt was made to do that.[117] Frank Cave was later to tell the manager of Askern Coalite there would be no coal in or Coalite out until the Grimethorpe situation was resolved. The manager warned us that shutting Askern Coalite would stop the production of coalite to our own concessionaries, and we should safeguard Askern Colliery as far as possible within the developing Grimethorpe situation.[118]

20 June. The situation is resolved with a return to the 'status quo': the output is to be used solely for NUM beneficiaries, and all coal will be transported by union rail and not road.[119]

Bill Ronksley, the regional leader of ASLEF, notes:

STEELWORKS
There was pressure from the ISTC and the National Union of Blast Furnacemen for the NUM to release enough coal and coke to prevent

damage to the blast furnaces and coke ovens. Approximately 6 meetings were held in Scunthorpe and representatives of the NUM, NUR, ASLEF, ISTC and the Blast Furnacemen's union, with Danny Wall the manager of Scunthorpe Steel Works. I represent ASLEF. Finally, it was agreed to release 15,700 tonnes of coal to prevent damage to the coke ovens – not for production. In my presence, the Scunthorpe Works Manager shook hands with Sammy Thompson of the NUM and said 'Thank you – that guarantees the protection of the ovens for the duration of the strike.' On my insistence, it was agreed there would be two men in the driving cabs of the coal trains – one man driving and the other holding a giant NUM Form indicating the trains were sanctioned by the NUM. Then after about 11 weeks, the NUM received a telephone call on a Tuesday from the Scunthorpe Steel Works indicating the Works required 5,000 tonnes of coke from Orgreave for the blast furnace but did not request the agreement of the NUM.[120]

11-30 David Douglass reported Orgreave Coke Plant has taken coke out to Scunthorpe, the agreement with ISTC has broken down and they are moving all fuel available.
Action: Inform all branches to deploy all available pickets there. Orgreave is near Treeton Rotherham.
12. Noon. 30 lorries heading toward Scunthorpe under police escort from Orgreave Coke Plant, all branches informed.[121]

At that time, neither I nor anybody else had any idea what had happened; we presumed they had simply stabbed us in the back.

I did not agree with Arthur's 'told you so' conclusion that Sirs[122] was manipulating our exemptions and quotas to steelworks. In fact, both we and the steel unions up to that point had played it straight. Sammy Thompson, the most revolutionary Area official, a firebrand militant vice chair, along with Mr. Clark, an Area agent, carried out regular and spot inspections of the Scunthorpe steelworks to ensure no more coal than our permitted quota was allowed through, and no commercial steel was being produced. Sam had reported to the SCC on 2 May, after an exhaustive investigation of the site: 'Scunthorpe had no coal at all other than that delivered by Yorkshire under dispensation.' He also reported that BSC Scunthorpe was losing £1.5 million per week as a result of our action and their solidarity.[123]

We had agreed to allow the steel ovens to tick over with enough coal to stop them being damaged by cooling and inaction. I believe that that had been a genuine deal, and one that the local regions and branches had signed up to; it was preventing the production of steel, which was their side of the bargain, and it wasn't breaking the strike and therefore causing us to open up a second front of picketing operations. I believed at the time that Sirs tore up the agreement and launched his lorries into the Orgreave coke plant because the deal *was* working in our favour and stopping them breaking the strike.[124] Their workers were being paid, steel production had stopped; the agreement was keeping the steelworks tied down without thousands of pickets and great financial and physical costs to us. It is only in writing this work, 25 years later, having discovered it was our NEC who scrapped the agreement, really without serious consideration of what it would mean, that I have to pause. The first 'scab' run into Orgreave would seem to have been on 24 May. We know from the evidence that the furnaces at Scunthorpe were in a perilous position and that BSC had asked for further amounts of coke and coal. Then comes the scab run. The manager of the plant issues a letter explaining that the request has been rejected and they have to take direct measures to secure the future of the plant. Formally, the NEC assumption of control of dispensations, in reality an end to them, is reported in June, by which time the request for a safety dispensation is passed not to us coordinating the Yorkshire Area but to them. Some authority 'higher' than our Area body, and our vice president, turned them down. Ken Homer's report from the NEC is on 13 June; he is talking of a previous decision made by the NEC to end dispensations. I have assumed from the evidence that the crisis at Orgreave was sparked by our decision on dispensations. For me picket lines are non-negotiable. Even if you consider them unfair and to be disproportionately affecting you or your workers, you still don't cross them, but have the argument from the strikers' side of the line. In the case of Scunthorpe and its declared desperate need for coke to save the furnaces we certainly didn't do anybody, ourselves included, any favours.

STOPPING THE DISPENSATIONS

On 13 June, the Area Coordinating Committee hears a report from Ken Homer that the NEC had decided no coal or oil would go into steelworks or power stations, and all requests for considerations for dispensations would be handled by the National Office.[125] It appears Arthur had successfully argued that in order to get continuity of treatment for unions we were seeking solidarity from, all fuel would be blocked unless on proven safety grounds. We could reflect long and hard on this move, on its authority for a start. The Yorkshire Area was on *Area* strike, albeit in a national context, so the NEC had actually no right to take control of how the strike was conducted from the Yorkshire Area. The Yorkshire leadership, however, by a process, which isn't at all clear, yielded to the authority of the national leadership. Whether the full implications of this were foreseen is uncertain. Few of us at the time appreciated what had happened and would now happen as a result. Am I going soft now to think the dispensations should have been continued? I have always considered that they cost us nothing. In the case of the steelworks they ensured no steel was sold; more particularly, the last steel tunnel supports (arches) to the scab coalfields left Teesside in mid April and no more were going to be supplied. The dispensation kept the unions sweet, cost BSC millions every month, stopped the supply of steel and kept the whole operation under our control. Ending the dispensation opened up another front in a battlefield we were already fully engaged in – that's the way I thought then, and nothing I've seen over the last 25 years persuades me I was wrong.

14 June. I'm happy to report that my efforts to hold the line down at Immingham with the TGWU are still being successful. I report first that the

'pulverised coal' essential for steel manufacture is coming in from Durham and is probably non-union opencast. I am engaged with the TGWU to stop this. At Immingham a Polish ship with 50,000 tonnes of coal for Scunthorpe is blacked by the Immingham dockers; all offloaded coal is reloaded onto the ship and it sails away.[126]

21 June. Another of my road blockades succeeds in blocking all approach roads to and from Flixborough and preventing the movement of coal and iron ore. The cops are caught totally off guard and cannot get their own vehicles in or out by the time we are in place.[127]

MacGregor hits on his 'second front' strategy. First, the Nottingham breakaway, which he will return more attention to later. Then our withdrawal of the dispensation for steel in general and BSC/Corus in particular handed a 'get-out' to the ISTC, the steelworkers' union, to abandon their support for the NUM and start using unlimited supplies of scab fuel. This gives rise to Orgreave. Bill Ronksley in his 'Diary' appears not to know that the NUM NEC stopped the dispensations, and to be right neither did I until I started this work. He writes that following the Tuesday telephone call to the NUM, 5,000 tonnes of coke was needed from Orgreave.

> On the Wednesday, the following day, a large number of lorries operated by Consolidated Land Services – a non-union firm – arrived at Orgreave. This same firm went through the picket lines when the docks were on strike in 1972. Coincidentally crane drivers at the Immingham Docks broke their union's agreement and commenced to assist unloading imported coal from ships and loading it onto lorries.[128]

(I think Bill means 'simultaneously' rather than 'coincidentally'.)

The Battle for Orgreave

On 21 June had come a remarkable resolution from the ISTC at their national conference:

Resolution Carried by ISTC Conference 21 June 1984

Given the deteriorating situation in the coal industry and the effect this is having on the supply of fuel for the steel industry and the additional effect on community relations in South Yorkshire, South Wales and Scotland between the miner and the steel worker, this Conference pledges support to the NUM in their fight to securing jobs and the safe future of their industry.

However in pledging its support this conference calls upon the Executive Council to seek urgent meetings with the NUM Executive in order to reach agreement for satisfactory fuel supplies to steel works.

This conference also calls upon the NUM to recognise the precarious state of the British Steel Industry and in particular the effect on the mining communities should any works suffer irreparable harm either of a mechanical or commercial nature relating from the inadequate fuel supplies. – passed unanimously.[129]

But what did it mean, respect for the picket line, a black on all scab fuel and transport? Did it request a return to the previous dispensations? If so, we as Area committees were no longer in a position to negotiate these and all decisions were now in the hands of the NEC, and more particularly Arthur.

Between the 23 May and the end of the ISTC conference it is clear that their NEC approached the NUM NEC to discuss exemptions.

They had laid before the union the present catastrophic state of the steelworks, in particular Scunthorpe:

> The furnaces have gradually also deteriorated with marked signs of thermal instability on a routine basis, and on occasions extremely serious thermal dips. Slips have become common place, and it is increasingly evident that the dangers of a chilled hearth are becoming nearer.
>
> This situation has culminated in an incident at Queen Mary during the early morning of Monday 21st May. During the night, the furnace became increasingly tight and cold. One effect of this was the coal injection then failed due to insufficient volume entering the furnace and slag appeared at all tuyeres. This gave rise to a highly dangerous situation where the ropes on the furnace topgear were stretching due to the heat giving rise to potential catastrophic failure and at the same time rapid reduction of blast would have led almost certainly to a chilled hearth. In the event first class work by furnace operating staff in which lengthy standard procedure was followed to the letter led to the emergency being alleviated.
>
> It has become evident that operation in such circumstances cannot be allowed to continue and the danger to plant is reaching an unacceptable level.[130]

In response to this they requested from the NUM

> sufficient coke … to keep two blast furnaces on blast at the lower outputs … These appeals have not been successful, [and] it has been necessary to take steps to obtain our own coke supplies from Orgreave.[131]

This was perhaps the explanation for the phone calls to the NUM and the subsequent scab fuel convoy.

Was any of this made known to me at the time? I don't think so. I can find no minutes of us discussing the merits or demerits of this. The flight to Orgreave was just a breach of our agreements, in fact the process now shows it was we, or rather the national leadership (the decision 'by the NEC' is unlikely to be the whole NEC and was probably the work of a special committee), who cancelled the concession, and who then took charge of decisions on dispensations. Most rank-and-file members think the dispensation was still in place and the steelworkers wanted unlimited supplies. It had been noted in the decision to take over dispensations that 'safety considerations' would be borne in mind. At pits across the country men were being allowed to work on heatings (or exempt NACODS so they could), ropes were being capped, boilers mended, pumps restored, places degassed, etc. Coalite had its dispensations to keep its furnaces intact.

We were allowing dispensations to our own industry. On the other side, it must be said, it takes two to tango; why should the NUM back down to save the steelworks? If the government was bothered about such an important economic asset why didn't they withdraw the closure programme, end the strike, and allow us all to go back to normal? The concession was being asked only of our side. Still, and very much now in retrospect, the situation with the steelworks and the ISTC was not perhaps handled as well as it could have been.

I have with the help of Chris Skidmore the Yorkshire Area president scoured the NEC minutes of the period to discover how this whole matter was presented and debated. There is nothing for April or May. The first we find is Thursday 14 June 1984, Minute 132, 'Triple Alliance'. National officials reported on a meeting held at NUR HQ on 7 June 1984 whereby the Transport Unions

> had unanimously agreed to recommend that they blockade the movement of oil & other fuels into Power Stations. Following a detailed discussion on the steel industry it has also been agreed to blockade the movement of all coal/coke into Steelworks until such time that the ISTC were able to accept the invitation to meet with the NUM & reach an agreement which would provide sufficient Coal/Coke to keep their furnaces intact & the industry safe, but not to allow any production. The Committee gave full consideration to the report following which it was agreed: That the actions of the National Officials be endorsed & that members of the Committee report back to their Areas in preparation for a National Agreement with the ISTC regarding deliveries of Coal/Coke during the present dispute.

Minute 153 from the NEC Meeting held in Sheffield 28 June 1984 informed of an impending meeting to take place with the ISTC to discuss solidarity action. A meeting of the NEC was also held on Friday 29 June at 10.30 a.m. prior to the Meeting with the ISTC. It was agreed the President present the Union's case. The Meeting with the ISTC took place in Congress House concluding with Bill Sirs (ISTC) stating that they could give moral & financial support 'but not what amounted to industrial action'. A decision would be conveyed to the Union by Monday. What is crucially absent is hard and fast evidence of who did what first. One can only extrapolate from the evidence such I've discovered it. I have concluded what happened was that Yorkshire NUM and ISTC and other steel unions in Yorkshire operated at least until the first Orgreave run (24 May) an amicable agreement. We supplied fuel and they refrained from producing steel. Neither Sirs nor Scargill liked this arrangement from opposite sides of the conflict. By the beginning of June, the NEC of the NUM had taken control of all exemptions and stopped unilaterally dispensations to Scunthorpe. It is clear to me these had been stopped by the end of May, which prompted the request from BSC ; this was rejected and a letter to the workforce confirming this issued on 23 May. The first runs to Orgreave happen the day after. Had BSC and ISTC unilaterally ended the agreement they would not have been requesting from the NUM approved exempted supplies at the end of May.

They had requested urgent supplies of coke to maintain the plants infrastructure. The NEC refuses, probably pending a comprehensive national agreement. Corus with the support of Sirs and ISTC start running scab fuel from Orgreave using scab lorries. Sirs sees the chance to end the agreement and restart unfettered steel production and supplies to the scab pits. The NUM NEC and the ISTC National Conference agree to reconstruct an amicable agreement; Arthur, and Sirs sit down to negotiate one. Sirs refuses to go back to our old agreement locally or agree a national scheme along similar lines. The fat is in the fire. If there is another interpretation of events, I have seen no evidence of it from any source. We can speculate whether the agreement would have held with Sirs against it anyway – we just don't know. In my view, the removal of the initial dispensation allowed us loose control of a situation, which up to that point we were on top of.

June. My cat-and-mouse tactics have from time to time run rings round the police operation, sometimes literally. We plan a mass picket at Coal House in Doncaster, and draw in cops from the entire country, with their elaborate infrastructure, parking, eating and sleeping arrangements. We storm up to the scab offices, the cops all march into position, inspectors with their loudspeakers and batons bark orders, riot police run about and form columns and defensive barriers. At 9 a.m. the pickets start to quietly disperse. By 10 there are only 20 pickets – and 1,500 police. The pickets making off in their cars via different routes are well on their way down south to Silverhill Colliery, where the mass picket descends like a swarm of bees amid a handful of terrified bobbies. Meantime, in Doncaster, as the townsfolk go shopping and kids dismount from buses for the baths, they discover thousands of armoured and rigid ranks of police, facing a tiny band of laughing pickets.

On another occasion, we let it be known we were heading for the wharves. The cops set up roadblocks, with hundreds of them along the route and stacked on every bridge and sliproad, while we were on our way to Nottingham. We'd covered the bulk of the route before we were detected and then it was too late for the police to countermand the elaborate countermeasures.

Second week of June. Joe Green, picketing at Ferrybridge Power Station, dies beneath the wheels of a scab lorry. A Scottish transferee to Kellingley, he was 55. Printworkers, from whom we had unstinting support and solidarity on picket lines, came out themselves in a solidarity action for the miners and in protest against the bias against the strike exercised in 'their' newspapers. The *Sun* and *Mirror* didn't appear.[132]

9 June. Scottish Miners' Gala, Holyrood Park, Edinburgh. I am invited as a formal guest of the Scotland Area NUM to attend their gala. We are accommodated at a plush hotel in Edinburgh, and a big executive dinner is organised for the preceding evening. Because I am a vegetarian, I am seated at the same table as two of the Greenham Common women, who have also been invited, in place of Bruce Kent, who was still secretary of CND and a bigwig in the Catholic church, but anyway couldn't make it. The women comrades were vegetarians too, so we sat discussing direct action, violence, and non-violence as we ate. Nearly at the end of the evening, Mick McGahey comes up to discuss the platform arrangements with the women and asks which one of them will speak.

'Oh, no, we both speak together,' they replied assuredly, and together.

'No, ye'll no,' says Mick. 'Only one o' ye can speak.'

'We don't do that individualist thing, Michael, we are a collective, we speak together,' they insisted.

'Well ye'll baith be on the platform, ken? But only one daying the speakin.'

'No Michael, we'll only use the same time as one, so it's not expecting anything more than any other guest.'

'Aye, well, OK then,' Mick concedes reluctantly. 'Now how should I describe ye? Coz I ken there's a way you dinnet like to be introduced, I shall call ye the Greenham Ladies?'

'No, Mick, call us women, or comrades is fine.'

'Women?'

'Yes, Michael.'

'Does nay soond very respectful.'

'Women is fine, Mick.'

When the gala wound its way through the streets of Edinburgh accompanied by pipe bands and brass bands, and the Scottish miners and their families, the whole of working-class Edinburgh turned out to cheer them on. The miners' fight was seen as Scotland's fight almost as much as UCS[133] had been. I am so proud to be in the van of the march, and to sit on the platform, although not of course as a speaker – I wasn't high enough in the union's ranks, and anyway Mick still regarded me as a bloody Militant supporter, something I was only able to disabuse him of in his last years. After every tub-thumping speaker, Mick leaps to his feet to lead the whole mass crowd in the 'Here We Go! Here We Go! Here We Go!' anthem of the strike. Then he turns to the Greenham comrades: 'I should like now to introduce you to the Greenham Women Ladies,' which I think was a slip no matter how hard he had tried to purge it from his language, but anyway was totally unnoticed by the crowd and ignored by the women as they rose together, hand-in-hand, to speak.

In June, I am writing to Paul Noone's *Workers Newsletter*, as

Leader of Doncaster Strike Committee, co-ordinating the Doncaster pickets, directing them to new targets, keeping one jump ahead of the law, keeping the flying pickets flying and the petrol tanks full and when possible actually getting into the field and leading men. I have been working every hour near enough for the last three weeks.

I describe the situation in the pit communities:

See the marks of battle on the faces of the community, the young pickets scarred and battered, men and women with their eyes around their ankles from days on end without sleep, some women too, with split heads and swelling bruises from defending the picket lines. The children, tired and anxious from waiting till early hours for Dad to return from the picket or else be released from prison, their small bellies knotted in apprehension about the present and the future. Three Doncaster pit villages have already had school strikes, with all the school students marching out in support of the miners' strike and their own futures. The police, true to their treatment of both parents, react in similar fashion with the pitmen's kids.[134]

Next, Mac comes up with the strategy of putting a scab into every pit in

Britain, not with the view to them actually producing any coal, but purely to force the pickets to fall back into their own backyards; in his words:

> All you had to do was to make it known that you were going to get men back at a particular pit and all the pickets from that particular area would disappear from Nottingham or the other areas to cope with it.[135]

The tactic of trawling up waifs and strays and getting them back to work became a daily chore for the NCB across the country. It threw the onus back on otherwise solid areas and fed the media the steady drip, drip of 'new faces returning to work' daily and sometimes hourly bulletins. The strike was, according to the media, always collapsing. NCB chiefs were being fed constant polls and surveys of professional opinion-takers testing the waters; but they *knew* it wasn't so.

In July, Ken Homer is complaining about the Doncaster hit squads, saying that we were here to *save* pits; and men at Hickleton and Rossington who sabotaged them were not acting in the interests of the union.[136] Just as well he didn't read the 28-page document the 'Working Miners Committee' (the scabs) drew up of riot, sabotage and outrage committed by strikers in the first 6 months of the strike.[137]

> On 2 July, Tommy Thompson of ORC (Opinion Research and Communications) told his client (the NCB) that almost no miner his team had interviewed thought the NCB would win. Many of them believed the strike would achieve a lot. 'Six out of ten Durham miners and 49% of Northumberland miners thought they themselves would benefit from the strike.'[138]

Although the press believed Arthur was the great master-mind deploying and planning picketing operations (and for a time he thought that that would be his role), it didn't work like that. The National Office in which Arthur sat had no pickets, only areas had pickets. Arthur had no funds with which to deploy pickets – only the areas had funds. Arthur had started out with a National Strike Committee and a National Coordinating Centre, but the truth was they couldn't deploy us – only on occasion field requests to us for pickets and cover. At first even the elaborate Area coordinating body in the old Executive Committee room with its banks of telephones and colliery maps looked like it might be the war room. But what evolved rapidly was that panels operated as they usually did in peacetime, as semi-autonomous centres of the four coalfield regions. The panel coordinators deployed their own pickets, planned their own targets. Obviously we coordinated between ourselves and Barnsley as to who would have what to picket. From time to time, Arthur would call for pickets here and there and we would consider it, but often these calls were at short notice and our pickets were working shifts and their deployments were tightly coordinated and highly secret. Men were not just sitting around waiting for something to do. At best we called on a few reserves to make what were usually small-scale incursions anyway. Arthur never knew where the pickets were until he read about it in the morning papers like everyone else. This no doubt displeased him; it certainly annoyed the Socialist Workers Party and Workers Power, standing with their tablets of gold and nobody to distribute them to. It is rather disconcerting to be the vanguard, but not know where the army is until they come back. After our daring motorway operation, Area officials decided to wrest control of the picket operations from the panels; they were particularly worried by the Doncaster and South Yorkshire initiatives, which were becoming more and more militant. The question of the legality of picketing was uncertain at this time, and we were now taking the widest definition of what it was and where it should be focused. They established an Area Coordinating Committee to vet targets, to control operations, to check expenditure. It would be responsible for the 5,500 pickets which was Yorkshire's flying contingent. We estimated we faced or rather tried to avoid 18,000 police who had been deployed to obstruct us.[139] Although we had arguments over the number of pickets being recruited and deployed, and Ken Homer had initially put the blocks on mass recruitment, by 11 June the Area Coordinating Committee had agreed, on a proposal by Frank Clark, to put out a leaflet 'imploring members to join picket lines in suppprt of the NUM'.[140] As I recall we also produced full-sized poster versions of the same message.

I thought the Area Coordinating Committee was aimed at putting us on a lead, but to some extent, they failed. For a start, I was on the Area Committee and had an input into tactics across the whole Area. In addition, I was always able to hold back a reserve of pickets, which I didn't declare and could deploy without interference by alleging this or that development had arisen between meetings. I also refused to hand over our picketing codes, which we used on the phones to deploy pickets between areas; I just didn't trust some of my fellow committee members. We continued to use the sealed-envelope deployment system, the target hidden until minutes before the pickets left their base. Despite this, I thought detection of picket targets and their subsequent obstruction increased after the development of the committee, but whoever was the nark was only occasionally successful – the overall plan of flexible, rotating and surprise mass pickets continued.

Arthur, for his part, didn't like it; he was convinced a mass showdown like Saltley, where we could rally our total forces and call upon the rest of the labour movement to join us, was the way to win this strike. As it turned out, Orgreave presented itself as the new Saltley. We saw Orgreave as one target in a host of others; we deployed pickets there as fallback positions or as occasional mass blockades. This wasn't the plan as Arthur saw it; and once he took himself there with the full flood of national publicity and called directly on every miner to turn out and shut down the plant, we couldn't stop the flood. Pickets alleged they couldn't reach the targets we had set them, and turned instead to Orgreave; many others just went without any direction because their greatly respected National president had called upon them to. We risked a public and damaging split with the National Office.

The situation was totally misunderstood and misrepresented by groups like Workers Power and the SWP. Workers Power complained on behalf of the pickets who *they said* wanted to go to Orgreave but 'found themselves being scattered all over Nottinghamshire.'[141] Put another way, they found themselves picketing the scab pits where coal was flooding out into the power stations and breaking the strike. We needed the pickets spreading through Notts and the Midlands in mass numbers to stop MacGregor's strategy, which centred on those coalfields. The Coordinating Committee, of which I was a member, saw Orgreave as only one of our targets, along with the pits where the host of blacklegs were working, the scab wharves and the power stations.

ORGREAVE[142]

4 June. A very long discussion took place with regard to the picketing of the Orgreave plant, and it was felt that politically we could not withdraw. It was felt therefore that the best solution to the problem was to hit Orgreave on an irregular basis rather than every day.[143]

The bonus of the tactic was that the police never dared muster their entire force in the field ready for a set battle, in case we didn't go there, and had always to be on the back foot as to where to station their men and over what period of the day or night.

One thing, which needs noting perhaps, is that Orgreave itself wasn't producing coke during the strike. No shipments of coal went into the plant after the dispensations were withdrawn and the scabbing started. Bill Ronksley of ASLEF informs us:

> What is not generally understood is that the use of road transport coke traffic from Orgreave Coking Plant to Scunthorpe Steel Works was due to Tinsley Train crews, ASLEF and NUR members refusing to work this traffic in compliance with instructions from their respective Trade Unions. Train crew members refusing to work these coke trains, were immediately booked 'off duty' without pay. This was also the case ... [at] other depots, where train crews refused to work coal, coke, oil and iron ore trains ... on one occasion when I visited the Orgreave picket line along with Ken Curran, a local GMB full-time officer, we managed to get through the three lines of police and enter the coking plant where we interviewed a number of plant workers. They assured us they were not producing coke, also that the lorries were loading coke from stock.[144]
>
> Actually, by 29 May, only 20,000 tonnes of coal remained at Orgreave; they didn't produce coal, only coke from coal we had allowed them. Now that was stopped, they were on a steady rundown to exhaustion anyway – we estimated there was about 21 days' supply left. It was the propaganda and inspirational value of shutting the site that was the imperative here rather than its strategic importance. But then it was reported to us (11 June) that coal was to come into the plant from Flixborough Wharf, in 45 lorries, which would then take the coke from the plant through to Scunthorpe.[145]

The far left saw Arthur's call for a mass picket of Orgreave as fighting militancy, and Jack Taylor's opposition to it as a sell-out. Many thought Orgreave was Lourdes: all our sins would be cleansed there; and a visitation of the Immaculate Conception in the shape of Arthur himself was known to occur frequently. It was in my view however a monumental mistake. Since Saltley we had lost just such showdowns, at Warrington and Grunwick. The police, knowing where we would be and how we'd get there, could move all their forces into preplanned positions, and reinforce them and change them at will. We on the other hand would be permanently tied down. The idea was that we would heroically fight it out here, before the nation's and the world's TV cameras. We would become a cause célèbre. Other unions in the heart of steel towns Sheffield and Rotherham would be forced to down tools as the Birmingham engineers had done and march to our side. Steel plants and factories across Yorkshire would see our beacon burning on the hilltops, strike, and bury this place in tens of thousands, hundreds of thousands of pickets.

That was the plan. Well not all of it; after a few bloody days of medieval jousting and no-holds-barred combat, down in that field, Arthur declared that he was going to get a grip on this; he had a plan to shut this plant once and for all. Meantime, our pickets were no longer on the pit lanes at Nottingham, were no longer flying around the country and hitting scab targets and holding the line on wharves and power stations. In the Nottingham coalfield, some collieries, which had managed only one shift coaling, now were able to start up a second coaling shift and in some cases the night shift too. Coal production started to rise, blacked coal started to get through to power stations, scab lorries started to breeze through motorways and even back lanes without escorts, unmolested. We were closing down the most important fronts of our picket in order to stake everything on one big push in that Orgreave field.

It was clear to me that this was an entirely symbolic battle with little strategic value. The wharves and the power stations were, on the other hand, vital blocks of resistance, which we could ill afford to weaken. If we were going to have a mass no-holds-barred showdown you wouldn't have picked Orgreave to do it, not least because it was wharves and power stations which were the jugular. That this was so was demonstrated by the fact that at every other picket in the country the cops blocked you from getting there. At Orgreave, they actually conducted you to the field, had actually set up road signs and diversions to conduct picket vehicles to the scene, actually told you were you could park, and waved you in.

So how far did we get with the Saltley Gate Mark Two? Sheffield Trades Council did call for a mass one-day strike and picket of Orgreave on 6 June. The Trades Council made sterling efforts to levy and collect money right through the strike. The rail unions were as solid as a rock in their commitment to the miners and solidarity. The CP-dominated mass engineering factories, however – Shardlows, Davy McKees and others – confined their troops to barracks. Well, actually, nobody on earth could have kept the workers at work if they had chosen to down tools and march; that they didn't wasn't helped by our CP comrades in Sheffield deciding not to make the stand they had made in Birmingham all those years ago.

Dockers had launched a national strike after their colleagues at Immingham had sanctioned the use of non-union labour to unload coal. This became necessary because railworkers respecting an NUM picket line blocked coke and iron ore imports to the Scunthorpe steel works. A method to break the boycott was arranged using fleets of privately owned lorries. The system could work only if dockers unloaded the minerals or allowed non-dockers to do it. For a period, they refused both, but then under heavy pressure they allowed non-dockers to load up. This effectively breached the long-established National Dock Labour Scheme and brought about a national dock strike, which was to cause a national crisis that could potentially have brought the miners victory.[146]

Bill Ronksley explained that the dockers at Immingham were a weak link in an otherwise strong chain:

Immingham docks was opened prior to the First World War but was a 'white elephant' until the development of very large freight ships following the Second World War. Therefore, the Immingham dockers did not have the strong trade union traditions of the dockers in much older docks such as Goole and Grimsby.[147]

David Normington, principal private secretary at the Department of Employment, decided that the rapidly spreading docks dispute must be settled quickly, 'and in favour of the union'; there was panic in the Cabinet ' in the event the strike was over by the end of the July'.[148]

Apparently, the dockers were persuaded after negotiations with the port employers and the government guaranteed the continuation of the National Dock Labour Scheme. But the actual issue of the scab coal and iron ore was not resolved, and presumably non-union dock labour continued to unload it. We do not know what negotiations were carried out in this period and by whom. Certainly none of the books written on the subject hitherto have attempted to explain or explore what happened. Bill Ronksley of ASLEF told me his insights into this crisis. He tells me he and Ron Todd (head of the TGWU) went to a mass meeting of the Immingham dockers. They were in a furious mood, and had fought with Hull dockers who were outside lobbying the meeting for them to stay in line. Bill says these Immingham men were not traditional dockworkers; they had come to dock work from factories and service industries as the port expanded with containerisation etc. He tells us:

In an attempt to persuade them to cease unloading coal and iron ore ships, the TGWU organised a Dockers Meeting in a large hall in Grimsby with Ron Todd, TGWU General Secretary, Wilf Proudfoot, NUR Organiser, myself the ASLEF District Secretary as the speakers. Dockers from Hull, Goole, Liverpool and other ports lobbied the meeting with the view to persuading the Immingham dockers to cease their activities and to support the National Union of Mineworkers. All three speakers were shouted down by the packed meeting, which ended in disorder.[149]

Rod Todd rose to plead with them not to break ranks and not to scab on miners, railworkers and seafarers who were all holding the line. Most of all he pleaded for them not to stab fellow dockers in the back and break the terms of the National Dock Labour Scheme.

Bill tells me he was terrified of the crowd of big burly dockers, who tried to knock them off the stage, flinging iron bolts at them. Ron, his head split open and blood streaming down his face, continues to plead with the Immingham men to respect themselves and the union. So, unless someone has evidence to the contrary (and I haven't seen any), I think we must consider the TGWU and particularly the docks section did their best to hold the line. A scab is a scab is a scab whatever their profession or union, and God knows we can't say we didn't have enough of them. Most of the docks in our region had held the line, without the need of our pickets. The exceptions had been Wharton Grove Wharf, which was infamous in every dispute of miners or dockers or anyone else, and Fosters of Barrow Haven; both of these were non-union, non-registered docks.[150] The dockers from London I have spoken to explained that their action was only sold to the members in defence of the National Dock Labour Scheme, and not as an outright solidarity action with the miners, although that was the clear motivation of the rank and file and the men at the sharp end of dock work. So as soon as the government is able to issue guarantees of the continuation of the scheme and its terms, the grounds for the dock strike disappear, and with it our major second front.

It perhaps needs restating that the withdrawal of the safety dispensation to the steelworks by the NEC opened up a huge breach in our wall of solidarity. At the point the dispensation was withdrawn, BSC was not producing steel. Gregson told Thatcher and the NCB they would make Llanwern and Ravenscraig a trial of strength; getting fuel into the plants, the defeat of the blacking operation, would be a 'substantial' blow against Scargill.[151] The withdrawal of our deal with the blastfurnacemen and BSC opened up the steelworkers to scab fuel and a second front against the strike. But this could only come about with the complicity of the ISTC, its general secretary Bill Sirs, the company and the government. On the issue of the unloading of scab fuel by non-union dockers at Hunterson for Ravenscraig, for example, Norman Tebbit, Thatcher's trade and industry secretary, agreed that this was a key turning point of the strike – 'If the dockers had come out and called a national strike, we would lose.' But the fact is, down at the Immingham operation to get scab fuel into Scunthorpe steel works, that's precisely what did happen. This was in July of 84. However, what occurred at Hunterston, and its relation to Immingham, is still unclear; and is either not mentioned or else totally misunderstood in other works, as if the two events are unrelated. The so-called definitive work on the strike, *Marching to the Fault Line*, in fact gets the history back to front, with Hunterston happening first and Immingham second. It was in fact in September that the dock strike reignited after the giant iron ore ship *Ostia* docked at Hunterston with iron ore for Ravenscraig. The TGWU dockers, in solidarity with the striking miners, blacked her because of the steelworks scabbing. Steelworkers scabbing on the dockers then unloaded her. This led to a second national dock strike. That excellent summary of the strike, with dramatic photos, *Unfinished Business*, tells us the fate of this action:

> A national strike followed, but again transport union leaders and the Scottish TUC cobbled together a shabby deal whereby the supply of coal to Ravenscraig was actually increased. The NUM immediately rejected the

sell-out deal, and continued picketing the port at Hunterston. The government once again survived, not at all through its own initiatives but through the cowardly behaviour of the union leaders.[152]

Steelworkers at the River Don works and Tinsley Park, meantime, have suggested we remove any pickets from their works, as they were blacking all scab fuel and supported the strike both morally and financially.[153] By this date, it was agreed all pickets be called off all Sheffield steel sites with the exception of Forgemasters, although a token picket of steelworks in Rotherham will continue. This is in appreciation for their solid support for the miners.[154] (Although this never actually reached the level the Birmingham engineers had at Saltley, and they never fulfilled Arthur's dream of striking and marching, banners flying, to shut down the Corus cokeworks at Orgreave.) By the following day, Forgemasters too was guaranteed to come off the list of targets.

27 June. The Coordinating Committee takes a nasty turn. First, I have my knuckles rapped for an ambush organised at Coal House, with Doncaster branches allocated various pressure points to disperse the scabs and block the route and disperse the main troop of white-collar scabs into the offices. My supposed mate Kevin Hughes takes it to Ken Homer, crying 'He's got to be stopped!' It is the beginning of a campaign to oust me from the Coordinating Committee and in the long term from the Executive Committee itself.[155] That original plan indeed makes fairly hair-raising reading and instruction, and still could earn me 20 years in nick for conspiracy, so I have declined to insert it in the archives but keep it to myself.[156] The other item is worse, if anything:

A discussion took place on the position of Doncaster Women's Coordinating Group, and the position last night where women were detained for picketing Calverton.

The Coordinating Committee endorses its previous decision, and the decision of the Executive Committee, that the Yorkshire Area are not responsible financially or legally for any women other than NUM members carrying out the directions of this committee.

Any women attending a rally should have the authority of Yorkshire Area or National Union as other members of this union.[157]

I will not indulge myself by recording my furious outburst in response to this matter, which, following hard on the previous one, won me no more friends on the EC. I declared myself proud of Maureen and the other women on this picket and I wished we had more men like them, and some of them on this committee!

LOSING CONCENTRATION

Arthur consulted with me from time to time on major points of his strategy and regarded me, I guess, as a comrade, as I did him. He was annoyed, however, that I wasn't just on call like a member of staff, and that I wouldn't confide in him operations which 'just seemed' to happen around me without prior consultation on my behalf. On one occasion, I was just getting down to it, relaxed and free in an empty house with Maureen and the bairn away, and a gorgeous, sexually gyrating Rachael on the living room couch, just coming to the boil, her jeans just starting to slip from her rising hips, when the phone rang. Jumping up and lifting the receiver too quickly, I had cried 'Oh bloody hell' as I lifted it. 'Never mind "bloody hell"!' an irate Arthur Scargill responds 'You're never in.' He went on to explain briefly the big push for Orgreave. My lads and those of South Yorkshire would carry the mission, I would head this up … this was a commission. This was the real class action, and the turning point of our history. Except Arthur was saying it all in a sort of coded message, and it was taking a wee bittie time. Rachael, at length, still laying on the couch, draws up her sweatshirt and reveals her magnificent thrusting breasts with erect nipples. I am speechless. Arthur notices the lull on the line. 'Are you listening to me comrade, this is important?' 'Comrade,' I reply, 'If you were looking at what I am looking at I assure you, rebellion or no rebellion, you would be distracted too.' By this time, the jeans were sliding down the legs, along with the knickers. 'Yes, Arthur, whey aye. Yis. I'll agree to be the bliddy bouncing bomb itself but just now I really have to go.' I put the phone down and dive in the couch and we knock hell out of the wall and the floor, until we abandon the couch and take to the rug, then up against the door.

At other times, Arthur would call using one of his disguised voices. Phone rings. Emma answers. 'Err, pardon, is Missure Douglass there, merci?' says the French voice on the phone. 'Dad! It's Arthur!' Ems would shout.

Arthur called a secret planning meeting up in the National Executive office. I was one of the esteemed conspirators, along with Sammy Thompson the Area vice president, and executive members from each of the panels, representatives from all the striking coalfields clustered around the table on which sat a big and actual plan of the Orgreave coking plant. The plan for 18 June involved mobilising all the pickets nationwide, and as many other workers as we could muster on the same day, at the same time, with the 'Close the Gates' determination which shut Saltley and battened down the loose corners of the 1972 strike. We would be split into three forces. Arthur would lead group one at the top gate, the rest of the country, North Yorkshire and Barnsley would attack the bottom gate, while I would lead Doncaster and South Yorkshire from two assembly points into the rear of the plant and take the loading bays. Coordinating the transfer and movement of groups would be Ted Millward, and high on a hilltop overlooking the whole scheme would be Sammy Thompson. Each of us was to be issued with a CB radio to coordinate the whole operation. I considered I had a lead role: I would command the most numerous and fiery section of the whole operation, maybe in excess of 2,500 pickets, led in units by their branch officials and executive members.

It was a good plan. Timing was of the essence; this thing had to be coordinated. Bloody Yorkshire impatience insured it would go off half-cocked. My section was instructed by secret orders from me to assemble around the little bridge at Orgreave village, with South Yorkshire further down the back of the plant, I think at 7 a.m. While my Doncaster pickets dutifully waited the call to action, bloody South Yorkshire pickets, seeing no 'leaders' and hearing the shouts of surges beginning down at the other gates, set off on their own, though they hadn't a clue what we were supposed to be doing. They set off above a thousand strong, round the back of the old Orgreave pit. I was furious, but rallied the rest of the troops and told them our aim was to take the plant while the comrades at the top and bottom gates sealed the roads and acted as a massive decoy.

Just as we approached the back of the plant, the great throng of South Yorkshire men appeared over the old pit tip and charged down to meet us, shouting 'Bliddy late as usual!' and, sarcastically, 'You got here then?' There was no time for ripostes, the back doors were open and in we charged, trashing trains and loosing the bottoms out of waiting trucks of coal and coke. Suddenly a thin line of short-shield cops, their long batons over their heads, marched in a single line abreast towards us. Barry Miller, the diehard Goldthorpe secretary, ran to a pile of abandoned fence posts and picked one up and shouted, 'C'mon lads – we can play this game,' and a number of us picked up lumps of wood and stakes and advanced towards the cops. Two or three of the police dogs were now bounding about and barking and falling over themselves and clearly scared shitless at the angry herd of men marching toward them, chanting 'Oot! Oot! Oot! Oot!' like a tribal blood bond. Barry addresses the cops: 'Look lads, we're here to do a job, you can have some of this if you want, but we can bury you, just fuck off out of the way.' Well the chief cop, whose Adams apple was up and down like hickory, dickory, dock, whispered some order and the cops melted away backwards, and to the side and out of sight, while we marchers went relentless on, or so we thought. Just ahead were the loading bays.

The empty lorries were beginning to arrive, having fought their way through the determined lines of fighting pickets and police on the front gates. We could see them and they could see us. They were terrified – there was nothing between us and them. As we started forward at a trot, some of the drivers jumped from their lorries and fled. I was taking it all back – we were going to win this one, we *had* the base, we *had* the loading bay. We were inside and had spiked their operation. Then the police re-emerged from the side, dogs on long leashes, their batons pointing forward. 'I told ye pillocks,' Barry began, and the chief cop shouts back, 'The odds have changed lad, look around you!' We were down to 25 or 30 men, the army had melted away without sound or reason. 'Now I'm returning the favour, drop your sticks and fuck off!' We did so, swearing and cursing the useless bastards we had had with us. We marched back to the back gates pursued by increasing numbers of police ensuring we didn't do some death-or-glory counshercharge.

Two thousand pickets milled around aimlessly at the gate, throwing the odd useless and stupid pieces of coke at the cops, which more often than not were blown away in the wind. I mounted the heap of rubble and pleaded with the men to reform and get stuck in and let's take the plant. Despite cheers and 'Let's gaan!' and choruses of 'Here We Go!', we were actually going the wrong way. Hundreds were drifting around the side of the plant to join up with the fearsome charges on the bottom gates. I tried with Barry and the others to lead by example, to shame the aimless mob into action. We rushed back into the plant with a hundred pickets and heaved and punched and kicked and were likewise kneed, belted, punched, stamped on and kicked by the police, or bitten by their dogs or whacked with batons. But still the crowd drifted off to the bottom gate. Black and despondent, we had no choice but to join them.

At the end of the day these were pitmen, not soldiers. They wouldn't just do what we told them. They didn't follow orders. They did what they thought was best, no matter what we said. They didn't like being inside the plant, didn't like to be this far in front of what everyone else was doing, preferred to be along with everyone, doing no more or less. As they emerged round the side of the plant, they caught sight of an ill-coordinated rabble of police from various parts of the country being marshalled into a line to attack the bottom gate pickets from the rear. With a roar, they fell upon the scattered cops and for once, the forces of law and order scattered, fell, and took a merciless kicking. Then the selfsame men, who stood resolutely refusing to take the open gates at the rear, charged full-bodied into the armoured ranks of police and horses on the bottom gate. I called up Arthur in the thick of this and told him we were no longer inside the plant and were backing up the effort at the bottom, but my request for air cover went unheeded. All day the fighting was furious. There were numerous casualties on both sides. Up at the top gates a police portacabin had been pulled into the road as makeshift barricades and set on fire. Police vans and buses were ambushed from railway bridges with bricks and steel poles. The whole scene was something from an epic film set, but the fighting and blood and gore was real.

At length, the chief constable closed down the plant for the remainder of the day. Arthur can claim something of a victory, but where were the northern industrial working class in their millions? They are still on their way. Nesbit, the chief cop, declares that if he had to meet this every day, he couldn't sustain it and would have to face surrender. Truth is, we couldn't sustain it either. This was a mighty one-off, meant to light a distress signal and cry for solidarity from the massed ranks of labour watching with detachment in the main.

The labour and trade union movement in Britain and right across the world responded with massive material and financial assistance to the miners, their families, and the union. Labour councils ensured that miners' children would not go hungry by maintaining schools meals throughout the school holiday periods – a feature which made a huge difference to the welfare of the children. Meantime, MacGregor had written every striking miner a personal letter. It was June 1984:

> This is a strike, which should never have happened. It is based on very serious misrepresentation and distortion of the facts. At great financial cost miners have supported the strike for fourteen weeks because your leaders have told you this ...
>
> That the Coal Board is out to butcher the coal industry.
>
> That we plan to do away with 70,000 jobs.
>
> That we plan to close down around 86 pits leaving only 100 working collieries.
>
> If these things were true, I would not blame miners for getting angry or for being deeply worried. But these things are absolutely untrue. I state

categorically and solemnly. You have been deliberately misled.[158]

THE MINERS AND IRELAND

From June, I couple up my strike work and political agitation with a whistle-stop tour of the country, speaking at meetings at various venues and with various titles. Essentially, I am trying to link the war of resistance in occupied Ireland with our war of resistance here. Privately, I hope to make stronger organic links with the ordinary class fighters on the street. I have worked with Chris Reeves and Platform Films to make a series of red-hot agitation films on the miners and their communities and the fight under way. My piece, 'Only Doing Their Job', deals with the cops. I make the connection with the troops in Ireland, the repression in both lands. At the end of June, I am speaking on the platform 'From Northern Ireland to The Miners Strike', at Coventry Lanchester Poly, together with the Irish Republican Socialist Party. I speak to a packed fringe meeting of the Labour Party Young Socialists at South Cliff Hotel, Bridlington, on the miners and Ireland, and I quote as my title bold James Connolly's 'The Cause of Ireland is the Cause of Labour, the Cause of Labour is the Cause of Ireland'. The speech is a belting, flem-flecked 45 minutes which has the Militant team squirming and restless, more so since it captures the young crowd and quite a few of the miners and their families on holiday at Brid who have seen the street hoarding adverts and turned up.

In July, I and the Women and Ireland Group speak to an assorted mass of colour, dress, religion and dialect at the West Indian Centre, Leeds. I begin to feel the risen peoples will start to see the link, forge a link, launch a joint rebellion together, not just emotionally and figuratively similar, but actually coordinated and organisationally linked. *The Leeds Other Paper*, a widely read alternative journal, gives me the full inside pages under the heading, 'Self Defence Is No Offence – The Miners, the Police and the Lessons from Ireland':

> I'd like to take this opportunity to disassociate myself from the people who disassociate themselves from our men defending themselves against the murderous assaults by these people. We don't ask anyone's permission to defend ourselves. We don't ask anybody's authority to defend ourselves. We claim the right to use violence against people who are trying to kill us, and run us down. We claim that right, we don't want anybody's permission.[159]

I try to fuse the Stop The City anarchist movement with our hit squads and riots.[160] They are so 'anarchist' and at this time out of touch with the working class; even in the middle of this strike they have no organic connection, and miss the chance to make one. I had tried to link them up through formal NUM structures, albeit the striking ones, but fear of arrest for riot, fear of being off our own coalfield patch, fear of being left isolated from the support offered for picketing as such, damned the initiative. Not entirely though – the idea was proposed in the name of the Doncaster branches and had the hearty support of some South Yorkshire branches like Maltby.[161]

TAKING THE COMMUNITY HOSTAGE

A striking miner's family with two children received £11 per week supplementary benefit. The striker himself was allowed to receive nothing. The rate should actually have been £27 per week, but the government issued an instruction to deduct a further £16 per week from the family's benefit as 'assumed strike pay'. Strike pay was not in fact being paid and wasn't paid even during sequestration of NUM funds when the government had direct control over them. It was noted at the time of the arrest in 1981 of the infamous 'Yorkshire Ripper' for mass murder that his family were not having any deductions from their benefit and were £16 per week better off in hardship benefits than the family of a striking Yorkshire miner in 1984/5. To make this stick even harder, DHSS snoopers were encountered trying to find evidence of the £1 payment to pickets and workers doing safety work and exemption work for pensioners and dependants, in order that this too could be deducted from the families' already reduced benefits.[162] We had previously encountered police searching picket vehicles finding payment slips for petrol expenses, and issuing 'producers' in order to assert that the licence and insurance was invalid for the 'business purposes' which the vehicle was being used for. Evidence of £1 picket money payments was being passed on to the DHSS. Snoopers were later identified at Welfares, getting evidence of families receiving food parcels; when challenged they confirmed 'They are quite within the law to offset payment to families receiving food parcels.'[163]

Family Income Supplement was likewise denied to strikers' families. This was despite the fact that government-declared levels of subsistence stood at £40 per week. Regulations on assessment of income level stated the income should be an average of the preceding 10 weeks *before the date of claim*. Government instructions dictated that the last 10 weeks in *employment* would be used instead, thus preventing the minimum income supplement being paid for children in families where the parents had had no income at all. Housing Benefit had been denied to single striking miners, something to which all other single claimants would have been entitled. We had successfully challenged these decisions, and by November of 1984 it had been accepted that a single person living as a member of another person's household was entitled to claim a rent allowance from the local authority. The government responded by rushing through, in December of that year, new regulations to prevent further payments to single striking miners. This was done without the obligatory consultation with metropolitan councils; accepting they hadn't complied with the law, the government then ruled that this lack didn't invalidate the amendments.

In 1982 they had sent out instructions to employers saying that tax rebates should not be paid to people on strike, or people who would benefit from a strike or people laid off by strike. It meant that the massive overpayment of tax by miners, and incidentally by those who retired or became redundant before the start of the strike, would not be refunded until after the dispute was over. It should be borne in mind these were *overpayments* of tax, and clearly belonged to the taxpayer, but were being withheld in order to punish strikers.[164]

The Leeds Other Paper week by week runs a practical helpline, listing the things desperate striking families need, and reaching out to individual readers to come forward and sponsor them. The lists are heart wrenching:

> Nine-year-old girl, 28" chest, needs summer coat and short jacket. Nine months old baby needs suit, short trousers, socks, coat. Five year old needs trousers and cardigan ... For Garforth Family 1st size baby shoes. For Barnsley family push chair, car seat, baby clothes 6/12 months. For a miner in South Leeds size 7 shoes ... (6 July 1984, p. 9)

Many thousands of older miners who had gone out of the industry redundant, prior to the start of the strike, found themselves deprived of unemployment benefit and other benefits for a full 12 months as the law held them to be parties to the dispute, despite having left the industry altogether.[165] One of the regular financial appeals to the panels is from penniless strikers asking for funeral expenses to bury the dead in their families. Every branch has a Death and Benevolent Fund, but these were only ever intended as supplements to the funeral expenses, not to provide the whole cost. The grief is bad when it is a parent, but when it is the child of a striker and there is no money to bury them the knife goes even deeper.[166]

Some would conclude that these facts demonstrate that an all-out war was being waged against the mining community as a whole and not simply the NUM or the strikers.

BY THEIR DEEDS SHALL YE KNOW THEM

30 June. Conference 'From War in the Third World to Third World War' – no, not a conference called by the Posadists but by Sheffield Latin American Solidarity Front, in solidarity with the Sandinistas against Yankee imperialism. I am a guest speaker and I am 'privileged to speak for the fighting NUM and to bring solidarity greetings to this conference, the neglected world in general and Nicaragua in particular'. The conference is hosted at Sheffield University Octagon Centre and I think I just let rip in a fierce polemic against the stagnant, sterile left theorists and their aloof detachment and never-ending, nit-picking criticism of the whole Latin American revolution. I link it to the attitudes of the left 'vanguards' towards us the miners, to our struggle on the streets in action and their inaction from their theoretical armchairs. I see the vulgar ignorance on Nicaragua, on Cuba, on Chile as the same snotty middle-class political snobbery. They start this way with the miners but soon they will not dare to lecture us for risk of being seen as the enemy by the young lads on the picket lines keen to distinguish who is with us and who against, and not too arsed about the reasons at this temperature of the fight.

The left theorists and armies of paper-sellers, the gangs of bearded prophets in their various factions, have descended upon us from the hills clutching their tablets of stone and the word(s) of their respective gods. I am commissioned by the NUM Yorks Area EC to write a quick confidential resume on who they all are, so that Branch officials are not completely in the dark as to where they all stand in the world scheme of things in theory and, if they have any, practice. Sadly, the document gets leaked to the press and a number take up the theme of 'outside agitators', missing completely the theme of the document, which is basically to analyse their usefulness to us. I warn the miners and their leaders that political theory is vital to us; theory and practice are two arms of the boxer and we shouldn't be afraid of debate, but also not to be cowed by people who on the other hand have nil experience and a bag full of arrogance. The section on the anarchists reads:

> It will come a surprise to many but the Anarchists have in fact been far more helpful than many of the self-proclaimed saviours of the working class. Since they are against telling other people what to do, they have in fact spent what time and energy they have actually helping us, in the ways we ask to be helped ... in addition you will find that when push comes to shove in dangerous situations on the picket lines, the 'left' are way back with an arm full of papers while the Anarchist is stood to the end with you.

Of course, the press doesn't actually quote any of that, they just try and pick bits out to hit the left with and, in the process, they actually conclude I'm a Militant supporter which really does ingratiate me to them even further.

ENTER THE SECRET STATE

Into this situation came the well-oiled arm of the secret state. Recent revelations by Seumas Milne in his book *The Enemy Within* now prove that any explanation of seeing the hidden hand of the state as some wild 'conspiracy theory' or simple paranoia was grossly unfounded. The roadblocks, the police surveillance, the phone taps, the undercover agents, the interception of mail, the eavesdropping, the spies were to be expected perhaps. What was unexpected was the actual partisan involvement of the state's counter-insurgency forces and 'dirty tricks' department, manipulating the media and actually setting up situations and individuals for public opinion backlash and PR catastrophes. As I will discuss later, in the chapter on the Scargill slander, in my long-considered opinion the explosion of lies and falsehoods directed at discrediting Arthur Scargill and Peter Heathfield, and now demonstrated at every turn to have been completely unfounded, were a late detonation of an anti-strike device which events had rendered unnecessary by that time. These dirty tricks were analogous to the red scare set loose in the 1926 strike and earlier, and were meant to rob the miners of the oxygen of public support. Few members of the public to this day know the true extent of state involvement in defeating the strike.

On 18 July, in talks brokered by Stan Orme MP between Mac and Scargill at the Rubens Hotel, the two sides came within a wisp, actually one word, of agreement.

Arthur tells us that, given the new imperative for a settlement, a deal was in sight – we virtually had the whole shooting match – but NCB chair Ian MacGregor went off and phoned Thatcher, and when he came back, everything agreed hitherto had been taken back.

Another example. Neil Kinnock tells us that he and Stan Orme MP came up with a plan, which would have saved the bulk of the British coal industry and allowed development of all 'beneficial reserves'. The NCB accepted the plan. Scargill, sleeves rolled up and prepared to talk it out, all day and night if necessary, felt we were down to the last nuance of the fine detail of a settlement, which would have conceded the bottom line of the union's position. Day by day, we watched the negotiations until disagreement centred on a single word, 'beneficial', and how to resolve conflict over its meaning. It was MacGregor who walked away when, Arthur swears, everything was all but signed and sealed.

Mrs. Thatcher may well have been convinced by forces to her right, who it seems encouraged her to stop negotiations and go all out to defeat and break the NUM. One might need to read between the lines of her autobiography when she says:

> But further talks were difficult to avoid, although Mr. Scargill's intransigence would probably ensure that they went nowhere. Using Robert Maxwell as an intermediary, key figures in the TUC were anxious to find some way of concluding the strike, which would allow Mr. Scargill and the militants to save face. In fact of course it was only by ensuring that they lost face and were seen to be defeated and rejected by their own people that we could tame the militants.[167]

The problem for all of us was Thatcher, who turned hot and cold during negotiations, kept switching between her need for a settlement and her desire to crush the miners. Mac, left to his own devices, actually conceded much of the NUM's case, until suddenly grabbed from behind by direct representatives of the cabinet. The talks had progressed to the point where the only sticking point was around the term 'beneficially developed' – i.e. that all coal reserves which could be beneficially developed would be so. Scargill and the union obviously saw this as meaning 'economically' in terms of the NCBs profit-and-loss yardstick. In other words, 'uneconomic pits would close'. The point of the strike. It's worth just stressing, though, that we had made some movement, agreeing that poor geological conditions and poor-quality coal would be classed as 'exhausted' seams. In fact, of course, they aren't – only on a cost balance sheet. In this sense, we *had* agreed to some closures on 'economic' grounds. The NUM tried to remove the word 'beneficially' from the agreed text, but the NCB insisted that something which addressed the question of 'loss-making pits' would have to take its place, so there is no doubt what they meant by 'beneficially developed'.

Many commentators then, and more since, have said this was the nearest to victory, the NUM could hope to get 'That a pit would not be closed so long as reserves could be beneficially developed.' This was a long way from the previous NCB position that they would be closed if they were 'uneconomical'. Nevertheless, frankly, it would have represented a draw. Perhaps more than a draw – the closure of the five pits, which sparked the strike, would be rescinded, all sacked men reinstated, and all threatened non-agreed closures withdrawn.

But it would have left us exactly where we were before the closure list. It would have left the door open to future negotiation pit by pit, area by area, but with the management in control of what 'beneficially' meant to them, and the threat of renewed action from us if we failed to agree.[168] Had we come this far, at such cost, to simply go back to the pre-strike battle lines? Scargill thought it was not a commitment to ensure the survival and expansion of workable reserves. In truth, all the armchair commentators and allegedly 'skilled and seasoned trade union negotiators' that have been wheeled out to say Scadge[169] should have signed, admit it would simply be an exercise in gloss, a way off a hook, a means of looking like you've achieved a great victory but knowing you actually haven't. The TUC, we are told, was now blaming Scargill for the failure of the talks, that the words formed in the manner quoted would have allowed us to proclaim a victory:

> Had Scargill been a proper negotiator, they said, he could have grabbed the chance before Thatcher had time to whip it away from him. The EMA leader John Lyons, who always maintained that Scargill had been offered the nearest thing to a victory that any trade union leader can ever expect, most forcibly expressed this view. 'It was 95% of what they were after.'[170]

Journalists and labour historians also have since suggested that Mr Scargill should have signed the deal, 'beneficial' and all. This would have been fudge, but only on very close inspection. It would have allowed the NUM to claim a colossal victory; it would have seemed like a massive defeat for the government and concession by the NCB. It would, however, have left a gaping hole where Arthur and the NUM wanted steel-clad agreements. The logic of those who suggest Arthur should have settled for an apparent victory is that Mrs Thatcher, having been given a bloody nose, would not come back again with the same pit closure programme. Such a view cannot be based upon the miners' history hitherto. Fudges of this description, as demonstrated in history, had only ever allowed the opposing side to gather strength and increase their resolve to weaken the union's side. The words 'beneficially developed', when applied to a threatened pit's reserves, would beg the questions 'Says who?' and 'On what criteria?' as it would be decided upon only via the NACODS agreed review procedure, which gave the defining decision solely to the NCB management. At such a point of disagreement the union could, of course, in theory have wheeled out its forces again. In practice, the NCB would have had other irons in the fire. The breakaway organisation would now be in existence, and Mrs Thatcher had declared, and set it in concrete, that a condition of any settlement would be that 'Nothing should be agreed which would undercut the position of the working miners.'[171]

We also know now that the deployment of enhanced redundancy packages was waiting in the wings to bleed the strength of the NUM to the point where manpower could be cut down and pits left unmanned and unworkable.

Did we want a draw in July with the first 7 months of the year already gone and autumn on the way? In August, the supplies of coal were becoming scarce throughout the UK, and especially in Ulster. Rising electricity prices were threatening to hand the miners the PR victory we were looking for. Supplies in Northern Ireland were said in fact to have 'dried up completely'[172] and they had gone over to oil, at an excess price of £800,000 per month. They were debating raising Ulster electricity prices by 3–4% to cover it; that would bring bad publicity and protest. 'Contrary to public statements, [the strike] was biting already, even in high summer.'[173]

It's clear Thatcher needed a settlement. When we refused to settle, the government then decided to turn the heat up on Scargill as an individual, and let the press hounds loose. Press conferences were convened; 'Ministers had launched a crusade to destroy Scargill and all he stood for.' Walker: 'This is not a mining dispute. It is a challenge to British democracy and hence the British people.' The signal to the press barons was now to unleash a deluge of black propaganda against Arthur, the pickets and the union in general.[174]

Then follows Maggie's 'Enemies Within' speech, a declaration of war on the coal communities, with members of the cabinet lining up to condemn the strike and its leaders across the whole of the media. That this was orchestrated and fed to a compliant media is established in *Marching to the Fault Line*.[175] The line was that Scargill was asking the impossible – no closures, no matter how expensive the unit of coal production. But who on that side of the table, or among those who have come to judge us since, actually considered that British coal had the lowest operating unit costs on average of any of the deep-mined coal industries in the world, and particular of Europe? British taxpayers subsidised through the EEC all the coal-producing countries of Europe to help offset their high-cost production to allow it to come back to Britain, subsidised and 'cheaper', to displace the lower-cost British coal. This wasn't about import controls, or being anti-European or of being chauvinistic or, God love us, 'patriotic'. It was about recognising what game was being played here: the attack on the coal industry was cover for a concerted attack on the NUM. The excuse was economics and high-cost coal production, but in fact this was a myth. British coal was always the cheapest deep-mined coal in the world. By this yardstick, there were NO uneconomic pits in terms of an overall operating average (although, obviously, to have any average, some are going to be marginally more costly than others).

THE STRIKE AT HATFIELD

I can't allow myself the indulgence of recording here the dynamism and heroism of the Hatfield miners and their wives, some of which I have touched on elsewhere. I am often asked about the level of physical response and disciplined organisation of the Hatfield troops. The BBC2 programme made for the twentieth anniversary of the strike records interviews with terrified police officers who are deployed to Hatfield. This village was regarded as something like the 'Russian front' of the strike. Our organisation and the politicisation of this community shines through this work hopefully.

The August (21st) Invasion

Hatfield had been 100% solidly on strike for 5½ months. It never really crossed our minds that this pit would fall victim to MacGregor's second-front plan. Our flying pickets were already in position ready to leave to targets in Derbyshire and Notts, when word came in that two or three scabs had gone into our pit. The news spread like wildfire and so did the indignity and fury. We as usual had only a small picket composed mainly of our older or less fit members on the gate.

The police had likewise only a handful of coppers on what had been hugely uneventful duty.

The Branch secretary and I walked down into the pit yard and asked to meet the management, to get permission to talk to the men who had gone in, with a view to getting them to come out before things got out of control. The strikebreakers refused to meet us. Light the blue touchpaper then. While the secretary withdrew men away to the Welfare for a meeting, I launched a tour of the villages in a loudspeaker car, rousing all our members to come down, defend the picket line and demonstrate our feelings to these scabs.

While I was so engaged and the crowds were gathering, the pit gates pickets simmered and concluded that they had failed in their duty, and allowed the scabs to get in on their watch. They resolved to storm the pit on their own, and drag these scabs back out. With numbers so evenly matched it was a quite a short and bloody fight with the cops deploying their truncheons without caution and our pickets wading in with fists and boots. As the men retreated bloody and injured back up the lane and the cops dragged their injured away, the Greater Manchester police started pouring in reinforcements, with horseboxes and endless lines of riot vans and tooled-up cops. Within minutes, they were deployed, advancing up the pit lane and pushing and kicking anyone in the road. In the style of the National Guard in Harlem, they shouted 'go home' to the men who had been born and bred on these their own streets.

The loudspeaker cars were massing an army from Thorne and Moorends and the surrounding Dunscroft, Hatfield and Stainforth villages. Masses of people started to flood in. A gang of teenage boys on their BMX bikes set off from Moorends. Buses from those villages suddenly found themselves full with old lads and young 'uns and not a few women. From the neighbouring houses crowds of women and children were descending on the pit lane.

There were many atrocities that day; Adrian Simpson was beaten almost literally to death. His heart stopped and had to be revived. He was permanently incapacitated, but found himself, and not the police, charged with malicious wounding and jailed for three months. There were many acts of absolute selfless courage from the Hatfield men.

As the crowds gathered and the long-shield units formed up right across Emerson Avenue, a little old grey-haired women, with a wonderfully lined and strong face, marched alone toward them, shouting loudly. 'There's nen o' ye would come oot from behind there and fight our lads one to one like men! Any one o' wor men could fight ye lot, in fact ah dar fight ye's mesell!' she cried out, amid a great cheer. An old chap in his cap covered in his NUM badges comes to her side, and waving his stick at them denounces them all as 'the bosses' lackeys, and Thatcher's lackeys'. It is deeply moving stuff and the air is charged with emotion. As more and more police vehicles poured into the villages from all directions – a big detachment of the Met we are told – women and children stood in their gardens and jeered. Men came out of the pubs and clubs, everyone dropped everything and shouted at the passing vans, sticking two fingers up at them, bricking them and moving in a mass after them toward the pit.

Myself and Peter Curran the Union secretary have quite a few heated words between ourselves as to how we will handle this. Peter is fearful of what could become a massacre of our people – deaths, serious injuries. The cops agree to allow him back through their ranks to speak to the personnel manager, Eddy Smith, a man with whom we have always had the best of relations. He succeeds in convincing one of the three scabs to come back out, on his own feet, if he is allowed to rejoin the strike unmolested. We agree and he is led through a narrow open column, through the silent pickets, and off toward home. The womenfolk though feel no constraints and loudly tell him what pain and suffering he has caused to his mates and neighbours. He stays loyal the rest of the strike. It is only halfway through the shift.

The rest of the day, while the crowds massed and waited the return of the scab bus bringing out the traitors, there were many sorties and skirmishes, too many to tell here.

The crowd surged up the pit tip and outflanked the police right along the pit lane. As the crowd massed toward the colliery offices and the pit yard, the riot police deployed in ranks up the tip to disperse them. There were volleys of stones and police charges. Sometimes there would be standoffs with both sides now sweating and black from dust and shale on the tip. A renewed charge of young lads towards the pit washer and stockyard is met by the police Land Rovers with the crash barriers on the front, charging from cover and trying to run them down, swerving here and there and being hit by great stones. The cops retreat, chased by an army of little kids, some as young as five or six, throwing stones. There follows a concerted counterattack by short-shield riot police. This one is for real. Panic spreads and the crowd runs off in confusion and comedy thrill and terror. Half of them rush down the side of the tip where police with clubs chase them across the busy railway lines as amassed passengers aboard the passing trains see police charges and hand-to-hand fighting on the lines. Police have clubs held over their heads as they come screaming down the side of the tip. In among all the running bodies – pickets, children and police – travellers' horses have broken free from their stakes and run in terror among the crowds, through the streets, or onto the railway lines. As a mass retreat of teenagers and children and women come streaming down the side of the tip toward the village a big convoy of police vehicles is entering via East Lane. The cops looking out of the windows think it is an ambush as the crowd descend upon them. Many of the back doors of the vehicles are open, and into the packed ranks of sitting police come point-blank volleys of bricks and sticks. A motorbike escort is knocked from his bike, which goes spinning along the road and is at once captured by some inspired young lads who mount it and drive it off up a back lane laughing uncontrollably to cheers from their neighbours.

Meantime in the main street the riot police are marching in formation, trying to club people off the streets; they are meeting charges, bottles, catapults and bricks. There is a lull, they fall back. We take stock – the bus will soon becoming out.

Well, I usually come up with something unexpected and this was unexpected.

I mass the ranks of pickets, and urge them that we will sit down in front of the lines of riot cops just as the scab bus comes down the lane. It will force the cops to move us, it will halt the bus, it will give the community time to let these spineless bastards know we hate them and to get back in line before we discover who you are. It is not a popular proposal. It is though mostly accepted and the men, loyal as the day is long, follow me to the front of the riot shields and sit down as the bus comes down the pit lane. There are masses of cameras upon us – some media, some press (*News Line* has a massive collection of shots from the day taken by Peter Arkell and Ray Rising, who stayed in the thick of action to get their photos) and lots of ordinary folk. The chief cop is wrong-footed, confused. He orders his men to lower their long shields to move us from the road. The bus is already standing, the crowds are starting to surge, snatch squads with short shields start to move in from the sides. At once all is confusion as hell breaks out.

They start to grab the sitting miners, some of the kids who are here along with us, an old bloke. Then the bricks start to whiz over our heads. The lads take to their feet; the riot police break through the ranks and start charging forward, clubbing people. There is heroic hand-to-hand fighting. We retreat. I take off with three snatch squad, who have been eyeing me all the while, on my tail. It takes some dodging through gardens and back lanes to lose them, and probably avoid the sack – NCB management were known to give lists of the Union men they wanted nicking at scenes just like this, so they can sack them whatever the courts later decided.

Throughout the day, there are cavalry charges through the street. A horse goes down. Cops are injured. They hold the ground at the top of the pit lane where we had erected a big marquee as a picket hut. They set fire to it while we watch, by kicking the brazier over. They march through the street. Women with their children stand in their gardens, mock and jeer them. At times they are driven back and crouch under walls of long riot shields as the world rains down on them.

There is no bus the next day. The scabs will not be coming in. Within days we know who they are, and have given them a call. One is profoundly sorry. He has lost everything, his house is empty of furniture he has sold, and both he and his wife have medical conditions. They are suffering, though they never sought help from the community. Now we take him and them back, and he too stays loyal to the end. The third scab, out of fear, bides his time. For now, he will not be back.

The invasion force moves on to Markham (Armthorpe) the next day, then Rossington and over successive days and weeks into all the Doncaster pit communities. From now on, though, the riot police will stay, will be an alien force in our village, will be banned from shops and bars. From now on, nightly, Hatfield will be at war. It will not be with our organised picket teams – they will be flying again. It will be a battle sustained by ordinary folk, young and old, men and women in the community. There are now no scabs at this pit, but the police are still here, attacking us night on night, day after day. The strike is their enemy and so is this community.

A small manufactured break had occurred, but we managed to reseal it and it held firm for a time. By the next time, we had managed to organise counter-surveillance and spies within the police ranks themselves. This way, when the second front was opened up against us in September, we knew when it was coming; we knew the date. This allowed us to plan a level of response, which the police were totally unprepared for. There were three routes, which the scab bus with its handful of occupants and escort could take. On each of them was a reception equal to anything anyone had experienced anywhere. We didn't know which way the bus would come. As it turned out, it hit our team led by the COSA branch. The COSA-led defenders had assembled a massive barricade of cars from the scrap yards, and suitable inflammable gas bottles and part-filled petrol tanks. As the scab convoy came face to face with the roadblock, the barricade was torched and a huge volley of bricks met the bus and the convoy. The cops retreated and only just managed to keep the scabs from jumping screaming from the bus and running in terror through the streets; it's as well they did. Terrifying though that encounter was, it was less severe than the one, which had awaited them on the Barnby Dun approach road. This was the squad I myself led with some hugely heroic men who of course I cannot name – all volunteers who knew the score and the potential for very long prison sentences; they know who they are and I will never forget their selfless bravery. Had the scabs come that way, it is likely the vehicles would have been destroyed, and scabs and police seriously injured, if not killed. That ambush itself had two backup ambushes, which would have proved potentially lethal for any police vehicles that sought to disperse or chase and capture the team from the initial attack. Say ney mer. Except maybe this perhaps. As police, violence moved toward going up another notch, with the use of tear gas and plastic bullets, so our response was already in preparation. The road from Stainforth to Belfast was already mapped.

Big Harry (Harle) was arrested during the police riot; enthusiastic police smashed his arm in the process. When he appeared in court, with his arm in a plaster and sling, the rather curious Mr Lumley, a Doncaster solicitor, represented him. Lumley, a small man with some odd court mannerisms, sits on the table in front of the judge and dangles his feet in the course of his presentation.

The judge asks, 'If your client was innocent why was he running away from the police?'

To this Lumley replies, 'Everyone in the coal communities run away at the approach of the riot police m'lud'.

This clearly surprised the judge. 'Really?' he asks.

'Yes', elaborated Lumley. 'If you m'lud were sitting on the wall reading your newspaper and the riot police were coming toward you, you would run away.'

'I would run away?' the now irate judge asks. 'Why would I run away?'

'Because they would knock you over the wall m'lud,' Lumley answers.

The judge is clearly shocked and repeats, 'If I was sitting on the wall, reading my newspaper, the police would come and knock me over the wall. Just like that?'

'Yes m'lud.'

It is an impressive discourse. It totally convinces the judge, who not only finds Harry innocent, but goes on to award him damages for his injury. Harry is able to buy a new car from the proceedings. Weeks later the police pull him over in his new car. 'Do you mind if we inspect your vehicle?' they ask. 'No problem,' answers Harry. 'You bought it for me.'

TUC SOLIDARITY?

Scargill met with the TUC leaders and the leaders of the strategic unions involved, and asked simply for respect of our picket lines. David Basnett, leader of the GMB, the principal power union, and speaking for the TUC delegation, said he 'could not accept the demand to respect picket lines. It would divide unions without achieving its objective.'[176] After hours of discussion prior to the TUC Conference, they agreed they would stop moving and using scab fuel if that had the support of the TUC. On the floor of the conference, Gavin Laird and John Lyons of the engineers, Bill Sirs of the steelworkers, and Eric Hammond of the electricians all spoke and voted against respecting picket lines. Basnett's GMB voted for it. Bennett and Hencke declare 'It was of course meaningless, because it was undeliverable,'[177] but just why we are not told. Given that the victory of the miners in 1972 and 1974 came about not because the miners had held a national ballot, as our critics seem to think, but because the pickets were respected across steel plants and power stations, wharves and transport, why should it have been 'not deliverable'? In straight, practical, common-sense terms, a decimation of the coal industry was bound to lead to the destruction of steel and power generation. The closure of coal-fired power stations put power workers at those stations in the same dole queue as the miners. We weren't asking for some act of superhuman selflessness. The miners were asking simply that our fellow trade unionists not burn or use fuel produced by scabs or transported by strikebreakers. We were not demanding solidarity action as such: workers in every industry were not being asked to refrain from using the fuel they already had, just not replace it with strikebreaking replacements. Our own support for the earlier steelworkers' strike had been lukewarm, but we had at least not allowed any new steel to replace that we already had on site.[178] We had further banned the movement of steel supports between colliery sites.

NACODS

The National Association of Colliery Overmen, Deputies and Shotfirers were pivotal in the strike. No mine could work without their presence. Their jobs were affected, along with those of the ordinary miners, from whose ranks they all had graduated. Considerable controversy and debate remains on the efforts to draw this union into joint action alongside the NUM, and the efforts to prevent this. They twice balloted with clear majorities in favour of strike and this was clearly a popular view among rank-and-file members of the union nationwide. The first ballot was not acted upon because it failed to achieve the union's two-thirds majority rule, which had spiked the guns of the miners' union in days gone by. Despite this, the union's NEC and leadership were heavily lobbied by rank-and-file members demanding they join the struggle against closures.

At work, where they were still deployed among the working miners of Nottingham, something of an unofficial work to rule was developing, which ultimately nearly brought around a total halt to ongoing production in coalfields which were still working. A deputy who had been injured by a fall of ground as he checked the unsupported area in advance of the 'gate' (tunnel) was held by the High Court not to be due any compensation because this wasn't 'a normal working place'. NACODS members quickly responded by refusing to inspect or supervise unsupported ground in advance of supports, which rapidly brought production to a halt in those pits still working.

Although a rapid compromise on injuries sustained in such circumstances was produced, deputies continued to assist the NUM's action by refusing to cross picket lines 'where they could not do so with dignity', i.e. walking or in their own cars. This severely restricted the employers' attempts to maintain any coal production. A second NACODS ballot produced a 'yes' vote of 82.5%, and Mrs Thatcher was said to have 'wobbled'. A nationwide strike by NACODS alongside the NUM would stop every mine in the country and prevent any further supplement to diminishing coal stocks. Mrs Thatcher was later to record that she had been told that NACODS members could not be much longer restrained from joint strike action. She describes the October NEC decision not to take strike action after all as a 'hammerblow' for Mr Scargill. She claims why they came to this decision is 'unclear'. NACODS settled by November of 1984 on the basis of an agreement to institute 'a review procedure' for each individual pit closure; the weakness of this agreement, and the reason why the NUM wouldn't also accept it, was that the finding of the review would not be binding on the NCB. Two of the mines that subsequently went before the review, Cadeby in South Yorkshire and Bates in Northumberland, and proved their case for continuation of operations, were to have the recommendations of the review body overruled and the mines closed anyway, thus demonstrating the NUM's justifiable dissatisfaction with the terms of the NACODS settlement. Mrs Thatcher is less than coy in her memoirs, recognising that the right to close pits regardless of any 'review' was central to her strategy:

No matter how elaborate the process of consultation, the NCB could not concede to a third party the right of ultimate decision over pit closures. This, although generally understood, was best not set out too starkly.[179]

This might have been advice to the NACODS NEC, since NACODS members seemed genuinely shocked the first time they tested the procedure with a favourable review result, only to find the colliery closed anyway. Ten years later Arthur Scargill, reflecting on the events in the April 1994 edition of *The Miner*, observed:

The Tories twice came within a hair's breath of settling on the NUM's terms – but the deal was sabotaged both times. The closest the Tories came to capitulating was in October 1984.

Terms of settlement were worked out between leaders of the NUM and the pit deputies' union NACODS whose members had just voted by 83% to strike.

We agreed these terms were 'the bottom line', and handed them to ACAS (the government's arbitration service). In the next 48 hours, the emergency cabinet met, with Thatcher in the chair, and agreed to them. But then there was a further meeting. Everything changed. It was reported that the 'under managers' union – they meant NACODS – had agreed to settle for a mess of pottage: the Modified Review Procedure.

A former Cabinet Minister has said he could not believe the 180 degree turn made by Thatcher, in rapidly agreeing to settle. The tragedy is that in those crucial hours we could not get anyone from NACODS to meet us. By the time we got back to ACAS, any possibility that the government or the NCB would back down had gone.

In the paper Arthur comments further:

The first time NUM and NCB negotiators agreed to settle the strike was 3 months earlier, in July 1984. The deal was that the five pits whose closure sparked the dispute would stay open. The *Plan For Coal* would form the basis of future energy policy. Victimised miners would be reinstated. Prime Minister Thatcher and her agent David Hart intervened to stop the settlement.[180]

Mrs Thatcher's memoirs[181] and other contemporary evidence would seem to suggest that both of these descriptions were accurate, though the motive for the NACODS unilateral settlement for terms far short of the joint demands remains open to speculation and assumption, for want of any factual explanations.[182]

24 October. The NACODS executive had agreed to accept the NCB proposals, albeit 'modified' but not so modified, they were not going to proceed to decimate the industry and tear up the terms of the *Plan For Coal* as formally agreed with regard to investment, development and exhaustion.

A short 4 months after the strike and 10 years before his reflection on events recorded just above, Arthur had been less clear on NACODS support for a joint demand to Thatcher; he reported it, at the Annual Conference thus:

On the 23rd Oct 1984, talks once again resumed at the ACAS headquarters and it became clear the concentration of effort was to get NACODS to call off their strike threat. The NUM team were left kicking their heels for hours. That evening the Union side met briefly with NACODS, who had in their possession a document of that date setting out amongst other things a proposal for revising the Colliery Review Procedure by setting up an independent body at the end of the procedure. The NUM side explained the idea had been floated previously, but it really did not tackle the issue at the centre of the current dispute, namely, colliery closures. On the question of the five pits, the proposal contained in the document was less favourable than those contained in the Board's document dated 18th July 1984. Secondly, it was pointed out that the proposal contained in the Board's document dated the 23rd October did not make any reference to withdrawing the closure programme. Moreover, its reference to 'market objectives' was a clear indication that the closure programme would be proceeded with.

It was – said the NUM side – tantamount to accepting the butchery of the industry. NACODS left the NUM with the impression that they had taken on board what had been said, and would stick out for withdrawal of the colliery closure programme. Next day, however, they announced they were calling off their strike threat, and claimed that the Board's proposals regarding The Colliery Review Procedure met their requirements …[183]

This version of events leaves no impression that NACODS had been very convinced about standing firm with the NUM at all – or that's my reading of it anyway.

NEGOTIATIONS

The fate of negotiations, of which there had been many, swung from indifference to concerted efforts to reach a solution. Who was responsible for the hot and cold reactions to a settlement has never been explored in any depth. The press during the strike and 25 years on have suggested Arthur refused to negotiate; this is far from the truth. Initially having to some extent at least set the strike up, in the belief that a confrontation was not only inevitable but desirable, the government – and, vicariously on their behalf, the NCB – was prepared to test the metal of the strike and wait to see if it would come together. Soon after, as the strike takes on a national dimension and starts to sweep all before it, the imperative to explore some sort of settlement is engaged. Rapid progress towards a settlement in July had been well in hand, until the government decided to scupper any early deal deciding instead to stick it out.

As the NUM Conference in July 1984 was taking place, the strike seemed to be rolling all ahead of it. The pound had fallen sharply against the dollar in response to the strike.

KEEPING THE STRIKE ON THE RAILS

Beginning of July. 'On one occasion a group of miners hung a flag on a bridge over a railway line and deemed there to be a picket line. As we shall see, the actions resulted from that gesture nearly paralysed the entire country.' (I. MacGregor)

I am proud to say the action was one of mine, and the pickets Hatfield's. If the winning or losing of the strike could be narrowed down to two crucial events, then this picket line, and the 100% solidarity of railworkers as a result, with the consequential challenge thrown down to the dockers nationwide, would be one of them, while the NACODS strike vote and date for all-out action was the other.

We drape a banner over the wall of the bridge over the main Immingham railway line into Scunthorpe steelworks. It reads 'NUR/ASLEF Stop All Fuel And Iron Ore – Official Miners Picket – Hatfield Main NUM'. The crew of the first train from the docks see the banner, stop the train. There it stood for 12 months, not a single train was to enter the steelworks. It caused a major crisis, would in time lead to a national dock labour strike and near enough a generalised strike alongside the miners. That little banner came closest to being the catalyst to a total victory for us and the dockers. It would all fall on the shoulders and backbone of the Immingham dockers. Would they stand by the TGWU policy and neither allow scab fuel and ore to be loaded into scab lorries breaching the rail blockade; or allow non dock labour to load it, in breach of the National Dock Labour Scheme?

Dockers had launched a national strike after their colleagues at Immingham had buckled and sanctioned the use of non-dock labour to unload coal. This had become necessary because coke and iron ore imports to the Scunthorpe steelworks were blocked by solidarity action by railworkers respecting our NUM picket line mounted on the bridge overlooking the train track. It was to cause a national crisis which, later evidence would show, potentially could have brought the miners to victory. Dockers from Liverpool heading over to talk to the Immingham dockers and persuade them to stick to defence of the dock labour scheme, then came up against the arbitrary 'laws' being made up on the hoof by the 'National Reporting Centre'.[184] Few dockers made it across, not because of weather or their vehicles but because the police blocked the M62 and M18 motorways. Dockers were turned back almost as soon as they set off, on pain of arrest, their vehicle details like ours fed into the 'stolen vehicle' police computer and monitored around the country.

COAL STOCKS, POWER STATIONS, NEGOTIATIONS, THE COUNTEROFFENSIVE
Some sections in power plants across the country joined regional strike days of action and others ensured no power joined the national grid for the duration of the strike. Widespread solidarity action of the kind that ensured the victories of '72 and '74, though, was not to be forthcoming; and without joint secondary action the miners were heavily overmatched.

Considerable efforts were made to ensure that power stations did not stop producing power and that there would be no power cuts. The government had previously made considerable efforts to ensure the supply of energy during any miners' strike. In particular, power stations had been converted to 'dual-burn' so they could switch to oil from coal if necessary, and massive stocks of coal could be stored at power stations in anticipation of just such a strike. However, there were a number of localised power cuts, particularly in the south of England, and big voltage reductions, though these were put into effect during the night hours so they wouldn't be noticed. All of this was safely kept off the TV screens and newspaper pages.[185] However, supply hovered just off the brink of total collapse on a number of occasions, with nuclear stations sailing well into the danger zone past their shutdown period. On 8 January 1985, the CEGB had boasted of meeting a demand of 42,000MW, but actually only a further 800MW were in reserve, and that was with all emergency generating systems on overload and a battery of aeroplane jet engines bolted and welded to the floors – the final-final-back-up-all-else-has-failed system.

At Bradwell Nuclear Power Station in northern Essex, the station went into 'preliminary meltdown alarm'; the workers tried to flee the plant, but were stopped by the Nuclear Energy Authority Special (armed) Constabulary. Most of the big coalfield power stations, in strikebound coalfields like Yorkshire, did not accept scab fuel, and ASLEF and NUR ensured picket lines were respected, even when our bored pickets took off and abandoned their posts. Drax, Thorpe Marsh,

Ferrybridge and Eggborough all blacked scab coal and oil. The same was true in other strike coalfields like Scotland and South Wales.[186]

COUNTEROFFENSIVE

PICKETS

The miners' flying pickets had been something of working-class folklore in the '70s, though actually they had been around with great effect in most previous mining strikes, especially in 1912. MacGregor concludes that in, '84, these pickets were mostly young and from Doncaster.

'But at the core of most of the trouble was a hardened group of miners who had obviously been trained well in advance in the techniques required to force dissenters into line. We had reports of these cadres mainly of young miners based in the Doncaster Area being created and trained, but we did not realise how effective they could be until the battle for Nottingham was on in earnest.' (MacGregor)

It is quite clear Ian is talking here about our EMC camps and training sessions, and our long history of preparing the miners for confrontation on picket lines etc.[187] Doubtless Ian's 'reports' are those in secret NCB files or else reports shown to him by the Special Forces.

BACKBYE FROM THE STORM

Ron Rose was a South Yorkshire playwright, to whom I had suggested some time before the start of the overtime ban preceding the strike that he should write a play about the illegal though widespread wildcat pit strikes during World War Two. He came up with *Bread and Roses*, a play set in South Yorkshire during the rash of 'pit lad' strikes in the middle of World War Two. Ron had collected loads of first-hand, anecdotal evidence from Tom Mullanny and Dave Glover, both pit activist Union officials and subsequently Doncaster councillors. Maureen got her first shot at live acting on stage, as Ida Jones, almost the leading lady you could say. The play toured the strike-hit coalfields of North and South Yorkshire to mass crowds of striking miners, their wives and children, for whom all such entertainment and collective togetherness were now much sought after. It was her first step down a new road to acting, for following this came *Enemies Within*, a powerful story of the '84/85 strike itself, which went on to tour the country, ending in the Young Vic to mass acclaim.[188]

Me, I run myself ragged with a nationwide tour, down one side of the country and back up the other. I address mass meetings of all kinds of workers and groups, talk to local radio stations, field heated phone-in debates, sing at socials and headline mass open-air rallies. I stand at factory gates, dock gates and local working men's clubs. In February and March of 1985, in conjunction with Workers Power, we run a 'Miners and the Struggle in Ireland' tour, where I make the connections, demonstrate the similarities, draw the conclusions for common struggle and common recognition. I plan to fill in the gaps on a tour with the Direct Action Movement; I am told I spoke to the biggest assemblies of anarcho-syndicalists in Britain since prewar days, arguing for workers' direct control of the strike, the Union and the industry. At Burnley Labour Club I call on the crowds to stop debating direct action and start *taking* direct action, which wasn't completely appreciated, but Christ, this wasn't some academic debate; we were hanging on by our finger tips. If ever there was a time for thousands of syndicalists to appear over the hill singing 'Hold The Fort I'm A-Coming' now was it. I am speaking at the History Workshop in Leicester on the role of the media during the strike; I had by this time a little pamphlet out addressing the question. It also gave me the chance to call for solidarity pickets at the beleaguered Leicester collieries, which were badly split between strikers and blacklegs.[189]

I carry on through Nottingham and back down to Festival Hall for a rally, picket and Ewan MacColl's birthday. By the end of February I have lost my voice, which is utterly frustrating, and I gurgle particles of blood from my throat as I try to make it work.

In January I addressed the Direct Action Movement's Congress for Industrial Action in Otley. It boasted one hundred and fifty delegates from rank and file bodies and anarcho-syndicalist groups. We take in Bridlington, Camden, Chesterfield, Cambridge, Cardiff, Bradford, Burnley, and Manchester. In Birmingham, I tour with the Red Guzunders, and other Sheffield folkies, in fundraising socials where the old Brummy folk crowd turn out in huge numbers, including the Ian Campbell folk family and their lads from UB40. We stay with their grandparents. Since we haven't got a collective name I come up with 'V & The Spitting Lizards', which is duly posted around the city. (It is based upon a current sci-fi drama on TV about invading alien humanoid lizards.) It causes some confusion, as a big gang of punks turns up, drawn by the title. They leave after the first session; I hear one say, 'I knew it wasn't a new wave gig man, when I seen the accordion.' I speak at the Sparkbrook Labour Club on 'Ireland and the Miners Strike'. At Kersley, I address a mass kitchen, food and clothing distribution session packed with strikers, their wives and kids. It is teaming with optimism. In the evening I am at Coventry.

There was clearly some long-term strategy by the Labour Party leadership, in cahoots with the civil service and probably the special forces, to ensure Labour would not have a left leadership during the strike and could not therefore swing the substantial weight of that whole apparatus behind the miners. The rank and file of that party, however was strongly in our support. In little quiet middle-class backwaters where the Labour Party was regarded as the local Angry Brigade and couldn't gain a council seat, it suddenly found itself the centre of political agitation. Right-wing areas of seaside conservative reaction found local parties at the cutting edge of social agitation and revived political interest and protest. Nowhere was this more marked than down at Whitby, where the local party's weekend school on 'Socialism and the Media' suddenly became the major political event in the town. I was to be the star speaker, exposing the role of the media during the strike, and presenting a couple of Chris Reeves's *Miners Campaign tapes*. The local party had adopted the Clipstone miners, and they and their families were to be in attendance. The local media had made the whole thing top billing, and announced the participation of the local MP, the national secretary of the TGWU and members of the NUJ at the prestigious Metropolitan Hotel. It was typical really of the way in which the Labour Party rank and file in the constituency and ward parties stood, in total contrast to the parliamentary leadership, who were everywhere distancing themselves both from the strike and their members' hearty support of it.

By October 1984, 6 months into the strike, the future of Thatcher's government hung in the balance – when there were less than 6 weeks' coal stocks left. As mentioned earlier, at this point Frank Ledger, the CEGB director of operations, revealed that they had only planned for the strike to last 6 months. Power supply by this time was 'catastrophic', while the former chairman of the Central Electricity Generating Board (CEGB), Sir Walter Marshall, spelt out what this meant: 'Our predictions showed on paper that Scargill would win certainly by Christmas. Margaret Thatcher got very worried about that ... I felt she was wobbly.'

Ian MacGregor was summoned to Downing Street, and recalls Thatcher's comments in his memoirs: 'I'm very worried about it. You have to realise that the fate of this government is in your hands Mr. MacGregor. You have got to solve this problem.'

Marching to the Fault Line in many respects not only confirms the above impressions of government, police, and press involvement, but also underpins many of these notions with facts and new revelations. Less helpful is the authors' obsession with nailing Arthur Scargill as somehow culpable in the failure of negotiations. In the fury, not least from Arthur himself in the pages of the *Guardian*, following the publication of the book, the authors insist the settlement was in the bag and Arthur kicked it into touch. They say on the *Guardian* comment website:

According to the diary of the late Bill Keys, he met with Lord Whitelaw in the House of Lords on December 13 1984 to discuss the terms of the settlement. He then met Mick McGahey in Edinburgh on January 11 1985, gave him Whitelaw's terms, and took from him the minimum terms of an honourable settlement, for transmission, with McGahey's agreement, to Whitelaw. These discussions produced the deal that Scargill rejected on February 20.

This diary was given to one of the co-authors, Francis Beckett, by Bill Keys before he died. The general tenor of it was also verified by John Monks, a former TUC general secretary, who was already working at the TUC during the strike. It may be that McGahey, a loyal deputy to Scargill, never told him where the proposals came from. But it's quite inconceivable that Keys, a one man ACAS and one of number of go-betweens during the year-long strike, should have made it up.

Of course Mick is himself dead now as well as Keys, and who actually knows what 'McGahey's agreement' was? 'Yes, give it a go,' and/or 'We've nowt to lose,' perhaps? Speculation aside, Arthur refused to sell short the aims of the strike, but at the same time clearly entered into these negotiations suspicious but prepared to take them at face value, in the belief that a settlement was not only achievable but being sought by both parties to the dispute. Negotiations were always tripartite, although they were presented as being bi-partisan; the third party, the government was the missing face at the table but it was never far from MacGregor's shoulder or ear. David Hart and his more extra-curricular agenda, expressing total hostility to any negotiations let alone settlement, occupied a further invisible chair at a crowded negotiating table. No wonder Scargill was frequently confused by the variety of voices and personas, which addressed him through the medium of Mr MacGregor; it must have seemed at times like a scene from *The Exorcist* as the body was possessed by different entities at different times. But there were other disembodied forces around this table. Both sides believed this clash to be more than a sum of its parts; believed it to be much more than about pit closures. Mrs Thatcher carried the spectre of Ted Heath and his crushing defeats in '72 and '74 at the hands of the miners.[190] By Mr Scargill hovered the memory of Arthur Cook and 1921, 1926, and all the injustice done to the miners then which he would never allow again. In the 1920s, the employers had sought to lengthen the miner's working day and reduce his earnings; now they had come to take away the work altogether. Raphael Samuel poetically suggested: 'In one aspect the strike was a war of ghosts, in which the living actors were dwarfed by the shadows they had conjured up.'[191]

Nothing the authors of *Marching* have produced in any sense suggests that Thatcher and her government had actually withdrawn the closure programme as such, or that they had agreed a union veto on pit closures; at best, we are told that they stepped away from the table. Withdrew to pre-existing borders as it were, but what for? We can speculate forever as to whether such a peace treaty would have lasted and whether it would have made us (the miners) stronger or weaker. Certainly, the people round the table were playing for high stakes; both sides announced this was a 'winner takes it all' gamble, but its outcome would lie in the hard material forces in existence on the ground, not in the ether. Everything was still to play for right up to the end; the result was never a foregone conclusion.

For her part, Mrs Thatcher confirms that she would never have allowed such fudge in any case:

> I do understand your fear that the NUM leadership may yet evade
> responsibility for the misery they have caused – but I believe that the Coal
> Board have been, and are being, resolute about their position. For my part,
> I have made clear that there can be no fudging of the central issue and no
> betrayal of the working miners to whom we owe so much …

– Mrs. Thatcher calming the fears of a strikebreaker's wife that negotiations might go in favour of an NUM victory.[192]

One fascinating aside which Beckett and Hencke's book *Marching to the Fault Line* reveals for the first time is the fact that Norman Willis, who had now succeeded Len Murray as general secretary of the TUC, clearly got MacGregor drunk, and in the process Mac agreed to sign away the Coal Board/government case – lock, stock and barrel. In a private hotel room meeting in February 1985, Mac had agreed no pit would close unless the reserves were 'deemed exhausted'.[193] The document waited to be signed the following afternoon when he was to re-meet the TUC team. Until, that is, the ministers Walker and Hunt discovered what he had done. It meant no pit actually with workable reserves could close without the union agreeing they were not practically or safely recoverable. Mac was probably not as stupid as they make him out; he probably knew that in the wings there were hefty redundancy packages waiting which might have caused many pits to be so deemed, unless the union at a higher level was given the power to make the judgement. The two horrified ministers, under Maggie's instruction, whipped the agreement off the table and retabled a suitably useless one in its place. Thatcher, we are told, never forgave Mac for nearly handing the whole shooting match over to the TUC and the NUM. It was one of Willis's better days, if not his only better day in the whole 12 months.

Another of our Hatfield pickets, Jeff Budworth from Stainforth, is jailed for 6 months (there were three of our men given jail sentences). Jeff is a remarkably good-looking, tall, quiet and dignified man. Were it not for the strike, Jeff would never have seen the inside of a court. Well, that and the fool of a policeman he encountered while approaching Harworth Colliery at the head of a long column of pickets. PC Ian Sunderland was the sole upholder of law and order that morning, the picket target having been successfully kept covert and a decoy deployed to the Midlands. Another cop would have looked on in dismay and maybe had some breakfast backbye somewhere, then called for reinforcements. Not PC Sunderland. He leaps in front of the lead car and stops the line of pickets. Jeff is pulled over. As Jeff gets out of the car (he here continues the story in his own words), 'Constable Sunderland decided (for reasons only he could know) to get me in what I can only call a bear hug. He pinned me against the car; at this two or three cars pulled up full of pickets, who asked PC Sunderland to let me go; he was having none of it. So they decided a few kicks would do the trick. This went on for a couple of minutes, which at the time seemed much longer. I myself was taking kicks by well-meaning but not very accurate pickets. I noticed a ditch by the side of the car and managed to manoeuvre myself and Sunderland to the rear of my car, by this time he was starting to loosen his grip. I managed to break his grip and pushed him into the ditch. The pickets returned to their cars and drove off (job done). I stood looking down at this pathetic figure looking up at me and remember saying to him, "You've just taken a kicking for nowt there pal," and I turned and walked back to my car. I was about to reach for the door handle when one of the lads who was with me shouted: "Look out, Jeff! He's got a stick!" I turned to face him … I remembered seeing the damage done to pickets at Orgreave, so as soon as he came within striking distance I gave him a right cross. It hit him on the left side of his nose. He staggered back, looked at me pointing his stick, and said: "I'll see you later."

'Apparently PC Sunderland was found later slumped over his steering wheel by his colleagues.'

My own Harworth experience was a lot more comical, though not without some aspects of guilt and regret. I had been at the head of a mass convoy of pickets en route to the wharves. We pressed on through undetected until a hurried single line of cops slung itself across the road at Gunness, the entrance to the main dock roads. In these numbers, we should have steamed on through. My driver however stopped, and we being the lead car so did everyone else. Speed was of the essence here, and I was fuming – everyone was getting out of their cars, lighting up fags, and bunching together for a chat. The road to the wharves with hundreds of thousands of tonnes of coal was just up ahead. Fleets of unsuspecting scab lorries with their bloodsucking soldier-of-fortune drivers, were cruising along, draining our strength away, unmolested.

Only this pathetic line of cops stood in the road. We should charge now, before they get the riot cops on site, before they can be reinforced. I yell at the men, 'Ha'way, lads, lets gaan!' and make a run for the line on my own, thinking they will surge forward and follow me. I'm grabbed and pinned to the floor, before the bulk of the pickets realise I've been lifted. I'm furious we didn't keep going through the line and scatter them off the road. I'm furious they didn't dive out of the cars, punch through this line, pour onto the wharves, and scatter the scab drivers. They on the other hand accused me of 'giving myself up' before the fighting started. Yes, it did start – they waited until vanloads of riot police, kitted up, formed up, made ranks and advanced towards them. Then when the advantage of time and equipment was with the cops, they charged into them and fought a fierce battle during which both sides were knocked down ditches and through fences. It was as if they had wanted to give the other side time to get ready – like there was a proper way to do this battle and sneaking through when they weren't ready wasn't it. I was always going on to anyone who would listen that the cops were an obstacle to the target but they weren't the target – we hadn't come here to fight them, we had come to stop the coal and the scabs, sometimes that got lost sight of.

My unthought-out 'suicide' charge was stupid of course, it earned me, a thumping and my arms pulled behind my back and plastic tie-bands slip-knotted over my wrists; these they call 'plastic handcuffs'. I was left in the back of a transit on my knees, in the sweltering heat, while they fought it out with the lads. By the time they came back for me, hours later, my wrists had swelled up, my hands were drained of blood, my arms felt like they were bursting with pressure and I was on the verge of unconsciousness from pain and heat exhaustion. They drove me to Scunthorpe police station where they tried to cut loose the ties while I laid on my face on the floor. The flesh was so swollen and the tie bands now biting so tight into my skin that they couldn't find which was which to cut them. Then they sent one of their colleagues off to B&Q and bought a set of long-handled garden shears, which they positioned between my wrists and forced my hands apart. Only then did they succeed in finding and cutting the bands. My hands were like raw meat and the pain of the blood surging laid me out cold. I was charged and let go, late in the evening.

I mention this because the next morning I had no intention of joining any day shift flying picket. I was sitting this day out. Or so I thought. I didn't know today was an afternoon picket, and it was at Harworth, and they sent one of the vans to come and pick me up, so I had to go. Once at Harworth the lads massed up and set off for the pit gates. Not me – I was going to sit on this wall in the sunshine and have one off today.

Then I see the armoured scab bus coming along the road, and I pick up a half brick and run toward the bus, to 'persuade 'them not to cross the picket line. As I get within throwing distance, I see it's not the scab bus, it's a bus full of the Metropolitan Police, and they have seen me too. They dive off the bus with their short shields and clubs as I exit stage left and through the main street. Normally they give up, but not these buggers. I shoot down a side street and down the path of a house, where a bloke is up a ladder painting the brickwork. I know the black-clad, armoured men are not far behind and seen me come up this street. I'm in the back garden, and I whip my shirt off, pick up a garden folk and pretend I'm digging the garden. I'm up by a patch of rhubarb when I see a pair of feet sticking out from under the leaves. 'Bugger off!' a voice whispers – it's another fleeing picket! Just then, the riot police come down the path and round the corner. I fake what I think is a Nottingham accent, 'Ahl right lads?', and walk toward them, sweating – I hope they think from my garden exertions.

At that point, the bloke is coming down the ladder and I walk toward him.

I whisper: 'I'm all right, aren't I ?'

'That depends how you look at it, youth, I'm going work in that pit in 10 minutes.' He was a bloody scab, I look at the cops still suspiciously eyeing me up, clubs in hand. I think of my trembling tortured hands and wrists from yesterday, a possible jail sentence and out the corner of my mouth mutter, 'Look, I've problems of me own at the moment, do you want your garden digging or don't you?' That, dear comrades, is how I come to be digging a scab's garden at Harworth. It is a major indiscretion, second only to having shagged a young nubile Nazi in London in the late 1970s (see *The Wheel's Still in Spin*).

SHEFFIELD OCTAGON CENTRE, 4 DECEMBER 1984

Some years later Alison Aiken (née Sharp) writes to me asking if I

> remember the benefit for the miners' families with Linton Kwesi Johnson at the Octagon Centre Sheffield on 4th Dec.? You gave a 'Great Oration' and also discussed with LKJ at great length … it was a very inspiring occasion which united black struggle with that of the miners. Linton Kwesi Johnson gave a charismatic and fiery performance, and the roof came off when you spoke of the unity and solidarity of the strike and the tremendous support it was receiving from everywhere. There were hundreds upon hundreds of people and the concert raised £600, which went to the Hatfield Women's Action Group.
>
> The concert was organized through Retford Music Co-operative (but I guess that was principally me as coordinator and Steve Aiken as co-director). I was pleased to help the strike effort in such a positive way … the Anti Nuclear Campaign benefit with Benjamin Zephaniah was another concert we did.[194]

GENERAL STRIKE

Almost from the word go, we had been lobbied by left groups, particularly the

Workers Revolutionary Party, demanding that we demand the TUC call a general strike. At first, we strongly resisted their call. With memories of 1926 still deeply indented in the coalfields, this is hardly surprising. We were fearful of any plan that would hand over control and direction of the strike to the TUC General Council. We didn't need a general strike as such, we needed basic solidarity at this stage: don't cross our picket lines; don't use scab fuel; black scab lorries. That would in a nutshell have clinched it. We thought the demand for a general strike as such should be held as a bigger gun in case of the army coming in to move coal and oil stocks or ports and power stations. By November, however we were running out of options. We needed to take the movement by the scruff and shake them from their indifference, inaction or worse – scabbing.

The first formal call comes to a Council meeting from Darfield Main. Their resolution urged that the TUC recognise that the attack on the NUM was the prelude to war on them all. That what was going on was nationwide – with anti-union legislation, common law, and militarised partisan police being used to break and roll back all the rights and achievements the whole trade union movement had made over decades. The resolution was more mature than the bland call, though; it urged that if the TUC refused to mobilise such action then the NUM should directly make that call to all the members of all the unions, over the head of the TUC. And that the call for a one-day general strike should be the prelude to a general fightback. A few days earlier, the Northumberland Area had proposed a similar resolution to the NEC, calling for a 2-week general strike by the whole movement, as a prelude to ongoing action. Darfield's resolution was heartily supported by all the Doncaster branches, who urged the EC and officials not to reject this motion out of hand unless they had some strategy just as good to offer in its place.

Indeed some suggest *any* strategy offered from the leadership would be an improvement on where we were now. Delegates urged that it was obvious the NUM couldn't win this dispute on our own and that other sections of the working class must be drawn into the fight. They said that we couldn't wait for the TUC to move. It was added that we should make concerted efforts to make direct appeals to the unions, and failing that direct appeals over their heads to their members; this should not just include those in fuel and power, but all workers everywhere.

For a moment, we had a flash of a vision of a new and bold strategy – we could see where we had to take this movement. All the officials, however, rose to tell us how impractical it was; that we hadn't been able to get the Yorkshire TUC to take part in a Yorkshire-wide general strike/day of action. The moderate North Yorkshire Area delegates all spoke against, saying that we could alienate the unions who were supporting us, and end up with no support whatever. When it came to the vote, only 19 branches voted for the resolution: all the Doncaster pits plus 7 others, mainly South Yorkshire and Barnsley branches – though not all, or we would have carried it.[195]

15 January 1985. A closed Coal Board meeting at St George's, Doncaster, reports that, of 12,698 men in the Area, 240 were at work; 29 had started that

week. 50 men had already been sacked as a result of the strike 'and there were many more currently within the disciplinary procedure'. They also reported that a BACM (British Association of Colliery Management) member called in to fight an underground fire at Rossington Colliery, which the NUM refused to supply safety cover for, had died of natural causes while fighting the fire.[196] 240 men out of 12,698 more than 10 months into the strike wasn't a bad score, even supposing that was a true figure and not an inflated one.

REARGUARD ACTION

We can't let the picketing strategy go, but we are highly curtailed as to our ability to break out of our backyards. We are frankly a defensive force now, operating a rearguard action and resting the solidity of the strike upon basic trust and loyalty rather than militant picketing. I spend a great deal of time speaking across the country to try and spread solidarity action. I have a regular spot on BBC Radio Sheffield, which never fails to draw widespread phone-ins from miners' wives, striking miners and our supporters. I am also trying to spread and hold our support by singing, in bars, at folky clubs and socials and on occasion from platforms. Sometimes I have the backing of Red Guzunders, and a host of radical folksters; other times it's just the larynx and me.

A SPECTRE OF THE RETREAT FROM MOSCOW

8 February 1985. Yorkshire Area NUM Delegate Council meeting heard a National Executive Committee report given by Johnny Weaver. He raised a spectre, which would come to haunt our union. There had been outrage on the NEC by rumours that the South Wales Area was about to propose a return to work without settlement, that we call off the strike without conclusion. South Wales was equally outraged. They explained that this idea had been floated by a staff member (Kim Howells),[197] that he had anyway been taken out of context, but whether or not this was South Wales policy, they were bitter that this was being said. They said it was one man's view and obviously had been seized on by other areas. The NEC confirmed this was not a proposal which would ever be contemplated.[198]

14 February. The most sweeping of court judgements on picketing. A South Wales judge had ruled that more than six pickets on a gate was *illegal*. References to 'six pickets' had previously been recognised as simply a code, advice, not a law. Apart from this, more than the officially designated six pickets did not debar any number of others 'demonstrating' at the same locations. This new judgement held that demonstrations at sites of trade disputes were now *illegal*. Allowing financial penalties against the South Wales Area and injunctions to prevent further demonstrations, it was now held illegal to organise pickets of more than six, or demonstrations of any sort, even *at your own place of work* as specified in the relevant act. This judgement rendered picketing as we know it illegal; planning mass pickets and organising pickets were also now illegal and the Union at every level was open to writs at common law; plus fines and criminal action in criminal law. We should note here that this entirely new law was created in a court, not in

Parliament. It represented the view of a privileged and partisan judge, and was now enforceable by the police and the criminal law as well as being subject to financial retribution through common-law action. It meant we, as an Area coordinating picketing, still organising mass pickets across the coalfield, were now acting illegally. We had eleven writs pending against us as an Area already. We reluctantly agreed that at those pits neither the Area nor the Branch would organise picketing. That organisation of mass picketing would now stop. *At least that organised by the NUM*. There were no such constraints on women's support groups, nor on our retired members, nor on our members acting off their own bat without organisation. From now on in, masses of women would coordinate their actions and carry out picketing at 'their own' pits and those of their sister collieries, signing up and organising other sections of the pit community in the process.[199]

Tuesday 26 February. Council Meeting, Barnsley. Hatfield had put forward a resolution confirming that one of the conditions on which we will return to work is that all sacked men are reinstated; and that there will be no return without this assurance. Briscoe, the general secretary, talked it down, saying it was too wide – there were people who had done things off their own bat and not as part of the strike action.

Grimethorpe admitted that they didn't usually agree with me, but on this occasion they did, and we had an obligation to those lads who had lost their jobs fighting for other people's. Henry Daly, the moderate delegate from Nostell, said all this resolution would do was to ensure the sacked men, and all of us with them, would stay outside the gates while everyone else drifted back to work. Frickley delegate Johnny Stones said he didn't like the way this was all shaping up; people were trying to back out of commitments.

Jack Taylor, the Area president, urged me to withdraw it, as it shouldn't really be on the agenda anyway since it was already the Area policy. My fellow Doncaster delegates whispered that I should in fact withdraw it because a straw poll indicated if we went to the vote, we'd lose. That would mean Yorkshire no longer had an 'amnesty first' policy.

The next Council meeting saw a stream of resolutions from North Yorkshire demanding we organise a return to work. Eleven branches from North Yorkshire – the whole of the area really, including all the Selby branches – supported these propositions. Many said the 'majority' of men were already back at their pits, and branches were talking of going back on their own. The Area officials moved a resolution noting the fears of the Area and promising to convey these to the next NEC, but confirming our efforts to reach a negotiated settlement. It was passed with only three against, but with North Yorkshire, talking of going back alone; Selby and Shireoaks reported 80% of their members had already gone back.

After that, things started to fall apart rapidly. The NEC meeting had in fact turned itself inside out and had lasted 'several hours'. The Board was now dug in and not moving. Areas were wavering. Northumberland reported 60% back at work. In Durham 'floods of men' were reported going back. Easington Lodge had voted it would go back 'Monday under protest'. While Kent argued to 'stick it out', in North Derbyshire, Cumberland and Leicester the situation was 'untenable'. The balance fell to South Wales and Yorkshire. The situation in Scotland was unclear at this time, but actually they turned out to have more belly for continuing the fight than even Doncaster did, refusing to go back until an amnesty for their sacked men could be agreed. Midlands argued that the NACODS deal now looked more promising in the light of the current loss of resolve, although it was noted this was no longer on the table. South Wales said if we don't do something we are going to make scabs of 19,000 good men.

The Yorkshire members, following our last Council, urged that we stick out for an honourable settlement – an amnesty for the sacked men. COSA said their Executive Committee had given Bell, the president, 'one week more'.

When this report came before the emergency Area Council meeting in Yorkshire on 2 March, we had before us the decision of what to do next, where to go. When it came to the vote, on a show of hands, returning to work unconditionally won by 8 votes, against the platform's recommendation; the vote being 31 in favour of sticking out until an amnesty, 39 against. We called for a card vote and swung it, just – by 561 to 557. Yorkshire, by skin of its teeth, was voting to stop out for an amnesty.[200]

March 1985. The tide of opinion towards a return to work without an agreement began over a few hectic days beginning Friday 1 March, when NUM areas in Durham, Lancashire and South Wales voted in favour. Scotland's vote was 'conditional' on an amnesty for sacked miners.

The day after Yorkshire's Council meeting, we travelled to London, utterly wretched, to a special NUM Delegate Conference held at the TUC headquarters; it resulted in a 98–91 vote favouring a return to work. A Yorkshire resolution for an amnesty for sacked miners was defeated 91–98 at the delegate meeting.

At the end of the strike, at that final Conference, Scargill comes in for one more word of criticism from the academic pundits – namely that the NEC would go to the decisive Conference without a recommendation. The NEC had been split evenly down the middle. Scargill should have used a casting vote to recommend staying out, or going back. But a recommendation was problematic. This was after all a movement of area strikes, not a national strike as such. The NEC could declare an area strike official, but it had no authority to tell an area to call it off. The National Conference was convened to coordinate a return or continued action. Given that the areas were roughly divided, the NEC was likewise divided. Had Arthur cast his vote to make a recommendation, which way would the recommendation have gone, to stop out or go back? Whichever way the NEC went, with his casting vote swinging it, he would be damned as the one man holding all those starving miners out on strike, or else the treacherous bastard who led us up the garden path then sold us out. The rules of chairmanship actually dictate that a casting vote from the chair should always be cast for the status quo, which would mean Scargill would have been damned as not only inventing the strike, denying the miners a vote, organising the picketing, but also pushing through an NEC recommendation to continue the strike. He declined. The Conference ultimately voted for a return without a settlement, and without an amnesty for the sacked miners. The announcement of this decision was shocking to the solid ranks of miners and their families who had stuck it out for so long. Outside, the fury among the lobbying groups was tangible. These were miners, their families and supporters, only a tiny fraction of them in organisations of the left. Scargill was jeered and jostled, and called traitor. 'We're not going back!' was the united chant of the crowds.

Since the end of the strike, some 'left' commentators have tried to separate the views and strategy of Mick McGahey from those of Arthur, have said that Mick was for calling off the strike, and had been for some time. But Scotland voted along with Yorkshire *not* to return unless an amnesty could be gained for the sacked miners. After losing the vote and the acceptance of the resolution for an unconditional return without agreement or amnesty, Scotland didn't in fact go back to work, and stayed out. So did Kent, and so did pits in Doncaster. Would it have been feasible that Mick couldn't swing his own area to such a strongly held viewpoint in an area still dominated in lodges and districts by the CPGB? Unlikely.

The Area Council meeting was reconvened to endorse the National Conference decision and organise a return to work in Yorkshire. In fact seven branches, all of them from Doncaster if I recall correctly, voted *not* to endorse the Conference decision and that Yorkshire should stick out as we had agreed previously. This was moved by Goldthorpe and seconded by Hatfield.

In fact Hatfield and Armthorpe Branch stayed out, and, along with the Kent pickets who also did not withdraw, continued to picket out the coalfield, spreading to almost very pit in Yorkshire. But Hatfield surrendered two days later, realising that men were now being branded scabs after having had a full 12 months on strike, and the once solid branch was tearing itself apart. Markham Main, our comrade in arms, stuck out till the end of the week, and Kent finally withdrew.

I was furious at the way people were talking of 'it all being over'. It wasn't all over. We hadn't decided to give up and just go back. We decided to go back and fight, carry on guerrilla struggles, maintain the overtime ban, regroup and rebuild our strength. That was what was said. I had stood on the steps of the Yorkshire Area HQ and proclaimed to the TV cameras: 'There'll be no coal turned in Yorkshire, I'll tell you that – the Coal Board will wish we were on strike.' I addressed the men in their muck before going to work on the first day back at Hatfield. I was asked, 'Do we turn coal, Dave, or not?' I replied, 'Aye, but only about two bucketfuls and whatever you empty out of ya buets.'

We tried various coordinated efforts to keep the fight alive while at work. Silverwood in South Yorkshire became the clarion of the sacked men. They demanded at the Council meeting of 18 March that a ballot be conducted to withdraw from the incentive scheme, and therefore minimise coal production until the sacked men had been reinstated. They further called for the Area to urge all other areas to adopt the same policy. The danger was in the ballot part; if we lost it, it would make for the withdrawal of all guerrilla resistance, and a return to normal working. I pointed out that it ought to be unnecessary anyway: nobody should be earning any bonuses, as we shouldn't be turning enough coal to warrant any. Nonetheless, 20 branches voted for the resolution. Then came the counter-attack resolutions from the North Yorkshire branches, calling for an end to the overtime ban and the return to normal working. We were horrified that men should want to work seven shifts when their victimised mates couldn't work any. When put to the vote, all 14 North Yorkshire pits voted to call off the ban and return to normal working.

19 March. The Yorkshire Area unanimously calls for the expulsion of the Nottingham Area of the NUM.[201]

Ian MacGregor's autobiography is interesting. Full of venom and hatred for the NUM, Scargill and the strike, at the end he nevertheless concludes that we came 'within a whisper' of winning. It is quite a contrast to the latter-day armchair industrial relations generals who now conclude that the strike had been forlorn all along and futile. That – historically, factually – is just not the case.

Even when we were defeated, we weren't really defeated – not then, and not yet.

Ken Loach produces and directs a wonderful film about the strike, *Which Side Are You On?* Perhaps it was too late to do the job it was intended to do, to present the truth and justice of the miners' stand and perhaps inspire others to stand out with us. We show it to a packed audience in the Broadway, with Ken in the audience, then again over at the Fox at Stainforth amid great cheering – and much laughter, despite the often poignant message of the film; the lads feel they know about all that side of it, and just enjoy seeing themselves and their cause on screen.

For all that – and despite all the wise words, after the fact, that we were in some heroic, savage, forlorn battle against 'progress' – we came to within a hair's breadth of winning on a number of occasions.

The first of these was in July 1984. The deal would mean the five threatened pits, which had sparked the strike, would stay open; the *Plan For Coal* would be reaffirmed; and all victimised men reinstated. The NCB negotiators, including Ian MacGregor, then found the deal vetoed by Thatcher on the advice of David Hart, who urged her to hold out for complete victory over the NUM.

Perhaps the closest was October 1984. The actual terms for a settlement were worked out once and for all by the NUM and NACODS leaders; the latter's members had just voted again, this time by almost 83%, to join the strike and in so doing close every colliery in Britain and kill the scab movement and the bulk of overt police operations dead. We had nothing to lose by a joint agreement with NACODS – just the contrary: if NACODS didn't sign up with Thatcher they would join the strike and within a month or so shut the power down nationwide. The unions agreed a bottom-line deal and handed the terms for our settlement over to ACAS. It would effectively mean no pit closures on simple economic grounds, and withdraw all the pits on the list from closure, etc. It was secret insofar as it was just between the NECs and leaders of the three mining unions (NUM, BACM – the management union – and NACODS), and was to be presented to Thatcher's side, with every indication they had accepted the terms. Within the next 48 hours the cabinet met, with Thatcher in the chair, and agreed to honour a settlement on those grounds. But between then and the signing of the united agreement something quite unfathomable happened. The Cabinet was recalled and told that NACODs had agreed a unilateral deal without the NUM. Their deal as we lived to know and regret was the so-called Modified Colliery Review Procedure. Arthur Scargill searched desperately for NACODs reps to find out what on earth they were doing and why they had stabbed the NUM in the back, but they had gone to ground and couldn't be found until it was too late to pull them back from the edge, too late to stop their deal going through.[202]

REFLECTIONS

The difference between where we are now and where we were then is huge. Now there are maybe 8 working branches of the National Union of Mineworkers; then there were around 180. In December 2004, with the third closure of Hatfield Colliery, the NUM had 2,500 members nationwide and falling; in 1984, at least 150,000 had been on strike. For every miner's job, some 10 others were dependent on it – for example, coal accounted for 75% of all rail freight.

Taking into consideration wives and families, you are talking about a very considerable number of people – not spread across the country, but concentrated in key industrial areas built around real, fixed communities where men had worked down the pit for generations.

If anyone has won, it has been the miners who stayed at work, the dockers who stayed at work, the power workers who stayed at work, the lorry drivers who stayed at work, the railway workers who stayed at work, the managers who stayed at work. In other words all of those people who kept the wheels of Britain turning and who in spite of a strike, actually produced a record output in Britain last year …

Yet the coal strike was always about far more than uneconomic pits. It was a political strike. And so its outcome had significance far beyond the economic sphere. From 1972 to 1985, the conventional wisdom was that Britain could only be governed with the consent of the trade unions.

No government could really resist a major strike, still less defeat; in particular a strike by the miners' union. Even as we were reforming trade union law and overcoming lesser disputes such as the steel strike, many on the left and outside it continued to believe that the miners had the ultimate veto and would one day use it. That day had come and now gone. [203]

The meaning of the strike would not be determined by the terms of the settlement – if there is a settlement – or even by the events of the past year but by the way in which it is assimilated in popular memory by … retrospective understanding both in the pit villages themselves and in the country at large.[204]

END OF THE STRIKE AT HATFIELD

Diary entry:

The feeling going down the pit lane knowing that we had been out a whole year and not succeeded started to become overpowering. Many of us wept.

For the first time, the full impact of defeat, the fact that we had battled in the most magnificent heroic and unstinting manner and come back to where we started.

It was unthinkable, but here it was. Utter wretchedness. Miners stunned, befogged. The men strangely quiet, everyone deep in reflected thoughts.

Evening. Passing the top of the pit lane, a glance previously saw the flickering reassurance of the picket fire. A symbol, which had burned without exhaustion 24 hours a day for a whole year. Its light showed the picket in place, the battle continuing. It gave a reassuring glow to the masses of miners and their wives passing by at night on the late-night buses.

Tonight, a glance brought back a blank stomach like a sharp winding blow. The light extinguished a feeling of emptiness floods in.

The strike perversely had become almost a way of life, or a life of its own; its loss touches the village like bereavement. Something quite important, abstract yet somehow personal had died. There is a sick emptiness. While something quite vital has gone. There is almost a desperate feeling of loss, not in any material sense, but like a disorientating social compass spinning away now from its cardinal points.

THE TRUTH WILL OUT?

It is easier to be wise after the events, if only because you come into possession of facts withheld from you at the time. Nowhere was this truer than in the struggle surrounding the government's attempts to 'keep the lights on'; the BBC documentary *Who Kept the Lights On?* helped to lift the veil a little higher and show us aspects of the operation that hadn't been revealed.[205] The battle for the power supply was of course the core struggle, not simply in that 12 months, but for the long-term future of our respective perspectives. We certainly tried in the 12 months of that strike to close down the power stations. In retrospect, it is now clear we hadn't given them the absolute priority which the state had, and in that sense we failed to give this target the kind of impact it deserved. Behind the scenes, the government had constructed a war strategy, with the power stations as 'the keep'. Following the 'body swerve' which Maggie had given us in 1981, they had spent £80 million building up coal stocks and mass-storing bottles of hydrogen and other gases to withstand any outside siege. However, the storage of oil supplies was not so easy. It was essential that we stop all new supplies of coke, coal and oil reaching the power stations, and that we pull out all stops to gain solidarity action from the power workers. The 'back to work movement', that fifth column which was fostered and nurtured among our own fellow miners, had done the desired job and distracted us from the power stations.

I had had furious arguments with Arthur and the left over the focus on Orgreave, which was distracting us from constant pressure on the scab coalfields. In fact, I now think my own preoccupation with those coalfields was a distraction too. We needed to keep pressure up on the scab miners, but the jugular was the power stations, and we were neither hitting them nor blockading them with anything like the impact deployed at Nottingham or later Orgreave. Whereas the scabs were producing 24 million tones of coal, the added oil burn was 40 million tonnes equivalent. Many of us had concluded that the power stations were a dead loss from the beginning and a waste of time. It didn't dawn on me till much later we had been led to believe this and it was utterly untrue. The mighty northern power stations of the northeast and Yorkshire, where power workers lived in close community with miners, had almost from day one marched to the cause of the miners. At Ferrybridge Power Station, the last shipment of coal allowed through the gate arrived as the strike began; no more shipments were allowed through. The same was true of Drax, Thorpe Marsh and many others.

Granville Camsey, CEGB operations services engineer, informed the programme *Who Kept the Lights On?* of how they had been covertly preparing a 'plain-clothes' convoy or army of vehicles and handpicked drivers for years prior to the strike. These would run any gauntlet and ensure supplies of 'light-up' oil. Fleets of helicopters were prepared to outflank road, sea or canal blockades, to transport the thousands of tonnes of chemicals needed to keep the stations running. They had already sounded out British Airways pilots and concluded that solidarity action was a likelihood, so private scab helicopter firms with lucrative inducements were recruited. The whole plan was based on being able to stand off a 6-month strike. The whole thing came close to collapse as, despite all attempts to kick-start the strike at the desired time, the miners didn't rise to the bait, but instead started a long-term overtime ban which started to dramatically reduce the carefully constructed coal stocks. See my earlier references to CEGB predictions of doom.[206]

Through a combination of inertia and discipline, the miners had refused to rise to the bait on earlier occasions, until a particularly humiliating public smack across the face at Cortonwood caused what we can now see was a premature launch of the strike. This is not to say there weren't many of us who saw this was a time that favoured the state rather than us; but we couldn't see a way of avoiding the challenge. The overtime ban after Cortonwood no longer seemed an adequate response. We could never have held the line and bit the bullet while the collieries closed around our ears and we waited till we saw the whites of our enemies' eyes, holding onto the overtime ban and nothing more despite the provocations. We would have got to the optimum November launch date only to find that collieries had already been closed in every coalfield without concerted resistance and the miners would have asked, 'What's the point?' Like it or not, the ball was at our feet. The miners' rank and file were determined to take up the challenge, regardless of what super-wise leaders and strategists might have urged. As things turned out, despite setting us off prematurely, Sir Walter Marshall of the CEGB and the Cabinet were still not certain they could outlast the strike, and bought oil at twice the price of coal to burn in the power stations. It burned grossly inefficiently and at terrific cost. In turn, it pushed oil prices to astronomical levels. The BBC documentary revealed that £4 BILLION was spent on this contingency alone. The operation was kept strictly secret, and nobody in Her Majesty's Loyal Opposition even mentioned it in Parliament; presumably, because on this occasion they actually didn't know. Before the start of the strike, the CEGB had been buying 30,000 tonnes of fuel oil per week; by mid strike they were buying 600,000 tonnes per week.

The plan to recruit 'good non-union lorry drivers' had been part of the anti-NUM strategy laid out by Nicholas Ridley in the years following the defeat of Heath and during Labour's brief period of office, 1974–9. This strategy was given its head, taking precedence over and giving exemption from trivialities such as the Highway Code, the MOT test or driving licences. Any driver with his own lorry would expect to make £2,500 a week profit. An army of rust-buckets and clapped-out vehicles salvaged from around the country ferried coal from wharves and scab pits. Coal lorries were making 25,000 journeys per week. Cottam Power Station was reported to have taken 1,289 lorries in a day. There just weren't that many serviceably lorries in the country, so literally anything that could be kept rolling was allowed on the road and given police protection, despite the fact that many of the so-called drivers actually couldn't drive, couldn't reverse, couldn't stop properly in what were anyway dangerously unroadworthy vehicles.

Despite all of this, stocks were relentlessly falling, except at northern and Scottish stations were they were huge but untouchable. A four-man war cabinet met to discuss an even higher-risk strategy: moving those stocks from northern and Scottish power stations and strike-bound colliery yards. CEBG chairman Walter Marshall had outraged and shocked Thatcher by telling her that if the miners held on through the winter without major breaks in their ranks then, by autumn, 'Scargill would win.' This was her much-famed 'wobble' previously mentioned, but sat down to plan the feasibility of using troops to move the stocks. We had actually planned for this development, some of us anyway. We drafted huge posters and covered army towns and barracks with them. It was the most subversive poster of the whole strike. It read:

Soldiers
This is Britain 1984
(violent scenes from the coalfields)
Your Class Needs You!
140,000 miners and their families have been on strike for over eight months in defence of their jobs and communities. They have suffered daily attacks by riot police.
Eight thousand miners have been arrested with two killed and over 4000 injured – many seriously. This government of millionaires and their hired

thugs are prepared to spend any amount of money to batter and starve the
miners back to work and an unjust settlement.
Refuse To Move The Coal
Shortly you may be ordered to move coal from the pitheads.
The miners, their families and other workers will not sit back and watch
their further attempt to defeat their fight for justice.
By moving coal to power stations you will lengthen the strike considerably,
condemning the mining communities to even more hardship. You will
undermine hard-won gains of centuries of bloody struggle. A victory over
the miners will ensure further destruction of communities and certain
return to the days of unprotected sweated labour!
You Must
Ignore the lying propaganda of your officers and the government
Refuse to move the coal or report sick en masse
If you are forced to go to the pits, sabotage the loading equipment
And lorries, individually or in small groups.

The CEGB chairman is reported to have told Maggie that intelligence from
all the power stations was that the power workers would walk out the moment
the army came in, and the lights would go out within a week. Doubtless, too,
someone must have stressed to Maggie that a civilian population confronting
troops on the street of Britain, perhaps in scenes similar to Ulster, would force the
hand of even the most reluctant trade union leaders into solidarity action. We
ourselves were preparing our forces for tear gas and plastic bullets and had
resolved that a response with something harder than bricks would be not only
called for but also forthcoming.[207]

Our particular strongly politicised community had been getting warned of this
development for that last 10 years, and we had been preparing teams to respond
to it for almost that long; we had already set out the links and contingencies for
drawing in friends and comrades well used to this form of engagement, from a
variety of sources. Our community had also been under close and constant
surveillance for a decade, and we were the feature of more than one Home Office
report. The violent and revolutionary consequences of moving in the army and
using the army to protect itself in the process must also have been well known to
Thatcher and her advisers. Thatcher was at a crossroads here. One way led to
certain civil war, maybe the road to hell. The other looked like outright surrender.
It is more than clear that she toyed seriously with both. Walter Marshall (and
probably a litany of others, doubtless on their knees with their hands clasped)
urged her to caution:

So I sat down with the Prime Minister, told her straight that she mustn't
bring in troops, and I was certain we could keep the lights on. And she
showed me her graphs and I said well that maybe so, but I guarantee we
will keep the lights on. (Walter Marshall, CEGB chairman)[208]

Instead, less controversial, though still covert and dangerously irresponsible,
actions were given their head. Nuclear stations, as already mentioned, would be
given the green light to keep running well into their danger zones and shutdown

periods. The 'back to work' campaign funded and fuelled by extreme right-wing millionaires was seen as Thatcher's fifth column, although we now know there were others in her pay closer to home. The media was given almost daily instruction on how to report the dispute and put over only the government's spin on things. It has even been suggested that Geldof's 'Feed the World' project, if not conceived of from the start in government circles, was seized upon as a means of diverting charity and funding from the miners at home[209] All of this elaborate plan, which touched the four corners of the state and utilised every department and desk, was aimed at defeating a union and its social and political aspirations; it demonstrated the same absolute commitment of the state to smashing the miners' union as they had done in 1926. As time has moved on, we uncover more and more of just how far the state was prepared to go to defeat us, and the realisation of how right we were to take it on.

Just 20 years on, we see this start to happen. People now have time to look around them and discover where we have now arrived and how far from where we were we have been driven. The strike, in the greater context of time, becomes clearer, at least in perception and meaning, with each successive year:

> Just spare a thought at this conference 20 years on, for miners who were killed on the picket lines supporting the union. I mention Joe Green and Dave Jones and others that were killed ... 20,000 miners were hospitalised, thousands arrested, thousands convicted and hundreds jailed. There were 1,200 who were sacked and victimised, many who have not been able to gain any employment since ... we learned how to love and hate, we learned the spirit of friendship, hardship, comradeship; and we encountered brutality, victimization, discrimination and corruption on a scale never seen before within our movement; but comrades, we should be extremely proud that we did it. The only other option would have been to roll over and die at the feet of the Tory government.[210]

Labour Party wards, constituencies and councils across the country had rallied to the side of the miners; those in positions of local power were able to exercise great assistance to the pit communities with meals and clothing grants, and the non-pursuit of rent. Many saw the struggle of the miners as the barricade from behind which the Labour Party would resurge and re-emerge. Old decrepit Labour Halls, which had scarcely had the lights turned on or the chairs dusted off in 40 years, suddenly had felt a rush of blood, an infusion of principle and activism. The betrayals by the leadership are now legion, but they do not characterise the rank and file or even the middle echelons of the party.

20 May 1985. I am invited to address the Bradford Council Labour Group in the lavish rooms of City Hall. This is what I said.

> The vote to return in Yorkshire had been taken as result of the decision of a Special Conference of all the areas to do so. We had voted against it – but we had done so against a divided feeling – in Doncaster only 2% were scabbing, the strongest coalfield in Britain – while in Selby 80% had crossed the line. At Kellingly, above 1,000 men were defying pickets and

working. The whole of North Yorkshire seemed poised to return unilaterally. Despite this, when the return was agreed it was a ragged retreat. After a year of struggle, there was still a strong spirit – perhaps among a minority, but a sizeable minority that wished to fight on.

Pickets from Armthorpe and Hatfield continued to stop pits, Kent miners tried to maintain the effort, but overall the gesture caused a lot of bitterness.

Hatfield had voted, despite the National and Yorkshire decision, to fight on for the sacked lads, as did Armthorpe in the next village.

Initially we tried to carry on the dispute by other means; work-to-rules, and the continuation of the overtime ban. It was just a brief month later when a Special Delegate Conference endorsed a recommendation of the NEC and called the overtime ban off as well. Not that it altered the reign of terror below ground. Over 100 men had been sacked since the strike ended. In Scotland and Kent, no man has been re-signed on no matter how minor the offences committed during the action. Meantime, the massive debts they had run up were heavy on the minds of the miners. Some of the debts would take 2 years to clear, with consequential loss of earnings now.

Some could not, would not go back defeated. The long-distance fundraisers living in London, life and soul of every left soirée, drifting in and out of the parties of the middle class and intelligentsia, some would not go back, not to work, not to the village. Round inner cities and at time abroad on distant shores and in holiday locations were a smattering of 'deserters'[211] who had 'gone native' and never returned. Some of the bikers had taken the golden handshake and now camped out in woods and in tents at every festival and rock gaff in the country – they would not return. New ways of living had been encountered; new relationships combined with impossible pressures had resulted in widespread marriage break-ups, broken homes, new horizons, new loves, new locations. On the other hand, those who had doubted the strike call, and only with the utmost reluctance joined it, had become more and more sullen as the year went by. They ignored the morale-boosting parties, ignored the community bond but stuck out, wretched and neglected. Now they spoke open heresy, about 'a wasted year', that 'strikes never got us anywhere'. They read the *Sun* and the *News of the World* and believed we had been betrayed and misled. They wanted nothing more to do with militancy and unions, wanted just to get back to work, put their heads down and do as they were told. At the other extreme were those who bore all of this with an air of inevitability – this was a miner's life, it was always like this, trial and hardship, struggle and trouble. It was pointless to expect anything different. With strikes and rag-ups it was us calling the shots; without them life would be a drudge.

Despite the grossly weakened position of the men, the dictatorial attitude of the management led to walkouts at nearly every pit in

Doncaster and many in other coalfields. In one week, the Board announced 2,000 redundancies in Doncaster, all to go before July; although these were voluntary, the subsequent weakening of the Union would soon lead to involuntary redundancies and compulsory transfers and pit closures.

That threat had already been made, and elsewhere in Britain the Board's closure programme goes ahead with the shutdown of six pits within the next months, with none of the consultation or the independent adjudication supposedly guaranteed by the NACODS agreement.

This had led to the imposition of an overtime ban by NACODS, recognition that their deal – so boasted of in newspapers and even by Thatcher in the Commons as the best deal anyone could get – was in fact a totally cynical exercise to get NACODS out of the dispute and stop them adding their considerable weight to our elbow …

In conclusion, comrades, it seems the miner's lot since time immemorial has been the razor path of uncertainty and danger. If we are not facing the abstract apparent conspiracy of the earth to crush us, burn us, drown us, or bury us, we are facing the subjective and vindictive assaults of owners, employers and the ruling class to push us back down our holes like rats, to collectively gibbet us, jail us or kill us.

Our spirited response to both, our determination to match blow for blow in accordance with our abilities is something they have never understood – drives them to distraction because they will never understand – but will remain so long as we remain.

For some time after the ending of the strike, ragged resistance rages across the country. The cause keeps going. At the beginning of March, I am speaking on a common anti-war platform at Brid at the regional Labour Party conference, with the theme 'Close the Bases Not the Mines'. A little later, I am down talking to the unions in Camden, one of our greatest sources of financial and occasional solidarist support. The History Workshop is host to dozens of mining families reflecting on where we are now and where will we go. Neither us nor the movement has a clue, really.

Throughout the strike, numbers working, breaking the strike or defying the strike were a huge cannon in the armoury of the NCB and the government. Figures were polished, enhanced, elaborated and manipulated for the daily and sometimes hourly news programmes and news flashes. It was a drip, drip effect to demoralise the strikers and persuade them that the strike was collapsing; or, near the end, that it had already collapsed.

In July (1984), Peter Walker had told the Commons that 60,000 striking miners were already back at work. When the Board took on its independent auditors Thompson and McKlintock to analyse numbers working, they could only find by all sources 51,000 working in November of 1984, some 4 months later. This is including ancillary workers, like cokeworkers. The figures at 19 November show: manpower 196,000, striking 144,428 and working 51,372. There is a discrepancy in the figures of 200, most likely due to the 196,000 having been the result of rounding-up, or else perhaps because the 200 are people neither working nor striking. We do not know how many of the non-strikers/non-workers were included in the 'working' category. The thousands of deputies not crossing picket lines are not counted, but are included in the 'working' figure. Hundreds if not thousands weren't actually working but were not on strike – men off 'sick' for example, and men being picketed out. 'Working' only means 'not on strike'; it doesn't mean actually at work. Even so, the figures demonstrate that, after some 8 months, nearly two-thirds of the miners were still on strike. Bear in mind also that perhaps 20,000 never struck in the first place, or only for a short period. In real terms, something like 30,000 had abandoned the strike over the period of 9 months, but 144,428 had remained on strike throughout that period.[212]

German TV have made a terrific film of the strike based on the lives and struggles of the Hatfield families. They fly me to Hamburg at the end of March to see the cuts and the final edition before it goes out on German TV and to give me the right to correct anything I think is wrong. It is the only time a TV company anywhere does this, and incidentally the film is brilliant in its grasp, both educational and sociological, of the situation. It was never shown on British TV, but we showed it to mass audiences in pubs and clubs around the Hatfield mines villages. It was greatly acclaimed and bootleg copies circulated with more potency and expense than any blue movie.

Twenty-five years down the line, and Beckett and Hencke claim to have found another of those cupboards in which Scargill keeps various skeletons. They tell us that the first thing Scargill did at the end of the strike was to bring together all the big unions who had stumped up millions in loans to the NUM in order that we could keep operating through the strike and sequestration.

Scargill allegedly tells them our lawyers say it would be unlawful to pay any of it back. (Scargill does have an unlimited supply of such lawyers ever ready to back him up in rough moments). None of the union leaders were going to let this go, however; and all the money was eventually, 5 or 6 years later, paid off. But the charge here is that Scargill tried to dupe the very people who had put their necks on the line to assist the NUM financially.[213] The source for this story is given as Ken Cameron of the firefighters' union, the FBU, in an interview with the authors; sadly he too is now dead. This is a nasty revelation. It is part of what would become a whole stream of such allegations of breach of trust and mishandling of support funding. Bad though it is, it doesn't actually minimise the importance of the strike, or indeed Arthur Scargill's outstanding contribution to it.[214]

MacGregor ensures that his deformed UDM baby continues to crap in the crib for years after the strike is over, and to play the role of disunity and collaboration he and Thatcher set out for it, almost from the beginning of the strike. The switchover of authority and rights and recognition from Nottingham NUM to the UDM is done illegally and was in breach of countless binding agreements, but enough sand was being thrown into the NUM's eyes in this period to allow it to become a fait accompli.

Files now held at National Archives reveal the extent to which the UDM is a creature of government invention. So too is the fact that the special relationship between the NCB, privatised industry and the UDM continued with the approval of the incoming Labour government in 1997. The UDM were uniquely granted a 'Legal Claims Handling Agreement' on the millions of industrial injury compensation cases for hand arm vibration syndrome (HAVS) and chest diseases which the NUM had applied for and been refused. It meant everything the NUM and anybody else did had to be through private solicitors. The UDM set up its own legal firm called Vendside, and then undertook a nationwide newspaper advertising campaign under that name and signed up tens of thousands of former miners and their dependants to run their claims. The profits from the claims, as well as the government's direct payments, turned the UDM into a highly profitable organisation, with its leaders paid fortunes and the organisation featherbedded with a massive war chest. The UDM, through Vendside, were paid 'disbursements' from the government; all their costs and fees. Then they charged a percentage for everyone who won a case. They also charged fees for membership of those claiming through the UDM or an equivalent for those going through Vendside. (So they paid themselves twice and three times over.) This ensured the scab outfit would survive as Thatcher and Mac had promised, but was done with the indulgence of the incoming New Labour government.[215]

> Falconer's advice – given either jointly with Dehn or sometimes solely to the NCB's legal department – played a crucial role in the creation of the Union of Democractic Miners (UDM) ... for Falconer, the work was particularly lucrative, as he went on to advise the privatised British Coal before joining the Blair government in 1997. [216]

A court ruling decided that the UDM could not invent itself or abolish the Nottingham Area of the NUM and take its assets, and certainly not without a ballot of all members of the Nottingham Area and a legally constituted organisation. The NCB privately admitted that their ongoing support to the move and their decision to recognise it was unlawful and in breach of its own national constitution and national agreements with NUM. This didn't stop them conducting the whole legal setup on behalf of the UDM, or advising that it should merge with another smaller breakaway organisation, the Colliery Trades and Allied Workers Organisation. NCB lawyers advised Lynk, the UDM general secretary, throughout the process. Government lawyers urged the NCB to allow favourable wage increases and incentive payments to miners joining the UDM. All of this was happening outwith the terms of the legal judgement and before any legally constituted organisation existed – or, laughably enough, without a ballot!

> Peter Walker endorsed the strategy on the same day. The collusion between the breakaway union, the NCB and the government was complete.[217]

On 4 December 1985, the government certification officer granted recognition to the UDM as a bona-fide trade union.

TOTALS

There have been many attempts to summarise the statistics of the strike at its conclusion. Using figures taken from all sources including police, government and unions I conclude as follows:

9,808 arrested, 10,372 charges, including 3 killings, 4 criminal damage with intent to endanger life, 3 explosives charges, 5 threats to kill. 200 given prison sentences.

882 sacked for 'violence and sabotage', 967 for striking.

20,000 miners hospitalised.

2 killed on the picket line.

1 scab driver killed.[218]

1 killed by a scab years later. [219]

3 died digging for waste coal.

3 suicides rather than break the strike.

Total costs in financial terms including redundancy, benefits, policing, courts, lost revenue, decommissioning, closed businesses, etc., etc.: well over £5 BILLION (up until this point).[220]

Yet they hadn't won. The political aim was not met. The NUM was still dug in deep and power was still coal-based. We lost 100,000 jobs and more than 100 coalmines, but when the dust settled, the miners were still here, and so was the Union, even if it was crippled in one leg with the presence of the scab organisation.

3

AFTERMATH OF DEFEAT

At the beginning of April 1985 the Direct Action Movement (actually the renamed Syndicalist Workers' Federation – a name I had preferred), the British section of the International Workers' Association, holds its international conference in Hackney. There are delegations and speakers from Norway, Denmark, Sweden and West Germany. Together with official observers from Italy and the USA, I address the main topic, which is the epic struggle of the miners, its triumphs and weaknesses. DAM was good enough to publish two pamphlets of mine on the police and the media, which were very timely and well received. [221]

At the end of March, I had addressed a similar conference hosted by the Leninist faction of the CPGB.[222] The conclusions of the two organisations, two ways of assessing the world, couldn't have been more different despite addressing the same set of facts. To the Leninists, the problem lay in the lack of a functioning mass Communist Party, although I was quick to point out we had had something like that in 1926 but it still didn't save us.[223] To the Syndicalists, it was lack of rank-and-file control and democratic structures within the working-class organisations. Of course, there was something in that, but you didn't need an embossed invitation from your well-heeled union boss not to cross a picket line, and it was ordinary workers crossing picket lines which in the end defeated us, of course ably assisted by the class assassins in the TUC and at the head of most unions. Yes, the CPGB without doubt was better placed, better staffed and more up for it in the '70s, and this made a crucial difference to the results of the miners' actions then. But those things had been symptomatic of the combativity prevalent in the class anyway, and that was what at base had been missing. Mind, it hadn't just upped and gone of its own accord; it had been battered out, bribed out, betrayed and disillusioned out mostly as conscious actions of class war or class treachery.

On 27 March I received a most remarkable letter, thanking me for my contributions to their conference – I had submitted a written paper – and also greatly sympathising with our current position, both as a union and me and my family as human beings. The response, though, cautioned me against ongoing 'guerrilla warfare' as outlined in my strategy, and called for a more moderate and cautious period of consolidation. The letter was remarkable in the light of earlier and then later experience because it had come from the Spartacist League, who were now entering a period of appreciation of the quality of the British working class, and in particular the miners' rank and file and families. The letter included the following:

> We recognise the heavy workload and difficult task facing you and many more in the union at this point. Your statement was read to the day school and your vivid description of what we describe in our propaganda as vindictiveness in victory on the part of Thatcher and the Coal Board was

very powerful. We plan to run extensive coverage of the day school in the next issue of the paper and if you have no objection, we would like to include your statement in the coverage.

One thing which would have been interesting to discuss is the course of action you outline at the end of your statement which you describe as 'immediate guerrilla response'. While we are not in a position to give direction on particular day-to-day activities our stance is much more cautious and conservative than what you outline. What guides that is the overriding need to preserve the struggling capacity of the union and most immediately to avoid further victimisations ...

Comradely Greetings,
Eibhlin McDonald[224]

April. I am up in court on public order offences during the last day's picketing down at Hatfield. It is potentially quite serious; if I get convicted they could sack me. We had held a big rally at the Dunscroft Miners Welfare with the local MP, Lynne Clegg for the Hatfield Women's Support Group, and myself. We were, as far as anyone could tell, en route for a further 12-month strike. The hall was packed to the rafters and quite a number of the Markham miners and their support group had turned out too, along with many other union members. I made my 'Barbara Woodhouse' speech. ('Thatcher might think she's Barbara Woodhouse but we won't "Sit!" just because she tells us to.') It was a powerful call to continue resisting, not to be stampeded back to work. At Hatfield we had, even at this late date, 20 scabs; 1,500 others were on strike and had been for almost a year. In Doncaster we had less than 1% at work; in Yorkshire, despite the haemorrhaging up at North Yorkshire, only 5% were back at work.[225] We marched from the hall, our banners flying, into the thick of a snowstorm – up Broadway, through the miners' streets. People stood in their doorways and waved, lads came to the pub windows or outside and waved their pints in salute, kids came to the fences of the schools and crammed to the gates shouting what was suppose to be 'The miners united will never be defeated!' but which they interpreted from listening to marches and pickets over the course of that year as 'The Miners, The Miners, will never be defeated!' – which was actually a much better slogan. There were hundreds of us, maybe thousands. I think the cops thought nobody would be out in a blizzard and hastily threw up a single blue line across the pit lane, although we had actually been given permission to march there. We had timed the demonstration to coincide with the scab bus coming out, so the bastards could see we were still strong, still determined. I ran into a nearby garden, which overlooked the pit lane, and a number of lads came with me; I was in truth trying to outflank the cops, but with little more intention than trying to show how pathetic their little line was.

The men came out of the club opposite as the scab bus came up the pit lane. Suddenly, a snatch squad shot out and grabbed me round the head to pull me over the wall. The men grabbed me round the waist and started to pull me back. Police and pickets now ran into each other, and a furious kicking and punching battle started. I was pulled through the wall. My trouser leg was split from my bollocks to my knee, my leg was gashed open and bleeding as I was wrenched across the road by two cops. Once down the side of the pit lane they dragged me down the side entrance of the bookie's office and punched hell out of the back of my head and constantly kneed me in the kidneys and ribs, calling me 'little gobshite'. This was seen from over the road by a couple of the lads and started a great surge forward, the crowd crying 'Free Dave Douglass!' Well, I felt suddenly heartened as the fighting continued around the police van they were throwing me in. It transported me down the pit lane to the management offices. The police were now installed in the deputy manager's office and in many of the other offices. The pit nurse was actually serving them tea and being a right little ray of sunshine. She did me the courtesy of telling the cops who I was and that I had done been for drugs previously – thanks.

Soon to join me was a NUPE member who had come up from Camden with a delegation to show solidarity. A big black cockney lad, he had got stuck in and ended up in a flying neck tackle of a cop which any professional wrestler would have been proud of. As they lined us up for photographing, he insisted in putting his arm round the shoulders of the arresting officers like they were mates on a lad's holiday. The cops took it in good stead, although they ignored the torn trousers and the blood running down my leg onto the floor.

The case, when it came before the magistrates, was laughable. The statement made by the cops was as usual just a dialogue they had made up: 'There's enough of us now, let's get past these black bastards and do for the scabs!'

'Do for the scabs'? Pure TV crim twang, but that wasn't all I'm supposed to have shouted while summoning the troops to charge: 'There's not enough of them. Come on, they can't hold us! Kill the scabs!'

As to the accusation of me saying 'Lets get these black bastards now,' I informed the court that although Yorkshire miners' pickets described the police as 'black bastards' because of their uniforms, I was a Geordie socialist and would never use 'black' in that way as a term of abuse in case anybody thought I was being racially disparaging, something which was anathema to me. They were simply lying. The dialogue was laughable.

Well, my case was thrown out; but one of the women, Sonja Hopwood, also grabbed that day, one of the Thorne Women Against Pit Closures, was fined as she admitted 'scabbing' the people on the bus. The judge had asked the lad from London if he was a miner too and he caused a laugh round the court when he answered, in broad cockney, 'Not me guv – I'm a dustbin man from Camden.' Sadly for him he was actually being sought by cops from another town and although he was found not guilty on this charge he remained in custody on another one.

That cop who did me travelled all the way over from Sheffield just to sit in the court in the hope of seeing me sent down. He was disappointed. However, 5 years later I ran into him in a bar, out with all his loud and violent off-duty mates. I recognised him, although I couldn't remember really from where. As he was leaving he said, 'I arrested you, cock, and I gave you some of that – showing me his fist – forgotten already?' I thought, no, not 'black bastard' – just bastard.

The Panel meeting of 17 April heard Area Agent Frank Cave report that the NCB was threatening to withdraw delivery rights from Home Coal schemes unless we started delivering scabs' fuel by 26 April. Frank warned that the Home Coal Societies could collapse. Hatfield had proposed that it was our society and these men had rejected us and the union so we shouldn't deliver coal to them – let them make their own arrangements. Only three branches voted for this proposition. Hatfield went on to propose a one-day strike across Doncaster in retaliation to the current phase of jackboot management imposed on the Area. Only two branches voted for this, the rest deciding to explore legal redress.[226]

In May, I am privileged to be one of the only white speakers or white member of the audience at a massive 'Black Workers Conference on the Police'. I speak alongside Paul Boateng, a militant black legal academic then, later a glib apologist for the Blair government.

Following the end of the strike, Arthur came up with one of his flashes of brilliance. His idea was to incorporate the women of the pit communities into the NUM. The mothers, wives and daughters of the miners would become part of the organisation of the NUM. It was a brilliant concept; it would mean the NUM uniquely was moving up the evolutionary chain, and developing from a 'trade union' as such to an organisation based and structured on an industry and community. We would not simply be a 'union' for work – actually, we never had been just that – but would now formally start to incorporate the communities in which we live, and the people with whom we lived and shared our lives. It always amused visitors to the pits during the strike to hear the women talking about 'when we went on strike' and meaning themselves too – as of course they would, because with the man on strike, the family was on strike; it was a collective household decision apart from an industry one. Our mass branch meetings were held not so much at the pit, as in the community, on playing fields or in mass welfare halls, with the women and kids standing around the doors. Throughout the strike, I reported back to the branch mass meetings, and then to mass meetings of the women; at Stainforth, Dunscroft and Moorends.

This suggestion of Arthur's came on the back of a much needed Rule Revision Conference to take stock of the post-strike situation. Arthur had won the approval of the NEC to include the provision of associate membership for women. Of course, at this stage, that membership did not suggest voting or speaking rights, but both supporters and opponents knew that wouldn't be long in following.

The union, which had always been based upon the community and drew its strength from there, had never organisationally given any representation to that quality of our existence. The proposal would have incorporated all the strengths and vision, which that colossal women's movement had brought to our strike. It would have sunk our roots still deeper into the villages and areas and ethnic cultures, from which we had sprung and drawn our power. The NUM would de facto no longer be simply 'a trade union'; it would have evolved into something like a social industrial movement based on the pits but with the wider political aspirations more focused. To me, a person with deep syndicalist convictions, the plan seemed like a stroke of utter genius, and a truly qualitative response to the world as it now confronted us. It was Arthur at his most visionary. Not that the NEC had fallen over with delight at the proposal; in fact, it had severely restricted its scope so that the women had no voting rights, no speaking rights and couldn't influence the direction of the NUM through Conference or internal elections. For Arthur, such a compromise at least kept the tub on the rails and allowed for incremental changes further down the road. The Hatfield branch and I enthusiastically welcomed the new perspectives and anticipated they would be popularly hailed throughout the coalfields, and in Yorkshire particularly, where the women had made such a magnificent stand.

The Area officials in Yorkshire however were fiercely opposed to the proposal – they too saw it as the first rung on a ladder leading the women into full participation in the union. At first, the officials tried to vote out the proposal without any consultation with the branches or the membership at large. The disagreements broke at the Council meeting of 20 May, where the minutes of the previously convened Rule Revision Conference of 19 April were about to be confirmed. Had this gone through, all the decisions of that meeting, including the decision to throw out the proposal on women, would have simply gone through on the nod. On behalf of the Branch I objected to the minute. I suggested that the meeting of the 19 April had in fact been unconstitutional, since less than 12 hours notice was given between the meeting being called and it taking place. Nobody was informed even within that 12 hours as to what the meeting was, or what was on the agenda, while few would have suspected, given the nature of the way the Conference was called, that it was of serious importance or dealt with rule revision. The delegates in Yorkshire were all working miners, most on shifts; they couldn't simply drop everything and run, so many didn't get to the meeting and didn't get to know about it until it was over.

For those who did make it, they hadn't a clue what was to be debated, and as such their branches and therefore the members hadn't discussed the issues or mandated the delegates which way they should vote. The meeting had been sprung, and those in attendance asked to vote on important rule changes just off the top of their heads, without any recourse to the men they were supposed to be representing. That same meeting had voted to support Kneel Kinnock (as we called him) despite everything he had done to stab us in the back during our life-and-death struggle against Thatcher. I moved that the minutes be not accepted. Jack Taylor badly misjudged the mood of the Council, and when put to the vote the challenge was carried, 44 votes to 22.

I hoped to buy us time. I hoped to get the women's groups lobbying the branches; it was scarce one month since the end of that strike, which would never have sustained had it not been for these women.

However, after referring the question back to the branches, it was me who misjudged the mood. When we reconvened on 17 June, the Council voted to accept all the rule changes except those dealing with Associate Membership and Honorary Membership for women. Throughout the heated debate, the platform misrepresented the proposal and said that women would be better off in the union than our retired members. It was true the new rule changes left glaring ambiguities and voids on the rights of our retired members, but these were not clarified or improved by disallowing membership rights to women. When it came to the actual National Rules Revision Conference, Yorkshire was the lead area in voting down the proposal, a shameful page in its history in my view.[227] Only five branches had voted in favour.

Yorkshire was at the head of the reaction arguing against the farsighted visionary change. I will never forget the comment of Briscoe to me and Ken Capstick, who had been supporting the proposal: 'I'm sure you two squat to piss.'

A SEA OF DISCONTENT

Divisions within the union nationally were opening up; there was a strong backlash against Arthur, and there were attempts to snub him. For the first time, he wasn't invited to attend the Yorkshire Miners' Gala – not to sit on the platform, never mind speak. Hatfield invited him to march with us. When it became known that he would be attending, at the head of the rank and file, he was formally invited onto the stage, though not as a speaker. Much of the problem was of Arthur's own making; he was refusing to acknowledge the incredibly more difficult terrain we were all trying to operate in, and seemed too often to overlook the fact we had just lost a punishing 12-month strike. But the divisions were wider and deeper than the miners themselves. The strike had been a bitter resurgence of industrial struggle, which much of the old left, 'the communist left', had previously designated as belonging to the dustbin of history, both tactically and as a social feature of class struggle. On the other hand, for the traditional industrial cadre of the CPGB the strike had been a clarion call to return to the outlook and focus of the 1940s 'proletarian' strategies. The remaining industrial cells and branches threw themselves into the fight, especially in the power plants, the docks and the print. The Communist Party had been riven between factions (The *Morning Star* and *Marxism Today*), neither of which espoused the old-time religion of industrial class struggle. 'Eurocommunism' – in fact a sort of popular liberal search for mildly 'progressive' policies – had been the flavour of the period. The *Marxism Today* tendency, which dominated, had much more in common with the new SDP right break from the old Labour Party than any new working-class expression. It meant, in short, we were, as a union, defying their new rules of gravity. Like the bee, we had been told we couldn't fly; but for 12 bitter months, and in the teeth of their opposition, and sideline backbiting and cynicism, we both flew and stung as well. As mentioned in the previous chapter, the rank-and-file Labour Party members nationwide were reborn during the dispute; and the whole ancient creaking organisation, long consigned to dark and forgotten corners in favour of the party's shiny new middle-class model, suddenly emerged, flexing muscles its members had forgotten it possessed. Now the strike was over, the party managers and new modernisers couldn't wait to tell us how it could have been foreseen, how naked class war, and especially industrial conflict, no longer held resonance; indeed, some would proclaim, never had. My esteemed Ruskin tutor and comrade Raph Samuel was to launch a blistering counter-attack upon the contemporary trends and failings within the party of his childhood, family and cultural traditions in *The Lost World Of British Communism*.[228] The CPGB not only was unable to gain any members during this most visible and dynamic expression of the class war in Britain since the twenties; it actually lost members. Because of the 'party's' lacklustre support for the strike and its implications, leading rock-solid members like Malcolm Pitt and the legendary Jack Collins, the president and general secretary of the Kent miners, resigned in disgust. Some of the those who stood with the Labour leadership, or who stood with the 'old left' or 'Euro left', influenced the bitter mix of conflict following the strike; as time went on, the divisions got worse, but it was never simply militant against moderate, class warrior against social democratic reformer. As time went, on the struggle to maintain class democracy and rank-and-file control over bureaucratic excesses eclipsed all other political and regional conflicts, and for both fundamentalist factions 'had been what the strike was all about' in the first place. (I speak here as a senior supporter of one wing of that fundamentalism and not some neutral, of course.)

BALLET IN PIT COMMUNITIES

March is Emma's Dance Show. She has continued to go to dancing right through the rigors of the strike. Ms Pat Pye, whose ballet school it is, and who is the daughter of a coal miner, has deliberately built her dance studio here, not in any of the prestigious upper-class sites in South Yorkshire which her acclaimed dance school could easily have done, defers any charge on the miners' kids for the duration of the strike. The show of April '84 broke my heart. There was something poignant about all the kids on stage, as the strike raged round the town of Doncaster, and Emma was a butterfly in the frog song, as they all sat in a solid crowd of swaying ranks singing 'We all stand together, one thing is certain we'll never give in.' The dual meaning was lost on few, and not just the mams and dads from the pits. I wept like a blushing bride.

This time she was a swan-like creature, in a beautiful and demure long ballet dress doing the most moving and graceful of ballets. After everything, we had all been through; her emerging still like a butterfly through the smoke and hardships was and remains touching in the extreme. Incidentally, given some of the debate around the excellent Billy Elliott production, this dance school had a number of male students, any one of which could have been a miner's son or indeed a young miner. The presence of so many spectacularly beautiful girls in the school, and respect for athletic fit young men among their martial arts, rugby and mining peers would easily neutralise any charge of being 'a puff'.

When I went on demos I felt proud to march with the miners. Glad that my Dad never scabbed. I think it was demonstrations that made me realise just how many people were on strike. Marching with the band (or in my case *riding* with the band on the banner) getting to the top of a hill and looking back gave me, and everyone else I expect a sort of happy feeling, even though we went through hardship I felt that I (a child) was one of the community, I felt that I was contributing by being there. I think that being on Demo's were my happiest moments and will stick in my mind for ages. (Emma Douglass, aged 12)[229]

THE OVERTIME BAN

April 1985. A Special Conference of the NUM is called to consider the situation in the industry, and in particular a clamour to the NEC from a number of areas calling for the overtime ban to be lifted. This came against a background of ongoing subversion by the scab areas and 'Working Miners' Committee' to create a schism. It came as blackleg leaders in Nottingham sacked and locked out of his office Henry Richardson, the left leader of the Nottingham miners who had supported the strike and the minority Notts strikers. Following the strike, the working miners as they called themselves moved to take control of the Nottingham Area of the NUM and oust its loyalist leaders. Other areas were engaged in the same struggle. They felt that lifting the overtime ban and allowing the men – strikers and blacklegs – to earn money in overtime would be used as a recruitment issue to potentially breakaway areas and factions. Many felt the miners would start simply to work the overtime and defy the ban and the Union, and we would effectively lose any control over conditions in the mines. The NEC had recommended to Conference that we call off the ban, and Arthur, as its spokesman, had the thankless task of moving that resolution. Despite his obvious opposition to it, he did so faithfully.

The first person to his feet and to speak in the debate was me. Speaking for the Yorkshire Area by poplar decision of the delegation and the Area officials, I rose to speak against the NEC resolution. I am in good company, with Jack Collins, the tub-thumping 'gunslinger' of the Kent coalfields, and Sammy Thompson, Yorkshire vice chair, following me. Sammy made the best speech of his life; in a deep, gravelly growl of anger demanding time and again 'So what are we going to do?' as he went through the catalogue of injustices and indignities which had befallen our miners and our union. 'So what we gonna do when we call it off?' But call it off they did, after a card vote of 122 in favour and 74 against, with Nottingham not attending. As far as I recall only Yorkshire and Kent voted to maintain the ban.[230]

NATIONAL RANK AND FILE MINERS MOVEMENT

The sacked, victimised miners see the Union boats starting to sail away from them, life on board returning to normal, flags starting to fly again and the odd verse of chanty wafting back to them on the tide as their own frail craft are cast adrift and the Union boats start to disappear over the horizon. Our brave words and intentions to carry on the fight at work, with work-to-rules, with overtime bans, had been swamped with calls for normal working. The national levy to pay the wages of the miners still at the gates was defeated in a vote by selfish men counting every penny for themselves now and careless of their one-time heroes. In Yorkshire, we have carried the vote for an area levy; it pays the men a grant now and again, or sometimes a bit of coal. The Justice Campaign for their reinstatement manages to raise enough money to give their kids a present each

Christmas. Many of these men are the vanguard of the vanguard, highly political, anti-bureaucratic with JUSTICE written through their veins like BLACKPOOL in rock. It was they who decided to start the National Rank and File Miners Movement; it will struggle to unite all the sacked lads nationally together with the rank-and-file activists and militants at every pit in every coalfield. It will stand outside the official restrictive strictures of the branch and area, even the national leadership; it will seek to maintain its political independence and not become controlled or directed by the left parties trying to seduce it or distract it. It soon develops its own national newspaper, *The National Rank and File Miner*. Neither the national nor area leaderships like any of this. The organisation, by experience and response, veers toward anarcho-syndicalism and the politics of left communism and/or anarchism. The sacked Hatfield men and in particular Tony Clegg are prominent in its leadership. Many of the branch flying pickets across the coalfields and hit squad members fall in behind its banner. Most union officials will see it as loose cannon. These are desperate men with nothing to lose; toeing the official union line and relying on formal union structures have got them nowhere.

After the miners, the government moved in for other strong sections of the trade union movement, particularly those who had supported the miners. The seafarers were facing deunionisation, and had struck. The action was thickest down there at Dover. Terry French, one of our lads who got a harsh jail sentence during the strike and was sacked and blacklisted from hell to breakfast time, had become the backbone of the victimised miners' organisation. Now he stood up to be counted with the seafarers; the *Daily Mirror* ran a scurrilous campaign against him and no one was too surprised when he ended up jailed again.

The National Rank and File Miners Movement aim to retain the power and confidence which the rank and file seized during the strike, and everywhere now was on the retreat, as management pulled on the jackboots, and the Union bureaucracy went to war against each other in something reminiscent to the Wars of the Roses or some other feudal stand off.

From the start, the rank-and-file organisation sees Arthur as 'pure' and the area leaderships as self-interested. The latter see the rank-and-file movement as Arthur's fifth column in their army. Its members from the word go are under threat of being cut off from the Union and left isolated. Actually, it is entirely a creature of the rank-and-file activists and at its core are the hundreds of sacked men determined that they should not just 'fall on their swords'. Key to this movement was the dynamic Hatfield loco driver Tony Clegg. More than 6 foot, an able street-fighter, he had been catapulted into activism by the strike. His wife Lynne had been one of the founder members of the Women Against Pit Closures; almost as tall as Tony, she was just as capable of landing a left hook on the nearest scab or policeman's lug. Strikingly beautiful, with a number of rebel songs, she, like Tony, threw herself heart and soul into that movement. Tony had had quite a strike; sacked for hitting a scab in Nottingham, he was himself stabbed by one creeping past his back garden at the end of Abbeyfield Road. The scab wasn't so much as charged. Tony had become the dynamo driving the National Rank and

File Miners Movement. It took some of its inspiration from the National Minority Movement of the late '20s and early '30s, which had arisen following our defeat in 1926. Seeing area funding gradually drying up and seeing the failure of a national levy ballot to support the victimised men, Tony and his comrades had set about keeping the national support collections goings. At first they established an office in London and then one in Liverpool to keep the issue of amnesty and welfare alive. He had succeeded in winning the Doncaster NUM panel's endorsement of the drive, and in issuing authorisation letters to the collectors, something Barnsley would never have done.[231] On 17 May, Tony addresses the Panel directly and tells them it costs £200 per week to run the offices, and that another was to be established in Birmingham. By 18 September the Panel has agreed that all Doncaster branches place a regular order for supplies of Rank and File Miner, the NR&FMM paper.[232] That meeting also gave notice that management were now moving against the Doncaster Priority System and were refusing to recognise it at Rossington. Vic Lindsey warned the panel that Rossington might soon be looking for support on this issue and the coalfield could stand, once more.[233]

CAMBRIDGE: ALLEN GINSBERG, TOM PICKARD, TOM RAWORTH

A most remarkable and historic poetry reading; proceeds 'will go to the families of miners imprisoned as a result of their fight for their jobs and communities during the 1984–85 strike'. I am appalled that I couldn't move heaven and hell to take up the invitation to speak at it, but it is too close to the end of the strike, I am too poor, and the management are strictly implacable. In the event, it raises £250, which, considering that very little notice was given, wasn't bad.

But me, I had missed the opportunity of a lifetime to meet in the flesh a poet who had so influenced our side of the generation and the Tyneside beat anarcho movement in particular. However:

4 May 1985. One of the greatest honours of my life: I am invited to be the guest speaker on the official Tyneside Trade Councils May Day rally at Leazes Park in Newcastle. I am on the platform along with Jim Slater, the president of the NUS. Ann Lilburn, the Northern chair of Women Against Pit Closures, is a magnificent dialect speaker and a women so full of fight she scared half of the Northumbrian potential scabs into staying out rather than risk her wrath.

I think this is the first time I have ever spoken on a big official public platform like this. I have spoken to bigger crowds I am sure, but this crowd, on this platform, in this city, me toon, is priceless. I speak as a miner, a Geordie miner, albeit one now working in Yorkshire and a member of the Yorkshire Area Executive Committee. The march has converged from three directions into Leazes Park, over from Gateshead, doon from Byker, and up from the Bigg Market. It is largely organised by Mick Renwick, who has become an indispensable aid to the Tyneside Trades Councils. I speak in dialect, as I am able to on *this* platform. I end, and recall I am talking to the whole of the Northumbrian trade unions here, not just the miners: 'It is time to take the offensive. It's time to seize this time. Tyneside tek a' had.'

WILDCATS

Wildcats raged across the coalfields in May. Pits in Doncaster were striking against new management attitudes; in Derbyshire, Ireland Colliery strikes when five Doncaster scabs are transferred to the pit; Renishaw has been on strike over cutbacks in payment agreements. The picture was fairly common. In the 52 weeks ending 29 March 1986 there were 414 disputes, losing 1 million tonnes of coal. 166 of these were in South Yorkshire, 56 of them in North Yorkshire, 55 of them in South Wales, 36 of them in Nottingham. Of the 12 collieries with the greatest number of disputes nationally, half of them were in Doncaster, 3 of them in South Yorkshire, 1 in North Yorkshire and 2 in Scotland. [234]

LETTERS

Russel Shanklin and Dean Hancock, two of our Welsh pickets, are sentenced to life imprisonment for the murder of Wilkie, the taxi driver taking Williams, the region's solitary scab to work. The verdict was met by strike action in the Welsh pits. From the day they are imprisoned, I keep up a correspondence with them, about the events in the Union and the coalfields, sending them a stream of leftist papers. They favoured *Workers Press* and the *News Line*. Russel told me Arthur had sent him *The Enemy Within*, our History Workshop book edited by Raph Samuel. I was over the moon. I was later a bit bothered to read that they weren't getting much sleep, but then found out it was only because they were passionate rugby fans and the matches were broadcast at 2 and 3 a.m. on the radio so they stayed up to listen to them. It was quite an eye-opener that, while at Shankland prison, they made friends with the IRA prisoners, who swapped books with them and discussed their mutual situations.[235]

2 June. Dan Jacobs, my old comrade and sometime polemicist, writes:

San Francisco, CA 94112

A few weeks ago I saw you on television here, being interviewed on a program on the miners strike aired over a public broadcasting station. I really enjoyed your remarks – brilliant agitation! The connections you drew to Ireland were really sharp, and I thought your ideas were the most politically advanced ones put forth on the program. In general, I was excited to see how much political and intellectual ferment seemed to arise among British workers and youth who participated in the strike struggle.

Me Dad writes:

You will be surprised to know your Mam flew over to Eire on Tuesday 23rd July coming back August 6th, which means a fortnight from leaving to coming back. It is hard to believe that a fortnight today, your Mam was very poorly, in fact David your Mam's heart almost stopped beating, if she had been another ten minutes in a blackout we would have lost her. I was deeply shocked. The doctor explained that due to her blood condition, the blood wasn't circulating properly and explained it could happen again, now your Mam was advised that once she had her injection she would be able to stay for a fortnight, just as long as she made sure to be back at least a week before her next injection. Your Mam dearly wanted to see her family even though she isn't able to get around much, it means an awful lot to your Mam and you have got to admire her will power. You see David I honestly think this will be Mam's last visit to Eire, and I am happy for her sake she was able to go ...

He also tells me my DAM pamphlet on the media and the strike was selling well: 'The men that bought them thought they were very true.'

This month I am up for re-election; a redundancy candidate, who campaigns solely on the basis 'Vote For Me and I'll Get You Your Redundancy', opposes me. He actually receives 40.5% of the vote. This is a creeping cancer; now that the strike is lost, and the carrot of redundancy is offered, men have given up the fight. Some are looking to have the money and then a job at somebody else's pit; some have had enough of the industry, the new regime; some have clearly had enough of us, with their visions of glory gone they are now penniless and disillusioned. It is a feature that will fester, as time goes on, right across the coalfield.

The National Conference of this year concludes with a huge wad of proposals for rule changes. Arthur is trying to shift the ground of control within the union, widening some areas of influence, cutting back on others. His central aim seems to be to rein in the autonomy of the areas, so that an Area like Nottingham couldn't defy the majority view of the NEC to support the strike. The problem with that whole concept, though, was that it was the autonomy of the Areas that allowed Yorkshire and Scotland to call Area strikes and seek NEC approval in the first place. This amounts virtually to a total rewrite of the whole of the rules, devised by Arthur and accepted by the NEC. It is fiercely contested. In the end, despite speeches from Greatrex and Roy Lynk, and the South Derbyshire and COSA delegations, the rule change proposals are passed. At this point, the Nottingham Area announces that it is mandated not to accept this new rulebook and leaves the Conference, leaving their amendments and resolutions redundant. One man from the Nottingham delegation, B. Smith, a Nottingham striker, stays. He announces that the Notts delegation have not got the authority of their Area Council to walk out of the Conference – it is their own decision. He declares that 7,000 Nottingham miners who struck deserve a voice in this Conference, and he isn't leaving. Conference agrees he has no need to. It's the start of the most decisive split in the union's history since 1926. The rule changes themselves are such a godalmighty turmoil of change and soft-shoe political shuffling that babies are thrown out with the bathwater. Not least among these is Yorkshire's decision to stop associate membership for the miners' wives, daughters and mothers. This was a long-sighted proposal, but in the melee is struck down for purely bureaucratic and sexist reasons. In order to achieve a two-thirds majority to strike down the proposal (because the whole new rulebook has been accepted pending amendments), Yorkshire insists the potential votes for Nottingham be taken out of the equation, since they have left. It is an unprecedented demand – the rules and amendments changes always requiring two-thirds of the potential vote. Arthur on this occasion, and against his better judgement, no doubt fearful of another walkout, rules that it will be two-thirds of the votes actually cast, giving

Yorkshire its amendment and robbing the women of membership. Dennis Murphy, president of the Northumberland miners, is up and down like a yo-yo. His hard Northumbrian is difficult enough to understand for most delegates at best of times; he is going off particularly at random on this occasion and basically making up proposals for changes to how the rule should operate as he goes along. At length, after his haranguing of Peter Heathfield about Tony Benn's record, Peter responds:

> The trouble is Dennis, you and I have got a problem. I'm stone cold sober. I have not been and had a pint or two at dinnertime, and I have to conduct myself with dignity and decorum in the interests of this conference, and I wish you would. (Applause)
>
> Mr D. Murphy: It proves you are not human.[236]

Other controversial proposals were those for the new category of honorary members, and that these honorary members, who were not miners and hadn't been full NUM members but have the blessing bestowed upon them, could be the Union's trustees. Sammy Thompson, for the Yorkshire Area in particular, doesn't like this, seeing the members losing control of their own funds and their own trustees by giving the power to people outside of the union's membership and unaccountable to them.

Resolutions start with a host of congratulations to the NEC for either the period since the strike, or the strike and since, or since the inception of the overtime ban in '83; Nottingham's amendment demands removal of 'congratulates' and inserts 'condemns'.[237]

However, Notts clearly still had some faith in the NUM, since further down the agenda it demands we seek parity with the terms and conditions enjoyed by BACM and NACODS 'for full pay for sickness injury and compassionate leave … ' It then goes on to call upon the Conference 'with utmost urgency' to seek increases for unsocial hours on nights, after[noon]s and early mornings in parity with other industries. It then again 'calls upon the NEC to have immediate negotiations with the NCB over national concessionary fuel allowances, and in particular towards men forced out of the industry by ill health and injury before the qualifying period.[238] And there, bold as brass, nominated for the NUM's NEC, and as the Union's trustees, are D. Prendergast and Roy Lynk from Nottingham, the men who did the government's dirty work in keeping their pits working throughout 12 months of strike, deaths, cavalry charges and murder. The men who broke the NUM strike – 4 months since its bitter defeat, largely at their hands – are seeking power on our National Executive Committee. Intent on making this a national referendum on the strike, they stand Roy Lynk against Mick McGahey for vice president of the union. Of course, the precedent for this had been Spencer, the man who led the Notts miners out of the 1926 lockout and back to work against the wishes of Miners' Federation. The Spencerites had broken from us and then years later we were persuaded to accept them back into a reformed NUM (1944), and onto the NEC of that body, as part and parcel of the new nationalised coal industry and the 'new epoch' we had been promised with nationalisation of the coal industry (1947).[239] On this occasion, they backed themselves both ways, with a decision to walk out if the new rule book were accepted, whether or not you could amend the proposed changes, but, in case it fell, a raft of resolutions and nominations to influence the union.

Two or three resolutions and umpteen amendments and debates and clarifications later, Dennis Murphy gets up on a point of order:

I think I have to clarify the situation. I think, Conference, it is totally unfair what the General Secretary said today. He implied that Dennis Murphy was out drinking and that *he* was totally sober. I will tell you what it is. Dennis Murphy left this Conference along with one of my colleagues, and Peter; we went to the Crown Court to see where the lads were being charged.

The fact I like a pint, understand, does not mean I am any lesser a person than yourself. The fact that you drink Coca Cola that is your matter. I will tell you something, I didn't like it. It hurt. Somebody said 'Take it up with him privately.' I said 'No.' I think it is totally unreasonable that the General Secretary of this Union should imply that one of the members went out and had a drink. Peter you are totally wrong.

A Delegate: Apologise or withdraw

Chairman: I think Peter has taken the point.

Mr D. Murphy: He has not withdrawn the statement, and he should, it is unfair and unrealistic. I have been to meetings when Michael has been there and three Officials …

Chairman: Colleagues, is it agreed we adjourn and recommence at 9 o'clock tomorrow morning? (Agreed).[240]

Also massively controversial was a proposal that would have meant Arthur Scargill coming up for periodical election. He was voted in as president under the rule that said he was there for life. Arthur had always canvassed for 5-yearly elections of officials, but now he was in, the rule was the rule! Delegates coming to the rostrum to speak in favour of the rule change were accused of advancing the newly proposed Tory anti-union legislation.

The arguments for not bringing Arthur up for election were highly unprincipled in my view; control by the membership over their own officials was not a tactic, but a solid principle. The members' right to decide on who was their president wasn't determined by the fear they might make the wrong political choice; the right to do so was a far stronger class principle than the danger of voting out a progressive leader. That wasn't however the view of Conference, who saw defeat of the proposal as an act of solidarity with a great militant union leader against the machinations of the anti-union press and state.

UNION OF DEMOCRATIC MINERS

Next, Nottinghamshire, South Derbyshire and sections among the North East Area break away and form the Union of Democratic Miners; it is listed with the registrar from December. The NCB, under government instructions, immediately starts to graft the breakaway faction into all consultation and conciliation arrangements and bodies. At length they will negotiate with it alone rather than the majority NUM.[241]

INTERNATIONAL MINERS ORGANISATION

In September, a new international miners' body is established, the International Miners Organisation. It is a breakaway from the previous miners' international, the Miners' International Federation, which refused to accept as affiliates organisations affiliated to the WFTU, including the French CGT miners' union. (The World Federation of Trade Unions was a Moscow-oriented communist international with union leaders from all the Moscow-aligned nations affiliated – the other was pro-western.) The new international started as a bureaucratic alliance of miners' leaders and state unions, and never moved on from there to a point where the miners themselves could control the organisation or have a say in its operations.

THE DONCASTER (NO) OPTION

August sees the Doncaster NCB management still at war with the Doncaster branches over new impositions and restrictions. It is clear the Doncaster management have formed themselves something of an unofficial 'panel' too, and have drawn up a programme to take on and confront the NUM in this, the most belligerent outpost of the union. Trouble centred at Markham, where the Branch had almost uniquely refused to adopt the new 'Doncaster Option' incentive scheme. The problem was that it wasn't actually an 'option'. Yorkshire Main Colliery (Edlington) had refused to accept and had stopped producing coal in retaliation to non-payment of bonuses; the pit closed, decades ahead of its time. A sign of things to come came when management started sending disciplinary letters to men engaged in ragups or walkouts. Now they were using the Mines and Quarries Act as a form of punishment for industrial relations problems, something unprecedented and dangerous. Frickley branch's Johnny Stones reported that the same process was underway at Frickley, and that NACODS Doncaster officials had told him management were planning a wave of dismissals to tame the Area.

A meeting the with the Area industrial relations officer proved the new invective did not come from him. A most kindly sympathetic and humanitarian man, David Holmes, the AIRO, was most unsuited for the new jackbooted management style. The panel agreed that, in the case of any such sacking at any Doncaster pit, the Area would stand.[242]

11 October 1985. Hatfield Miners Welfare Hall is full to capacity and overflowing. It is like the scene at the mass strike meeting prior to the strike. The doors are open and people crowd into the doorways. The whole of the pit – NACODS, COSA, APEX and the NUM – are here, miners, officials, and their wives, even some children. Here and there are interested members of management, electrical engineers and mine mechanics. Top of the bill is Arthur Scargill. Next to him on the platform, myself, and, by guest invitation, a Salvadorian trade unionist.

The meeting is titled 'Where Are We Since the End of the Strike? How to

Fight Now!'

There hadn't been a meeting called anywhere to asses where we were now, and where we went from here; we decided to organise our own and it clearly struck a cord. With Arthur on stage, before the eyes of thousands of miners, it was my chance now to have a say – have a say about the lack of direction, about the insults thrown at Doncaster for the adoption of new incentive arrangements and much else:

'It's true to say wor strike ended in confusion and disarray – despite the alleged order with which we withdrew. We were supposed to have went back to work with "work to rules" and a continuation of the overtime ban. Which is why I came out of that Council Chamber crying "there'll be no coal turned in Yorkshire" (As Yorkshire ratified the decision to end the strike, the TV cameras and radio reporters were reporting "it was all over", but it wasn't supposed to be.) We were supposed to be going back to work but carry on a guerrilla "ca'canny", work to rule, work safely, generally the "act the goat but still get paid" tactic. I was fuming they were reporting it "all over", and the TV cameras just homed in on me as I angrily stormed from the building and told the cameras "No Coal In Yorkshire! You gaffers will wish we were on strike by the time we've finished!"

'It was a statement which some later compared with the captain of the *Titanic* saying "I don't think it's too serious."

'Because it was only weeks before we mustered again and the overtime ban was called off. Attempts by the Doncaster branches to get the ban continued in Yorkshire failed, and we were all thrown very much into our own backyards – to mix a metaphor, to sink or swim by ourselves. People can deny that now if they wish, but the truth of the matter is, for the first year after the strike, the Yorkshire coalfield as a whole was disjointed and uncoordinated, pessimism and redundancy fever swept through the pits and the organised right wing started to become and more assertive.

'Against such a backdrop, with the Doncaster coalfield as a whole threatened with closure, with at least one pit cutting its own throat and the Board closing in for the kill, the Doncaster Option was conceived – and if people now feel so lily white themselves that they feel they can judge the Doncaster coalfield then they must at least look at the situation which gave rise to it.

'It is a simple matter of fact, that nobody in the National leadership or the Area leadership set down an analysis of where we as a union had been, what were the mistakes or what improvements could be made, how do we proceed without throwing the baby out with the bathwater? There was no Special Delegate Conference to map out the road ahead. Instead, we had the old British business adage of muddling through.

'A post-strike strategy was not forthcoming when it was needed, immediately post strike.

'However, Doncaster was pulled back from the precipice – has retained its position as top of the national disputes league, has led the way with 24-hour stoppages for the reinstatement of the sacked men, and with colliery overtime bans for the same reason.

'At the same time, the character of the North Yorkshire coalfield in general and Selby in particular has been dramatically changing, becoming stronger, more cosmopolitan and more militant in its trade unionism.

'The Yorkshire coalfield has consolidated and returned to its strength and commitment, although largely this has been the result of the rank-and-file and branch leadership's native wit and class instincts rather than any pre-planned tactics and strategy.'

The speech, which proceeded to outline all of the problems facing the union and suggested how we meet them, then moved into the global and national questions of class struggle and politics. It was a resounding success, which drew a standing ovation, from Arthur too, every bit as enthusiastic as that for his own. Nobody recorded it, nobody filmed it; however, in drafting this text I did come across a tape of my rehearsing the speech for timing, so much of the text and content is at least preserved, albeit on very old tape.

At the end of the whole meeting, I had ensured that men escort Arthur from the hall to his car, and that cars accompany him in escort until he left the village. He wouldn't be attacked in this neck of the woods.

ASBESTOSIS

Me Dad wrote:

> 23 Joyce Close. Wardley.
> This is just a few lines to congratulate you on your wonderful success in the claim for the widow of the miner who died from asbestosis, this is fantastic, for all miners concerned that may have similar problems. I do hope the top officials recognise the wonderful thing you have succeeded in doing ...

Well, it had been a long hard to fight to prove that miners worked with asbestos. The NCB had denied any link between mining and asbestosis. I now had Bill Christie, dead in his grave, and the post-mortem showing asbestosis. I attended the inquest and caused the case to be adjourned pending evidence from me that miners did in fact work with the stuff. Bill was a Hatfield miner, a heading man, a face man, had worked with me frequently, one of the old militants, 'one of my men,' a *Mineworker* supporter. I was determined to nail this thing. I set off on an exhaustive study of all the suspects and followed up all the men's pet culprits. My own doubts had focused on the water range. Miles of pipes had been made by a firm called Everite. I had questioned Jimmy Ramshaw, the safety officer, about this pipe range and he had assured me it was 'composed of a matrix of fibreglass and cement'. It was a few weeks later, and following a locomotion collision which had smashed up many meters of the pipe range, that I requested our S123 mine inspectors, under cover of the loco investigation, bring me out a piece of the pipe. This was sent off for independent survey, and the result was it was 100% white asbestos. There were hundreds of miles of the stuff at Hatfield, and thousands of miles of it in Doncaster.

When we reconvened the inquest, I had summoned the mine manager Ken Deeming and the Area purchasing manager to the stand. Ken had tried his dry wit and sarcasm in response to my questions: 'I don't suppose heading men were dancing on the pipes,' he suggested; at this, the coroner warned him to take these proceedings seriously – this was a court of law and this was an investigation into the loss of a man's life. He was suitably slapped down. The Area purchasing manager agreed there were hundreds of miles of this pipe throughout the coalfield and no special arrangements had ever been made about its installation, salvage or disposal. Bill would have crashed his way through miles of abandoned pipes and broke them up with the Eimco (a sort of underground bulldozer) or the big hammer. I had proved without doubt Bill had asbestosis, that this killed him, that he worked with it down the mine, and that the mine had extensive areas of asbestos. However we were all too optimistic; although the verdict of Death from Industrial Causes was established, the subsequent common-law claim against the NCB wasn't. Asbestosis has a specific and lengthy gestation period of no less than 15 years. Bill's lethal asbestosis must have been contacted prior to coming to the pit. He had previously worked at British Steel Scunthorpe, a place described as 'wick' with all sorts of the stuff.

As a direct result of the death and inquest, we now called in independent specialists to commission a thorough and extensive survey of asbestos in the mine. The result was surprising perhaps: blue, red and other asbestos throughout the baths, and the boilers, the winding house etc., and white in engine break pads, and throughout the Everite system. It was strong evidence for other cases.

Following the closure of the mine, and repeated requests by solicitors for evidence of asbestos in coalmines, I deposited the entire report with the verbatim inquest proceedings and specialist firm analysis in the County Archives. Soon afterwards it disappeared. It had in my view been stolen; it never resurfaced, so it wasn't taken by anyone fighting the corner of the miners and their widows and dependants.

To Russia – Without Love

15 October. I lead a delegation of miners from all over Britain to the USSR as guests of the Soviet miners. We will undertake a study tour at the Higher Trade Union Institute in Moscow, and sit for a certificate of competence and understanding. It will be a 5 weeks of Soviet hospitality and education; for them it will a month of culture shock and non-understanding, but more of that later.

The original document,[243] coming from the NEC, inviting applications had noted: 'It is important that the representatives finally selected are of the highest calibre, and are able to effectively participate in numerous seminars which will be held during the school'. As it turned out, few had taken any notice of that stipulation.

Really there are two tales of the Russian visit experience. One was positive, the other deeply negative. Russia had been since my pre-teens a source of wonderment and inspiration. I had, within the Marxist-Leninist milieu of two generations, poured over its history, read everything, and argued over the trajectory, development, aims and ends of its working-class movements, like a born-again Christian over biblical chapters and verse. I felt I knew something of its leaders lang since deed, knew many of their words by heart, knew many of their major polemics and those of their opponents. The nature of the USSR had split the world communist movement, as had the question of the state previously; we argued, discussed and hated each other on matters of its composition and the minutiae of definitions.

Now I was there, I was walking the pavements of streets I knew as if they were my own; I scarcely needed a guide on many of the thoroughfares – I knew their history so well without ever having been there. Amazingly, I could understand Russian, or some of it; I had absorbed so many of its words since early puberty. I could use the massive Metro system and understand the names of the stations as they were announced on the trains. In the heavy classroom lectures from Soviet professors, I was able to home in on crucial turning points of issue and matters of disputed history. I wrote notes furiously on the current trends, the economic positions, what were the actual organs of power, to what extent could workers influence anything. We politely debated, though we both knew these were not random, unfocused questions.

I had come out of the big lecture hall at the Higher Trade Union Academy in Moscow. One of the young girls from the Komsomol – the Communist League of Youth (whom I had christened The Consummate, for their strong inclinations to sleep with the delegations from abroad) – asked me what the professor had said. I replied: 'Well, he explained the difference between western capitalism and Soviet socialism. Under western capitalism we have the exploitation of man by man, under Soviet socialism it is the other way round.' She let the English words sink into her brain, then suddenly said: 'Did he?' 'No, not really, it's a joke.' She laughed heartily. 'That is a good joke,' she responded emphasising that there was more to these words than humour. Actually, I had refused to let go the question of the Soviets, of the heart of the revolution, control and ownership of the revolution. Professor Popoff (I think was his name) wearied of the dispute as did most of my fellow students, half of whom were asleep during most of the lectures anyway – the others thought I was just being hypercritical. But this wasn't an academic discussion. This was a debate within a Moscow university, albeit out of sight and sound of the Muscovites, and these were serious political questions.

At my side, almost everywhere, was a huge bear of a man with a face like granite and thinning ginger hair. He was going to seed now but once had had the build of Arnie Schwarzenegger, with whom he shared a strong facial resemblance. This man was a 'retired' officer from way back. He was a young officer in Stalin's regime; now he was a special attaché to foreign delegations. He was either supposed to guard us against the Russian people, or them against us – I was never sure. One thing I was sure of was he had adopted me like a son. He listened hard, and strained to understand what I said to the party officials and professors. His English couldn't always keep up and he would sidle up to me, away from the crowd; I was waiting for a theatrical 'psst', but no, he didn't do that, but these conversations were private, maybe dangerous – he should know. He would ask to me to explain more slowly not just the questions I asked and what I thought of the answers, but what was the point of the question, what was the point of the answer. What was I driving at, what were they actually saying?

He had been, in his youth, full of invincible pride and certainty. Being hard-nosed in the face of death, assassination, arrests and jailings was a mark of the cadre, a mark of commitment; what was to question? It was obvious how to proceed. Mother Russia, patriotism and the verbiage of Marxism-Leninism were all rolled into one. He genuinely had loved the world's workers, sort of felt they weren't served by all this argument and debate by the left intellectuals. Stalin was a worker, a practical man who did things – of course he got frustrated with the intelligentsia and petit bourgeois theorists and pushed them out of the way; 'Don't you?' he asked. But now he was confused; confused and displaced, he couldn't see where anything was going, and the path that had took them there had long been ploughed over and lost; you could no longer retrace your steps to see where you went wrong; if you had gone wrong, you could no longer tell – he no longer knew whether they were going in the right direction or not, and he didn't think anyone else did either. He spent many nights with me, drinking wine, vodka, probing this issue, that issue, suddenly coming up with profound insights and reflections on the great and small of Soviet political movements and leaders. I don't think he had his KGB cap on, although I got the impression he kept it in the drawer, as did tens of thousands of his former comrades, still waiting the call to impose some real direction and security back to the system. His questions, I thought, were sincere, as he sought to gain his feet again and get some firm ground on which to stand.

Down at the HQ of the Soviet miners' Moscow office, we met the whole staff and officers of the union and received a long lecture on soviet coalmines, wages, conditions, history. I asked what the death and accident rate was. The Soviet miners' president answered that such information 'wouldn't be helpful'. Pressed on the question, he explained, 'Well, our coal industry is much bigger than yours and we have many more workers in it – the figures would confuse you.' I pointed out to him that international figures on fatal and serious accidents in mining were counted in 100,000 manshifts, so were internationally weighted to convey the correct balance for these variants. 'Well, I don't know,' he responded. 'We are not as bad as the American mines, but not as good as the British mines.' When at last, a couple of weeks later, we visited the coalmines of Tula, we found them modern and safety-conscious, though these may have been specially selected. Mind, we had planned to see the Ukraine mines, and the seasonal weather was already bitter. I was looking forward to the visit very much, but some of the pillocks who had come with us told us that, despite instructions, they had brought no warm clothes, no duvet jackets or boots, and since the temperature was 30 degrees below freezing, the visit was cancelled.

Some of our fellow miners' motives for visiting this country were dubious, to say the least. They had no intention of going along with the plans, but were awkward and non-cooperative; they had come merely for a joyride and holiday. It was to get worse. Some of them – a couple, anyway – had political objections, being members of the SWP and thoroughly hostile to the whole paraphernalia of the USSR. There was nothing wrong with that politically of course, but the scepticism and hostility bordered on rudeness to the ordinary Soviet workers too, who were showing us nowt but hospitality.

A number of us were of course rightly cynical of the mighty bureaucratic apparatus and aware that leftist visitors were often overcome, like visitors to Lourdes, with an all-self-deluding urge to believe and embrace the faith. Luis was a character and a half, an exiled Chilean hard-rock, usually gold, miner. An organiser of the migratory, solitary gold miners who took off like early American prospectors and worked in the mountains for months, even years on their own, mining for gold with basic, hand-held technology. These miners lived only on their wits and what they could grasp from the mountains. Luis was nicknamed 'The Puma'. Starving in the freezing mountains, having a run of bad luck such that he couldn't come down until he struck enough gold to feed his family for the year, he was attacked by a likewise starving puma. Luis had killed and eaten the magnificent beast with only his knife and his axe. He told me that even in the midst of that desperate encounter he loved the animal still, always had; this was not a killing by choice. He had earned the name 'el Puma' among the Chilean trade unionists who knew him well. When the 1973 coup led by Pinochet happened, 'el Puma' led a guerrilla struggle from the mountains, sometimes with a small band of miners, sometimes utterly alone. He dynamited roadways, he derailed army trains. When tracked by a team of army rangers parachuted into the mountains with the sole task of catching and killing him, he ambushed them one at time. 'I jump from cave, tha knaas, knees in back, twist head, snap neck, tha knaa?' Luis had the most endearing mix of Derbyshire pit twang, which he picked up while working in exile as a heading man, and his native Spanish. Luis's politics had been close to the Leninist organisation the Revolutionary Left Movement (Movimiento de Izquierda Revolucionaria – MIR), but he leaned toward syndicalism in his nature and experience. As we walked through the broad Moscow thoroughfares, we would frequently see the big black limousines of the Soviet bureaucracy. Luis hated them; he would shout at the blacked-out windows speeding by: 'Capitalista! Bureaucrata!', or words to that effect. 'Bosses!' he would shout toward me, smacking his fist into his hand. Until one black limousine pulled along side and Luis was about to give them more abuse, when the door slid open, and there on the back seat, in a suit and dark glasses, was one of the exiled leaders of the Chilean trade union movement. With arms outstretched, the man in the black car shouts 'El Puma! Compañero!' with obvious genuine emotion and joy. Luis dived into the car to embrace the long-lost comrade – each had thought other killed by the army. After a few minutes, the limousine swept off through the snow-brushed streets. After that 'El Puma' was often an occupant of the bosses' cars. I ribbed him about it a lot but he used to tap his nose with his finger and say 'tactica', as if he was secretly planning an anti-bureaucratic coup on the sly and he would put up with this unusual privilege for the cause.

TULA

The visit to Tula was a week of close contact with the Russian miners; we would stay at a nearby hotel, but go down the mine with the miners and spend the shift with them. We were heartily impressed by the underground travelling roads; these were specially constructed walkways separate from material roads and belt roads. The lads in the headings drove the giant stone-cutting machines not unfamiliar to us, in fact we were told the heading machines were made on licence to British mine supply firms, from Soviet mining equippers. Mind, I was less than impressed when two of the safety lamps hanging in the chock line had been knocked out, and the deputy came along, unscrewed them and simply lit them with a box of matches from his pocket. I had placed my hands over my ears in mock anticipation of a massive explosion. I was speechless; what was the point of having Davy lamps, to avoid a naked flame coming in contact with explosive gas, if you lit them with a naked flame? An official told me later that the exposure time of this one ignition was not the same as working with a naked flame all day; these were not anyway very gassy pits and the lamps were just an added precaution. I wished I'd had the presence of mind to take a gas test while I was there, as I for one wasn't convinced of the logic of this process. It was the one slip on an otherwise very impressive visit.

We had visited a huge mining supply establishment, and I noticed the range of chocking equipment ranged from the giant seam supports to clever, thin-seam hydraulic chocks smaller than those manufactured in Britain. In Britain, the remaining thin-seam mines had generally been hand-filled and had hand-set timber, as no mechanical system had been devised for seam heights of less than about 2½ feet; the trouble was that support occupied too much of the precious space. The Russians, it seemed, had cracked this problem, with lightweight, durable thin- seam supports and tiny disc cutters aimed at rapid turnover and advance. The Soviets were using every nut of coal they had, not writing off vast reserves as either too large or too thin, as had been done in Britain. In the UK, the Union to its shame had agreed with the NCB that a coal seam would not be a workable proposition if it was less than 30 inches. Emley Moor, the last hand-filled pit in Britain, the most westerly Yorkshire pit, worked 14-inch seams last off, but the men were confident it would rise again to its full height of 18 inches. They filled the coal as they had always done, lying alongside the coal, driving the shovel in flat from their stomach, filling and turning it up past and over their heads, launching the coal onto the belt running behind them. Their bodies moved in a wave with their feet sliding back and their buttocks thrusting forward, tensing with their stomachs, drawing their arses back, dropping their head and shoulders forward, then thrusting in an upward body movement of neck, spine, head, stomach, arms and chest, generating massive power in a confined space which allowed minimal movement.

The seam was jib-cut and fired, the full face shovelled away onto rubber face belts. Amazingly, the pit had never made a loss, and its high-grade, large, house coal was top of the yuppie market choice. The branch wished to resist the closure; there was masses of good quality coal left, and although the hewers were no spring chickens, they had no desire to give up their working lives and take redundancy. The Board however ruled the pit was exhausted and 'the Union' agreed; by accepted definition it was exhausted. It was another of those issues which seen me support the common-sense aspirations of the rank-and-file against the blind autocracy of Union officials who were working from some other form of logic and motive that I have never understood. Despite the complicity in the closure of Emley, scenes of the last weeks of production on that tiny face, the men captured forever in their horizontal toil in the last such scenes we will ever witness, hang around the room of the Yorkshire Area's executive room. This was a method of work I had first encountered all those years ago in the thin seams of Wardley pit; it took a special aptitude, a particular physical focus now gone forever; and though some would add 'Thank God', it was also an adventure, which granted a great and unique sense of achievement every day you laboured, perhaps something like reaching the summit of a small mountain every day.

The president of the Moscow CP came to give us a lecture, explaining something of the political history of the City, and its current standing. At the end of the lecture he announced: 'Now comrades you may ask me anything you wish.' One of SWP blokes gets up and with great flourish asks, 'Why are there no birds in Moscow?' The president, whose English was very good, nonetheless looked puzzled and asked in Russian the group translator what this British miner had asked. 'Why no birds in Moscow?' He looked almost helpless as he replied, 'I have no idea, you must ask an ornithologist, when I say, ask me anything you want, I mean on the subjects that I have spoken on of course.' I curled up in embarrassment, although the comrade thought he had scored a really good blow against the Stalinist bureaucracy.

Mind, the iron hand of bureaucratic malfunction was everywhere, and plainly evident when I tried to coordinate stuff for the group. Hotel Sputnik had a small café bar, which we all would return to before forages further afield, or after coming back in. They served beer, the miner's staple diet. The hotel, however, ordered only the same amount of beer each week. An influx of British and now also Australian miners drank them dry in a week – ney mer beera, again. I go to the manager and ask him to order us more. This produces no outright refusal: the Soviet bureaucracy in all their shapes and forms react to everything with agreement, but then don't do anything. It's like trying to enter a building through a constantly revolving door, nobody says you can't come in, but you won't come out the other side. After 2 weeks of failing to reorganise the managers order lists, I got onto the brewery manager but discovered that apparently the brewery, like the hotel, only produced the same amount of beer each week regardless of changes of demand; when it was gone, it was gone – the plan couldn't be altered just because demand had.

At length, I took the occasion of a lecture by the head of the Central Committee of the Communist Party of the Moscow region to illustrate the failings of the Soviet system by the beer crisis in the hotel. This speech, unlike the earlier complaint about the birds, struck a resonance with all the delegations, and put the PB on the spot. 'You are right comrade, we do not get so many changes of demand on our productions because we plan it in advance, we are used to cutting our cloth according to our width as you say,' although I thought at the time this just meant going without. 'But in this case, I shall personally intervene to ensure an adequate supply of beer for the mining guests, as much as you can drink,' he said to cheers.

Well, my hotel room fronted the building and a few days later, I heard the expected rattling of bottles like a milkman's convention. Looking out of the window I saw a large flatback brewery lorry, with masses upon masses of crates of beer. Unfortunately I also saw teams of Australian miners with hand trolleys, wheeling stacked high crates of beer into the hotel. I was at once suspicious and dived out to see what was going on. The bastards had hijacked the load; they were diverting hundreds of crates into their rooms, where they stood piled high to the ceiling, the group's puffler,[244] paying load by load to the café manager as they arrived and were wheeled away. I roused the sleeping miners from Britain and we piled downstairs only to see that a mere 50 or so crates had actually made it to the café. World War Three was about to be unleashed as we charged down the corridor to the Australians' rooms. They had locked and barricaded the doors. Well, we knocked and banged and shouted and sang, much to the consternation of the floor supervisors whose normal role is to make sure you don't have any loose women in your room after dark. We squirted CO_2 from the fire extinguishers under the doors, and through the keyholes, and occupied their landing prepared to wait it out in a siege. Peace negotiations seen us agree to split the supplies three ways, half between us and them, the other half back to the café for communist distribution – well, actually, first come first served; though jealous eyes scanned with scorn any Soviet citizen drinking 'our beer'.

Our hosts were kind to a fault. Almost as soon as we arrived, they sized us up and fitted each of us out with the KGB overcoat, that long greatcoat so loved by Russian politicians. They are undoubtedly the warmest piece of apparel I have ever come across, although because of their weight and thickness the buttons need constantly sowing back on again. The classic Cossack hat too was being distributed; when he got to me I declined, it was obviously real fur. 'Niet, comrade,' I said holding up my hand. The distribution official looked surprised, 'Hat keep head warm, very cold out,' he said trying to put the hat on my head. 'Niet, comrade, I'm a vegetarian.' 'OK,' he replies 'Put on head do not eat it.' I took the damn thing amid much hilarity from my comrades at his double-quick wit, and gave it away to one of the moaning comrades in the hope he might actually find something to his satisfaction since his hat was too big, and his coat wasn't right. He didn't, but later as we stood in the snow and wind in Red Square watching the great October parade, my head near froze solid. I had a little woolly hat, and then a scarf wrapped round the back of my head Arafat style, but the biting sub-zero temperatures made me ponder on how wise the decision had been to 'niet hat' it.

Since being a starry-eyed boy of twelve, I had watched the Red Square May Day parade; I had dragged myself out of bed every year at 6 a.m. to watch it blow by blow on the aud black-and-white telly. At school I had earned a swipe roond the lughole for drawing the parade as my portrayal of May Day, when actually it should have been the Blessed Virgin. Now I was here, in that square. I had joined the thousands upon thousands of excited families heading for the huge square, decked and adjourned with massive revolutionary slogans, and portraits of Marx, Engels and Lenin, the hammer and sickle, red stars, and giant red banners streaming in the October breeze. It was like a miners' gala multiplied a thousandfold. Happy children skipped along with their folks, ranks of schoolchildren marched into their designated places, Pioneers and Komsomol, seaside Mams laded down with picnic stuff, old men in their mufflers with their memories, and lines of medals from that war against the Nazis which cost them 60 million lives of their comrades and families – but this was anything but grey. Light tanks stood at junctions and entrances to the square. In the turret of one stood a resplendent tank commander in his grey fur Cossack hat with the red star and hammer-and-sickle badge, his double-breasted greatcoat buttoned across his chest. I asked in sign language if I could come up into the turret and he come and take a photo of me in his place. He laughed, and began to dismount from the tank. I could see the photo now, me arms spread peering into the future from a gleaming Soviet tank. It didn't happen. Just as I was climbing up to the turret, an army general glistening with medals and ribbons, his wide-peaked Red Army cap firmly in place, waved his hand theatrically and shouted 'Niet!' I mean, I could have been a maniac taking over the tank and running amok through the people. The tank commander shrugged so I gestured for the general and the commander to stand in front of their tank for a photo. The general broke into a wide-beamed smile and laughter, and the two of them stood, stern-faced with their arms folded across their chests in front of the tracks and gun, while two other occupants unseen by the gaffer waved two-finger peace signs out of the turret.

As the crowds gathered and milled around, I was convinced Yuri Gagarin strolled along in front of me. I loved that man – he was among my first heroes. A small man in stature, with a firm though constantly smiling face, was picking up children and having his photo taken with them. Aud lads and women were coming up and shaking his hand, and he smiled at me as he went by and for a moment I nearly grabbed him to have a photo taken with him, arm in arm, me and Yuri. I let the moment go, and he was lost in the crowd. A year later I told the tale to someone and they ridiculed me, saying Yuri had died years before I went to the Moscow May Day parade! Was that true? I don't know, I could have sworn it was him.

I was to be interviewed by Radio Moscow live from Red Square, in a broadcast throughout the USSR. I have a photo of me, standing there in borrowed fur hat (for the publicity follow-up), two great mic stands and microphones in front of me and the Soviet journalist translating by my side. Except he wasn't actually. He had come to my room the night before and asked me to go through what sort of things I would say. Well, I hadn't actually written a speech, as they only wanted 6 or 7 minutes, so I thought I'd do it off the cuff mainly, but I outlined what sort of things I was going to say and he made notes. What I didn't know was that he didn't trust his English to translate me simultaneously, so he went away and wrote a speech he thought I would deliver. I didn't realise this until I was rabbiting away down the mike, and coming to the end, when he indicated me to keep speaking, keep speaking! Well, I had said what I wanted, so I just started plucking things from the air to add. He, on the other hand, spoke earnestly on in Russian to the nation. Only proper English speakers, listening, would know that what I was saying was nowt like what he was coming out with. In fact to this day I haven't a clue what he said I said, only that it was 'nearly the same, nearly'. Still, quite a coup I thought, bringing the fraternal greetings of the British coalminers and the British working class to our Soviet Socialist working-class comrades and friends.

Actually, this journalist was most concerned about the political situation in Russia; and had talked late into the night with me about what it was all about. In particular, he couldn't understand why ordinary workers in the west didn't realise what a sacrifice the young Soviet soldiers were paying in Afghanistan, a sacrifice for the progress of the world against the barbarism of Islamic medievalism, in defence of education and equality and science. He asked earnestly, 'Do any of them know what this war is about?' I confessed that I did see the struggle as being of epic dimensions and importance but no, it was presented as Soviet aggression against brave little tribesmen. He confided that, within the USSR, the death toll was causing despair; the Soviet authorities refused to call this a 'war', refused to allow the young Soviet troops to be honoured at the war memorials or to have their deaths formally marked and respected. Young soldiers' widows protested to bring the war to an end, as nobody cared that their lads were dying. 'We should pull out,' he demanded. I suggested gravely that I understood that, but that a pull-out of Afghanistan would be a prelude to pulling out of more and more of the USSR, and finally they would 'pull out' of Russia too. He understood my inference; these were the last days of whatever the so-called USSR had become: 'Maybe, then, it is time to,' he countered. But it was not yet and not now; and the massed ranks of Soviet troops marched in lines hundreds wide and tens of thousands deep, arm in arm, shoulder to shoulder, through the drifting snow, their heads turned in salute toward the mausoleum, their lips curled in that strange barrister's snarl, which they adopt in this position. The voices of the officers ring out across the square, and massed harsh voices, like a staccato choir, shout back in great furores, as cannons too blast across the square. Trundling forward, squeaking and crunching across the cobbles, the multitracked iron fist of Soviet armour pushed forward in mechanical precision and power, like one great iron machine, bristling with heavy guns – the force that pushed 19 crack German divisions across the continent and to utter destruction in Berlin in World War Two. My heart and head were in appalling conflict. My heart swelled, something in my head, despite everything I knew about this parasitic, lying system, something said 'Get that up you, you bastards!' This was our side, this was our force, these were our flags our heroes, this must be our army?

My reason questioned: was it all a lie then, was everyone in on it? Did the generals go away and have a good laugh as soon as the crowds went? Did the Politburo know they were pissing up our backs, or more importantly the backs of the millions and millions who fought and died under this system in the belief it was all a genuine and honest effort to liberate the world? Certainly the 'communism' of the leaders, the well-heeled, sated, bloated, parasitic bureaucrats was not communism of any description; maybe they were just there because they were there, were singing to an old hymn sheet from a chapel that long ago had fell down. What none of us realised was that a new regime was being fashioned 'in the belly of the old' in the way we thought socialism would emerge from capitalism; but now, whatever this system was or wasn't, capitalism – full-blown and stripped of any illusion of social justice and radical verbiage – was being cobbled together and perfected. The old guard were now on borrowed time and all this, whatever it was, would soon be gone, replaced by the Mafia, rampant crime, dog-eat-dog and gross poverty unseen since the starvation days of old Stalin, but this time without any comforting thought that it was for anything more than to keep the new rich rich and getting richer. They wanted capitalism – they would soon have it again, red in claw and tooth.[245]

Forbye, that was the knowledge of hindsight. Just then, I was still in the square, and still hadn't quite decided what this Soviet Union actually was. That it played an often progressive role in anti-imperialist struggle, albeit for its own agenda, was a fact; that it kept the naked clutches of the World Bank and the free marketeers out, that it put a break on unbridled American expansionism and Victorian gunboat imperialism was also true. Was it socialism? Certainly not, not by anyone's definition. The workers didn't run this system and never had since the first few years of the revolution. The scales had fallen from my eyes halfway through the strike, when everything was up for reassessment and change. Lenin had presided over the abolition of the Soviets (the workers' councils), and Trotsky had put down their last defenders in an orgy of blood when the anarchist and left-communist sailors, the vanguard of the revolution, were eliminated at Kronstadt. I knew what it wasn't, but I was unclear what it was. Capitalism as such, the kind we knew didn't exist, was waiting in the wings. When it came there was little resistance: the population had had 70 years of inoculating decay and transition back to bare-faced capitalism, through varying graduations of it. 'Soviet socialism' hadn't so much failed as been defeated; and a crude impostor of a system based upon power elites and privilege had assumed its place, its clothes and its slogans. The regime went through the motions, continued the deception, and millions of its citizens, its soldiers, its workers and rank-and-file party members still believed they were working for the same cause. Why did the regime maintain the deception? Was it a conscious deception, or just some massive organisational dysfunction? I don't have the answer.

Nobody can have anticipated the utter contempt with which many on the delegation treated our hosts and the ordinary Russian workers. It began almost from the first night. We were staying at Hotel Sputnik. It hadn't been my idea that we would be off on a tour round drinking establishments on the first night, but some of the men, those from Durham and parts of Yorkshire, considered from day one that this was going to be one big 'boys' night out'. As we swept through the darkened streets from the airport, towards Moscow, I was absolutely thrilled, thrilled to be here, in this land of the first serious and sustained go at workers' power and revolution. Others on the bus took the piss at everything they passed, contrasted everything with Britain almost from the moment we landed. It was to get worse and worse and time went on.

The first I became aware of a problem was within 2 days of getting there. Our delegation coordinator came and told me one the hotel staff had been assaulted, the night before, 'by one of the British miners'. I couldn't believe it, in fact didn't believe it. How could it be true? 'Da, da, true!' The old doorman at the hotel was there to stop crooks coming into the hotel basically. He had stopped one of the British miners, he said, who was coming into the hotel with a Moscow prostitute on his arm at 2 a.m. He had told the bloke he couldn't bring her in at this time of night, it wasn't allowed. The man had then smashed his head into the doorman's face, kicked him on the floor and ran past with the girl, who was by now struggling and protesting she didn't want to come in. He let her go and she ran away, as did the miner. Who was it? He could guess, but a couple of the British miners looked the same – he didn't know. How could this happen, how would anyone know where to go on the Moscow streets? Would he really have gone off on his own, and why? It didn't make sense, but as time went on it became clear it was all true. A little later I became aware that a petty Russian criminal was visiting one of the rooms and holding court with a cabal of apolitical miners from the delegation. He changed roubles for dollars, he sold Soviet military surplus, well, not always surplus, just items sold by disillusioned Soviet soldiers desperate for money. He bought jeans and cigs; finally he started lining up prostitutes and fixing up visits to girls on the game. His patter was shot through with counter-revolutionary criminal crap; it amused this particular group of miners that someone could be counter-revolutionary, iconoclastic, criminal and useable. In one encounter with girls on the game at their flat, the lads ran out of dollars and paid with their wedding rings, then refused to hand them over – then their minders came round and the lads escaped using a pair of kitchen knives; and even then only escaped by stopping a passing police car and pleading that they were innocent victims of a criminal scam.

In the end, perhaps 30% of the delegation was involved with prostitutes, drinking throughout the day, marching off arm in arm to drunkenly pace the streets of Moscow to loud choruses of 'Get your tits out for the lads!'

Evening of November 7th/morning of Nov 8th

The worse incident of a sorry saga. Not surprisingly, it involved three of the people who were an active source of problems throughout the visit; two of the three were people involved in the previous trouble.

The night ended with a hotel bar being smashed up, drunken brawls, and eventually four of the delegation arrested. One was subsequently released to hospital with a split head as a result of the brawl.

The survivors informed me at 4-30 am. From then until 8 am I was phoning staff and officials of the Education Ministry and the Soviet Miners to get them to intervene. They too had less sleep and a worse night then the men in cells. Instinct would have urged that they be allowed to stay there, (my own view was that they should throw the key away or put them directly on the next flight back to England), but a residue of the dissidents were threatening to go to the British Embassy, which in my view would have thrown even more discredit upon the union and the Soviet Union. It could have pressured the police into taking stronger action against the men, and more importantly it could have got into the national press in Britain, with particularly bad results for the NUM and the USSR. For that reason, I headed off that demand in exchange for immediate action down other channels. My KGB mate was furious, more that they were treating me with lack of respect than the lack of respect they were showing them. 'We can deal with unruly comrades like this,' he snarled, nodding at me for approval. I was sorely tempted to tell them to lock the buggers up and we'd collect them on the way home.

The four protagonists: K—on, St—son, Pl—er; and S—ds, who was sent to hospital.

One of the worst things of the issue followed on the morning of the 8th after I and the guides had been at it all night trying to sort things out. At the late breakfast held at 10 am S—ds turns up with his head stitched, telling glorious tales of the struggle, while at least a quarter of the delegation laughed, swapped stories and gave the impression that the previous night had been one hell of a hoot. Our guides coming back into the room looked speechless and shocked.

Subsequently, as a result of long, exhaustive representations by officials of the Trade Union School and the Soviet Miners Union, the three were released about 3 p.m. despite the fact that a police officer was still in hospital as a result of head injuries. The officials concluded that the whole incident was caused by gross drunkenness; and the delegation would now not drink and not go round visiting international hotels and nightclubs. I made the point that, despite everything, most of the party had behaved themselves and if they could have a drink in our own hotel without drunkenness we would comply with the request not to go to the night clubs etc. However when I put this to the delegation, the people who had been the source of the trouble thought it unfair, and the events of the previous night neither here nor there. Two of the arrested men asked if they could bring women in their rooms; surprisingly enough they were told that guests were permitted until 11 p.m.[246]

I had hoped the activists, the militants, the politicos in the delegation, even those with just common courtesy, would prevail upon the antis; that they would actually start to appreciate all that was being done for them, the open kindness being shown them. It was not to be – the rotten apples continued to fester.

Our visit to Tula, to our fellow miners, I thought would smarten up the antis; these were pitmen like ourselves, in pit villages, with their families. At first, the crack, sustained through sign language and mime was canny. We had been invited to 'a miners' breakfast' at 5.30 a.m., before going underground. Essentially this miners' breakfast so called was every item of food they had in the canteen, including mashed potatoes, and beetroot. No miner ever ate a breakfast like this and did a hard day's work, and neither did we, though that was mer to dey with lingering hangovers from days on the bevy.

On the Friday evening we were all invited to the shindig at the local miners' club. The miners and their families were there in their hundreds for their weekend night out. A rock group of sorts was booked for the night and a Russian disco, which sort of incorporated a mutated rock'n'roll, with traditional Russian-type dancing, not the Cossack dance of course (though years ago in the early Sixties jack the lads back yem often did it to impress the 'burds') but the whirly arms and clever skip movements that the Russian girls performed.

The first couple of hours of drink were to be free, but this brought little cheer to the sullen clique, who noted with grimness that the whole poxy place had no beer. No beer again. There was vodka, or Russian champagne, the choice drink of the Russian miners. Still, things perked up as they got more of the booze down their throttles and there was much backslapping and handshaking and camaraderie. The Russian miners were sitting at our tables, groups of our lads were with families, there was much coal being cut and timber set underneath the tables, while doscos of all descriptions were being drawn on beer mats. I was no fan of either vodka or champagne; I decided to call it a night. I visited all the tables and warned the lads, 'For God's sake behave yasells here lads, dey as ye wad be done by.' I was assured I was fussing, bureaucratic even, they were fine. I went to bed, worn out from the pit and the non-stop talking and visits and strain. I drifted quickly into deep sleep.

I don't know when I first became aware of the sirens, sirens, lots of sirens and a vague hubbub. I didn't wake up, I slept on, until the loud banging came to my door about 5.30 a.m. The local miners' officials had been looking for me. Some of them were bleeding, and all dishevelled. They were breathless, speechless, they took me down the stairs and across the road back to the club, where cars were parked and lights were on. Angry voices could be heard on the streets, people stood around mumbling. I went into the club concert room. It was scene from a Wild West bar brawl – overturned tables, chairs, smashed bottles, pools of drink, splatters of all sorts on the walls, ripped curtains.

'What the hell?' The lads had got bladdered, had got up dancing, had went round the tables getting the miners' wives, girlfriends and daughters up, danced with them much of the night, ney problem. As it got near lowse, their respective partners or parents came to take them by the hand or walk them back home. 'Oh no you don't!' Suddenly these had become 'our women'. 'We had danced with them and bought them drinks all night, then they wanted to walk off with other blokes!' one vociferous fool had used in defence. Fights started, and because we had a team of berserkers with us, it soon went beyond control and became unrestrained hit-everyone-with-anything fighting.

The Russian pit communities do not have cops as such; instead, there is invariably an army camp, the troops charged with keeping order in the mining villages. The authorities might well have supported the British miners, but they had no intention of letting their miners mount any national offensives. When the call for help went out, dozens of army trucks and jeeps, packed with conscript

Russian soldiers, armed with batons and pick shafts set off for the club. They walked into the middle of a riot. Their young officer asked what the hell was going on? 'British miners fighting Russian miners,' he was told. That was it. He ordered the troops back into the trucks and drove off, saying he would be back in the morning to pick up the dead and survivors. Truth.

What could I say, to the men, to our hosts, or to the miners themselves? Bernard Jackson, a militant Yorkshire miner from Cortonwood and a veteran of the Orgreave battle, battered and jailed, had stood in tears, telling our so-called comrades how much he was ashamed of them, how disgusted he was and how he wished we had never been invited to the country at all – we were a disgrace. He was right.

There was a different climate from now on, a coldness which you couldn't blame anyone for. It took time to crack the Russian depth of hospitality but if you persist, you will get there – they do recognise cynicism and abuse eventually. By the last day, things had started to recover; the miners hosted a big farewell meeting, no booze this time. It fell to me to make the speech of thanks and farewell. It wasn't an easy task. I handled it in the way I would back home. After the thanks and a résumé of what we had learned (well those of us who were interested) I conceded that we had had the chance to work with the Russian miners, live with the Russian miners, eat and drink and dance with the Russian miners, and some had even fought with the Russian miners. The local president of the Tula miners, presenting me with a wonderful stainless steel shield, behind which a windy pick in a lump of coal occupied the foreground in miniature, said, 'You should not blame yourself comrade.' (As my profuse apologies had made him quite well aware of just how ashamed and embarrassed I was.) 'The Tula miners do this every Friday, they do not wait just for when you are here.' It went down well, though I think the weekend brawl was never on the scale of this barny.

The Soviet students obviously all receive a grant. They had concluded we too were due a grant, as official students at a Soviet academy and studying for a certificate validated by the Soviet education system; this was more to dey with the fact that we had so recently been on strike and had suffered such financial hardship. To allow us to buy presents to take home, they awarded us each £200 in roubles. A lovely touch, I thought. Despite this, as we sat on the coach waiting to go to the airport, the hotel manager came out and told me that two comrades had not settled their bills. 'Bills?' 'Da, phone calls home.' Few of us had phoned home even once; we were well aware of how costly that was, and far too much to expect our hosts to pay for. Two of the Durham lads had phoned every day, sometimes for hours on end, then just left and not paid. The £200 they had been given would have met the bills which they knew they had; they spent it instead. I hit the roof, called them all the selfish shits under the sun, and declared that the bus wasn't leaving until they paid their bills. After 30 minutes of showdown (and I would have been prepared to miss the plane and have us all sleep on the bus until they paid) the Russian miners' leaders took me by the arm and, shaking their heads, none the less said it was OK – they would pay. They had paid our airfare and everything else; they would pay this bill too. I was and am furious. My report to Arthur produced a demand from him to 'name names, comrade, names, branches, areas. I shall ensure they never get to represent our union on overseas work again.'

Cartoons by Tony Hall featured in *The Morning Star*, 1984-1985

4
The Struggles Continue

The post-strike period is a historical black hole. Many of the events have gone unrecorded, and evidence of what happened between the end of the strike in '85 and the next great offensive against us in the early '90s by John Major is lost. Inter-union battles between factions and areas, between branches and lodges and within branches and lodges have ensured that minutes and Conference reports have been suppressed, and accounts of what took place are hotly contested to this day. [247]

The dust had scarcely settled when a new calibre of manager started to take up office at Area and pit level. MacGregor, commenting on the onslaught against the NUM's standing in the industry, the abandonment of procedures and agreements, the wave of sackings and victimisations, commented that we were 'learning the cost of insurrection'. The new breed of no-nonsense managers given the reins of the industry had been led to believe that they faced a dispirited and defeated foe, which had now been fought to docile standstill. They were soon to be cured of such a perspective. The miners had marched back, not victorious; but Thatcher's central objectives had not actually been achieved. They never understood that the miners' battle on the street and others just like them throughout our long history were ancillary to what being a miner meant: the ability to control your own work, to exercise 'the miners' freedoms' as self-regulating and self-motivating workers, and to claim the right to fight injustice, down the mine and in society. The right to be a miner was only partly about the right to mine coal; the right to fight, to use our social strength and power within industry was a far greater imperative. The new management formula required that the NUM and its local, area and national leaders were humiliated, rendered impotent. Ancient freedoms, longstanding agreements and work practices were set upon, with a view to clearing out the whole tradition of 'Spanish practices', as they now termed them.

Government and management never understood that without freedom to control our own work, to pick our own workmates, to work the seam as our knowledge and the skills of generations had taught us, without our human rights as mineworkers – without these they could have the pit. We didn't want it anymore.

Wildcat strikes spread throughout the coalfields, massed pickets surged between collieries, and some took on the role of suicide bombers – determined that, if we couldn't keep the industry as we knew it then they, the gaffers couldn't have it either. We would sink the pits ourselves first.

As the strike closed in 1985, management started to pull on their jackboots and get their self-imposed 'prerogatives' polished up again. Another decade of war was about to be unleashed. Amazingly, it is one hitherto unrecorded.

The strikers in the scab coalfields had had it the hardest. Throughout the strike *they* were the ones in the minority in their own pits and coalfields. They were the ones attacked by mobs, who had their cars wrecked, had their walls daubed in anti-strike slogans, had their kids victimised at school. Many suffered serious injuries, some survived murder attacks. The police never so much as went through the motions of protecting their rights, their right *not* to work. Crimes against strikers were not crimes. The police were boldly partisan, telling complaining strikers, on the odd occasions they turned out to the scene of an attack; 'Tha should get thasel back off to work, mate. We can't be everywhere.'

The press and TV never attempted any 'balance' on this score. Maggie never talked of 'terrorism and mob rule' with regard to the scabs' treatment of strikers.

Throughout the strike, police had moved into colliery offices, shared strategy with pit managers, transported scabs, protected them in areas where they were the minority. Parts of the pithead were arrest holding centres, arrested strikers were processed on colliery sites by police sitting behind colliery desks in colliery offices. Police would show managers photos of pickets, and the managers would identify militants and men who they assumed would be behind any rammie and getting stuck into any fighting. Police snatch squads would be briefed on who to look out for; and as soon as the pickets arrived, they would charge the crowd, pull out the militants identified by the manager and from then on justice was done. Win or lose in court, the man would be sacked *for misconduct*. Where the court found the lad innocent, the police would release details of statements and charges to the management, who would use this as the basis for sacking and blacklisting the man, regardless of his established innocence.

Over 700 men were sacked before the strike ended. After the strike, the gloves were off, to see how far men could be pushed, how much flesh and blood and pride could be forced to stand before they left, took 'voluntary' redundancy, or were sacked. In the scab areas, face and heading men were nowhere allowed back to that proud place at the point of production, but were busted to the low-paid backbye work with the old men and young lads, and robbed of their pride and social standing in the community. Attitudes to scabs – at work, in the club, overheard, alleged – were taken as grounds for instant justice and summary dismissal. The scab union was moved into place, the NUM ignored, rendered impotent.

In the strike-solid areas, things were just starting to hot up. My spies in St George's, the Doncaster NCB Area HQ on Thorne Road, informed me the Area management team discussed a memo from Hobart House, the NCB national HQ in London, to discuss the possibility of sacking me and Johnny Church, the Bentley branch delegate, for misconduct based upon statements made during the strike, on TV, in the press and in front of witnesses about scabs, about management and continuing resistance. I am reliably told the Doncaster team of managers agreed almost unanimously the coalfield would stand indefinitely if it happened. The minority view was that – worse – the miners in Doncaster would instead elect me to a senior position at Area and then put me in a more dangerous position vis-à-vis the new strategies for the NCB. Sacking me would be the best career move they could ever make for me.

Other than individuals, whole collieries, whole communities would be pushed to the limit in a make-or-break endeavour to maximise production. A war was launched against agreements, customs, and the high level of indulgence shown to the union by local management.

Back at Hatfield Main, the screws were turning on the whole colliery. We would only survive by producing coal at £39 per tonne, £1.50 per gigajoule. We required 15,000 tonnes per week. At that time Hatfield coal was £52.92 per tonne.

TERRORISTS?
24 November. Manchester Martyrs Commemoration
Support Irish Republican POWs in English jails!

Stop Strip Searches!

Ban Plastic Bullets!

Repeal the PTA!

Speakers: Sinn Féin. IRSP. Women and Ireland. Dunnes Stores Strikers. Pakistani Workers Association and myself for the National Union of Mineworkers.

We were in good company right enough, and the state's special forces were only too well aware of it. That they regarded us as the same genre of enemy as the Irish Republicans became plain in later years, with Stella Rimington of MI5 admitting that the Provisional IRA and the National Union of Mineworkers were the main fields of activity for the service during her reign. But we weren't really expecting the quality of 'dirty tricks' and media manipulation usually preserved for 'foreign wartime enemies' to be directed at us – more of that later.

January 1986. I am invited to speak at a big public rally against the arrest and detention of Maire O'Shea, a middle-aged academic lady, under the Prevention of Terrorism Act.

The defence committee had written to me:

The Maire O'Shea Defence Committee in Manchester is holding a public meeting the day before the start of the trial, Monday 13th Jan. Speakers have been invited from her trade union ASTMS and the Irish in Britain Representation group, along with organisations active in the campaign. It was agreed to invite a speaker from the NUM ... we particularly wanted you to speak after hearing you at the Manchester Martyrs Rally.

Ah, the Manchester Martyrs Rally. I had persuaded Emma to come along with me on the promise of doing some Christmas shopping in Manchester and having a meal in the big city after my speech. We took a taxi from the railway station to the university where I was due to speak and attend the rally. As the taxi drew close, two great crowds of struggling people fought with cops on either side of the road. One side, festooned with Union Jacks, chanted 'National Front, the British Front, Smash the IRA!' The other, led by uniformed bandsmen from Glasgow in their bonnets and drum straps, surged against the police ranks, and to the accompaniment of booming base drums chanted 'IRA, boom, boom, boom! IRA, boom, boom, boom!'

'What the hell is that lot?', the taxi driver asks.

'I'm sure I don't know,' I reply. 'Can you find us a back way in? I'm here to lecture on ancient pottery.'

BACK THE PRINTERS

The Area leaders at Barnsley have nailed us to the floor in an effort to frustrate the growing demands from the branches for us to flood London with miners' pickets in support of the printers during worsening violence down at Wapping at the printworkers' dispute. The printers were alongside the miners in every way they could be; it was our turn to return the favour and give the forces of law and order and massed ranks of TNT distribution lorry scabs some direct action from the coalfields. Finally, after one obstruction after another, the militant branches started coordinating for joint action together, without the approval of the Area leadership. Armthorpe, Hatfield and Silverwood agreed to jointly fill six coaches with our finest. The Area leaders went ballistic. Branches were contacted and instructed that we were on our own. If anyone got arrested, the Union would not defend them, wouldn't pay their fines, nor treat them as men in the 'victimised miners' category as we had done in our strike. We were shocked to now have to confront Sammy Thompson, the Area vice president and soon to be National vice president, who we had regarded as the left's voice at the top table and behind the mighty closed doors at Arthur's Castle. He had written to all branches about an unofficial Liaison Committee of Print Chapels (i.e. union printworks assemblies), which had written to branches asking for support, and condemning the Area leadership of the NUM for failing to respond to requests for mining pickets. We next tried a front-door assault, with Askern and Hatfield tabling resolutions to the Area Council calling for the Area to send pickets when called upon by the printworkers' unions. A similar composite was then counterposed by the leadership themselves, so it wouldn't look like they had been forced into it. At the same time, we went on to move heaven and hell to get those leaders of the printworkers to make such requests and to actually let us know when they had done so, so that nobody could get out of it. Following the next meeting of the Liaison Committee for the Defence of Trade Unions, Sammy Thompson and Frank Clark reported that they had had meetings with the leaders of the print unions SOGAT and the NGA and that they were making no calls for flying pickets from Yorkshire. Instead, we would spend £6,500 on a solidarity walk and rally round London on a Sunday afternoon.

As it turned out Hatfield raised its own fighting fund and made its own contingency arrangements and got involved down at Wapping a time or two, both officially and highly 'unofficially', as some of the scab drivers found to their cost.

BACK OUT

9 April. Hatfield Pit walks out. The great strike has been over one year, the feeling towards those who stabbed us in the back is as raw as ever. We thought we had discovered all those who scabbed at Hatfield. None remained at this pit, and they had all been transferred away. Suddenly one of our crack development teams

discovers, I am not sure how, that one of them, Ken Firth, had scabbed. As the team ragged up and headed for the surface, the news went around the pit, and machines came to a stop. The whole pit stood idle. Ken stands shaking with fear and guilt in the Personnel Officers' office. I am called down to the pit, which hangs in sullen silence. Ken had went back to work two days before the rest of the pit, he has been on strike for 12 months all bar 2 days. Those 2 days have cost him his friends, his reputation, and his life as he knew it. I break the news to the afternoon shift and then the night shift; they walk off the job too. The pit is out solid. In pits elsewhere in Yorkshire and all over the country, with the exception of Wales, where they couldn't find or invent enough scabs to put one in at every mine, scabs are working, not normally, and not without abuse and sometimes violence, but they are working. Jack Taylor, in his address as the Yorkshire Area president in 1986 made the point that, despite people going back to work, these people hadn't joined the UDM and remained with the union:

Certainly in matters of policy, the Area Union has taken this stance. In future there can be little distinction in our view between one NUM member and another. Each is entitled to the benefits of the Union, and assistance from this Union. Of course, there are still individual cases of difficulty and there was a stormy period immediately following the return to work.

This expression of ill will was understandable in the circumstances, and even now. However, nobody can seriously expect the Union to exert total control over one individual's feelings toward another. Many people were bitterly disappointed and angered by the fact that there was a Return To Work Movement – whatever the reasons behind such a movement … nobody can fail to accept the advantages of a unified workforce in our coalfield![248]

The Hatfield miners however don't see it that way. The men want to make a point, they want to leave an impression; scabs at this pit, in these villages, will never be forgotten and will never be forgiven. We shall not work as if they did nothing wrong and let bygones be bygones.

10 April.

Trouble-torn Hatfield Main started production again today as most pitmen returned to work – except the miners at the centre of the strike.

The six underground men went down in the pit cage, but returned to the surface.

The coal board claims the men could not agree among themselves whether to carry on working, so they walked out.

We had called a mass meeting at the pit, with the Area agent brought in to troubleshoot, but he couldn't solve this one, and told them so. The ball was at their feet, but there was nowhere to go with it. At the same time the NCB had issued dire warnings about Hatfield's massive financial losses. The pit was already living in borrowed time. There were no NCB indulgences left.

With the knowledge that this dispute could close the pit, since it wasn't going to be resolved by anyone else, the painful medicine to swallow was that we had to agree, someone had to agree, to work with this scab. It was agreed to put him on a dead shift, with a scratch team, off his own team, away from his former mates. We weren't happy – he was still in this prestigious heading, and a new scrap team had been invented just to accommodate him, but with assurances that the contract would be worked out without this team in the divisor, we agreed. It was a bugger and a half when on the first shift back on afternoons, I landed with him – Firth.

There were three of us in the distant heading, including him. It was possible we could have injured him, but it would have very hard to argue in the circumstances it was an accident. As it turned out, the bastard nearly killed us. Not intentionally I suppose, but just because he wasn't a bright spark in the first place. Me and the other bloke had lugged the backbreakingly heavy 'hollybank' support down the gate, got up on the belt and lifted the end of the hollybank onto the miniveyor (conveyor) which runs down the middle of the big road heading machine. We trust him to sit at the controls since neither of us will work with him alone in case he gets injured and we get the blame without any witnesses. He is supposed to run the miniveyor in reverse to feed the hollybank down to the face of the heading. I have buckled and bent my knees, bent my back and slowly rise, lifting the rear end of the support up level to the miniveyor; my marra has put his shoulder under the front section and has threaded the end onto the conveyor. Firth fails to engage the conveyor in reverse and it sets off outbye, throwing the hollybank back into my stomach and near ripping me marra's shoulder off. The support lands across both of us, who are thrown backwards onto the belt, helmets flying off, lights being pulled off, into darkness and pain. In the concussion and confusion and pain it is hard to tell what has happened, except I am unable to breathe – there is no air left in my body. I am suffocating, and helpless to move, on my back. The other lad has fallen in a heap off the belt, his face swelling already, his shoulder bleeding with friction burns and raw meat exposed from the metal thrust of the support. He staggers around and finds his helmet and lamp and comes to me. He and Firth lift the great weight off me legs. I am still gasping, I am put into a crouched position, my head between my legs, I am urged to keep throwing my head back to try and force some air into my winded belly. At length they throw cold water from their bottles over my head, and it seems to get me breathing back in order and my heart starts to slow a little. Firth is apologies, apologies, confusion, thinking of the problems, the grief, apologies. We are not working with this bloke. We set off out, not on strike but injured, quite genuinely injured, and having had a near-death experience we are in no mood to work with this man again. He is quietly dispatched to some tranquil backwater of the pit, and then transferred. Most men at the pit think we staged this: another of my many wheezes to take industrial action without taking industrial action, fighting for your aims without seeming to. Well yes, that is my philosophy where possible and one I had instilled in the men many times, but my marra's ripped and bloody shoulder, the big rusty burn mark in my belly and the mass of lion claw marks and swelling around me calves would suggest we were either bloody good makeup artists or damn fine actors – or both. The pain and the memory of nearly being impaled on a huge iron roof support, by a stupid scab I had just urged the men to work with, was little compensated for by having got rid of him as a danger.

DID WE WIN?

In February, Arthur is reflecting on the strike, and the 'mistakes' and lessons we were supposed to learn from it as instructed by the armchair left generals – mainly the not-so-left social democrats of Eurocommunism. Firstly he chides me for referring to the strike as a defeat and then goes on to show up the inconsistencies of the strike's critics.

I do not accept that the strike was lost and feel that there are too many – inexplicably – who are prepared to refer to a defeat, setback etc. when the very opposite is the case.

One has only to look at the current situation in the printing industry to recognise that all the baloney about the NUM getting support provided they had

1. A ballot
2. Had total support from their membership

was unfounded and incorrect. The print unions have had a ballot – they have got the support of their union and still trade unions like the EETPU and scab lorry drivers continue to do to their union exactly what they did to ours during the 12 months miners strike.

This in itself demonstrates the shallowness of the arguments against the NUM and of course at the same time the incorrect attitude that the miners suffered a Defeat.

One final point – the Coal Board's intention was to close 50 pits between March 1984 and March 1986. They have in fact closed 25 (seven of which were agreed closures prior to the 1984 dispute and the others unfortunately, apart from Horden, have been pits that have accepted closure rather than fight).

I am convinced that if all the pits had continued to resist, the most the Coal Board could have closed by this point would have been about eight.[249]

Arthur's point, and one which is increasingly proved correct as time goes on, is not that we didn't lose, but that we didn't lose per se or absolutely, although his insistence on describing the strike as 'a victory' robbed it of its authenticity. The fact was, although it wasn't clear at this time, that we hadn't been smashed out of existence, and the review procedure, damned though it was to the ultimate veto of the NCB, was a stalling process by which we could totally gum up the executions of collieries and make mass closures in a short period impossible. Provided, that is, that branches agreed to take the appeal procedure to the wire.

In retrospect, I don't think we argued this tactically; going through the review was being presented as a principle in place of redundancy money or transfer to 'long-life' pits. Had we argued that going through the review prevented the closure of pits further down the line and thus saved other people's jobs, had we argued that we were buying time and rebuilding our strength, perhaps for a secondary offensive, perhaps for a political alternative to Thatcher, we might have done better. Such is speculation. Certainly Arthur's conclusion that we didn't 'lose' as such – or outright, let us say – is true, but it was greeted with incredulity. Like with the comedian, 'It's the way he tells them.'

HOLDING THE LINE

May brings one of the stormiest, potentially violent mass Branch meetings of my life. We have thrown down the gauntlet to the countervailing forces among the men who are trying to drive the pit onto the rocks and shut it in order to get what they call 'their' redundancy. It is a tendency that is spreading like a cancer through the Yorkshire coalfield. It takes on a number of guises, some of them having the flavour of militancy, aimed at shutting off all production, 'fuck the pit', rejecting work and wage slavery. In reality, these are not tactics for any aim other than having the pit sink and let those selfish and shortsighted individuals get paid redundancy money. We have tabled a three-page resolution, titled 'A Time For Straight Talking'. It is hard-hitting and tells the truth about the caucus trying to shut the pit, and why we as militants oppose them. It calls such men worse than scabs, which lights the blue touchpaper, and ensures an angry meeting of virtually everyone at the pit. We want this thing fought out here, right here, right now – enough of the slogans written on walls, the sabotage, the backstabbing, the jealousy.

I am confronted in my presentation of this resolution by a big heading man who jumps up to shout me down. I face him down, saying: 'The last bloke of your proportions who come here to shut this pit, had a riot shield and a club, and he didn't scare me, so ye'll not,' to cheers and feet stamping.

'You have said this resolution calls the men at the pit worse than scabs. It does no such thing. It says in fact that those who call for the pit to close are worse than scabs. That is a simple matter of fact and here's how. Every pit in Nottingham was wick with scabs – you couldn't get more scabs than Nottingham had – yet all the scabs in the world couldn't wipe out the Nottingham NUM branches. Every pit in Nottingham has an NUM branch today.

'There's no NUM branch at Edlington. So from the point of view of survival of NUM branches, the people who want to close pits have far more devastating effects than the action of even a lot of scabs … "fuck the pit" might sound militant, but what it means is "Let me out, I've given up."

'Our resolution spells out that we haven't given up. If we intend to live to fight another day we have to survive now! You can't fight if you're dead.'

We were sticking to the branch policy, we will offer redundancy to all men over 50, who will be going out on the best terms possible, and to long-term-sick men who will benefit and for whom we will apply for incapacity retirement. But we were resisting any general change in the direction of closure or men stamping on other men to get out.

SUMMER OF '86

Anyone who has ever played 'What time is it Mr Wolf?' will know the purpose of the game is for the crowd to try and creep closer and closer to 'Mr Wolf', asking, 'What time is it Mr Wolf?' The wolf, will in order to allay suspicion, turn and say, '11 o'clock' and you will creep a little closer. Each time the wolf turns to tell the time, your fears that he will nab you are dispersed and you may creep a little closer. Only when the wolf thinks you are within grasp will he turn and answer 'Dinner Time!' and grab you.

My association with the Spartacists gets into print, writing to their paper *Workers Hammer* and long theoretical historic pieces for their theoretical journal *Spartacist*. I appear on joint platforms with them, never in agreement, but fraternally, comradely. I am perilously close to 'Dinner Time'.

The period following the defeat of the great strike, as it was becoming known among the left and progressive academics, was decisive in determining the long-term fate of the industry, more so than the strike itself. For a time following our defeat and the colossal impact of that upon communities, surviving or abandoned, the NCB and government started to unfold its strategy for actually claiming its victory:

• Undermining of the NUM at national level:
— Isolating the leadership
— Talking encouragingly to area and local leaders
— Increasing the tensions between area leaderships in a game of hard-cop–soft-cop.
• Outside of the NUM, the UDM would be given privileged status and credited with sole 'negotiating' rights for the industry.
• New incentive arrangements would be introduced to break pits from area bargaining mechanisms and conciliation structures.
• Pay negotiations would become decentralised as local contracts determined the real level of income with national rates as a fall back, sometimes in the absence of any national rates.
• Local branches resisting the poisoned chalice were circumvented as managements went straight to teams and groups of men to lay offers of 'gold pigs' at their feet.
• New American-style business school consultants were brought in with their arguments about 'new cultures' and 'excellence'.

All of this was aimed at delivering up a highly profitable, streamlined, non- (or marginally) unionised industry up for privatisation – and super profits. Major changes in the energy market were not at that time the front runner; it was not yet the time of the long-term replacement of coal's sovereign power by nuclear. Coal's monopoly could be offset and balanced, but still allowed pride of place only if the privatised industry was non-union and the NUM was no longer a threat. Having defeated the NUM in the field of battle, the planners in government and industry saw little obstacle to implementing the rest of the plan.

Reality was to confront this vision, as the miners almost universally stuck firm, not simply with their Union branches, but to whole swathes of ancient job controls and 'restrictive practices'. New 'get-rich-quick' schemes were almost everywhere blocked by disciplined rejection of any schemes not negotiated by NUM branches or sanctioned by the area union. Pressure upon local management and area industrial relations teams to get the new incentive schemes implemented often meant that major concessions and safeguards were drafted into schemes that were designed to do away with just those features. Skilled branch negotiators often 'subverted' the schemes' new standards, which resulted in greatly enhanced payments to their members, while these in turn further strengthened the standing of the miners' local lodge. While the spectre of nationwide, all-out strike action receded, widespread guerrilla industrial action raged, despite increasingly draconian anti-strike legislation. Flying pickets, particularly those from the militant Doncaster coalfield, were persistently ignoring such legal restrictions and imperatives for ballots and non-secondary action. Clearly the problem of 'Scargillism' and the NUM culture had not in fact been adequately dealt with. The coming 5 years' events would demonstrate to the powers that be that a large, even privatised, coal industry was too dangerous to have around; and that something of 'a final solution' would have to be found.

A year after the end of the strike saw us enter a period of conflicting tensions and contradictory trends. First had been the massive onslaught of pit closures: ruined villages with their heart and soul ripped out. Having expended everything flesh and blood could muster in that stand against the closures, and still to fail, took away any cheery or morale-boosting perspective of any further resistance. Hefty redundancy terms with more money in one go than men had ever seen or would ever see again in their lives was destroying any chance of slowing down or even blocking the closure programme with appeals to the independent review procedures. On the other side was the new managerial regime that the rebranded British Coal was trying to impose in efforts to take away our 'Miners' Freedoms' – job controls, customs and agreements. The combination of lack of resistance, at least in the first year or so, and the new jackbooted management robbed the young miners of their self-respect and led them to conclude that mining for them was over. Perhaps, further than that, we should sink the remainder of the industry ourselves, take the redundancy money and make this our final act of defiance. There had, however, been strong countervailing trends, which insisted that the industry must survive for the Union to survive to regroup and continue. This meant an acceptance of new incentive and coal-working techniques, and collaboration with delay analysis and efficiency schemes, to take pits into profitability and increase our bargaining strength. This was particularly true of Doncaster and South Yorkshire, where there was a confusing combination of rising productivity accompanied by rising strike figures reaching pre-'84 proportions. Between the two trends was an ocean of animosity between men, and between men and branch officials. The 'shut-the-pit' tendency was pernicious, crazed with 'redundancy fever' as we called it; they lived, breathed, loved and would kill for 'their' redundancy – a sort of 'My Precious' obsession. They wrote odes to it in whitewash round the pit: 'Shut the Pit' 'Give me my money!' They sang 'Shut the pit, shut the pit, shut the pit!' to the tune of 'Here

We Go!' wherever management, Area directors or even Union officials conducted inspections or came within earshot. Tannoys resounded with the song. While saving the pit was the obsession of most branch officials, closing the pit was a big bag of money to others. They didn't just come out and say it, they dressed the cause up as militancy: refusal to allow any change, any flexibility and new ways of doing things. 'Non-collaboration' slowdowns, and outright sabotage of belts and machines and pumps, were the forward tactic of the shut-the-pit merchants; the issue brought us into often violent conflict among ourselves.

All these elements were present in all coalfields; pit closures were side-by-side with rises in productivity as increasingly heavy-duty chock lines, faster bi-directional cutting machines, often remote-controlled face lines and increased numbers of fast retreat faces all combined to offset production drops caused by the mass closures. Men who had manned picket lines tore into survival schemes for their colliery, while other men who had also manned picket lines to stop pit closures now slashed belts and punctured oil supplies to get it closed. The overall control of contracts and payment and efficiency schemes remained in the tight grip of the NUM, despite all efforts to prize them free. The energy market itself, at least for the next few years, would remain overwhelmingly supplied by British Coal, at least 80% of it still delivered by unionised rail transport.

Ironically, the Coal Board's use of outside contractors to displace their own employees placed an industrial hit squad at the command of the NUM. If that sounds difficult to appreciate, let me further explain. These 'outside' contractors were the ex-employees of the NCB/BCC; and in the main, big heading men, tunnellers, and 'tackle anything do anything' big hitters. These were the men who had either innocently been caught up in a pit closure which they had fought hard to stop; or, they could be the men who had run their own pits onto the rocks to get out. They had become obsessed with the redundancy money, the Coal Board (in order to speed up the closures) kept dangling new revised and escalating offers, then whipping them back off the table if you didn't take the offer and agree to shut the pit then and there. While this was bad enough, men at pits and on jobs which were not threatened would turn heaven and hell to stop production, slow down developments and create a situation of run-down where they could get out, or else sink the whole dam pit around their own ears to get the bag of money. Once out, with the biggest stack of money they have ever or could ever own in the bank, they were safe. The obsession was then cured. They applied to any of the multiplying contract firms, who were being employed on short contracts to come and do specialist driving work, much needed developments or high profile infrastructure work. Of course, this was the work they were doing at their own pits, and which at an earlier time the NCB/BCC had employed them to do directly. But in this maelstrom of pre-privatisation, part privatisation, run down and restructuring, these men were being given a sack of money to leave British Coal, only to be re-employed as contractors doing the same class of work if not always at the same pit, sometimes at the self same pit. We didn't like what many of these men had done, though some had stood their ground and fought, and all of them had been through 12 months of strike. Many of them were the hard front line flying pickets, many had sold the pass to take the 'redundo' as they called it. The dichotomy for the NCB was, once these men had the safety net of the big money already secure, you couldn't bribe them or threaten them anymore. All of these men were still NUM members; when the union called for strike action in ballots, they had nothing to fear and voted almost 100% to back the union's call, while those still directly employed were more cautious of being finished without the golden handshake and into a world of declining mining opportunities.

Whichever way you looked at it, despite the strong counter-currents already explained, the NUM and its place in the industry and the place of that industry in the politics of fuel were almost as strong as ever. We laughed one and all when Arthur on mass meeting platforms declared that we had won the strike, 'Thank God!' we said. 'Because if that was winning what would losing be like?' It didn't take too long however to observe that really Thatcher hadn't won. We might have lost that strike but we hadn't lost the war. She had not achieved her objectives.

MEXICAN STANDOFF
Within the Union, a several-sided fight was shaping up. The alliances and perspectives of the respective sides were not always clear; certainly not as they were presented by their countervailing oppositions. There were right-wing anti-Scargill forces trying to mount a moderate, non-militant, non-confrontational approach to the current situation and industrial relations, while also there was an air of war-weariness on behalf of Arthur's previous comrades, who now no longer snapped to attention as he thought they ought. A kind of pragmatism and realism which was not of itself reactionary or 'moderate' nonetheless called for a new leadership and a repositioning of our forces and objectives.

26 August. Hatfield Main strikes in protest at the continued victimisation of men sacked during the '84/85 strike. We are the only pit in South Yorkshire where nobody has been reinstated; our three sacked men remain sacked: Adrian Simpson, Jeff Budworth and Tony Clegg. It is the second anniversary of the invasion and occupation of the village by an army of riot police, and the day the first scabs went in.

SEPTEMBER – NUM YORKSHIRE COUNCIL MEETING
The mood to restart concerted resistance is growing. There were calls for industrial action in the Area from Hatfield, Wooley, Armthorpe, Silverwood, and Shafton Workshops. Durham Mechanics were already well into their series of one-day strikes and work-to-rules. At the Council meeting I argued for support of my 'disruption plus production' policy, which I saw as a national perspective. The idea was to let those pits in profitability, which were operating with full-on production, take up the issues which were pressing across the coalfields, allowing those pits under immediate threat of closure to dodge the firing line and avoid making things worse. This was already being seized on, as the profitable pits, which could see their production targets being met (to cheers from management), slammed to a dead stop as the miners walked out over aspects of the new post-strike regime. A round of pit stoppages was in progress over the fate of the men

dismissed in the strike and the demand for amnesty.

14 November. I am a principal speaker at the Irish Solidarity Movement public meeting. I share the platform with Maire O'Shea, and relatives of the Birmingham Six and the Guildford Four. The fight for their innocence and release had not at that time been won.

DINNER TIME!

Hatfield is quite consciously putting itself forward as a political organiser, the centre of class war issues in the region. The struggle against apartheid is one that has united the whole branch; we are particularly involved with the struggle of our comrades in the NUM in South Africa. We have supported the Revolutionary Communist Group, and its City of London Anti-Apartheid Campaign (it was expelled from the Anti-Apartheid campaign as such because of its questioning of planks of the ANC programme), both in London and at Conferences around both wings of the movement. When we discover South African coal coming into Immingham, at those same damn wharves which bled us dry during the strike, that it was being stockpiled in South Kirkby, and was being shipped as 'Dutch Coal' when there were no coalmines left in Holland, we took it upon ourselves to organise a mass miners' demonstration down to the wharves. Dave Nixon was the Branch's resident coalmining banner-maker, a lad with an eye for detail and striking reproduction of scenes. He was commissioned to make the lead banner showing two black South African miners struggling with a boring machine boring holes, with the slogan 'Stop Apartheid Coal – Victory To The South African NUM!' Other banners said 'Solidarity with the Black South African Miners'. The young multiracial singers from the City of London AA choir sang and toi-toied all the way to the wharves, leading an army of miners, mostly from South Yorkshire, with their branch banners, struggling through the wind and hail and snow. Every branch in South Yorkshire and Doncaster and many Barnsley and North Yorkshire branches were there.

We had had quite a job getting permission from the cops, so soon after the strike, so soon after all the bad blood, to march past these scab dockers on these scab wharves, and they knew damn well we wouldn't do it quietly. As we surged past the wharves shouting abuse and gesticulating, they were all under cover and out of sight. The cops guarded the entrances and broken fences in case we surged through, which would have been a real probability had just one of the gutless wonders shown up. The only near flashpoint came with a scab coal lorry cruising down the opposite side of the road to fill up on the wharf; there was quite a bit of argie-bargie as it realised its mistake and just kept going – had it tried to turn into the gates just where we were passing those windows were going through and I think it would have been over, given the mood of the lads. First they scab on us, then they scab on their mates in the docks, and now they let in South African coal, fresh with the blood of black South African miners.

We had parked lorries from the Home Coal Society opposite Grove Wharf, and set these up as platforms. I spoke of the struggle of the miners' union in South Africa, of Hatfield Main's opposition to import controls, but support for any boycott called for by the workers and unions involved. The snow swept across the rally and banner poles broke under the strain, then we marched and ran and sang all the way back to the coaches.

The rally in the Miners Welfare Hall that evening was moving and inspiring. The singers were all teen and 20s fresh-faced, 'nice' young people of all races. They did the black workers' toi-toi, a kind of Knees up Mother Brown, they did collective dances and sang like the Red Army rather than a choir of angels. Big Harry commented that if these had been in the van at Orgreave, we would have bowled the cops out of the way.

Dinner time? Throughout the day, the Sparts had pestered everybody about this being a racialist march, about there being scabs on the march, about us going to a scab wharf. I was just too busy and too preoccupied to listen much to them today, bought a paper, nodded and carried on.

The bones of their 'scab' argument was that a man who scabbed was on the march. It was true, although we didn't know this until a later event when we tried to merge the Doncaster Miners Panel with the South Yorkshire Miners Panel. Not just a bloke, but a bloke who had scabbed and now was the branch secretary of a South Yorkshire branch.

Jock Nimmo, the old Bentley militant and secretary had just been elected chair of the combined panels, when it was brought to his notice that a scab was in the room, forced the issue. The bloke got up and admitted, 'Yes it was me'.

The Doncaster miners, with Tony Clegg, one of our sacked and victimised men in tow, stood up and walked out.

We got into the car park and called a halt. We had had months upon months of strikes at the Doncaster pits in general, and Hatfield in particular, over the presence of scabs at work. The NCB wouldn't pay them off, but threatened to sack any of us who didn't work with them. In the end we agreed: we didn't have to be mates, we didn't have to talk to them, but we would bite the bullet and work with them. They continued to be attacked – at work, in the showers, on the way home, their cars, their lockers – until most of them left, transferred to Nottingham or just left. That was fine for Doncaster – only 2% of men had scabbed there. However, there were branches in South Yorkshire where a third or more of the entire workforce had scabbed. At first we were keen for a policy of expelling them, but as the UDM was pushed more and more as an anti-union, anti-strike formation in the industry, it was decided we would be giving them a gift on a plate by no longer representing these strikebreakers. Half of North Yorkshire would be signing up for the UDM, a number of South Yorkshire pits might be 50–50, while nationwide we would be allowing them inroads into areas and regions they didn't exist in. So, difficult though it was, we agreed to allow them to stay in the Union, and be represented by the Union. This was fine when there was only a few of them as in Doncaster; but what we hadn't perhaps realised was that in other places they might actually form the majority, and when it came to elections they would elect other scabs as Branch officials; they could even stand scabs as Area officials. But that was the road we were on. We agreed we could be on line to break the Union through our own hasty reaction. Tony agreed, but said he for one wasn't going to sit near the bastard. Old Jock was the shortest serving Panel chairman in the history of the Union – he had his sons still in jail for fighting folk like this; he couldn't treat such a man with civility, and resigned. So now the bloke had turned up on the march at the head of his branch at their Union banner with loads of men, prepared now to do the right thing. So that was that matter explained.[250]

Or so we thought. But the following week or so we had another mass branch meeting and who should be there but two or three Spartacists selling papers outside about *Hatfield Miners scab racialist march, to a scab wharf!!?* According to them, the call for boycotting South African coal was 'racialist import controls'. Of course it was no such thing. In an earlier statement for the Chesterfield TUC bulletin, I had made a statement on behalf of the Hatfield Branch:

> We wanted to hold the demonstration to show our solidarity with South African miners, not because we support import controls. I am an anti-imperialist, and I would never support import controls ... we made a point that this was a solidarity demonstration, and the call for the ban is directly related to our internationalism.

As to the charge about this being a scab wharf – well, that was the point of us being there: it wasn't because they had invited us, as implied by the Sparts. The paper and its accusations were outrageous. Actually, for a host of cultural and historical reasons, there are very few black or Asian miners in Britain. One of the few mixed-race Caribbean miners at the pit, a young militant and fearless picket, 'Eggy' Palmer, took one look at the headline in the paper, heard the slander, and went got the fire hose and hosed them down, to cheers from the drinkers in the bar and men waiting to go into the Union meeting. Now the fat was in the fire; and the following edition of *Workers Hammer* screamed about 'Anti-Communist assaults on the Spartacists at Hatfield NUM'. It was to get steadily worse from then on in.

5 February 1987. As part of my strategy to make Hatfield a central feature of bringing together trade union and political struggles across the piece, the Branch organises a 'Common Fight' meeting, bringing together all the fighting unions and issues to a mass public meeting. Terry Flanaghan, a victimised SOGAT 82 member, spoke about their stand. We also had speakers from British Telecom, Terry Wilde, a longtime CP member, and Dan MacCormack, a sacked Silentnight worker for Silentnight strikers, as well as myself for the NUM. Flanaghan as I recall was a wee bit optimistic: 'They [the Labour leadership and TUC] want to talk about everything except Wapping. But we will win the print dispute at Wapping. The printers will show you and everyone else the way home.'

Thatcher now imposes rule amendments on our Coal Industry Social Welfare Organisation, a body established by the NUM and the NCB way back in 1945. CISWO sat at the heart of our whole social organisation, from village bowling greens to national athletics and brass band contests. Thatcher knew too well the social standing of the miners' union in the communities and the authority we exercised there. First she sought to snatch this away from us by grafting the UDM into joint running of the schemes. Next the old CISWO limited company is wound up and a new one established; it grants the NUM 8% of the controlling votes. It rules that all monies held in Welfare Trusts and Schemes must be used to fund 50% of any project being developed or supported, rather than 100% funded from government sources into CISWO's national coffers.[251]

NATIONAL VICE-PRESIDENTIAL ELECTIONS OF THE NUM

The politics of the post-strike situation are hidden within the struggle for the vice presidency. Hatfield miners are great fans of Arthur, but we will not slavishly follow whoever he deems should be his deputy. Sammy Thompson has the nomination of the Yorkshire Area, but that doesn't necessarily mean our Branch will canvass for him, or that the Hatfield men will vote for him. The SWP and its coterie thought Sammy was Arthur's right-hand man in Yorkshire. They were way out of touch. After the strike, Sammy had become highly critical of Arthur, and he began to take on something of an alternative left stance against him, especially in the influential Miners Broad Left, which wasn't so broad at all and really was the Area leaders and potential leaders. Sammy had mercilessly attacked Arthur and the National Rank and File Miners Movement. He saw this as Arthur's own invention, an attack by proxy on the 'left' Area leaders like himself and Jack Taylor.[252] Me and Sammy had had quite a few words over his trajectory but remained mates, more or less. This was a multifaceted war whose outcomes and directions were far from clear. Arthur for his part saw the main assault as coming from the 'new realism' of the old CPGB and its Kinnock-Labour leadership whose candidate was Eric Clarke. Sammy was thought by Arthur to be the safest bet. We wanted a discussion of the politics involved here, and where we are going, with what in mind. The NUM as a ship has a fine captain all decked out in his gold braid, but we have no rudder and nobody understands the radar; we are just sitting becalmed and helpless or worse, cruising round in circles. The people on the bridge, like Nelson, can see no ships, but unlike Nelson they really can't see any problems either.

We call a national meeting for all miners and their families to hear all the candidates address them on where they stand on the issues facing the miners in 1987. The SWP calls us 'traitors' because we are not following their line and rooting for Sammy. They just don't get it; that's not what class politics or any politics is about. As it turns out, all the candidates turn out: Eric Clarke from the Scotland Area, Sammy, the candidate from the Midlands; only Terry French, our jailed miner who is running with the endorsement of the Kent miners and the sacked miners, cannot make it, although their lass does. Terry had written to me from Northeye Prison, and told me of his intention to stand. He told me that Jack Collins had urged him to do so before he died. He also told me that if I had actually stood as I had earlier indicated he wouldn't have bothered. 'But one of us must stand.'[253] My money was on Terry – Terry was the anti-career candidate, the rank-and-file hellfire candidate. If I'd thought like a bureaucrat I'd have got Hatfield's support for Terry, no problem, as the activists and the other officials supported him. But this was meant to be about the rank and file and their views, and discussion and debate, so it would be up to them.

The meeting is mobbed to the rafters. I am proud to make the opening address on how we see it, and point up some of the issues we think need addressing. I nearly stood myself. I had potential nominations from Leicester and Cannock, and had been told I had a strong chance of getting Northumberland; Dennis Murphy and many of the EC were great friends of mine. Frank Watters, I think acting on instruction from Arthur, made sure I didn't get Yorkshire. That didn't mean I wouldn't get the vote from the Yorkshire miners – once the names were on the ballot paper the men would vote for whoever they thought suited their mood and inclination, and not simply follow the Area's recommendation. 'You're jumping on the bandwagon Davie,' Frank had told me. 'Frank, I responded, 'You're not even in the bliddy Union.' So anyway I had decided not to run, although I had initially been determined to make this a political campaign; I had now, with the endorsement of the Branch, to do it by proxy. This was one of a series of national initiatives we had taken, given the lack of any from the national office or anywhere else. It was wildly successful and everyone, at length even the SWP, thought it had been a good idea.

In the end I think the Branch formally endorsed Sammy, who we knew well of course, but a good number of the rank and file went for Eric, and the militants voted for Terry, as I did myself.

CUMBRIA

Following the closure of the last pit in Cumbria, Haig Colliery, the ancient coalfield closes and the NUM Cumbria Area is wound up. Coalmining and iron mining had been wrought along the Celtic coast of Britain, from Cornwall and Wales up through to Cumbria, since iron and Bronze Age times. The miners of the west of Britain had mined gold, silver, copper, lead, iron and coal; they had worked in pitch-black rock caverns with bone, antler and wood tools, they had wrought huge galleries supported by cathedrals of timber or in hard rock. It is nigh impossible to convey the meaning of this end, this abrupt and premature stop. It is the end of a race, and of an era in history almost as old as humankind on this island.

AN IRISH NUM?

Around this time I thought I spotted the chance for a growth in NUM membership. My information was that 'Northern Ireland' was on the verge of a coal expansion to fuel a new generation of solid-fuel power stations. The coal was lignite, a sort of poor relation to the hard black stuff we knew, but one which was heavily mined in Germany and other places, where I am led to believe its soft brown crumbly texture has allowed it to be cut solely by high-pressure water. 500 million tonnes of the stuff had been revealed at Crumlin–Lough Neagh alone, while reserves in the south were discovered to be enough to render the 26 counties self-sufficient in power supplies. All of this was coincidental to plans to construct a new £500 million, 450-megawatt coal power station, with a planned life of 30 years, using just 20% of the northern reserve. I at once thought the NUM should be the organisation to organise the miners, whether these were deep mines or opencast.

First I went to Arthur with the plan and suggested we get the OK from the Provos, which he heartily agreed with. I next went to Sinn Féin and asked them if they would have a problem with a British-based trade union organising in Ireland. After consideration, they informed me that we would be welcomed and supported by Sinn Féin, and the NUM would be an admirable addition to the labour movement of Ireland, north or south. That our political positions on the question of British presence in Ireland would be added weight both sides of the border to getting the troops out as well as demanding a totally non-sectarian recruitment policy for the new plants. The only caveat they gave us was that we should affiliate to the Irish TUC as well as the British one. Well, we were all set ... and 20 years down the line we are still waiting for something to happen. To the best of my knowledge, neither of the regions went ahead with the plans, for internal political reasons, some of which might well have been the prospect of introducing the NUM into Irish politics and society, more likely the clamour on global warming.

NORTHUMBERLAND

March 1987. I am invited to the Northumbrian Miners weekend school at their regular venue at the Windsor Hotel, Whitley Bay. Its always a great weekend and I have been on previous occasions. This time I am in the bar having a general crack with the lads, reverting back to me pure twang in the company of such dialectic-efficient speakers, when Mat from the Northumbrian NUM asks me if I'm ready? 'Ready?' I was the speaker!! 'Ney body had actually telt is that! Had on,' I says, 'Ah'l be 15 minutes,' and whipped upstairs to write me speech.

Actually it was simply a matter of fleeing doon some headlines; the crack in the bar had made it clear we had days of things to talk about, mainly the respective situation in the coalfields post-strike. What fascinated the lads was what the truth was behind the new bonus schemes in operation in Doncaster. The Doncaster Option we had actually moved on from, to an individually negotiated Hatfield Main option. None of this had pleased Arthur and Peter, who thought we were breaking ranks, when actually we were just trying to stay in the game. The Union had sorely lacked a national stock-taking conference, to analyse where we were and how we fight back. We needed to analyse what ground we had been forced to let go, and what we could together fight to maintain. Instead Arthur and Peter have insisted that despite everything we didn't give an inch. Those forced to bend to save breaking were denounced as traitors at worse or at best selling us all short. It had been grist to the mill of the post-strike disunity and infighting. South Yorkshire was now the most profitable (though strike-torn) coalfield in Britain. Wistow colliery in Selby had turned 53,000 tonnes in a single 5-day week. In the oldest coalfields, here in Northumberland, in South Wales and Durham, dramatic productivity drives and development performances were achieving what many would have thought were impossible. These performances had been facilitated and often initiated by the NUM trying to regain its feet, digging itself back in.

So a chance to actually discuss where we were, and truthfully explain how things like bonus were paid, how much we were paid, what terms and conditions, how much had the Union held, how much now was gone, were vital and interesting subjects. I drew a full house, and the discussion crept well into the evening dinnertime. Of course a neet on the bevy with the Northumbrian miners in Whitley Bay is for me almost a religious experience. The breakfast time is aye a revelation for me though, the lads all to a man get up for the Sunday lecture no matter how much the worse for wear they were the neet before. More than that, at 8 a.m. with their bacon and eggs and fried bread they are suppin cans of Broon Ale. It takes some digesting, and I'm only watching, having dispensed with the broon dog years ago in me vegetarian purge of un-Kosher substances.

1 May 1987. The sacked miners had established their own victimised miners' organisation, totally outwith the control and direction of the NUM formally, although they were all members of the NUM from every area of the country. They decided they had sat in isolation long enough. As production returned to normal and men started to earn big bonuses, they sat at home with nowt, facing a blacklist from hell to breakfast time. They decided their mates needed reminding now and again, and set up a flying picket column that toured the country stopping pits in full production. First on their list had been the big Midland collieries. On May the first, in joint celebration of May Day and the tradition of laying workplaces idle that day, the Doncaster pits were picketed to a total standstill – Goldthorpe, Hickleton, Frickley and South Elmsall, Brodsworth, Markham, Askern, Rossington and Hatfield standing from the day shift. At Bentley, the pickets, who were from another area, couldn't find the pit, and arrived after the men had already gone underground; they worked the day shift, but the pickets were able to pull out the rest of the shifts. This allowed Doncaster to maintain its 'most militant' status in the coalfields.

From Doncaster, the pickets moved onto the Durham, with their eyes on Scotland as a chaser.

OUT AGAIN

7 May. Hatfield walked out again. The management had added all the strike shifts into the bonus divisor and thus killed off the high bonus payment which would otherwise have been received. Mine bonus schemes are complicated things, but basically think of it as a pot of money per number of strips of coal on the full length of the coal face, divided by the number of bodies or face workers put into the divisor. Up until Thursday of last week the cuts against the numbers of men meant a high face bonus and a high pit bonus, which was an average of the individual face bonuses and accumulation of strips cut. When the sacked men came to call, the pit went home, which to our mind meant OK: we don't get paid for the strike, and since we didn't cut any coal we don't get paid any bonus for that day. But the management wanted it to sting a bit more and included all the potential man-shifts for the Friday into the pot, thus knocking the bottom out of the accumulated bonus Monday to Thursday. When we got the calculations the pit ragged up quite spontaneously.

VILLAGE RIOTS

For 2 years, and out of the glare of national publicity, the villages of the coalfields had been on and off at war with the police; mini riots had raged ever since the end of the strike. At Stainforth, the police station came under regular attack, while on one occasion late-night buses were seized to block the roads to prevent police reinforcements coming in. In July, disturbances at Edlington had reached a crescendo, with 100 rioters laying siege to the local cop shop. 'In the disturbances police station windows were smashed and police vehicles damaged. Policewomen Denise Crooks, who tried to prevent further damage outside the police station, was injured and had to go off duty.'[254]

British Coal formally ends its commitment to the joint 3-year day-release courses at Sheffield and Leeds universities. I had valued greatly my time on day release, and hundreds of Union activists had found them gateways to more active roles within the Union or a path into higher education and the academic world. The old NCB was now shaking off the last of its paternalism.

TOWARDS A GULF WAR

CND is still the biggest peace organisation in Britain, although its core membership is old and basically the same group of Quakers, old hippies, middle-class liberal 'do-gooders', reconstructed Stalinists and old-time-religion Labour Party socialists. Its youth wing and student wing have short flashes of growth and decline. The NUM is affiliated both to CND directly and to the trade union section, TUCND. The general secretary of that organisation is a man called Jimmy Barnes, a Geordie, former printer; a kind of organisational soldier of fortune, he looks the image of the later ill-famed mass-murderer Dr Harold Shipman.

TUCND bring together the vast bulk of all the major trade unions in Britain to work out a working-class and labour movement analysis of the world of war and warfare, and the struggles for peace. Jimmy persuades me to become the Yorkshire and Humberside secretary, the NUM nominates me to the NEC and Conference elects me. I am, in that position, also on the National Council of CND itself. My comrades in Class War will not at first understand the membership of 'peace man' middle-class CND, as they would see it, but it is an important standing committee of unions in its own right. CND, disagreements aside, infuriatingly bureaucratic and pedantic though it is, is an important, well-connected and well-organised anti-war organisation. When the Gulf War breaks in August 1990, it is able to swing into life, and those old creaking bones and joints feel the sudden rush of rejuvenation as thousands join. They are able to lose their historic conservatism and isolation and join with the Joint Stop The War Committee, which has united most of the anti-imperialist far-left groups and parties. Its credentials ensure the Communist Party and the Labour Left with its handful of faithful anti-war MPs will also be part of this coalition.

To understand the background to this war, one would need to enquire further than the remit of this book, but suffice it to say that the whole region of the Middle East had, since the inception of imperialism and earlier, been dominated by the politics of plunder and manipulation by the superpowers. Firstly the crusaders, seeking spices, silks, and trade routes rather than any holy grail; and then the power divide-up following World War One, when the ancient nations of the Middle East were carved up to suit the political aspirations of the European powers. International capitalism, particularly in the form of America, Britain and the rest of Europe, needed cheap and accessible oil, and half of it came from this region.

Within the Arab states were mutual conflicts, a struggle for forms of political power, religious interpretation and expressions of government. Notions of socialism and pan-Arabism conflicted with fundamentalist visions of medieval Islam. Pro-western puppet states and oil-rich sheikhs were in conflict with impoverished and deprived Arab workers, peasants and nomads. The presence of Iran was a counterweight to Iraq and Syria in terms of how Muslim-majority states should be run. The Iraqi war with Iran had been a war of ideology, interspersed with socio-political religious conflicts; the 'west' didn't mind stirring the pot and letting the conflict reign – it kept the heat off Israel, their racialist-supremacist client in the area.

When Em and I visited Egypt before the start of the war, we were struck by the gross and vulgar poverty of the people, people who had literally nothing at all. Little girls sat making dolls from strands of wool to sell to tourists for pennies so as to eat. Kids were selling a few handfuls of sunflower seeds in a twist of newspaper for less than a penny. The only thing these countries had was oil; oil was the only source of income that had to fuel the whole society and life of these countries. Leave aside the ill distribution of wealth within these nations, it was the price of oil which would determine the standard of life throughout the whole region. Saddam had been a catalyst in getting the oil-producers of the Gulf to stand together, to regulate the flow of oil, to seek a fairer price. This resource had to last long enough and be paid for at a high enough prices to fund the development of an economy and infrastructure which could operate after it had gone. The arguments for greater conservation, for higher prices, for redevelopment and standing together were logical ones. They did not ring any bells in the White House or Downing Street. Additionally, Saddam looked very belligerent on the subject of justice for Palestine and getting tough with Israel.

The flashpoint was not to come there though, but over his efforts to tighten the alliance. Kuwait was severely out of line. First, they refused any common pact on oil production and price, and churned the stuff out as fast as the west wanted it; second, Iraq argued that the Kuwaiti side of the oil field was exhausted and they were actually tapping into Iraqi reserves. I don't know if this is literally true, or whether they were making a mathematical calculation of the proportion of oil the Kuwaitis were entitled to take against the amount Iraq was entitled to take, but Iraq thought it was being robbed. As it happened, Saddam was having tea with the American ambassador, and he mentioned his displeasure at the role Kuwait was playing. He was told that that would be regarded as an entirely internal dispute and nowt to dey with America.

On 2 August Iraq invades Kuwait. It is, of course, by international law and international standards of behaviour, illegal. As the condemnations pour in, the west mobilises the United Nations for action. We pull out all the stops to mobilise against any war on Iraq. I am called upon in my capacity both as an Area EC member of the NUM, which is opposing any war, and the regional secretary of TUCND to address conferences and public rallies throughout the region. I make the point that the politics of this war, much more than the Falklands or Vietnam, is marked by hypocrisy and double standards.

On the steps of Sheffield City Hall, to a mass rally of unions, peace protesters, and left parties I make the most impassioned speech of my life. A little of which:

'Saddam has illegally invaded Kuwait and therefore must be ejected because otherwise he'll take over Saudi Arabia, and then Europe. With a population of less than 17 million, without a single satellite (the USSR had stopped all logistical support as soon as the invasion happened), with a collection of second-hand, mostly post-war equipment, with the notable exception of a few prized pieces sold to him by the west, and a third-world economy, he is poised to march through Berlin, Paris and London – defying atomic bombs, and notwithstanding the fact that the geriatric scuds have, had so much explosive removed from them so they can fly a few miles further have only an effect in military terms that is little more devastating than a crisp packet being blown up and busted. A nasty shock if you're not expecting it, or if you've a weak heart fatal, but at the range it's being used at, it has proved less intimidating or deadly than an automatic rifle at short range. It is not a weapon with which Saddam can threaten the Middle East, let along Europe and the world.

'Hypocrisy, insofar as Western European imperialist wars had first cut up and divided the Arab world, and then re-divided it and reshaped it according to the results of military force and thus created the problem. That they should now deem to solve the problem by further military force, re-division and then assert that 'military force cannot be allowed to succeed' is pure idiocy and hypocrisy.

'Hypocrisy in the ignorance of the plight of Palestine – invaded and occupied by Britain, then divided and handed over to Europeans and Americans while the Palestinians were forced more and more from their homelands with the full consent of Britain and the United States.

'Hypocrisy as Israel invaded Syria, Lebanon, Egypt and the West Bank – where is the task force? Instead the United States 2 weeks ago dispatches $3,000 million, a vote of thanks for the thousands of unarmed men women and children murdered by Zionist forces in a genocidal anti-Semitic pogrom against the Palestinians.

'Why aren't we saying they illegally invaded and occupied these sovereign states? Why aren't we saying they've got 200 nuclear bombs and they threaten world peace?

'What's the difference between Iraq invading Kuwait and America invading Vietnam, and Cambodia? They've invaded tiny Grenada and Panama. Where is the world's task force, why didn't they apply the same yardstick?

'Because it's nothing to do with objecting to illegal invasions and illegal occupations. The USA has a murderous record of invasion, occupation and abuse of human rights second to none ...

'*The Daily Star* – "its a right riveting read"; it's a right riveting read all right if you happen to be a National Front supporter sharing a solitary brain cell with a slug.

'The *Sun* – do we ever learn, after what that bastard done to the printers, after what he said about Liverpool supporters causing the Hillsborough disaster?

'Why do we still buy it? "Send a message to our boys in the Gulf" – I'll send a message to our boys in the Gulf:

'"If you want to fight for decency and justice and rights, bring the tanks home! Bring the tanks home and take them to Parliament, take them to Downing Street.

'"Demand a National Minimum wage, old-age pensions based on the national average wage. A maximum 4-day week, a maximum 6-hour day. Restoration and extension of the NHS and the education service. An end to the Poll Tax, and an insistence that if the ruling class want to go to war, let them do the fighting. Why should the poor pick up the tab for the rich and powerful?

'"Let the rich give blood, it's their bloody oil. It's their bloody war. Let them give their own bloody blood."

'Put this in your window to support the boys.

'"Put the *Sun* and the flag on the fire.

'"If you can't bring the tanks home, leave them there – after you've sabotaged them of course; we don't want to be irresponsible. Or come home without the tanks, you'll be welcomed home by millions.

"And if you can't come home, Refuse to Fight! Strike Against the war.

'"And if you really want to know ... then the last place to look is the *Mirror*."

'Will we at last lay to rest the scandalous lie that the *Mirror* is a labour paper?

'It was lie before the Zionist anti-union millionaire took it over and it's a lie now.

'"Give blood," they say.

'"Save blood," I say. Don't join the army, close down the recruitment offices.

'Don't spill any blood, least of all that of the working class and oppressed. Don't spill any blood and you won't need to give any.

'Stop the war, unconditionally and immediately. Let the warmongers and millionaires fight their own battles. The working class has a war of its own to fight.

'No War but the Class War!'

Well I'm not certain what they would have thought of it down in the CND offices, but on the streets of Sheffield it went down like a hurricane. Old socialist workers and Arab workers came up to shake my hand. A party of Yemeni workers, who form the largest Arab community in the City, came and hugged me.

Monday 18 May. Me and Peter Heathfield, the dynamic general secretary of the NUM, are the guest speakers at Chesterfield and Derbyshire Anti-Apartheid Movement's rally, on 'The Need for Workers' Action Against Apartheid'.

June 1987. I speak in Church! Under the title 'Coal and the Church For the 1990's', the coalfield vicar the Rev Anthony Attwood hosts a seminar for his chaplaincy. It is a detailed seminar actually hosted at his little church in the solidly militant Goldthorpe Colliery village. His chapel is a monument to the miners and their community. I speak on 'Hopes and Fears for the Future Among Mineworkers'. Actually, Tony, in full God get-up, was nicked during the strike. On his way into Derbyshire, in the early hours of the morn, he hits a police roadblock, who drag him out, and accuse him of being 'a picket in drag', something he amused folk by telling them ever afterwards.

THE PRIVILEGE OF THE EXECUTIVE COMMITTEE

19 June 1987. Barnsley Metropolitan Borough Council hosts a 100th Yorkshire Miners' Gala commemorative dinner. It is all pomp and circumstance, with lord mayors in shiny golden chains of office and the Union bigwigs and their wives out in full regalia. My partner is Emma now. She always accompanies me to these dos; in her glittering necklace and bonny dresses she is always the belle of the ball and I am so proud to have her on my arm. I love the way she casually discusses the latest issues for the Union with Arthur, which she follows horse's-mouth from me and from overhearing the ardent discussions with the men as we meet on the street on the bus, or round the supermarket. Arthur is courteous to a T, introduces himself to all the guests and their ladies. He is quite the gent, but can't resist a dig about 'those bloody contracts of yours, David'. Are we important? We are the executive of the coal miners' union – of course we're important, we're bloody famous, I suppose. Yes, this does somewhat raise you to the level of something of an officer class and install notions of leadership and your own crashing self-importance.

Ted Holloway, *Miners' Heads*, Oil, 1954

5

WAR ON ALL FRONTS

The industry is in a strange state of flux. The dust from the great strike has settled. Despite swingeing cuts and closures, the industry as such is still standing, still powerful, the Union is still deeply entrenched. The National leadership is becalmed and singing from last week's hymn sheet. We are meantime turning to meet the next wave and the next and see our way forward – it's a badly mixed metaphor, but one that reflects the disjunction. The Board seem genuinely to have plans for new long-term developments and investments. They are talking of £2 BILLION on 13 pits and 9,000 new jobs. At Area level, we are desperate to re-establish some security and consolidate our grip both on the members we have and on the coalfields we sit on. To a large extent we are cooperating with productivity schemes and efficiency schemes. Team-building, face conferences, delay analysis, troubleshooting, weekend efficiency meetings with bags of statistics and facts. One of the wags said that previously their organisation plan was drawn like a mushroom: they kept us in the dark and every now and again they would throw shit on us; now they have the lights fully on, but they still throw shit on us.

The Board are looking for 'flexible working', which means continental shifts (working weekends as ordinary days of the week), extended shifts, forced longer hours, and an end to concessions and agreements. We are determined that production can rise, that new seams can be developed, but we want to keep our national agreements. The Coal Board says that if the NUM aren't prepared talk to them about new terms they will go to those who are. In other words the NUM areas will be allowed to die while the UDM areas, which were expected to roll over and accept the new hours and shifts, would expand and grow. Where did that leave us strategically as a union; how did that impact on our 'historic mission' and our will to survive to fight another day? But if we accept such blackmail, where and when would the blackmail then ever stop?

Areas under the cosh are offered expansive and long-term developments, but only on certain conditions. The Welsh Area is offered Margham, a new super-pit development, but first they must accept 6-day working. In West Wales lies a vast area of untapped anthracite reserves. They waver. There is internal war between the Areas and the National leadership, pressure from all sides both for and against. While the National leadership hints at expulsion, Wales hints at disaffiliation, and others totter too. Our giant silent neighbour Thorne Colliery is suddenly the attention of new development interest. A third shaft had started some time ago but been suspended, work on new head gear had been completed and the old colliery now boasted the most prestigious industrial architecture in Britain; it was still recognisable as a pit, though like something from the kids' SF series *Triads*.

Thorne sat at the gateway to boundless reserves. Coupled with Hatfield, with our underground connection greatly enlarged, the two mines could become the centre of a new coalfield to rival Selby. The plan was to develop the Snaith and

Pollerton coalfield, an as yet untapped area of coal lying between Kellingley and Askern, Hatfield and Thorne and up to North Yorkshire – more than 70 miles of coal. And across to Lincolnshire, perhaps to the coast from Thorne and under Goole, lay a bonanza larger than the old Durham coalfield, which in its heyday had boasted 140 collieries. The NCB and secret government reports referred to it as the East Yorkshire Coalfield. It was an area of untouched coal probably bigger than the entire Yorkshire coalfield and containing more coal than had already been mined since the inception of the coalfield 200 years and more previously. Unlike Margham, which is just a plan, Thorne will be the first pit in the country to reopen and absorb new investments, with an existing reserve of 140 million tonnes and 700 jobs initially. But only in return for 6-day working for 3 weeks then every fourth week off. Suddenly it's on our doorstep. The Executive votes never to accept it. Ted Horton, the Area director and a genuine believer in the industry, believes that behind closed doors at Area level, and without national interference from either side, we can do a deal. This month's Conference at Rothsay in Scotland will nail the scheme to the floor and ensure we don't. Arthur was warning that the cost of 30 pits and 40,000 jobs was flexiworking at new super-pits. He warned that the policy was designed to break national unity and turn area against area in a scrabble for investment crumbs rather than a united fight for overall security. He pointed to the fact that the Union nationally was de facto derecognised; none of these plans would be put to the Union nationally but would instead be introduced through areas or individual pits, or even over the heads of the branches, going directly to the membership in an aim to further destroy the united stance of the NUM.[255] The Conference of 1987 was a masterpiece of scholarly speeches and informed passion. The speakers were all giants of the movement and each occupied highly principled and vital positions. This Conference was about the direction of the Union, probably as important as any previously hosted on the survival of the industry itself, and how we meet the relentless attacks and weasel plans of the Tories and the NCB. There were hints at a break-up of the Union, and Areas going their own way. Sammy Thompson the Yorkshire vice president made a brilliant speech – about technology, about the meaning of 'progress', about control of the future. He tried to place into a combative perspective the plans of the NCB to increase output, how we should view theories of progress and technology and what were our goals.

The Durham Area had advanced a far-sighted though controversial resolution calling for us to take back into organisation the opencast workers and the workers at the private drifts and shallow mines. The urgency of tying down all coal production during the strike had pointed to this fundamental weakness we had allowed to develop. The Union's steady growth in opposition to opencast work had developed in many areas to total opposition to that form of mining. It had handed those workers, our allies really, into the hands of non-mining unions and non-unionism. Davie Hopper from the Durham miners skilfully tried to square the circle, talking of long-term aims and principles set against immediate imperatives and tactics, and not least the need to preserve our industrial unionist principles and structure.[256] The leadership were caught facing in two directions on

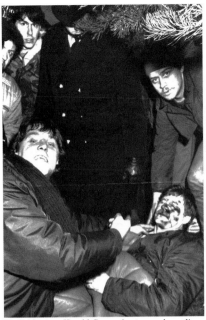

Hatfield miner Harold Cruzac beaten up by police at Thoresby Pit, March 1984. © John Harris

Arthur Scargill arrested at Orgreave coking plant, May 1984. © Syndication International

Miners picket Parliament. © Ken Wilkinson

Hatfield Main Colliery, Stainforth, 21 August 1984. © Ray Rising, *News Line*

Mansfield Colliery picket line

Mass picket at Babbington Colliery, 25 July 1984

Hatfield and Armthorpe miners' picket. © *News Line*

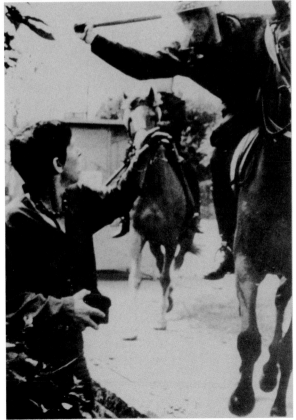

Unprovoked attack on
photographer Lesley Boulton
(at Orgreave) by the 'Blue
Cossacks' under the
command of Assistant Chief
Constable Clements. © John
Harris

Arrest of George Foulds and Bernard Jackson at Orgreave. © *Rotherham Advertiser*

Arrest of Eric Newbiggin at Orgreave. © *Rotherham Advertiser*

PITMEN MOURN PICKET'S DEATH

3,000 mourn dead picket

Three thousand mourners turned out yesterday to attend the funeral of Yorkshire miner Mr. David Jones., who died on a North Nottinghamshire picket line nine days ago.

Pitmen from all over the country united at South Kirkby, near Pontefract, to follow the coffin of the 24-year-old trainee deputy.

At least 3,000 men strung out for half-a-mile paraded with the banners of more than 30 mineworkers' lodges from Yorkshire, Wales, Cumberland, Northumberland, Co. Durham and Scotland.

Other unions, including the Public Employees, Boilermakers and Engineers, added their weight to the tribute.

Following the hearse on its mile long journey from Mr. Jones' home in Saxon Avenue, South Kirkby, to the centuries-old Parish church of All Saints, were five limousines and three coaches containing family and friends.

A respectful distance behind came the nation's miners led by NUM president Mr. Arthur Scargill, who took no official part in the service. The Yorkshire leader, Mr. Jack Taylor, and the MP for Bolsover, Mr. Dennis Skinner walking alongside.

In the forefront of the banners was Mr. Jones's own NUM branch — Ackton Hall, Featherstone.

As the cortege reached the church the dead man's mother, Mrs. Doreen Jones, broke down and had to be supported by her husband, Mark, and other members of the family who included David's five brothers and sisters.

At least 300 mourners packed the church and some had to stand to hear the service conducted by the Vicar, the Rev. Phillip Wright, assisted by the Rev. Dennis Hibbert, Vicar of Ollerton, where David Jones met his death.

In a brief eulogy Mr. Wright said: "We are here for many reasons, the predominant reason being one of grief."

A drummer, closely followed by NUM president Mr. Arthur Scargill and Yorkshire miners' leader Mr. Jack Taylor, leads the miners' procession through South Kirkby.

Mr. Scargill, left, and Mr. Taylor wait to enter All Saints' Church for the funeral service.

23 March 1984. Over 3,000 mourners attend the funeral of picket David Jones at All Saints, South Kirkby. Picket David Jones, from Ackton Hall Colliery, died on 15 March after injuries received on the picket line at Ollerton in Nottinghamshire.

Hatfield Main, 21 August 1984: Dave Douglass and Branch secretary Peter Curran prepare the pickets for the one remaining scab to leave the pit in the protected bus.

Preparing to block the route of the scab-carrying bus

Hatfield Main, 21 August 1984: after initial fighting management allow union secretary Peter Curran to go in and talk to the two scabs. One of them agrees to rejoin the strike, if he can walk out unmolested. The picture shows Peter Curran and the former scab, walking through silent ranks of pickets, myself at the rear right of the photo. © Ray Rising, *News Line*

Pickets attacking scab convoy at Rossington Colliery

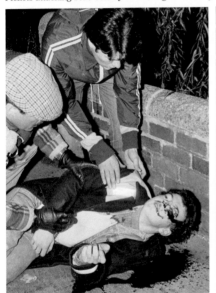

Above left: Darren Price seriously injured by police vehicle which mounted the pavement in an attempt to disperse the pickets. © Peter Arkell, *News Line*

Above right: the late Betty Corrigan, wife of miner Dickie Corrigan, attacks professional strikebreaker Walter Sharp, leader of the Doncaster working miners, with her shoe. Sharp, employed as a power house attendant, left Rossington after the strike to work for area security. He was killed at Thorne Colliery trying to stop an off-road motorcycle. © Ray Rising, *News Line*

Police escort pickets into Orgreave. According to prosecuting counsel Walsh, 'Their aim was force and violence.'

Orgreave was policed by 'unprotected officers', according to Assistant Chief Constable Clements (seen here briefing his 'unprotected officers' prior to their assault on the miners' pickets).

© Sheffield Newspapers Ltd

Miners fleeing before the advance of Assistant Chief Constable Clements's 'Blue Cossacks' into Orgreave Village. © Martin Jenkinson

the issue, and Arthur, at this Conference anyway, was quite sympathetic to the need to organise these workers, or so it seemed. When he asked that the question be referred back to the NEC for consideration, Durham agreed. However, the war against opencast and by extension opencast miners continued.[257] The issue resurfaced again the following year, with moves by Jack Jones of the Leicestershire Area to get some real effort into taking these workers back into NUM membership and that, inexplicably so far as he was concerned, the opencast miners had been handed over to the TGWU and a deal signed to allow the T&G rather than us to organise them. But the Union was still left opposing opencast mining, while supporting superficially at least efforts by COSA to recruit them.[258] At the same time, Conference was being told that while the NCB wished to develop 18 million tonnes from opencast, the NUM's policy was that it should be wound down to a tickover capacity of 5 million tonnes.[259]

The NCB had revealed meantime that its 'technically recoverable reserves' (not its 'economically recoverable reserves') were 45 BILLION tonnes.[260] It had no plans to actually mine these reserves, or to search for new fields beyond the existing coalfield areas.

The major crux of the passion and debate however was around the Margam proposals. Although most speakers said they weren't in fact talking about Margam, clearly inter alia they were. George Rees was at a crossroads:

> This problem between South Wales and the National Union should never ever have blown up to the proportion that it has. It was completely mishandled from the start and I put the criticism to the President on this, that he did not have the courtesy to consult South Wales Area before he made his press statement saying 'They are not to have it.' That is what you call a national Union? I call it a dictatorship when you reach that, I am not prepared to be dictated to nor my area by any individual in this Union. We are part of an organisation and if we had been consulted in the first place, we could have made a joint approach to the Board on the problems of Margam without getting into the mess that we are in at the moment ...
> In South Wales we have always held the view, not just in my days, in the days of Horner and Painter, Dai Francis, Dai Evans, that the best way to represent your members is to be able to talk to the employer and if you cannot talk to the employer you are not doing the job you have been elected to do, and that is the problem we are faced with today (Applause). This is the basic function of any trade union, to represent his members and to talk to the employer, whoever the employer is. No, Chairman, you have made many statements over the years. We have supported and given support to you as the President of this Union, and when you were the President of the Yorkshire Area in your campaign for Presidency, but we do not have the luxury of being able to say 'I will not prostitute my principles' because there is not a lodge secretary or delegate or official in this Area here, in this Conference, who has not at some time or another had to prostitute his principles in order to achieve for his members what his principles demand, because you are elected not for your own

principles, but you are elected to carry out the principles of the membership you represent. If you are not doing that then you are not doing your job ...

Comrades, in conclusion, we do not live in a society that we all want. The society that we want is a million miles away from us. Do not let us live in a dream world, where we can dream about things that do nothing to achieve the dreams we set out. We live in a cold, cruel world. The world of Thatcherism. We have had 9 years of it and we have got another 5 years of it to come. You won't defeat Thatcherism unless you are prepared to talk on behalf of the members you have got. Let me say this to you. Take off the blinkers, stop having tunnel vision. Look at what is happening around because if you do not get involved in the discussion with the Board on new technology, then the Board will impose it over your heads, like they have done with wages. We have seen to our costs what is happening on that one. Unless we are prepared to get into discussions, all the Board's proposals will come to fruition, and to the cost of this Union, because it will destroy us. (Applause)[261]

The Conference resounded to well-argued, passionately felt speeches, not least that by Mick McGahey, addressing his last Conference, and in the capacity of vice president:

... I want to make it clear there should be no division in this Conference, that Haslam[262] must withdraw his blackmail. He is not entitled to be inflexible by demanding that this Union must agree before. Who are they to invest? Whose money is it? He is not taking it out of his pocket. It is the British people's money, and who are they to demand that this Union must agree before they invest to develop the needs of the nation? So I must make it clear, Haslam withdraw the blackmail. Yes we will negotiate ... I am prepared to say to Haslam 'We will discuss new technology. Are you prepared to discuss retirement of mineworkers at 55 underground, 60 on the surface? Are you prepared to agree to a radical increase in pensions? Are you prepared to agree that new technology is the product of past labour? Are you prepared to agree that the new technology brings shorter hours to the working miner? ... a shorter working week, what about holidays? After all, why do we have longer hours in this extractive industry? So our strategy, we are not against new technology. We are very flexible, provided it brings benefits to our members.[263]

SIEGE

The NCB have elaborated a response to our 'production plus disruption' tactic. Recognising that, despite everything, the Union was rebuilding and militancy was mounting, they aim in a make-or-break effort to bring the miners to heel and control the influence of the Union.

First was the total severance of all contact with the National leadership under any circumstances at all. The NUM had last negotiated pay in 1982, and wasn't allowed back since the end of the strike. All pay 'negotiations' have been conducted by the yellow-dog minority scab organisation the UDM. These are then imposed upon NUM members nationwide. The NCB's aim is to cut the head off the beast and allow it to flounder round in all directions. This had certainly posed a problem, which was compounded by the National leadership simply sitting with folded arms in a sulk and demanding: 'What's to talk about?' The leadership clearly expected that the Union from top to bottom should likewise adopt a posture of total non-cooperation and hostility. We as a body should boycott the NCB management apparatus. This might have looked tough from the officials' desks at National Office, but at pit level the miners demanded: 'What do we pay the Union for?' They demanded progress on the pressing issues that confronted them. Pit closures via poor production and non cooperation were a weekly fact; some strategy had to be found to maintain our relevance while holding fast to what we could of union principle.

This had been the reason I had devised the industrial equivalent of 'the ballot box and the Armalite'. We were forced to try and bargain on new contracts, new bonuses, new production incentives just to stay on our feet in the ring. Peter had seen this as collaboration and loudly condemned the new bonus scheme that I had jointly devised at Hatfield. This had seriously increased the income of all the pit's miners, put the colliery back into profitability, and almost at once had shot the pit into the top ten for industrial action also. For this reason, as the NCB tried to impose radical new shift working times against the existing national agreements in key areas, we had some understanding and sympathy with them. But this was an NCB strategy aimed at driving a wedge into our hard-won terms and conditions. Central to this had been the floating of new shift times and working week lengths. Nine-and-a-half-hour shifts for the North East coalfield, 'because of the distance we are having to travel to get to the coal'; without longer shifts the North East coalfield as a whole is unproductive and therefore threatened. In South Wales, Margam was offered as a great modern expansion of their coalfield, a replacement for all those jobs lost in older hand-got pits and a secure place in the coming century for Welsh coal. South Wales had lost 50% of its entire workforce in the 2 years since the end of the strike. Margam's existence would only be offered however by acceptance of 6-day working. If this wasn't accepted Margam would not go ahead.

THE CARROT OR THE STICK?

Arthur argued:

> Margam was promised to our industry in the 1974 *Plan For Coal* – on the basis of the Five Day Week Agreement ... now the Board argues that Margam could not operate profitably on a five-day week ... If a pit with 2,200 men, such as Wearmouth in Durham, can produce a million tonnes of coking coal at a profit before interest, then I submit there is no way that a project such as Margam with only 650 men can avoid making a profit producing the same tonnage. Indeed the difference between the two pits in manpower alone equals a £15 million per year saving at Margam – working a five-day week ... British Coal is trying to use Margam and other

major projects as a 'sprat to catch a mackerel'. Their real purpose is to establish the principle of 6-day working, smash the five-day week and weaken the National Union of Mineworkers. Their intention is to refuse to negotiate with the National Union and seek to reach 'deals' at Area level.[264]

Des Dutfield, the area president, felt that the existence of the miners' Union, with its potential still to bring the working class together in all-out struggle, was vital not just for Wales but for the whole labour movement. Arthur saw this as sectionalism and indiscipline. Wedges were being driven into the solid ranks of the NUM as a whole, and the National leadership didn't help by looking like King Canute with its face set against the tide. Worse, Arthur started to manipulate rules and Conferences to force the areas into compliance with his vision; as time went on, this meant an active war to displace the areas and their officials altogether. The first of these manoeuvres, the reader may recall, had come at the end of 1985 when the rule book was changed to forestall any necessity for him to come up for election again and effectively to render him president for life. Government legislation was to force him to stand anyway, despite the bureaucratic rule change.

Forbye, this third plank (if we were to say that isolation of the National Union was the first and decentralised contracts and bonuses was the second) of NCB strategy proved an own-goal. The terms of the National Disciplinary Code were a red rag to a bull, a tired, bruised and bloody bull but a bull none the less. Given the fierce independence of the miners at work, our self-controlling skills and resistance to supervision, our propensity to 'rag up' or walk out of the mine on strike, this 'code' sought to break us and essentially render us different animals. Worse still, it sought to invade our communities, our attitudes and actions off pit premises, what we did based on our attitudes to members of the community who worked at the pit. Wherever the political and social voice of the union was heard in the village, at every level, this code sought to intervene. It had, by August of 1987, 13,000 miners out on strike in South Yorkshire, flying pickets spreading to North Yorkshire and the NEC trying to hang on to the movement's coat-tails by calling a national ballot for industrial action. The miners were back on their feet.

It has to be noted here that our strength came from two things. One: coal still provided the bulk of power generation in Britain. Two: it was the NUM that overwhelmingly controlled the production of that coal. (In 1987 total coal use in Britain was slightly higher than it had been in 1981.[265]) By the beginning of 1987, the South Yorkshire Area had made £50 million clear profits after all costs were met. At the same time, rumours had been circulating of a new NCB offensive in the form of some new disciplinary code; a union official in Derbyshire had been disciplined for talking to men in the pit yard and a secretary sacked in Nottingham for putting a notice on a notice board. Furious correspondence had passed between Heathfield and Hunt, the NCB chief industrial relations officer. Peter had made the point that there could be no unilateral adoption of a new code outside of the existing signed, sealed and delivered agreements.

The Board appeared to have backed off; although raised at Conference, the

National officials thought it a low priority, and that the clash, internal and external, would come over 6-day working. There was something of a perception gap here, between what the pit yakker considered the final straw, how the man at the point of pick saw the world changing and what the formal union officials had perceived as the next strategic target. There was a further misperception of what this former rank and filer would take on in terms of strength of reaction, and what the leaderships of all levels thought the potential strengths of the union ought to be kept for. When the struggle broke, the miners took up the issue head-on and were prepared for an all-out effort, whereas our full-time leaders thought this a diversion to be sidestepped as far as possible. They sought to save our energies for something more important like flexible working, holiday arrangements, new technologies etc. There was to be a critical failure to mount the re-engagement we so needed, and which the members overwhelmingly were up for.

WILDCAT MINERS

Wildcat action[266] against British Coal's new Disciplinary Code started at Frickley Colliery in the Doncaster Area, although it nearly started at Hatfield Main in the same Area, where two matters put the issue firmly on the agenda. One had involved a team of heading men, working in thick mud attempting to repair a broken dosco. To do this, a man and a fitter[267] had to work in a height of 2 foot, beneath the jacked-up section of the machine, with the massive machine groaning and easing in the thick floor mud right over their bodies. The men take turns working under the machine. They lie flat in a sump formed in the mud by their bodies rolling back and forth and twisted from one side to another. The sump is filled with a mixture of oil dripping from the machine and mud. The men had demanded that they complete the job but be allowed to ride the pit as soon as they had done so, to wash the caustic oil from their bodies, and change their soaked overalls ready for the next shift. It was a common practice but if the charge overman was a meanie he would allow them to do so, but then fix them up with some time-wasting job on the surface so they didn't knock off early. If he was a good'un he'd let them off home as soon as they were bathed.

This customary practice was obstructed with the intervention of a newly arrived undermanager who would allow only the fitter, plus one workman, to ride. The men contended that they had all taken turns digging out under the machine and making a working space and they were all equally soaked and oiled up. Negotiations between the undermanager and me, summoned from inbye to sort the problem out, reached deadlock; the men rode up the pit in dispute having finished the job anyway. A small, not unusual incident in the life of a colliery. I had arranged an immediate site inspection to validate the environmental conditions, in readiness to take the issue up on Friday at the regular round of dispute meetings held with each undermanager. I operated a book for each undermanager, as well as a thick wad of social welfare issues pursued with the personnel manager.

The following day, a Thursday, a similar dispute arose, and an hour before lowse the men ragged up and came out of the pit to present themselves in their soaked and wretched condition to the undermanager. By this time, however, more sinister events were unfolding behind the scenes. All of the men were sent registered letters telling them that this constituted a formal written warning and that they were in breach of contract, and had left work without permission, which was a breach of the new disciplinary code. The offences would be entered in their employment records, and any further offence would result in their dismissal. Meantime a second case had arisen, when a fitter had questioned his deployment from a priority job to one previously deemed unimportant. An argument ensued and the local dispute procedure was entered into; after the intervention of another Union official the fitter reluctantly accepted the deployment. The following day he too received a registered letter with a formal written warning, and instructing him to see the colliery engineer before going below ground again because he had failed to carry out his deployment, a breach of the new code.

The fat was perilously close to the fire. These were not disciplinary matters, these were industrial relations disputes, usually resolved or anyway debated through the conciliation machinery; discipline was usually to do with illegal or unlawful breaches of health and safety laws, or attendance. A mass branch meeting was convened which agenda'd possible strike action at the pit – Hatfield was shaping up to be the first pit in the country to take action against the new rules – while a meeting was convened with the manager. For his part, the gaffer blinked first, saying the situation of the code 'would be investigated' and the letters suspended.

Meantime, news was circulating that a secretary up in Selby had been suspended for breach of the code.

At Frickley, the manager had went ahead and sent out disciplinary letters, on the old flashpoint of snap time. A team of heading men were caught having snap after the designated snap time, halfway through the shift, was over. The men explained that they got their snap when they finished the last cycle of work; they couldn't just leave the roof hanging in the hope it would stay there while they got their snap. They were sent out of the pit. Another group were sent letters for the old custom of 'job and knock' (fill off and fuck off) prior to the annual holiday – basically you complete the expected work cycle and then go home. The men virtually pick the coal cutter up and carry it down the face in order to ride early. This practice was now deemed dangerously illegal and the team sent letters. All of these letters demanded individual interviews in a disciplinary setting, and not the first-stage industrial relations dispute meeting, as had been the case since nationalisation. The Frickley men, realising that this was a feature of the new code, refused to attend and were suspended forthwith. Frickley's mass branch meeting saw an explosion of anger focused against not simply the code but the new-style jackboot management which it was a symptom of. The branch voted to strike, but rejected their official's proposal that they seek the support of the South Yorkshire Panel following meetings of the other branches.

AUTONOMOUS WORKERS?

Instead they decided to picket out the rest of the South Yorkshire coalfield from the night shift of Wednesday 15 July. There was among the Frickley men what could be called a climate of 'worker autonomism', which suddenly subsumed all customary official and unofficial practices of the Union and resolved almost from day one to heed neither official nor unofficial bodies of the Union. Firstly they hit the traditional Doncaster Panel pits and each one stood completely. Hatfield and Rossington, both with Executive members, called an emergency Panel meeting. This was heavily and violently lobbied by the Frickley men, many of whom argued fiercely that we (the branch reps) didn't matter, and they should be lobbying the miners of Yorkshire directly. Some expressed the view that they 'have had it with officials of any sort in this Union – you always try to keep the lid on it'. Despite the clear hostility even to this semi-official body of the Union, and one that represented the branches and membership directly with no full-time officers, the branch representatives met the Frickley men with warmth, comradeship and support. The Frickley men rejected this embrace and suspected that this was just a long way round to stopping their action. When the Panel meeting was opened, branches went through a brief history of how the code had so far been tested at their own pits, and came to a united conclusion that the code had to be fought. A number of branches, however, expressed the view that they couldn't guarantee support for all-out, open-ended industrial action, and their members were not yet incensed enough to match the mettle of the Frickley men. A more limited form of action would have to be contemplated.

TED SCOTT AND NORTH YORKSHIRE

The action in any case would have to be carried into North Yorkshire where, the code was already being implemented against a Branch official (Ted Scott); an appeal to their North Yorkshire Panel meeting should be made. I as acting chair (I was formally vice chair of the joint South Yorkshire Panel and by all previous practice ought to have become chair when the previous chair finished, but strong political pressure from Barnsley ensured that didn't happen, despite the unofficial nature of the organisation) had to try and span the mixed strengths of the meeting with a united resolution and at least make a nod in the direction of industrial relations laws, most of which we were all breaking:

It is the opinion of the South Yorkshire Panel that the coalfield will continue to be subject to disruption until such time as the Coal Board withdraws its unilaterally imposed disciplinary code. This Panel supports the stand made by the Frickley Branch and calls upon all its members' Branches to convene emergency meetings to discuss the situation. We formally request a meeting with the North Yorkshire Panel to review the situation.

This resolution was passed unanimously.

My idea was that we hold a joint panel meeting of all the Yorkshire branches, outside the formal NUM council structures, which would be severely restricted by the legal requirements of the anti-union laws and the pressure upon the Area officials to conform to them. This meeting would have been outside the control of the Officials and the Executive and agents, and therefore protect the formal

Union from sequestration and prosecution. In the event, the North Yorkshire Panel pre-empted the request by inviting all South Yorkshire EC members plus the Frickley officials to the Panel to put their case.

The meeting was again heavily lobbied by the Frickley men and a growing gang of leftist paper-sellers. However, despite the apparent warm reception by the North Yorkshire Panel, it soon became clear that a dramatically different response to the code was being enacted. We had discovered that true to rumour Ted Scott, the Stillingfleet branch secretary, had been suspended for carrying out his union duties. He had actually pinned up a notice making men aware that it was against NUM policy to cut coal at weekends and in overtime. This was a far stronger issue, and one worthy of national action, than the one being taken up by the Frickley men and the rest of the South Yorkshire pits. Yet there had been no response whatever, even at the man's own pit. An unofficial pre-Panel meeting of the Executive members present, north and south, was then told of the shocking sequel – that Ted Scott had actually now been sacked, yet all the North Yorkshire mines were working as normal. This would clearly not have been the result had the same situation occurred in Doncaster with me or any of the other officials anywhere in Doncaster. It was also true that we actually had a National Conference decision to oppose the new code, yet here we had one of our Branch officials sacked under it and no action!

We were speechless. Perhaps the lads at Frickley had known far more than we did when they launched the action. The North Yorkshire Area agent (arch-moderate Johnny Walsh) had advised the branch to play it softly-softly and he would see what he could negotiate while they worked normally. In Doncaster the response one and all would be 'bollocks' to such a recommendation.

The officials at Barnsley had decided to take the question of Ted's sacking through the appeal procedure! We were furious. Here we were as a union putting the conciliation agreement which was being ignored through the conciliation procedure to argue that we wanted to conciliate. Someone was severely missing the point in all this. I violently stated that I did not want to argue about having a fair trial for being a Union official, since it wasn't a crime; the procedure being used to prosecute me or anyone else wasn't the issue. It's the existence of the charge that we oppose, not the means by which it is tried.

The North Yorkshire branches had already been advised prior to this meeting to do nothing which could jeopardise Ted Scott's appeal. To us this was de facto acceptance of the new code; it conceded that they had the right to take actions like this, for union activity, with the possible right to appeal against the specific circumstances or penalty. It made us party to the new code from the word go.

Well, OK – so where did this leave us now with the Frickley dispute? We hadn't come to advise them on how they should handle the dismissal of a branch secretary, although somebody should; instead we would stick to the point at issue. We were already on strike against the code as it was being applied in South Yorkshire; where did North Yorkshire stand?

Frickley put its case, although conscious that a much bigger issue was on the doorstep of North Yorkshire. My own contribution was that this was not an action for Frickley; it was an action against the existence of the code. Frickley had simply provided the initial flashpoint. We recognised that the issue of Ted Scott was a specific issue being handled in a specific way following specific advice, rightly or wrongly. That didn't hamstring them from taking action on this issue; the root cause of all 'prosecutions' current or forthcoming was this code. The North Yorkshire officials argued that Scott's appeal was being heard the following day (Friday) and with this in mind the result would be known by the weekend and a special meeting of the North Yorkshire Branches followed by a recalled meeting of the Panel would convene to decide on what action to take in the light of this, with the possibility of joining the action as of Monday day shift. In the meantime, it was requested that the pickets stay out of the North Yorkshire coalfield in the intervening period to give the branches the chance to debate and decide the issues for themselves.

To the South Yorkshire representatives, given the 'queered pitch' that had been presented us, this was a clear victory and better than we could have hoped for. It seemed to suggest to us that either the code would be withdrawn or the whole of Yorkshire would stand on Monday. When we reported back to the mass Frickley pickets it wasn't enough. Nothing now would be enough for Frickley, short of the whole Area out now. We were dodging the issue by given them too much rope to get out of fighting the code. 'What if Ted Scott got his job back Saturday? Then support for Frickley could hang on Monday.' We argued, against a tide of abuse, that all the indications were that if the Ted Scott issue was got out of the way, it would strengthen the case for action on Monday against the code as such. I wasn't the most popular man in Yorkshire when I argued, true to our word, that the pickets should not go on into North Yorkshire at this stage – for God's sake, the difference between us was one day. If that one day strengthened the resolve of men to strike in support and not be picketed out reluctantly it was a far stronger action and more sustainable. We were trying to win united action here – that was what we were trying to achieve.

Keep On Keeping On

The pickets reluctantly agreed to stand down from North Yorkshire but hold South Yorkshire for the present. The pickets however were back across North Yorkshire on Monday, and the TV channels showed they were rolling all before them. Murmurs among the Derbyshire and Nottingham men suggested that the strike would soon pass their boundaries. It is interesting here to note that the blackleg miners who worked through our strike against closures were far from happy by this turn of events and saw the code as an attack on them too. The UDM might not take any action, but they could.

Although the Frickley men were violent and unruly and in my view undisciplined, as it turned out they had been right to be suspicious. At the height of the unofficial action, the National Executive Committee met at Stillingfleet NUM Office with the strike raging all round them. In 1984 they had sanctioned just such a strike movement. Since then, the laws had been utterly clarified and such actions were unlawful unless preceded by a ballot. Failure to do so meant sequestration of the Union's already vastly depleted funds and potentially offices. The threat of the arrest of our Area and even National officials to be right didn't cut much ice with us, though clearly it did with them. Once the question of the unofficial strike appeared formally on the agenda of the NEC, the Union had to make an official response (Jack Taylor and the Yorkshire Officials up till now had managed to escape all mention of it) and the ball would be taken from Frickley to the NEC.

WHY WERE WE WAITING?

Actually, the NEC had already been given authority by the last Conference to authorise action against the code. Many of them were running scared of the force of the picketing action, and feared with sheer terror the total collapse of their areas from all-out strike action. Nobody at the National Conference had argued for all-out strike action – such would have seen utterly unobtainable. The truth was, fear of another prolonged strike was evident in many a Yorkshire branch, not to mention more moderate coalfields. Even in the South Yorkshire coalfield the Panel meeting had heard branches were not ready for unlimited strike action. More moderate voices were talking of something less than all-out strike action, and that only on the strength of a ballot.

Arthur came from the meeting and announced to the assembled media that a national ballot to seek to impose a national overtime ban was to be conducted. The carpet was whipped not only from under Frickley's feet but also the feet of all those branches now on strike against the code and the feet of those of us on the Executive who had been arguing for strike action. Following the NEC decision, the Yorkshire EC met on 18 July. The question, like it or not, was now formally on the national stage. Frickley branch could not realistically hope to run a national action from the Welfare at South Elmsall; neither could it unilaterally dictate the measure of the tactics to be deployed, even though some of us preferred their tactics rather than the NEC's. This was and always had been a national question; it was inconceivable that Frickley could continue to mount all-out strike action while the rest of the Union marched at a slower pace. The Frickley action was commendable, as was the solidarity strike action by the rest of South Yorkshire; it had built a head of steam, it had got the basic issue widespread national coverage and all the other issues involved were already receiving widespread airing, with much popular opposition in the media to the code.

But the action couldn't continue as it was. Even without the NEC taking charge of the issue, the branch officials at Frickley were on borrowed time from the legal sanctions imposed by the Trade Union Acts on secondary action, and unlawful strike action passed in anticipation of the great strike, during its process and after its defeat, sealing off every legal right we had to just strike and picket as we had done for centuries (though not always lawfully of course). The Barnsley officials could only play hide-and-seek for so long; sooner or later the injunctions would start to land on the steps of the Barnsley offices. Was the Union as a whole, as an organisation, ready to say 'bollocks'? Jack Taylor had clearly given the action its head – had 'turned a blind eye', had done nothing to stop the strike or the picketing or the unofficial meetings; he clearly supported the strike but officially couldn't be seen to. This is why we had never presented the question before him or the formal structure of the NUM. Others, however, were not so inclined. Disgruntled branches had flooded the Barnsley offices with formal letters of complaint, demanding an official Council meeting be called to discuss the situation.

The weight of these demands was now so heavy that neither the officials nor the EC could ignore them further, and once this meeting was called and the issue agenda'd, the membership would have had to be balloted if the strike was to continue. That was the reality of the situation. We had no choice but to recommend a return to work, pending the national ballot on the national overtime ban.

Frickley, picketing out South Yorkshire, and starting to call out North Yorkshire, had the NEC cornered. They (the NEC) had been extremely reluctant to sanction strike actions in their areas; many area leaders felt benevolent managements were settling industrial relations matters and hadn't implemented the code. On the other hand, the hounds were running, and the wildcat now loose in North Yorkshire was poised to cross area boundaries. Their choice was now to take control of the action or lose it to the rank and file. They agreed to call a national ballot, but for action short of an all-out strike. The form of action was to be left to the NEC.

Having called for it, the Yorkshire Area Executive Committee, including myself as a member of that leadership, felt obliged to win a national vote in favour of a national action. We reasoned that tactically, as well as purely economically, a national overtime ban would be stronger than any patchy unofficial action that was shaky to say the least, and holding the line purely out of respect for the picket lines and not actual agreement. The NEC in my view didn't expect to win the ballot; they thought the rank and file would turn it down. They were wrong. The men had lost much dignity since returning to work, and many old concessions had been torn up, with new disciplines and attitudes imposed. The men wanted their pride back. At first, the prospect of renewed all-out action seemed implausible, but then as the idea took root it began to look like we might just pull it off. The wind was in our hair again. The Yorkshire EC with me as a member called for the Frickley action to be called off during the course of the ballot; we should let people vote on the basis of the issues not the picket line. It was not a popular call among the Frickley men, many of whom were wild and militant it was true – a number had no time for union nor management – but some, it must be said, also had redundancy fever in their veins and hoped perhaps to close the pit with some dignified rationale rather than greed.

In the week we called for the Frickley men to go back pending the arrangement of the ballot, Hatfield was on holiday. There was no coal production and no development work; only outstanding safety work was being undertaken. Frickley continued to deploy its pickets, including to Hatfield. This had caused quite a row down on the gates – the other pits were being allowed to let safety cover workers work. At Hatfield, these were already the only men working, and picketing these out meant making the action stick harder here than at Frickley, and was in any case directly against the decision of the Panels and the Council and the EC.

HATFIELD MINERS SCABS?

I was on afters, having decided to work me holidays and take them later on when a trip abroad was cheaper. I was to work repairing a massive hole over a manriding belt. I received a phone call at 6 a.m. from the men at the colliery gate telling me about pickets. By the time I arrived a furious row was taking place, although to their credit not one of the Hatfield men had actually crossed the line and gone to work, despite their disagreements. The pickets also had a flock of leftist paper-sellers with them. Brian Roberts, a large committee man who lived across the road, had come down on his bike in the middle of the dispute and told the men to go to work as that was the branch decision. When I arrived I addressed both pickets and men. I told them that branch policy was you didn't cross anyone's picket lines, even the ones we didn't agree with, and if anybody did we would bring them before a disciplinary meeting. I told Brian he should be ashamed of himself and should resign from the Committee. But I also told the pickets in no uncertain terms that they were misguided in general; the issue was now a national one, and we should be working for the maximum ballot result now the NEC had finally got off their backsides and organised one, but that in any case Hatfield was already not producing coal or new faces or developments. The pit was on holiday, and I had formally notified the Frickley branch of this. We were stood already, the only men at these gates were men doing essential safety work as agreed between the Union and the management. These were the terms that applied at Frickley itself and every other pit in Donnie and South Yorkshire. When this was explained the pickets withdrew. It wasn't however the end of the story.

NOW IT's ME IN THE CROSSHAIRS

The ever malevolent *Spartacist*[268] then produced a front-page slander saying that I had told the pickets to withdraw or I was leading the Hatfield men through them to work. They actually quoted Brian's words as being mine; 'someone' had told them Brian was me. Outside the mass delegate meeting at Kellingley, the Sparts sold their papers, and delegates laughed, taking the piss, saying 'Dave Douglass is a right-winger' and buying the paper with great enthusiasm and mockery. The following edition quoted these delegates confirming I was a right-winger! The slander ran on for weeks and to this day has never been withdrawn, despite all the facts to the contrary. We regarded Spartacists as a hostile body from that day on and they sometimes got the blunt end of Hatfield miners' tongues, inluding that of Eggy who you will recall had turned the fire hose on them, thereby earning his own piece in the paper as being the author of 'an anti-communist attack'. (They had got off easy; Eggy was also a grade 1 street fighter (and dancer by the way)).

The NCB clearly thought a firm stand was necessary, and sent all 900 men at Frickley registered letters, warning them they were in breach of contract and could all be sacked. Frickley were furious. They resolved to defy Scargill and the NEC and Yorkshire Area Executive and the decisions of both the North Yorkshire and the South Yorkshire Panels. They continued to picket out all the pits in Yorkshire amid many bitter scenes and conflicting loyalties. The furious South Yorkshire Panel, meeting at length, decided we had no choice but to recommend a return to work pending the ballot. Four Branches voted to stop out: Goldthorpe, Hickleton, Bentley and Frickley. Frickley refused to go back and resolved to carry on picketing despite or maybe because of a personal face-to-face appeal by the four Area leaders plus the well-regarded Area agent Frank Cave.

The mood of hostility to the Union leadership at all levels was extraordinary when compared with the far cooler response from the other seven South Yorkshire branches. They resolved that they would strike indefinitely, even at the risk of the pit shutting around their ears. Stopping the picket, which had defied all levels of authority, formal and informal, took another Council meeting, and growing bitterness on the picket lines, as men strained to keep their principles of not crossing the lines, despite unanimous votes to return to work before the Frickley wildcat picket was called off. After much brow-beating and pleas from all the other branches to Frickley to hold off the action, they resentfully returned and awaited the result of the national ballot.

Meantime at the pit, each of the men was interviewed individually and given a warning over their future conduct, but all suspensions were lifted. At least one was found not actually to have done anything he had been charged with and given a complete vindication.

BACK WITH TED AND NORTH YORKSHIRE

Much of the focus now swung back to North Yorkshire. Theoretically, if the Board went ahead and rejected Ted's appeal, the North Yorkshire branches could still strike. We on the South Yorkshire Executive thought the overtime ban a wholly inappropriate response now, given the letters to every man at Frickley. Vic Lindsey from Rossington commented that 'perhaps if the NCB were to sack a branch official every week maybe the NEC would consider it serious enough to call a one-day strike. But save our energies in case something important happens.' When they reached their verdict it was wildly provocative: Ted Scott was to remain sacked at his own colliery, but could be reinstated at another pit. In other words, the NCB could now decide if someone would stay the branch secretary at a pit, or be removed through dismissal and sent somewhere out of the way. An emergency Executive Committee meeting met to review the verdict, and, wrongly in my view, now decided that like it or not they were fully committed to the impending national action, as a total response to the overall implementation of the code and not a specific instance of it. They decided Ted would not be the main focus of the fight – that would be the code itself. We thought the ballot result and the rising tide of hostility to the code might steel the nerves of the NEC.

When the result came, the strength of feeling couldn't have been more determinedly shown: a Yes vote of 75% just 2 years after the ragged return of '85. As the result came through, it was tannoyed underground; wild cheering could be heard from the colliers on the faces and in the drivages. 'Right, ye bastards, lets have a right go this time!' was Morris's[269] comment as he came out of the pit beaming. We were already working on our new strike song from 'Here We Go! Here We Go! Here We Go!' it would be 'Here We Go Again, Happy As Can Be…'. But the news was not taken like this in area offices up and down the country; the NEC didn't have much hair left to let the wind fly into, and called an 'overtime ban', which effectively meant nothing at all. It would demand 'no coal turning in overtime or at weekends'. Nobody in Yorkshire, Durham or Northumberland or most other places we could gauge ever cut coal then anyway. Disgust and ridicule greeted officials of the Union from Branch to Executive. Dave Bathurst, an agitator of highest degree, a rule book memoriser, knower of every safety rule and mechanical and electrical regulation in existence, a man who wielded safety locks like a gun slinger, applied with deadly response to management harassment, but who always kept within the letter of the law, was also the world's biggest piss-taker of authority. Me included. 'Ha!' he shouts as I stand among all the shift waiting to go underground and mocking my accent, 'Let's hev an overtime ban lads, but you can work all the overtime ye want! And if that doesn't work we'll gaan on strike, but you can all come to work!' – which was vaguely based on my address to the mass meeting just weeks ago. The NEC would struggle to ever get us to believe them again. Billy Etherington, an NEC member representing the North East, was later to put it bluntly:

> There has been reference made this morning to that infamous overtime ban that was instigated by the NEC over the disciplinary code.
>
> Certainly, the North East, following that charade, made one important decision. Never again would we involve ourselves on motions that left things to the NEC. That is an awful thing to say but that is the way it was.[270]

In 1990, with no movement on wages or any other question of conditions, with no negotiations and virtual derecognition of the Union, proposals for an overtime ban were once more mooted. Nigel Pearse spoke bitterly for the rank and file:

> Now I am not going to argue against other Areas that they say it might have been effective, but it was not effective in Yorkshire because the majority of pits did not produce in overtime and the majority of the pits now don't produce in overtime. So it never affected us in Yorkshire. We thought it was a joke. We did more overtime when our overtime ban was on than when it was not. (Laughter) We voted it off, we did not even know we had one on.[271]

I note that I sat throughout this Conference on my hands, which indicates to me that I and the men I represented had no realistic prospect for a successful fight on this issue in this way. I would never speak against the Area view, which we had argued and decided upon, but I couldn't bring myself to talk up a fight I didn't think we could get into, so I had said nothing.

Subsequent action never took place. Management ensured the code if it still existed wouldn't be applied; no more flashpoints on this issue would be allowed to develop. For the Union, and perhaps the industry, this had been a potential turning point; the chance was not so much 'missed' as deliberately sabotaged. While we struggled to convince Frickley to call off its action, exercise some discipline and respect the views of the rest of the Union, I had demanded: 'Do you think your branch is the only one that's right and everyone else is wrong?' As it turned out, they could have correctly answered 'yes' – the Area Executive Committee, myself included, had been fooled and the whole membership betrayed. I think it was the point when the mass of the men decided we wouldn't find a collective industrial response to the growing problems of the industry at colliery and national level, and that they would seek individual solutions, mainly getting out. The decision to fall into line behind the Area EC decision and to urge Frickley to call off its action was the biggest mistake of my trade union life, and while my sticking out with Frickley's delegate would not have swung any votes, I certainly would have slept better at nights.

ONLY ONE ARTHUR SCARGILL

Towards the end of 1987, in view of pending legislation, on 12 November Arthur announces to the NEC that in accordance with legal advice, he was resigning as president in order to seek re-election. He had held office for 5 years and had always campaigned for the principle that the president should come up for election on five-yearly intervals.

Had there been no entrenched right-wing opponent I might well have sought nominations to stand to Arthur's left. The rank-and-file in Doncaster phoned me the whole time about it. Other Areas also had heard rumours and offered me backing. What would have come of all this is daydreaming really? I could not have won the Yorkshire nomination because Arthur's machine was too big and too entrenched. Had I followed up those other area offers and got on the ballot paper, I think I might have had a chance though of winning Yorkshire's miners' vote, if not the branch nominations. It would have been an overtly pro-strike, pro-mass-picket, militant and left political platform. It would not have been an 'anti-Scargill' platform, at least in the sense of acting as condemnation of the strike; never in a million years. I would have shouted Arthur's strengths from the rooftops as I always have, but offered new initiatives, deeper rank-and-file control, less bureaucratic shenanigans, and new determination for the sacked lads and a perspective on the growing body of contract workers. It's matterless now. The right advanced Johnny Welsh, and behind Johnny undoubtedly stood those forces of the UDM who would have expected his victory to usher them back into seats of power in the NUM. A victory for Johnny would have meant a return to the days of abject surrender, the pre-Gormley days. In such a contest there was no real contest actually for any class-conscious mining militant; the campaign to re-elect Arthur was a campaign for a vote of confidence in our stand and an endorsement of the strike.

WORKERS' CONTROL

1988 – the year is scarcely open, indeed only 6 days old, when a line in the sand is drawn at Bentley pit. Despite all the grovelling terms of the NPLA to accept deployment and manning organised by the boss, to accept interchangeability and to get rid of all restrictive practices; despite the fact that this had been sealed and signed back in the early 1960s, many areas and pits had ignored the provisions and held on to wide areas of ancient job controls. In the Durham and Northumberland coalfield 'cavilling' still prevailed. In the Doncaster coalfield the pit operated 'priority systems'. These ensured the constant break-up and reassembly of teams, and jobs, markets and regular men. It ensured the Union had control of manning and who went where, and that there should be no blue-eyed boys or blue-eyed teams given the best pickings of headings and faces.

Since the days of the private owners, these systems ensured all face-trained men would be given an equal chance to earn a good living and not end up with the dirty end of the stick time and again (except by chance, anyway). Separate lists of cutters, colliers and rippers ensured that the men of these skills kept to these tasks first. The men running spare and surplus to requirements this time round would be the full-time team members next time round. No manager had the right to move anyone or hold anyone off. Over the ensuing years, the priority systems in their 'pure' forms had eroded at some pits. At Rossington, for example, the management reserved the right to vet the face team lists and object to a limited number of men.

This issue had never been fully settled at Rossington when the strike broke out at Bentley. At Bentley, the heart of the priority system had gone some 10 years previously when the pit was on the verge of closure. Since that time faces and headings had been manned on the basis of 'consensus'. Meantime, the pit had, through a failure of forward planning, found itself with the lack of face room. All eyes had suddenly fell on B42s, a forgotten drivage which had been left to its own devices, plodding along for years in atrocious conditions with a battered in machine going through a 1-in-6 drift through solid rock. The men working in these conditions, long since fed up with fruitless complaints, had plodded along, earning 65% of the anyway pathetic pit bonus. Management in earlier reviews had agreed that the combination of geology and the lack of funding for re-equipment had blighted the heading.

As the drift neared the end of its gradient and the level became more even, good news arrived in the shape of a brand-new Mindev state-of-the-art roadheader. It was the first chance in 5 years for the men to earn some money and get stuck in with some prospects of making progress. The management, in the normal eternal wisdom of such positions, decides then to take 'the red shift'[272] off the job and disperse them through the pit. Their long-suffered heading, now shaping up to be a plum job, would be given to a hand-picked team selected on the whim of the manager. Despite this, that hand-picked team refused to take the places of the existing team and the old team refused to be dispensed with. The issue went through the first stage and then the second stage of the conciliation machinery, when the men decided: 'Sod it – we've talked enough!' The pit struck and after 2 days dispatched pickets to all the Doncaster pits, which stood to a man. The following day Bentley pickets swept across into the old South Yorkshire

Area and halted every pit. A hasty South Yorkshire Panel meeting was convened and despite the SWP paper-sellers prophesying betrayal by massive majority, we agreed to stand with the Bentley men. My old pal Ted Houghton, the Area NCB director, came on TV to berate the Doncaster miners as 'lemmings' but also, in mixed metaphor, as a kind of virus which was contaminating the rest of South Yorkshire. Worse still, the now very much enlarged flying pickets, joined by men from the halted pits, now flooded into North Yorkshire to halt the giant Kellingley Colliery, the biggest pit in Europe, and then on into the jewel in the crown of the NCB – the Selby Complex. Solidarity action was total, even in the usually moderate North Yorkshire coalfield. Haslam, the national director of the NCB, was furious and promised a final settlement of accounts with the Doncaster coalfield.

Ted Houghton, probably the nicest, most genuine area director of the NCB and considered a liberal outsider among the new management regime, was now forced to act. With his own version of the 'director's cut' he tells us all in an internal newsletter we will no longer be developing the sleeping giant which is Thorne Colliery. Ted, the director, had taken a special interest in Thorne and had put his weight behind its development. He had been prepared to compromise on the flexible shift requirement imposed on all other developments, so long as we demonstrated our commitment to turning enough yardages to develop it, and enough coal to pay for its modern infrastructure. Our spate of South Yorkshire and mainly Doncaster wildcats had put paid to that. That pit would now be mothballed. He put it all down to our coalfield stoppages, the lack of an agreement on working and the ongoing overtime ban.

It is deeply disappointing. Ted tells me, in his straight-from-the-shoulder style, that with current relations at rock bottom we are struggling to keep the collieries we've got; MacGregor could see no justification for the entire Doncaster coalfield. We had pointed to the vast reserves of coal in the Doncaster take and beyond, and MacGregor had responded: 'Well, gee, they've got gold in the Scottish mountains but only a fool would try and mine it.'

All eyes are focused on a settlement at Bentley, which is reached between Area negotiators from the Union and the Board at the Disputes level of the procedure. The pit returns to work well satisfied, having given the Board a bloody nose. I was immensely proud of the Hatfield men, who voted in favour of my resolution to stand the pit until Bentley returns and no sooner. We refused to commence work until Bentley's first shift was back at work.

At that stage the dispute is over; it has been a victory for the militants. It is bad medicine for the camp of Johnny Walsh, the North Yorkshire Area Agent, candidate of the moderates and right wing of the Union, seeking election on 21 December. Someone in the offices of the NCB in London decides it can't be left like that. They send out warning letters to all those who took part in sympathetic action, and all those who took part in secondary picketing, telling us all they will not hesitate in dismissing all who were involved. They had had a mysterious photographer who rode with the pickets to Hatfield and Kellingley and identified pickets; with telephotography each of the pickets received final written warnings that any future conduct of this sort would result in instant dismissal. The photographer turned out to be a freelance mercenary hired and on call to the Board. It was a lesson I didn't forget. In future, all our pickets would be masked and camouflaged; and all flying pickets would be accompanied by a camera spotter and dismantler.

February 1988. South of Scotland Electricity Board without warning announces that it would take no more deep-mined coal from Scotland and instead would use exclusively imported coal. British Coal then sought and obtained an injunction compelling the SSEB to keep to its agreement of using Scottish coal in its named Cockenzie and Longannet power stations. The SSEB responded by burning imported coal at its Kincardine power station instead.[273] This was a prelude to privatisation of the electricity supply industry nationwide. We were forewarned as to which way the sell-off would go, and to the fact that British coal and British miners would no longer be given special status in fuel supply to the energy producers; also that a widespread turn away from coal from any source was on the cards as privateers looked for 'get-rich-quick' schemes.

LETTER OF THE LAW

The South Yorkshire Area of British Coal decides to make the wearing of protective glasses a condition of employment. It was 'tekin a mell tiv a wallnut' somewhat, for although eye injuries from dust and stone and splitters of all sorts were a problem, wearing glasses all the time wasn't really practical on many jobs. The men, in usual fashion, showed their disapproval. I was with Jeff Ainley, acting manager at the time, as we went below ground on an inspection on the first day of the total obligation to wear glasses. At bank the banksman greets us with a pair of children's kaleidoscope swirly coloured glasses. The loco driver has a pair of those eyes on springs hanging out of his specs and all conceivable forms of comic glasses including mirror sunglasses and pantomime masks are everywhere in evidence. I can't stop laughing and even Jeff has to smile. Further inbye we see the serious side of the protest. An FSV driver with his goggles totally covered in diesel spray caked in thick mud attempts to drive his vehicle down the gate. I ask him how much he can see. 'Not a bat,' he replies nonchalantly, but 'they' (lifting his elbow toward the manager) 'will send yi oot if yev not got them on.' I suggest sets of spares, or something like 'wet ones' to be carried to clean the damn things.

ROCK AGAINST THE RICH – JOE STRUMMER AND CLASS WAR ON TOUR

July. We link the miners and the sacked men into Class War's 'Rock Against the Rich' tour by Joe Strummer and the Latino Rockabilly Band. We hold it at the Brodsworth Miners Welfare, all funds to the victimised miners. I give Joe a Hatfield miners' badge, with which he is chuffed to wee bits. The concert was mobbed with punks and heavies, many of them young miners and more than a few of my key pickets. Outside is an extreme anarcho punk crowd from Crowmen. They are heckling the band and the punters as 'Rich scum bags' and 'Sell outs'. I think they thought the fact that people were wearing shoes and that Strummer had made few quid marked them all out as traitors to real hardcore anarcho punk. They came sauntering up the aisle with their Mohicans and dangling chains and big boots with no laces.

'Where ye gaan?'

'We're going to boycott the concert.'

I explained that if they wished to 'boycott the concert' inside they would have to pay, otherwise they could 'boycott' it outside for free.

'These are sellout scumbags and fakes and rich fuckers!' they screamed.

'OK, maybe, but this concert is for the sacked miners and I don't care if its Cliff Richard on stage, you pay to come in!'

Next thing I know BOOM! one of them does a flying head but into my face and my lip explodes in blood and skin.

'Ye fuckin bastard!' I shout, and catch him a glancing blow as he dives away. I grab him in a head lock and he falls on the floor with a crash. Other lads come diving in to drag the Crowman up and his mates down the corridor.

Suddenly, from being pains up the arse and universally hated, they become an oppressed minority. This SWP bloke shouts 'Let them go – they're entitled to a point of view!'

'Point of view!' I scream, my face a mass of blood and a big titty lip swelling up in the corner of my mouth, 'He just nutted me!'

Not deterred, the SWPer goes outside to debate the question and ends up with the Mohican and his mate occupying his car and refusing to get out until the 'State Cap' had driven them back to town, which under protest he did, but then they wouldn't get out until he had also given them £5 each 'to get home'. The SWPer was clearly a rich scumbag too. When he arrived back late and cursing, I asked him: 'What about the bloke's point of view?' 'Fucking twat!' he responded; but it was too painful to laugh.

I had told Spot he would get in free if he did me the stage security. Ten minutes before the start of the show, beaming and laughing and bumping along the corridor, dead drunk, swagger Spot and his bikers.

'Bliddy hell, Spot!'

'Why, what tha want me ti dey like?'

'You were supposed to be guarding the stage!'

'That's OK, Dave,' he says, rushing off to the front and shouting 'Ah'l make sure no bugger steals it.'

Later, as punks are trying to climb onto the stage, Spot is having a whale of time, dragging them off and trying to clamber up himself in a kind of King-of-the-Castle game, and amid the pogoing, bouncing, bumping car dance of the punks, Spot's body is seen leaping up and down and demolishing the hysterical crowd at the front like some kind of doped-up Masai warrior.

SELLING OUR LABOUR POWER BY OTHER MEANS?

By 1988, most men over 50 with the maximum service had gone out redundant; they had financial packages worth up to £40,000, in some cases more. They were allowed to draw unemployment benefit without the need to look for work (the exempted mineworkers clause); they were allowed to draw their pensions early;

the ones over 55 were guaranteed concessionary fuel for life. Ironically, without the strike against closures and redundancies, they would have had none of this. Most of these men retired on terms, and at ages, they could never have dreamed of before our action. Men retiring at the normal 60 and 65 tended to have few years left and little money before sudden death. We had forced the Board and government to deliver up improved terms in order to get the closures and job losses through. Though this wasn't our aim, it wasn't a bad result.

We had insisted on drawing up criteria for redundancy to stop a clamber into the lifeboats which would have sunk every pit in the country. First came all men over 50 according to length of service. Next were long-term sick, or those in danger of dying or never working again. This had always proved controversial, as many men patiently standing in the queue to get out felt others were dodging to jump the queue. (Mind, it was occasionally remarkable the recoveries men made once they got the money in their hands; the effect the lump sum had on men who were drawing their last breaths one week and rocking and rolling at the pit club the next.) The effect of controlling the exit was, overall, to strengthen the core membership: the average age was now down to around 32, an age when men would wish to keep their jobs and not sell them.

TIME TO GO

On a national level, there came an 'anti-Scargill' backlash. Its was joined by those who, although not anti-Arthur, thought it was time for him to go, and let us draw up new plans and new perspectives for the post-strike period. As I said, I even had a sudden rush of enquiries from a number of pits and coalfields as to whether I, as a credible left alternative, would stand in Arthur's place, against him if necessary. As could have been predicted, Arthur was faced instead by his right-wing and moderate nemesis Johnny Walsh, the North Yorkshire Area agent. There would be no chance of me opposing Arthur from the left with a potentially successful candidate from the right. Hatfield was evenly split, with some of the men furious I wouldn't oppose Arthur. Worse, a TV crew decided to use Hatfield as the weather gauge for the election. It was a bit embarrassing: Hatfield was well known as a militant pit, yet here were men, pickets, militants, calling for Arthur to step down or be replaced. Onto this programme came Pat Bennet, a most remarkable, comical, dedicated miner and Union man with a heart of gold. Unfortunately his tongue had a habit of starting before his brain was in gear. 'I love Arthur,' he started, 'I've got pictures of Arthur Scargill on my wall ... but I am not going to vote for him.' I think every miner in Yorkshire watched that programme and boy did I get some stick over it. Hatfield pit bottom had, in huge whitewashed letters, the slogan 'Pat Loves Arthur ... BUT'. Worse, at the pre-Conference Yorkshire AGM, I had risen to speak in support of Hatfield's motion to the National Conference and given it some hellfire and brimstone. The room fell silent. Then Howard Wadsworth, Kellingley branch delegate and court comedian, rose with a twinkle in his eye 'You know, I like Dave Douglass, I may even have a picture of him somewhere, but I'm not going to vote for this resolution,' he said to cheers and laughter. There were to be many varieties of this over the coming months.

14 August 1988. Sammy Thompson, a comrade, friend and occasional sparring partner, in whose company I had spent many interesting times, has died. It seems strange, gathering in the potatoes in the sunshine this Sunday afternoon, and experiencing a feeling that is more than something I really know, that Sam is not there anymore. The things he till so recently did are now of no concern to him. I am still here, he is off on that journey, or is off in a far-off distant place never to return again, never to see his garden or set his clock for work. God speed, Sam lad.

Sam had fought an ongoing war with cancer, but never let on. Arthur knew, of course, and quite sensibly allowed Sam to go out redundant from the position of National vice president. Once more I allowed myself to flirt with the idea of standing for the position. Northumberland indicated I was popular with their officials and could get their nomination, Leicester asked me if I wanted theirs, Cannock did too, Staffordshire said they were almost certain they could swing it behind me. Would I get enough of Yorkshire to get my own Area nomination and appear on the ballot sheet? Frank Waters, the Communist Party 'kingmaker', for an emphatic second time made it clear I was not on his selection list, although oddly some moderate and 'right-wing' branches in North Yorkshire looked like – really out of friendship and respect – coming up with nominations.

It wasn't to happen, because Arthur declared the position no longer existed. In heated rows, he informed us that positions are made redundant, not men. Of course, allowing Sammy to go redundant wasn't in question here; Arthur had in our view used this tragic situation to start pulling up the ladder behind him and narrowing down the top table. The whole of the Area Executive Committee was against the abolition of the position. The situation was made worse then by the decision by Jack Taylor and Ken Homer to appoint Ken to the position of general secretary of the Yorkshire Area, Sam's Area position, without reference to the members, the Council or the Executive Committee. It hadn't even been cleared on a branch vote. Democracy and rank-and-file control were being washed down the plughole without a second glance.

The arguments raged. Our demand for democratic control produced an even worse and at the time scurrilous backlash from the bureaucracy. When we published in the Hatfield branch newsletter, in full, the arguments behind the bad blood between the branches and Arthur, someone (I have no definite proof who, but suspicions are rife) then went to Sammy's family and told them I was kicking up a fuss about him having gone out redundant. The family was incensed. Sammy's wife, with whom I had always been best of friends, stopped talking to me, and his brother came out round the pubs I visited in Doncaster looking to knock my block off.

It was a scandalous lie, of course; I couldn't believe that some erstwhile mutual comrade was, especially at this sensitive period of time following Sammy's death, using our opposition to the arbitrary decision to change the rule book and the constitution as a source of personal complaint about a dead comrade's conduct. I wrote a long and sincere letter of explanation to the family and apologised for any misunderstanding, but I also made the point that this matter was being exploited by someone for their own political ends. In the end, the Doncaster Area agent, Frank Cave, and the Armthorpe Branch delegate, Alan Bailey had to go to the family and explain the real situation and my motives for raising it.

By the following Durham Miners' Gala, Sam's widow, along with Ann (Scargill) was talking to me again, so I assumed the matter had been set straight. But what a totally unprincipled and mean trick; to try and muster someone's personal grief and sense of injustice against a political opponent in such a heartless and cynical manner.

THE SPIRIT IS WILLING – THE FLESH IS WEAK

November 1988. The Union calls a Special Delegate Conference to decide on forms of industrial action to force the NCB to negotiate wages and other matters with the Union. It was a soul-searching Conference, with delegates telling it just as it was, and not how we they wished it to be. Following the stupid NEC response to the industrial action ballot on the disciplinary code, few had any confidence in them anymore. An all-out national strike wasn't on the cards, but the members didn't trust overtime bans following the last fiasco. Nonetheless, something had to be done to force the employers to meet the Union. Subsequently, it was agreed to ballot the members for authority to call a full overtime ban with minimum safety cover. The record shows I attended the Conference but didn't speak, a clear sign that I didn't think the resolution was achievable and therefore had little enthusiasm for it. That wouldn't prevent me canvassing like mad back at the pit to have it accepted.

Despite this, by the end of 1988, miners were still 30 times more likely to strike than any other British worker in any other industry. This leopard hadn't changed any spots, and somewhere in Whitehall a more radical 'final solution' was being found to this mining problem. In the wider industrial arena, Tory anti-union legislation followed closely the actions of the miners from '83 onwards. For every law we broke in '84 they drafted in new penalties to stop defiance. For every loophole we discovered they blocked the gaps. For every manoeuvre we found they brought in counter-legislation to stop it. Increasingly draconian actions were adopted against unofficial strikes, while at the same time rendering formal official strike action more and more difficult. Previous legislation had demanded that if any employer wished to take action against strikers he had to punish them all or none at all. Now he could selectively dismiss; and that didn't mean, as one would think, the militant being given his cards; no, mild and moderate workers obeying a strike decision could be sacked, in a parallel with wartime killings or punishment shootings to discipline the militant by sacking the innocent. Industrial action could now be sanctioned only by postal ballots.

Whereas previously we would host mass pithead, canteen or welfare meetings which were packed to the rafters and everyone could get up and speak their piece and argue the toss before voting together to take action together or not, now it was the individual in the private and isolation of his/her own home, inevitably with the influence of the TV and the newspaper. The vote is in private, no one else can see what you have decided or why. Vital issues, sometimes highly complex and requiring explanation, reports, discussions and clarification, are undermined by the private postal ballot. The mass solidarity of the show of hands, and the common resolve of all, are neutralised. The same will be true of Union elections at area and national level, campaigns will still take place, debates can still take place, but the private vote at home is aimed at breaking the election from its very context. To both these forms of 'democracy', greatly weakened responses and participation are the result. 'Giving the unions back to the members,' Thatcher had said in a doublespeak for actually taking the unions from the members. All of our previous alternatives to strikes – work-to-rules, ca'cannys, sick days, acting the goat – are now themselves deemed 'industrial actions', and disciplinary measures can be taken against them. Absenteeism comes as ruthlessly under scrutiny as wildcat action, and equally ruthless is the disciplinary action in response. A concerted effort is made to undermine the standing of the branch at the colliery. First, the workforce is now seen as independent from 'the union'; this is a new and huge departure from all previous practice. The workers themselves will be consulted, 'leaders' will be selected by management for consultation meetings. Team meetings will be called without us, and serious attempts made to negotiate contracts and schemes direct with the workforce and without union involvement or restriction.

1988/89. Ted Houghton, quite the most reasonable and honest Area Director of the NCB, announces '88/89 profits and productivity up and accidents down. With an operating profit of £70 million and a further £8m from 'other operations', and with an all-time-low operating cost of £1.40 a gigajoule (GJ), South Yorkshire was producing the country's cheapest coal. Hatfield had made record profits and Goldthorpe was producing coal at 82p a GJ, the cheapest coal in Britain. Ted was a man I could do business with, a man I could sit down and talk to as well as negotiate. At this time I was still confident that we all had a future and our living standards and conditions could still improve.[274] Noteworthy was the fact that average incentive earnings were up by 36% on the previous year, and three-quarters of the pits were now operating local colliery versions of the scheme, taking the incentive earnings to workers outbye and on backup and supply.[275] Arthur and the National leadership hated these schemes. We, myself included, felt obliged to intervene and take control of them, negotiate them, keep them under the province of the NUM and not have them handed out from some gaffer's bottom drawer to the blue-eyed boys. They were certainly putting more money into pockets as well as increasing the standing and relevance of the Union, albeit at Branch level. Management didn't by any stretch of the imagination get all their own way; the modern 'butty' contracts and schemes aimed at displacing nationally agreed wage rates were kicked into touch almost everywhere. At Hatfield we fought hard to repel all boarders: the backdoor, sealed-envelope schemes the management were pushing at the men to get them to abandon union control.

By the time of the NUM annual report of 1989, we were reporting that some 154 miners remained sacked and out of work as a result of actions during the

1984 strike; we had started off with 579 at the close of the strike. Areas had whittled away, trading this or that concession to management to get as many men as possible reinstated. Some directors were fiercer than others and refused to budge. Many of the lads at length gave up trying to get back to the pit and found new careers with their heads held high.

ENTER DAVID GARDINER

At each pit new challenges were taking place, new moves set by some distant higher body aimed at breaking up 'cosy' industrial relations – in-house community-based management by men from the village or coalfield who now sat in the manager's chair with their feet still in the miners welfare and their relatives still in the miners lodge. Hatfield can be taken as a microcosm of this.

In this month David Gardiner, a somewhat fanatical manager from Derbyshire, (although a fiery Scot by birth and education), starts a whole series of initiatives to break the Hatfield workforce, particularly the face men, from the authority and control of the Union. The priority system is anathema to him; the fact that he cannot deploy face men where he wants, or man up headings as he wants, drives him crazy. The fact that he can't say who works overtime and how many men are required to meet a task is something totally alien to him. His attempts at plucking men's names out of the hat and offering gold pigs to others invariably has the pit on strike, officially and unofficially, from now on in.

We had got off to a flying start. Mr Gardiner, after all, apart from being a Scot with whom we Geordies are blood brothers, was a fellow graduate of Strathclyde, with many forward-thinking plans, many of which I had cooperated with at once and fought to bring the branch with me. However, the last straw for us was our sacred priority system – without that the pit could stand forever. Still, in between periods of war there are periods of peace when Gardiner had his collar felt by Mr Houghton, the Area director who you could reason with and never lose your temper. He was, in the words of the aud colliers, 'a gentleman', although there are few other such directors of the NCB; perhaps in the pre-strike generation like Mr Tuke but few since if any.

THE PIT WIT CONTINUES

In the Union office I was now growing a number of tomato plants. One in particular, in the outer office, was basking in the full beams of sunlight shining in the window. It had been a particularly boisterous and crowded office prior to the afternoon shift, with men in shouting the odds about this and that, telling the tale, sharing tabs. The Union had rarely been so well sorted, and the current batch of officials were generally well regarded. After the rush, I took the order for teas and set off to the canteen, noticing how bright the outer office was. Too bright: my plant that had been happily installed in a big plastic bucket by the window was gone. In its place was a note:

> We have the plant and unless you pay the ransom (which will be told to you by phone) by twelve p.m. Monday the plant dies!! We hope you will cooperate. We don't like to kill the innocent … signed Nabih Berri.

'The bastards!' I screamed, 'What? Who? What they done now?' – they all ran from the office thinking the management had come up with a new imposition 'Me bliddy tomata plant, they've stolen me tomata plant!' Well half an hour later comes a phone call from down pit. In a fake Arab voice, the demand is made: 'Three pints in the Abbey tonight or the plant gets it.' In the background someone is making the tiny voice of a frightened plant: 'Don't let them kill me Dave, give them what they want!' 'You bastards!' I start and the phone goes dead. I am jumping up and down. That plant is covered in tiny tomatoes, they are just ready to be fed and nurtured, they'll be all bent and bedraggled, and where are they? The phone rings again. This time the voice says, 'Thees time you will not blaspheme and curse or we don't negotiate.' 'OK, OK,' I agree. The phone goes dead. About 20 minutes later, the onsetter rings the office: 'Dave, is this your bloody plant doon here?' It's doon the pit?' 'Whey aye, think I recognise a tomato plant when I see one, and you don't usually get many of them queuing up to ride the pit, not on this shift anyway,' he explains. 'OK,' I say, 'Just stick it on the cage and send it up and I'll get it from the shaft side.' 'Can't do that Dave, I've got material raps, and coal raps and men raps, I haven't got tomato raps.' 'Just rap manriders and rap it off!' I scream. 'It's not a manrider.' 'Bliddy hell!' At length another call tells me to look behind the bike sheds, and there still beaming in all her glory was me plant. That night I strolled along in mystery to pay the ransom and discover who the hijacker was. I was standing at the bar when in walks Elmo, an ace electrician and picket veteran of most of our campaigns, a pillocker of the finest order. We laugh our bollocks off and drink the ransom. The plant went on to give fruit to masses of tomatoes despite its ordeal.

MUTINY

A complex set of uneven responses and mishmashed perspectives prevailed among the areas and their leaderships. We were all in a struggle to survive, in a battle to preserve our pits and jobs and standing as a union among our members. The Board was weighing down and weighing in with different degrees of hard cop and soft cop, investment and non-investment. Proposals and plans for the future engaged the areas, but not any overall national plan. The National officials were cold-shouldered out of any negotiations and any involvement. Arthur and Peter watched from the National Offices and saw local and area agreements being brokered, in their eyes seen proposals for 'flexibility' as surrender of sacred principle. We rarely came up to Arthur's expectations; he felt we had abandoned him and the ground we stood on. We, on the other hand, felt the ballot result we had given them had opened the way for out-and-out resistance and a regeneration of struggle, but it had been 'pissed up the wall', or as Bathurst would have said, 'up our backs'.

Much of this was to break into bitter hostility at the November 1989 Conference. The National leadership was calling for industrial action in support of wages, and, second, against the move toward flexible holidays as against set annual holidays. Yorkshire had decided to oppose both actions. Arthur and Peter would be proposing the respective resolutions; the Area decided that myself and Ken Homer, the Area general secretary, would oppose them.

Ken decided that he would take the wages one, and I should take the flexible holiday one. I was stunned rigid when the platform announced that Peter would propose the wages resolution and Arthur would propose the flexible holiday action. 'I didn't know, mate, honest!' Ken assured me. It couldn't be helped. This was to be a clash about a lot of things really; conference was quite happy for me to take up the cudgels for a number of reasons. First, there was no way on earth I could be described as a moderate or a right-winger; neither could it be said I had any record of being 'anti-Scargill'. I had covered his flank on numerous occasions in the media and before mass assemblies of the miners, defending him from spurious attack, breaking concerted middle-rank union officials' attempts to isolate him or keep him out of the coalfield. I mentioned earlier that in 1985, when the Area officials refused to invite Arthur onto the platform even as a guest or to march with the lead of the Yorkshire Miners' Gala procession, Hatfield invited him to march with us. He had addressed a public meeting called by the Branch in a pub near the field; this was a de facto rival platform. When the Area was holding policy meetings, we invited Arthur to public meetings called by the Branch to address the whole Area over the heads of the Area leaders. We knew who was doing what, we knew there were moves to get rid of or undermine Arthur, we would ensure this didn't happen.

But there were differences now, differences to do with proximity of struggle, perceptions of how we moved forward, more particularly what was the ground we conceded and what ground did we dig in to and defend to the last. We thought we knew the strengths and weaknesses of the men, we knew what they liked in the proposed changes in working, and we knew what they would battle to the end for.

It was like two blind men examining an elephant from opposite ends: we would draw radically different truths from the same object. To Arthur, we were conceding when we ought to oppose every change, we were being flexible when we ought to be rigid. To us, Arthur now only had one answer to every question – 'strike'; not only that, but he sincerely believed the members at large were always in favour of a strike on each and every issue; it was only us, the Branch and Area Officials, who no longer had faith. We were coming to this conference 'with excuses' as to why we shouldn't fight and he would say just that from the platform. To us on the sharp end – frequently in action, ducking, diving and regularly taking it on the nose too, in our individual working and financial circumstances – we were stung by Arthur's frequent cry that we should 'Stop making excuses' and 'Get off your knees.' The verbatim report of that conference [276] is illustrative of these deep currents and tensions.

It would be far too self-indulgent to record all my speech that day, except to say in all modesty it was a powerful contribution. I came to the platform at boiling point:

> The first thing I want to say Mr Chairman is I don't come to this platform
> with any excuses. I come with mandates, and the mandates we bring to
> conference are the mandates the membership has given us, and if you do

your job right, go in the canteen, get men to come to meetings and hear the views of the members you come here with a mandate. My mandate is no less a mandate today for no action than it was in 1984 when the mandate was for action … I am here to represent the membership and the views of the membership whether I have individual views opposing them or not. So I resent any implication that we do anything other than respond to the true feelings of the members. ….. about the flexible holiday question … there is little resistance to it. Because we believe that the perspective for resistance was flawed in itself. But also because there was little account taken of the actual state of play and the balance of forces and bargaining position. I am afraid that if a person has in his back pocket the SWP's book of strategy he will not find it a very thick book. It will probably only have one word in it: 'Charge'. Well that strategy is not very good, particularly if you're standing at the edge of a cliff … Strategy does not mean one thing all the time. What was right yesterday doesn't mean it is right today. The clock does not always say 12. Although even a stopped clock is right twice in a day … A boxer does not always go forward. Sometimes he has to go back, and sometimes he goes down as well.

The other part about the flaw in the situation was 'The Traditional Holiday'. I listened with tears in my eyes, and I read in *The Miner*, of this traditional miner's holiday down at Cleethorpes with a bucket and spade … I tell you what. I would have loved to be able to do that at traditional holiday times, but in their wisdom, my colliery always took holidays outside the school holidays. Those were the holidays they picked. If I wanted a holiday with my kid I used to have work the holidays in order to go somewhere else, because as a matter of fact fixed holidays are not necessarily in the school holiday period.

I would like to come back to the thing about Rhyl … Has anybody been to Rhyl for a fortnight? Do you know how much it costs? I can have a holiday in Turkey for a fortnight and a holiday in Greece for less money than going to Rhyl for a week. Somebody ought to get the travel brochures out for you, because I can tell you the men are looking at a situation where they can go away in September for a fortnight in Greece and lie down on a beautiful island somewhere for £130 apiece. If the same man wants to go down to Cleethorpes or Scarborough in August and he doesn't have the fortune of being at a conference, then he is going to pay two or three times the amount of money to take himself there. So things *have* changed.

Things have changed. 41% of the men at my pit always work their holidays because it suits them to do that. I am one of those for the reasons I have said. The difference is of course that we have not produced coal in that time. We had a dispute this year over that. The members have looked at the situation and they say: 'I have heard it said if it is good enough for Officials and Staff to have salaries etc. then it is good enough for us too'.[277] Well I am told officials and staff also have flexible holidays, and I know that the Board members and management also have flexible holidays and our members have looked hard at it. What they have said is that the bulk of the men say £100 and the potential of holidays when you want it, although there is no guarantee, I am not saying that. There will be categories of key men, onsetters, banksman, who knows, who will not just at the drop of a hat be able to go and get their holidays when they want. It is not anyway a matter of fact that we like flexible holidays. It is a matter of what have we got the capacity and the ability to do. It is not where we want to be but where we actually are …

We have also got another problem, by the way, and that is a hell of a lot of the members can't wait to get out of this bloody industry, and the problem we have got as Union officials is holding back the flood and trying to show that we have got some relevance to the membership and that the Union can do something. I am fed up with people saying to me 'Why can all you buggers do is take money away from us and never put anything back in our pockets?' And that, at a time when we are trying to convince people that the Union has a cause and there is still some life in the industry, is a very, very difficult task. For these reasons, there are many, many reasons why we are not able to hold the line.

I would like to say this, and I have wanted to say this for some time. The membership has been in continuous struggle in this union for the last 8 years and nobody, but nobody, has got the right to tell men 'to get off their knees' when we are in a 'backs to the wall' situation, and my men and the men in the rest of this Union have never stopped fighting since 1981. (Applause) It is not a lack of the wish to fight. It is not the lack of the will to fight. The men have not changed their mettle. It is a question of the ability to fight and the right time to fight and the members have given us our marching orders that this is not the time to take on this particular question.

I want to say in conclusion, I don't know if anyone seen that film *The Alamo*? It was one of my favourites. You know when Davy Crockett was on that last wall and the Mexicans knocked the wall down and the lads inside pulled the cannon away so they could take up a second position? Davy Crockett didn't stand on the wall and say 'Come back cowards, get up and fight!' He didn't shout at Bowie, lying down with his legs broken, 'Get on your feet and fight'… (and nobody can argue with me about his film because I've seen it ten times) (Laughter) You had to take account of the situation as to what lines were falling and where you had to form new lines. I am afraid that it is an irrefutable fact that the Union is in its present weakened state and Thatcher is still triumphant, we are not able to hold on to all the lofty heights and hills that we set ourselves as targets since the Union was started. It is a simple matter of fact we will have to retreat from some of the positions that we would dearly love to hold but are not able to hold, because … the price of not letting go of some positions is to lose all positions. The price of not cutting your cloth according to your width is that we could lose the entire Union, and that Union is far more important than any other thing at this precise moment.

I have heard Socialist defined as many strange things and many people define themselves as Socialists in many strange ways, but I have never in my life heard a Socialist described as a person who believes in the last week in July and first week in August. That has nothing to do with the definition of Socialism. When you take your holidays is a tactical question. Whether you are a Socialist is a principle question, and you can't be a Socialist in this Union without you see fundamentally the defence of this Union.

In conclusion, Mr Chairman, this is not where we would like to be, it is not where we think we should be, but it is most definitely, where we are, and in these circumstances Yorkshire must oppose action on the question of flexible holidays at this period until such time as we can consolidate the Union as a whole. (Applause).[278]

Well any notion that Arthur would see the humour in my simile was soon cast aside in his withering response to Conference, and in particular

Of course that brings me on to the third point made by Davie Douglass Crockett. I am no brilliant student of American history but I tell you one thing, I know a little bit about Davie Crockett and Jim Bowie. I know a little about Wounded Knee. I feel as though I am down on one knee after your contribution. I tell you where I'd rather take my inspiration from, David. I would rather take my inspiration from people like the Vietnamese who fought against American Imperialism rather than the Davie Crocketts who were a bunch of gangsters trying to pinch someone's else's territory. That is the Socialist approach and I hope you don't use it in speeches again. (Applause)

Despite the applause and a reassertion that it was us, the delegates and officials, who determined the will to fight among the members, Conference overwhelmingly rejected both proposals for strike action.[279]

A THOUSAND WAYS TO DIE

In July came another fatal accident in the Yorkshire pits. This one was memorable because it has never left my nightmares. Mr Mick Shaw, a 38-year-old fitter, actually a surface fitter who, following a request that day, had gone underground at Wistow, died after going through a coal crusher, unable to get off a conveyor belt on which he was illegally riding. He never came home to his wife and three children again. Illegally riding everything down the pit was always taking your life in your hands. Men rode on empty material vehicles at high speeds behind locos, or clinging to the loco itself. In Durham we had ridden on ponies and haulage ropes, at Rossington men rode on the moving face conveyor blades. Riding the belts was everywhere common. This belt however fed into a crushing drum. He had been riding back out of the mine with his mate, unaware that a mistake on this belt would be fatal. Seeing the approach of the end of the belt his mate had dived off, but Michael, clearly aware now of the danger, was unable to crawl back or get off despite the fact that his mate had yanked on the stop wires and the belt was slowing. After going through the crusher, fully conscious, he actually spoke to his mate who had rushed to help him: 'I'm dead, Brut, I've gone through the crusher.' He died minutes later.

The Union's safety engineer Charlie Brabbins reported:

The first thing I have to say is that ever since crushers were first introduced underground, men up and down the country have been fatally injured due to passing through them, and that it is the type of accident no-one survives. All Mining Engineers know this.

There used to be a reluctance to utilise crushers, but their use has increased over recent years in order to promote and maintain the smooth and uninterrupted flow of huge outputs of coal along networks of belts and out to the Coal Preparation Plants ... but the crusher has shown itself to be lethal.[280]

Hatfield at this period is war-torn. Industrial relations have come to the level of physical confrontations; Pat Bennet, a member of the committee, offering Mr Hurst, an undermanager, 'out', and Hurst jumping up and shouting 'Top of the pit lane now!' Heated meetings between the manager and Union officials saw Ainley wang his phone through the window in temper, and the fiery Branch secretary pick up his teacup and shout 'We can all fling things about, mister' and wang his cup through the pane next to it, as secretaries ran for cover. David Gardiner had previously had a similar run-in with Tommy McGee, whose younger brother Steve is our most dynamic post-strike Branch secretary). Tommy, on suffering an accident underground, had been directed to light work operating a 'tap' stopping and starting a conveyor belt. David hated seeing men standing about as he put it, even when that was what they had to do. 'Here,' he says to Tommy and hands him a shovel, 'You can clean up spillage while you're standing there.' Tommy grabs the shovel and flings it yards up the gate. 'And you can fucking follow it,' suggests Tommy. As the authoritarian weight came on, our wild and anarchic cadre came into sharp conflict with the management's front line. Tony Larner had stuck fast to the basic ripper's principles on supervision – he wouldn't accept it. Like me and Jim in the heyday of miners' freedom and job control, he refused to work when any officials were within eyesight of his rip.

Tony's eyes would flash like a tiger's in a rage as he would forcibly tell any unfortunate undermanager to 'Get fucked off! We've got work to do!' Things came to a head with the appointment of George Edson as undermanager, a man used to taking hands-on control and snap decisions. He was rapidly nicknamed 'bungalow' (since he had nowt upstairs), because of his often furious and instant (wrong) assessment of situations and blame. Tony had challenged Edson's decision to end early ride water notes for men working in wet conditions. Tony rode out of the mine anyway and presented himself soaked to the skin in George's office, lighting a tab from his locker on the way. Edson would have none of it and, in the process of a furious row, shouted that Tony should stub that fucking cig out, which he did – in Edson's face!

I was at home when the van came for me to represent Tony at a serious disciplinary meeting with the manager. Telling Tony to behave hissell and bite on the authoritarian bullet at least for the course of the meeting, I tried to conduct what defence I could.

'He', cried George, 'has been ridiculing me since I came here!'

'How?' I ask.

'I wear my stockings on the outside of my overalls tied with string. He follows me round wearing his the same way,' he moaned.

'But George, he respects you, he's just trying to emulate you,' I suggested.

'And then he stuck his cig in my face.'

Tony stands up and leans over. 'Where?' he asks.

'Here,' he says, pointing at a slight red mark on his cheek.

At this Tony grabs the piece of cheek with his finger and thumb and nips his face like you would a naughty child. 'There's nowt there,' he suggests.

'Look, look, he'd doing it again!' screams George.

'Gi' ower George man, it's just a bit o' pillock,' I defended.[281]

'I don't even fucking smoke,' Tony had insisted.

Another instance, which sticks in my mind, was the attempt to stop men on the night shift parking in the management car park. They started chaining up the gates and padlocking them. A forgetful senior night shift overman, having forgotten to do this until too late, when vehicles were already parked in there, decided to lock it up and them in anyway. Big mistake really – one of the vehicles was an old Land Rover belonging to a fitter. When he came out of the pit early next morning, he simply wrapped a chain to the vehicle's winch, round the gates and wall, and pulled the lot down, leaving a convoy of cars to follow him through the now gaping hole. The car park was truly open after that time.

Gardiner, my Glaswegian fellow graduate of Strathclyde, though amusing when things went his way, was a demon when in a temper, which was frequently. Relations round the pit were at explosion point when the Area at the end of 1988 introduced Cooper & Lybrand's to do a human relations and communication study and to teach us all how to react to each other constructively. I later set about penning an assessment of their study and course of treatment. I titled it 'The Babes in the Wood Meet the Bull in the China Shop: Cooper & Lybrand Meet the Hatfield Miners'. The surly, unshaven heading teams assembled, boozy and bleary-eyed, in the canteen are confronted by a bright young wee Scottish girl in a power suit before her flip chart, asking 'And who are we taking to the party today, boys?' Dull silence stares in utter confusion: 'What the fuck are the bastards tryin to pull now?' And Dave Bathurst, the iconoclast of all things sacred, a kind of twisted intellectual whose talent is piss-taking, susses out their LIFO communication survey in one minute, awarding himself Franciscan-like correct answers of reasonableness and flexibility, while the management team, faithfully ticking all the boxes with their responses, identify themselves as a gang of psychopaths. Their exercise in good communication, for all the heading teams, brought forth 9 men, including us branch officials, while 25 were knocking,[282] despite the offer of double time, and a full Sunday lunch. The exercise is booked for 9 a.m. on a Sunday morning; it failed to recognise that all the lads were out boozing till the early hours, and a week's money or a whole pig on a spit wouldn't roust them out of bed.

The firm was given access to the whole workforce in a mass education day, but are not allowed to discuss actual problems at the pit, actual behaviour styles of actual undermanagers; and in the end I tell them they are vicars in a brothel. I also suggest to any of them that they stand at the bottom of the staircase to the manager's office of a morning and listen. They will then discover a miraculous enlightenment about skills and techniques at this pit. The bottom of the stairs was daily regaled by Gardiner getting into full stride, cursing and abusing his team and describing them in terms none of us on the Union side would ever use to another human being, but indicating that the undermanagers were both illegitimate and of old and solitary sexual orientation. As it went, the firm couldn't help but accumulate a whole tonne of evidence of discontent and disharmony, which they dutifully presented to the Area Director and his staff. Had he acted on it he would sacked every manager at Hatfield and opened up a whole range of negotiations with the Union to redress the outstanding issues of pay and morale. But I guess such a brief would conflict strongly with the changing perspectives of his gaffers; it wouldn't be long before he too was being shuffled off stage left as too liberal, and Cooper & Lybrand's would give way to fait accompli and regulation jackboots.[283]

Meantime the closures march on. Shireoaks, Brodsworth, Treeton, and Allerton Workshops, Woolley (Arthur Scargill's own old branch) and Royston close. Already scheduled for the following year were the closure of Barnsley Main, Dinnington and Denby Grange, with Houghton Main and the whole of the Barnsley coalfield looking bleak. By July 1991, 101 pits were gone, and with them 115,000 jobs. The steelworkers who worked through our strike and ran scab lorries through to Orgreave and Ravenscraig and elsewhere in the stupid belief that siding with Thatcher to close our industry would save theirs, found they had lost 150,000 jobs in 12 years; the rail workers who had stood with us, fell with us – 100,000 rail jobs went in the same period, and knock-on jobs in engineering, textiles, motor cars, shipyards, docks and general manufacturing were felled in similar proportion.[284] There was a little cheer with the opening of a new branch at North Selby; who would have dreamed realistically that the worst was still to come, or that North Selby and the rest of the Selby coalfield would be closed entirely within 6 years?

July 1989. The floor of the Conference saw for the first time a resolution on Ireland from Kent. It had given me the chance back in Yorkshire to try and submit a pro-Republican amendment, but this was heavily defeated. Nevertheless, I was able to win support for the Kent resolution and to speak on it. It achieved the full support of the NEC and was passed unanimously.

On the fifth anniversary of the great strike, 5 years to the day, in March 1990, the entire South Yorkshire coalfield, combining the old Doncaster and South Yorkshire coalfields, is at a complete standstill. Against a flurry of writs and injunctions, million-pound lawsuits and threats of the sack, even jail for contempt, Hatfield holds the coalfield out in defence of union recognition. All of the officials including myself are the subject to some of the first enactments of new anti-union laws. The Hatfield action comes as the third such mass coalfield strike, the first at Frickley against the disciplinary code, the second at Bentley against management interference with manning. Despite anti-union legislation and a loss of about 50% of our workforce, the spirit of resistance and combativity remain. With the Bentley pickets, pit CCTV, mercenary photographers and security men hidden behind walls and in cars photographed the pickets, who were given final written warnings. We learn that our pickets are wearing ski masks and army camouflage nets, which added a certain diviknaawhat to the ranks of Hatfield pickets in army fatigues and boiler suites. Writ after writ lands on my and the other Branch officials' doorsteps, charging us with organising the pickets, illegally stopping the pits, action without a ballot, secondary picketing and much else.[285] So we change tack. Branch officials at collieries expecting our pickets to arrive are phoned up, and told we won't be coming, the NCB is threatening to take away our houses and cars and seize our bank accounts and jail us if we deploy any more pickets, so the pickets will not be coming, but … It was a baffled Area director who receives reports of the strike spreading colliery by colliery, as men turn up for work, then go home, with NO pickets anywhere to be seen and none deployed. 'Let the phone book do the walking,' the ad had said. Local activists got up in the canteens and announced Hatfield pickets will not be coming, because of the writs 'but if they had come, I know which direction I would be going in'. It took a short piece of logic to reason that they should take the action as if we were there, and home they trudged. The ongoing writs and affidavits from NCB officials and security guards which now litter my collection of mining materials for 1990 testify to the bitterness of the dispute, and the concerted effort on their parts to jail us and bankrupt us, and us to take the thing to the wire.[286] The serving of those writs was particularly bitter, since it had to be done by hand by solicitors' agents protected by security guards waiting for us to come home, or sticking the envelope through the letter box.

At Steve McGee's house, his wife was in alone and refused to open the gate to let them in, so they forced an entry and then barged into her kitchen. Steve was a volatile man in the face of injustice, and a very handy lad at any time. Those security men got a gypsy's warning, but by that time we were looking at the edge of a chasm, and that is all that saved those two particular blokes from the hiding of their lives. The officials were being personally held responsible for the financial losses suffered by the Board. We were on the cusp of being jailed for contempt. The NUM at Area level was forced to repudiate the action or risk confiscation of the Union's funds. We were in clear breach of the law: we had held no ballot and the Branch officials, myself included, had refused to call off the action and repudiate the strike as ordered at the Old Bailey in London. Mass sackings were being prepared, without compensation, for the whole of the workforce. We felt we had made an honest stand. Amazingly – but then maybe it isn't – the tiny International Communist Party (British Section of the

International Committee of the Fourth International)[287] call us traitors and sellouts, me in particular! Not that any of them work at Hatfield or indeed any pit. None of them would face a lifetime of the blacklist, thrown out on the cobbles with no compensation of any sort, face eviction, bankruptcy and jailing. They called our decision 'a treacherous and cowardly capitulation'. Eh whey, meantime back on Earth ...[288]

The whole thing was given a grand finale at what could only be called a mass meeting of Area gaffers, the colliery management, NACODS reps, all our union officials from Area, COSA and the Area industrial relations staff. We, the Branch officials, turned up to this star chamber, unprecedented in any industrial relations proceedings hitherto, and prompted by a desire on both sides not to lose Hatfield. We each knew who we blamed: to us it was this new belligerent management – Mr Gardiner, who had come in to kick-start the pit, to generate greed; as he once admitted, 'greedy men are the best workers'. He couldn't do this with the union vetting every agreement and present at all and any meetings between management and workers. He and the deputy manager, Mr Ainley, were if anything more religiously anti-union than anybody on that side, with the possible exception of Ian MacGregor. They had a mine to run, they had objectives, the Union was an irrelevant distraction, they were the employers – who the hell were we? It had become, not to put too fine a point on it, a personal affront to their management rights.

The meeting would be a no-holds-barred, everything-on-the-table, let-it-rip, free-for-all. We, the four Branch officials, dressed in white shirts and ties and smart suit trousers, strode in like the four just men. I would open up for our side.

Boy, did I let it rip – but not without fierce and bitter interruption from local and at times Area management, with NACODS from Hatfield pitching in about the unprofessional way they had been treated by management and how all civilised accords had been tossed aside. We accused the management of a death-wish, of driving us onto the rocks for ulterior motives. The personnel manager who had carried the can for the new management culture, and had been selected because he suited the style, came in for quite a bit of flak. Ken Homer, who headed the Union side of the team, stood back in shock at the ferocity of the exchange, as did his counterparts on the Area management team.

Into the usually calm and restrained world of the body of industrial relations we came like a possession, a demonic kicking and snarling pair of spirits. They let it go on until the Area director rose to demand what we were going to do with this situation, how we were to progress. We adjourned to draw up a list of minimal demands to do with Union recognition, contracts and negotiations, but I was forced to add the demands for redundancy from our heading men 'and everybody who wishes to leave to be allowed to leave'. It was a demand which stood in complete contradiction to everything we ought to have stood for, but I was here to reflect the core demands, and, truth was, on our side we would never square this circle – we couldn't force them to stay. I had to admit, too, that by now the other Branch officials had also decided to leave, along with half the Committee. I would for some time be the sole NUM Branch official at the pit.

We cleared the log-jam, and for a time things improved. But the peace would not last – too many other agendas were unfolding, both within and outside the colliery.

THE POLL TAX: THATCHER'S WATERLOO

There is not here the space to devote an in-depth description of the anti-Poll Tax resistance movement. In a nutshell, the miner's strike of '84/85 can be seen as the embryo of that resistance in organisational terms. It was our elaborate system of support networks, community participation, and the revival of political interest on the left, from the anarchists to the local Labour Party ward, that laid the foundations upon which the resistance would be mounted. The embryonic networks were already in place, had remained throughout the printers' struggle.

The tax itself was ill-conceived, unfair and grossly unjust. Thatcher knew this, but in her class arrogance, having just smashed her way through the miners' resistance and broken the printers, having fought wars and put her tyrannical stamp on all branches of government and the state, she felt invincible.

When the resistance was at its peak, there was massive and widespread local and individual resistance, with millions upon millions of ordinary folk making a stand not to pay the tax. Everyone could be a hero – and without leaving your living room. It was at once a point of class pride, and community identity. Not paying the tax was a 'strike' everyone could participate in, and growing numbers were doing just that. In Scotland, the resistance was near total. Legal penalties and manifold threats were failing to move the strikers.

It reached a culmination in the most remarkable march and riot on 5 March 1990. This militant demonstration united the unions and the whole of the left, from the anarchists with their bold new Class War tendency through to the moderate social democrats of the Labour Party and CPGB.

Pensioners were out in force and the young 'uns saw this as their day, their stand. By the time the March had reached Downing Street, many in the crowd had decided this wasn't enough. A big statement of discontent had to be made. The spark came firstly with a sitdown at the gates of Downing Street, then an attack on the gates, on the police barriers; and the whole thing took off from there. The police, who had cut their teeth on the miners and the hippies and the printers, felt untouchable. With ferocious and misjudged savagery, they laid into the crowd with riot police and mounted sections.

But there was something in the spirit of this crowd that was different in quality from almost any since the last century. Perhaps their embryonic cadres hardened from the coal strike and Wapping, perhaps it was inspiration from that violent resistance, but the crowd responded with unchecked and unrestrained counter-violence. That the police had no overall plan was obvious – they attacked and regrouped and ran about, leaving themselves at times exposed and their units isolated. Resistance spread out in all directions and across the whole field, from Whitehall up to Trafalgar Square, where it reached its apex. The most heroic fighting took place this day, fearless and heroic – chilling in many respects, in that people were prepared to die in this stand. Women were mown down by rampaging horses, police vehicles were driven into the thick of crowds at high speed with clear intention and design to cause major injury or death. The demonstration turned like an angry bull and set on the horses and riders and tore apart police vehicles with their bare hands, while surrounding wooden structures started to blaze and improvised barricades were thrown up.

The fighting this day matched anything of the coal strike, including Orgreave, where, despite our heroism, we took a pasting. It surpassed anything dished out at Wapping. It was unprecedented in this century, indeed it was something of a mass urban riot at the turn of the nineteenth century, it had that quality and popular support. The cops were shocked rigid; we saw real mortal fear in their eyes and utter confusion among their officers, we saw unmatched and selfless heroism in the hearts and bodies of young and old, men and women, black and white; though this was largely and mainly a white working-class riot.

The Poll Tax would fall, and the writing was on the wall for the 'Iron Lady' too. Would that we could have sparked this second front during the coal strike; though some of us had tried to organise it, it was 5 years late in coming. For the first time in decades, the far left had met in conjuncture here; with the solid resistance of the working class at large, it demonstrated what was possible if we could actually organise that consciously. Not just the violent resistance of course – that would have been impossible without the mass civil resistance and popular opposition generated by the Can't Pay Won't Pay movement. It put to bed once for all the notion that 'the British' don't do things like this. Push us down in the gutter enough, prod us and rob us enough and oh yes, we bliddy well will!

JULY 1990 – NATIONAL CONFERENCE, DURHAM

Off my own bat I propose, and it is accepted via the NEC, that we organise an official Union delegation to the graves of the founder members of the Union, Martin Jude and Tommy Hepburn, to lay wreaths and mark their contributions.

No problem with Hepburn of course, since the Durham Area hosts a pre-Gala wreath-laying ceremony every year (and now an annual Tommy Hepburn Memorial every October) at St Mary's Church, Heworth. With Jude the question is more of a problem, and in all honesty the Durham research officer phones me to ask where Jude is buried. 'Elswick,' I say. 'But where aboots?' he persists. I have to confess I have never been there, he neither. So I start on their behalf a quest for Jude's grave, knowing only that Fynes, a contemporary historian of Jude's, says he is buried in Elswick. The old Elswick Cemetery is at the top of Westgate Hill (or so I thought; actually that one is Westgate Cemetery), with many ruined gravestones, crumbling tombs to the city merchants and gentry. I walk among the fallen stones, as the city buses cruise by; there are not many visitors to this cemetery these days. It stands a little walled-in piece of the past surrounded by dereliction and slums. As I peer about I become aware of a squad car parked under some trees, with the occupants transfixed by my meandering. A little while later I am aware that a cop is standing behind me.

'What ye'deyin?' he asks without further introduction.

'I'm looking for a grave,' I reply.

'You're acting suspiciously,' he declares.

'No, if I was looking for a grave in a supermarket, or someone's back garden, that would be acting suspiciously,' I retort, 'but this is a graveyard!'

He laughs and the ice is broken. I tell him about Martin Jude and the commemoration and he takes me and shows me the desecrated graves.

'Whey, man, the kids are digging skulls up and takin them yem, they're hammering wooden stakes through bodies and ah'l sorts, man,' he tells me to my horror.

'The little bastards! They had better not have dug up Martin Jude mind, or there will be bother on.'

As it turned out, Elswick Cemetery is near Benwell. This is properly maintained and vast; here I find a park-keeper who takes me to the well-maintained monument to Martin. Our ceremony gaans on, though Peter Heathfield who is doing the address gets it a little wrong and tells the tale of Tommy Hepburn – non of us interrupt him of course.

'HOY OOT! HOY OOT!'

10 July 1990. The Durham Area has organised a huge social/reception at Sacriston Working Men's Club. The big revelations and exposé of Arthur's hidden funds are rife in every medium. Loads of kids and young people are hanging around the club to see the famous comins and gaanins. As Arthur Scargill's car arrives the kids chant 'Hoy oot! Hoy oot!', just as I arrive too. 'What are they shouting, David?' he asks. 'They think you've got some money, Arthur,' I reply.[289]

The 1990 Conference was in many ways my Conference. I took centre-stage on a number of issues, not least in defence of a woman's right to choose, against a resolution from North Western Area which aimed at changing the Union's policy in support to one of neutrality.

This year's Conference had seen me in opposition to Arthur and the NEC's proposal to change our annual Conference to biennial. This issue was taken on by Howard Wadsworth, a brilliantly satirical and comic wordsmith. He had made the point that the NEC resolution was about as popular as Aids and he was surprised it had got a seconder. It was rejected with the help of Yorkshire's block vote. I had made the point earlier that if we wanted reasons why it should be opposed one should simply read Arthur's speech to the TUC a few months ago, opposing plans for a biennial *TUC* Conference. Still, Arthur was to experience a little local difficulty which was waiting in the wings and consequently the issue was let go, or so we thought. It wasn't long before Arthur convened a 'Special Conference' of only the NEC and EC reps, and changed the decision of Conference. He was to get his Biennial Conference rule after all, and when we in the Yorkshire Area delegation refused to endorse it he accused us of not abiding by Conference decisions.[290] But this year we were more in agreement than not, at least for now. I got to move the most serious and thoroughgoing organisational reform in the history of the Union. Originating from the Hatfield branch, it became Yorkshire's main resolution to Conference and later Composite Motion G. It proposed the rapid movement to a single union serving the whole country, and the winding up of the Area Unions. There would be a monthly delegate meeting of all branches in Britain, in truth a sort of standing National Conference, to which all branches could submit resolutions and at which branches would vote as branches without the distortion of Area block votes. Whole swathes of bureaucracy and elitism, rules and exposure would be removed and the National Union would rest almost directly on the democratic branches of the members.

That was the vision that I presented to Conference. But there were mixed measures and motives of support. I had moved it in direct opposition to the idea of a merger with the TGWU or any other union at this stage, while those in the leadership saw this as a step toward an easier life:

> Many of the members see this composite as an alternative to proposals to going into the Transport and General Workers Union, because at the end of the day the thing that has held the members to this Union, even though we have not had a serious negotiation since 1983 and all the pay rises have been imposed on us and all the lot, is because they still believe in the National Union of Mineworkers and all it stands for, is more important than joining some fly-by-night organisation or going into another organisation because it has half dues like the T&G. An alternative to that has got to be a small but efficient Miners Union, and I believe we can stand on our own two feet with that.[291]

The Biennial Conference proposal from the NEC had been in truth an attempt to harmonise the Union's practice to be more like that of the TGWU. I was opposed by Scottish and Wales areas, who argued for their independence. I thought they were missing the point, and the debate was at times quite furious. When I got back up to sum up the debate and reply, I addressed this issue directly:

> I want to address myself to the people that talk about this independent Union all of a sudden. Independent union? Independent of what? Who do you think the employers are that you are independent of? Have you got independent employers? Do we have a Derbyshire Coal Board which is separate from the Yorkshire Coal Board which is separate from the Welsh Coal Board and separate from the Scottish Coal Board ... in my foolish way I thought that British Coal, trade name for the National Coal Board, was a single employer, and I did believe that the representatives of the National Coal Board in Wales, Scotland, Derbyshire, Yorkshire, Durham and Northumberland etc. all came out of the same basket, and they are all paid by the same people and they all take their orders off the same gaffers, so let's get rid of that. There are no independent employers. There is one employer, one gaffer, one marching order. How they apply the different ways, playing hard cop, soft cop with different areas, giving different areas a kick up the arse one week and another area a pat on the back – are we so foolish as not to realise what they have been trying to do, dividing bloody areas up? ... that is the game they are playing. (Applause)
>
> We have got a single enemy. All right, there might be a nice gaffer behind one table. There might even be a nice Area Director. Some of them

are taught to speak very nicely, but who do you think it is stands behind the Area Director? It is Mr Haslam. Who stands behind Mr Haslam? Do you think he gets out of bed one morning and thinks, 'Well I think I'll talk to Arthur Scargill this morning. Then again maybe I won't.' Of course he bloody doesn't. Margaret Thatcher gives him his marching orders, and Margaret Thatcher tells him how far to push in Wales, how far to push in Yorkshire, how to deal with Scotland and how to deal with imports into Ravenscraig or anywhere else. Their marching orders are determined by the Tory government, unless you really, really believe that British Coal have got some independent right, independent of Margaret Thatcher, to decide what to do. It's a lie. Its a myth ... I want to say this finally. Nobody will ever accuse me of not being an internationalist. Just for the record I am a passionate Celtic nationalist. I support independence for Scotland, for Wales, for Brittany and Cornwall, by the way (Laughter) and I think the Geordies have a strong argument, but I don't see why we can't all belong to the same union while we are fighting different employers, unless you think that Rio Tinto Zinc, Amco and Anglo American Mining are also going to desegregate themselves internationally. They are international structures, international power relations, and we have an international Union represented by a single NUM. (Applause)[292]

We had proposed in any case, joint panels of NUM branches in each nation and region, which would meet to discuss its particular positions and promote its specific outlooks, only it would be done under the structure of a single union. I little suspected at that time the growth of monolithic bureaucratic functioning at National Office that would develop later, and against which Areas clung like grim death to their own identities as a block to undemocratic practices. The vision of the National Union adopted that day was never to become reality, because in truth the vision which Arthur and the National leadership had was initially for an easy passage into the TGWU, then, later, when this collapsed and his control-freakery went up several notches, for less democracy, less control by the membership rather than more.[293] What had appeared in theory like a joint purpose was later to be revealed as two absolute opposites, but meantime we were linked in an even more life-or-death struggle with the state and its misinformation counter-insurgency team. This would ensure that, disagreements aside, we were still on the same side, at least for now.[294] For now, though, we weren't finished with the NEC and the National officials.

Howard Wadsworth strode to the rostrum with a twinkle in his eye. The Conference was laughing in anticipation before he reached the podium. He was getting up on points arising from the NEC reports; everyone knew what he was taking on.

In March 1987, NACODS had had a dispute, the result of which was that the NUM members couldn't get down the pit and so were laid off. There were assurances that we would be paid and that it was well in hand. By the Conference the previous year, we still hadn't, and Howard had mercilessly lampooned the National officials and the NEC. He took the rostrum again, 'continuing where I left off last year.'

This morning I am rather in some sort of difficulty on this issue, because yesterday I was approached by a member of the National Executive Committee who I think a great deal of, and he came as some sort of emissary from the National Executive Committee, it would seem. He said suddenly yesterday the NEC had realised we had not resolved the NACODS dispute, and suddenly realised it would be incorporated in the NEC report and even more suddenly realised that it would be debated today. Their fear was that I might have something to say on the matter. He said he really did not ask for the NEC to make excuses, but he said he hoped the Yorkshire Area and myself understood, and he looked at me with his big brown eyes and he said 'Howard be gentle, wont you?' (Laughter) It's years since anybody said that to me.(Laughter) ... he goes on amid terrific humour to give the background to the dispute, that we had been on strike and NACODS couldn't go to work, so they got paid. So now here we were, NACODS were on strike and we couldn't get to work, so we would get paid? Wrong. 'When the dispute was over, and I can only speak for myself as a local official, but I am sure that every branch official at the pits did the same, we dived straight into the manager's office and said 'We've come for us money.' 'Ah, so,' said the manager. At least that's what I thought he said (Laughter) ... 'I'm afraid you can't have it. I am under instructions from my Industrial Relations Officer that it is an Area problem ... Therefore the problem was passed round our Barnsley Area Offices. It was looked at by everybody in those offices, including the caretaker and the Area then decided that it was in fact a National Question because the Deputies nationally had taken that kind of action ... So it went as a national question and our National Officials then put the problem to British Coal. In fact it was the National Coal Board at that time ... It was only after a year, with pressure from some Areas and from the membership, that in fact we decided we ought to make some movement. Therefore, we had the historic day in the Council Chamber where in an NEC Report we were given the information that our lawyers had got their act together and we were ready to go to court within 2 weeks. That is why I talk about 2 weeks being a long time. The following month when I went to the Council Meeting where I was given the NEC report, I was told, as the other delegates were told, 'On the question of the NACODS dispute, we are almost there, and it will be ready to go to Court within two weeks.'

Well after three or four months of this I got the feeling that my members weren't believing me (Laughter), although I have got to say I tried to change the situation slightly by not repeatedly telling them 'within two weeks'. I used to sometimes tell them it was a fortnight. That seemed to settle them on that occasion. (Laughter) ...

When I was a little lad – no, I was never a little lad – when I was a lad I used to get a comic and it was called *The Wizard*. In *The Wizard* there was a cowboy character and his name was Tex. Normally cowboys only ever carried one gun. If you were right-handed, you carried it here. If you were left-handed you carried it there. But in this case Tex had two guns, and when he used to walk down the centre of Dodge City the people would point to him and say 'There goes two-gun Tex.' When I walk down the car park at Kellingley Colliery they say 'There goes two-weeks Wadsworth. (Laughter – Applause)

Our membership and my membership find it difficult to believe the reason for the delays. They feel in fact that if our lawyers have got hold of the problem, even if they are unable to resolve it themselves, there are other avenues they could go down, they could go to other lawyers, they could even go to the Nabs lawyers. At last gasp, they could go to the Citizens Advice Bureau. (Laughter)

The other day I went to Beamish open air museum, which is not far from here. The Museum revolves around life in the past, and they have got an old pit, a station, and they have an old town with shops and offices and houses. In the row of houses, they have a singing mistress, a dentist and other people, but they also have got a solicitor's office. There among all the dusty documents was our case. (Laughter) It was not on top of the pile ! We have some advantage in the delay, certainly for me at Kellingley, because had we took the opportunity then to have made a commemorative plate. You know that since the strike there have been commemorative plates for everything. We at the pit shops had a commemorative plate for the settlement of the NACODS dispute but we have been unable to put the years in it. So what we have done, we've sold the plates with a blank space and a felt tip pen and you can write in it when we settle. (Laughter) …

Strangely enough, we get there on 16 May ready to put our case before the judge. The judge says, 'Unfortunately I am not competent enough to take it. I specialise in divorce cases … [295]

There isn't space here to do justice to Howard's ongoing Conference oratory; he requires, like many of the people I have highlighted in this work, a biography of his own. Howard was on the right and a moderate; we crossed swords on platforms and across pub tables and welfare halls throughout our respective lives in the pit and the Union, but it was without rancour and with great pit wit and pillock. The NEC and the leadership cringed before his tirades far more than they ever did before mine.

6

THE SCARGILL SLANDER

22 October 1989. Ewan MacColl – the Red Megaphone they had called him – fell silent and died. The gap left by his enormous presence was chasmic. I miss his voice, and his thoughts, his cautions and advice, and I miss his friendship and his certainty. It wouldn't have surprised him one iota when, through the limited Freedom of Information Act, national archives were opened in March 2006 to reveal that he had been the subject of M15 spying and surveillance. The old tie-up between the establishment media and the state's Special Forces ensured that the careers and public exposure of MacColl and his partner at the time, Joan Littlewood, were blocked and suppressed. Ewan's Communist Party membership, drama skills and great public resonance made him a dangerous man. It seems ludicrous today, but Ewan's talent was considered in much the way that armed units of the revolution in preparation would have been regarded some time later. His house was watched; his every word recorded, his plays monitored. Joan would never be allowed to work for the BBC.

THE SCARGILL SLANDER

In July 1990 had come a low-level pincer attack upon Arthur Scargill and Peter Heathfield. It was a coordinated assault by Central TV – *The Cook Report* – and the *Daily Mirror* launching a simultaneous screaming headline and TV documentary on the Union officials who it was asserted had fiddled the miners out of millions. Arthur Scargill and Peter Heathfield, to pay off their mortgages, had allegedly grabbed large amounts of money from Libya and the USSR destined for the destitute striking families. The money from the Russian miners' weekly levy had never got to the NUM funds and had been siphoned off for private gain. In the doorstep confrontation style, which is *The Cook Report* forte, they collared Arthur as he drove into the NUM HQ and asked him about missing Russian millions, sent for the miners during the strike, which Arthur had redirected for his own use.

Along with this came the revelation of the big ranch, the luxury detached house Arthur had built on the proceeds, and the extension Peter had done on his house, during the strike when men were losing theirs. Arthur was caught in the headlights, ashen-faced. 'Put your question is writing and I will respond to it,' was all he could say to the mics thrust into his face. It was a bombshell.

Arthur and Peter were suspended by the NEC while they called in an independent QC, Gavin Lightman, to investigate the allegations of misappropriated funds, and missing millions. The rumour machine did its own work; men stopped and questioned whether they had been duped. At the Durham Miners' Gala that year, as Arthur took the platform there were shouts from Durham miners, of 'Ye'r a thief, Scargill!' And 'Ye'r a crook!' They were a minority, they had had a good drink, but it was painful. One man sang 'Ye'r a crook! Ye'r a crook' Ye'r a crook!' to the tune of 'Here We Go!', a cutting irony.

Among the wider public there is a certain element whose lack of principle and thought, whose humdrum, lacklustre lives made them need to believe it. Nobody ever does things for principle; there is always a corrupt self-serving angle – notice the joy among the media hordes when the vicar is found in bed with the choirboy, the scoutmaster with the boy scout, or the politician with the schoolgirl. Or the union man with his fingers in the till – there is something satisfying and self-assuring that everybody is really in it for what they can get. In every crowd that puts a principled person on a pedestal there is an undercurrent of raw cynicism, of those who can't wait for the mud to fly and the hero to be pulled crashing down into the dirt. That cynicism had been severely tested during 12 months of selfless endeavour and mutual aid and communal strength; the hacks couldn't wait to present it all as a fool's game.

The honour of the strike, perhaps of all strikes, the honour of our Union, maybe all unions, the integrity of solidarity and selfless donations – all were now in question. By extension all Union officials, especially those close to Arthur, were also now suspect, me included. In the Regal, Butts, a twin, a miner I had worked with, whose common law claim I had taken up, who was now incapacity-retired, in a permanent temper because he hadn't been paid, thought we weren't pursuing his claim fast enough, and now thought we had stolen money from him, had pissed up his back, went for me. 'Ye robbing Scargill bastards!' – he dived at me, and I dodged him, and since he was in a thick of his mates, all well served, fresh from the TV screens, I thought it best not to take this on here.

But I seethed with indignation, couldn't wait to get on that platform in front of the mass of Hatfield miners and tell them just where it all fell into place and ask them what side they were on. When I had taken on the accusations, taken on the argument, fought the lies of the media, then if someone wanted a go I wouldn't mind, because I would feel morally vindicated whatever the physical outcome. The strike had been lost on the street, but not in the hearts of millions around the world, its place in history was assured, and this assault was upon that. It was a dead strike that wouldn't lie down or go away, this attack was meant to be the wooden stake in the heart of the restless, undead miners' strike and its immortal reputation. Emma asked, 'Could it possibly be true?'

It stormed onto the TV right at the start of the NUM National Conference in Durham. I watched the programme with Mick McGahey, the vice president of the Union, and George Bolton, the secretary of the Scottish Miners, at their accommodation; neither of them had seen the revelations in detail, and neither had seen the programme. Mick watched in stony silence. At the end of which he stood up, silent and grim.

'I knew nothing of these things at all, not a word.' 'I don't think they are saying you did, Mick.' He looked at me like I was five years old and I suddenly felt stupid because I realised what he was on about. 'I'm the vice president of the NUM, Davie, and I knew nothing about parcels of money and trips to Libya, and dividing up stacks of poond notes.' Mick never said another word in public on the subject right through the whole scandal, and I believe he thought the best thing he could say would be nowt.

I make the front page of the *Doncaster Star* in defence of Arthur and our Conference decisions and against the NEC decision to essentially hand over the whole enquiry into the Russian gold affair to a firm of lawyers, suspending Arthur and Peter, and announcing that they are to 'sue' the two men for repayment of moneys donated by the Russian and other miners during the strike and which we never, allegedly, received. We had had a right battle royal over these allegations. The National Conference just 2 weeks earlier had decided to call a one-day Special Conference on the whole subject, to examine all the evidence and the report back by Gavin Lightman, a senior and progressive solicitor brought in to conduct an enquiry into the whole affair, and then decide what course of action the Union should take. Two weeks later the NEC moved to pre-empt that decision, on the advice of the legal firm. To some large extent we had been sequestrated again, this time by a law firm brought in to conduct an enquiry, but who were now calling the shots.[296]

For us, there was a side to take and we sprang to Arthur's defence, mounting a huge campaign to expose the press and media set-up. We knew what side we were on here. Public meetings were called all over the coalfields and Peter and Arthur spoke out for their integrity and honour and principles. It was a sad and soul-destroying period. We held a mass public meeting at the Broadway, Dunscroft, on 30 August – myself and Arthur together with Jack Boyal, the president of the Offshore Industry Liaison Committee, with which I had been trying to get the NUM to merge as another body of militant miners who had been abandoned by the formal trade union movement. The lads themselves crammed to the rafters, the men who had stood and slogged it out in the dead of winter, bloodied and unbowed. They sat there, watching the man they would have died for if necessary. We wanted to believe, we couldn't believe any other. I made an impassioned speech drawing parallels from history, when our leaders had been vilified in this manner before. W. P. Roberts, 130 years earlier, the pitmen's advocate, branded in the press as thieving and deceiving the poor miners; Arthur Cook, the general secretary of the miners during the 1926 strike, his name mud from hell to breakfast time in the annals of the bourgeois media. Now Arthur Scargill and Peter Heathfield.

The upstairs room of the Broadway was packed, mainly with Hatfield pickets, many with their wives. They listened in deadly silence, not laughing as they usually would in almost any other situation. Arthur was forced, under intense public scrutiny, lies and innuendo, to lay bare his private domestic arrangements for any who wished to review them:

> Months after the end of the strike I wanted to buy a house and sell the one I had lived in for 20 years. I was not receiving any salary (because the Receiver would not pay me) and there was no chance of my getting a mortgage or bridging loan from a bank or building society. I had 'lost' my two and a half percent mortgage with the NUM Yorkshire Area through no fault of my own, and I had had to pay out of my personal monies (in respect of that mortgage) a sum of £22,255.45 to the NUM in August 1984.

A total repayment made by me to the Miners Trade Union International (including interest and the donation of eight months salary to the NUM for the period of March/November 1985) in respect of the temporary loan is equal to an interest rate of 16%.

The loan – which has been fully repaid – was not obtained from the NUM and I was assured no NUM monies were involved. My house was and is being purchased by the proceeds (£50,000) from sale of my previous house, a £50,000 Co-Op Bank mortgage and from personal savings.[297]

Kinnock was banging on tables, demanding to know if money had been sent from Libya to the miners, and Norman Willis wrote officially to the NUM to ask for assurances that none had been sent. I angrily made the point at the Broadway meeting: 'We know where Gaddafi was in 1984, but where was Willis? Where was *his* assistance, that we had to trail the four corners of the globe begging for aid? We got more support from poor black miners in South Africa who didn't have two pence to scratch their backsides with than we ever got off Willis. He has no right now to ask anything of our union, because when we asked him in 1984/85 we got nowt.'

The fact was that all of our fundraising and distribution was against the backdrop of a union in the grip of sequestration. All of our official bank accounts had been seized. Injunctions, writs and damages claims were hog-tying the Union, or trying to, so that it could neither spend nor receive money. Yet the infrastructure of the Union remained intact and kept operating. Common-law claims were still being processed, tribunals were still being attended, in fact owing to the host of issues raised by DSS regulations and entitlements during the strike these had multiplied a hundredfold (not that we accepted any payments for attending these tribunals or preparing our cases, I must add), pickets' petrol was being paid, an army on the move, welfare to food kitchens, 12,000 men had been arrested, lawyers had to be paid, fines paid. Did anyone seriously imagine that we could apply to the sequestrator for funds to pay for all this? For mass picketing in Nottingham or at Orgreave? Likewise did anyone think we were so stupid as to raise hundreds of thousands of pounds from British unions and unions worldwide just to hand it over to the sequestrator through our official bank accounts?

It was patently obvious that we had to set up ruse accounts, had to hide the money in different countries, under different names, with the quite explicit intention of defying the law. Most of this money was being distributed in wads of cash – our money-raisers in London, Birmingham and other big cities in Britain and across Europe were collecting wads of cash for distribution to the impoverished miners' families back at home. I have mentioned earlier how I regularly carried a poly bag, full of picket petrol and expenses money, on late night rowdy public transport back to the village from Barnsley.

The real reason I was safe, and the reason why the accusations were at once suspect, was that had money been our motive force then we wouldn't have been putting ourselves through this in the first place. I was perhaps aware that our collectors in London ate more than the £5 per day we allowed them expenses and that doubtless more than a few hot meals came out of the bucket rather than my allocation, but I was equally confident that every penny piece more than that was faithfully dispatched home. The lads were giving up more than £200 per week in wages for principle; they didn't have to – this cause was their cause, they would no more gain from it personally than scab. Of course this is not to suggest that this was a slack or woolly operation, far from it – every single penny was accounted for, every sandwich and £1 expenses signed for, every vehicle and mileage clocked, receipts for petrol, oil, repairs, sandwich fillings, my bags on the return journey to Barnsley were three times greater coming back, with receipts and records, and doomed to face the most tight-fisted of all tight-fisted treasurers in the shape of Ken Homer, who vetted each and every £1, signature, and mileage account, then checked them through the clerical staff in the Finance Office. Every penny claimed had to be meticulously justified.

I was tirelessly making the point that, uncomfortable though this whole thing was for Arthur, it was not solely aimed at him. It was an effort to rubbish what had been for 180,000 miners, their wives and families a most noble stand, the most important and principled and valued year of their lives, our lives. We suspected Kinnock's fifth column, in the shape of Kim Howells, Kevin Barron, and his sidekick the media king Maxwell, owner of the *Daily Mirror*, who were still fighting the strike, the ghost of that strike and everything it represented; though defeated in material terms its spirit was as bothersome as ever. This seemed to be confirmed to us when Kinnock himself came forward to publicly present a British Press Award to the very journalists who had run the smear story.

Fifteen years later the whole thing is raked over again with an abject apology from the new editor of the *Daily Mirror* and a third edition of Seumas Milne's book *The Enemy Within*: we had actually only touched the surface of what was going on.

For there was more, much more. The degree to which the state, the secret state, MI6, MI5 and the Special Forces intervened into this struggle was also unprecedented, and although much of it is in the public arena, it is invisible. How is that possible? People do not yet know how Thatcher through special forces set traps and public relations high-explosive bombs to destroy the NUM leadership's reputation and with it the strike's reputation, and rewrite our history as futile, a pathetic endeavour manipulated by well-heeled leaders with criminal agendas riding on the back of noble savages being led up the garden path. Then the *Daily Mirror – Cook Report* exposé, following the strike: the missing millions, the criminal intrigue, the shite that sticks whatever you do.

Remember Libya? The shock-horror during the strike which had everywhere gathered sympathy and was touching the conscience of the public at large – then, suddenly, the outrage that greeted that much-publicised visit of our executive officer Roger Windsor to get money from Gaddafi during the strike, before the specially invited cameras of the world, that embrace, Gaddafi and the NUM executive officer exchanging pecks on each cheek. That picture of the shot policewoman laying in pool of blood, shot we are told by Gaddafi's gunmen on the streets of London, while the miners seek money from them. And then the money itself, creamed off to buy a luxury mansion for Arthur Scargill, and an extension for Peter Heathfield and a bridging loan to that same executive officer, Mr Windsor.

The heat of the story was to run cold on the river of facts; neither Heathfield nor Scargill had mortgages during the strike, but who knows the sequel? The most serious and it seems now proven scam was concerning the Libyan donations. It is surely not necessary here to retell the serious financial and social hardship being suffered in the coalfields by the striking miners and their families, or the financial demands upon the structures of the Union at all levels to keep the fabric of our operation running on all fronts? Thatcher had moved in to sequestrate all our funds, to choke the Union to death. Money was needed from anywhere and everywhere for all purposes.

We, speaking for the rank and file, most of the branches, and the women's support groups, if not the apparatus officially at Area or National level, would have taken money from the devil, with or without receipts in any currency he cared to offer. We were fighting, we believed, an evil more direct and threatening. Assistance from Libyan unions, or the government, posed no problem to us; many of the militants had no sympathy for the British state's animosity to them, and even the shooting of the policewoman didn't ruffle many feathers in our camp to say the least. We could see through all the crocodile tears, double standards and hypocrisy.

I could well see Arthur dispatching Windsor, his appointed executive officer, off to Libya to raise funding for 'the fabric of the Union' and Windsor himself not being buggered who knew it. Alternatively I could see Windsor going off on his own initiative on Arthur's approval but with orders to keep the meeting quiet, because the state and the press would not take such fundraising as pragmatically as we did. Arthur insists he did not authorise or organise the visit and didn't know about it until it was over; if true this seems remarkable adventurism on behalf of the mild-mannered, almost timid Windsor. Arthur seems to have been very slow to cotton on to the man's treachery. Des Dutfield from South Wales makes the point at the Special Delegate Conference:

> The pre Conference Executive at Scarborough, which was the end of the two year term for those National Executive Committee members when I was still on the NEC and we were told at that pre Conference Executive in Scarborough that Roger Windsor, the Chief Executive Officer, was not in attendance at that Conference because his wife was ill with salmonella poisoning. There were no words of anger or acrimony associated with Windsor at that time, and I am talking about July of last year ... In September of last year, two months later ... and at the back end of that meeting we had a brief oral report not a written one, a brief oral report, dealing with Roger Windsor, the Chief Executive Officer. We were informed he had left the Union's employment in August and that the President wanted to report a serious issue concerning Windsor which had involved the Union in certain financial debts.[298]

Why does it matter? Because the state's forces knew that a donation from Libya could be a propaganda coup if they disclosed it with enough 'shock-horror' sensation at the right moment. Seumas Milne, author of *The Enemy Within*, now in its third edition, is utterly convinced that Windsor was an MI6 plant, and this scheme was central to bashing a hole in public support for the strike, maybe even the miners' own support for the strike. The fundraising trip was not supposed to include a meeting with Gaddafi, let alone a public and televised, then worldwide broadcast, meeting with Gaddafi. Nobody, regardless of how fearless they were at accepting funds from anywhere, would have signed that on without thought for its PR consequences back home and nobody surely would suggest Arthur would have sanctioned that development? The meeting with Gaddafi and the TV broadcast was, the Libyans now say, at the request of, or at least with hearty approval from, Windsor.

The impact of the publicity from that did indeed impact hard on our fundraising efforts among the public, at least for a time. 'Get your fucking money from Gaddafi you bastards!' London taxi drivers would shout to fundraisers following the 'revelations'. It took us a week or two to start combating the revelations in the press and exposing the truth about increased oil exports from Gaddafi that Thatcher had requested and received.

But there was more. The question whether we got money or not from Libya was a further part of the story, and for the Special Forces, aimed at discrediting the strike and its leadership, this was to be perhaps even bigger than the Gaddafi embrace. The involvement of Mr Abbasi, a Kashmiri political militant, with international armed struggle connections, who swears he carried through caseloads of money to support the strike; the link in with Windsor, who says he brought it up to Arthur's office where it was divvied up for various projects involving Peter Heathfield, Arthur Scargill and Windsor's living arrangements, as well as the Nottinghamshire NUM members' legal defence fund – all this becomes a fascinating and confusing paper chase.

The Lightman inquiry commissioned by the NUM to investigate the allegations of corruption found no evidence that money had come specifically from Libya. Parcels of money had arrived right enough, and it wasn't always with a 'from me to you' gift tag on it. Lightman concluded that if Libyan money had been sent in among a consignment of cash dropped off at the office by Windsor, then it had all been accounted for. Arthur had indeed divided up parcels of money for the four respective purposes, but these purposes themselves were subject to bitter accusation and denial. But perhaps much more importantly and startlingly, Milne is able to demonstrate that in fact Libyan money didn't get here, and what's more the Libyans themselves can account for every penny of their proposed donation. Windsor did not hand over tens of thousands of pounds from Libya and Mr Abbasi had not, as he had stated, walked through customs carrying it all in his briefcase, which was then opened, inspected and cleared through, and him sent on his way.

The allegations launched by the *Mirror* and Cook were a broad blunderbuss of allegations of corruption and theft, covering many areas of donations and funding. These smears were class-motivated and politically conceived of. What they did, and they perhaps didn't understand it, was unearth an unexploded bomb which the state's security and counterinsurgency team had left in the field, undetonated and perhaps abandoned. What had been disclosed could have been the biggest press exposé of the state's dirty tricks department and the criminal lengths it would go to defeat the miners. But so blinded by class hatred, and so determined to pull Arthur from his throne were the hacks that they missed the real meaning of the whole 'Libyan Cash for the Miners' scam. I do not think Cook or Pattinson, the reporters central to the whole exposé, were part of the plan. I think they set off with a simple piece of gutter journalism to show Arthur was a fat cat who bought a big ranch while the poor miners got raggy arses. They then started to discover bits and pieces of a far more involved device which in fact had been set by the state itself, to explode in the NUM's face and defeat the strike. In my opinion they were not clever enough to understand what they had discovered and just swallowed, whole, the hook line and sinker that Arthur and the NUM leadership were creaming the funds off for themselves and accepting money from terrorist agents.

THE LIBYAN TIME BOMB

That Libyan time bomb was Plan B for the Thatcher government if all else was failing – if NACODS had carried through the successful ballot result and struck with the NUM, the lights were going out and the miners were riding to another crushing victory against another Tory government. The exposé of boxes and briefcases of cash coming from Libya, with the good wishes of Colonel Gaddafi, carried into Britain by a convicted armed fighter, presented on Arthur's desk by a chief executive officer who had been kissed before the eyes of the world by his Libyan master, the head of a government which had murdered a hapless British policewoman. The cash, apart from funding an anti-government, anti-democratic, anti-British strike as part of a worldwide terrorist conspiracy by Marxists and God knows who else, was also being used to keep the NUM leaders in the manner to which they had become accustomed. All of that was meant to go boom! at the eleventh hour of the miners winning the strike. It was meant to pull the rug on the strike, demoralise the strikers, cut off our support, discredit any case we had. *Key to it all happening of course was that money had to arrive from Libya.* The truth was, as we can now prove, that it was raised and was sent, to assist the great struggle of the miners, without any strings or ulterior motives, on behalf of the Gaddafi government.

What catches the state's special forces in a trap is their own impatience and their own belief that the victory of the miners was imminent. The money gets held up, *it doesn't arrive*, in fact Libyan security forces now say it was seized by criminal elements in a purely internal scam. *Their money never leaves the country.* But money comes out the other side all the same! It is paid into Abbasi's bank account. Although it is the selfsame amount, paid into the account set up for the purpose, it is not Libya's money, but money put in by persons and parties unknown to bait the trap for the British media to spring in the event of the miners' impending victory! The conclusion is that the special forces decided: 'The bloody Libyans have made a bollocks of baiting our trap, so we will do it for them and pretend it was their money all along.' The money was never drawn in fact and as far as we can tell is still sitting in that account, while the Libyans know exactly the source of their own money, which never in fact arrived at this end. *That*, regardless of any other feature of this story, is a remarkable revelation. That it hasn't blown the roof off Parliament and the British media goes to show how far they all piss in the same pot.

Incidentally, the Milne book, also for the first time to my knowledge, makes clear the heavy involvement of David Hart (already mentioned) and Thatcher in derailing the NACODS joint national action. Thatcher had always expressed the view that she was 'unclear' why the deputies had suddenly settled and saved her and her government's skin. The book discloses a plan for splitting the NACODS Executive, and actually bribing some officials with backhanders, jobs and special concessions overall on pensions. The pulling of the plug twice on joint NACODS action was absolutely crucial to the defeat of the miners; it is a little discussed and researched area of the whole dispute and one which still stands begging for answers.

The story of the missing Russian millions, which Arthur supposedly 'diverted and withheld from the striking miners' is an entirely separate event, though not one that occurred without deliberate state interference. If this was another shot against the NUM leadership then it misfired. Misfired, because the press got the story wrong again and cocked up its impact. The Russian miners did indeed get levied, from their wages, money to support their British comrades, who they had seen on TV fighting it out with the cops and making a stand for the survival of their jobs. The donation was a magnificent act of international solidarity and was much needed by the striking miners and more importantly their families. We never received it. The story went that Arthur had nabbed it, and used it either for himself or for his own political whims.

Originally the whole central allegation was that Arthur had paid off his mortgage with it, during the strike. The middle stump went when Arthur was able to demonstrate quite easily that he didn't have a mortgage during the strike. The fact though that something to do with Soviet money and Arthur's (as it turned out subsequently) mortgage was known about, and this information was privy to perhaps three people at most, shows that very secret communications had been intercepted and fed to the media. The fact that they were too stupid to build on the information they had been given and in effect 'dropped the ball' doesn't take away the lengths the state's intelligence services had gone to in order to publicly crucify Arthur, and to a lesser extent Peter Heathfield, on a similar charge.

Chasing these Russian millions and unearthing their fate has been a sound piece of detective work by Seumas Milne. Mrs Thatcher had sought and received assurances that no money would come from the USSR to assist the British miners; this would be unwarranted interference in an internal matter. The Soviet politicos agreed. As a consequence despite everyone's best efforts in the Soviet miners' union to get the money (2.2. million roubles) moving, it got spiked. Eventually 2 years *after* the strike was over it landed, but was redirected, so as not to offend anyone and cause any international incidents, as 'aid for international purposes' and sent to the Miners Trade Union International which Arthur had set up some time before, one of the recipients of which could be the NUM ... The MTUI later becomes the International Miners Organisation, with Arthur its joint leader. Milne says that the MTUI 'dissolved', along with its funds, into the IMO.

Arthur has argued throughout that he was not party to the decision either to delay sending the money, or to redirect its purpose. He had made direct NUM fund account numbers and those of the women's support groups available to the Soviet miners but they, not he, had chosen not to use them.

Likewise the money donations from the eastern European miners' unions, raised during the British miners' strike, had been designated 'for international purposes'. There are few of us in any doubt whatsoever that these moneys were raised for the British miners and their families as a result of the hardship of their struggle, and for the NUM as an organisation under siege by the state. 'International purposes' was doubtless a cover used to prevent any international incidents or incurring Mrs Thatcher's wrath. It may also have been a bureaucratic device by the miners in those countries to outwit the official party and state line on the matter.

Where we do have serious disagreements with Arthur is in that, having got custody of the funds, now titled 'for international purposes' and directed to his organisation over which we the miners have no control, he concluded that the money never was the property of either the miners or the NUM. He was free along with Simon, the IMO (which was to become IEMO) secretary, to dispatch that money to any purpose they wished, some of which he assures us would have been the miners' hardship fund or even the NUM. He also still insists that since that money was never ours, he never would have released information about it to the Union, were it not for the revelations.

What gives grist to the rumour mill and lays him wide open for accusations of corruption and double standards then is made worse by the fact that he borrows money from this (MTUI) fund – £100,000 – to buy his big ranch at Barnsley, 'Treelands'. 'Treelands' cost £125,000 at a time when the miners were living in houses valued at £15,000 and less. This wasn't during the strike, but it was only 6 months after the end of the strike. Peter Heathfield too was allowed to borrow money from the fund to assist with his living arrangements, although that transaction is less explicit. Peter insists that repairs were necessary to the house he and Betty were living in at the time and some modernisation was undertaken at the same time, *but the house wasn't his* – it belonged to the Union and any repair or improvement which was undertaken was for the benefit or the value of NUM premises and not his personal gain.

Nobody can say either of these things, anyway, was illegal, or given the self-governing rules of the MTUI or IMO, unconstitutional. These were privileges of the type which had been enjoyed by miners officials' in the NUM and probably its predecessor the MFGB almost since the Union started. The press and TV had never previously been outraged by privileges enjoyed by Joe Gormley or Sidney Ford or any other of the miners' leaders; certainly they had never conducted any campaign to democratise the functioning of the NUM or its international affiliates before. The concern for 'justice for miners and their families' was not something one would normally find tripping off the lips in the editorial rooms at Fleet Street, or in BBC Broadcasting House before – quite the opposite during that epochal struggle of '84/85. All of this 'fat cat' and manufactured outrage was aimed at discrediting Scargill and Heathfield because of the strike. It was an attempt to take away the legacy and dignity of that stand, and rubbish its status in the eyes of the working class and for future generations. That was its sole purpose.

My close comrade Bob Anderson of the Midlands Area NUM was to put the whole issue into class perspective at our soul-searching Special Delegate Conference on the subject:

I watched *Panorama* on Monday night, £15 million the Tories had, £15 million come into their funds for the election, and the Tory treasurer turned round and said when the interviewer said to him 'Do you think you should know where that money has come from?' 'I have not got a clue.' 'Do you think you should know where that money came from?' 'Yes but it does not matter,' and Norman Tebbit said he didn't give a damn. He did not give a damn because he does not care where the money comes from as long as he has got money to fight for his class. That is what this is all about.[299]

To be right, not one of the areas condemned raising money from any source or the efforts to keep it from the sequestrators; it was the period *after* the sequestrator had left, and the funds and accounts still not revealed, which was their bone of contention. As the Scotland Area's Nicky Wilson said, 'The Officials were quite correct right up until June 1986. But why did it continue until December 1989?'[300]

Arthur paid the loan back at a high interest rate within 3 years of borrowing it, which benefited the fund, BUT it had been borrowed the year after the most bitter strike in union history when miners and their families had given their all. To be enjoying a privileged position like this, and to be engaging in lavish consumption like this, on the back of that strike, was not only politically stupid, it was seen by many as grossly arrogant. Certainly it laid the way open for him to be discredited and mud to stick which had had no actual basis in fact. Even today round and about the bars in Barnsley or Doncaster or South Shields former miners will repeat the allegation that 'Arthur bought the big hoose while we were on strike.' He didn't, but *he did* buy a big hoose soon afterwards, which to class fighters doesn't sound a whole lot better.

In the course of writing this chapter of the book I have again looked exhaustively at this question. It is too detailed to give an account in more detail than I have here. I can do no better than to recommend researchers to read the verbatim report of that Special Delegate Conference where all of those matters, investigations, anomalies and principles were thrashed out openly and without compromise. Of course we knew little of the state's input at that time, but the central issues then are clearly presented in full in that text.

In part this comes down to arrogance, rooted in Arthur's Stalinist view of socialism as a top-down action carried out by wise leaders on behalf of the workers. *He* will decide what is best for the money, not the miners. As Des Dutfield for the South Wales miners said at the time,

We are not pointing fingers at the strike or the aftermath. We are pointing the finger after. We do not believe it is right and proper in any democratic organization that such secrecy should ever prevail, because when you come down to the point of individuals saying 'we know better than you and this is why we are doing it,' that is autocracy and not democracy, and that is why we feel so angered over this matter.[301]

Although I have nothing but praise for the scholarly manner in which the facts of the whole situation were explored and exposed by Seumas Milne, they are not presented as plainly. The turn of phrase and the choice of presentation hide another agenda in my view. I would be very surprised if Arthur, in fact, didn't write a couple of chapters of the book or greatly edit their content personally. There are telltale phrases and descriptions of Arthur himself, and that egocentric knack he has of turning history around his personality and presence, rather than being simply a part of its process. The phrases include 'The Troika' to describe himself, Heathfield and McGahey, which he hoped would catch on, but never did – in fact only he calls them that. The descriptions of Saltley in his own image and likeness are a giveaway as to who wrote these passages, and the book says *he* masterminded the whole operation. 'In 1974 Arthur and other left wing area leaders'…'pushed through a strike' which helped bring down the government of the day. There is the old favourite that Arthur 'invented' flying pickets and even mass picketing. Jones was editing the *Yorkshire Miner* not for the miners or the Yorkshire Area of the NUM *but for Scargill.*

Describing the situation following the strike when there was a mass and often aimless scramble for survival among the areas and real tactical and political divisions with Arthur, Milne says 'Traditional left wing areas like South Wales and Scotland made common cause with the right wing against Scargill.' He doesn't tell us how, or about what or why that should be. This is Arthur's view of perfectly valid disagreements about the way forward after the strike. In fact Arthur tended henceforth to see any disagreement and tactical dispute as a sign that his comrades were turning against him and being treacherous. From this point on, Arthur's political and tactical vision starts to become very refracted, but this wasn't in fact what was really happening.

Worse still in my view is the almost Jesuitical logic which leads, through a defence of the miners and the NUM and their leaders in 1984/85, to support for the IEMO. It's the kind of reasoning that starts with support for the Russian workers' revolution of 1917; then, because of the need to defend that, the abolition of Soviet democracy in 1921; and finally through to Stalin and the purges of the 1930s. Defence of our stand in 1984 and 1985 is not in any way linked to support for either the IMO or its successor the IEMO. Milne, echoing Arthur, calls the IEMO the biggest and most important union international in the world, which if it were true is crushingly sad for the others. In fact the IEMO, even more so the IMO, is simply a bureaucratic social gathering of union chiefs with no rank-and-file involvement or control. It is not a working-class organisation at all. Of course it could be that Milne is simply totally sycophantic and has started to see things through Arthur's eyes himself.

Reading Milne's book, and its account of the lengths to which the state and its intelligence services went in signing up spies, agents and the media, gives us some idea as to their determination not to let us win.

There was more. David Peace's novel *GB84* isn't a fiction at all – it's a set of facts without footnotes and evidence, but there was more, as the state has moved to bury witnesses to worse. There was a plan to implicate striking miners with the murder of a police officer. The officer was in fact murdered, though not by us. Indeed the death was reported on the news, with the mining strike background denoting a feature involving a strike broadcast. Some of our pickets with military training were set up as the fall guys, but the real assassin caught on an unauthorised venture of his own threatened to spill the beans. We can't prove any of this, but I have talked to the key actors and a man called in by the assassin as protection, in case they should decide to permanently dispose of his services.

It maddens me even further that we lost; had we been aware as to the extent of the state's involvement against us, I'm certain we would have stood out more determinedly to win. As it turned out, although their efforts to discredit our strike by discrediting the leaders was proved to be a setup in one case, and a mishmash of lies, fabrication and distorted fact in the other, the mud still sticks – in part because of the bureaucratic and entirely egocentric world Arthur inhabits, and his view of the world from the lofty heights of his own importance. The two things together have damaged us, and the events are not easily explained, although in the heat of the slander and attack the vast bulk of the miners stood shoulder to shoulder with Arthur and Peter, and not simply because the accusations were in fact discovered to be fabrications and distortions. We knew the reason for the attacks – they were intended to break all of us and send a message of despair to the whole working class not just here but worldwide. One wonders how much of the truth of the story followed the original exposé round the world. One wonders if your average Russian miner for example knows the truth behind the story or whether he thinks his magnificent gesture was futile and would be wary against doing such a selfless act again. This was the true purpose of the slanders and why we repulsed them so energetically.[302]

The state is indeed in final analysis a room of armed men, with a highly efficient propaganda vehicle in the shape of the press and TV ready most of the time to print whatever scandal and anti-working-class propaganda they are asked to, regardless of its truth or lack or integrity. It is a team with its own agenda and its own programme which has nothing at all to do with the wishes of parliament ner mind the people.

A week or so after the attack on me in the Regal, I was standing at the bar in the Abbey, when in marches Butts. OK, I think, only me and him here this time, let's slag this out then go outside if necessary. 'Areet Dave?' he says cheerily. 'Well, OK, I think, he obviously wants to let the matter go. 'Aye, champion, fancy a pint?' 'Ehh aye, gaan on then,' he says. I buy him a pint. We chat. 'Not many in the neet.' 'Nor, whey its early yet.' He downs the pint. 'Anyway Dave, I should look out for our kid, he's gonna rip your head off !' Damn! It was Butts's twin brother; I was still on alert. Actually when the dust settled, and some of the truth of the story started to come to light, he apologised and explained the pressure he had been under. Soon afterwards we started to settle his claims and his Union badge was shone up again.

We were standing in the crowded Welfare, listening to a rock band, people dancing, and groups of people talking, their pints in their hands, me and the Butts twins, when a fight started right in front of us, a resurgence of some earlier incident elsewhere. A bloke takes a swing at Butts's brother, who dodges the punch and lays him out with a double handed smash on the back of the side of his head and follows it up with a knee in the face; he goes sprawling. Suddenly, the bloke's girlfriend, who is a regional taekwando champion, tall, thin and dark and dressed in black, vaults the little veranda and in a bound, is in the middle of a spin kick turn which will see her leg unleash like a whiplash and smash his head and face with the most powerful kick in the taekwando arsenal. Butts's brother jumps back, the kick flies past his nose, he dives back forward and smash! – lays her out with a straight punch to the face. He is then led away back into the crowd and toward the bar. It looks, I must admit, very comical, although extremely painful. I can't contain my laughter, though, when a little later someone complains to Butts's brother he didn't fight fair because the girl was using taekwando, and he was just fighting 'ordinary'. I said, laughing, 'And you didn't bow, you bastard.'

January 1990. Me and Maureen receive the final decree absolute on our divorce which had been submitted in November of '89. It is a painfully hard piece of paper from which I have no pleasure. It had been a long and torturous road to hell made worse perhaps by attempts to cling on, to just believe that like some wound it would heal itself. I think in the end it had started to fester and a final break became the only answer for everyone involved. As it is Emma agrees that she will stay with me permanently. I am ecstatic. Losing your wife and comrade of 23 years is one thing, losing your daughter is not credible. On 22 November I go before a judge in chambers along with Emma and apply for 'formal custody' – what a description. Emma has to state who she wishes to stay with and she announces she will stay with her Dad – I was so happy and so proud. Well, as I walked from the court, I could see nothing at all wrong with the English legal system, nothing at all, it's quite fair.

I promise Emma by way of light relief that the house will be ours now and we can make some changes. 'Not an inside toilet, Dad?' I remember her asking and me replying 'Whoa, wait on a bit, are ye trying to mek wi middle-class like?'

'Dad if it means your bum can stay warm when your having a pee, maybe there's something in this middle-class thing,' she had countered. So in the year of 1990 we had an inside upstairs toilet installed. For the first time in her life Emma had no more to brave the wilds of winter snow flurries to go to the bog in the pitch black of night outside. Well, I was spoiling her, I suppose! Emma becomes my close friend and companion. We study together, we go round the world. Oh aye, we argue too; she will regale all who will listen about my cruelty imposing my weird stews upon her and standing her at the bottom of the garden when she wouldn't eat them. She says too I was strict on bedtimes and she was in bed far earlier than any of her mates. We disagree about the details of this stuff as I do with Veronica about our formative years, but our trust and love grows stronger over the years. I treasure the time we had together as I raised her as a single parent.

Maureen moves away, first to a flat in Doncaster and then down south. She meets another person and falls in love again (the cheek of it!) – a member of the Royal Shakespeare Company, from a pacifist war resisters' family. Nice bloke, Vivian.

Mind, I do not regret the past – falling in love, getting married. We were together for more than 20 years, 20 years of revolutionary passion, love and sex; we were walking the wild side, I suppose. There is Emma. Emma has been my life and now through Emma and her love I have Caitlin too. If there had been no me and Maur then would have been none of this. And the road since has not been one of regrets and looking back in anguish; we have both looked forward. Today, another 16 years down the line, we regularly bump into each other at Emma's or Caitlin's dos. Her new husband didn't know either of us at the time of the breakup, and is a nice bloke with reasonable politics. So we get on, even enough to have the odd political argument still and disagree with how the world should proceed, as we always did. We have no hard feelings anymore and haven't had for some time now. But back now in 1990 it is hard to be that philosophical and the gap in my emotions is still a raw hole.

CRUNCH TIME

1 September 1990. NUM Branch Meeting. This was crunch time again. The industrial relations at the colliery had gone from sour to utter contempt. This mass Branch meeting would hear a full analysis of what was going on, and debate how it should be met. Half the men at the pit – that being all of our heading and development men – had taken redundancy and gone. I was the only remaining Branch official and only two members of the Union committee remained. Meantime the management were staging their old attempts to break collective bargaining at the pit with 'butty' non-negotiated contracts. I was at constant war with management and the few shortsighted men who thought they could make hay while the sun shone and damn everyone else at the pit. I had drafted the two committee men in as pro-tem treasurer and president. After meeting us in that capacity, the management then cynically refused to pay any time off work to them to act in those roles. Next they banged us all on the three-shift cycle to

make it ever more difficult to represent the men and monitor what was happening across the colliery.

NUM CONFERENCE IN BLACKPOOL, 8 JULY 1991

On Social Insurance the regulations on deafness rattled me in particular:

> DSS regulations on deafness, pneumo, emphysema and bronchitis are a travesty, in the case of these four they completely abandon the otherwise straightforward criteria for disability used in other forms of injury and instead invent mystical and magical formulae ... in the case of deafness we are told a man must have 51db loss of sensorial hearing in both ears before he is disabled. Bad enough that a 14% disablement is the first trigger for payment –we are told 51db is the trigger level for deafness. Just how 51db is related to 14% disability is as I say quite mystical. But then we have the proscribed list of tools criteria. You might think any tool that makes you deaf must be proscribed. Not so. You could stand under a gigantic fan for ten years and be made stone deaf, 51db and more, but you cannot claim, because the gigantic fan is not on the list, which I believe was drawn up in stone age times and takes no cognition of modern machinery.

DROWNING IN THE TGWU?

At this Conference I was to clash most forcibly with Arthur and the areas he had managed to gather round the flag of merger with the Transport and General Workers' Union. It was widely reported that Arthur had been offered a deputy general secretaryship and he expected to move rapidly to the leadership of the giant union. A number of NUM officials were also doubtless happy at the idea of having their jobs and salaries underwritten by the T&G.

Actually and ironically it had been a resolution from Hatfield and then the Yorkshire Area to the Conference in the previous year, 1990 (composite motion G), proposing the development of a single national miners' union constitution, as against our federated one, and the construction of 'an energy union', which had given licence for the tangent of merger with the TGWU to be pursued. This proposal had been in direct contrast to and in opposition to our loss of focus and industrial unionism in any general union merger.

The resolution under the heading 'Organisation' had been put forward by the tiny North Wales Area which in a sense reflected the narrow base of support for the merger. Arthur accused us who were against the merger of being 'dinosaurs'. I countered: 'as opposed to lemmings'. My arguments were basically in support of industrial unionism. The NUM was an industrial union, the TGWU was not and what was being offered here essentially was that the T&G will absorb our union. It was not, as the other side had argued, 'an energy union'. All the other union mergers that they quoted from had been with associated unions: NUR/NUS, rail and maritime transport; NUJ/SOGAT, printers and journalists; NUPE/COSE health unions. This I argued was a totally bureaucratic concept; it was to do with office and offices, cars, officials and salaries. It was not a dam to halt the tide of pit closures – it was a Noah's Ark for the Union officials to sail off on while the industry sank. The resolution, with the support of the NEC, and an amendment that no merger would take place unless the terms were right and the membership was in favour, was passed. I was not the flavour of the month with the guests at the top table. Arthur had asked from the platform whether we could not see the benefits of being with the TGWU. I had replied 'Only one': we could be run over by members of our own Union.[303] I am bitterly opposed to the move as are the bulk of the NUM membership. Elsewhere sincere comrades like Michael Hogg, the humorous and dedicated leading light of the Scottish Executive argued: 'My sole concern Dave is what is best for the members and how best do we give them value for money and how do we guarantee to ex members who have been loyal contributing members for over 40 years.' As it turned out when word got out that Arthur might be in line to start leading a brand-new union with over half a million members, maybe three- quarters of a million members, the Labour Party leadership shit its collective breeches and the plan to give him an automatic position was scotched. (At the end of November the TGWU presented a formal paper to the NUM NEC; it was alleged they had changed their position on two major issues from that initially outlined when the leaders of the two unions had first met.)

The TGWU had been unwilling to accept that the president of the NUM should become a joint deputy general secretary of the TGWU but had 'offered' the vacant position of assistant general secretary with responsibility for the Energy Sector following the departure of Larry Smith. The TGWU had agreed with the National Union of Mineworkers that there should be an Energy Sector for all energy workers; however in their formal presentation these two proposals had been withdrawn and the TGWU were now only offering trade group secretaryship to the NUM National president, and a coalmining group consisting of NUM members and TGWU opencast members, but only if at a future date the opencast workers voted to become part of such a group.

That being the case the plan was quietly put to bed. I however started to campaign instead to start recruiting all miners in Britain which included the offshore oil workers who were at that time cut adrift by bureaucratic unions and operating in their own isolated though highly efficient organisation outside of the TUC. I had met up with the leaders and members of OILC on a number of occasions and put the suggestion to them and they were enthusiastic about the merger; the Offshore Oilworkers were by any definition 'miners' and militant to boot. We were made for each other. On every occasion the question of mergers came up at Conferences I had been on my feet promoting the idea. We wouldn't even have to change our name and we would expand easily to absorb another 20,000 to 25,000 industrial workers in mining and energy. To their credit, people like Frank Cave, general secretary of the Yorkshire Area, enthusiastically got behind this idea and I believe even Arthur on reflection quite liked it.

Talks progressed quite far down the line until the TUC told us we would be expelled from the TUC if we embraced the oilworkers, who were personae non gratae to the cardboard unions that had failed them so badly previously and now wanted them isolated and abandoned. My view was we should call the bluff, if bluff it was, and sod the TUC. I even suggested to Frank we consider affiliation to the IWW as a joint organisation and as an alternative militant union centre. Now that *would be* union reorganisation. In April (1995) the OILC made a formal approach to the NUM for a merger, actually a transfer of engagements. We then made a formal notice of intention to the TUC that from now on we would be organising workers in the North Sea. After formal consideration the TUC threatened to expel us from the organisation if we took them into membership. It was not to be. It threatened too many vested interests in the Labour Party and trade union bureaucracy and local authorities, too many bigwigs and well-heeled officials. In fact Arthur and Frank were, I think, ready to take this matter to the wire if we had had the support of the middle ranks and area leaders. But we didn't.

The Conferences and their wit and humour, their rancour and anger would make a study all of themselves, I have reluctantly decided not to included them in anything like the glory they deserve, but, this one is memorable because Nigel Pearse, the young up-and-coming former supporter of *The Militant* and Branch delegate for the giant Stillingfleet Branch, instructed Mick McGahey, the veteran communist vice president of the Union, in the meaning of Marxism, in his Conference speech – Mick in his benign amusement commenting, 'Is that right?' Frank Cave too, the bluff former Brodsworth delegate and Doncaster Area agent, now the general secretary, instructs the Conference 'We don't want to get bogged down with logic do we?' He wasn't being sarcastic.

Ee, Nigel was a good comrade, with a heart of sheer gold and irrepressible optimism, but given to speeches which built themselves on faith and wishful thinking. I never ever stopped ribbing him over his 'sleeping pig' speech. He had taken the floor on the Special Delegate Conference of October 1990 to urge Conference to take up the cudgels against the NCB again. To get back up on our feet and fight again. His speech was well received with much foot-stomping and applause and had he ended it where he had scripted it, he would have sat down to acclaim. Instead the cheers and enthusiasm spurred him to improvise on the hoof and give it some welly by means of an encore. I later characterised this part of his speech thus: 'And the NCB is like a big fat pig laying asleep, and we have to creep up on it and stab it!' This I accompanied with tiptoeing and dramatic stabbing gestures. It had the crowd in laughter and Nigel embarrassed – 'Gi ower, wi ye?' Actually in writing this text I revisited many of the Conference reports and reread Nigel's speech and discovered his 'big fat pig' wasn't sleeping after all and he had urged that it required 'slaughter', not stabbing. But why spoil a good bit of pillock with cold facts?

In writing this work I also came across a big doodle obviously drawn 3 years later, at the Conference of 1994; it is drawn on the back of Emergency Resolution A, and shows a blissfully happy sleeping pig with Nigel's knife hovering over it and the enjoinder, 'Give Us The Big Fat Pig Speech, Nigel', which I had held up. I liked Nigel's speeches usually; it gave me the opportunity to play the straight hard-nosed factual analyst rather than the raving anarchist Kamikaze. Like the time in 1988 in the Yorkshire Council chamber, when Nigel announced 'We have never been stronger!' and I had to remind him of 110,000 lost members and 100 closed pits and a workforce with its head in the sand and its arse sticking up in the air. Whatever we were, we certainly were not as strong as we had been in 1984, though that didn't mean you still couldn't get stuck in if you timed it right and chose the issue carefully. But the days of gung-ho charges were gone.

COAL, CULTURE AND COMMUNITY CONFERENCE, SHEFFIELD, 1991

This year Powergen imported over 650,000 tonnes of coal through Gladstone Dock in Liverpool for Fiddlers Ferry power station, and over 1 million tonnes through Medway for Kingsnorth. National Power has imported 2 million tonnes through London for its Tilbury and West Thurrock stations. Now they are involved in the construction of coal handling facilities on the Humber, Tees and in Bristol, making possible the import of an additional 14 million tonnes of coal each year. When their contracts with British Coal run out in 1993, the two generators have loudly proclaimed their intention to halve their take from British Coal. The Government stand silently by whilst the generators only plan to add to the fuel trade deficit which soared during the first six months of this year, way above the deficit for the whole of last year.

From January to June Britain imported 12.8 million tonnes more fuel than was exported – six months deficit with a value of 333 million pounds. The deficit for the whole of 1990 was 11.5 million tonnes. Coal exports for January to June fell to 0.9 million tonnes whilst imports shot up to 10 million tonnes almost doubling the deficit in coal trade alone.

This was part of the contribution of Kevin Barron MP to the conference in Sheffield in 1991 while sitting in the capacity of Labour's coal spokesman under a Tory government.

9 December, Bristol. Mass demonstration by dockers and miners' supporters against the building of a 10 million tonne capacity coal import port at the Avonmouth Docks.

Britain's mineworkers need and deserve to know that they have a future they can rely on in an industry that is no longer regarded with 'hostile eyes' by government. Britain's electricity consumers deserve to know that they have the safe, secure and economical supply that our own coal can provide.

No pit was immune to counter-currents and changing perspectives. Brodsworth ('Brodie') was fairly typical of Doncaster pits. Militant, its pickets had led the field all over the country during '84/85. It had been a world production record-holder and a big hitter at tunnelling yardages, but now falling morale had eaten away at its resolve and placed it under threat of immediate closure.

Interviewed on *Look North* as to the possibility of a Doncaster-wide strike in support of Brodie, I had issued the challenge: 'If you come for Brodsworth this coalfield will stand! It's an attack on every Doncaster pit!' That evening as I perused the pubs of Doncaster market place I was met with hostile and unexpected comments: 'Yi want fuckin, you, yi little bastard!' and 'What's tha mean, save pit? Get the bastard shut!' It was a noisy and violent caucus of shut-the-pit merchants from Brodie and Hatfield, not pleased with my endeavours that threatened to foil their dreams of untold wealth and a life without mining.

The 'give-me-my-money-and-shut-bastard-pit' crowd were becoming more violent and desperate as time went on. However, some never lost their sense of humour. On a joint inspection with the Area Director, a choir of rippers sang: 'Oh we've got to go away, its impossible to stay, but you keep me hanging on before I go ... ' This scheme had been drawn up by Ian Biggs, one of the young militants who had previously graced the pages of *A Year Of Our Lives* with poems against closures including 'Coal Not Dole' and 'An Ode To Mr MacGregor'. The joy of mining was our force as social resistance, industrial and political rebellion; if that was taken from us, the pit was just dry and cold, thankless slog – it might as well close, that was their new perception.

In 2004 as coal imports and coal import facilities expand massively, and mines with long-life reserves continue to close, it is a Labour government which now presides:

> There still appears to be a view that the scenario envisaged in Energy Paper 68 should not concern the government unduly. In that report it projects that fuel use in the electricity supply industry (ESI) in 2020 will be nearly 70% from gas, 8% from coal and just over 9% from nuclear. (DTI Energy Paper 68, 2000)

As it turned out nuclear was unready to step into the breach because of costs and determined public resistance, while gas-fired power stations generated power far dearer than existing coal ones and gas only held its share via mounting imports; against this backdrop coal proved resilient, if only because developing countries saw their production and export of coal as cornerstones to their own economic progress. To this end they were 'dumping' coal by the million-tonne bucketful at a price far lower than the production cost of mining it, in order to secure hard currency and market share. For generators this was good news, but it wasn't for British Coal, which continued to be killed off, regardless of future fuel markets pointing back firmly in their direction. The whole process was relentlessly killing off indigenous power sources, and transferring dependency abroad, regardless of import costs, balance-of-payments imbalance and insecurity of supply. In my view the ground was being laid, well in advance, for arguments in support of a new generation of nuclear power stations. Without the effects of the former process they would be utterly senseless.

IF YOU CANT BEAT THEM ...

The NEC agree to start up an official NUM website. It is constructed by a professional website company and will be strictly under the control of the officials: www.nationalunionofmineworkers.com. Although ideas and sections are lifted wholesale from our website there is no reference to us, or any links to us, except a prominent disclaimer that they are not responsible for anything appearing on 'any other unofficial miners website'. Fair enough.

20 April 1991, London. Commemoration of the Irish Uprising of 1916. This is against the backdrop of the first Iraq war, the patriotic jingoism, and bashing the patriotic drum, which has the whole country swathed in union jacks. I make a storming speech, centred on the role of that flag (I am forced to buy one secretly from a shop and hope no one sees me), which I have positioned in front of me on the rostrum above the crowd.

By heck, hasn't it been promoted? Everywhere from the corner shop to Woolworths selling them off by the bucketful. (Me? It was like buying me first packet of Durex – 'wrap it up quick'!) Loads and loads of young working-class lads and lasses are wearing this damn thing now. For the first time in their lives they've been persuaded to identify with the flag of the class enemy.

The butcher's apron my Ma called it, for it wasn't just pushed in the face of Asian people during century after century of oppression, not just pushed in the face of Africans from one end of the continent to the other. It was waved in the face and stuck down the throats of the Irish people, the Scottish people, and as the class war intensified throughout this island, it was rammed down the miners' throats too, in 1912 and 21 when Churchill ordered the troops onto the streets and miners were clubbed to death, and in 1926 as tanks clanked over cobbled streets and gunboats sailed up the Clyde and the Tyne and marines with fixed bayonets charged the crowds in George Square Glasgow and The Bigg Market Newcastle. It wasn't our flag then, and it's not our flag now.

Black and Asian people in Britain have had it as an overt threat every bit as sinister as the burning cross of the Ku Klux Klan, as nazis and National Frontists, fascists and all sorts of racist scum have taken this flag to their bosom, as well they might embrace its gory and bloodstained crimes.

'These colours don't run!'

(And leaning over with a cigarette lighter I set the flag alight.)

The bastards burn easy though!!

Victory to the International Working Class and All Oppressed Nationalities!

It was quite a crescendo. I had been livid at the *Daily Star*'s widespread use of a colour poster showing the union jack and the stars and stripes and the slogan 'These Colours Don't Run'. The danger with actually setting the big plastic union jack alight was it melted and had the potential of burning the whole crowded hall down. It was a trick I decided not to use again at indoor rallies, no matter how incensed I felt.

SPECIAL CONFERENCE

October 1991. The Union calls a Special Delegate Conference in line with the Annual Conference decision to do so if we hadn't received a satisfactory pay offer. Actually the Board simply refused to discuss anything with the Union at National level so the pay negotiations were going nowhere. There were three responses, one from Yorkshire for an overtime ban without safety cover, one from the North East for an overtime ban with safety cover and one from the Midland Area calling for one-day strikes with pits selected by the NEC in succession. Peter Heathfield, the National secretary, on behalf of the NEC had said this resolution would give them problems. My mate Bob Anderson with his broad Stoke accent responded with furious sarcasm:

Chairman, Comrades: I am flabbergasted. I don't know where to start. I don't know whether to come around with a hat and have a levy for the NEC (Laughter). Problems? You know a one day strike will give you problems, a series of one day strikes. What do you think we have got at the pits, Peter, problems? We have got problems day in, day out, and we are not on, and I am not talking about you personally, but we are not on in excess of 20 grand.

Strangely absent from the list of Conference speakers is myself, although I am listed as being in attendance at the Conference. As I recall there was no belly for a fight over wages at Hatfield; we were clinging on for dear life to the pit. If we had ammunition left it shouldn't be spent on any wages issue. So I had no heart for this fight and wouldn't pretend I had. The NEC clearly didn't have any either, with Bob Wills from the NEC offering us only the prospect of a Labour government as the solution to our problems. Tyrone O'Sullivan the 'jolly green giant' from Tower gave us a potted history of Tower Colliery and its militant past and determination to resist redundancy, but over this matter he could see no other option either than the return of a Labour government, although he couldn't have much confidence in them either:

I am telling you the boys in Tower at the moment see the only way to survive is at least wait until the return, we hope, of a Labour government. We can't possibly in any way see ourselves going out on strike.

Even a Conference like this, in the eleventh hour, we might say, of the Union's life, with our backs to the wall and little in the way of options, was alive with wit and character; the House of Commons couldn't hold a candle to it:

J. A. Scott (Yorkshire): Mr Chairman, delegates, there are five things up to today I am proud of. One, I am a Northumbrian. Two, I am a member of the National Union of Mineworkers. Three, I am the only one in the Midlands that supports Berwick Rangers. And four I support Scotland. The fifth one is my members at Manton Colliery. For the past 3 weeks we have had exactly what we have been talking about on at Manton Colliery over one of our colleagues that has been sacked. We have got a total overtime ban with no safety cover, fair enough it has hit some of our lads on a Monday morning and it has also hit the Officials because the only way they can get back at us is to threaten to sack all four Branch officials. I today have been told that if I didn't come to work this morning, I would be marked as absent and put in front of a Disciplinary Committee on absenteeism. I didn't go to work. I didn't intend to go to work. We cannot stand by and let a manager dictate what our Union Officials do at the pit.

We have got the support of the members. (Applause)

The Union launches a nationwide strike ballot, aimed at securing a majority for a biting overtime ban without safety cover or flexibility. It is aimed at securing negotiating rights on wages and conditions, something we had been deprived of since the end of the strike. The National Conference of 1991 had put forward the pay demand, along with the realisation that unless it was to be a pious resolution, as so many had been previously, it would have to be fought for.

Was pay the right issue to canvass support on at this time when the members were hanging on for dear life? Many just wanted out, many others seen the pits as on a knife-edge. They complained bitterly about the loss of negotiating rights and declining wage values at most pits, but actually stopping overtime work in protest was a risky business. Even among the militants there was mistrust of the NEC, after the last time when they had voted for action and been humiliated by the leadership's response. We got whacked as many of us predicted, but there was an air of self-righteousness about the areas and branches – that we at least should be providing the leadership and issuing the call to fight, even if the troops would not rally. I had been appalled by this attitude; we couldn't afford to lose ballots, especially ones on which we had campaigned and tried to inspire – it made us look weaker than we actually were. But at the same time was the union going to stand up for itself or just let events wash over it? I would have preferred a straight fight on recognition but that didn't capture the imagination of the Area.

When it went to the vote, the resolution for an overtime ban without safety cover was carried on a card vote 36 to 22 with 1 abstention. Sadly it didn't get past the members when put to individual ballot. Only 36.6% voted in favour of a ban without safety cover. When it came to the ballot even at Hatfield we lost by 111 in favour to 119 against, the fiery Frickley likewise voted 315 for to 381 against and the Yorkshire Area as a whole went down to a 45.2% yes against a 54.4% no. Only the tiny Nottingham NUM voted yes by 62.6%. Scotland and South Wales voted by more than 80% against action. It was a thunderous 63.1% nationwide defeat.

The wages issue, although tied to the question of derecognition, was about wages during a time of mass rundown and ongoing pit closures. It wasn't a feasible proposition; a resolution on the question of Union recognition and respect itself would have had a far better chance of success but that hadn't been the view of the summer Conference.

15/16 November 1991. The national strike ballot for action on Union derecognition takes place. It is lost by 43.2% to 56.8%.

November 1991. Orgreave coking works is closed and the site demolished. Not a picket in sight. Arthur phoned the police when the works closed and asked them if they knew a group of people were stopping workers at the plant going to work? Why weren't there any police with horses and riot shields stopping it happening? It wasn't their business they said – strange, it had been when the miners had tried to close the plant.

During this period Terry Norman, a well-placed fellow-travelling Welsh academic was closely watching and commenting on events. Terry had been a loyal supporter of the strike and an official of the Justice For Miners Campaign. He was to be influential again in the re-emerging support groups in the final stand on the miners in 1992. He had a particularly amusing turn of phrase and in one letter to me observed:

> I remember once being button-holed by a particularly intense member of one of the tiny Moonie-like sects that proliferate the left and asked what my politics were.
>
> Upon replying something to the effect that I was 'a revolutionary Anarcho-Marxist Trotskyist Syndicalist with a touch of chapel' I was somewhat nonplussed when I was next asked where I stood on the Irish question, how could I reconcile Christianity with Marxism and was the chapel influence Methodist or Baptist.
>
> I left my interlocutor to attend a funeral service to the memory of Irony, swearing never again to trifle with those of an ideologically sombre cast of mind.

John Bird, *Years of Victory*, Oil, 1947 (courtesy of Durham Miners' Association)

7

1992: The Miners' Last Stand

Following the end of the strike of 1984/85, initial closures, and job losses that amounted to more than a third of the previous workforce, there came a brief period during which NCB management tried to take advantage of the situation to break old agreements and enforce new disciplines, as they had following the 1926 lockout. When the dust started to settle and the miners and their Union started to take stock, the shock of defeat started to subside a little. The miners were still a dominant force in the British economy and industrial society, comprising more than 100,000 men in over 100 mines and supplying the bulk of Britain's energy requirements. Badly bruised, the NUM, at least at pit level, started to recover its energies.

In the national statistics for tonnages lost through disputes during the first quarter of 1986, South Yorkshire was top of the national league with 38 disputes. The ratio of tonnes lost per 1,000 tonnes of saleable output was 20:30. The Area was responsible for 41% of all disputes; 5 South Yorkshire pits had the heaviest tonnage lost and 6 the highest number of disputes.[304]

The scene was set, at the end of the 1980s, for renewed open conflict. It began with pickets at Frickley stopping the whole Yorkshire coalfield. Then Bentley Doncaster stopped South Yorkshire. The Coal Board was furious at the continued picketing, which took place despite disciplinary codes, dismissals and threats, cameramen and spies. Then came Hatfield's mass pickets stopping Doncaster who withdrew after a flurry of writs and injunctions. South Yorkshire brought themselves out in sympathy, much to the bafflement of Mr Houghton the Area director, who referred to 'invisible pickets.[305]

New incentive schemes and bonus systems had required the active participation of the NUM, and rebuilding profitability at colliery and area level produced new bargaining strengths for the Union. While at National level the Union was ostracised, at area and branch level the NUM was starting to recover its strength. In the late 1980s numerous local strikes swept the coalfields and whole areas stood, mainly around questions of job control. The biggest flashpoint however with British Coal (as the NCB had now renamed itself) was a stringent new disciplinary code. This had produced a rash of colliery strikes and the Yorkshire Area was poised to relaunch a national offensive when a national ballot was called for. The ballot on whether to take industrial action against the code produced a massive 'yes' vote – much to the surprise of the government and British Coal; it also shocked many area leaders. It demonstrated that the NUM as a force was far from dead at this time. The NEC of the NUM, however, fearful that the miners couldn't sustain another all-out strike, implemented only minimal sanctions but achieved 'an understanding' that the code would not be implemented.

In 1989/90, the number of disputes at colliery level continued to be high, especially in the Yorkshire coalfield, where abrasive management caused a serious morale problem. Overall, there were 173 disputes throughout the entire British coalfield. The Yorkshire coalfield accounted for 93 per cent of these and a number of pits in that coalfield had the highest number of disputes. On 6 March 1990, a High Court judge banned the miners from taking action over the redeployment of seven colleagues at Hatfield Main colliery (*Financial Times*, 7 March 1990). In July the same year the Frickley NUM Branch and its four officials were held in contempt of court and threatened with jail because it was claimed they had not disassociated themselves from the strike action taking place at the pit regarding a dismissal issue.[306]

The government now prepared to take the initiative again and launch a renewed assault upon the remainder of the coal industry. This it did initially with CEGB deregulation in 1986. Basically it meant the CEGB no longer had any obligation to buy coal even if it was the cheapest or most conveniently situated source of fuel. Next came the privatisation of the whole power supply industry. It was coupled with almost carte blanche approval for new generation sources in what was called the dash for gas, without any requirement to demonstrate an energy need or a market requirement. Worse for any overall conservation or energy strategy, burning off huge volumes of a relatively scarce domestic energy source was massively inefficient and wasteful, and had then the added impact of driving existing coal-powered generation out of existence at the same time. The overall energy pool was therefore allowed to be squandered for quick and easy profits to power speculators. The regulations such as they were had existed to prevent just such an occurrence. Twelve regional electricity companies and two all-powerful generators had been created, it was said to 'break up government monopoly and create cheaper power'. We look back now with not only the benefit of hindsight because we had foreseen the falseness of this prediction, but also from tonnes of statistics. Within the first 2 years of privatisation energy prices rose by 40%; this was despite falling coal prices, though British coal was being everywhere marginalised and its market drying up regardless of falling prices.

It might be speculated that this was due at least in part to the failure of 'Plan A', which involved:

– Closure of 'marginal capacity' and reduction of the whole industry by about a third.

– Increased utility of contractors, who it was expected would be non-union.

– Breaking the workforce at large from the control of the NUM by individual and group contracts negotiated directly with miners and excluding the Union.

– An end to strike action in the industry through contractor employment, imposition of strict discipline, high motivational contracts directly agreed with the men, and derecognising of the NUM at all levels.

All of this was a prelude to privatisation of a still large and highly profitable industry.

If this had been the Thatcher core strategy it failed spectacularly, as the NUM proved itself highly resilient and both contractors and direct employees overwhelmingly stuck to the Union. The wildcat had not been driven from its lair, and strikes, unofficial and quasi-official, still raged at many collieries and in a number of key areas.

Arthur was still telling everyone the strike had been a victory. But in many ways this isn't a totally mad conclusion. Thatcher certainly hadn't won, not in her core objectives. I suppose if you're expecting a hefty kick in the balls and you take a punch in the face instead then it could be called something of a victory. But then they came back to deliver the kick in the balls.

By August the NCB/British Coal itself came clean on plans for a further 20 pit closures and 20,000 job losses. Compounding the idiocy of the decision came the simultaneous figures that the Board had recorded record profits for 1991/92 of £170 million, up by £72 million on the previous year. Increased productivity for the year stood at 13.1%, with a production of 71 million tonnes, just 2% less production than the preceding year with 15 less collieries and 16,000 less men. The current workforce stood at just 41,000 men. From now on the red light was flashing. 80% of British Coal's market was in danger of disappearing. If it did, there could be only one consequence. The Department of Energy couldn't really ignore the light and commissioned a secret report under Lord Rothschild, who concluded that less than 12 of the remaining 50 pits would survive within 12 months. His forecast proved devastatingly accurate,– probably equating to less than 14,000 miners nationwide and going into free fall.[307]

It is my assertion that 'the market' which 'conspired' to rob the miners of their living was in fact inanimate. It was said that 'blind market forces' had taken away the fuel environment in which the mines lived; the market however was a vehicle that could be free-steered or run along tracks. This change in market direction was far from blind and it was aimed quite deliberately at getting rid of the miners. There can be no one, surely, who would argue that the events of 1984/85 were anything other than the result of a deliberate government plan to crush or neuter the miners. The government spent, lost or cost itself between £15 BILLION and £20 BILLION to complete the plan. It is my contention that the aims of that plan, demonstrably unfulfilled, required a Plan B that was more thoroughgoing, more drastic. It came through 'rigging the market'.

In work I undertook for Ruskin College, *The Last Days of Coal*, which was part of Raph's proposal to form part of a requirement for me to become a Fellow of Ruskin and which has sat unloved and unpublished following the chronic illness and death of Raph Samuel, I think I got quite close to telling who rigged that market and how.[308] My autobiography is not the place to tell that story, or to publish all my unpublished works by stealth. However something of it should be said about it here. That plan wheeled out by Major, but cobbled together in several backyards, produced the most extraordinary backlash from the public at large. The realisation that the miners, with whom the whole adult population had had a love–hate relationship for generations, were finally on the very last roundup, struck a raw nerve. Something important was happening here and people suddenly woke up to it. The backlash was surprising because the measure had been publicised even before Major's election. The BBC current affairs programme *Panorama* had spelt it out quite clearly in its thoroughgoing investigation 'Crisis at the Coal Face' (with the making of which I had cooperated). The programme trailed the fact that government plans would throw the coal industry into the deep blue sea of economic fortune without a lifebelt, to sink or swim alone. At the same time the newly privatised generators were announcing they would give no special importance to native sources of energy supply, regardless of costs, long-term supply or the wider impact on society.

Roy Lynk, whose ability to read, let alone reason, gives rise to serious doubts, reacted to leaks of the report by repeating what Mrs Thatcher had assured him: profitable pits, which included most of his Nottingham base, would stay open; it was the others, mainly NUM pits elsewhere, which would close. He didn't see that the old rules had changed: profitable pits could be profitable if they could sell their coal to someone who wanted it. That that 'someone' wouldn't actually want the cheapest fuel on the market does take some understanding for people with common sense.

In the teeth of a viciously anti-union Hatfield Coal Company run and owned by the hard-line anti-union Jeff Ainley, I conduct a straw poll of our NUM membership, which is a minority among the otherwise non-union Hatfield workforce. Across the rest of the privatised industry there is lack of conciliation, lack of Union recognition, imposed pay awards. (The situation applies particularly in the case of RJB Mining, a firm named after its owner and then major share holder Richard Budge. Richard was later to resign from his own company, which had been re-titled UK Coal, and set up shop on his own, buying Hatfield Main Colliery.) All this has meant the Union has had to throw down the gauntlet, first to our members. Across the much-battered industry we ask if they would be prepared to enter the breach once more dear friends, or fill the shafts with our unemployed members. I am determined that whatever the difficulties, if the rest of the coalfields strike, or even just the Yorkshire coalfield, our few diehards at Hatfield will be at the top of that pit lane with as many of their unemployed former colleagues from the village as we can muster. Hatfield will not scab, no matter how many members we don't have. The poll assured me that at least those who returned the ballot papers would not be changing any spots, but sadly the bulk of the men were gripped in fear and longing for a quiet life. Truth was, the bulk of the men remaining at the pit had been handpicked for this reason, with the Union militants and even moderates carefully weeded out.

31 January 1992. Hatfield Pit threatened with closure. This was, we thought, a final warning to improve performance, although by this time the pit was operating profitably. By 13 October government/NCB announce the closure of 31 pits, including Hatfield.

March 1992. The TUC Women's Conference, surprisingly, was to cause me to clash with COSA and the NEC. The NUM had sent delegates; at Hatfield we had chosen two canteen women who were keen members of the Union, and Bentley had sent a female member of the NUM branch committee. The leader of the delegation was however Vera Wasilewska from COSA, who wrote up a report of the conference without consultation with any of the other NUM delegates. In it she was most scathing about the conference decisions, particularly the one that agreed that women should represent their respective unions at the TUC Women's Conference. She claimed: 'The NUM delegates voted against this motion.' This wasn't accurate – they voted, all except her, for the motion. Remarkably, women being delegates for their unions at the women's conference hadn't been the case previously and a number of men represented their women members at the conference. Our industrial delegates all agreed that of course women should be the delegates at the women's conference, although men could be observers if they wished.

Vera wasn't aware of this and drafted a report condemning the women who voted in favour of this resolution as lesbians:

> Equality is not the one-way system that some of the Lesbian Delegates would have you believe ... I would hope that in two years time a Heterosexual Delegate would place a Motion on the Agenda to redress this situation.

I didn't get to read this report until the NUM Annual Conference of that year, when it was contained in the section on the year's NEC meetings and reports. I strode to the rostrum to berate the report and the fact that it had been accepted without comment from the NEC. Davie Murdoch, the fiery Scots leader of the Yorkshire Region of COSA, then leapt to the defence of his delegate Mrs Wasilewska. Peter Heathfield in the chair threw petrol on the flames by ridiculing my objections and asking if I attended in drag to laughter from the delegates and a shout that I didn't need to go in drag and more laughter. I was bright red when I stormed back to the stage to attack what I considered to be gross sexism and a lack of seriousness over the issues which affect our female members. I charged that the youth conference didn't have pensioners as delegates, did it? That a retired miners' conference wouldn't have youngsters representing them, would it? It was damned obvious that a women's trade union conference would draw delegates from female trade unionists. It caused quite a lot of bitter exchanges and Vera came into the Conference to ask what I was complaining of and why – the NUM women delegates were happy with the report. No they weren't; I had checked with Hatfield and Bentley's delegates before I came. I was seething that Peter had tried to make a joke of it, and even more so that I had blushed like a bride and took offence over the reference to my hair probably and being able to pass as a female delegate. It was harsh but simple pit pillock but I wasn't used to it in this arena.[309]

Mrs Wasilewska was nominated by COSA for the TUC Women's Gold Badge and became the NUM's nomination too in 1992, and as far as I know she was awarded it.[310] Incidentally, she did better than Arthur, who was nominated for the TUC General Council but failed to be elected; the word was that 'the candidate wasn't known'.

In June Paul Foot in his *Daily Mirror* column had run an exposé on the blacklisters. These were the firms which gathered information on militants and sent out CVs to prospective employers telling them just what working-class vipers shouldn't be held to the tender breast of capitalism. I checked and lo and behold I was on; just as well really: I'd have been most offended not to be on the list – I mean what the hell do you have to do to get on it if I wasn't there? (I am less blasé about what the state's possible lists might say about me, or, worse, do about me.)

The rumour machine was in overdrive. It invented the date on which the pit would close, or be partially closed. It dreamed up spectactular offers to reduce the manpower: early retirement at 50, then 45, then 40. It strove to cover everyone's interests. First the pit should not close – no, no closure, but all the men who wanted to leave must be allowed to leave, and they would get massive redundancy payments, enough to fill Aladdin's cave. Those who wished to transfer from less-secure pits could do so, and be paid massive transfer fees. All redundancy terms would be copper-bottomed; nobody would get less because of poor pre-closure performances. The dream was added to each week, each day, each shift. Until, that is, a new management initiative would burst the bubble, or the Union would develop some new confrontration or plan to spoil the dream. Sometimes it was just sheer wishful thinking: how could they get out and save their dignity, yet not be redundancy scabs?

Some of the rumours I tracked down to two lads in the surveyors' office, who would make up a story on a Monday in the canteen and see how long it would be before we were telling them their story as certain fact. The new greeting down t'pit was, 'Have you heard owt?' It was a cue for 'Tell me something I want to hear.' Someone's wife or daughter always worked at Coal House, or was the secretary to a top NCB manager or director. The source was always impeccable – people wanted to believe it: 'Their gaan shut Hatfield, and mine coal at Thorne. We get redundo for leaving here, but set on again over at Thorne.' The Board added to the confusion by raising then dropping the lump sum for redundancy in an effort to get men to jump at the most advantageous time for fear of missing the boat. Stick and carrot came in full measure. Confusion and demoralisation.

From the Union point of view the rumours were poison. They sapped morale, they stopped us developing any confidence in winning, they made all talk of a fightback seem futile. My response was humour or fury, depending on where the challenge was coming from. On the fury side came denouncing 'money grubbers' – short-sighted job thieves not simply selling their own jobs but offering up ours as well. We had to try and form alliances. We couldn't condemn the man who just wanted out – God knows, who could blame him? – but any man who wanted to sink the ship because he believed he could get to a lifeboat first was worse than a scab. At the same time we invented jokes about the freaks, and my 'Rowie's Song' was a great success at all events organised by us or the colliery. Not that Rowie was a real redundo freak himself; it was just that as an onsetter he was the first to greet you with the latest round of rumours when you got off the cage. I wrote the song in September '92:

Rowie's Song
(Tune: 'Football Crazy')

Oh you're sure to knaa wor onsetter, the feller with the smile,
A funny looking character with pound signs in his eyes.
He scans the morning papers some snippets for the find,
He reads that much between the lines,
He might as weel be blind.

He's gone redundancy crazy,
He's gone redundancy mad.
They say redundo's robbed him
Of the little bit o' sense he had.
For he dreams of piles of money
Piling up on high,
But all I think he'll really get
Is a Big Pie In The Sky.

Early in morning, when he is underground
He'll set the jaws a-clacking at twenty thousand pound.
By snap time it is twenty-five, its thirty-five at lowse.
With a time share out at Tenerife and a private yacht at Cowes.

He's gone redundancy crazy (etc.)

He's dreaming of a payout, one hundred thousand grand,
And twenty thousand for his coal that's placed into his hand.
A big posh hoose at Hatfield, with twenty living rooms,
With a landing strip for his aeroplane and ninety metre pool.

He's gone redundancy crazy (etc.)

Now the Queen she came from London, to give Rowie his cheque,
And place a big gold medal around his bloody neck.
She says: 'Phillip and I were thinking; now you've got the dough,
'Wor Fergie's after another man if you'll take her into tow.'

He's gone redundancy crazy (etc.)

Weeks later came the shock announcement that 31 pits would be wiped out in one go, an event more seismic than even the redundo freaks could think up.

Some of the physically biggest blokes at the pit were the 'heading men', 'the big hitters'; these were the Trojans, the single-handed lifters of heavy-section girders, the carriers of huge junction beams, the drivers of monster machines, and the biggest earners. Among these, the wish to get out was greatest; their skills were much in demand among the private contract firms which were growing in number and size as British Coal sought new strategies of control. The heading men reasoned that if they could get the money, they would soon be back in employment doing the same job on high wages – albeit perhaps at a different pit. Some used direct threats to 'go-getting' coal cutters: 'One and one ...or you'll get some of this!' In other words: you do one cut and cut plough, you reduce coal production; you throw the mine into jeopardy. With those miners coming from the opposite direction attempting to maximise production to save the pit to restore bargaining power meant there was a deep clash of perspectives and sometimes bodies.

Canteen meetings were often charged with violence; in one confrontation, as I spelt out new efficiency plans and increased incentives I was challenged: it was stand-your-ground-and-state-your-piece-or-crawl-away time. Both sides however claimed the strike as their legacy; *we* had changed, it was argued, *we* had let the bosses on top, we had lost our bottle, coal was collaboration. 'Fuck 'em, let it shut!' was a sort of Molly Maguire[311] response without the gunpowder but with the same intention. In the Branch Meeting the room was regularly packed to capacity with shouting, contesting parties. Some were trying to vote to shut the pit, or else refuse to accept survival plans. Others seen the survival of the pit as the survival of the Union and the principles of '84. At Edlington Colliery (Yorkshire Main), the first post-strike Doncaster casualty, a belligerent management and a workforce torn by contradictions ensured the death of the pit. Those who transferred to Hatfield determined not to allow the tragedy to be repeated, but everywhere they could see similar symptoms.

At length we finally agreed together with the Area director to let out all the heading men who wanted to go redundant. Only one man chose to stay. We passed a resolution that no man who had taken voluntary redundancy at any Doncaster colliery would be employed at Hatfield pit in any capacity. We were determined that any of our 'mates' who had taken the golden handshake and in the process tried to drive us all onto the rocks would not return to the colliery through some back door as a contractor. The big contradiction for us now was that we had to accept that outside contractors would now man all of our headings. Hatfield would be already one-third privatised. We no longer now any had control over manning and the operation of shifts and overtime in these headings; it made a mockery of our bold strike in 1990 when we stood the pit and picketed out the coalfield to prevent a single shift of heading men in a solitary heading being moved. A worker at the nextdoor Markham Main colliery said of one of our heading men: 'The last time I seen that bastard he had a balaclava on picketing to defend his job. Next time I see him he's a contractor and he's come for my bastard.'

July 1992. NUM Annual Conference. It would be far too self-indulgent to log *my Conference* contribution – 'up and doon like a bride's nightie', if there was any Conference which was 'my Conference' it was the Conference of 1992. Miners' Conferences always have been highly political; this was no exception, except that in essence it was the politics of the far left rather than the Labour left. I'm not of course talking here of the minute little sects that inhabit the theoretical world of left politics, but the issues of far-left politics debated within the workers' movement: capitalism and socialism, the Labour Party or the industrial movement, direct action, energy and the environment, nuclear weapons and the state. However, it is issues of safety and job control which dominate the Conference, which is surprising in many ways given the impending assault of pit closures now rushing towards our communities. I think we were unaware that a major new assault was almost upon us.

I was to more or less open the Conference, not officially of course, but by accident, though Arthur swears I did it on purpose. As luck would have it a coaster had collided with the Meccano-like bridge at Goole on my way to Conference. This caused me a considerable delay, as the bloke who was driving me had to make a long detour. As all too often, I arrived, late. Nobody was about as I wandered down corridors and round the little pokey corners and turns of the Spa Complex, Scarborough. Arthur was in full flight as I burst through the doors onto the stage behind where he was speaking, amid cheers and jeers from my comrades. Oops! Exiting rapidly stage ahint, I at length found the front entrance and walked down the aisles of delegates, while Arthur, looking menacingly at me, continued to give it some welly and profound utterances. I genuflected on one knee and made the sign of the cross, to titters from them that knew what that was, before inching my way along the line of cursing delegates.

We had just started on the approval of the past year's NEC reports when I rose with a matter arising. Actually it was a very big matter arising. I took issue with the NEC, and both the pro- and anti-TGWU merger factions who were refusing to further the decision of the previous Conference on bringing about a single constituted NUM based upon the branches and a monthly, all-Britain standing National Conference of delegates. Both factions had used this policy either as a sprat to catch a mackerel or else as a block to achieving a single structure which could more easily make a passage into the structure of the TGWU. I was furious that this merger thing was being seen as the only show in town, when in fact that policy decision was directly motivated as a *stand-alone alternative to merger*.

The guest speaker at the Conference was Rodney Bickerstaffe, at that time president of the TUC. For those who've never heard Rodney he is a hilarious speaker and at this Conference he was at his best with the delegates splitting their sides at his stories.

At the end of his contribution Arthur presents him with a memento and tells the Conference: 'People don't know this, but we and our families go out together each Christmas for dinner and have done that for more years than I care to remember. The arrangement is that one year I pay and he pays the following year, except he's never paid yet!' Rodney responds: 'It's a lie, he keeps telling me his money is tied up abroad!' We roared.

It was at this Conference where I made a stab at analysing what was happening to us and why:

So the Tories' nuclear mission is a vision that is based on playing in the political big boys' league. It happens to coincide with the need to knacker the coalmines and the coalminers. The trouble was and is, though, that in order to have the bombs in order to play in this big league you have also got to have a civil nuclear energy programme, and that nuclear programme is so fantastically expensive and non-competitive when compared to coal that an elaborate long-term strategy had to be developed which would ultimately justify the dominance of nuclear energy as Britain's main fuel supplier.

You already know the rest of the story. Run down the British coal industry, allow in cheap coal from abroad. I have made the point frequently that the coal from South Africa is the dearest coal in the world in terms of flesh, blood and bones ... all of the coal ... that is brought here is actually dearer than British coal: it is only sold cheap ... To get where we are now coal is dumped at below cost prices: the coal generators buy it; the coal generators don't want British coal: British coalmines close and on the road to there in my opinion privatisation is a very small spur line which leads from a great industrial complex to a blackberry bush or maybe a scene from a heritage tour.

Nuclear energy, once we have gone, is then cranked up as the patriotic British fuel. They will then be using the arguments that the coal produced abroad is far more expensive than nuclear energy produced here. They will then be making the arguments about the premium nature of gas production and we need to conserve the gas. They will then be using the arguments about dirty fuels and how we have got to be kind to the environment because nuclear energy will be better and safer. It is a long-run self-fulfilling philosophy that will lead us to the nuclear-based industry Thatcher dreamed of. No more mass divisions of the class war, the proletariat, three-day weeks or riots in Westminster. That's what it is all about. It is what it has been about.[312]

My mate Davie Guy, president of the North East Area inter alia, believes I have it wrong, and thinks imported gas will be our main assassin.

A future Labour Government needs an independent source of supply of energy. David Douglass's scenario about it being nuclear fuel in my view is a non-starter. There are too many reasons against that. But Davy, another time.[313]

The debate is joined by I. Morgan, the Welsh leader of the Cokemen and NEC member:

Looking at a comment made by David Guy referring to David Douglass. There is a lot I think in what David Douglass says. Coal power generation is much cheaper than nuclear. Everyone now, after years of argument by the NUM have come round and agreed. They have to agree to it because they could not sell it[314] for that particular reason. If coal is the cheapest form of electricity production, if you shut down the British Coal production then nuclear now becomes the cheaper form of production. It is now necessary to have nuclear production. That, I think, is what he was looking at: if we lose the argument on privatisation and the industry is sold off, he is looking beyond that and I could see that. It has now become far more attractive to have the nuclear industry if you can do away with coal … I think that is the type of argument he was putting.[315]

I was. We disagree, but we both live long enough for us to see Blair pick up the vision where Thatcher and Major laid it down, and plough on with the task of constructing a nuclear-energy-powered Britain, constantly upgrading her nuclear weapons while expanding the civil industry to the total detriment of coal and the miners. In later years they are cheer led by an army of 'greens' who fall lock stock and barrel for the 'environmental' argument, although their option is to cover the island with wind turbine estates (far more environmentally destructive as it happens than either nuclear or coal) that are never going to be the alternative to coal in reality.

At this Conference I am moving the Yorkshire amendment to a Scottish resolution on anti-racialism. I am talking about tackling endemic racism in the working class at large and also among our own members. I am calling for support to and praise for the Anti-Nazi League and the far-left Anti-Fascist Action. The amendment is opposed by Scotland, despite an NEC recommendation to support the amended resolution. Scotland accuse the Anti-Nazi League of being an opportunist SWP front, although they can find no argument against AFA, the hard-line, mostly anarchist and revolutionary communist frontline physical opponents of the NF. I think in reality they don't know who they are. The debate is widespread, with North East and Derbyshire speaking firmly in support, at the end of which all bar Scotland vote in favour of active work with ANL and AFA and in rooting out racialist attitudes in clubs and at work among our own ranks.

A little further down the agenda I return the favour. Scotland's resolution on Peace, Disarmament and Trident is severely iffy, calling as it does for all sorts of trust in the United Nations. We can't amend it as we had used our amendment allocation up already, but I did speak in support 'with grave reservations'. It opened up an in-depth discussion on the nature of the UN and the 'New World Order', but also some reflections on the 'Old World Order' – the nature of the imperialist manipulations in the Middle East and the selective hypocrisy of 'genocide'.

Peter Heathfield retires. He will be the last general secretary of the NUM; although others following him will have that role, there will no longer be a full-time position. I think it true to say none of us knew that that massive change had taken place until such time as we came to try and replace him.

The Conference of '92 I believe stands as a naked rebuttal to those who say workers in unions can only develop 'trade union consciousness', that political awareness and class consciousness cannot be furthered within the unions as such. The wealth of debate and range of subjects, the quality of the debates which are there in the records prove just how ignorant that belief is. Few formal political-party conferences would have touched the pulse of world power and understood its operation in the depth that this Conference as one of hundreds has.

13 October 1992. Heseltine, the energy minister, announces another 31 pit closures and minimally 30,000 job losses, with 10 pits to close forthwith. This would leave only 19 working mines. It is a move to checkmate in the age-long

battle between the miners and the ruling class; it is a move which is a prelude to removing all our pieces from the board. This is no longer the game Thatcher embarked on, but the next rung up from that. It can only be achieved by vital changes in the regulation of the way in which power is generated. It is illogical in any economic efficiency sense; it is not about new or modern developments replacing old and tired coal plants; and it is not about unprofitable energy sources being replaced by profit-generating capacity. Like the politics of coal since the turn of the century, it is a politically directed, class-motivated move.

Imported coal is overall 30% more costly to produce than British coal; it arrives here cheaper at the ports because the producers' governments give it massive subsidies. The EEC allows its own coal producers to subsidise their own coal. The Germans give £3.5 BILLION a year to their coal industry, whose output costs on average £110 per tonne, while Britain refuses to do so, and British coal is produced virtually without subsidy for £42. The 'dash for gas' is not a drive to efficiency: the cost of generating electricity from coal-fired stations is 2.2p per unit, but at the new gas-fired stations it varies from 2.7p at best to 3.3p per unit. Gas is a premium fuel, a domestic fuel for small-scale domestic consumption; there are ample supplies, but they are burned off in huge, wasteful, unnecessary power production; the resource is bound to rapidly deplete and the costs rise incessantly. The 'dash for gas', which was given a clear-sighted go-ahead, was aimed quite consciously at producing a 60% over-capacity in power generation; this over-capacity would be taken out exclusively by pit closures, but the new capacity was not required – it was more expensive and was wasteful. It was the catalyst in the new round of closures, aimed at destroying the power of the NUM by destroying the dependency on coal. (The global energy scene is a constantly changing one of course. At the time of writing (2010) world demand for all fuels is threatening to outstrip all sources of supply. At the same time as the climate change lobby continues its ongoing attack on coal and coal production, coal looks to be the fuel of choice around the world.)

The end game, however, was the end of coal production, the exhaustion of gas, and the long-term major dependency on nuclear power. The nuclear industry received a 'fossil-fuel levy' from the coal producers, a subsidy in all of £1.3 billion. Nuclear generation was over a hundred times more expensive than coal power generation and vastly more dangerous, while nuclear power station decommissioning costs, at present times incalculable, are taken out of any financial assessments.

The closure revelation produces a stormy emergency National Conference of the NUM held on 15 October 1992, along with cries of betrayal from the UDM, who despite promises on Nottingham pits now found they were equally on the closure list. Mrs Thatcher's public acknowledgement of the UDM had come during the Lord Mayor's banquet on Monday 12 November 1984:

> The courage and loyalty of working miners and their families will never be forgotten. Their example will advance the cause of moderate and reasonable trade unionism everywhere. When the strike ends it will be their victory.[316]

An appearance in the New Year's honours list followed for Roy Lynk, leader of the breakaway movement, but what guarantees on the survival of Nottingham pits were offered in reality, or whether it was a tacit understanding, we shall perhaps never know. Certainly, the division between the strikers and strikebreakers had been consolidated into an organisational break by Mrs Thatcher's advisers and allies. It would condemn any efforts by the NUM to recover its hegemony after the strike was over. Mrs Thatcher in her memoirs makes it clear that her involvement with these 'working miners' continued after the defeat of the NUM on the streets:

> In fact I remained in touch with representatives of working miners ... I accepted Peter Walker's advice to this effect, but told my Private Office that when the strike was over I would have representatives of all the working miners and their wives to No. 10 for a reception – which indeed I did. (I met some also at a private buffet hosted by Woodrow Wyatt at the end of March the following year.)[317]

The non-strikers had good reason to feel betrayed as the axe now fell almost as heavily across Nottingham as it did in Yorkshire.

THE OCTOBER MOVEMENT: A WIND OF CHANGE THAT REFUSED TO BLOW

The challenge could not have been more direct or immediate: 31 pits to close, many by the end of that week. The heartless and autocratic fashion of the closure notices presented the miners this time as hapless victims rather than the red-ragging bully-boys of the press machine's early caricatures. It was to produce a massive public backlash. This turnaround in the public perception of miners and the poor pit communities in general left many perplexed. This wasn't actually unusual – at times of mining disasters the press had traditionally changed its presentation of the miners, from 'the dupes of labour dictators' to hardy and brave sons of toil beset by danger. It was to this image responding to the quite spontaneous public outcry that the press now surprisingly sprang, with all the blackened, coaldusty, grimy and care-worn faces of the miners and stark pithead scenes they could rapidly splash across an ocean of newsprint. Of course it was just the stuff we needed, and Brenda Nixon the Hatfield secretary's wife had made the bold front page of the *Daily Mirror* with her 'Miner's Wife's Letter to John Major'. They were to lead the way with screaming banner headlines and pull-out posters for houses, shop windows and more importantly an army of bus windows as the nation mobilised in defence of the miners. We were suddenly 'Our Miners' again. The daily news programmes on the TV now fell back on archive material of coalfaces and headings, and the clatter and violence of pit work and human flesh pitted against the unforgiving earth. They repeated the warnings they had made in numerous documentaries as to the fate of the mines and the trajectory of Tory energy policy. The only Tories we now seen on TV were 'rebels' prepared to confront the government (they said) and bring about a defeat of their government if they forced a backdown. Major, Heseltine and Heseltine's deputy Eggar were men under siege, fending off arguments from all sides about rigged markets, nuclear subsidies, coal imports produced under near-slave conditions, and the depleting gas reserves.

A Special Delegate Conference was convened on Thursday 15 October 1992, at the new NUM HQ in Sheffield. The scene had all the trappings of the old days: a sea of cameras, sound men and journalists with mics and notebooks, little packs of left evangelists with their prescriptions of 'Launch The General Strike'; or 'Immediate All Out Strike Action The Only Way'. Lobbies of branch militants crowded round their besieged delegates as they pushed their way through the crowds 'Ha'way lads, we're not letting this one go!' 'Come on, Dave – ge'them some wellie!' The miners were back in national focus again. The press and left clearly thought this was the start of round two of the '84/85 strike, and it was, but between now and then had been a sea change of resolve among the miners themselves – what could we actually *do* ?

It wasn't just as easy as calling for action as the Trotskyist groups were now doing; the government had had wise counsel and had boosted redundancy payments by a further £10,000, while the deep despondency described earlier was widespread. 'Fight For Your Job!' had been the rallying call in '84. It had caught the combative spirit of the young miners; now it often would draw the response 'Fuck the Job!' The miners' rank and file didn't spring forward into action like a wounded tiger as they had done for a decade or more. This time they were more analytical. Slogans were neither swallowed nor regurgitated whole. Tactics were questioned and debated. At our emergency Special Delegate Conference when Arthur took a formal roll call of areas prepared to state their objection to the closures plan in order to take a case under Section 99 (of the appeal procedure), Gordon Butler, speaking for the Derbyshire Area, informed the Conference:

'As far as Derbyshire is concerned we have no mandate from our men to put any of the pits into the Colliery Review Procedure.'[318] He was followed soon after by Lancashire and then North Wales, who said the same thing. Fortunately COSA declared that it would oppose the closures at any pit where they had members, and that was all of them of course.

Despite the massive scale of the destruction being prepared, the questions wouldn't go away as to what to do about it, how to meet the challenge. Were we stronger or weaker than 1984? If we didn't win then, how can we win now? To this caution we pointed to the groundswell of public support, an outrage which never manifested itself in '84, a sympathetic press we never had in '84, and at least in terms of verbal opposition a united body of miners opposed to the closures, even though we doubted the UDM would walk out of the pits even if they were on fire. We had to determine how to play this skilfully, and carefully bring the men with us, not drive them into a corner or against us.

Who are the 'us' in this circumstance? It is a good question. We were miners too, but those of us with a mission, those with a political, class direction, and there were many such in leadership, official and unofficial, were a composite separate from the ordinary pitlad in many ways; it would be foolish to pretend otherwise. We were 'the militants', the communists, the political visionaries, the fighters of social corners and seekers of justice. Not everyone in the pit thought like us, so there was a 'we'. *Those* 'we' were worried that Arthur, seeing the clamour at the door, the flash of cameras listening to the chorus of voices, might, like the leftist groups and the press itself, misunderstand the quality of opposition among the rank and file. We would have to grant permission to the NEC to call industrial action, authority to call a ballot for strike action, but the launching of that ballot and the preparation for that action had not yet been done. We were worried that Arthur, with the wind in his ever-fading hair, would launch straight into an all-out strike ballot, when despite the furore at the doors the climate for militancy was a cold one. This might pull the plug on the public head of steam and leave us alone again. It would turn the tide in the media, it would burst the bubble before we had convinced the men of the chances of actually winning this time, and that was fundamental to the whole strategy. NO – the press wouldn't dictate our actions, and fickle 'public opinion' wouldn't either, but we would need to use both of these to get the position where we could launch a stronger and self-reliant resistance. British Coal was playing their £10,000 card for all it was worth, threatening to withdraw it if a strike was launched. Thus we would face pit closures regardless, but without the added 10 grand. We had stuffed more than £10,000 down their throats in '84/85 and lost; doing it again would be more than flesh and blood could even contemplate at this time.

Howard Wadsworth took up my earlier theme as a word of warning to Arthur:

> Arthur – as a friend. Stop going on television and telling our members to get off their knees and fight. I find that insulting, because they have been fighting since 1985, and if they are on their knees it is because they have been hit over the head so many times they are perhaps not on their knees, it is just that their legs have got shorter. (Laughter) Our members resent being told by anybody that they have not fought. We fight every day at the pits and we are not on our knees.[319]

In my contribution I chose to focus on two things, one that delegates avoid their instincts to treat the press with contempt by either ignoring them or abusing them. On this occasion we had to seize the opportunity to speak to these cameras and through them to millions upon millions of homes all over the country. You didn't have to be a star, the more plain-spoken and natural you were the better would the message come over. We have to use the media's new-found sympathy for us, to get people off their armchairs and settees and onto their feet. Next I demanded:

> Here and now, next Wednesday, we should mobilise for the big debate in Parliament, we have to pull every man, woman and child down to London and outside Parliament, not just from our communities but from all of the other communities that are going to be affected, together with all our friends in the trade union and labour movement. We need to march on London and make these people in the City of London wake up and show them that we are mad, and show them that we are angry … Let us decide that we are going to London next Wednesday, mobilising by the trainload and the busload and let us make that city rock with the anger of these communities.

To my mind that call was clear, this was to be a mass mobilisation of communities, of miners, of industrial workers of all sorts, of the trade union movement and our allies on the left and progressive movement, that we would block the City of London by the sheer weight of our numbers and we would demonstrate that if the City and its supporters could close us down, the miners and our supporters could return the favour. The reality of the situation was, though, that I was making this call THREE DAYS before the proposed date. But the Conference, enthused by the need to do something big dynamic and NOW, voted unanimously in favour.

The platform passed the gigantic demand on to the administration officer. He wasn't a politico; he had no staff, he had no well-oiled machine which would swing into action. Although I presumed that behind the scenes there was such an organisation, actually, as I should have known from the strike, there wasn't. Only him. His expertise was in organising the Miners' Gala or the Annual Conference, not the Vietnam Solidarity Campaign. Truth was he was overwhelmed by the urgency of the situation and hadn't a clue where to start. When the police suggested they take over the planning of the route he was relieved, he even thanked them; it never occurred to our naive comrade on which everything had fallen that they would channel the march safely round Kensington and the upper-class suburbs of London, rather than through the heart of the Square Mile where we could cause maximum disruption and maybe a bit of sabotage and confrontation.

It was not what I had envisaged or proposed but neither mind was the half a million people who turned out on 3 days' notice to march with the miners from every corner of Britain. The Union, area by area, opened its heart and its bank accounts, a damned near unique combination, and let it rip, turning every stone to ensure the miners and our bands and our families and extended communities would be there together, shoulder to shoulder, probably for the first time ever. We offered buses and trains free to anyone who wished to use them. Pit communities the length and breadth of Britain emptied, classrooms stood almost deserted, shops lay forsaken. The miners stayed off work, defying threats of disciplinary action; at Hatfield the manager walked up to the endless line of buses filling with miners and their families and begged for enough safety cover and deputies and even overmen to staff the mine. Volunteers, with the utmost reluctance, left their wives and families to go on the greatest demonstration any of them would ever see, to do their duty back at the mine ... London was indeed besieged, it was a crushing success, the biggest demonstration then ever held in Britain, but it had not been what either I or Conference had intended.

Three days later came the TUC-organised demonstration. Once again the capital was filled and overflowing with a waving sea of banners, and the strains of brass bands and singing voices. Lodge banners from the union movement, many of which had never seen the light of day since the 1920s, proudly struggled through the surging streets. The movement was at last moving again and, at the head, ranks upon ranks of the miners, in branches and areas. A confidence, anger was surging through the tired and long-dormant veins of British trade unionism.

It began to look like a real force for unstoppable change. For the miners, the vast bulk of whom, although on strike for 12 months in '84, had never actually manned a picket line or marched a step, were now out, on the street, active and involved. Confidence, that long-lost relative of ours, was coming back over the horizon after a considerable absence. A million people at least had marched within that 3-day period. There had never been a mobilisation of this force and dimension before. But it wasn't being controlled by us – essentially it was being mobilised by the attention the media was giving it. They were fickle friends; we had a tiny window to take over this movement before the press dropped us for Arctic seals or African elephants. Our comrades on 'the left', particularly the far left, were infuriated by this 'people's campaign'. Everyone knew that what you were supposed to do was actually go on strike, then send out pickets, then call out the rest of the trade union movement, or call upon the General Council of the TUC to call a general strike. Others were telling us we should be occupying the mines. They had told us in their papers this was what we were supposed to be doing, so we were doomed. The miners were being betrayed and misled. We were leading a campaign based upon 'popular frontism' where we collaborated with other social classes, in particular members of the ruling class, or its agents.

The tactics which this section of the left dreamed up were plucked out of their book of 'best things to do when faced with closures' slogans. If such a book really existed clearly the instructions had been lost, because they surely were not meant to be all-weather, all-seasons, one-size-suits-all scenarios? The actual balance of forces involved had to determine the tactics involved; otherwise, it was just self-serving sloganeering and did nothing to alter the situation on the ground or address the actual material conditions facing us, not least the gross loss of morale among the miners. None of them recognised that we had to try and build a majority among *the miners* for action – any sort of action, never mind all-out strike action, never mind winning other folk to join that action. We hadn't convinced the miners there was a point in fighting, or that victory was a possibility if we did. The miners' support groups which rapidly sprang up all over the country and were essential to building the campaign, political and industrial, became battlegrounds between the miners and the Trotskyist and far-left communist groups who smothered agendas and the floors of conference rooms with dynamic and fiery resolutions calling for strikes and days of action. They even passed resolutions deciding when *we the miners* would call these days of action, and surged off to tell everyone else that that was when everyone should down tools and march to the side of the miners. Great!

The only thing was, as miners from each and every area of Britain kept telling them, the miners were not convinced of action yet, and hadn't decided if and what, let alone when, this action would take place. Miners' support groups, no matter how well-intentioned albeit infuriating, could not call out the miners. Even the NUM couldn't 'call out the miners'. Miners bring miners out, when the miners decide to, if they decide to. They cannot be called out even by their own leaders – it doesn't work like that. To the left in general the miners were chomping on the bit to get back onto the streets and back onto those picket lines but were being held back by 'the bureaucrats and the leaders'.

This model of the worker always being ready to fight, always under constraint by 'the leader', who permanently sat on his aspirations to rebellion and revolution, was a caricature which actually bore only passing resemblance to the nature of the forces involved, especially in this instance. In fact the NUM Special Delegate Conference *had* passed a resolution in favour of calling a ballot for industrial action, but we had been acutely aware that this had to be at the right time, and right now was not that time. We had to be sure that if we went to ballot we would win the ballot, otherwise we were voting *in favour* of pit closures, or at least to let them get on with it. This 'people's campaign', I suppose, was actually *my* idea; it had been my proposal which had launched it from the floor of Conference and precisely for the reasons outlined above. It hadn't come from on high or from some cowardly top table of class traitors, unless I was suddenly in that category now. It escaped the attention of our comrades in the camp of Lev that these were *our own* actual jobs we were debating here. This wasn't some exercise in charity; if we got the tactics wrong here, it was us, the delegates, who would be on the cobbles alongside the rank and file who elected us to represent them, so we had no earthly reason to sell short the struggle or seek anything less than a total victory.

A straw poll held across eight major NUM areas of Britain in the 25 October edition of *Weekly Worker* predicted that if we went to a ballot now it would be massively defeated. In fact our public resistance campaign was surging ahead, although I had actually planned it to be a bit more like Stop The City than a miners' gala. The impact was felt within Parliament; Heseltine announced a 90-day moratorium on closures and withdrew the lot, for the present. A commission was set up to hear from all involved parties and accept detailed reports and studies. No, it was never a U-turn and we didn't think it was. When Thatcher had done something similar in the face of widespread industrial action in the mines in '81 McGahey had called it 'a body swerve', a rugby manoeuvre to avoid a physical impact from which you would come off the worse, I believe. In this case and in my humble opinion this current manoeuvre was the quiet construction of an escape hatch through which the government could extract itself *if* all else failed.

But it was what *we* did next, the miners and the rest of trade union movement, which would determine whether those original closures were reinstated or the whole plan withdrawn. For the latter to happen the government would have to make a complete change in energy policy and, essentially, undo the work that the Thatcher government had done in trying to neuter the NUM. It would require direct intervention into the energy market and declaring a ring-fenced central area for coal. Meantime the closure programme was proceeding as a guerrilla action; non-compulsory redundancies were being offered at ever increasing sums of money and bribes; widespread restrictions on the activities of Union officials and the standing of the Union in negotiations and conciliation were trying to either sicken the individual activist or official to the point where he too took the money and ran, or else push us as a union into premature action as they had done in '84.

The relaunched *Daily Worker* had been constructed from the *Weekly Worker* to give daily reports and orientation of the unfolding struggle across the trade union movement. They had opened up a regular column for me to comment and report on developments. By 31 October I was reporting:

The ten pits which were scheduled for immediate closure have all closed. Developments have stopped; coal production has stopped. The men are forced to accept redundancy. At the other 21 pits, supposedly reprieved pending the inquiry, a similar process of sabotage is taking place ... Meantime British Coal employees have been subject to the most inhuman treatment by colliery managers. Shift times have been changed to the most anti-social schedules possible. Wage rates and bonus payments are being slashed to the bone. Subsidised transport arrangements have been scrapped. To every complaint, the management respond by pushing redundancy under men's noses, cajoling them to take the easy way out. The miners are bleeding to death. The jobs are gushing away like blood from a severed artery...

The rallies were quickly followed by the construction of support networks and a relaunch of Women Against Pit Closures, reminiscent of the heady days of '84. Miners' support groups were being established in every city and town and many villages the length and breadth of the country. This time, though, there was a far, far greater involvement by a far wider spread of folk than even participated back then. Support for the miners was widespread and often star-studded. I was surprised to receive a call from Jeremy Clarkson. I don't think we got off to a good start. I didn't really know what *Top Gear* was, had never seen it, and had no real idea who he was either. In terms of self-opinion and arrogance Jeremy would probably trounce Arthur, and I don't think this put him in a good disposition toward me. They produced an accompanying magazine, also called *Top Gear*. The focus of his article was to contrast the featherbedded British specialist car makers with the coal industry being thrown in the deep end of the market, not so much without a lifebelt, as with two lead weights wrapped round its ankles.

Jeremy was of Doncaster stock and his granda was a coalminer, who had written a book in 1938, *Old King Coal*. He had predicted his grandson wouldn't be throwing the last nut of Doncaster coal on the fire, so vast and vital was our industry. The current situation had prompted that grandson to report on the fact that the last Doncaster mine had just now closed. He thought to accompany his article with some very arty shots of the coalfields, the miners set against shots of a top-of-the-range Aston Martin 'Vantage'. He makes the point that Aston has made a loss every year of its operation with the solitary exception of 1987. That Ford is hopelessly outdated. He lands outside my door in a Vantage, having tested his driving skills getting it turned round at the top of Abbeyfield Road. The splendour of the car was lost on me of course – just another car, a little shinier than most I suppose. This wasn't the reaction of the teenagers in the street, though, and they gathered around as if a flying saucer had just landed at the house. He explained what he wanted, in the process of discussing the current situation. He wanted shots of the pithead, and miners in their muck. Well, relations at Hatfield wouldn't let me get close to the pit yard and men in their muck with or without this car. Nonetheless he achieved it at one of the Nottingham mines, where the grimy miners are photographed leaning on the prestigious body of the sensuous Vantage. It was artistically a very good shot, black and white, headgear, star status car, and two miners in donkey jackets with their oil lamps.

Theoretically at least this was a progressive endeavour Clarkson was engaged in, but despite being a native of Donnie, it was clear he couldn't fathom the depth of the events. Mind he was no lover of this particular car; as he arrived in Highfields as part of his visit to Brodsworth he declared:

So it had tried to kill me, deafen me, and now in Highfields it was doing
its level best to embarrass me to death. I mean this was £178,000 worth
of car in a place where a three-bedroom terrace house only costs £15,000
… until very recently every man who lives in these two mile long terraced
streets was a miner.

But he was infuriating in repeating shite some official had told him, that there was 30 years of coal left in Doncaster!! The coal in Doncaster actually extends far into other counties and even within its existing borders there must be around 350 years of production; of course, the NCB directors would say that that's because of the slow rate at which we mine it, but that wouldn't be true of our last great thrust at mining ourselves out of danger. Coal was coming out of Donnie mines at £1 per GJ and less. What Clarkson said was it was the equivalent of finding an Aston Martin Vantage that did 900mpg (it actually did about 10).

I suppose most of his article was OK – until that is he declared that 'I talked to lots of ex-miners on my two day visit and although the wit is still there, they are a pretty sad bunch.' He then goes on to quote from my interview, although nothing of the important parts. He goes on to suggest that the closures are a sort of con trick and they will burst back into life:

I stopped by Markham Main – famous for being the last pit back to work
after the 1984 strike – although it's closed, the lights are still blinking on
the winch-gear control panel. The giant 8,000 horsepower motor is oiled
and primed and ready to rock and roll at a moment's notice … There's a
chance, just a chance, that this pit closure programme is in fact, a political
ruse to smash the man with the Shredded Wheat on his head. A move to
erode the power of Arthur Scargill.[320]

Nationwide the last stand of the miners and the pit communities produced the most dynamic public outcry ever seen in British popular political protest hitherto. At least a million people took to the streets, on two occasions, and public opinion swung sharply behind the miners. 70 coaches and four specially chartered trains left Doncaster alone. The pits were left with skeleton crews; everyone from every pit union including head engineering and electrical staff joined the NUM. National papers, in contrast to their treatment of the '84/85 strike, took up the cause of the miners, and the government was forced to stay its hand, promising a thorough review of the future of the coal industry.

Scottish miners start their 636-mile march from Glasgow to London, dressed in overalls and their helmets; they plan to march and hit all the major cities on the way down. As night falls, and they enter the cities of Britain, hundreds of town trade unionists are waiting to greet them and join them; they march through the dark, their cap lamps beaming an evocative image to the watching people on the pavements.

'GET THEM OOT LADS'
In Hyde Park a million people gather and hundreds of miners' banners and bands assemble for this final push, this final stand of our race. A clump of exiled aud Geordie pitmen, in big cloth caps, and mufflers, like they had just walked up a cinder path from the pigeon cree, are shouting: 'Get them oot lads, get them oot!' They looked like they had been here since 1926, like they had joined some hunger march in the 'thirties and stayed, as a number of our flying fundraisers had in '85. They had been waiting for this day, when thousands and tens of thousands of their kith and kin would descend in strength on this alien place and show we were not figments of some playwright's imagination. Here with our bands, our banners, and down in force, men women and children, we were taking the city, and reminding the politicians we were still here and angry. The city, the folk of the city, rich and poor, if not the institutions, had risen with us, almost surprising itself.

Concerned by the force of outrage and taken aback by the scale of its own backbench rebellion, by Tory MPs suddenly saddened by the passing of an ancient and suddenly now cherished way of life, the government called a halt. It responded with 'An Inquiry into *British Energy Policy and the Market For Coal*' by the House of Commons Trade and Industry Select Committee. There were shades here of earlier government actions seeking temporary diffusions of explosive mining situations. True to its form from the 1920s onwards, the government allowed for heat and press and public opinion to tire of the issue then totally disregarded the findings of its select committee which had established viable short-term solutions for the bulk of the threatened collieries.

I was speaking at union and labour and left meetings, in crowded welfares and standing on me hind legs in packed bar rooms, speaking from the floor, urging the 'lads not to sell yasells short, stick with the fight, lads, we're just beginning'. So powerful in fact, that one of the lads (Russell Telford), who had anguished for days because first off he had taken redundancy from Markham Main, and been working as a contractor at Rossington until they paid him off with the advent of the closure programme, went back that night to occupy the Armthorpe pit. He gathered some pit duds and got into the cage on night shift, only he brought a shot gun with him, to make the occupation stick.

He was later to tell me, following his court case, 'It was thy bliddy "Deen sell yoursens short lads" speech that did me.'

For us, tactics needed to evolve. It was me who had moved the resolution on the mass public relations campaign, the mass protest movement. It was a means of developing public awareness but more importantly building the confidence of the miners themselves who had not been ready to take it on. But now we needed to up the ante. The NEC however were now clinging to the public protest policy like a fig leaf for non-action, and this included the leadership at Barnsley. Hatfield moved a resolution calling for a concerted though covert mass 'stop the city' action in London planned to coordinate with the anarchist Stop the City protests. Our mass influx, miners and the women against pit closures, together with the intervention of thousands, maybe tens of thousands of London trade unionists and their left supporters, could seize the city, and stop its financial arteries. This was bold, dynamic thinking. It struck a chord and gained the wholehearted support of all the South Yorkshire Panel branches; when it came to the Yorkshire Area Council meeting those were the only votes it received. Our resolution to convene a convention of all trade unions at all levels, to organise a general strike against unemployment and government policies, didn't even receive a seconder. Markham had more success with support for its call for 'days of action' across the trade union movement; the element calling for the 'TUC to Call a General Strike' was withdrawn 'for the moment' after pleading from the platform and some knocking knees from North Yorkshire.

Two months after the Hyde Park demonstration a prosaic and complex volume, British Energy Policy and the Market for Coal (HC 237), was published by the House of Commons Trade and Industry Select Committee. All eleven committee members including Conservative MPs endorsed its findings and recommendations. The Thatcher government flagrantly rigged the energy market as a prologue to privatisation, this report said. There was no need to close all 31 threatened pits: at least 20 could enjoy a viable future. There were enough Conservative MPs ready to defy the whip and defeat John Major's government on the issue of Coal Not Dole. But Labour was split. Saving two out of three pits was not enough for some left-wing MPs. So there was no vote, the Tory government survived and all the pits shut.[321]

Allowing a third of the threatened mines to close, despite the fact that both the NUM and the UDM on this occasion argued strongly there was no case to close any of the mines, simply would not have satisfied the mass resistance movement being mounted both inside and outside parliament at this time.

For the miners themselves, though, the response was muted. Many miners now hated the new British Coal regime and loss of Union power and had had enough of the industry. Others felt unprepared to contemplate an open-ended, all-out strike as they had in 1984 and felt a lone fight would be futile. I had written in my resumé of where we were at the mass NUM public meeting at the Broadway, Dunscroft (30 August 1990):

It has been for the last two years almost continuous struggle against blatant attempts by key sections of the management to bypass and undermine the Union, and when they couldn't do that, to take up the cudgels in out and out industrial conflict. It has been likewise a bitter and demoralising struggle against those of our members so desperately sick of management tactics and continuous warfare and low money who called for the pit to close so they could get out, the people who wrote 'shut the pit' on every available notice board and who kicked the Union office door on every occasion they could in an effort to knock the bottom out of the boat.

At Elmfield Park in Doncaster, we organised a mass Trade Union and Community March to save the Doncaster coalfield. Our bands and banners, all the old unions of the town, the rail workers, the plant workers, the rail drivers, the bus drivers. The Sikh temple, the churches. I couldn't resist, when I got to the stage for my spot, thanking all the divergent forces, social, political and religious: 'The National Spiritual Church, what a magnificent blue silk banner, and nobody carrying it. Just floating along there!' Well it drew a laugh, especially from the spiritualists, whose lead bloke was a former Hatfield miner. He was well into his element, and I charged with him with being the 'happy medium' I kept reading about. But my serious head was to appeal to the hundreds of young married miners, many there with their families, kids on their shoulders, wives by the hand:

'I want to appeal to wa lads in the Doncaster pits.

'Keep ya nerve lads. Get hold of your principles and values and hold on tight.

'Don't be bullied.

'Don't be bribed.

'Don't despair.

'The money isn't what we want. We want wa jobs, we want a regular income, we want stability in wa communities. We want a social framework with education and health care and future for wa kids. And you won't buy them things with the money... we are tottering on the brink of a chasm here, every man that stands with us comes back from the edge, those that go over, dead-end the future for themselves and tha families and tha mates.

'Jesus Christ, lads,

Ah knaa what's going on.

'I understand the mind-blowing indecision, insecurity and   frustration.

'But don't leave us now –

'We are too close.

We are within sight of taking back off them what they stole from us 1984/85.

'The time might come when we might have to speculate the ten grand in a do or die fight, to finish these Tory scum once and for all.

'Who wouldn't among us trade that paltry redundancy sum, if we knew we could rid ourselves and our kids of this government?

'We have that chance now. You have been given that opportunity.

'DON'T SELL YOURSELVES SHORT LADS.

'YOU'RE WORTH MORE THAN THAT.'

Well, the crowd cheered and clapped to the four corners of the field, a crowd of young Caribbean miners from Markham pit spontaneously starting swaying and clapping and singing Bob Marley's 'Get Up. Stand Up. Stand Up For Your Rights!'

It is slowly spread through the crowd ready until then to disperse: 'Get up stand up, stand up, no, don't give up the fight!'

It gets louder, everybody clapping, singing, 'Don't give up the fight, Don't give up the fight!'

Nobody now wants to go home, we want to stay and win right now!

Well, it was powerful stuff.

21 October. Labour motion in the Commons demands NO PIT CLOSURES (unless on grounds of exhaustion or safety). It is the moment for all 'our friends' across parties who have stood on our platforms and beat their chests to stand up and be counted. It is defeated by 320 votes to 307. The Liberals under the leadership of 'Paddy Backdown', as he was to be christened, crossed the floor to vote WITH the Tories FOR the closures. This is bought for a mess of pottage: 21 of the threatened pits are to be placed into 'a review process'.

By the end of November, despite the Commons vote fiasco, and with the public campaign still large in the media eye, the High Court ruled that British Coal were acting illegally in dismantling the pits and stopping developments during the 90-day review period; this was an important though temporary victory. How to take the campaign forward was now the crucial question one month on. The Doncaster Branches were aiming at pulling off nationwide generalised strike action by the end of January when the government came to the end of the 90-day period, and were due to reassess the situation. In this vein Hatfield had submitted two resolutions, one trying to pin down a commitment to mass civil disobedience and direct action, the other to prepare for all-out inter-union strike action against all threats of job losses, redundancy, layoffs and deindustrialisation. We envisaged militant national unions, joined by local branches of no-so-militant unions, joined by the army of the unemployed already on the dole queues, launching a massive joint industrial and street protest campaign with the miners at their heart. For the former we had proposed the slogan 'HALF A MILLION FOR THE MINERS – STOP THE CITY'.

On the theme of the industrial miners' own action we proposed that strike action be taken at the pits that *were not* among the 31 threatened collieries. In other words, we hit the pits they wanted to keep, while not exposing further the ones they wanted to close anyway.[322]

Neither of these resolutions caught the imagination of the Council. The first one was argued down by delegates on the grounds that we'd be battered from the streets, or the buses would be blocked, impounded or re-routed. Maltby's Ted Millward, supporting the resolutions, had countered the arguments, urging that all we needed was the will to do it: 'We aren't on about forming up with bands and banners in Hyde Park, we just all make our own way to the Square Mile, as individuals and groups, on foot, on buses, or drive there, we can choke off every approach.' This was how the anarchists had organised their various Stop The City protests which had only really never been fully successful for lack of numbers. *We* could supply those numbers. Council didn't agree and only the seven South Yorkshire branches voted in favour of it.

Our second clever piece of strategy also failed to win acclaim; this time they argued that the non-threatened collieries would not vote in favour of strike action if they were not themselves on strike, and that other workers in other industries wouldn't respond to a solidarity strike call unless all the miners were already on strike. In any case, the platform assured us, 'Talks are taking place under the auspices of the TUC to achieve a united form of industrial action, between all the unions in Rail, Coal and Power.' If this were true and if it could be pulled off this would indeed take us to somewhere, or at least to the start of somewhere we wanted to go. It dropped the question of nationwide generalised strike action firmly in the lap of the big, powerful unions, none of which had so far made much of a stir about unemployment and the relentless march of redundancies and closures in their own industries. Something was stirring, with even the TUC General Council finding its way to Doncaster on a fact-finding mission and 'as an expression of solidarity'.[323]

By 12 December I am writing in my column that

the momentum is going out of this campaign. What was novel and dynamic is now (as my mate Dave Nixon described it) chocolate cake for breakfast, dinner and tea. The leadership has picked up one of the tactics that we generated, and is now using it to stifle others.[324]

There were too many 'miners solidarity rallies' too many demonstrations, too many rounds of applause and standing ovations and impassioned speeches.

16/12/92 23 Joyce Close
Wardley
Gateshead

Just a few lines ... how did you enjoy China?[325] You must still be feeling tired after that tremendous journey. Well David things are still very serious for the miners. I don't know how it will all work out for them. This government doesn't want miners any more, it is a very serious situation for you all.

Your Mam is still struggling on, she doesn't have any pleasure at all, nothing to look forward to, but at least I still have her here with me.

Love from Mam and Dad to you and Emma

In December our NEC had called basically an unofficial general strike, a 'stay away from work day' on 19 January as a national protest of all workers, in unions or not. It was based upon the action South African workers took in the teeth of anti-strike laws over there. Workers would take sick days, just stay at home or actually down tools and walk off the job. The suggestion came originally from Arthur and his call was flashed across every TV screen in the country. Again the media seemed to be doing a job for us. The ITV *Ten O'Clock News* came over as a party political broadcast on behalf of the Stay At Home Party. The leaders of the other unions however didn't like this date being thrust upon them and wanted to demonstrate that they were running their own show and were still very much debating not only when but 'if'. There was much to-ing and fro-ing. The 19 January date came and went, and we persisted – we needed to move them if at all possible, and – although it caused muckle pet lips, and tantrums among some of the left groups – there was nowt sacrosanct aboot 19 January as a date, anyway.

We had also appealed to the TUC General Council to endorse the call. They however shied away from anything that seemed to be breaking the anti-union laws prohibiting secondary action. When the TUC finally decided to dey something they presented Parliament with the biggest petition ever in the history of the trade union movement. 500,000 people signed the demand to halt all pit closures. They were delivered in huge coal sacks. In retrospect we may as well have put them on the fire.

The Union meantime had once again tried to assemble a Triple Alliance based upon related industries which would suffer the knock-on effects of the new round of closures: rail freight and power generation. They had formed an alliance: Unite (Unions In Transport and Energy). Power workers were destined to lose almost as many jobs as the miners and coal accounted for the bulk of rail freight. Despite this vision of a renewed Triple Alliance it again became a 'crippled alliance' as it emerged that the GMWU would not endorse industrial action of any sort to save their coal-fired power stations – in concert with miners and railworkers or otherwise.

A Golden Re-encounter with Amsterdam

Across the world, the old international miners' support networks were starting to come back to life; the phones were alive with calls in many different languages. I was in the crowded Hatfield Branch Office, full of cig smoke and the babble of people going to work and coming out, black and tired, clutching steaming mugs of tea. Folk from the left groups with their armfuls of radical-sounding papers, miners collecting their identity tokens and dozens of women from the support groups, journalists and trade unionists who were fast coming to use our office as an HQ for the miners' support groups nationwide.

Over the noise of the din I hear familiar Dutch accents on the other end of the line. My face is lighting up.

'Oh aye. Aye, that's me. Aye, I'll dey that.'

'Who's that?' they yell.

'Nor, I'll deal with this one!'

'Who is it? Where do they want us to go?'

The Union committee and some of the women hated to miss out on some exotic or well-heeled venue to be invited to speak at.

'No, you wouldn't like this, this is Dutch squatters, lang platted hair, smoking dope, bisexuals, all sorts of gaanins on, all night parties and wild sex ... you wouldn't want this, I'll do this one.'

It was the Amsterdam Miners' Support Group. It had been massive during the '84/85 strike. I guessed they thought something of the same order was about to kick off again, and wanted to be on the starting blocks. They had an active committee up and running, mainly the 'krackers', the hippy, anarcho squatters, many runaway teens and twenties British kids fed up with the sexual and drugs repression in Britain, rock 'n' roll emigrants, digging the old hippy culture still, working in bulb-packing factories, packing boxes of flowers, cleaning windows, working in coffee bars and shops. By beloved Amsterdam, I am requested to come and speak at big meetings of the youth and the squatters in gigs all round the city. Can I come?

Can I come? Where's me slavsacken?

Friday 11 December. I am sitting on the ferry sailing out of Hull and heading for Amsterdam, my sleeping bag is in the traditional roll with the polythene wrapped round it and supported by a sling of string. I am wearing my (extremely good fake) leather biker jacket festooned with anarcho and revolutionary badges. I feel like the reluctant hobbit off on an unknown adventure and really thinking I should be enjoying the security of the Shire perhaps. I don't know where I am going, couldn't make any final firm arrangements. When I land, I resolve: 'Shite – stop being so damn conservative. I can hack this. This is Amsterdam, man! I head for the Mouseshit; I haven't a clue what that means but it's what it sounds like. It is the new downtown squat centre. I actually remember these streets.

I land at the squat and they mostly all know me. I am soon in the throng of a warm, hairy, woolly, pot smelling, lentil-cooking, Amstel-supping crowd of anarchists. I am home, home in body and soul. The Hoggatat Café, on Damstraasen, is the social krackers, anarcho, eco movement café. It is something like a day-and-night Bridge Hotel. Here, everyone comes, everyone will come.[326]

The agenda though is a full one. I am whisked to squats, concerts, cafés; I speak everywhere. The city is covered with posters:

Strike Hard with the Miners, Hatfield Main Benefit, @ De Dirk. Dirk
Van Hasselsteeg
Veganistisch Eten
Speaker David Douglass

I spoke on Free Amsterdam radio, had extensive interviews with the underground press.

De Dirk was the major squat in Amsterdam, a huge block in the heart of the old town, which was due for demolition. The 'krackers' had taken it over. Opened bars, doss rooms, child care, food halls. It was run by a council of groups and individuals. It was actually making money, though that was by sheer accident.

I was to be given star billing on the main night of the week, the night when the big underground bands played, when the city hippies and revolutionaries let it all fly, when the alternative culture of the greatest alternative city in the world came together.

Huge wall posters announced:

De Dirk December
Non-Exit (onafhankelijk, vrif and heavy)
MINEWERKERSBENEFIET
Met SUPERTOUCH e.a.
Spreker Dave Douglass van Hatfield Main NUM/ Class War
Videoos en veganisties eten …

ANTIFA AVOND Met de Tribez Of Idiotz (skabaal)
DANCE CLEOPATRA (ska)
Dirk Van Hasseltsteeg

It is like the Doonbeat only a thousand times bigger. The crowds fill every stairwell and room. I am given free beer – all night; not sure if that's a good idea. I start to get into the music, the rave, the lights, the night, until 2 a.m. I have forgotten why I am there. Suddenly boom, smack, the music is off, the lights go on. Two thousand white faces, and squinting red eyes, two thousand swaying fields of corn are stilled, and a man is announcing in Netherlands, der spreker David Douglass van Hatfield Main. I climb on the stage, the lights shine at me, I can't see the crowd any more. A Glaswegian voice shouts, 'Fuckin' good lads the miners!' And I am back, I let them have both barrels, I tell them the score, I drive it home, but not ower lang. I bow and say Danker.

The crowd stamps and cheers, then bang, the lights are back off, the disco restarts and the fields of corn are tossed and swung across the expanse of shaking heads and writhing bodies.

Great! In what other city in the world, could you stop a rave at two in the morning, on a Saturday night out, when the booze and dope have settled in, when the music is coursing through the veins, and give a political speech and not be hung from the glitter ball? Only Amsterdam, and Amsterdam had adopted Hatfield.

I make a tour of the Irish and Scottish bars, giving out papers. The scene is set if the conflict deepens for real activity, including a blockade of the coal import docks and dockers' solidarity action.

I leave Holland, with pledges to everyone that I will return 'to chill' and just 'live the city man'. I certainly will.

19 December. Call for all lights across Britain to be turned off for 10 minutes in solidarity with the miners' struggle and to symbolise the future danger of power cuts if the closure of the mines is not halted. Cities and towns across the country shut down their Christmas lights, some big department stores do likewise, while households and estates demonstrate very publicly they stand with the miners and their cause It is a now-or-never stand, using all the forces we can, no matter how puerile they seem to outside critics. The action is to coincide with the Scottish miners arriving in London after the march through 636 miles of Britain, wearing their pit gear and their helmets and lamps. A national switch-off was called by the Scottish TUC and the TUC. It was organised that the whole island would, as far as we could control it, fall black at 8 p.m. as a gesture of solidarity and a warning to the government. It was a weak-kneed gesture which would have had real impact if the power workers had walked off the job for a hour and every trade union worker in Britain had joined them. *That* would have been a warning. Mind, it is a long way from when our strikes actually cut the power of their own action regardless of the impotence of the state and all its strength to stop us. It is a mark of how far our own power is now on the wane.

Terry French, one of our picketing, victimised, jailed miners now suffering the heavy hand of the blacklist, gets admitted to Kent University to study law. I am thrilled for him. He applies to the Union for a grant toward his study and this is referred to the Justice For Miners Campaign for them to make a donation. Not the response I would have expected.

7 January. BBC2 interview. Live programme with two government ministers and Tony Banks the left Labour MP. I got off to a faltering, stammering start but soon found my stride.

13 January. Did a TV documentary piece for Channel Four.

20 January. I received an eye injury down the pit. A piece of ancient metal stuck in my eyeball but so small you couldn't see it, only feel the excruciating pain. Things in the eye down the pit are a regular problem; mainly it's thick lumps of black dust, or hard shards of stone. Surface folk would never comprehend the first aid applied in such circumstances. With black and filthy hands and clothes, all sorts are used to howk the particles out again – pieces of coal or bits of stick used gently to catch the foreign body. Not what you would call sterile procedures. With this little swine all efforts had failed, from washing it out with a dudley[327] to pulling my lid back into my forehead or pulling the lid almost out of my head. I rode, and against my terrified urgings was taken to the hospital where, clearly used to heroic miners like myself, they strapped my head into a vice so I couldn't pull away and sat me in a chair clamped to the floor! The FBI light was shone into my eye, and the bastard detected lurking on the pupil. This big monstrous probe advanced toward my captured body, my eye clamped wide open with a damn screw. My toes were curling into a ball as the doctor got it out. An African, he giggled constantly, murmuring: 'It's all right, it's all right. Swear if you wish, but keep still.' Course, after it was out, it still felt like it was in; it had scratched the surface of my eye. I don't think it has ever recovered fully. The joys of pit work.

Actually, this period was my swan song in terms of pit work. I was a free agent. We identified broken lengths of tunnel and I repaired them. I was quite into it, and gave it heart and soul, braying out the loose rock, fashioning new boards and supports, salvaging the road and securing the top. We had worked out a series of contracts for such work and I was earning the best money I had ever done in my life. The other side of this meant I was now always early down the pit and I lingered late after I came back, collecting tools, selecting timber from the timber yard, getting Bomber in the joiners' shop to cut up planks and half tree-trunks to length for me. I arranged for mine cars to be waiting outside the joiners' shop and loco drivers, shaft men and underground drivers to pick them up and drop them on site. I worked me balls off during this period, usually working on my own, drilling, jiggering. The big hammer was specially made in the blacksmiths' shop. I was like Thor – it was a 10-pound mell with an axe blade welded into one side, quite a formidable weapon. I wielded it into rock and stone intrusions bursting through the roadways, often working at heights of 20 feet and balanced on two planks, swinging the hammer with one hand and arm and clinging on with the other.

I was no better thought of. Efforts by the management to break the officials from the industry started to get worse. We were now banged onto the 6 p.m. and midnight shift. From 'Go anywhere, do anything on contract,' it became 'Do anything we tell you or up the road.' Numbers of shifts allowed off for Union duties paid or unpaid are getting less and less. Even the secretary is now back on shifts and back down the pit.

The burden of the struggle meanwhile had been taken up by the women of the coalfields, who launched their most ambitious protest movement to date. It would take the form of civil disobedience, pit camps on the lines of the women's peace camps, lobbies, marches and occupations.

The massive Markham Main Colliery at Armthorpe in Doncaster was one of the mines threatened with immediate closure. Women Against Pit Closures staged an occupation at the mine. At first they planned an underground occupation, but after fears were expressed for their safety they occupied the control room at the colliery:

> On 11 December, Aggie Currie, Ann Scargill, Hazel Pedalty, Gwen White and I [Brenda Nixon] walked straight through the colliery grounds and into the control room where we barricaded the doors and chained ourselves to anything that wouldn't move. Our occupation had begun.
>
> After 48 hours we ended the occupation and walked out to a large crowd of cheering supporters from all areas. With about 100 bouquets from NUM branches, WAPC groups and trade unions we marched through the streets of Armthorpe to a meeting at the Miners Welfare. I have never seen or felt anything like that before in my life.[328]

From the New Year of 1993 the women constructed pit camps on the lines of the Greenham Common camps; these were built at Markham and Grimethorpe and took the form of a 24-hour presence on the pit gate. These camps were the permanent focus for protest and rallies, hosting barbecues and open-air socials and dances. Thousands of supporters visited the camps. By January the attempt of Women Against Pit Closures to seize the initiative with pit camps at threatened collieries is having mixed responses.

Little canvas or wooden encampments, with braziers burning wood, and women huddled in coats and scarves, now guarded the entrances of Grimethorpe, Houghton and Markham in Yorkshire, Trentham in Staffordshire, Bickershaw in Lancashire and Vane Tempest in Durham. It was a bold initiative and set away with much support, all-night parties and rallies at the gates. They became points of pilgrimage for coachloads of supporters from all over Britain, many overnight in sleeping bags and survival bags. Women kept 24-hour vigils at the gates. But there was a flaw. This was not a picket line. The miners were going in and out of work. They themselves were not engaged in this protest. Many actually didn't want any protest and deeply resented having their consciences pricked on the way to the pit every day. Many also thought this deeply undignified, not the stuff of the miners' wives at all.

Most daring of these endeavours was the construction of a camp right at the front door of the DTI offices in London:

> When we arrived there, we just jumped out of the mini-bus, did the jobs
> we had to do and in about 3 minutes we had a pit camp, complete with
> crates to sit on, posters stuck on the walls and windows, tent up and we
> were sat around the fire drinking tea and singing our songs. It didn't take
> long for the press to start gathering. In fact the press were there before the
> police, including a camera crew from ITN ... I think I will remember the
> next step the police took for the rest of our lives. They sent for the fire
> brigade to put out our fire. There we were, stood around the brazier,
> singing our hearts out, when we spotted the fire engine coming up the
> road towards us. When the fire engine stopped in front of us, Ann went
> up to the firemen and handed them some leaflets explaining that we were
> WAPC trying to defend our pits and communities and families. At that
> point they wished us well and drove off, returning a short while later to
> park on the opposite side of the road. The police asked them to come and
> extinguish the fire but they refused, saying the police could use their
> equipment but that they would not do it.[329]

Internationally the regeneration of the old support networks was starting to
bring money into campaign funds. On 8 January, as part of our attempts to pull
out every conceivable stop and push the campaign forward in imaginative ways,
we had 'Racing for the Mines' at Southwell Racecourse, Newark. Tens of
thousands of racegoers mingled with miners and their families with their lodge
banners, and a band, and listened to speeches from Robin Cook, Alan Meale,
Richard Alexander and the Bishop of Sherwood in defence of the coal industry.
They then watched a full day of scheduled racing. Popular support for the cause
of the miners had never been stronger, but was strangely impotent; we had to give
it some muscle.

In the midst of the campaign, Heseltine, the author of the closures, decides to
make his way to Carr Hill Industrial Estate in Doncaster where he will open an
extension to some engineering works. It will offer 100 new jobs, no doubt to
replace the tens of thousands of jobs being threatened in Doncaster pits. We are
there to greet him. As his car sweeps round the bottom gate of the plant the
Women Against Pit Closures have forced their way to the entrance to confront
him as he comes through.

We, meantime, rush in behind the car and after him. It all comes together in
a general melee. As he gets out of the car, the women are face to face challenging
him just as we arrive, and a shower of bricks smash over our heads into the glass
above the door. There is a confusion of bricks and showering glass, as he is pulled
inside white as a ghost, shaking near to drop. Mind, my legs are none to steady
as one of the smaller bricks catches me in the side of the face. Ann Scargill and
the other women are hit by flying glass. As the police force us back into the road
there are more bricks and fighting. Ann and the women are furious and a big
public argument ensues with the crowd of mainly young miners and activists at
the gate and Ann and the others.

'He's a get, he's a swine!

'What's his name?'

'Heseltine!' we all shout.

30 January. Mick McGahey died. He had been a full-time official of the Scottish miners since 1967 and National vice president since '73. Mick was more than a man in position. Mick was a legend in his own time, a hard Scottish communist with a magical power of oratory. To be in Mick's company was to be one of the honoured guests; for him to deign to speak to you, still more engage you in argument or discussion, separated you from the mass also.

I remember the first time I had been brought into his company. Billy Matthews, the communist cutter man from Hatfield and my frequent sparring partner, was a great friend of Mick's. We were down on a lobby of the TUC Conference, in I think 1978, when Billy led me through the throng up to the bar in the Winter Gardens. We waded through crowds of delegates and arguing groups or laughing clumps of people telling the tale and standing with their drinks. A great encircled crowd sat in an alcove. It reminded me of being brought to Santie's Grotto – the dark hush, then emerging into the alcove and there sat Santie, only now it was Mick. Mick sat like Jesus in the Temple, dispensing his pearls of wisdom. Folk sat on the outer of the circled chairs and strained to hear what he said, or join in the laughter. Those closer got to make some point, add some supplement and have Mick either nod sagely, or else with an inclined hand suggest a subtle twist or improvement. I too sat on the outskirts with the disciples. As the crowd thinned slightly and people got up to buy drinks my shape fell to view and Billy shook hands with Mick and introduced me to him, although he did so as 'a student at Strathclyde university' and not as a fellow miner. It was one of a number of misimpressions Mick was to get of me over the years. For a while he was given to ask: 'And what does our young intellectual comrade think of that?'

Later as he got to know me better he would bounce outrageously Stalinist suggestions off me, and draw me like a fish on a hook to 'expose' my position 'as a Trot'. Only to Mick, sadly, a Trot or anything that sounded like 'a Trot' was a supporter of Militant.

'Listen, my young Militant comrade,' he would start.

'Mick, I'm not in the Militant.'

'Aye, you all say that.'

'No, Mick, I really am not in the Militant, I hate the bliddy Militant.'

'Aye whey,' he would say, as if I was lying. At length many years later Mick identified me as an IWW supporter and in jest and otherwise would hail 'The Industrial Workers of the World'. He actually had strong memories of and respect for the Wobs.

I missed Mick's funeral – I didn't know it was on until the evening before it took place. Billy went up as did a couple of the other Hatfield miners. I was sad not to have gone. I spent many interesting days and weeks in Mick's company, arguing the toss or listening to his real-life encounters and reminiscences of men who had been giants of the movement. Mick met and had known many of the founding Wobblies as well as those from the early communist movement. Mind, he was no pluralist, he had dismissed most of my arguments as 'blether'. At times as the areas divided up during the bitter faction fighting following the end of the strike, he would grab me by the arm and demand to know what Yorkshire was playing at. It was a truly sad period when comrades even refused to sit with comrades and areas sat in their own corners or even rooms of the same bar.

In February 1993 I spoke in Glasgow to one of hundreds of miners' support groups which had re-emerged as soon as we took up the campaign. These we tried to use as alternative mobilising centres since we couldn't move the TUC or some of our closely allied unions:

'We at first, given the flush of public support and media compliance, thought we could get the TUC General Council to actually call a stay away/strike day on 19 January for the whole movement. This was meant to rally support for the miners join the general opposition to cut backs, job losses and pay restrictions: at the same time signal a mass defiance to the law, by breaking it, with a mass non-balloted strike action.

'Finally in February the General Council told wi, under ney circumstances would they call for mass strike action, balloted or otherwise, even for a day.'

The chance to offset the betrayals of 1984/85 is ignored.

March 20. The IRA bomb Warrington. It is a 'bad' bomb and kills two kids, Jonathan Ball, 3 years old, and Tim Parry, 12. Fifty other people, all just ordinary folk going about their business, are injured. It is meant to demonstrate that the IRA still has the capacity to hit British commercial targets and stop life going on as normal while the war is waged over the water. It is milked for all its stupidity by the press, while the RCT[330] say we, the workers of the imperialist oppressor, have no right to criticise it. At the same time four workmen from republican districts are shot dead by the UFF. The press are impassive, or else somehow blame the IRA for 'the troubles' at large – so making them carry the blame for the deaths in their own community too. Hypocrisy and the crocodile tears of the media manage to distinguish between kids' deaths, though. From 1969 till now the RUC and the British Army have killed 42 people under the age of 18, some just weeks old, often deliberately firing plastic bullets at point-blank range into young demonstrators, or firing with cavalier abandon into the houses occupied by civilian families. That's a fact.

I feel however that it is not only a right to criticise counterproductive tactics, tactics in which the people we are fighting for, or in any case not against, are killed by badly targeted bombs, it is an absolute revolutionary duty. Apart from everything else such devices play straight into the hands of those forces in the movement trying to disarm the struggle and take us to the right toward bourgeois Irish constitutional nationalism. I ponder whether that wasn't the hidden agenda, of right nationalist forces or the British state's counter-insurgency teams in the first place, to discredit the armed struggle and the progressive movement with murderous antisocial actions. I dismiss it as just too conspiratorial. After the Omagh outrage I am forced to ponder the question again. Of course neither should one underestimate the capacity of all sorts of self-declared left saviours for stupidity.

GMWU YOU ARE THE WEAKEST LINK !

After it emerged that the GMWU would not endorse industrial action of any sort to save their power stations, nor the TUC General Council back any call which seemed to be breaking the anti-union laws, RMT, NUM and NACODS instead called a simultaneous ballot for 5 March. The ballot would be the test of whether we had done enough to win our own members to action, or whether the miners would be the first to fall and bring down the railway workers with us. In emotion-charged pithead meetings I urged that we 'would die of shame' if we voted down the action and 'pissed up the backs of millions of people who had publicly supported us'. Platform speakers were everywhere urging: 'This time! ... This time! ... We can do it!'

5 March 1993. We ballot our members on joint action with NACODS and the railworkers against the pit closure programme and the knock-on job losses on the railways. The steel and power generation unions had bottled out, leaving it to spontaneous action at some power plants. We achieved a 60% 'yes' vote, including almost 100% 'yes' among the myriad of contractors. It was proof that our mass public campaign had worked, using the external support to power the internal resistance. When these closures were first announced, despite our sabre-rattling few would have given you odds on winning the lads over to any form of industrial action. We managed to stop all coal production in Britain at every colliery nationwide – it was not that the UDM had found some bollocks, rather that NACODS had taken the decision they should have done in '84/85 and struck along with us, shutting down the industry lock, stock and barrel.

When the result was announced we breathed a long sigh of relief: it was a very clear that yes, the miners would once more sign it on,[331] with a 60.4% majority for a series of 24-hour strikes beginning 2 April, a total of 12,913 for and 8,465 against. The results by area are illustrative (see table).

Against

Area	Yes	No	Spoilt	Total
COSA	581	1,321	12	1,914
Leicester	24	73	0	97
North Wales	60	169	0	229
Scotland	331	547	3	881

For

Area	Yes	No	Spoilt	Total
Midlands	792	369	2	1,163
North Derbyshire	799	687	2	1,488
North East	1.880	1,861	6	3,747
Lancashire	262	78	0	340
Nottingham	586	154	2	742
Power Group	304	143	0	447
South Wales	561	79	5	645
Yorkshire	6,581	2,961	13	9,555
Cokemen	72	1	176	249

Among the contractors nationwide my previous opinion was justified that now, with the safety net of previous redundancy money in the bank, usually with the mortgage paid off and all debts cleared, they had emerged as the most militant miners in the country. This was demonstrated at Hatfield, probably the pit with the most contractors in the land. Of 33 contract firms at the pit not one voted against industrial action. 22 of the firms' workers voted 100%, with the contractors overall voting 99% 'yes'. These swelled Hatfield's overall vote to 75%. (The NCB workforce comprised 40% of the entire workforce.)

Elsewhere this pattern was repeated. But what does the vote in Scotland tell us? It tells us that demoralisation had taken the very soul out of the once fiercely militant area, while conversely at the eleventh hour areas known for their traditional moderation decided it was now or never for a fight.

It was a stomping vote, and the Yorkshire Area of NACODS, perhaps now fully aware of the sand that had been thrown in their eyes in '85, this time voted in similar percentages for industrial action. RMT, voting at the same time, also gained clear majorities for joint action, while over the country militants and activists across the trade union movement tried to bring their own unions into action alongside the miners and railway workers. We were painfully making the point to one and all, that if we were to win we could not be confined to the law; the law was designed to stop us taking action. The NUM now ignored the TUC and appealed directly to workers in other industries and other unions to take action alongside us. I addressed a mass meeting of Hull Trades Council and urged all the delegates to get behind the movement and walk off the job wherever they worked. The Trades Council responded with a magnificent full-size poster posted in every unionised plant, firm, dock and office across the city:

Day Of Action April 2nd

Strike Alongside The Miners And Railworkers In Defence

Of Theirs And Your Job

Attend The RMT Mass Picket

Paragon Rail Station

5-30 am – 2.00 pm April 2nd

Rally 12-30 Cenotaph

Time For Action Not Words.

NUM/Hull And District Trades Council

The leadership of Hull Trades Council were syndicalists and IWW members and this was a blessing, but the vote had been unanimous and many other trades councils took up similar stands, including Doncaster who issued similar notices and letters to its branches. We called on workers one and all to take this up. Despite all the conflicts and battles I had been in, in my life, this moment was to be one of the most exciting. In the open air, I called out workers in their muck, or uniforms or white shirts, I called on all of them to walk off the job on 2 April.

We toured trades councils, open-air street meetings, the NUM activists and Women Against Pit Closures, calling on one and all to join the strike movement. There was certainly 'something in the air', something of the old IWW was abroad. I felt like we could do anything if we really wanted to. As Davie Guy, the powerful leader of the North East miners pounded away at rallies: 'I wish I had a quid for every time I have heard people say, "If we'd struck with the miners in 1984 we wouldn't be where we are now." So history is giving you a second chance, don't let it slip this time because there really won't be a third chance!'

Everywhere the Union's call seemed to be going home.

When the day broke virtually the whole British coalfield was at total standstill. At four of the UDM majority pits – Thoresby, Ollerton, Bevercotes and Asfordby – coal production was halted, while at the remaining eight it was highly restricted. The entire rail network hardly witnessed a single train moving. 1,200 bus workers struck against wage-cutting and longer hours while many London taxis struck work too. All NALGO offices in Bradford, Wakefield, Sheffield and Rotherham came to a standstill as office workers struck in support of the miners, so too the workers in the Doncaster offices, who were perhaps most threatened by a knock-on domino effect of job losses in the pit-dependent town. It swelled my heart and made me cry as my daughter Emma proudly turned up with all her colleagues, 'on strike for me Dad'. It was the most moving day maybe of my life; all the other office workers in Doncaster, in solidarity with the miners of the town, marching to the pit gates at Markham where Emma rushed to join me. If I didn't cry then, I did just now remembering it. Thorne Grammar School seen picketing by the sixth form and the school coming to a standstill, as school students, many of them sons and daughters of miners, struck school to join demonstrations through Doncaster. Similar actions occurred at Armthorpe, Edlington and Mexborough schools. The fool of a headmaster at Thorne Grammar School says to the reporters he can't see what it all has to do with them! Contract workers at Drax Power Station walked off the job and elsewhere nationally, because they couldn't find a single way to get to work, or were suddenly too ill to turn up; 6 million workers were not at work. The stoppage received nationwide publicity and also across Europe as millions of workers launched strikes against job losses and redundancies.

The miners and the railworkers and their allies in the support groups and on the left call for a rank-and-file general strike, with the miners and railworkers, against redundancy, rundowns, attacks on our Union and living standards. We make the call across the piece, to unions officially where they will respond, to all levels of the unions from executives to shop stewards' committees; where they are reluctant, which is most places, we appeal over their heads to the workers directly, in unions and out of unions. This is the line in the sand. This is the stand we are making – will you all stand with us, for all our futures, for a radical change in direction? At Markham Pit Camp, at the colliery pit gates, we all gathered for an evening disco by the braziers. I got drunk and danced mesell silly in the pouring rain. The CP comrades were quite impressed – not a side of me they were used to seeing.

Nineteen coal power stations were down for closure along with the collieries. The amount of support from the GMB and other power workers' unions on days of action, through industrial action of their own, would be crucial. It never came.

Be it ever so minimal or humble, it never came. From moving to draw into a new Triple Alliance of rail and power workers and miners, industries and workers associated with the pits and therefore the knock-on of the closure of pits, we moved to make the miners the catalyst for an overall generalised strike movement across industry. Yes, striking *for* the miners, but, more importantly, we called on those who would strike to time and link their own struggles against cutbacks and pay restraints alongside our own actions, in an outright challenge to the government, in outright defiance of their employment laws and the authority of the TUC General Council.

We toured industry, advocating joint industrial action. I toured Humberside speaking to customs workers, bus drivers, food process industry workers. I spoke to trades councils packed with delegates at Doncaster, Rotherham, Hull and Scunthorpe. By this time, April '93, we were 6 months into the campaign. Of the threatened collieries on threat of minimal redundancy pay and no prospect of winning, 7 had been blackmailed into accepting closure among the most heart-rending scenes of despair and soul-searching. But the fight for the other 24 was still on. The NCB and government had been blocked in the courts and blocked in Parliament and upon the streets from introducing compulsory redundancies at least until July.

I was speaking in a public workers' campaign for joint action against compulsory redundancies: 'In the coal industry, on the railways, in mine and rail supply and services, in power stations, on buses, in council offices, the DSS, the civil service, the NHS, and Timex, on building sites, in factories, shops, banks and everywhere else …

'A quarter of the total British workforce stayed home that day and the city of London came to a standstill.'

Despite this, and barking at our heels, little snappy leftist groups berated us for not calling an all-out strike in the mines, as if it were we, the leaders, the branch officials, the activists who were somehow suppressing the surging tide of miners trying to launch an unlimited strike action. Would that it had been true – our biggest effort was in demonstrating to the men that we could move workers, that there was a fight to be made, that it wasn't futile.

But at this point the sympathetic Tories, the liberals, the wets started to fall by the wayside, and condemned the strikes and blamed us for spoiling our nice harmless and peaceful movement. By the second day of action, following rapidly on 16 April, the press and TV had all but abandoned us. TV channels chose to report solely on the action on the railways and totally ignore the nationwide strike by the miners and others, despite the action being slightly larger second time round. Our support groups in Europe reported that no mention was made on any TV programme of the ongoing strikes of the miners. If we were to succeed the actions needed to be stepped up – it had to spread across millions upon millions of other workers.

Just at this time countervailing forces went into overdrive to take the momentum out of the core support. British Coal started threats of loss of redundancy, premature closure, pits going on the hit list that currently were not on it. Men at the collieries where production had already ceased pending the inquiry were offered further greatly enhanced redundancy terms but only if they agreed to leave en bloc and by the end of that week. At the 'reprieved pits' management was everywhere applying the screws: bonuses cut back and transport arrangements and local agreements and practices ended. This drove men out one by one, especially those travelling from remote locations with no personal transport. It sickened those who had resolved to stay and fight it out into giving up. Were men prepared to cut as much coal with less men for less bonus? More usually the men turned off the tap and production collapsed to a trickle. A double subversion started to affect the pits, with complaints that the action was either too frequent or else ineffectual and should be stepped up. On the railways the British Railways Board brainstormed for days on finding a deal that would effectively buy off the railway workers and leave the miners isolated once more. For the men being offered a fortune to leave together by the end of the week, the lack of certainty and confidence and no sign of any TUC cavalry – or even a raggy-lad militia from the rank and file across Britain – proved too much to bear. On 27 April the *Doncaster Star* was reporting that Markham at Armthorpe would be joining Rossington and accepting closure.

At Hatfield management took the offensive with a newsletter and a two-page personal letter from the colliery general manager Jeff Ainley.[332] It claimed that we were succeeding in saving the colliery by working together to turn coal and cut costs, but now:

> Our costs of production have doubled and we are in danger of not producing enough coal to supply our established customers let alone those which we have recently won … what is right for Hatfield Colliery must be our only consideration. We cannot afford one day strikes or any restrictions on performances.

Just to be sure we are all working together he then announces an end to all Union control of face manning, and agreements on staffing and protection of earnings:

> We will have to continue on four shifts until F105s is ready in August. The face teams will be reduced considerably from our present staffing with only 8 men per shift required which will also include the gate end preparation, dinting and packing as required. I will therefore, have to select 8 men from each team which will mean some more men will be asked to cover the jobs outbye, presently staffed by overtime and contractors … It is also important that we open our thoughts to more flexible working time on our units. Future pits will need to consider adjusting working arrangements so that they can react to customer needs. The events of the last two months have now unfolded and I consider that it was time I informed you of where I see us going. I make no apologies for treading on previously 'sacred' ground, but what I have put into letter needs saying …

J Ainley, Colliery Manager.[333]

This was nothing short of opening up another front against the Union at

Hatfield. To many it finally killed any idea of fighting to stay in the industry; basically what we were being offered was ongoing war at work, or eat shit, or take the money and go. We responded with a furious flurry of leaflets and newsletters, the tone of which marked the increasingly bitter relations between the management and the Union. We suspected that all this macho management and scrapping of our national and local agreements was more to do with Ainley's plans to buy the mine following closure than saving the pit now for British Coal.

Two weeks later the second day of action was launched, the British Railways Board were in overdrive to settle with the railwaymen and break the alliance. We had won large swathes of NALGO workers, particularly in the mass coalfield labour councils, to take solidarity action with us and the rail unions, but this wasn't an ongoing commitment. While the fight went on, the divisions between the miners – the divisions over where we go, whether to fight, how to fight, who is to blame – were exacerbated by management divide-and-conquer tricks. They knew collieries at this stage couldn't stand and fight alone on their own issues, so let disputes and divisions fester.

The climate at the pit was on the verge of meltdown. We called a mass stormy and angry meeting in April. I addressed the men, from the shoulder so to speak, and in the manner by which some of them had been addressing me over the previous couple of weeks:

'Anyone who thought, when we took up the cudgels with British Coal and the government, that they would allow us to take action without retaliating, must have been brain dead for the last 20 years. Yet still men are moaning and groaning about all the dirty low-life tricks management are getting up to, as if the industrial terrorism we are experiencing now were not the stock in trade of modern British Coal management. The whole response of management to our actions is to turn the screw on and start kicking us in the bollocks in the hope of either forcing men to leave the industry or else making us abandon the action we are taking. In many respects limited action such as one-day strikes are more painful to our side than all-out action, where at least the bastards can't do anything else to you.

'Current attacks at Hatfield include reducing the Union secretary's time off for Union duties to two days per week. This to administer a Branch of 400 members, in four different firms and 1,000 pensioners plus their dependants and widows etc. If we use NUM paid shifts to make up the shortfall we are getting the old "mark you as absent" trick. This is currently being employed against the NUM officials, the aim being to record enough of these to sack us. Ainley [the colliery manager] has his head full of ideas of being a private coal-owner in a non-union pit, where the workforce stand on their toes and tip their forelock as he goes by. Getting shot of the Union is key to his plan; he has already said "when" he gets compulsory redundancies he will pick who stays and who goes. Does anyone actually want to be one who stays under a reign of private ownership with a gaffer who thinks he's a cross between Captain Bligh and Napoleon? We have to win this fight, on our terms; if we stop accommodating and grovelling to the bastard that'll be a start.

'Tactics in the Yorkshire coalfield as a whole are aimed at splitting men up and sowing divisions. We are told the Selby coalfield gets paid four-fifths of its contract for the pit bonus and face workers, while in Doncaster the pit bonus earners get nothing, while the face worker gets four-fifths of his bonus earnings.[334] Let's be right lads, we're in a life and death war here, we shouldn't be turning enough coal to warrant bonus payments, especially since it's being deliberately used to sow divisions among our ranks.

'It might be said some face workers are working like fuck to increase bonuses to offset the loss of the day's earnings. Can't you daft buggers see, that you are producing the same amount of coal in four days that you normally produce in five? You are undermining the very action you voted in favour of. Stop expecting to earn any bonus in weeks in which the action is taking place.

'At Hatfield, face workers accepted an increase in their contracts of one third of a strip to pay for a face fitter and electrician to receive the face bonus. Now management have stopped the week's bonus for these fellow face workers, in any week when action is taken, but the rest of the team gets paid four-fifths. Are we going to carry on flogging our guts out turning coal while only some of the men on the face, to say nothing of the poor buggers outbye, get nowt at all? It is time to turn the tap off.

'Similarly, safety men are being used as an excuse to bring to work totally unnecessary bodies, just to create jealousies and try and break the strikes. Safety workers need to be tightly vetted and cut back to absolute minimums. Likewise, the ban on weekend coal production is essential if our days of action are to make any sense at all. What is the point of striking Friday if you turn the same coal in overtime or at weekends? The gaffers are pissing up your backs, lads. Stop all overtime and weekend coaling. So-called safety exemptions are being exploited by management to play face against face and pit against pit. Is it absolutely life-threatening not to turn coal? If it isn't, then we shouldn't be doing it.

'Latest management exhibits from Jeff Ainley's box of poisonous concoctions is his scheme to get rid of twenty-plus face workers. This is despite the fact the pit will be going from one face to two and will be two face teams short. He will "offer" them outbye work, or replace "odds and sods" of contractors doing "bits and bobs of jobs". At what rate of pay? At what bonus? And of course if you don't want it, you can go redundant. He told the Union this week: "Compulsory redundancy will be available and I'll pick who goes and who stays."

'As a matter of fact it is NUM Yorkshire Area policy, it is indeed NUM national policy, to ballot for all-out strike in the case of compulsory redundancy in the industry; as a matter of fact, that resolution came from Hatfield Main Branch. The time is sharp coming when we've got to stop shadow boxing with British Coal and their tinpot führers in the management and give them some industrial knuckle, in an all-out strike. It's a bit like swimming in the North Sea – once you get into the water it's no se bad, but the longer you run up and down the beach complaining about how cold it looks, the harder it seems.

'Remember the old adage lads, if the boss keeps grinding you down, don't just get mad, get even!'

But some had had enough already, some just wanted a quiet life and to be left alone, but that wouldn't happen. Some wanted to stop running, some wanted out with redundancy, so stop trying and get the pit shut – this was not 1984.

May Day rallies all over the country seen a renaissance. They were bigger than at any time in decades as the miners and their bands and banners now took the lead in every coal city and town in Britain. At places far removed from the coalfields the miners and their families and their banners were asked to lead parades or share platforms or both. At each of these our message was the same: 'Stop talking about solidarity and the meaning of trade unionism and start doing it.'

The reality however was painfully unfolding. It was familiar. We could now feel defeat in the stagnating air, see through the fog of words that nothing was happening. The heroic women of the Markham Pit Camp watched the men walk past them and out the gate, the redundancies in their back pockets. They nailed their pit boots on the hut the women used as a shelter. Meanwhile the women chained themselves to the railings to prevent the low loaders taking away the machines and the pit's vital electronic infrastructure, but they were alone, a thin line of cold, demoralised and now crying women. There were no men here holding the line. They were led helpless to the side of the road as the lorries ploughed on through the gates to carry away the ripped-out heart of the pit, and men stood and hung their heads and announced they were 'ashamed'. The tear-stained, grief-wracked women gathered up their stuff, and hung a wreath on the gates of the pit. It read: 'RIP – We Fought. We Lost. Sorry, Markham Main.'

Elsewhere the women were still engaged in dynamic actions. At Trentham, the giant Staffordshire pit, the women occupied the shaft. At 2 a.m. the miners' wives took up position in the back of one of the shafts. Chaining themselves to machinery they demanded that the colliery stay open. British Coal management reacted as they had done to all previous such actions, 'putting boards and barbed wire around the top of the shaft and depriving them of light, food and water'.[335]

There have been countless occupations, rallies, vigils, meetings, conferences, including an occupation by Ann Scargill, Ellen Evans, Dot Kelly and Lesley Lonas at Parkside Colliery, Lancashire – underground for 5 days in freezing conditions. 'There isn't anything we wouldn't do for this industry, no lengths we wouldn't go to; such is our belief in the survival of the collieries and the NUM.'[336]

Kevin Perry Secretary of the National Union of Mineworkers Power group told *News Line*:

> Three women who are miners' wives and supporters of Women Against Pit Closures, went into the pit at two o'clock this morning, and they are now occupying the back of one of the shafts.
>
> They have chained themselves to machinery, and are demanding that the colliery stays open ... The women are in the dark, they have been denied food and drink, and they are now allowing us to get food and drink to them.[337]

That there were no men to occupy the pits was due entirely to British Coal anticipating the demonstration and threatening to withdraw all redundancy terms from those involved and even sack all participants – as they had done in the Kent Area in '84. A conflict had also raged between the rank and file and NUM officials in Staffordshire, with the latter holding the line against talk of redundancy and the miners en masse demanding that they recognise the reality of the situation and gain support for a campaign to copper-bottom the best of the redundancy terms in the event of the review failing and the pits closing. I had much sympathy with this demand; tactically it favoured us and not the Board. The closures could never have gone through had it succeeded, as every pit would have gone through the review knowing the safety net of the money was in the tin and they had nothing to lose.

To Arthur and his loyal lieutenants, though, it would seem like the NUM was taking action *for* redundancy and not against redundancy, which would rob us of the moral high ground. To Arthur all talk of redundancy was unprincipled; but it wasn't – some of the best men were actually trying to tie into a strategy and use it tactically to stop the rush over the cliff and spike the NCB's biggest gun. The dispute rumbled through the Staffordshire Area for a full year and brought good rank-and-file lads into conflict with the Union officials. The view of the men was much misrepresented and misunderstood, though nationwide the rank-and-file militants could see it clear as day.

The end of May seen another cruel blow to our attempts to build generalised strike actions. RMT voted narrowly in favour of calling off the days of action, having got an agreement that there would be no compulsory redundancies for 2 years. The question of the struggle against privatisation would be left instead to a political campaign rather than an ongoing industrial one linked to the fate of the mines. We looked to a second front from the firefighters, urging them to bring forward their ballot for action against the ending of their pay formula. We turned to the mighty Unison to bring forward action against the 1.5% pay offer. Two or three unions in concerted joint effort could force a government backdown or even their outright defeat. This was the straw we were clinging to, trying to hold our increasingly anxious and weakening rank and file in check as we entered June. But one thing was coming back to the NEC loud and clear: the miners would not take industrial action alone. Either we won over new allies or the industrial action in the mines was futile. Having lost our allies on the railway we desperately sought to link in other workers in joint demands. I was banging the tables urging 'all those groups of workers coming up into conflict, the firefighters, council staff, Gatwick cabin crew, and aerospace workers to join with our action now, we face a common enemy, the so-called recession, the relentless growth of unemployment … it is crazy to fight individually as sections when we can fight together as a class … I've heard it "sack the government not the miners" but what if we apply the "market forces test" Heseltine keeps preaching at the miners – after all there is a national stockpile of MPs with thousands more waiting to be sworn in; there is an unlimited supply of unnecessary MPs. Say we give them away to the old age pensioners – but would they burn? There is just no market for them, and the taxpayer is fed up subsidising them.'

Me Da, who had been a pit lad in the '26 lockout, who knew these coalminers and the struggles of this industry in the way other people know famous battles of British rulers, after telling me how much of a struggle me Ma was having, but that we were keeping her at home, chose to describe what went on in a style and parlance which could have been drawn from the twenties:

Well David, things are not so good for the miners. They... members of the government are devious people not to be trusted. I mean Heseltine and his cronies. Do you really think you will gain anything with this strike? You may lose a lot. Well David I hope some sort of Tory backbench revolt might support you. I am disgusted at the Liberals, traitors to the working class. Mr Heseltine and Mr Major what do they know about coalmines and how they operate? The miners wouldn't have any problems selling their coal if this government hadn't issued permits which allowed coal from Colombia, from Australia, from all over the world – 40 million tonnes last year. The Tories are really showing their true colours, they are out to smash the miners. David the blackleg Democratic Union (so called) helped break the NUM in 1984, and now they know what it's all about.[338]

In many areas, there was a desperate fight to save mining – as a way of life, as an instrument of the class struggle, yes certainly, as a means of fighting for a social and political vision. It was wedded to what we were and what we had been and what we did and for generations had always done. Monktonhall Colliery near Edinburgh had been sold, one of the first 'lease and licence' mines disposed of by the former NCB. (I ought perhaps to explain that at this time, the nationalised coal industry still existed, the coal was still nationalised. So prior to the wholesale sell-off of the industry, mines could only be worked privately on licence from the government. The first group of pits to be sold off under the terms of the Lease and Licence were the ones the government considered little-hopers. The rest would be sold as a package later.) At Monktonhall, the miners pooled their redundancy moneys and bought it, determined not to let the colliery close and end with the rest of their lives on the scrap heap. 160 men sunk £10,000 apiece into the venture, and laboured to win coal from the narrow seams, often with windy picks and shovels, working on their knees. Despite the winning of a large order from Scottish Power, new faces and machines were stalled and the men were forced to handfill coal.

Then the bills came in and their wages couldn't be met. They worked on, without wages, willing the mine to work, tearing the coal from the ground. William Gorman, 35, was buried alive in a face fall, working to save a vision. He died then and there. The colliery, despite blood and sweat, never turned the coal it needed and died, leaving the men bankrupt. We were reluctant to go down the road of workers' buyouts, even before the heroic failure of this noble endeavour.

We are still searching, praying almost, for two or three big unions to launch simultaneous actions which we can link alongside our own struggle for jobs, and collectively force the government to back down. This is the only image that sustains us through June.

News of closing collieries drifts in, along with the associated power station losses; worse for Doncaster, and Bentley in particular, comes the closure of Thorpe Marsh power station near Barnby Dun. It stands yards away from Bentley Colliery's backyard whose main market it had been. The power station announced no more coal would be bought and existing stocks run down to exhaustion. This was disaster for Bentley; by the time it and Hatfield came into the firing line themselves 4 months later, Bentley pit was surrounded by a black mountain of unsold coal, ironically with the cheapest production cost in Britain, and without state subsidies, the cheapest deep-mined coal in the world. British Coal announced that it was now stocking one million tonnes of coal because of the failure of power stations to take up their customary orders.

July 1993. NUM Annual Conference. A major issue is the question of contractors. It is a problem – they are universally hated, sometimes unfairly. Many Union branches will not represent them; branches fight against their introduction. They are called 'bushwhackers' and 'ninjas'. They are often treated worse than scabs. They are the fulfilment of preparatory work by government and British Coal to introduce privatisation by instalments. They are the 'farmed-out' section, already operating side by side, private mine firms along the core nationalised one.

These men are no 'outsiders' though, these men almost universally are not scabs – not the conventional sort anyway. These are miners, usually the cream of mining miners, they are sought for headings, prestige drivages, important spot work, they drive the major mine machines, the giant tunnelling beasts, or they work with the ancient silver threes drilling in hard rock and sandstone, stripped to the buff and soaked. These are the bonus-chasers, but that is not why they are resented. The cancer of redundancy fever takes miners to sabotage and go-slows, not for any cause other than to shut their pit and get their redundancy pay-out, then they are free, they think. They can then apply to the contract firms to come back to some other pit as a top earner with money in the bank. The heading men at Hatfield, to a man, strong militants, good Union men with visions of the future and dignity, after the defeat of '84/85 and the loss of Union power, want only the wad of money – they can see no further than that. Our efforts to save the pit confound their efforts to get it shut and get off with their money. They are an anti-union cancer, with union-sounding slogans. In the end we are forced to let them go so they will not sink the pit; every single one of our heading teams, on every single shift, with the exception of two men I believe, leave.

We now have no headings being driven. As the coal is consumed on the existing faces the pit is dying – to live, a pit must ever expand. We are offered, ironically, private hire contract firms to come in and drive our headings. We have no option but make a stipulation: no contractor can be from a Doncaster pit. These are the men who by and large knocked the bottom out of many of those pits, had them shut, damned any campaign to keep them open, just to get out. They would not be rewarded by coming here. But it was clear they came from elsewhere, and our men now would be going to displace some regular worker at another pit.

The pool of pits, the number of headings overall, was continually declining;

we were collectively allowing ourselves to bleed to death, we were cutting our own arteries or worse still our mates'. This was the reason for the resentment. But what were we to do, not allow them in the NUM? Allow them in the T&G instead? Allow non-unionism to develop? It was a bitter pill but we took them into the Branch. Fought their corners, fought for their conditions. At other pits they were given the cold shoulder and the NUM would not deal with them. Areas were split on the issue. This Conference would see that thorny subject fought out.

At the end of his contribution Tyrone O'Sullivan, a much prized Welsh Conference speaker, a huge blond man with a permanent smile and sincerity beaming from his blue eyes, said in that beautiful Welsh lilt: 'And I would urge every man here to read the *Ragged Trousered Philanthropists*, for it is a real guide to socialism.' I got up just after Tyrone and started by saying that 'I would recommend every man here to read the *Kama Sutra*, that way we might have an idea what the Coal Board are going to do to us next.' Well it caused a great ripple of laughter, but my aud marra Tyrone wasn't too pleased. 'You spoiled my speech, David,' he said without laughing and I couldn't help but laugh. 'No, you did, David, you made fun of my speech.' I assured him it was an unmissable cue, it wasn't personal. I told him that I loved all his speeches, we all did.

At the Conference of '93 I made what was said (by everyone who got fed up listening to me) to be my longest speech to Conference ever. We had been told there was no time limitation on contributions, since we were talking here of privatisation and contractors and what the attitude ought to be. I gave a potted history of what was happening at Hatfield. All our headings were privatised as was the washer, something like 65% of the pit. I knew also that all my former comrades in the headings were now working at other collieries as contractors.

Some branches wouldn't entertain them, either denying them membership or treating them as if they weren't members. I thought it was vital that while on principle we fought to keep all work 'in house' and directly employed, where contractors came in we were duty-bound to take them into full and active Union membership. They were actually the Union's strongest members, they had been the best pit militants, the vanguard of the strike, but they were also highly money-orientated. They wanted that redundancy money while it was on offer, even if it meant running against the Union's strategy, even if it meant at times running their own pits onto the rocks. Once out with the money in the bank and a nice bouncy safety net, they would take employment back at the pits as contractors, voting loyally 'yes' in every Union strike ballot they were asked to. In the last ballot on national action against Major's closure programme they had voted all but 100% 'yes' and doubtless swung the whole Union into action. So the position was ambiguous, because we also had lads who had fought against the closures, whose pits were closed against their wishes, and were now seeking work in the only trade and the only way they could, as contractors.

It took a little telling; at length Scargill was flashing the light at me to wind up. I was admonished for taking advantage of the leeway. Cheek! Actually my speech took up three pages of the '93 report, Arthur's presidential address ten!

Howard Wadsworth made his final contribution on the deputies dispute:
Somebody has just asked me, 'Did it have a happy ending?' (Laughter) It
is a final contribution – some may say it is an epilogue – it is a final
contribution because of two reasons.

The first reason, of course is that some useless sod lost us the case in
Court, and before we get black looks from the National Officials or before
our lawyers – Stephen's Innocent – OK? (laugher) send a hit man to do
me over, can I say that the useless sod was a bloke called Blofeld, the
judge, because you see, he did not let justice get in the way of finding
against us. (Laughter)[339]

This Conference seen me moving the Yorkshire resolution in condemnation
of the US-led invasion of Iraq and the whole hypocrisy of the rationale for the
war. It had followed straight on from the Scotland Area's resolution condemning
Israel and the genocidal war against the Palestinian people which I had seconded
for Yorkshire with great gusto. Taken together these two pieces on the Middle
East and Zionism and imperialism produced some great contributions and were
both passed unanimously.[340]

The Palestinian guests in the audience must have been impressed, as a year
later me and the family, on a Branch night out to a Palestinian play, were
welcomed from the stage as we came in and they announced that I was the
gentleman who had spoke so forcibly in their support, so the speech made it back
to Sheffield and probably to Palestine without any of us knowing, which was
quite a privilege in itself. I am not sure it actually changed anything, but at least
they knew that the miners knew.

By August the local papers were predicting: 'Rotherham could be left without
any pits if the latest British Coal closures go ahead.' This would continue the
pattern of systematic localised closures, rather than the all-out simultaneous
massacre, which would prompt further public revolt. 'Miners at Kiveton ...
believe they could be among 15,000 miners set to lose their jobs under the latest
scheme to close 15 pits in the run up to next year's privatisation' (*The Star*,
Saturday 14 August 1993). Evidence that we were now utterly spent as a force
was clear in October's issue of the Union's own paper *The Miner*, which focused
entirely on the issue of privatisation and dropped the closure question
completely. The truth was there was nothing at all they could have said to further
rally the troops, let alone point in the direction of renewed resistance.

Between March and August, when the energy markets were supposed to be
given a close inspection to see whether the pit closures were justified, Heseltine
sanctioned the construction of five new gas-powered stations, ensuring the
existing markets of ten more collieries would vanish and ten more pits hit the
deck. In the first 4 months of the year overall electricity generation fell by 2.9%
while nuclear generation rose by 15.7% and coal-fired generation fell by 14.7%.
National Power announced the closure of three big coal generators, decimating
more of coal's markets regardless of the unfavourable costs of generation from
nuclear sources. In clear sight of Parliament the market is being skewed and
manipulated to a fait accompli on coal. It hardly needs saying that these are

political considerations, *despite* fuel economies, efficiency, profitability or actual market requirements.

October 1993. On the back of the 'Scargill–Heathfield' financial corruption allegations (Chapter 6) comes the counterattack in *The Miner*. If it can be believed, almost everyone who worked for us in Arthur's office or with his indulgence is in on the conspiracy. Maurice Jones, the former editor, and friend of Arthur, communist and lover of the GDR, is charged with having stolen documents from the president's office to hand over to the *Daily Mirror*'s owner Robert Maxwell and Roger Cook of the scurrilous *Cook Report*. Jim Parker, Arthur's bodyguard, driver and general dogsbody, a man who recruited Arthur into the CP, was paid £50,000 by the *Mirror* for his inside knowledge. Roger Windsor, the main informant, also £80,000 – scarcely 30 pieces of silver, really, but then he got a loan off the Union too, which as I write is still unpaid.

At the same time, the Yorkshire Area has agreed to transfer engagements and become one with the National Union as such. It is not happening in the way I had envisaged when I spoke heart and soul for it at the Durham Conference in 1990. We are starting to do all sorts of stupid things. Our Yorkshire Area specialist legal department is to close and the work handed over to Raleys, one of the legal firms we have used to handle some cases. The staff most specialised in the country at dealing with miners' claims, a staff which is part of our actual Union organisation, is being paid off. Arthur argues that we can't afford a specialist legal department. I argue that we have the capacity to take in work from other areas, from other unions actually. My opponents, who include most of the Area officials, now retiring themselves, argue it isn't cost-effective any more as we don't have the volume of claims. I argue that we are on the verge of an explosion of common-law claims for vibration white finger (VWF) and bronchitis, that we are on the verge also of financing the Union for the rest of its life if we get behind these claims and take possession of them before every hick lawyer in the country jumps on the bandwagon and makes a fortune on the back of our members.

Arthur has steered us away from 'overinvestment' in the VWF claims; he fears it will bankrupt the Union and indeed I get the strong impression there is a blackout on information and a cold shoulder on processing the claims. The changes go through, the legal department closes, our best solicitors are taken on by Raleys and a sort of 'near group' relationship develops: our members but their clients, our members' claims but the property of an outside legal firm. Teams of outside people start to flood in and fill the gap left by our not being on the ball with the VWF claims. In some areas ad-hoc relationships are developed between legal firms and Areas or sections of the Union; at first these are allowed on a nod and a wink, but then as the Union realises it is missing the boat, such ad-hoc arrangements are condemned as unconditional, corrupt even. In Doncaster, COSA and its leader Davy Murdoch will be eventually expelled from the Union because of his relations with the Yorkshire Area Compensation Recovery Unit, in part funded by the Doncaster Metropolitan Borough Council (DMBC). Our Advice Centre, after being almost alone in processing thousands of these claims for the Union despite their initial reluctance, will also come under close scrutiny.

But the roots of the intrigue and years of bitterness start here, with the dual decision to backpedal on VWF and COAD (chronic obstructive airways disease) and to simultaneously close down the legal department.

A Thin Seam

I am working on the 122's retreat face. The seam has thinned, the chocks are down on the collar and we struggle to clear rubble and coal which crushes in between the chocks. I am almost laid flat between the travelling run. There is scarce room to move. When the weight comes on we are periodically closed in and have to shovel a way through. I am cramped between a cast-iron scraper chain and a giant steel chock canopy, with tonnes of fallen rocks crammed into every space around both, 150 yards from the nearest point of exit, a mile inbye, and under 1 mile of rock and stone. The rock is packed like a solid wall of stone in front and behind. I have no means to tell anyone where I am and all round me come great weight bumps which now are crashing down into the metal of the chock legs already squashed and down on their collars. They can yield no further – from now on they are being crushed. They will in time bend. Before that happens, I at least have to make enough space to get out of here. I position my shoulders, and squat-push the rocks. I dig and pull with my hands. I use the shovel shaft as a lever. At one point I am forced to crawl over the top of chock canopies against the naked and unsupported hanging and rolling roof. It's not just my head on the block; if it comes in now or weighs down on my wriggling body then I'm dead and no-one will ever find me, or I am crushed and alive but crippled.

The shift isn't over, the battle is still on. Meeting up with Keith, we now struggle to bore forepolling forward of the chock line to hold the seam ahead of the cut. It means kneeling in the exposed ground with little chance of escape as the rocks bounce down on the left and right and we are forced to dook back under the canopy soaked in hydraulic oil and sweat, knees and back breaking under the strain of the boring machine. I am working with Keith Robinson, the Branch treasurer, member of the Communist Party and a supporter of 'Straight Left'. The management don't really intend to kill us; but they are throwing us consciously into the most unforgiving of work, but in reality in this shift alone we avoid death two or three times only by sheer accident, agility and luck. I come close to death twice more in this week on this face. It takes all the courage you can muster to pick yourself up and dive back into the fray. As aud Pete Elliott was to comment in one of his last songs, 'Fight for jobs? Why these jobs?'

I once expressed my deep concerns at working in advance of the supports, in unsupported ground, when still shaking and white as a ghost following nearly being pinned down and crushed. I felt it reasonable not to suffer or fear in silence and mentioned the events to the overman. I did not know then, or for 13 years afterwards, that he had passed this on to the management. Thirteen years later in the process of my claim for loss of earnings from my vibration white finger, they dig out a Mr Northcliff, some minor undermanager at that time, but later to be the acting manager under Hatfield Coal Company; he makes a statement that he wouldn't have re-employed me anyway because I was awkward and complained too much. I was furious, not simply at the vindictiveness since this level of spite requires a special kind of skill, but also that putting my life on the line on that face was regarded in such a cavalier and heartless fashion. I should add that although I did make the comment, I carried on working, with Keith, in the jaws of hell, risking death from rockfalls and weight bumps.

It says something too for the quality of the management who ended up running these one-off mining firms. Northcliff, who gave a lacklustre, uninspiring performance at Hatfield to the point where it closed, ended his career being wheeled out to blacken the name of good men, and as an outbye deputy at Rossington – so someone clearly spotted his true talents. It's hard to believe that Coal Board managers would continue to harbour pure hatred for me after all this time – I clearly left a lasting impression. I had argued that were it not for this condition (VWF) I would be still working in the industry or some similarly well-paid manual occupation, which was the truth, after all. He has made a statement saying they would never have employed me anyway, because of my poor working record and poor attendance. I am deeply hurt by this, outraged in fact – it's utter lies, of course. I had a regular stockpile of bloody NCB Hatfield holdalls, which were given as prizes for maximum attendances together with Hatfield 100% T-shirts, given for having no voluntary absences. My work ought to have spoken for itself really – I used to flog me guts out and up till now I would have thought that was one thing nobody could throw at me.

The statement from Northcliff seemed based upon pure venom. It was he who was frequently called before the HMI to explain various alleged lapses and ruses in reporting accidents, and it was I who passed the information on to the HMI. The claim, though fully justified, is a hard one to establish and this vindictive statement certainly went to make things harder. In the end, rather than risk this hostile witness blowing my whole case in court, I settle for less than half of what the case was worth if I had won it; testing the good judgement of the court could have left me with nowt.

15 October. *The Doncaster Courier* announces: 'More Gloom For Last Miners.' British Coal, the paper states, is pessimistic about the future of Hatfield Main and Bentley Collieries. Neil Clark, the new head of British Coal, says he has no hope for the remaining 30 pits, and experts are predicting as few as 15 collieries will be left by March next year. The paper notes that Hatfield made an operating profit of £5 million last year.

Despite angry scenes in the Commons, and a cross-party alliance pledged to save the coal industry, the closures went through. This was followed on rapidly by the privatisation of the remainder of the industry, and strict 'market forces' being applied to their survival.

'Betrayed?' Aren't we always? 16 coal-fired power stations are to close, along with the mass bulk of the coal industry. Did anyone see the GMB in the thick of this struggle? Not a bead of sweat, not a minute of lost production, not a minute of overtime ban. Amazingly, at the following TUC Conference I see a lobby of GMB power station workers; they are protesting in favour of nuclear power! 'What do we want? Nuclear power ! When do we want it? Now!' Well, it takes 40 times more workers to run a coal-fired station, quite apart from the question of the coal industry, so why did we never hear or see a pro-coal station lobby? Why, that's politics, son – politics and cowardice.

Although National and local leaders urged men to reject the redundancy terms and take each and every closure through the extended Colliery Review Procedure, British Coal's tactics were to offer greatly enhanced redundancy terms on condition that the workforce agreed to the closures without further delay, or else only basic redundancy money would be forthcoming. Knowing that the extended appeals procedure gave an absolute veto of closure to the company regardless of the decision of the appeal enquiry, and that the only two successful appeals had already been overridden, the miners were faced with heartbreaking decisions.

The company knew the miners had to weigh the chances of success against the loss of many thousands of pounds in enhanced terms, which would have to last them either until new work was found, or failing that, as it turned out in most cases, for the rest of their lives. As mines closed the pool of redundant miners increased, and widespread unemployment, which was to become long-term in the majority of cases, started to spread quickly across the once prosperous coalfields.

MIDDLEBROOK MUSHROOMS

Behind the scenes of our mass anti-pit-closure struggle, a nasty little strike is waging. The women workers of Middlebrook Mushrooms, many of them wives of the Askern miners, have taken enough of the bullying and poverty wages, struck and joined the TGWU, in that order. It is a bitterly anti-union firm, with lots of little tinpot gods strutting around the women workers, keeping them in line. There are a number of scabs – stupid, short-sighted and hard-skinned. The women have a 24-hour picket on and they have a caravan across the road from the Middlebrook entrance. It is attacked and then set on fire by company guards. A miners' hit squad repays the compliment. They challenge the point of a big heave-ho picket line down at the gate, and ambush the scabs miles away from the plant as they drive up the country lane.

The police are getting more violent, trying to stop miners coming to picket with the women. In one confrontation I am standing in a clump near the gate, when a police car drives straight at us. I jump to the side, and boot it hard as it goes past. A great crumple boot mark appears on the driver side door. They stop the car with a jerk and dive out. I meantime am rolling around on the ground, screaming 'You bastards have run over me foot, you've run over me foot!' The crowd all join in 'You've run that bloke over, you bastards!' The cops assume the dint is the impact off them hitting me and dive back into the car and take off. It is a trick I learned from Sammy Thompson years ago. With the other cops on the gate looking on. I hobble off down the country lane, assisted by Dave Nixon, then we get to the corner and leg it. As I lay on the floor of the car to escape, Dave reports that the booted-in police car is now cruising up and down looking for me, having suspected at length a scam of some sort, or to arrest me anyway in case I made a complaint. There are many scuffles and another picket hut fire before the TGWU calls off the strike they didn't even call in the first place. The women are given some token settlement, but we hold each other in mutual respect and admiration.

FIGHT OR DIE?

27 November. A week after the announced closure of Hatfield together with the rest of the Doncaster coalfield there follows the most emotional meeting of my life.

Fight or allow the pit to close? It is a tragic meeting, packed with the men I worked with most of my life, have fought alongside, men who knew and trusted me and I them. Called at the St John's Hall, Stainforth, the biggest venue in the twin villages, it stood at the top of the pit lane. The morning was bitterly cold as the men, wrapped up in topcoats and anoraks, assembled outside while the committee made their deliberations. There was no comedy at this meeting, as was usually the rule, prior to the general meeting. This was the trusted leadership of the Branch, the men's directly elected workmates. The room was no longer packed to capacity. It had once taken all 1,800 men at the pit, but everyone left was here, 150 or maybe 180 men. It was reminiscent nonetheless of those boom years, filled with earnest faces.

At other branches the committee had come out with a pious resolution calling the Branch to reject all redundancy terms and stand and fight, knowing damn well the rank and file would reject the resolution. The effect was to divide them – the rank and file – from the men they had trusted with their care. It was self-serving and made to appear that you, the leaders, were the principled and dedicated fighters to the last, while they, they were all money grubbing traitors. We would not go like that, we had come too far together. Calls to go through the review procedure would be an empty act of defiance, with the loss of £10,000 per man in the terms he would receive, or, put the other way, a saving of £2million for the NCB. When we walked from the committee room, and into that sea of anxious troubled faces, this time I had no box of tricks, no magic manoeuvres that would save the day at the eleventh hour.

Opening the meeting, Luke Carling asked was there any feeling to fight on, to reject the terms, to go to the wire and take this appeal through the review?

A man asks in response: 'If I throw all this money away, Dave, if I risk a much lower pension and a far smaller lump sum on the redundancy, and we go through the procedure and we win, can you guarantee that the NCB will not shut the pit anyway, and I'll have lost all that for nothing?'

I could not guarantee any such thing.

Another man rose and asked: 'Dave, tell me honestly, if we decided to tell them to stick the money up their arses, is their a chance we can force them to change their minds?'

In honesty, I replied that we had only ever had two successful appeals, with the review ruling against closure; the Board, as it is entitled by this appeal system, rejected that decision and closed them anyway.

'Would they restore the enhanced terms at the end of the review if we fail?'

'No. The enhanced terms are to stop you going through the review. If they paid it out anyway, everyone would take the closures right to the end, knowing the money was in the tin. They brought in the additional terms to stop you doing just that.'

'Will the pit keep working, and earning bonuses while it goes through the review?'

'No, they can't touch the infrastructure but will stop all coal work and developments; you wouldn't earn bonuses.' Which meant of course all severance calculations would be further reduced as would the pensions which are based on the last weeks of earnings before final closure.

'They have us by the bollocks,' someone suggested.

We couldn't argue that they hadn't.

I asked once more: 'If there is any feeling to take this on, the Committee is prepared to recommend that course of action.'

A man stood up, an ex-Yorkshire Main transferee, with tears in his eyes and open hands; looking helpless and lost, he said simply: 'We can't,' with a heart-wrenching honesty.

'In that case,' the chair said, 'I will call upon Dave to read a prepared statement which we hope you will endorse, and pledge to accept. Dave.'

I had composed a final statement, summarising where we had been as a Branch and where we were now and how we would meet the future. I had practised it the night before, with immense difficulty. I had steeled my brain to pass over the words as quickly but as clearly as possible, without thinking on their meaning as I read them – otherwise I knew I would never get through it. I was forced to stop two or three times to stop myself gagging on the words. I dared not even glance at the faces in that crowd, men who had faithfully hung on my words so many times before, men who stood like rock alongside their officials and the values of their Union.

STATEMENT OF FINAL BRANCH MEETING OF HATFIELD MAIN NUM BRANCH, 27 NOVEMBER 1993

The members of the NUM at Hatfield Main Colliery have been in continuous struggle against pit closures since 1983. In the year-long strike men from this colliery distinguished themselves as among the most loyal and valiant fighters in Britain. The period after the strike were years of dedicated commitment to pulling the colliery from the edge and bringing it back into profitability. Our efforts were frequently bedeviled by NCB management pursuing a different agenda, one that included ever-greater attacks upon Union rights and democratic working practices. In resisting this we fought alongside our comrades who had been victimized in the Kent coalfield and struck with them, as well as Frickley and Bentley when they had their disputes.

Despite our agreement to new incentive schemes and multi-skilling our cooperation was never enough and management persisted in attempts to break the workforce from the Union, resulting in Hatfield leading the South Yorkshire coalfield strike of 1990, in which our officials were prosecuted in the High Court, received damage writs for millions and suffered wall to wall injunctions.

With a new manager the Branch attempted again to find new relations for the sake of our mutual survival, only to be met by a government plan to wipe out 31 of the remaining collieries including ours and the rest of the Doncaster coalfield. It is to their utmost credit that the members of this Branch voted 75% in favour[341] with an easy majority among British Coal as well as our contract members. The Hatfield banner together with our wives and children have marched the length and breadth of Britain in protest at the massacre of our collieries. Women from Thorne and Moorends in particular have taken initiatives of the most heroic kind; while the chambers of parliament have rang with our voices. Our delegates have lobbied and picketed Union branches of all descriptions in an effort to bring around a generalized strike action against job losses; but with the exception of our comrades on the railways and in Local Government we failed. As members born and bred of generations of miners we were not surprised at the inaction of the TUC General Council or the leadership of the Labour Party, but our failure to mobilize the rank and file of the big and powerful Trade Unions is what ultimately damned us.

On the production front, our men have toiled in the most horrendous of conditions to turn coal and make the pit profitable. In this endeavour we failed, entirely due to management's acceptance of a scrap chock line which has crippled 122's face just when we needed it most, producing an £8 million loss. Despite this in the few weeks of operation of 105's and with reviewed efforts on 122's the pit was knocking off the debt at a rate of £1/4 million per week. To stop the pit at this stage when we could clearly be in a break-even position by May at the latest; when new well-equipped faces will be waiting and with access to over 200 million tonnes of prime coal reserves in sight is nothing short of an act of wanton criminal vandalism. Hatfield had fought hard to get out of the power station market and been totally successful in establishing new high proceed markets: indeed Hatfield's proceeds are already the highest in Britain. To be told by the Director that this colliery's markets will be filled by British Coal *importing* foreign fuel for our own customers is a national scandal.

The new Director says we are closed in part because of 'our attitudes'; he should know that faced with the murder of our communities and the loss of our livelihoods that 'attitude' is one of deep disgust. His lack of faith in us is mutual, given that in 2 months he has wiped out an entire coalfield and one with the cheapest coal and most productive collieries as well as those with the best commercial markets. Far from facing the sack for gross inefficiency he appears to be just the stuff of British Coal management in the 1990s.

So we come to today to decide on whether to take the colliery through the extended review procedure, knowing that no pit has ever been spared even in the event of winning the appeal, and threatened with the loss of £7,000 plus more favourable bonus arrangements; the imminence of privatisation and even more thoroughgoing attacks upon terms and conditions with the repeal of the Hours of Work Act 1908; we reluctantly agree to withdraw from the Review Procedure. Under no circumstances do we *agree* with the closure of this Colliery or the loss of our jobs.

We thank our men and their families for the magnificent support and strength of conviction they have given this Branch and the Union at large. We know that whatever they do, wherever they go, they will keep proud to our heritage, always join the appropriate trade union, never crossing a picket line of any worker in dispute.

Exhausted and demoralized the present has been taken from us: the past and future however belong to us and we shall guard them jealously. Mr Houghton, John Major, Margaret Thatcher and the rich folk you represent, this moment is yours – you shall never take from us our dignity as workers who have fought for justice and a better world. You may disperse us from this spot, this moment in time, but our conviction shall remain wherever we go and in the generations of post-miners' children who follow us.

The Future Is Ours!

This became the unanimous decision of the Branch 27 November 1993

Signed for Hatfield Main NUM Branch

Secretary: Dave Nixon
President: Luke Carling
Delegate: David Douglass
Treasurer: Keith Robinson

The impact of the resolution had scarcely settled, its meaning sitting like a heavy meal, when the secretary, who was labouring under problems, reported that his wife Brenda Nixon, a leading Women Against Pit Closures activist, had been arrested in occupied Kurdistan by Turkish army forces. The whole trade union delegation had been rounded up and put in detention. It was crucial that everyone here write or telegram or phone the MPs, the Home Office and the embassies before anything worse was allowed to happen. For Dave this was a week of double fear and uncertainty and it was clear in his voice, as he thanked the men who resolved then and there to get straight onto it.

Turkish forces had been carrying out a genocidal war against Kurdish insurgents and the villages the authorities held to be their bases. We had tried to throw some light on this dark corner of Turkey's operation by this delegation. Nobody on that delegation appreciated just what danger they were in, and the threat of being murdered became very clear when one woman attempted to phone the British Embassy and a guard fired his submachinegun over the top of the booth. For a time the whole delegation, trapped in an office, thought they were being set up for mass execution since weapons had been left in the room with them – it was a damn good job I wasn't there with them since the urge to fall for the bait and pick up a gun might have got me and them shot down as 'insurgents'. Brenda, the campaigner, had become nationally famous in the Women Against Pit Closures struggle and was along with Dave the star of a 'fly on wall' documentary about the last round of resistance to pit closures.

Meantime down at the colliery offices where the management were awaiting our formal reply, they were less than impressed by the statement they were given. They refused to accept it in this form and for a time we refused to give it in any other. They demanded a straight yes or no. We refused. At length we accepted to make an initial 'yes' to the closure, with 'full grounds and summary to follow', which they accepted along with the defiant statement which we released for broadcast in the media.

From our viewpoint the statement worked. It united us, across all the disparate and uneven forces at the pit, in an act of defiance and self-respect. We wanted to walk from here with our vision of solidarity, with visions of a brighter tomorrow intact and in not in tatters. This was the final meeting of our Branch, one that was potentially disastrous and explosive – whatever was said and done here would live with us for the rest of our lives. It ended in comradeship, a feeling that we had done all that could be possibly be required of us and more, and a resolution as to how we would meet new challenges of the future.

In the pit car park, this time for the last time, the shivering TV camera crews focused in once more on the pithead gear, as they had done so many times over the last 12 months. They knew everything about us, and we, the officials, fronting up what were often nightly TV stories of doom and desolation from the coalfields, knew them and their techniques. We had become quite proficient at TV presentation and knew all about 2/2 shots, 'noddies', talking heads and much else.

On this occasion, the situation was so dire and provocative it drew an interview from our camera-shy and moderate president Luke Carling. He was a strong, practical, no-nonsense pitman, more at home as a face chargeman, or driving a coal-cutting machine than addressing a meeting full of men. His physical strength, his pitwork and above all his honest pragmatism had got him elected. He explained to the camera and through those countless multiple screens in the living rooms across Yorkshire that he was the son and the grandson of miners who had moved down from Scotland when Hatfield first opened. He talked of his community and his family, his self-respect, the fate of the future. He had never done this before but he radiated honesty out through that camera that evening, as the headlines announced: 'And another of the reprieved Yorkshire collieries is to close … these are the last days for Hatfield Colliery, a pit where the closure has been most bitterly fought.'

Suddenly this was real. This was *my pit*, this could not be happening. The words impacted through my body, I felt sick to my stomach. My emotions going completely to pieces, I wept uncontrollably, for what seemed like ever. Later as I took the dog out across the fields and through the woods, years of Buddhist wisdom, which had offered calm and reason in the past, struggled in uneasy alliance with Marxist materialism to put this whole thing in context. This was a blip; this role I had played faithfully; it was now over. All things are constantly in the process of change and development, every new adversity is a new opportunity.

Then on a more earthly level I recalled the recent dangers, nearly being killed twice in the same week from rockfalls on that damn 122's face; or the torture of dragging my weary bones from my bed at 4.30 a.m. in the morning, or the injustice of leaving for work at 9.30 p.m. on a Friday night while the rest of the village boozed and raved the night away. I hated those things, the dust in my lungs, the aching back, the fear in the pit of my stomach. I could accept this new set of facts philosophically. I could do anything now. I am 15 again! The world is mine again.

Saturday 4 December. *The Doncaster Star* leads with 'Last of the Coal: Final shift for the miners as two pits are closed'. It featured photos of the Hatfield headgear, Dave Nixon and Keith and me, black as the ace of spades having just come off gate-end work, although stupidly the paper thinks I am Luke Carling. Hedley Salt, chair of the Coal Communities Campaign, said:

> The discrimination built in to the power generation market meant coal had lost out despite being cheaper than gas and nuclear power ... The miners of Doncaster have been sacrificed in the face of government failure while families face a life on welfare benefits and the nation can look ahead to dependence on energy imports while millions of tonnes of fuel lie accessible beneath our feet.[342]

My Last Day Underground

Friday 10 December. My last day in the employment of the NCB, now trading under the name British Coal. (Hatfield and other pits' markets will now be met from abroad; though the coal being sold will be supplied under the name 'British Coal', it doesn't actually mean it *is* British.)

We hold a 'Last Waltz on the Titanic' social at the Miners Welfare, with all the lads and their wives and girlfriends at the Ridings, as the Welly is now called. It is boozy and tearful and men let down their emotional defences and express sentiments which they have kept silent for three and more decades. Surface men, lower-paid men, and, to my mind, usually the least active of Union members, declared to me their conviction on the number of times, against their instincts and their dire financial situations, and the fact that I was a 'face man's man', they had always voted not simply for me, but for the Union's calls for action, 'no matter how fucking stupid they were.'[343] They asked, 'Did you know that? Did you know that's what we did?' and I, now beery too, confessed that I had not. I think we all realised in a way we hadn't before that we were more alive in the midst of those sacrifices and struggles than we were destined to be outside of them.

By Saturday night I am round town with my daughter and her boyfriend Paul. We are bumping into the ex-colliers from the other Doncaster pits which have gone before. Their words are more consoling than anything the Buddha or Marx had ever said: 'Sorry Davie Lad, we gi them a reet go, we *had* a go Lad, that's what's important.' And 'Its rough Dave, Ah'm still a collier in 'ere (pounding his chest), ah always will be, but tha survives ... tha survives.' So the lads from Markham, Rossington and Brodsworth did, in words, for me, what my statement had tried to do for the Hatfield lads. We'd survive.

On Sunday my sister rang. She was devastated and upset. She told me my Dad had been deeply wounded by the simultaneous announcement that Wearmouth, the last pit in the ancient Durham coalfield, was closing, and then Hatfield his son's pit and the last pit in Doncaster was closing. Grandson and great-grandson of miners, a miner himself and the father of a miner, it was almost certainly the end of a race, of 'his people'. I stopped the phone call dead, as the emotions of the previous day came back in all-consuming weakness, eating my ability to talk or stand. This was like a mass bereavement. It felt like real physical death, real tangible loss for ever and complete. What we were was no more, it had been killed. Whatever followed for me, I would never ever get that back. Something that I was and am down to my bones was never to be regained, and I miss it. Miss what? Put in parts, of pain, hardship, struggle, danger, injury, disease, or comradeship, meaning, worth, identity, ethnicity, it seems romantic nonsense, or just nonsense, but together it is worth incalculably more than the sum of its parts, the quality outweighing the quantity and even the substance massively. It is what I am and yet I can no longer be, my being is in suspended animation, my true self is on hold, unfulfilled, a thirst unquenched whatever I drink. All of this because I can no longer work down a mine? Can no longer sweat and scrawm on a coalface, or live within the pockets of thousands of others?

Is all of that the result of so relatively small a transaction, is this all I am worth then? It reads quite precious and absurd in the cold light of day and black ink. I expect that these words convey practically nothing of the emotion and meaning I am struggling to mould them to. Maybe only the miners themselves will appreciate this 'anomie', a growing nothingness, emptiness, meaninglessness; perhaps too those other folk robbed of their culture or past.

At Hatfield the pit is closed as a producing mine and we are all paid off. A group of men are re-signed under contract firms to carry on salvage at the pit while various bids are prepared by private coal-owners.

The Hatfield Main NUM Branch is still in existence, we still have men working at the pit, we are still financial members, still officials of the Branch and we are in the forefront of making sure the colliery survives. Cowboy firms begin to operate, offering 'self-employed' contracts where the firm is exempted from paying tax and National Insurance and dodges all safety duties. It is an indignity, but we are forced to go to the coal-owners and argue the merits of the pit and the workforce in the hope they will buy it. We fight the loss of employment contracts and face overwhelming assaults on health and safety and terms and conditions. Some private owners are interested, will talk to the Union, talk about guarantees on conditions, though not shift lengths and the working week. The only man who will not meet us is Mr Jeff Ainley, the current manager. He heads up a management buyout bid, and refuses to meet the NUM. We are banned off site and have taken up a 'government in exile' office in a scrapyard at the top of the pit lane. Some diehard members continue to pay their Union and continue to drop in every day, but as the rain and hail falls we look forlornly over the field to the pit. We have been ousted. By 10 December 1993 the last of the Doncaster mines were closed, including Hatfield. I had never ever thought we would go under, always thought we could talk, argue, kid, protest our way out of it. Thought if we kicked over enough tables, made enough noise, raised enough voices, evoked enough passions – aye, we did all that, but the axe still fell. To be confronted with it, on a personal level, was devastating. I was utterly clueless and in a state of anomie. The ground had opened up under my feet and I was in a state of nowhere, no fixed direction, or base. Still we were now clinging to the idea of privatisation by a big mining company, and starting at square one with Union organisation, while the bulk of British Coal carried on for now. We were in a flurry of meetings with Richard Budge, and Malcolm Edwards, joining the beauty contest, selling our pit and the virtue of the men as workers (which to be honest given the record of militancy was no easy game). Hatfield could turn coal, but actually not very often at a profit. But what difference did that make? They were closing Bentley across the field, which was producing the cheapest coal in Britain, at 88p per gigajoule; the imported coal price was £1.28 and the pit stood just yards from the Thorpe Marsh power station with no transport costs, who paid £1.50 per GJ for it. But it wasn't, anyway, the pit at any price. There would be no sense in the pit without the Union, it was the Union and its objectives in a wider sense, and our ability to intervene as workers, and impel our fellow workers in the labour movement at large, which at base we wanted to preserve.

For that reason we recoiled in horror from Jeff Ainley's plan for a management buyout. Jeff had been an arch-opponent of the NUM at Hatfield and the source of many a dispute and clash of powers. He and we NUM officials were not what you would call soulmates. From the beginning he set his face against any idea that the NUM as an organisation should play any part in his plan, despite the fact he was calling for our members to invest their redundancy in his scheme. We loudly condemned this idea and earned his wrath in the press, which we responded to in kind. Meantime the salvage operations were underway and we held onto the few dozen members undertaking this work. Even threatened strike action against the contract firm for paying under the agreed national wage rates. It was a sign of things to come. Meantime, machines and chock lines were being sealed in, but well oiled and always diggable out again. Jeff it seems was confident he would get this mine, and quite a bit of abandoned machinery even though the big low-loaders were trundling up the pit lane with our modern equipment, cutting machines, road headers and state-of-the-art chock lines. From our office at the top of the pit lane after being thrown off site, following the strike threat, we watched the pit being killed, every day. I fell into the depth of depression and desperation. I just couldn't seem to get to grips with the idea it was all over.

With the colliery now on the verge of privatisation the worst option on Earth for me and the Union was that Jeff Ainley would succeed in getting it.[344] Edwards and Budge had also expressed an interest, both promising protection of Union rates and Union recognition. But first they had to be sold on the viability of the mine. We had unrolled massive colliery plans, and explained to them the geology and the potential, but it was the site visits and the 'hands-on' feel of the colliery which would determine whether they bought it or not. Mr Ainley, their chief competitor, conducted the underground visits and laid open the books for them, although I don't know if they ever knew he was a far from unbiased arbiter here. Neither buyer was convinced; Edwards went on to buy the nextdoor Markham Colliery, an incalculably harder prospect, though with potentially far higher returns, while Budge bought every other pit in the coalfield when the whole caboodle came up for sale. At that time, though, the rest of the pits were bought as going concerns and as such the terms and conditions and Union standing were protected under TUPE. Those which had been sold as 'lease and licence mines' were sold as abandoned collieries with no protected terms and conditions; they were to remain the poor relations afterwards, with Hatfield eventually being the least-paid, longest-worked miners in the country despite our efforts.[345]

In 1994 the government throws in its final blow and privatises what is left of the coal industry. Pits closed under the Major plan of '93 are first put on the market for sale under licence. These are followed by the sell-off of the remainder of the industry. A fragile and weakened NUM now faces its most hostile old protagonist again. An opponent it had campaigned for a generation and more to legislate out of existence. The new coal-owners, although constrained to some extent by the terms of TUPE, had also been encouraged by repeal of a number of key mining health and safety acts and laws restricting hours of underground work. In the majority of cases they take over where the Board of British Coal had left off – isolation of the NUM at National level, and widespread restriction on the activities of the NUM branch at pit level. Numerous attempts at national industrial action since privatisation have been hog-tied in anti-union legislation, although industrial action, some of it diverse, long-lasting and bitter has raged at individual UK mines such as Rossington and Kellingley.

The *Yorkshire Miner* had published a special edition which went to every member's home in the Area, to every pithead, and every welfare and club. It called for a 'Vote Yes' for industrial action against the Major closure plan, with pleas from Frank Cave, the Area chair; Ken Homer as general secretary; and Ken Capstick as vice chair.

I am proud to say it featured an article by me, 'Vindictive to the Last', which filled a full page of the four-page paper. It dealt with the attempts by the management at Hatfield, still ostensibly NCB, to crush the NUM membership within the contractor firms operating the pit, and to help them force down wage rates among those workers; this they had succeeded in doing, with men working 40% and 50% lower than nationally agreed mining rates of pay, even though actually their terms and conditions had nothing whatever to do with the NCB anymore.

The local NCB manager Mr Ainley had informed the contractors that he would end their contracts and get someone else to do the care and maintenance and salvage if they so much as talked to us. But why should it bother him? It was no secret – Ainley and a couple of his management staff were about to put a bid in for the colliery; this would be the workforce he would inherit, and on these scandalously reduced rates of pay. He had no intention of having any Union input into this colliery when he took over and that workforce had better get used to it now.

Incidentally, the paper also carries a large advert for my new book of the time *Pit Sense Versus the State*, which they printed free of charge along with a facsimile reproduction of the rear cover and 'blurb'. In a way, the paper illustrates my position as a sort of 'minister without portfolio'. I had no official Area rank, but was acting as a de facto tribunal officer, taking on increasing amounts of Union tribunal and appeal work. I was frequently posted off to conferences and meetings on behalf of the Union and I regularly wrote for the Union paper and spoke on their behalf to the press.

My Dad writes:

> Things look very bad for the coal industry, everything said in parliament about keeping the pits open was just a con, and the miners fell for it, they hadn't any intention of keeping the pits open, on top of that, they are blackmailing the men into accepting redundancy, look what has happened up here David. All the pits in Durham are now closed, and as I understand, they are up for sale. This is a real scandal, it seems to me David, the mining industry as we knew it is finished. After all the efforts of the Union. I am very sad and bitter over the treatment of the miners. I rate the miners as one of the best class of workmen in the country. In my opinion they are the best. It is just unbelievable. I feel for you David and your Mam is also very upset. What is to happen at your pit, David?

Soon the news is flashing across the TV channels and my Dad writes further:

> I heard the very sad news on the telly concerning the three pits in South Yorkshire, Hatfield one of them, this is disgusting. It looks as if we may only have about 8 pits in the whole of England. What a shame, all the millions of tonnes of coal sterilised for ever and at what cost, the coal they are importing will jump up in price. People won't be able to keep warm, what with value added tax on top, here we are with coal to last for three or four hundred years, our own oil and gas, indeed one of the richest countries in the world with respect to fuel and this government has ruined the whole of the coal industry. A national scandal. Have you been informed yet about your pit? Your Mam and I are very upset over your future life, you have had about 29 years in the coal industry, 17 years of age when you started at Wardley Colliery and 18 years old when you went to Hatfield, you have devoted your life up to now to the mining industry. You are going to miss it David. You have done well at Hatfield and your Mam and I are very proud of you, we think you have done fantastic, but we worry about you. Do you know this government seem likely to build a nuclear power station at Druridge Bay ...
>
> Love to you and Emma from your old Dad.

It is Jeff 's bid in the long run which is successful. He becomes the first coalowner of Hatfield Main colliery since 1947. He revives the old name Hatfield Coal Company and he starts to recruit men. Both me and Dave Nixon the Branch secretary apply; we are not called to an interview. The office at the St John's Ambulance Hall at the top of the pit lane is busy with pensioners and ex-members but the numbers of men working at the pit rejoining the Union are pitiful and as the number of accidents increases there are no NUM safety inspections, and few are reported. Three accidents reported at the medical centre get you graded as 'accident prone' and a hazard and you're sacked. Men stop reporting accidents.

13 December. I turn up at Orchard Street, Thorne to sign on. What a humiliation. Worse, it is a public humiliation. 'My men' – that's the way we have regarded each other – are visibly shaken and sad to see me walk up the road to the dole office. One big heading man, standing with his mates, places a hand on my shoulder and with tears in his eyes says: 'I never ever thought I'd see the day lad, when you would be coming to this place.' It felt like the scenes after Culloden, when the proud and vanquished Jacobites seen all they had stood for and by, humiliated and dragged through the mud. We were the Native Americans being escorted to the reservation.

I have now to ponder here, looking for another job, how work without meaning, without force of social intervention, political challenge, love of a community, a people, a history, a culture, the Union, would be – just a job. Since I was 17, I had never ever contemplated such an empty way of life. But surely I could realise this truth again?

People are in constant struggle at work, in school, in offices, and industry. Scargill's message and that of all our labour organisers is to address the struggles of life as they fall. I cheer myself with Bob Dylan's words: 'Meantime life goes on outside all around you.' And that being the case, the spirit of our endeavours, that vision so hard fought, that speck of the whole reality must be carried in whatever we do, if we really believe it. I am convinced that I will remain a coalminer whether I am mining coal or not. If 180,000 of us, decapitated in that life-and-death struggle, carry that vision to the new earth, can we not be the dragon's teeth?

Are we so thoroughly defeated as Tommy Hepburn, our illustrious leader of the 1840s, beaten down by poverty, forced to sell tea door to door, his faithful men banned from buying it? He signs an undertaking never to work for the Union again and gains a job at Felling Colliery on point of starvation. When he dies only four men attend his funeral. Martin Jude takes up the torch, dies equally broken and impoverished, only two men at his graveside. We are not so defeated, and Arthur will never be carried to his resting place without an army at his side again.

But the intrusion of modern inspirations breaks through the boozy reflections with a hearty and unanimous rendition of Eric Idle's 'Always Look On The Bright Side Of Life'. The song is the very essence of pit humour and laughter in the face of tragedy. The photographer from the *Doncaster Free Press*, along to capture the final picture of the ill-fated Hatfield miners, has to ask us 'not to look so damn happy'. He is told, with Anglo-Saxon embellishments, that 'Ye deen knaa miners, lad.' Grief is taken on the chin, and if you can't dook at least you can grin; or, as someone was to say many years later, 'Am I bovvered?'

Asked in the middle of December '93 just where the great protest over closures had gone, Labour's trade and industry spokesperson Robin Cook told BBC TV that people had abandoned demonstrating because they had become aware that the government would ignore whatever they did. However, 'the public is just as angry now as it was a year ago.' He predicted that by April '94 there would be less than 10,000 miners left in the whole of Britain; 'less than the workforce at the Trade and Industry Office', he commented.

The great wind of change that for a brief moment stirred the banners of labour, and linked once more great sweeps of the British public to the miners, had failed to blow long enough or hard enough to change a government with its face set determinedly against it. In its own way, though October '92 to October '93 had been another 12 months' struggle, it was less dynamic than '84/85, though for those of us who joined it with every ounce of determination we could muster it is likewise etched into our hearts.

Malcolm Edwards, former director of British Coal, moves in to buy up Markham Main, the pit next door that the women in particular fought so hard to save. They are concentrating their work in the deep Barnsley seam, and are struggling to win out the vast reserves in new areas of the mine. The earth is stubborn. The weight sits down on the new roadways as they are being driven, the roof crushes the new tunnels, the men struggle to make progress, the pit is turning no coal; Markham is dragging down the other Edwards enterprise in the Midlands. In the end comes a big fall, and he too walks away from the mine. They abandon 72.1 million tonnes of the lofty Barnsley seam; the Hazel which ran from Markham to Hatfield and Hatfield to Askern lies in unmined – virgin seams in quantities of anything from 150 million tonnes to perhaps double that. Markham, a giant in industry, a legend in the annals of the NUM in Yorkshire, providing great leadership to the whole county over a century of struggle, a red-ragging, militant, far-left pit, closes. The village is abandoned and the headgear unceremoniously pulled down. Not a trace of the pit survives, although in its place there flourishes a wonderful nature reserve and expanded woods. We never had any argument with nature. We love nature. We just wanted to work as well as walk in the trees. Kevin Hughes, the former Branch delegate and one-time member of the Communist Party and then the New Communist Party, ended up the MP for Doncaster North. He said: 'The government seemed happy to inflict the cost of pit closures on taxpayers – a cost which could reach £1.2 billion.'[346] As time flew rapidly by, and the coalfield areas stagnated, new jobs and industry did not blossom as the foolish spokesmen far and wide had predicted, and the costs far exceeded Kevin's conservative estimate, especially as the newly 'saved' and then 'privatised' industry carried on to be ruthlessly butchered to extinction.

Across the country, the closures were swingeing, and the effects upon mining communities terminal. While miners had weathered many storms in their long and bitter history, this time the industry itself was all but gone and hopes of a revival dashed forever.

What we see in the communities at this time, in these mining communities where people quite rightly and quite proudly express the view that they used to leave their doors open, their windows open because of the friendship and the comradeship and the tight-knit communities which once prevailed throughout the coal industry, what we see now is high crime, a huge increase, and record levels of teenage pregnancies, drug abuse, alcohol abuse, debt, violence, all now common but they were not there before … this is the Thatcher legacy.[347]

In the 1950s a book regarded as a classic, *Coal Is Our Life*, focused a tight study on a pit town in West Yorkshire, the folk, their aspirations, their lives. In his book *Coal Was Our Life*, Royce Turner returns to the same locations now and confronts us with a devastating contrast.

It is as if the book has erupted from the suffocating swamp of PR sociology which has buried the decimated pit villages since the mass closure programmes. The book challenged the self-congratulatory business schemes, job creation schemes, retraining schemes, coalfield regeneration, reinvestment, reinvention schemes which everywhere tell us they are at work, which everywhere publish reports and surveys, and seem to be the biggest employment growth area themselves, though not for the pitmen or their families, yet still the deprivation and poverty and wretched loss remains. How can so many organisations, apparently awash with European and Lottery money, be running so fast and yet standing still?

Talking of housing in Featherstone in 1996:

The families that lived in them were beset by social and economic problems. On top of that the residents were struggling to survive in the face of a poor local reputation. It is almost as if the houses are a physical representation of hopes dashed, of a vision for the future turned sour. People had secure employment, brand new modern houses, what were seen as good prospects for their kids. Now 40 odd years later, the houses are crumbling, and the lives have crumbled too. Old battered cars sit on oil-soaked drives. If it's sunny people sit on the doorstep for half a day. There's nothing much else to do.[348]

And Maltby:

It was in one of the worst states of disrepair that I have ever seen any housing. Sean (a local councillor) told me that it had improved a lot from what it had been. Many houses were boarded up and dropping to pieces. Some of the youngsters had taken to breaking the gas pipes inside and throwing petrol bombs in. They'd completely lost a few houses this way. It provided the youngsters with a bit of fun. Sean took me to the derelict houses that had been occupied by his family and friends, where they had looked after the gardens and been good neighbours and helped each other out. The house are in rack and ruin, gardens like jungles, without the eerie charm of a jungle. A few yards away is the footpath next to a railway line where the smack dealer had threatened to kill Sean for trying to fight the drug trade.[349]

Even those of us living in the shadow of the former coal industry, as it struggles to survive and maintain a living and a tradition, cannot often explain what is lost, though its loss is massive, it is more than the sum of any parts, roots, job, pride, class identity, community, culture, ethnicity, politics, vision, one could chose to add together. Certainly grim toil, death, injury, disease and conservatism are also words and concepts which battle with the former as descriptors of pit life, no one here is looking for any nostalgic glow. The cold light of most poverty-strewn, heroin-addicted, crime-ridden pit villages would quickly damp any of that. Yet the change is real, the contrast inescapable, the loss of real life values, and the will and determination to intervene and fight back is everywhere visible.

In Featherstone there aren't many choices. If you get chance of a job at the packaging factory you take it. You think yourself lucky to receive what you see as decent money and a gold watch and to get an invitation to a dinner and dance at Christmas.

The pop factory represented the only foreign investment in Featherstone. Yet foreign investment we were told throughout the 1980s as deindustrialization savaged large parts of the economy was going to be the salvation of local economies. Looking at a small town like this gets you away from the platitudes and generalisations of national politicians who wouldn't even know where Featherstone is except when it's needed to provide a rock solid labour seat for some anointed rising star …

Yet these were the two themes of the 1980s and much of the 1990s. A newly rejuvenated small business sector, and inward investment by multinationals were going to transform the economy. Neither has happened in Featherstone, and neither will.

But the author is sucked down too deep perhaps by the depression and despair he sees all round him. He declares:

You walk around, and you want to help them. You want an economic and a social and a cultural revolution. You want to remember them as they were, full of pride and hope for the future. You want them strong, and confident. Knowing that their day is to come, but come it will, as they used to believe. But you know it isn't and you know that you can't really do anything about it … I remarked on this once to an older man who had lived in the locality all his life. He took his time before answering me, thinking about my words. Then he fixed me with his now watery but still steely blue eyes. 'What do you expect them to do?' he said. Riveting the position deep into my psyche. I suddenly realised of course, that I hadn't a clue.

Public ownership as it might have become as we approached the millennium had never simply meant 'Government Ownership' in the coalfields, at least certainly not back in the forties, when it first came in, or even in the fifties. It may never have lived up to its promise, but it had been seen as being about much more than that. It was about power. About moving power from the despised coal barons to the workers …

It is a spirit, a culture, a world that has passed. It was a fleeting moment in political history; a moment in which it was thought that the collective could achieve more than the individual. It will never happen again. All that is believed in the 1990s by 'Labour' and Conservative is that the successful entrepreneur is the 'key player' in the economy. There's nothing else. There are no grand ideas anymore. Nothing we can strive for, and be proud to call our own.[350]

Yet class anger remains. 13 years after the defeat of the miners strike in '85, MacGregor died. Someone felt enough to go to the site of a former Barnsley colliery and paint in giant letters on the walls: 'Rest In Hell. Ian MacGregor. Bastard. 1998. Rich Fucker!'[351]

So the effect of the 'rigged market' struck deep; it had laid low the coal industry as a large modern industrial operator, it would go on over the coming few years to fell the remaining pits struggling against impossible odds. Why was it done? After a lifetime in the industry and quite a number studying the very question I am now certain that the basic plan, with two or three variants, was laid back in the '70s when the NUM was termed 'the storm troops of the TUC'. The aim of both major political parties was to ensure the storm troops did not storm anyone anymore. A full-scale massacre had not initially been on the cards, only a systematic culling and neutering. When this had proved inconclusive then a 'final solution', by the destruction of coal's markets, was consciously and deliberately planned – that is, for political not commercial, economic grounds or those of fuel efficiency, still less care of the environment.

At the beginning of the new flush of militancy and confidence at the end of the '60s Barnsley, like many other traditional mining towns, was rooted through history and location to coalmining. The people themselves were inseparably linked to coal and mining and unions. Somewhere within a 15-mile radius of Barnsley town centre 70 pits operated, employing an army of miners. In 1976, 47% of the total Barnsley workforce worked in mining (21,000). By 1994 not a single coal mine remained. The shock of that transformation and the manner by which it was imposed still resonates on through those communities. It is as if a great machine was suddenly unplugged and fell silent. People are left 'aimless'. The characters are still around town. In the pubs and clubs the old lads will still tell the tale and draw on their immense reserves of humour and wit, on the weekend streets the young 'uns will still strut their stuff, but something at the heart has died. There is something of a collective social bereavement here, which is still so raw one hardly dare touch on it. Grown men, who have faced the most indescribable hardship and danger in their lives, can now be moved to tears when reflecting on the last two decades and how they have impacted upon them and more importantly their families, and their communities. These were more than just job losses.

The whole town has changed and run down; it's riddled with poverty, most people on benefits, or trying to work in the black economy. If you take the pit out of the pit community what is it there for? All of the things that people considered to be meaningful in their lives, their history that they'd literally heard from grandfathers, their parents, dads' grandfathers and great grandfathers, all working in the pits, they lost that. They emigrated to other coalfields to work in the pits and indeed went abroad to populate coalfields in other parts of the world. I mean, we are part of a mining race of people. So when you take the pit out you are left with nowt, really. That's even supposing they've tried to bring some kind of industry back into these places.

The mines are dead and gone and the coal communities buried, but the folk of the pit communities refuse to die, refuse to become something else that somebody's trying to make them. We still have traditions. There's still miners' galas where people turn up with bands and banners and their families and listen to speeches and talk about the way forward now, despite everything – 'them', 'us', 'the bastards'. Class on class. They still see it still.

March 1994. The Yorkshire Area of the NUM moved to merge with the National Union as such and be one constituent body. I had been an enthusiastic supporter of all the area unions transferring engagements into a single national constituted union. I had been the person who moved the resolution at the Durham Conference in 1990 and cast aside the objections of areas wary of losing their independence and identity. I had seen a single national union as a democratic body directly responsible to the members as such. It would have only one tier of bureaucracy, the National Executive Committee would function as a Branch committee and be elected on the direct votes of the branches with proportionate representation for the traditional areas; the NEC and the leadership would come under increasing control of the membership, the branches would be directly represented, with monthly meetings of every branch in the country. Branches could agenda any subject they wished, the members could have direct input into the National Union through the branches. It would be like an Annual Conference every month. That was the vision as I seen it, and had been led to believe it would play out.

June 1994. The International Miners' Organisation which had been started by Arthur and his mate Alain in France becomes the International Energy and Mineworkers Organisation. It claims 100 affiliates worldwide with a total membership of 30 million. In the main it is an alliance of old cold-war, state-sponsored 'unions' in the old Stalinist countries and their third-world, state-funded 'union' allies. It is a total invention of the bureaucrats and never ever had any rank-and-file input into either its creation or its functioning. It is awash with the affiliation fees from the hard-working miners and energy workers who see none of it. While those who junket across the world at its expense talk a good fight, it is all smoke and mirrors. There is nothing of substance behind the whole edifice. For sure, African and Arab and Indian miners' leaders are invited to the lavish table and at times jetted around the world, but for no real purpose other than to give credibility to the claim that somehow this organisation represents workers. In its entire lifetime it achieves nothing whatever at astronomical expense. Throughout the whole period of its existence I fight to either change it or dismantle it. I am not successful, mainly because the rank and file have little or no knowledge of it and those who get to sit at the lavish tables and international junkets have no intention of letting them know about it, or what is happening to their money. In its entire life I have never once seen a balance sheet, despite requesting at every level to see who contributes to what and what happens to it.[352]

REDUNDANCY SCHEMES

For a time I still had a wad of redundancy money in the bank. I had been awarded £33,422.45; it would have been more, but they deducted all the periods I had been on strike and then these had added penalties as they broke the continuous-service mark-up. My list of deductions read like a battle honour: '72, '74, '79, '84/85 and a month in 1990. I knew it would not last long, with little or no income coming from the Union, and none from the pit. I entertained for a time the idea of opening a vegetarian restaurant somewhere on Tyneside or in Northumberland, preferably Seahouses. I didn't consider this too much of a sellout, since I had to live and everywhere walls seemed to be springing up to stop me doing just that. Apart from the new coal-owners' and contractors' blacklist were the ongoing effects of 30 years of graft on the rips; the big air leg machines, the windy picks had taken their toll on my hands and wrists and I was soon to discover that the agony of pain and terror of paralysis creeping up my hands and arms was 'hand arm vibration syndrome' (HAVS). I might add this was a relief, as I had tried to suppress the growing belief that it was the precursor of a heart attack or stroke. Either way my days as a big hitter, slogging it out with sinew and muscle and gritted teeth with a pneumatic pick at the end of my arm, or my shoulders hunched into a boring machine, were pretty much doomed. In any case, Stokely Carmichael, one of the heroes of my revolutionary generation, had also gone on to open a right-on restaurant without the loss of too much street cred, although I think he also had gone on to abandon any belief in militant black struggle and communism; not so me – I could surely run a veggie café or restaurant without joining the ranks of the bourgeoisie? I started a business enterprise training course at David Hall's together with loads of potential gardening shop or paper shop proprietors and window-cleaners.

It was a thrill of an adventure, following up on places, visiting with Emma and Paul, getting excited at the possibilities. I even took my Health and Hygiene Certificate and gained a distinction. The women folk on the course were much bemused by this 'pit union man', who they recognised off the telly, sitting in the classroom or kitchen with them learning about what shelf to keep your cheese on and how to disinfect your mop.

It was not to be. Emma, God love her, and probably thankfully, was by now a skilled finance officer, knew her accounts and budgets inside out and could size up a financial future projection in a blink. She stayed my spontaneity and enthusiasm with cold analysis and calculation. Great premises at the Metro, and North Sunderland, became no-hope money drains and millstones under Emma's bucket-of-water reality treatment. I would end up broke, and out of work, and probably hundreds of miles away from my nearest and dearest and still have no work and the blacklist on my back.

So it hasn't happened and the money has gone here and there, supplementing what bits of work and employment I have been able to pick up along the way working for the miners and the coal communities in the last 10 years between the privatisation of the colliery and the closure of the Branch in 2004. I am able, like most miners, to have paid off the small mortgage for the NCB house, buy a bit of a car, and have holidays, but the gruel is destined to get thinner in the next few years.

January 1994. The Communist Party (*Weekly Worker*) are hoping to relive some of our class history and reconstruct the National Unemployed Workers Movement of Wal Hannington in the '30s with the launch of the Unemployed Workers Charter. God knows, with the mass redundancies in the mines across the country and all the knock-on effects at ancillary suppliers and servicers, there is plenty scope for it. They do me the honour of asking me to head it up, even offering to pay me a small salary to do it. The potential exists raw and smouldering in the bombed-out working-class communities of mines, docks, shipyards, steelworks and foundries. The formal letter from Mark Fisher ended on a personal note about the now unemployed members of his mining family; at his uncle George's recent funeral in South Wales,

> I encountered my uncle Peter. He told me he had recently been made redundant, but had got a good job almost immediately; 'management in one way', he had said. 'What do you mean "in one way?"' I pressed him. 'Well I've got three hundred people under me,' he said. 'Really?' Knowing my uncle Peter's work record I was a little surprised. 'Where are you working now, then?' 'Morriston Cemetery,' he said and laughed uproariously just as my widowed Auntie came into the room. The Welsh just can't get enough of death.

I thought long and hard about the project, and it had great merit, but life was uncertain enough as it was and the TUC pulled out every stop to outmanoeuvre this initiative, mainly with unemployed centres firmly under their control and with strictly limited agendas. Mind, many of the unemployed centres became the only resources for a fightback in many traditional working-class cities like Liverpool and Newcastle.

31 January 1994. I am awarded my MA in Industrial Relations and Law from Keele. It had been a hard slog, working nights, late afters, and studying mainly at home. The Branch had funded my fees as a final act of defiance to ensure my war on the gaffers would continue whatever happened in this mining arena. The ceremony with the gown and mortarboard and all the pomp and circumstance was fine. Ems came to watch. I sat at the front behind the new PhDs, but refused to stand up for the national anthem much to annoyance of folk making nice home movies. Em stood up, mind – she was sitting on her own at the back of the room and felt rather intimidated, so I couldn't blame her really. I'm quite chuffed. I got a B Plus, an excellent mark. St John's and the disgrace of the C stream seems vanquished now – not really, that particular burn is scorched too deep.

GIZ A JOB

February 1994. MA or no the list of application forms for jobs of all descriptions and types is endless. It reminds me of my period of endless unemployment when I first left school, but I am not yet desolate; in fact, I write: 'I suddenly have a good feeling about my chances for a job – it's rushing through me! I feel a strong feeling I'm coming out of this dive.'

Phoenix Press publishes my *Pit Sense Versus the State*. This is really my attempt at showing some of the internal workings and struggles within the Union during the strike. It is packed with minutes and notes, which confuses many non-miners apparently. I think it probably needs rewriting as the information which it contains, uniquely recorded in many ways, is lost or too obscure for many to appreciate.

18 June. Yorkshire Miners' Gala. We arrange one of our famous Miners Folk Music socials with The Elliotts, Tom Gillfellon and the North Staffs Miners' Wives.

NUM Conference Blackpool, July. The Conference of '94 seen something of an unusual clash between the Yorkshire Area branches and the National Executive Committee on how Yorkshire managed its own affairs. On the one hand this was the last battle of the old right in the Union and the currently dominant left. It was represented on the one hand by Johnny Walsh, of the traditionally moderate right-wing miner's leadership. A strong, fit rugby-player, quietly spoken, a reasoning and apparently reasonable man. He looked like a caricature of a miner – tall and muscled, he would not be out of place in a major heading hulking great iron girders. He was totally opposed to militancy and the language of militancy. He always seen 'the sense' of most of the projects the NCB came up with. He had opposed the strike, opposed mass picketing, opposed Arthur as a leader, and firmly believed the Union was on a wrong tack in almost everything it did. We had clashed throughout our Union lives, especially as he strove to stand for senior Union positions, sometimes up to the wire of violence as *Hot Gossip* lampooned him and the paper spread like wildfire through the coalfields. At length he had become one of the Yorkshire Area agents representing North Yorkshire. He had also stood against Arthur Scargill following the strike and came too close for comfort. During the strike he had sat on the Area Co-Coordinating Committee planning the Area's picket strategy; he was none too impressed with my tactics and strategies and I had sought to have a dual strategy, one public and one secret and not open to his veto, although I am sure he was well aware of this.

Grist to mill of the dispute was the freefall of membership; mass rundowns and closures had meant that the Union was becoming top-heavy with too many officials for the numbers trying to sustain them with their subscriptions. In 1986 we had agreed nationally a formula which, based upon the contributing members, that is full members, would decide how many full-time officials and staff we could support. As membership fell, so would the number of officials. In the first year after this was agreed, one official and four staff went out, but the Area was still substantially overstaffed. In 1993, with the agreement of the staff union it was decided to reduce the office by 13 staff members.

Each of these cost-cutting exercises was of course itself costly, since it involved severance and redundancy packages in line with NCB terms. January '94 seen us reluctantly agree to lose two of our full-time officials, and that the oldest officials would be asked to go first since this was the formula we used at pits, giving the best terms to the oldest men. We agreed at the Council meeting by 20 votes to 4 to take this course of action.

The two were to be Ken Homer and Johnny Walsh. Frank Cave was a sprightly 50 but had a child at primary school; he would, given his short length of service and age, be very much worse off than either of the other two in the event of redundancy.

Johnny Walsh stubbornly refused to accept this proposal; he wasn't against the formula – only against him being the one to go. Additionally he then turned his opposition to the fact that I had taken part in the vote when actually I wasn't entitled to vote since I shouldn't be a member! Basing his logic on the fact that Hatfield had closed, and I wasn't one of the men involved with the contractors doing salvage work, I shouldn't be in the Union. Well, first off, the contract firm hadn't taken me back on – on strict instructions; and second, the men at the pit and the retired members had formally voted to employ me as the Branch Secretary, at least so long as funds held out to keep the Branch together and be in a position to rebuild the Branch should an owner be found. This had been done with the full knowledge and approval of Arthur and the Area officials; indeed I had thought that they had suggested it, and some of the correspondence from the period strongly suggests they did. Johnny appealed to the NEC on 4 May 1994 and, obviously looking over their shoulders at their own declining areas and shaky employment prospects, they voted by 7 votes to 6 including all the Yorkshire members, to uphold Johnny's appeal.[353]

We were furious that this national formula had been established by them in the first place and accepted by areas. Mr Walsh argued that he didn't object to the formula, only to the selection process and to 'unconstitutional voting', i.e. me representing Hatfield, plus five other delegates who he claimed ought not to be there; presumably those pits had already closed and were up for sale, but still had operational branches and members. Hatfield for example had 150 members, so quite enough to constitute a branch under the rules. The QC later advising the Yorkshire Area to check the credentials and authorisation of its delegates did so, and found all of us legitimate voting members of Council.

When it came to floor of Conference it was a wild and bitter exchange. Speaking on behalf of the Yorkshire Area I demanded that the NEC had better come up with a way to pay Johnny's salary because the members in Yorkshire could not afford to do so. The NEC had ruled that areas were responsible for the salaries of area officials, but not apparently how many of them we were forced to employ or could afford. The salary costs were £54,000; our budget wouldn't and couldn't meet this cost.

The reason for the adoption of that formula was a simple and logical necessity.

We had fewer and fewer Indians and by virtue of what had become almost a guarantee of lifetime employment, more and more chiefs.

A smaller and smaller number of contributors were having to support not only all the services for our non contributory retired members, but by proportion larger numbers of staff and officials. The membership could not and will not continue to underwrite proportionately larger and larger cheques to keep people employed in the numbers and manner of life to which they have become accustomed. (Appeal to Annual Conference Rule 9M against minute 131 – NEC May 1994)

The Annual Conference report for '94 is one which is missing from my collection but I believe the minute was moved back to the NEC who accepted Yorkshire's decision.

Incidentally, no one at that time, among either Area or National officials, upheld the view that my membership, Union position or employment by the Hatfield Main Branch was in any way illegitimate. It had been a spurious and desperate tactic employed in a fit of rage to throw sand in everyone's eyes and overturn a decision which the old right didn't like. Amazingly, that same spurious argument was to resurface a little later when the new left leaders took on the role of the new right bureaucracy, at least on the issue of democracy and accountability.

Persistent, widespread unemployment dominates the former coal communities. Worse still is the loss of vision which had previously carried past generations over seemingly insurmountable hills. This is later confirmed by the 2005 Welsh Index of Multiple Deprivation, which is more detailed than previous studies. The report focuses on income, housing, employment, education, health, services, and the physical environment. It divides Wales up into smaller areas than a similar study in 2000 and the Assembly government said this would better help it identify pockets of deprivation. Merthyr Tydfil, the heart of the former coalfield, remains the local authority area with the greatest deprivation. By the 1990s 25% of the male population of 'the coalfields' (and that includes many major northern, Scottish and Welsh cities, so one shouldn't be deceived by how large 'the coalfields' so called were) had lost their jobs 'and almost half of all ex-miners had long-term illness or injury'.[354] By March 2007 it was being reported: 'Coalfield areas had only 13% of the country's population yet a quarter of all the derelict land in the UK.'[355]

It is interesting to note that in the Annual Report of the Yorkshire Area NUM, Owen Briscoe, the then general secretary of the Area, quoted a prediction from the Sizewell Inquiry held in 1983 (into whether there would be need for nuclear capacity) that by 2007 the deep-mined coal industry in Britain would be producing only 10 million tonnes annually.[356]

This has proved to be slightly optimistic but gives a lie to the oft heard suggestion that the pit closures were somehow Arthur Scargill's fault and there had been no plan to decimate the industry prior to our resistance to 'limited closures'. This prediction was made by government opponents of the coal industry to an official inquiry held in the year before the start of the '84/85 strike.

11 August 1994. Our dear friend Peggy Seeger, now on her own again without Ewan, writes to say she is closing their house of 35 years at Beckenham, Kent. She is returning to her family in the USA:

> I hope this note does not seem abrupt. You know what it is like moving house, the third most traumatic experience preceded only by divorce and the death of a beloved person. I am combining all three of these because in a way leaving England is like a divorce. I love this country and it will probably always be my home always. Hope to see you again … Peggy

September 1994. The Provisionals call 'a complete cessation of all military operations'. It is one more dramatic step from the uncompromising socialist republicanism which characterised their trajectory until about 1988 or '89; since that time they have been, often without the realisation of their cadre, going down another as yet unspecified route.

A New Career?

12 September. I stand on the edge of a new career opportunity. I had toyed with the idea of going into nursery nursing, at least as a nursery assistant or something along those lines. A position had come in Leeds with Kids Unlimited. It was only part-time and I was untrained of course, but I thought: 'What a wonderful idea, what a wonderful combination of roles, working 2 or 3 days in the nursery and 2 days in the Help and Advice Centre and as part-time Union secretary for the miners.' (Which is what I had been doing for a wee while.) Well, the manager of the nursery, Chris Lewis, a courageous and far-sighted manager who knew and understood children, with a radiance which shone from her eyes, was also a very good judge of character; she knew my qualifications were nothing whatever to do with this role, but I had had life skills, especially looking after Emma in her formative years. She had left me to go and answer some long phone call and I was alone, though still in view I hasten to add, in the main hall of the nursery, with a dozen kids ranging from 2 to 5. I can't see auras, but I bet this place was bathed in a golden glow from theirs; they shine with perception and burst with the full energy of the planet coursing through them. I love the way kids see life, the way they experience every day, the sheer joy of their existence and happiness of their being. The child in me isn't really hidden at all, it's still very much me as I am now and kids see it – I can be taken as one of them almost at once. By the time Chris came back I was the centre of the a growly, crawly, curl-up game, and the kids shrieked with enjoyment. 'I can see you've got to know the children,' she said, not entirely pleased with the lack of order. Remarkably, she set me on. I was to tear through the NVQs while working the 2 or 3 days per week they wanted me. What an absolute joy.

Although I was driving now an hour each way and setting off at 6 a.m., as I tumbled from my bed my heart sang. I was overjoyed at being in their company. I suppose at least some of the women, because other than me it was all women, regarded me as a lackey. I would arrive early, work through breaks, eat my dinner with the kids and have to be told to go home. Well it wasn't work, not real work, not to me. Of course it was to them, and my sheer exuberance must have annoying.

Mind, I didn't quite get the idea, it seems. I just thought, 'Whoopee, into the sand pit with the kids, over to the Lego, get the paints out, let ten thousand schools of play reign.' It wasn't long before I got my first bollocking. 'I look into that classroom,' said Chris, 'and I can't see an adult in there. The point isn't to be everyone's favourite Uncle Fred. Play must be educational, structured, part of a curriculum, it must be themed and planned, not spontaneous and disorganised.' Oh. Plus I was supposed to map out the next day's plan, time it, leave all the equipment out and clear it all away after every session. Well nobody told me.

In fact, I think, some of the female staff allowed me to head for that fall, to bring me down a peg. I had also noticed, and it shocked me, that there was competition between the carers, even jealousy over the allegiance and attention of particular children, like these were private projects. I also noticed that to some this was just a job, just looking after kids, a chore, work. Not that they were uncaring or undedicated but they could be quite cold and detached about the children. Not so me – despite the warning, I still got swept along with the mayhem and magic, despite now being more in charge and sitting up each night till late planning activity and ideas.

A little later, I think Chris thought I would be better deployed to the baby room, where the babes ranged from 4 to 18 months. I confess to thinking how this would be a very boring assignment; how ignorant I was. Babies are little knowledge machines, they consume knowledge the whole time, they assemble masses and masses of new information every second, every minute, every hour, and they are alarmingly intelligent; this they taught me during my priceless time in the baby room. I was working 2 days sometimes 3 days a week, the babies were in there 5 days a week plus 2 off for good behaviour. I had amused one little lad in his highchair by booling a big musical tomato around the floor, which made a pleasant music box type jingle as it rolled along. Six days later I come back into the room, and the little boy, who wasn't yet 12 months old, smiled and his eyes lit up and at once pointed with absolute certainty at the tomato. He remembered me and it, and was able to put them both back together.

I started to see babies in a whole different light. I noticed one wee bairn refused to be fed. He twisted his head away from the spoon every time, he refused to open his mouth, he-just-would-not-eat. Despite this he was clearly interested in all the other babies being fed. I got a chance to have a go a little later and I noticed that the other helpers had stood up and spooned the food out of the jar, then brought the spoon down to mouth level, but, if you sat down his highchair table was too high for him to see until he was confronted with the dreaded spoon. It was clear to me that he could see all the other bairns' food but couldn't see his own. I mean, imagine someone shoving stuff in your gob that you hadn't seen, couldn't see, couldn't touch or feel. I arranged his table lower and my seat parallel such that I could stand the jar within his line of vision so that he could see the jar, the food and what was on the spoon. He could, too, stick his fingers in the jar, stick the food in his own mouth, smell it, rub a bit in his hair to see what that did, a bit in the ears – and we were away: suitably tested he wolfed it down, occasionally stopping the splodge-laden spoon mid flight to check it was still the same stuff, before continuing. It was quite a coup. Two 6-month-old twins I could feed at the same time, one on each knee, cradled in the bay of my arms, listening to the contented suckling and feeling them nestle in my arms. Chris commented: 'You'd think you'd been doing that all your life.' Mind, when I did afternoons, I usually landed the after-dinner-feed nappy change: 14 nappies, all dirty, and by the time I'd changed the last one, the first one was ready for another change. I confess to having had early instruction in the art of changing as 4-year-old Charlotte, who usually followed me round and instructed me in things, informed me 'ducks to the front', a priceless guide in getting them the right way round. Babies are so fragile, so vulnerable, so prone to sliding off, falling over, bumping their heads, you need to develop terrific farsightedness to anticipate danger no matter how small.

Ee, I turned into a right baby-drooling git. Evenings in the bar while the big lads watched football and shouted loudly at each other, they looked at me with utter contempt and bewilderment as I prattled on for hours with the women behind the counter about the wonders of babies.

I had been almost universally known as a miner and a leading strike picket and militant. As our army was dispersed following on the first big round of closures the lads had been cast to the four winds, carrying their memories and pride with them. So it was that two big ex-heading men tramped along outside the nursery as part of the construction going on beyond the playground railings. They carried an enormous iron girder between two of them, their wellies squelching through the thick, track-churned mud of the site. I was pushing two plastic cars along with two little drivers, pursuing two speeding girls on trikes round the playground, when the big lads noticed me and stopped dead.

Bliddy 'Ell! Danny the bleedin Red here! What's tha deying in there?'

'Shhhh!' I say conspiratorially, 'Working on the next generation of pickets.'

They laugh, 'Aye whey, happen tha'd not be much use oot here wi us,' they charged as they tramped off laughing, the cheeky bastards.

I was actually in my element or one of them – Work? This was, just, well, life, another side of life, close up and new. Could I really have kicked over the traces and devoted myself to this new-found sharing of spirituality and wisdom? I hesitated too long.

MOMBASA

9 October 1994. We fly out to Mombasa, to Watamu Hotel on Turtle Bay Beach for Emma and Paul's wedding. What an absolute privilege – they have asked me to go with them, to the wedding and also on their safari. Emma is a princess in a wonderful dress her Mam has made for her. I am the proudest man in Africa. They sit sunbathing in their beach stuff until 45 minutes before their wedding. No rushing about, no daft pre-wedding panics and tomfoolery. They walk up off

the beach and out of the beaming sun, get a shower and get dressed for the wedding. Under the palm trees a little Christian children's choir sing traditional African Christian and wedding songs. The safari is a totally unreal experience. In particular we stay in a tree hotel, built into the heart of the dense jungle, with wooden and rope bridges strung into the trees and overlooking a waterhole. Deathly silence is observed and in the pitch black and silence of the jungle you can see truly wild animals timidly and silently come to drink at the water. The silence is like the moon, I suppose.

WOBBLIES AND ANARCHY

22 October. The Industrial Workers of the World hold their national meeting at the Broadway Hotel, Dunscroft, and as is the wont of the Wobs, members from other branches are allowed to just drop in. Two members from Hawaii come along. They were off up to visit Edinburgh and dropped off on the way.

21–30 October 1994. CONFLICT IN LONDON – ANARCHY IN THE UK – TEN DAYS THAT SHOOK THE WORLD. The Hatfield Main NUM Branch joins the anarchist festival in London, part of which was the mass levitation of the House of Commons. As we surged down the road toward Westminster we pass, near Big Ben, the ruin of some majestic building on the far side of the road. 'No, No!' shouts one of the anarchos, 'Not that side, the other side!' as though we had lifted and dropped the wrong building. We stood and concentrated on lifting the building. Lift! Lift! The cops stood in lines facing us, with their backs to Parliament, but couldn't resist the urge now and again to turn round, to see if we'd actually moved it!

This was an event thought up by Ian Bone from Class War. There was to be all sorts of singing, dancing, public sex, speeches, rude shows, banned exhibitions, challenges to censorship and consenting sex. When I heard about it and read out the programme to the Branch we all said 'The miners have got to be there.' So we went, we organised a miners' section of the show, at Culross Hall, Battle Bridge Road, films all day covering the history of the miners, speakers, along with Women Against Pit Closures and the Justice For Mineworkers Campaign, and a big barnstorming social in the evening just behind Kings Cross. I don't think the anarchists realised what a huge commitment the local NUM had made to this, determined to make a stand with an anarchist political event. We came down from the coalfields down for much of the week and in force over the weekend. We brought out friends and comrades from the Staffordshire Women Against Pit Closures, Geordie pit singers, folk over from Rotherham and Barnsley. It cost the Hatfield Branch a fortune, but it was well supported by the miners, their wives and kids. It stamped, we thought, a working-class input into the anarchist movement. It traded our class struggle and history alongside more diverse, not to say obscure elements of this movement. It is immortalised in the Chris Reeves film of the same name. Though the film itself takes some watching, featuring as it does sadomasochism, naked women pissing off ladders on men, and fearful sights of huge plastic live arseholes being crawled through and consuming people dressed as penises. It shocked me, though when I saw it presented at the Side

Cinema on the quay, at the Tyneside Anarchist Film Festival in 2004, the room was full of little kids, who I thought are going to be severely shocked at this, but roared out laughing all the way through. I meantime sat looking at the floor, like I used to in the scary bits when I was a kiddha. At the end of it all, I felt the anarchist movement was singularly unimpressed by our efforts; many didn't get this proletarian thing in the first place, but at the end of the day we did it because we ourselves wanted to be part of this. Not the weird stuff mind, no, we didn't get too involved with that. Honest.

200 of our former members work at the privatised Hatfield Coal Company. They work 12-hour shifts compulsory, and there is no overtime premium, no bonus and no pension contributions. Ainley tries to get round the 'non-union' tag by signing men up into BACM, the managers' union, which produces outrage from Arthur and protests to the TUC. Me and Arthur meet with the BACM president and EC at their South Parade offices in Doncaster on 16 November and go three rounds with them. They try to tell us they are now BACM-TEAM and are open to all supervisory layers of mineworker. Arthur calmly responds: 'Chock fitters and machine operators are not supervisory in anyone's definition, even yours.' Ainley backs off the BACM union drive, which dies a death, but the NUM does no better. It is a dig-in fight for a long haul to reconstruct Union power at Hatfield.[357]

Me Da wrote, to ask how I was bearing up and how the search for a new job was going:

> What a shame when you already had a job, a job which you enjoyed doing; with a decent standard of living, which may have lasted you until you reached retirement age, it annoys me very much when they stop peoples dole after 6 months; where can anyone find a decent job? Even if one does find a job, the money is useless, very low paid, unless you can hit on a better class job. I feel really sorry and sad for you, after 28 years working at Hatfield Colliery and now on the scrap heap, thanks to the great Paddy Ashdown voting with the Tories on pit closures. True you know, David, if he had joined with Labour instead of putting the party over to the Tory side, the 29 pits would still be open. His party is supposed to be between Labour and Tory. But his 21 members along with the Tories vote defeated the Labour amendment to keep the pits open.
> Well how is Emma getting on with married life? I hope they are both very happy … Dad

ME MAM – THE WORST YEARS OF HER LIFE

My Da takes the decision to put me Mam in a nursing home. I'm not sure she realises this will be for the rest of her life. Me Dad is exhausted; my Mam needs attention and care all the time. She always falls out of bed and me poor Dad has killed himself trying to lift her back in. He often has to call the police in the middle of the night to help him. Her leg is badly damaged in a fall and needs constant dressings. She is admitted to St Oswald's Nursing home on the Felling. It is a Catholic–based home. On the face of it, it's nice, clean, caring. She has her own room, with some of her things in there and photos, but she is there and not at home. It was a heartbreaking decision for me Dad. Me Da says the staff can bath and dress her and she gets better food in there than she did at home. He says:

I cant look after Mam now, I am too old for that David, I struggled on for the last 6 or 8 years, it was a very great worry and a lot of stress and strain, don't you think it is better for Mam to have someone available most of the time to see her? Of course David nothing is perfect, but I am much easier in my mind now.

COMRADE KILBURN

I had written to Tom in the April and told him about our forthcoming folky socials and political activities with the IWW and all. He replied to say he had mangled his arm up in a machine at work and was only just getting back on his feet, and being able to write of a fashion.

Speaking of writing, its a good idea of yours to use a printed sheet. It means that I can open the envelope and simply read the letter instead of rolling up my sleeves and reaching for my Rosetta Stone.

I must belatedly apologise for my very abrupt departure last time I was across in Dunscroft. My companion at that time (the portly McGarry) was and no doubt still is a fiercely self centred and semi-alcoholic chap who had to be back in Hull by opening time in order to knock on the doors of his local pub. The idea of him entering the pub a few minutes late was such a breathtakingly blasphemous concept to him that he panicked … Forgive me. Its now two o'clock in the morning and I'm in a garrulous mood, due to an infusion of strong cider and metal-polish.

My eldest daughter Ruth and her husband have moved to Newcastle, so my grandson will at least be spared the indignity of speaking with a Hull accent. They've got a place in Fenham just off Westgate Road, and it's a strange feeling going up to visit them. I only partly recognise Newcastle these days: taking a self-indulgent and nostalgic walk along Elswick Road (mainly to see how many memories of Ev Brown it would engender) I found nothing familiar. It was only when I came across the infamous Benwell Dwellings that I realised I was on Elswick Road at all. Perhaps the most depressing sight of all was the Bigg Market on a Sunday evening. With my (and our) memories of the Hyde Park soapbox meetings in mind I took a trip down there and witnessed the dreadful sight of idiot people in mass. Crowds of the Roaring boys and droolers, all jostling and baying at the moon. People tend to forget that in the term Homo Sapiens, Sapiens is an expression of self-assessment. Perhaps a more accurate description of our species should be Homo Stupidiensis.

By the way, Adamson (Radio Humberside) says if you want to phone his wireless programme, please do so. Your calls always generate a flurry of other conversations – some agreeing and others aghast. The more phone calls he gets, the longer he can stave off unemployment. He has nightmares of returning to busking outside cinemas and taxi-ranks, holding out his enamel cup to the punters after his saxophone solos.

I've started my old double vision now so I'll sign off before the voices start. Good look with the Gala and keep a sense of rage.

Tom Kilburn

I reply with the latest crack.

... Did you hear about the devastating plans to build a bloody greet angel at Gateshead? Surely this calls for direct action on a big scale, not least trying to make the hideous thing take flight, a small deposit of nitro should do the trick! Beats trying to levitate it by OM chants.

Yes Newcastle has changed, and then again it hasn't. It is still intensely political but not as generally so as it was in our hey day (or should that be hay-day?). Many of the focuses, foci? of industrial struggle have long since gone or are mere shadows of themselves, Swans and Ellington Colliery being two that come to mind, mainly because there are no others.

We went camping up to the Trossaschs at Easter. Cad? I had to be chipped off the tent floor of a morn. Mind in my drunken stupor and fearing my poor dog on the other side of the tent might be thirsty for some reason I picked up a pan and staggered to the river side perchance to take up a measure of crystal water for me hoond. The bliddy bank collapsed and I was plunged into the icy water up to me knackers, my screams of indignation brought little response from my daughter and her husband in a neighboring tent, only a murmur that 'It sounds like Dave fell in the river.' This being not an extraordinary event they didnt even stir. The sequel was worse, as having taken off the boots, socks and jeans and got dried and struggled back into the sleeping bag, the dog all the while snoring its head off under her blanket. Early morning I was bursting for a slash and sought to rekek, only to find the jeans frozen solid, the socks standing on their own and boots covered by a few inches of frost. Normally I would, as all campers do, bring a change of clothes, but on this occasion I hadn't. What to do? I was bursting. I had however brought a pair of swimming trunks in case the mood for a scheduled bathe had come to me; this was all that was left. I pulled on the swimming trunks and in me bare feet dove into the car, driving to the toilet block, and striking a frenzied pose as I dashed along at 6 a.m. in a snow and frost filled camp site toilet block. Of course this being bliddy Scotland the toilet/washroom was already full of happy campers at their ablutions. Pace into their midst, shout aloud 'Alreet?' Piss and swagger oot, leaving them not knowing if I had in fact just returned from a swim, which of course in a manner of speaking, I had. Anyway such was Easter; lovely place, mind. They nearly speak the dialect reet. They didn't appreciate me saying that Wallace was probably a Northumbrian who never wore a kilt in his life, mind. Brilliant film didn't you think? Emma had to sit on me to stop me jumping up and

327

down on the seat and running up and doon the aisle singing 'Scots Wa
Hae … and Geordies an'arll!' Of course Wallace was great hero of the
Northumbria and Durham Chartists, especially the miners. They (the
northern Chartists) used to meet in the pub that was 'The Post Office'
opposite St. Nicks …

Keep A'had
Dave

I win a tiny victory over state bureaucracy and cause the entire claim form for an
employment benefit to be changed. The form asks me my marital status and
whether I am divorced. When I challenge that this is entirely irrelevant to my
claim and has no influence whatever on either the amount or eligibility to claim
it they insist it's on the form so you must complete it. I refuse and take a case
under the Data Protection Act: 'Personal data held for any purpose or purposes
shall be adequate, relevant and not excessive in relation to that purpose or those
purposes.' Ha! The question is now removed from ES461 for the next reprint.
Awkward little bugger aren't I?

March. I start full-time work at the nursery. I have been doing 2 or 3 days a week
but now I am working almost every day. I couldn't be more delighted. Every day
I wake up and my heart sings. I just love the kids, love being with them, love
sharing their day with them. Mind, its not a weekly contract. I am employed and
paid hourly, £3.54 per hour, plus it takes an hour each way to drive there for
which I don't get paid of course and I pay the petrol. Still I love the job so much
I almost felt disloyal even mentioning wages.

At the same time a job custom built for me comes up. The Campaigns Officer
for the Coal Communities Campaign, which campaigns for resources, and
retraining for the former coal communities and preservation of existing jobs in
coalmining. They tell me at the interview: 'Frankly no other candidate and few
members of this panel know the coal industry from as many aspects and depths
as you do.' It seems to bode well, but it isn't to be. I think maybe the choice of
Arthur Scargill as my main reference and another glowing one from Brenda
Nixon from the current phase of Women Against Pit Closures doesn't assure the
selectors at all. The position is of course intensely political; the campaign is
funded by the MBCs in the coal regions nationwide. My interview is faultless, but
I am taken aback when asked why would I want this job? I reply that if I could
custom build a job that I was uniquely equipped to do it would come out looking
like this one. The main selector says: 'That's bullshit!' I am shocked rigid as were
the other members of the panel. Despite my assurances that this is transparent
honesty, I do not convince them. The weak-kneed rationale for not selecting me
was that they thought the job would be too mundane for someone with my high
profile! I reply that it has to be more fulfilling than carrying arch girders down the
tailgate on a night shift, which I had been doing, or wiping babies' bottoms,
which I was doing just now. They reply that 'Well, a lot of this job is just like
stuffing letters into envelopes and sending out leaflets.' I reply that for the salary

Handcuffed pickets being led from the field at Orgreave. © Peter Arkell

Jack Collins (left) represented Kent Area on the NUM NEC from '71 to '81; John Moyle (right) was Area president '81. Taken during the national strike of '81

1974: NUM NEC in Downing Street: Mick McGahey, Joe Gormley, Lawrence Daly, Arthur Scargill, Joe Whelan, Peter Tate. © Terry Kirk

Lawrence Daly (1924–2009): NUM general secretary 1968–84

'O.K., Sergeant, get their names' – Cartoon by Tony Hall (*Morning Star*)

Cresswell Colliery, July 1984: pickets shackled to a lamppost during mass picket. © P. J. Arkell

7 February, 1975: Peter McNestry, general secretary of NACODS at the NUM Executive meeting

Fankie Cave, NUM National secretary

Dave Douglass, 'Bobholeman'

Ken Homer: financial secretary of Yorkshire Area NUM

Reminiscing: Jeff Stubbs, Yorkshire Area agent, chats with former NUM official David Murdoch. © *Doncaster Free Press*

Miners' solidarity

Siege at Berry Hill

March 1983: Hatfield Women's Support Group
lobby the local NUM Branch for action in support
of Lewis Merthyr Colliery, South Wales

March 1985: still solid, still strong

1992: Women's Support Group take to the streets following the occupation of Markham Main Colliery.

© Martin Jenkinson

Supporting her dad and her Branch (Stillingfleet Branch, NUM Yorkshire Area)

Green/Jones Memorial: l–r Dave Douglass, Steve Kemp, Ian Lavery, Dennis Skinner

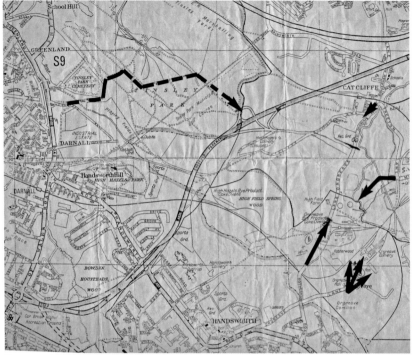

Orgreave: picket campaign map

Hatfield Colliery villages occupied by 'Blue Cossacks'

Orgreave: invasion of the 'Blue Hundreds'

NUM V-P Election Rally, 1987 (Stainforth): l–r Sammy Thompson, Dave Douglass, Brian Robson, Eric Clarke, Eric Lippet. © Martin Jenkinson

1982: Dave and Frances Brennan, Dave Douglass and Alan Robe (left) holding banner

Bad roof: the yard seam North, from *The Collieries of Durham* by Dave Temple, 1980

Brodsworth Colliery, 1992: end of an era

NUM 'Troika' at the 1984 TUC: left to right: Peter Heathfield, general secretary; Mick McGahey, vice-president; Arthur Scargill; and, behind him, MI5 plant Roger Windsor (with glasses and beard).
© *The Observer*

Miners march through Fleet Street.
© Ken Wilkinson

Police and pickets clash on last day of picketing at Frickley

1991: Hatfield/Thorne donation to DRI Baby Care Unit: Dave Douglass, Personnel Officer, Mr Gardener, Jeff Ainley, Nurse and baby not known

Roger Windsor, NUM chief executive with Arthur Scargill in November 1985. Two years later, in 1987, Windsor was exposed as an MI5 informer

Dave Douglass and his sister Veronica at the Durham Miners' Gala

The author and Arthur Scargill address climate camp protestors on cleaner coal power stations

Don't go down t'mine, daddy...

Wait 'til the next time, pal! We'll be ready for you!

Dave Douglass singing in a pub at the Durham Miners' Gala, 1988

Emma Douglass (age 12), Ruskin College Miners' History Weekend, 23 March 1985

Emma and Maureen Douglass, 1987

Dave's dad's 80th: with Dad, Emma, Dave and Mam

The author and the banner

they are paying (£17,325; the most I had earned at the pit was £16,000 and that was good money) I would stuff horse manure into envelopes.

I am left to reflect that this 'high profile' of mine, while great for pats on the back in the bar, isn't doing me any favours to get a job. I can only conclude the decision not to appoint me was ironically my NUM membership and closeness to Arthur. They had asked if I intended to stay in the NUM, and without thought as to who was asking the question or why, I had replied that of course, and I would have the opportunity to remain highly active within the Union, though of course I would keep the campaign officer's role entirely separate. They challenged me on a conflict of interests, that the NUM policy on opencast (to oppose them) was in contrast to the CCC which campaigned to save them and continue them. I had told them I would have no problem in continuing the campaign for all coal-extractive industries and locations.

It hadn't worked. It was one of a seemingly endless series of knock backs for this type of job. Actually and on reflection this all-consuming obsession to land a big-profile, big-title, big-role sort of job proved I wasn't really serious about making childcare my new career. I seemed to think I could somehow do both; the childcare career needed a serious commitment, and was low-paid and totally out of the limelight, and I obviously wasn't ready to accept all the implications of that. At first it wasn't apparent to Chris and the nursery but I think over time they picked up on it and by the time I realised that perhaps I should have thrown myself body and soul into this new vocation, I had blown it.

27 May 1995. A police car pulls up outside my house. Two cops peer in as they approach the door. Oh aye? What's this then, I wonder, I open the door. They are two local cops who know me. 'Can we come in Dave? I have some bad news,' one of them says, and my face drains of blood. He puts his hand on my arm in a kindly gesture and says: 'Your Dad's dead, Dave.'

A silence rushed into my head, then disbelief. I kept saying 'You're joking? You're joking?' As if the cops or anybody would actually joke about something like this. I couldn't comprehend it. They wanted me to go up to Gateshead to identify his body. They advised me not to drive, although stupidly I did, my face bathed in tears that just kept gushing and flowing down my face.

Behind a curtain was the wee body of me Dad, now shrunken, his teeth removed, his hair now white and wispy. He lay peacefully in the little chapel at the hospital. This body, this hard-working body which had toiled below the ground and in the shipyards of the Tyne, to feed and clothe us all. This wiry irrepressible man spent his money and his energies on us and us alone, never drinking nor smoking, taking little more than a nice apple as his special treat after a day's work. He loved his fruit, did Da, and walking, walking out in the good clean air. Singing his head off or head tilted back in open honest laughter.

I had to inform Veronica, and she broke into pieces over the phone, and resolved to come up the next day. I stayed at me Mam and Dad's house; we resolved not to tell me Mam who was by now full time in a Catholic nursing home, until we were both there.

That night I slept in me Dad and Mam's bed. It was like being a little boy again, and I felt utterly vulnerable and alone. I had drunk a good bottle and a half of wine, but that hadn't seemed to impact on my grief.

I awoke in the middle of the night. All around me was a glistening mist hovering and twinkling, like a transparent cloud with a rough elongated shape. All the while I had this tremendous feeling of calm, and my Dad's distant voice saying: 'It's all right David, it's all right.'

You will have gleaned from this book my attitude to Heaven and Hell and God and an afterlife. I am not a believer, but that experience was as real and profound as anything in my life. I have been drunk and tired before but I have never experienced anything like that before or since. I felt that me Dad, or his spirit, or his memory or his essence or whatever it was, came – in a form I don't think I could have imagined, although it did have a passing resemblance to 'The Guardian' in one of the Star Trek films I must confess – came and becalmed me. Assured me. Somehow let me know that it wasn't all over. In truth I don't know what I make of the experience. I don't know how to fit it into any of my adopted philosophies, but it was not on reflection the first time I had felt I was being watched over and helped, just the most touching and real one. There now, I've gone and shattered your illusions of me as a hard-nosed atheist anarchist with his feet set on good Earth alone. I am, mostly.

When me and Veronica and the lads and Emma go to break the news to me Mam, she is at once all smiles to see us all, then suspicious, then I tell her. They would have been 57 years married this year. 57 years of happiness, toil, war and strikes, ceilidhs, arguments, children and togetherness. 'What's going to happen to me now?' she kept asking. 'John, why have you gone and left me? God, why have you not taken me?'

I will never forget it, never ever forget the pain and loss. I am finding it extremely hard to write this piece, as the loss and pain remain raw again now I have uncovered it from my memory.

What is worse is that from this point on my Mam's care at the home goes downhill like a lead balloon. These are the worst years of me Mam's life. Neither Veronica nor me can consider looking after her; it's a full-time job. As time goes on and me Mam's treatment clearly gets worse, we cannot decide if this is her age, her infirmity or accidents combined with the two. She is frequently bloody, bruised and injured. They say her skin is thin, they say her bones are brittle, they have to lift her, they have to wash her. They say they have a regime to engage her intelligence which she thinks is harassment. She says her money goes missing, she doesn't get fed, and that as her eyesight gets worse she is left to feed herself but cannot find the food and eats with her fingers. I install a phone with an immediate get-through to me and Veronica. We are on the phone all hours of the day and night to the duty nurse. We have frequent meetings with the managers; they tell us: 'Take her out and put her somewhere else if you like.' In the end she says she doesn't want to go. The pain and distress continues.

2 June. Following Dad's expressed instructions, he is cremated. The service is held at the Methodist chapel on the Ellen Wilkinson Estate where me and Veronica often went as kids to shows and jumble sales. The chapel is full of his

old friends, his fellow Wardley miners. Men from the lodge, all the relatives from Jarrow and Hebburn, and Ireland. I am in absolute bits, I cannot stop crying, the loss is like space, unbridgeable and gigantic. Emma is by my side, though she too is lost in grief, mine as well as her own. She is the only thing which makes me feel life is worth continuing with. The pain of loss makes me consider for a time if it is worth the love just to lose it and feel it so badly. What is the point of putting ourselves through this? My Dad is dead, how can he be? How can my Dad be dead? I miss him, I miss him and his friendship and his counsel and his praise, aye and his harsh words and temper. I miss him with an emptiness which has never been filled.

Arthur Scargill who met me Da and made him so proud, writing in his diary that I should be proud of him, as he is proud of me. Arthur when he discovered me Da's death wrote a very kind letter, which I read out at the service, as me Da would have liked.

They sang his hymns, the inspiration of his boyhood and all his life, his 'endeavour' as he termed it.

In August the loss of my Da is still dumbfounding. Despite all the attempts I make to get on with life, I keep getting drawn back to it, and him, and us, and where are we all now, and what was it all for in the first place, was there a point?

Raph wrote in his usual kind and warm sympathetic way:

I knew what a mentor and inspiration he was to you and I remember the way he was your most constant point of reference – both by letter and in person when you were writing *Pit Life and Pit Talk in Co. Durham*. You have always sounded the finest combination of Durham and your Mother's Irishness; it is sad if it has come to an apparent end – but I am sure it lives on through Emma and Yourself.

Then almost in passing he tells me:

I have had cancer diagnosed. I had last term off – but my health seems to be getting better rather than worse. So I hope the chemotherapy had killed it. Alison has taken most of the strain.

Love

Raphael

Joel too wrote in deep concern:

I was so deeply sorry to learn of your Dad's death, and very moved by what you wrote. I have not had to experience this pain, but have watched a few close friends recently go through it and it ways seems very dreadful and surprisingly devastating. There are things that weren't said, worries about parents left alive, the sense of permanence of loss and your own mortality. I couldn't have helped much … it sounds like Emma was just wonderful in her love for you … but I wish I could have been there. How is your Mom? How are you getting on?

On a brighter note he invited me over to start a series of lectures at his college:

We are launching a new course for first year students which deals with some important themes in different disciplines like nationalism, colonialism, and racism, and the ideological and mythic claims about 'progress' whether linked to biological evolution or claims about industrialization as progress. The idea is to challenge these conventional views of progress by looking at the devastating human (and ecological) consequences of industrialization, the unevenness of it etc. Students will be reading parts of David Landes, *The Unbound Prometheus*; Hobsbawm, *Industry and Empire*, Raphael's article 'Workshop of the World', Zola's *Germinal* and last but not least *A Miner's Life*. It would be great to have you lecturing on your interpretation of what industrialization is all about, the experiences of work, how Zola's 19th century mining and your 20th century mining compare etc. ... I have moved in with a great woman (Carol); you could stay with us. Not to mention there are some great Irish bars in our neighbourhood. The college would pay all your transportation and related expenses and $1000 above that. Give my love to Emma will you and regards to Paul. It is a shame that they couldn't come for a visit this summer. Sometime soon I hope.

All the Best

Joel

Actually, my finishing at the nursery had been a little staccato. I had turned down an earlier offer to go full-time, because I was still doing work 2 days a week at the Miners Advice Centre, and was still almost weekly attending tribunals and appeals and processing claims for miners as well as running the Branch, which continued. The news that I would not be required at the nursery again was a sudden shock. It was put down to falling rolls, but I wasn't so sure. On reflection, I think it was because I had a very high media profile still. I was interviewed regularly on Yorkshire and national TV on all issues mining, and all pit community subjects. My revolutionary brand of trade unionism and politics went down well in the smouldering pit communities but would surely have been a bit disconcerting to the parents of the wee kids in whose charge they were being left. Personally, I think revolutionary Marxists make great child-minders and mentors, but your average parent probably doesn't see that. Violent revolution and feeding a baby on your knee would seem like not a good advert for your average nursery. So I think, falling rolls apart, that was the real reason. I much missed my work with the children, and the babies in particular, but how could I abandon my role as the public face of the workers' revolution? I think I could probably have played down my public appearances or even ended them, but I didn't think through what the PR for a trainee nursery assistant should be. I perhaps missed a chance here to move over into a completely new career and lifestyle, but only in terms of work. I could never unlearn the class nature of society, or not intervene strongly into it as a political activist, but perhaps at this stage I *could* have been a wee bit less the public face of the workers' revolution. Numerous times since, as new crossroads loomed in the direction the rest of my life would take, I seriously reconsidered this option. Working with kids isn't like work, its just like, well, being alive, living your life, sharing your day, having fun, experiencing something 'magical' and unique.

July 1995. NUM National Conference, Miners Convalescent Home

Blackpool. On behalf of the Yorkshire Area I propose a strong amendment to Scotland's resolution on South Africa. In true Stalinist tradition, it heaps praise upon the new South African state and its leadership, and welcomes the great 'democratic revolution'. We are a little more precise:

> Conference notes that the justified expectations of the Black population remain unmet on even the most basic levels of subsistence. We note that the Democratic phase of the revolution is now giving way to open multi-racial class war. Our allegiance remains with the Labour and Revolutionary Movement of the working people, rather than those who would seek to appease the White establishment and the emergent Black bourgeoisie; the rank and file of S.A.T.U.C. deserve our continued class solidarity.[358]

I'm not sure of the outcome of that resolution. That Conference was predictably a lively and contentious one and if for no other reason it is one of those of which I have no verbatim record of the debates – usually an indication that they weren't circulated in customary numbers. Not solely because of my contribution, of course, but because information somewhere in that Conference was likely to be contentious and best not circulated too widely. Doubtless we were also being urged that financial constraints now restricted the numbers at large, but if this was a decision it was made without any consultation with the members who mandated the Conference delegates. All NUM areas will however have been sent all Conference verbatim reports, if future researchers succeed in getting access to them.

The High Court and Court of Appeal rule that the Union's 83.4 % vote for 24-hour selective strikes against the imposition of non-negotiated wage rises is unlawful because they were planned to start a minute after the expiry of the deadline, the Union having interpreted the law as meaning you take action after the final expiry and the court ruling it meant a minute before the expiry and not the minute after the expiry. Most of the members' venom is directed at 'whichever daft twat advised us what the law was'.

In January 1996 Arthur Scargill launches the Socialist Labour Party. It is a moment pregnant with hope and expectation and optimism. It was at first flush another of his flashes of genius. I was summoned to the confidence of Arthur's office and told of the project and asked about my feelings toward the development of such an organisation. I had favoured more of a general 'movement' and alliance rather than 'a party'. Arthur and Frank (Cave) right from the onset gave the distinct impression that they didn't really know how the left outside the Labour Party worked; they were indicating that all the groups would have to give up their own identities and merge with the new project – no tendencies and no fractions.

Despite this I was overwhelmed by the speed at which the notion took off across the class. Arthur was the first major trade union leader to walk out of New Labour and nail his colours to an alternative organisation. He was rapidly joined by half of the RMT executive and Bob Crow its general secretary. Officials of

UCATT and other unions started to walk in the direction of the SLP. Press and media coverage set the agenda alive among ordinary workers, who were talking about 'Scargill's new party – is tha joining?' Working-class communities across the country suddenly started to sit up and show an interest. It was a moment which at once posed a real radical alternative to Blair and New Labour or even potentially to 'Old' Labour for the first time since the twenties. This is not the place to record the rapid and grotesque degeneration of the new party into an egocentric, bureaucratic, Stalinist cult; I and others have written at length about the steady degeneration elsewhere.[359] Suffice it to say Arthur's overbearing sense of his own infallibility, fed by his undoubted and sincere popularity among large sections of the class, ensured that he blew it. It was a tragic lost opportunity.

13 March 1996. A madman massacres a school of 5- and 6-year-old children in Scotland.

16 children killed.

16 5-year-olds, 6-year-olds.

Five years old! Six years old! Small bodies torn apart by wave after wave of bullets. Not from a machine-gun, but from handguns, exchanged one for another as they ran out of bullets and the victims, tiny little kids, fall all around. Five years old! Six years old !

Shot one, purposefully, after another. Tell me now the prayers at assembly on the curriculum were valid.

Hello, God? A madman is massacring our little children. Are you in? Are you watching this?

IF GOD HAD A NAME[360] IT WOULD BE BASTARD! AND I'D CALL IT TO HIS FACE AND I'D MEAN IT, I'D KICK HIM IN THE FACE AND DAMN ALL HIS SAINTS AND PROPHETS. GOD IS GOOD, YEAH? YEAH? GOD IS GOOD? WHAT GOOD IS GOD?

Later after writing this in fury and tears I reflect that if I don't believe in God, why should I be so mad? It's because I want there to be a God, and that I want that God to do the things they say he can, like save these little kids from such a disgusting and wanton death. That he didn't shouldn't come as a surprise to someone who doesn't believe in it anyway, should it? Or perhaps I think it exposes those who do believe in God to the reality of life without one and they need to see it. Why is that of comfort? The sad reality is the twisted individual who slaughtered these kids was a complete invention of human society so called, he was made, if not by us, than by them who have drafted its framework and architecture; he comes with the building. Looked at another way, someone once said: 'Jesus loves everyone, but some very strange people love him.'

GERRY ADAMS; MONICA LEWINSKY

It was the big NUM Council meeting in April. Before us among other things proposals for who would be the guest speaker at this year's Yorkshire Miners' Gala. We needed a big name, a dynamic speaker; no one had come up with anyone very sparkling. Well me and Hatfield had. I proposed Gerry Adams. At first there was a stunned silence, and then Arthur threw his weight enthusiastically behind the proposal. The Durham miners had once invited Peter Kropotkin the famous

Russian anarchist to their gala. Gerry was at the heart of the struggle against British imperialism in Ireland – he would make an honourable guest. There was no other proposal. Gerry was carried.

Light the blue touch paper and stand well back. Kellingley, who were furious at the proposal, leaked it to the press and the balloon went up. 'Be our guest of honour Scargill tells Sinn Féin leader Adams,' boomed the *Yorkshire Post*. The furore was predictable. Barnsley Town Council, who host the executive reception and helped fund the day, threatened to pull the plug and boycott the gala, right-wing Labour MPs were throwing tantrums, and Frank Cave our illustrious Area secretary was sticking to his guns and demanding why Bill Clinton and Labour MPs could meet and speak to Gerry Adams but the Yorkshire miners shouldn't? Hatfield Main published a defiant response:

> Everyone else is free to listen to and talk to Mr Adams, including John Major the Prime Minister, Dick Spring and Ian Paisley. Mr Adams is free to address meetings of Labour MPs, American senators and everyone from Senator Kennedy to Bill Clinton the President of the United States. He had frequent all party talks with all the Irish political parties and spoke to rallies across the world.
>
> Well pardon us! We just happen to be the working class, the hapless Joe Soaps expected to pull on a uniform and die in every war the ruling class dreams up, and do so without question. Not this time, we want the violence to end, and will not accept there is only one side to the argument, we claim the right to listen to other points of view about this war, we have every reason to suspect this government in particular in not being honest with ordinary people in this country, because they have been duplicit so many times with the communities we know them of old. We also know something of being criminalised and called 'The Enemy Within' ... This branch voted with 85% of all other branches in Yorkshire to submit an invitation to Mr Adams, as part of our long tradition of inviting radical and if necessary controversial speakers, it is notable nobody invited Mr Blair ...

Frank says to me: 'Do you think you could ask Gerry to walk with you David?' 'Why's that Frank?' 'Why's thee fucking think, someone might take a pot shot at him and hit me!' he responded in characteristic style. But all was saved; Gerry was booked elsewhere on Gala day so he let us all off the hook. It would have been an interesting Gala but we were having to plan for mass stewarding of the platform in case the fascists turned out in force.

This wasn't the last of my star-studded invitations. A few years later, prior to the National Conference of the NUM, nominations for positions in the Labour Party were circulated to branches. The NUM being affiliated has the right to put forward nominations and these are debated at Conference. In truth only the Labour Party activists ever play any role in this, and most branch members take little interest. We had had a mass and stormy Branch meeting over contracts; the hall was full when the item of nominations came up on the agenda and I could see the shuffling impatience. 'The bloody Labour Party? After what them twats have done for us?' they were murmuring. Leader of the Labour Party? I proposed Monica Lewinsky, which was passed unanimously amid cheering and stomping. Well, it was meant as a joke. What I didn't know was no other branch in Yorkshire had put forward a nomination; Monica became the Yorkshire Area's candidate for leader of the Labour Party! As it turned out only two areas had forwarded nominations to National Conference. The Scotland Area had proposed Tony Blair and Yorkshire Monica Lewinsky. It caused great mirth when the point was reached on the agenda; I took the platform in support of our candidate:

It appears to me that the only thing required to do this job is to have the ability to grovel round the nether regions of the American president, something Monica, we are told, is very good at, although since Tony is already doing the job he probably does it better than she does.

Well, amid cheers and laughter the Scotland president marched down the aisle his face ablaze. 'That's no funny, David, this is the leader of the Labour Party were talking aboot here, this is important business, this is serious business, Tony Blair is a man of vision and ability ...' I shouted: 'Monica's got nicer legs.' After the Scotland delegate left the platform still blazing, Arthur, who was in the chair, pulled his glasses forward on his nose, peered into the Conference and said dryly: 'I couldn't possibly comment.' Tony got the job and grovelled ever after – pity; I might have actually voted for Monica in a general election.

20 May 1996. Yorkshire Council Meeting. The agenda strangely has listed 'Medical Appeals Tribunals and Industrial Tribunals'. These were the work I had been doing over the last couple of years. Since I was appointed by the Area onto the ITS service and sent on training courses for DSS appeals etc., most of these appeals had fallen to me. With Arthur now back operating in Yorkshire, even though in my view he had no constitutional authority here, I believe he had started to grow concerned that the Area was becoming dependant upon me in this role. He also looked with concern at the number of shifts I was drawing from the Area NUM for this work.

None of this would have mattered had I been playing political ball with Arthur, but we were increasingly clashing around his growing authority and control of the Union and our loss of autonomy and independent Branch and Area functioning. It was the start of a shooting war between us which would get worse as the Union polarised between centralisers and decentralisers, which translated as a battle between membership and their branches and the bureaucracy and manic attempts to control the Union with rigid top-down direction.

This agenda item implied much bigger things. With the increasing number of DSS and common-law damages claims for the recently discovered vibration white finger and chest conditions for ex-members growing by the thousand daily, the number of 'limited members' being signed up was growing massively. Members is power, is votes, is a voice and an audience. Before the attacks and closures and run-downs, a limited member simply stayed in membership with the branch they had been in full membership of while working. As the number of mines closed, so these limited members were passed on to the nearest geographical branch, or whoever had been allocated to deal with them. In our case after the closure of

Edlington, and the transfer of the bulk of the Edlington working miners to Hatfield, we inherited their limited members too. Then as branches closed, and I fell into the role of attending all the tribunals for former miners all over Doncaster and then South Yorkshire, these miners were being joined to our membership as limited members. The same was happening at a number of other branches, none of which were singing off Arthur's hymnsheet. Arthur clearly seen this limited membership numbers game as a double-edged weapon; if he could wrest it from the branches and take charge of those numbers himself, the growth in limited membership numbers would accrue power to him and not to us. In order to do this, someone other than me would have to represent these men, and often miners' widows etc.

15 June 1996. We stage our Yorkshire Miners' Gala folky social at the Broadway, with The Elliotts of Birtley, Toe-In-The-Dark, Young and O'Toole, and 'The Hatfield Folk', who are basically all of us miners and our families who sing. It is packed, with many of the lads at least putting their faces in for an hour or so before heading off on their usual tours of the clubs and bars round the villages.

20 August. I am in London making DSS law! I have challenged the decision of the DSS to 'aggregate' the different disability awards received by Mr McNulty, one of the old cutter men. DSS regulations demand that you need 14% before you qualify for the payment of disability benefit – except in the case of pneumoconiosis, which because of its disabling and potentially lethal effects is paid at the rate of 10% for anything above a 1% pneumoconiosis diagnosis. Joe has his 10% award and is receiving his benefit. Then he applies for vibration white finger, and is awarded 3%. The DSS aggregate the figure and, it only amounting to 13%, then rule that he is no longer entitled to anything, because the aggregate figure isn't 14%. So if you only have pneumo you get paid, but if you are unfortunate to have more things wrong with you, you don't. So someone with a collective greater disability doesn't get paid while someone with a lesser disability does. Well that's what the rule said, the adjudication officer had said so, the medical appeal had said so, and now I was off to London with Joe in tow, to appeal the case to the commissioner for DSS law in London. The DSS was represented by their top DSS law QC. Despite this we won, and I got to change two pieces of law nationwide, which has benefited not just Joe but hundreds, perhaps thousands, of folk. First, they accepted my argument that the wording of the legislation was actually intended to benefit the claimant; aggregations were supposed to be undertaken only if the net result was an increase in the benefit payment and not a decrease, and it would be nonsense to read it any other way (not that that stopped them in other cases, mind). Next, in the process of arguing the different grades of award for pneumoconiosis the commissioner had challenged me to demonstrate where in the statute it said the definition of 'pneumoconiosis' was 1% or more. Actually though I could produce all the DSS advice material which said that, I couldn't quote the legislative chapter and verse. I suggested, 'Ask him,' i.e. the DSS whiz-kid QC, who blustered that he wasn't obliged to give me such information, as it was my appeal. OK – I then went out

on a limb and suggested that in fact there was no such stipulation of 1%; this was a definition the DSS had made up without any statutory authority. In fact pneumoconiosis was 'any' pneumoconiosis, be it ever so simple.

This forced the QC to call for an adjournment while he consulted his textbooks and the law and was to discover that my long shot was accurate. A week later we returned to a new definition: henceforth Pneumo was any Pneumo, which was found; it didn't need to meet the 1% definition, and would be paid at 10% from now on. It also, incidentally, meant that the NCB/NUM pneumoconiosis compensation scheme would now have to start paying out compensation from the word go and at a much lower level of infestation than previously. I returned home well pleased, if something of an unsung hero – since my law-changing challenge was never really given any publicity, unless you looked up our case reference, of course. Joe was well pleased; we had challenged an injustice and won.

DOBERFLAP

October 1996. My big, docile but utterly neurotic Doberman, a giant with huge paws but a steady, methodical, analytical brain, is outside by his kennel while I visit the hostelries roond Donnie. He watches with some curiosity the cat, coming and going through the cat flap on the bottom of the door. When I return I am at first surprised to find Satday standing in the kitchen looking rather proud of himself. Over his shoulder I notice a large, oval-shaped hole in the door. Satday had made himself a Doberman-size cat flap, without the flap. He looked up with a mixture of pride and foreboding; I collapsed in laughter. When I photographed the door for the insurance claim and sent it off I was surprised to receive a rejection on the basis that it wasn't an accident – clearly the dog had done it on purpose!

DEATH OF RAPH SAMUEL

9 December 1996. Raph Samuel dies. It seems impossible, that a man like Raph, vibrant, intellectual, gentle, full of passion, knowledge, wisdom and love, can be no more. His soft, cultured voice, like a cup of warm tea with sugar, saying 'Dave, … ', always welcoming, always supportive, always interested in everything you did and with a computerised memory bank which simply pulled out ancient insights and little-known facts of circumstance and no consequence which he could recall and update. A time-traveller, at home in this century or that, now 'dun roaming'. Shocking too to discover he was 61. How can he have been? He was always young, slightly built, energetic, jumping off his bike, his old railway footplateman's denim jacket on his back, his corduroy pants tucked into his socks. A coloured neckerchief round his neck. His hair is a great black wave over his face. I miss him greatly. His face and voice often come drifting through those mists of time, and I hear him yet whenever I have a history paper to present. I have sometimes caught myself sweeping hair from my brow, as he did constantly, even though I had none there.

He had had cancer, he had told me but I didn't know until John Saville had told me at a Ruskin do that Raph was dying. I thought, na, it can't be, and phoned him and asked him, expecting him to say 'Oh, Dave, there's centuries of future for me to visit yet,' or something, but he confirmed it. I stupidly said 'All them years of roll-ups, eh?' – like, rub me nose in it; and Raph: 'I haven't smoked for years, Dave.'

ANOTHER STRIKE BALLOT

December 1996. The Union successfully ballots for 24-hour strike action by a margin of 54%. RJB appeals to the courts on New Year's Eve that the vote is invalid as the membership figures are out of date. They were out of date because the employers refused to furnish the Union with lists of up-to-date membership contributors and not every member had been sent a postal ballot form as required by law. A further bit of internal politicking meant that COSA withheld the names of members eligible to vote because they didn't think it involved them, and in other regions COSA members were advised not to vote for the same reason. In fact when it all came out in the wash, a number of areas had not sent in lists of their members eligible to vote or in some cases had sent completely inaccurate lists. The company when it got wind of this was able to demonstrate to the court that all the eligible members hadn't been given the chance to vote. Apart from egg on our face again, it was an extremely costly exercise, the cost of a ballot running to tens of thousands of pounds, ner mind the court costs.[361] It was also a sorry admission that the NUM National leadership and NEC did not know who its members were and had no accurate record of their contact details; this was almost certainly a defensive measure by areas, 'blinding' the National Office to stop it going over their heads and dealing with the members directly. In this case it produced an entirely reactionary result in crippling a serious industrial action at a crucial time. The long-term effects upon the morale and faith the members would have in future ballots could not be judged, but there must have been some negative impact, as twice in recent times strong ballot results had been ruled unlawful.

FEBRUARY 1997. NUM COUNCIL MEETING: RESOLUTIONS TO NATIONAL CONFERENCE

I clash with Arthur over the totally undemocratic functioning of the International Miners' Organisation. A resolution from Hatfield:

> Instructs the NEC to draw up appropriate constitutional rule changes to the structure of the IMO in order that that body can become a delegate representative organisation under the control and direction of the mass affiliate membership at large. These changes to be pursued through whatever decision-making bodies exist in that organisation. Conference further calls for a plan of action to be reported to subsequent NEC meetings on what progress is being made.

Few of us had any idea how this IMO was structured or what means of influencing let alone controlling it there were. Arthur responded that the IMO was now the IEMO, that that organisation had been founded in 1996, 'and its constitution had been unanimously accepted with the support of the British NUM' – in other words when Arthur and a few of his mates in other mining unions had invented this organisation Arthur had of course agreed with its structure. No one else had any idea what the constitution was; certainly nobody had ever seen it, let alone approved it. Arthur went on to say the next IEMO congress wouldn't take place until 1999, and all affiliates would be circulated at that time as to suggested amendments to its constitution. That was an entirely spurious ground to rule the resolution, a statement of aims, out of order. There was no timeline drafted in those aims, no reason not to have them as a statement of democratising aims and principles. This was one of the opening bouts in a battle I would have until Hatfield Branch closed in August 2005; from that day to this, I never once succeeded in viewing a balance sheet or copy of the constitution, or seeing a decision-making conference which would give control to the members ever take place.

Rossington Branch also puts forward to the Yorkshire Council a resolution critical of IEMO and the costly world trips. Things had come to a head with the international conference in India. I had assumed this was an IEMO event, but Mr Lavery tells me it wasn't. In my view in order to secure the support of the NEC it had been agreed that all of the NEC who wanted to attend could do so. This same formula was then passed on to areas, with Council members being invited all costs paid. Attend what? I had demanded. Nobody I asked at the time seemed to know what this conference was debating and why it was so earth-shatteringly urgent. Ian Lavery informs me that the conference was hosted as a simple act of international solidarity, in the heart of one of the most deprived coal-producing areas of India: a fact-finding conference to let some light into the Indian mining communities.

The rank and file by and large didn't see it like that. When news leaked back out to branches and to the membership, there was hell on. The men at Rossington were still heavily involved with their branch, unlike most of the other pits; they demanded the whole question of even our membership of the IEMO be reviewed. I strongly backed the resolution when it came it up; I had been banging away about this in my view cardboard organisation since its inception. Remarkably, the resolution was passed and formed one of Yorkshire's resolutions to the National Conference. The NEC had asked us to remit it, which meant we could speak on it, but Conference wouldn't vote on it – it would be referred to the NEC for debate and consideration.

We reasoned that with a Yorkshire majority now on the NEC (C. Kitchen, K. Meloy, J. Kelly, N. Pearce, K. Rowley) we wouldn't let the subject be lost. I and Chris Skidmore, the Rossington delegate and now Area chairman, spoke on the spiralling costs and the lack of effective or indeed any results from this organisation. We were met by a veritable tide of red herrings from Ken Rowley on the platform in the capacity of giving the NEC international report. We were told of all the treats and loyalty we had received from the IEMO during our great strike, their selfless commitment to us, and here we were now, meanly begrudging support to them. I pointed out the IEMO wasn't in existence during the strike.

Well, its predecessor the IMO then, they replied. Neither was that, I countered. Having been told we should remit, and having accepted that proposal, we hadn't canvassed any support from other areas for the resolution. We were then shocked when Ian Lavery, the National chair, called for a seconder for the resolution.

In the middle of the discussion and the call for a seconder, Davie Hopper of the North East Area tries to get in on the debate, mainly to speak for the thrust of our motion, but he isn't mandated to second the resolution.

I tried to formally second it (which of course being from the same area wouldn't do). The chair asked for a seconder again,

just to clarify that Dave [Hopper], you are seconding the motion?'

Mr D. Hopper (N/East Area): We have got a problem.

Chair: Dave, hang on, if it hasn't got a seconder the motion falls. The North East is opposed to the motion?

Mr D. Hopper: We're not opposed to internationalism and being a member of organisations.

Chair: That's right but we've had the international report. If it is seconded, not a problem but if it is not seconded you cannot speak on it, it falls. Is there a seconder? Well the motion falls anyway. If it's fallen it doesn't need to be remitted, if there's not a seconder it doesn't need to be remitted. If it had been seconded the NEC would have asked the Yorkshire Area to remit it, but because it has not been seconded the motion falls.[362]

We didn't get a single other area to second our resolution and as such it fell with a deafening crump. It may seem a cynical view but the trip to India had worked.[363]

The counterattack following on my 1997 stand was not long in coming. Frank Cave had phoned me and tells me that I am no longer to handle any claims from any other branches, members or former members, and that I would not receive any payment for any outstanding or pending appeals coming up. He further tells me, and this is perhaps most shocking to me, that I will not longer represent the families of deceased miners from Doncaster or anywhere else at inquests and medical boards.

This particular arena had become quite a forte of mine. I suppose, in reality, I was now something of an expert on the subject of lung diseases, at least with regard to DSS regulations and appeals and the structuring of claims at common law and under the pneumoconiosis scheme, and the way in which inquests, and pathology, affected them. I had in fact been the guest speaker at a specially convened seminar at the Doncaster Royal Infirmary. Of all the 'gigs' I have played over the years this was to be my crowning glory, I thought, and though my colleagues and audience were small they couldn't have been more prestigious: the coroner and his officers, the principal chest physicians, their respective students, NACODS, BACM and me. In fact, I am giving the principal paper. It will deal with the history of industrial law and legislation; the occurrence of diseases; the fate of the victim and his family in case of death; welfare benefits and compensation. It is quite an honour.

The whole thing has come about principally because of the apparent clash of objectives among those different parties. We had had some trade-off arguments and polemics in the coroner's court, vigorous cross-examination of pathology evidence, and pleading of various features of the legislation and its effects. It wasn't always or even mostly helpful for the bereaved families and this was not the time nor the place to fight out the issues. The symposium was really a way of clearing the air, letting everyone involved know what the issues were and what we for our parts were trying to establish and why.

In fact I went on to develop the closest possible relationship with the Doncaster coroner, Mr Hooper, and his officers. Whenever a former miner died in Doncaster I was informed at once if there was any suggestion of death by industrial causes. This gave me the chance to meet the families and prepare them and the case for the hurdles ahead and assist them with everything they were entitled to. The paper I prepared and the place I was given at such a prestigious and important seminar made it one of the most valued occasions of my life.

At the Annual Conference 1997 I seconded the South Wales resolution on social insurance on behalf of the Yorkshire Area, Frank Cave advising the delegation meeting that I probably knew more about social insurance and welfare law than anybody else in the room. It was quite a compliment and when I got to the rostrum I went into great detail about the working of the law, especially in relation to the chest diseases and the great injustices now in the pipeline as a result of the so-called 'reforms' of the system.

I had made law, and altered law, on the question of pneumoconiosis, I had argued down the DSS legal reps before the commissioner and won, affecting the income and justice for possibly thousands of miners. I had never been paid a penny piece for my journeys to London or my loss of shifts, and the claimants were never well off enough to make a donation. The honour of seeking justice for my fellow miners and their families was always enough for me.

In this context I attended my one and only funeral of a police officer. PC Frank Cunnington was the Doncaster coroner's officer, a man of great sensitivity and practicality. He had come to respect my work with the miners' bereaved families and referred them always to my assistance. He would call me and discuss what dates for inquests would fit in with my diary and give a summary of the probable cause of death. He deeply regretted the great strike from all angles and believed the confrontations had done none of us any good. His compassion with bereaved families, in sometimes the most horrendous of circumstances, was remarkable. The day of his funeral, I arrived at the Crem amid a giant throng of uniformed officers of all ranks and trench-coated detectives. Apart from the police wives and Frank's family I was the only non-police person there. A huddle of silver-peaked officers with decorative batons eyed me up and clearly debated who I was, although they soon twigged. At length two of them sauntered over, 'You're David Douglass the NUM official, aren't you?' I was, and wondered what would follow. Actually their dad or in the other cop's case his grandad were former miners, struggling with mine-related conditions and not in the best of health; they hadn't a clue how to claim and who to claim to – could I help? Of course, it was the first time a police officer had ever taken out his notebook for my details in order to help their family; surprisingly, it wasn't the last. I had no problem attending Frank's funeral, I am bigger than petty bigotry against anyone, and Frank was a good bloke; he had died of a heart attack at only 50.

To minimise expense I had arranged with the coroner's officer to fit all the miners' inquests onto the same day of the week, so I would only claim a day's pay for attending all day, rather than allow them to fall consecutively and have to claim a full week. The visits to families' houses to speak to widows in an evening or at weekends of course I didn't claim for.

Now I was being told I would not be paid at all.[364] This was to be the main weapon used by the Area Office against my continued work within the Union. All loss of earnings would be stopped, even those when presenting evidence for deceased miners before tribunals or inquests.[365] The only way they could legitimately not pay me loss of earnings as per rule was to argue that I didn't have any earnings, i.e. I wasn't employed. Despite statements from the Inland Revenue, HMI Taxes, and all my tax returns demonstrating that I was employed by the Hatfield NUM Branch, first Arthur, then Frank and finally Steve Kemp continued to repeat the bogus reasons for rejecting my expenses 'as per rule'.

May 1997 sees the 'landslide' vote for a New Labour government, actually the 'landslide' was 43.2% of the vote but secured 63.3% of the seats. This was in line with the fact that when Mrs Thatcher was decimating the coalfields on the basis that she had a mandate to do so, in actuality no British government since before World War Two has ever won a majority of the votes under the current voting system. Further, had there been a system of proportional representation Labour would actually have been in office permanently since 1945. Arthur concluded that had this been the case, 'The Tories could not have closed the mining industry, destroyed the steel industry and reduced Britain's industrial landscape to something resembling the moon.'[366] That's true – 'the Tories' could not have, but Arthur is forgetting that Labour decimated the coal industry in the '50s and '60s along with the railways and steel, probably on a grander scale than the Tories did.

In August, Arthur comes up with another of his weighted schemes, this time to deal with the rising costs of the Union being a union and representing our old lads at DSS tribunals and appeals. He highlights the escalating costs of paying solicitors to go to these appeals although we didn't recover any costs – from the DSS or from the member. Frank Cave the chairman made the point that I attended all of these tribunals and didn't call upon the solicitors to do it. His point was to try to get other branch officials to do likewise themselves without calling upon Raleys, the Union's solicitors. Truth was many of the branch officials were new and not as experienced as their predecessors had been. Arthur's proposal was that we should claim back a percentage from the members' benefits to pay for our 'additional costs'. This caused some outrage, not least from me, and I pointed out that I had been called upon by the Area to attend these appeals where retired members didn't have a branch any more; I was quite prepared to act on behalf of other branches if they required without the expense of the legal firms. Maltby tried to make this into a formal proposal, but Arthur suggested you were some sort of a wimp if you had to call upon me to help you out; however he then went on to press his proposal. The minutes record that it was unanimously agreed; in fact, we had agreed to no such thing, and this became a bone of bitter contention for years following. We had agreed to a proposal that limited membership fees should be deducted, not that the member should then have an additional 5% on top of that.[367]

THE STRANGE RE-EMERGENCE OF TONY MCHUGH

Following the demise of the Socialist Union, we lost all contact with and knowledge of Mr McHugh, until the winter of 1997 when *News from the Borderland*, a journal which specialises in the exposing the workings of 'the secret state', comes up with an intriguing story under the headline, 'Still Spying On The Comrades: The Curious Case of the New Communist Party, *Searchlight* and the Nazi Honeytrap Run by a Hermaphrodite' – enough to catch your eye on its own! *Searchlight*, I ought to explain, is ostensibly an antifascist journal aimed at outing the Nazis, except the anarcho left universally believes it to be a police–MI5 front, doing as much inside work on the far left as they do on the right. Forbye. In June of 1996 a new nazi publication, from the previously unheard of British National Socialist Party, is sent the length and breadth of Britain to selected recipients. This BNSP was set up by 'self-proclaimed hermaphroditic Stalino-Fascist "Lady Athena McHugh" '. Surely no relation to 'our' Tony? At the same time McHugh was infiltrating the campaign 'London Against the Job Seekers Allowance', and using the Unemployed Centre in East London to collect information. The article took a detour to review the role of the Communist Party of Great Britain's leadership role in spying on what they called 'the ultra-left' – the anarchists and the Trotskyists. Since MI5 were practically built into the CPGB woodwork in order to spy on them this became a useful service, the information, photos, names and lives of the ultra-lefts flowing straight into MI5's files through the CPGB's. It becomes more torrid as Irish Republicans are located via the far left and then 'taken out' by the Loyalist agents of the British state.

Tony was at this time producing the East Anglian Maoist Institute's *Maoist News*. The address is as usual 22 North Market Road, Great Yarmouth – the same venue as the Unemployed Workers Action Committee which Tony was the secretary of. In 1990 wor Tony takes on female identity! He becomes Athena, actually Lady Athena, McHugh and declares he is a hermaphrodite. In case readers lost in my meandering through the matrix of the left think this is a form of Greek existentialism, I should explain rather that it is the physical property of having both male and female sex organs. Tony had been married to the daughter of the New Communist Party (a break from the 'old' Communist Party by the even more ultra-Stalinist supporters of the old team who felt abandoned and betrayed by the shift from Joe) organiser Bob Cooper. They had had a daughter. Her dad suddenly coming over all feminine and adopting a female name and dress must have come as quite a shock – even more so when under this female persona in 1993 he, sorry – she, joins the British National Party! One year later she, sorry – he, is East Anglian Regional Organiser! You couldn't make this stuff up. When publicly challenged on the changes – the political ones not the skirt and high heels – she said she was no longer a communist but a nationalist. The change must have been difficult since s/he seems to have worn both hats at the same time. At the Tory Party conference 'a woman' member of the BNP was giving out leaflets for the 'National Union of Unemployed and Workers'. She said it was on behalf of 'my other half'; this could be a reference to her left-wing persona but probably means his partner. Her 'comrades' in the BNP however considered her a pervert and she left, though still stayed right, if you see what I mean. But then it gets worse. In June 1996 Lady Anthony decides to help set up a rival, perhaps even more overtly fascist, organisation, the British National Socialist Party, which s/he advertises using lists stolen from a BNP computer during a violent attack on one of their party organiser's houses.

Now as the leader of the BNSP Lady McHugh intervenes into the London Against the Job Seekers Allowance campaign. The JSA was a harsh crackdown on claimants with penalties and the loss of all benefits as the whip. Some resisters were advocating equally harsh measures against job centres and staff who implemented the scheme with any enthusiasm. The state may well have thought this was going to be as big a flashpoint as the poll tax. Lady Athena became prominent and took part in the original organising campaigns and marches. What thickened the plot was the role of the New Communist Party and its front the National Union of Unemployed Workers throughout the whole period, who seem to have been well aware of their former comrade's dual identity and political cross-dressing, but did nothing to prevent it or alert the other organisation being contaminated and infiltrated.

One thing is now certain:; our very early suspicions of the man at that time (see *The Wheel's Still In Spin*) were more than sound. He obviously backed off a close infiltration of our group for reasons which can only be speculated upon. That doesn't unfortunately mean that there weren't some other of our erstwhile 'comrades' playing for the other side at that time, and God knows we had suspicions.

By '98 Arthur has taken over as resident not so much commander as commandeerer in chief of the Yorkshire Area, in a sort of ad-hoc coup; to this day I don't understand how it was achieved. His hand sat on everything we did. A sort of left opposition was trying to emerge and we had won a major victory, we thought, with the election of Nigel Pearse as the vice president of the Area. Nigel, a former Militant member and self-declared Marxist revolutionary, was not in Scargill's awe and stood well to his left politically. We thought through Nigel's election we could start to direct some energies back to rank-and-file struggles and fundamental first bases. Arthur was determined Nigel would have no such impact and denied him first an office, and obviously then a phone, and finally ruled that he couldn't just come into the offices and deal with things or respond to calls, and in fact should only come in if there was something specifically he had to do. Being Area vice president was not 'something specific to do', despite the fact that when Ken Capstick, a Scargillite, had had the position he acted like a full-time official.

To try and give Nigel some muscle and to jerk the Union back into action – recruiting miners to the Union for a start, since they had been leaving in droves – we voted to establish an Area Campaigns Committee. Onto this committee, to be chaired by Nigel, they elected me, Keith Stanley, president of the Nottingham miners (who now sat in at joint meetings) and Terry Harrison. When we actually met and started to draw up a back-to-basics plan, with a regular bulletin, posters, campaign meetings, membership drives, consultation drives, we found the shutters firmly down. We could not use any of the offices in the Barnsley building, even the empty ones, neither could we have a phone, nor access to printing or funds. So that effectively was that.

Things were getting bad: basic staff laid off, and fewer and fewer people to deal with the numerous queries and cries for help which still flooded the office from the abandoned and isolated pit communities. Arthur then presided over the closing down of the switchboard and its replacement with a tone-dialing, automated-answering service. This was quite useless to most of the aud lads and lasses who tried to phone in, and anyway even if you had a touch-tone phone the faceless voice asked you to enter an extension number so if you didn't have it you couldn't reach anyone, and anyway, there was increasingly nobody to take any calls that finally managed at the end of all that to climb all the hurdles. We were not functioning as a union.

The Annual Conference of 1998 was compressed to one day only and it was not at the seaside but in the Barnsley offices; this was a sign of the importance now being attached to the Conference. Worse than that, Arthur had staged another coup. He knew last time we had debated knocking Conferences back to a biennial basis the proposal had been roundly defeated in Yorkshire.

Unable to get his Biennial Conferences through the normal channels, he calls what he calls a 'Special Delegate Conference'; actually he just asks the NEC on which he has a controlling majority of fans to stay behind and reconvenes the meeting as 'a Conference'. At this 'Conference' he submits all the rule changes he wants including the Biennial Conference arrangements and to reduce the number of NEC meetings per year by fully one half. He would run the Union between Conferences with the backing of the much-weakened NEC. Remarkably, none of the National Executive members, including those from Yorkshire, seem to raise any objection to this at all and the rule changes, needless to say, go through. No branch, no area or anybody else has a chance to put forward any rule changes they might wish; no branch or area or member has seen these new rules let alone approved them.[368] Few delegates even know this change has taken place; at a far distant time, when it comes to light, Arthur claims we approved the report! If true, and Arthur is rarely wrong on dates, if they back him up, it was probably lodged like a naughty sin in amang a wedge of innocent ones to blind the priest or in this case the members, and we didn't notice it and waved it through with a wad of other meetings and reports.

The power was drawing to an ever smaller circle of people, with Arthur at its centre.

The Conference such as it was did its best to pretend we were still big, fit and healthy. Arthur set the ball rolling with a target of £50,000 per year for face workers, £40,000 per year for workers elsewhere underground and £30,000 p.a. on the surface, a 6-hour day and a 4-day week and retirement at 50 on a full pension.

In Arthur's words, there was only one note of discord in the whole Conference, and of course it had come from me. Raising a question on the Annual Report and Accounts, I had simply asked how, given the apparent financial constraints in our declining Union, with an operating margin of only £3,000, we could justify the ongoing £20,000 per annum affiliation to the so called International Energy and Mineworkers Organisation. How could we justify the laying-off of staff and the cutbacks in services to the members and retired folk when for £20,000 per annum all we got was a badly duplicated semi-English stapled news-sheet knocked off somewhere in a French office going on about the problems of fundamentalism in Algeria?

I suppose I should have known better, and since this could only be raised as a question, I had no comeback. The IEMO was Arthur's own baby, born in his image and likeness and totally a tool of him and Alain Simon in France. He was livid. He had never been so slighted, he was accountable, anyone could go to their conferences (I noted they were their conferences and not ours). He went into his fishmonger act wholesale, with barrow-loads of red herrings and charges of disloyalty and nationalism, no less! He had the floor now and I wasn't allowed backup as the red herrings and charges bit me left and right. All that was left for me to do was a sort of McEnroe 'What did I say? What did I say?' plea to my fellow delegates.

By 27 November 1998 the Union had called a Special Delegate Conference to consider forms of industrial action in the face of the continued derisory pay awards and lack of Union recognition by RJB, the new coal-owners for most of the pits. In the teeth of everything that had gone before, the Conference, by a vote of over 70%, said yes to all-out unlimited strike action.[369] Although that didn't mean the members would support such a call in an individual ballot, it was still a stamp of the industrial bravery, or perhaps wishful thinking, of the NUM, who just couldn't swallow its new weakened status.

Along with the sell-off of the mines to private coal-owners, or else their closure, came a parallel hiving-off of our national welfare scheme, CISWO. Government-appointed officials who had nothing to do with the coal industry were suddenly presiding over our welfare scheme, which had been patently built by the members of the miners' Union, first with benevolent coal-owners and then with the NCB. We had had a huge problem nationally after the end of the strike when Thatcher forced the UDM onto the government of the scheme despite the fact that they were not parties to it. We deliberated long and hard as to whether the NUM would keep its seats or refuse to take part, but this would have meant handing over the whole scheme to the scabs. The NUM had never had a majority on the scheme anyway; the NCB always had the casting vote, although we did in better times have a rotating chair.

They had moved against Arthur and Peter and then Frank, our National reps, to ensure they could not sit on the governing body. They were removed as trustees from the Yorkshire Miners' Welfare Convalescent Homes Trust and the Yorkshire Miners' Welfare Trusts. The grounds? They were biased in support of members of the NUM! Our convalescent home at Scalby, built 100% with NUM money, was nonetheless part of the scheme. They then decided that we, that is the Union, should pay the scheme for our members using it! It led to our home being disaffiliated from the scheme and us having to run it ourselves, outside the overall welfare organisation. Similar things were happening to our holiday camps and convalescent schemes all over the country; many, now without funding and assistance, simply closed, leaving our retired miners and dependants that much the poorer. The spite of the government against such schemes was a kind of social terrorism, another of their 'social punishment shootings' to make the communities 'pay the price of insurrection' as MacGregor had described it.

The Yorkshire Area Welfare Committee, which governed all the local welfare schemes, was abolished without further ado when they privatised the mines. At local level, although they tried to object to our representatives, it was the NUM that ran the scheme in the coalfields and across the pit villages the length and breadth of Britain. Following the sell-off, the schemes were struggling. Where we could, we tried to get sympathetic councils to take them over, with guarantees on their grounds and assets being kept for the communities and not sold off to speculators. I on behalf of the Hatfield Main Welfare Scheme had completed the handover of the extensive grounds at Stainforth to the Doncaster Metropolitan Borough Council for greenfield recreational activities for the whole community and was in talks to do the same with the Dunscroft lands when privatisation hit us, and control was wrested from my hands, despite the fact that I represented all the folk who had paid every week to secure and maintain all this property. I had opened up talks with Hatfield Council to take over the land, and was in the process of securing some copper-bottomed agreement that the grounds would not be sold off to speculators or built on. Speculators had previously offered me a fortune to allow them to buy parcels of land for prestigious house-building on Broadway fronts. One of the local high-flyers told his partner: 'I have never been so politely told to "fuck off" in my life.' Actually, I had told them, without malice, that the Union, the Welfare and I were not for sale to anyone. The council too had looked for a time to raise revenue from this big chunk of land which they would develop and trade us off with some other green fields. Nothing doing.

All of this was shuffled sideways when the new CISWO managers moved in, accountable to no one, and took up negotiations with the council. I was now no longer party to the talks: 'You have no more right than any other member of the public to have any more involvement or control or sanction over the fate of the Welfare Grounds,' Mr Maiden, operating director of CISWO had told me in December of '98. And then one Sandra Beighton, who was an assistant under the old regime, was suddenly in charge; she told me: 'Hatfield Council will have to determine whether you can be informed or not as there is a question of confidentiality.' I was furious. These were our grounds, this was the Miners' Welfare. True, we didn't have the funding any more to maintain them, but to lose direct control of their fate was a point of much local anger.

They didn't have it their own way though, and the local Labour Party and councillors were hounded by the retired miners and their families about the direction of these assets. We managed in the end to get the assurances that they would stay as green field recreation sites in perpetuity. A new children's park was constructed, the football grounds upgraded and the area generally smartened up. To the architects of the forthcoming revolution all this is small paternalistic beer, to us this is part and parcel of working people trying to take control of areas of their lives and resist all impositions from above.

SINKING SAND

The diary entries show almost every day back in Yorkshire filled with inquests and tribunals, appeals and presentations on behalf of the abandoned mining community inhabitants right across South Yorkshire, as well as meetings with the HMI and internal Union meetings to represent the lads still working at Hatfield pit.

But something of the 'nothingness', the all-consuming emptiness that is laying waste to the pit communities across Britain, is starting to thrive in Dunscroft. Large gangs of teenage smackheads start to occupy houses on onetime hardworking streets. The Welfare fields house nests of antisocial, alienated gangs.

Still, the end of January 1999 seen a visit by Joel and Carol and their little lad Nathan, which is a joy all round. I am nonetheless thinking the time is right to now leave Dunscroft, Stainforth and all that, and kick over the traces. Emma and Paul too have had enough. They are terrorised in their own house, by kids, by neighbours who saw down their trees, shoot their cats, poison the fishpond. Emma is attacked and I explode. We are getting toward major confrontation and the police have warned me and Paul we will be the ones who are arrested not the antisocial arseholes, if we take any violent actions against them or threaten them.

Thursday 1 April. Jeff Morley's badly decomposed and mummifying body is found at his house. Jeff, a 'marra', fellow Hatfield face worker, had been an awkward bastard at times; he could be cruel. Early on in our relationship he would grab my head in vice-like locks and try and squeeze my brains out. He could grip your hand and bend it back until it nearly broke and you were forced to stamp on his instep or kick him in the shin to let go, and he'd laugh. We used to have furious arguments about Ireland, but at the same time he could be a scream. A big daft bugger, skipping down the tail gate, with his little finger intertwined with Kenny Hodges the deputy's, singing Bay City Rollers fan club songs, from where I have no idea. He mellowed and started to think, and reflect and drink – too much. He used to collect matchboxes, and since I ventured to foreign parts on occasion he would always charge me with bringing some exotic boxes back. He frequently came into the Advice Centre, just for the crack and to update the claims I had running for him. Of late I had noticed he was gradually 'going bush'. His staid, normal, pitman style was getting more longhaired. He took to wearing headbands and growing a beard, he started wearing beads, he was now into Irish rebel music, and neighbours complained that it sounded like a full-blown Irish ceilidh. 'Yippee!' he would yell, 'Up the IRA!' he would toast. The word was he had turned a little gay, too. His wife (long-suffering, as Jeff could be a hard bastard at times) left him; she said she could handle an affair with a woman, but not this. Jeff used to drink at the Fox; it is no place for the thin-skinned. Someone suggested Jeff had turned gay; Jeff bottled him, badly did him over and ended up with 6 months in jail for GBH. When he came out, he called in once, didn't talk about anything to do with all that, just collected a load of matchboxes which had been accumulating.

He had, it seems, drunk himself to death; not eaten, starved and drank himself to oblivion. Mind, that is speculation; the body had been there so long that the pathologist could not ascertain a cause of death. There were no obvious signs, but the police had concluded that there were no signs of anybody else having been involved and no signs of any injuries. Bliddy hell, Jeff lad, I wish I'd known you were so alone. I would have gladly teamed up with ye, marra. What a waste. I miss him even yet.

KEEP FIGHTING ! KEEP FIGHTING!

On 15 February, the Union had launched a campaign to win the membership to a make-or-break battle to secure a negotiated wage settlement and de facto recognition of the Union with RJB, now Britain's biggest mining employer. RJB had taken over the bulk of the NCB when it was privatised. They continued with their divisive double-dealing, making fish of NUM members and flesh of UDM members. They had continued the NCB's 'minority/majority' conciliation strategy which debarred the NUM from negotiating for our members in UDM-majority coalfields, but didn't extend that concept nationally, where the NUM represented more than three-quarters of the entire workforce. The Union was out on a limb, really, calling for all-out strike action, but that had been the tactic the branches had rooted for; when it went to ballot 57% of the members votes 'yes'. Even the Rescue Brigadesmen, who we had to ballot separately as they were now employed by the private firm Mines Rescue Service Ltd, and with whom we had had great difficulty during the '84/85 strike, voted 54.5% 'yes' to strike action. It was an amazing testimony to the strength and resilience of the British miners, given the background of hardship, defeat and perpetual pit closures and job losses, along with the autocratic and arbitrary treatment by the coal-owners. It knocked the coal company backwards – they had not anticipated such a result. They were acutely aware this could be a terminal battle and once those chips went down the miners were prepared to take it to the end. They decided to talk. Arthur's view was that 'The NUM was able to win a stunning victory for miners, resulting in the largest basic pay increase since the end of the Second World War.'[370] Even given considerable spin that Arthur put on the result and repackaging the deal, it was a worthy victory and one we were sore in need of. At the eleventh hour, RJB agreed to consolidate a further 10% incentive/bonus pay into the basic pay. We were also able to negotiate this 10% consolidation agreement for the 'lease licence' mines, the poor relations of the industry. The men at these mines were far from satisfied with the package, especially at Rossington, where discontent raged until the colliery finally closed. The UDM deal negotiated earlier had offered nothing to these mines, whereas the NUM package offered increases of between £400 and £1,040 over that accepted by the UDM and marked a propaganda as well as a financial victory.[371] More importantly perhaps, RJB agreed to start negotiation on a conciliation scheme and collective bargaining agreement, which would cover all our members, including those in Nottingham; despite the high hopes, though, it was never fulfilled. Thatcher's bastard Tony continued as a dead hand on the remnants of the industry to the end.

Barrie Ormsby, *Miners' Strike*, Watercolour, 1980s

8

Barnsley Wars

I get up to speak for the Area on a number of issues – not least the one very dear to my heart and a great cause of annoyance, namely pensions. Hatfield has submitted and the Yorkshire Area has accepted our resolution to Conference on the anomalous way deceased miners' pensions are treated. In the last paragraph, it states:

> There is no practical reason why a contributor to the Mineworkers Pension Scheme ought not to have his next of kin or estate treated in the same way as widows with regard to payment of posthumous and residue pension entitlements.[372]

It bothers me that I, as a divorced miner, in the event of my death have all my pension contributions seized and confiscated by the NCB, whereas had I been married my wife would get the residue of my pension entitlement. A widow of course should indeed get the residue of the pension that her man had paid into all his life, but then why shouldn't my daughter get the residue of mine? Payments in the event of death should be paid on contributions and not marital status, surely? Why should my employer keep my pension contributions and not pay any of them out if I die after the first year of my retirement? After I made my speech, the platform asked me to remit it along with the supporting amendment from Nottingham to the Pensions Committee, which I did. The situation remains the same over 10 years down the line, despite the fact that I as an individual have tried to register a formal complaint with the Pensions Ombudsman and unsuccessfully tried to get the support of the Equal Opportunities Commission to run a test case on it.

10 September. Something strange develops down in Derbyshire. Readers will by now be aware the areas of the NUM are in most cases semi-autonomous. Following the collapse of the strike, some drifted off into doing their own thing, and more or less by the 1990s some had no working mines at all. That they were able to survive was due in part to the bonanza provided by the tidal wave of claims for chronic bronchitis and HAVS. Areas had initially gone off and started their own campaigns, frequently in alliance with legal firms outside the Union. I have expressed the view that under Arthur's influence a dead hand was put on the Union running the claims directly either in Yorkshire or nationally, at least initially, and this task had fallen to areas, advice centres like mine and ad-hoc arrangements like the Yorkshire Compensation Recovery Unit. Often the constitutional standing of the arrangements was very vague. Arthur didn't start tightening up on the arrangements and whipping areas back into line until an understanding of the full potential of the money, and the influence, to be made by these claims had been taken on within the Union as such, and 'official' procedures drawn up. It led to all sorts of attacks and allegations against the legal advice and representation firms IDC in the North East and YCRS (Yorkshire

Compensation Recovery Service) and the COSA section of the NUM in Yorkshire. My office and advice centre was under ongoing suspicion, but in September the Derbyshire Area bounces into the cross-hairs. Derbyshire had got behind the potential very early on, had set up a full-scale legal operation with Grayson's solicitors and were now advertising nationwide for former miners. They ran national press adverts and started to rival everyone in the business.

Suddenly it came to Arthur's notice, and at the same time the press started to run a spurious campaign against the Derbyshire Area officials as somehow doing something illegitimate. The gutter press ran features on how much money the officials were now on, when they didn't have a single pit. The truth was, they were gaining members hand over fist and the volume of work they were dealing with and service they were offering probably rivalled anything they had been able to do before. A similar press smear had been launched against YCRS and David Murdoch, and another was hinted at with IDC in the North East; allegations of mis-accounting and misappropriation were floated against the Durham officials of the NUM. Some thought these smears were coming from within the NUM and were part of an internal political struggle. In September the Derbyshire case came before the NEC.

The constitutional flaw seemed only to be that they hadn't signed up all these new and old members as official NUM limited members, which would require that the Area paid dues in respect of them to the National Office. The language of the NEC verdict was that of expulsion without doubt:

> ... that if the NUM (Derbyshire Area) and Messrs Butler, Gascoyne and Fairest refuse to give the undertaking required by the NEC, then the three individuals together with the NUM (Derbyshire Area) be reported to the National Disciplinary Committee with a view to it taking appropriate action against the individuals concerned and if necessary the Area.[373]

Now a great deal of pragmatic negotiation seem to have resulted from all this; Derbyshire signs up all the claimants to the NUM formally as limited members, the funds in the national coffers swell, while a deal is done which ensures that the whole of that area is represented by the Scargill loyalists on the NEC from Nottingham, which thus swells the National card vote of that, now, joint area for voting purposes. It also means that for a time Nottingham could use the card vote of both areas at National Conference, although when disagreements arose between Derbyshire and Nottingham over voting direction, Derbyshire was allowed to cast a card vote in opposition to that of Nottingham. Any former miners discovered in their national sweeps that ought to be serviced by other NUM areas were passed on to those areas.

The press smear against the officials in Derbyshire was quite scandalous. Both the area and the officials were in fact doing first-class work for the former miners of Derbyshire and for those of many areas that no longer had area offices. I frequently sprang to the phone-in programme and replied to press reports in their defence. In particular, I noted that this Mr Fairhurst, who they were slagging off, was the same man who the year previously had been awarded the MBE for bravery in going over the top of a collapsed roadway unprotected to rescue some trapped heading men, when they had hailed him as a hero.

TERRY FRENCH

25 September 1998. My dear comrade and friend Terry French is killed in Holland, it seems murdered. Terry, Kent coalminer and anarchist fellow traveller, has emerged every now and again in these pages. A fearless and skilled picket, he had gone down for an 8-year sentence for picketing of the more enthusiastic sort. His court case made it clear the cops had been planning to get him for some time and Michael Mansfield his QC accused the police of concocting 'a trumped-up charge'. As it turned out, he did 3 years hard time in jail. When he got out, he threw himself into the Victimised Miners Campaign and was a founder member of our rank-and-file miners' organisation. During the seafarers' strike, he made national news on the front of one of the tabloids as a professional picket and trouble-causer, arrested again and blacklisted from hell to breakfast time. The news of Terry's death and the circumstances surrounding it filtered through slowly. God knows what he had been forced to get involved with last off to make ends meet, but if it hadn't been for Thatcher and her bloody pit closure programme Terry would be on the coalface enjoying the crack and telling the tale. He was 49 when he died, leaving his wife and two doting kids.

KARATE

November. I grade for First Dan. It is intense, and hard, but I am totally committed and focused. Karate is now the most important feature of my life – other than Emma, of course. I think it has overtaken politics, at least so far as time and energy is concerned. The Karata in this school are now my only real friends; it is they I choose to go out with; it is their company I find myself in, it is they I am relaxed with.

FREE SPARRING OF A DIFFERENT ORDER

May 1999. A bitter internecine war has developed at Barnsley, the Yorkshire Area HQ of the NUM (and now, with the failure of the new 'state of the art' office at Sheffield), also of the National Union.[374] I see this as an anti-bureaucratic struggle; how Arthur and his team see it, I have never understood. This becomes the first of many in which me and my comrades will be on the opposite side of Arthur's table – I was going to say round table but he would never have stood for a shape that didn't allow him to sit at the head of it. Arthur's grip on the Union was tightening and as part of that process his influence and control over the Yorkshire Area started to become stifling. On this occasion, it was the long-running and sorry story of Barnsley Main Road Transport Branch, and the efforts of their secretary John Clarke to fight what they perceived was a naked injustice. This is not the place to retell the story blow-by-blow. Enough to say that, as the coalfield ran down, Barnsley Road Transport Branch, the drivers who drove the lorries, transport, and supplies between sites and workshops and collieries, were run down, and privatised along with the rest of the industry. An anomaly in the transfer of engagements between the new owners and part of the transport depot meant that when the new owners suddenly went belly-up the redundancy terms of the drivers should have been protected on a par with those of the terms under British Coal, who they had transferred from. Instead, the men had ended up with nowt.

A tribunal claim, taken by the Union's solicitors Raleys, ought to have covered all the points and all the workers covered by the appeal, but a key section of the claim was never presented, namely many of the men who had lost redundancy terms didn't in fact have their names submitted to the tribunal. The men still ended up with nowt. When the Branch complained and charged the Area Union and Raleys with effectively making a bollocks of their claim, Arthur and Frank turned the issue around and blamed the Branch officials for not presenting their claim correctly. Every time the Branch tried to agenda the issue at Barnsley for discussion, on Arthur's advice Frank Cave ruled it out of order; furthermore, they ruled that the Branch couldn't spend any Branch money on pursuing the charge. Every time the Barnsley secretary rose to make his protest, he was gagged. It produced embarrassing scenes of fury and passion, and loud accusations of betrayal and sell out. At one point, the Council finally agreed to a proposal from the Branch, that they and Arthur should go to London and meet with an independent QC, to review what had happened, if a bollock had been dropped and whether the men had a claim against the Union or Raleys for negligence. This was passed with great sighs of relief, as the Branch had agreed if the QC ruled that it had been a fault of theirs or if the claim was a no-hoper they would accept that and let the matter drop having done the best they could. It was agreed to applause, a unifying conclusion to a vexed question. Then Arthur simply got up, and announced: 'I ain't going nowhere, and I am not going to London. This matter is closed as far as I am concerned,' and walked out. I demanded to know, as he walked past my elbow, 'What sort of democracy is that Arthur?' While others jumped up to ask, 'Do we have any say in the running of this Union any more, or what?'

A short time later it was suddenly discovered that Barnsley Main Road Transport Branch didn't have the required 29 members to remain a branch (they had by this time declined to 12) and it was accordingly closed down, the issue unresolved. Anyone who thought the closing of this branch, which had operated without 29 members for some time, was unrelated to its clash with the officials was touchingly naive. Arthur later accused John Clarke of forging entries in the Branch minute book to make their case seem stronger; an enquiry led by Ian Lavery found the evidence. John was disciplined and I believe expelled from the Union a short time later, although I believe the saga continued with John then taking a case to an EAT against the Union.

Since the days when Arthur dreamed we would sail into the TGWU and he would be given the deputy general secretaryship and another almost million members to play with, he had tried to knock bits out of our rulebook to be more in line with theirs. Then it was just the bits which gave control to the rank and file or challenged the authority of the National leadership. A classic was his determination to have us go from Annual Conferences to Biennial Conferences. Trouble was, the delegates liked the Annual Conferences, because they brought us together, they kept a tight reign on the NEC, they governed the Union, and – to be frank – they were a bliddy good expenses-paid piss-up at the seaside. Yorkshire had opposed all attempts to get rid of them.

So on 1 July 1999 Arthur convenes a 'Special Delegate Conference'. It was so special that only members of the NEC could attend it and it was called without invite to all the branches and areas and was convened following the NEC business. There were only 11 NEC members at the 'Special Delegate Conference', in fact no delegates at all. Contrast this to the Special Delegate Conference just 8 months previously, which had seen the full 38 delegates and area representatives present.[375] Arthur's proposal, now an NEC proposal, didn't wait for it to be approved by anyone else, let alone the man at the pit face or the branch at the pit who knew absolutely nothing about it at all. The NEC, after approving it, simply closed one meeting and were declared a 'Conference' where they sat.[376] I couldn't believe that two of our comrades, one of them Nigel Pearce, our former Trot member of the NEC and my leftist running mate, didn't seem to raise a word of objection, let alone march out of the farce and expose it. As far as I could see, this Conference wasn't disclosed as such to anyone, until at least a year later some minutes allegedly alluding to it, though none of us knew what they were on about, were endorsed, probably on the nod as they frequently are, in among a lot of other NEC stuff. Arthur was then to argue, when we discovered the con, that we had endorsed the minutes!

The Anarchist and the Lord

July 1999. BBC had commissioned a series of 'fly-on-the-wall' real-life documentaries in which they placed two people of opposite lifestyles and political persuasion together for a week and more to see what transpired in terms of dialogue, and amusing confrontation. It was far more focused than the later and utterly banal Big Brother was. They contacted me the previous year during the making of the first series. They knew me as a representative for the miners and assumed I was 'old Labour'. They had pencilled me in to sit opposite one of Blair's New Labour supporters, a repellent yuppie character thrilled with the Thatcherite polices of New Labourism. I confessed I was broadly an anarchist, so the piece wouldn't work. The following year they were commissioning a new series and *The Anarchist and the Lord* seemed heaven-sent.

The thing about Lord Rowallan was that he was, as lords go, very progressive, certainly more progressive than many Labour MPs and certainly more than the New Labour yuppie they had tried to line me up with last year … He believed in unions, believed in a right to strike, and had supported the miners' right to fight for their communities and jobs. Agreed with the NHS and supported better pay and conditions for fire-fighters and nurses. Thought religion was divisive and sectarian. Defied the Tory whips and voted in favour of the equalisation of the sexual age of consent for gay teenagers. Believed in the defence of benefits. Was an anti-racialist. Had been against the withdrawal of student grants, privatisation of rail, coal and steel and believed most policemen were a waste of space and were ineffectual.

So he wasn't one of those blustering old Colonel Blimp, 'Get off my land you Bolshie bastards' types. Neither was I the kind of Class War member who would run through his living room swinging on his chandeliers and painting obscenities on his ranch wall. If we had been, doubtless this would have made better TV but we neither of us, despite our emphatically different outlooks and lives, were like that.

He shows me round the House of Lords and explains to me this is how things are done in peaceful constitutional England. In the process of walking through the marbled great halls, I notice a fine Greco-Roman type statute has a broken arm, which has been stuck back together. 'Oh yes,' he instructs, that was when one of the suffragettes chained themselves to the statue to prevent eviction from the House,'and they had to break its arm to get her out.' 'That,' I parried, 'is how we change things in England.' Mind, I was a bit disillusioned with this Palace of the Aristocrats; it was rather tatty and cheap. For instance, the great oak fireplace near the entrance contained a cheapo pretend red plastic mock fire, like something you would find in a bed-sit. We had breakfast out on the members' veranda, from which, he was proud to tell me, you got a clear view of the London Eye carousel wheel and the London skyline. I mentioned to him that viewed from the other way round, any anti-establishment marksman would have a clear shot at any member of Her Majesty's upper house and 'would probably get three or four of you before anyone realised why you were all falling in a pool of blood over breakfast'. He thought for a minute and looked at the wheel – 'Good God, you're right!' He resolved to eat inside in future.

We flew up to his 'mansion' on his Rowallan estate, and I was introduced to his family over dinner. In one of those odd coincidences of history I realised not only that his wife Claire was a Geordie, a working-class lass made good, a horsy person who had met the noble laird at a horsy persons' do, where he'd recognised a bonny lass when he seen one. She later confided to a paper that she thought I would launch a big attack on her as a class traitor, but why? She wasn't some self-declared revolutionary, or dyed-in-the-wool militant; ah well, more was to be revealed. We were sitting having dinner that evening and she asked me what pit I had worked at in Tyneside. 'Well you wouldn't know it, it was a wee colliery called Wardley.' You could have knocked me over with a feather when she responded, 'Follonsby Lodge?' How the …? Seems she was the former sister-in-law of Harry Dinning, the last lodge chairman, and incidentally a great friend of my family and as it happened the long-running lord mayor of Gateshead. I don't know what her former bloke had done or why they broke up, and didn't ask.

But then I went on to drop a bollock, as I am wont to do. They had gone in the kitchen and left me with the petite bonny daughter. 'So what ye gaan dey when ye leave school?' I asked innocently. Oops, she was left school and not only that, was that one of the top female equestrian athletes in Britain, famous in fact to all the horsy set. Well I bliddy didn't knaa did I? You know how wee these folk are.

He took me to his castle, which he had been forced to sell. I confessed to being a bit sorry for him losing his ancestral hall. The family were all Covenanters; this had been a Covenanters' castle. Mind, he confessed to total mystification of Scottish history and the turning points and issues of that warring country. He was fascinated when I started to explain the convoluted principles and causes of the Scottish ruling class and their working-class followers. The cameras stayed firmly off during this – boring.

We visited his family chapel, where he had his own special family pew in which the Laird and his family and special friends could sit during services. I met a fine upstanding Scottish aristocrat in there, singing heartily 'All Things Bright And Beautiful'; next time I seen him he was on the platform of the Countryside Alliance advocating the right to tear animals to pieces in the name of sport.

Mind, the chapel amused me. The poor Wee Frees of the parish needs must deposit some of their hard-earned cash into the coffers to support their local preacher; in turn, he preached his sermon. Somewhere lost in the realms of time when the Scottish Protestant masses were fighting for what they seen as common justice in their religion, they resolved that a sermon should be an hour. What was funny was that the chapel had a huge hourglass sand timer, like an egg timer. As the preacher took to the pulpit, a devotee swung the hourglass and started the time running. *Preacher or no, we had paid our penny and we mun get wor hoors sermon*. Only right, mind.

I cannot recount here the blow-be-blow tale of events with my noble laird, but the film crew ran up 190 hours of tape, from which only 45 minutes were to be used.

Needless to say some of funniest and politically charged and poignant pieces fell on the cutting room floor and are gone forever. I was actually in the cutting room when the final cut tape was down to 2½ hours; by this time the very best of the week was condensed and could seriously not be condensed further without abandoning the best bits. I tried to bribe the cutting man to make me a copy of this 2½-hour draft. I had visions of us putting it on as the full and unexpurgated version. Of maybe bringing it out as a Class War bootleg. Sadly, the company guessed that too and refused to save this longer version. It went, and with it some of the funniest bits. His Lordship had announced his main plank of argument, that there was no working class any more. Nobody was working-class, everybody was either upper-class or middle-class; there was no what he seen as 'bottom'. Mind, in part it was his crass ignorance of what class was. He thought working-class was a term of abuse, a derogatory term, and nobody would wish to be associated with it. 'Well where can we go to meet some of these workers?' both the producer and his royal laird asked.

We, for I was now in company with a little coterie of Glasgow anarchists, brought together for the event, stared speechless. 'Ye divind have ti gaan anywhere, workers are all over the place, there is nowhere yi winnit find workers; just ask the folk in this pub,' we had suggested. No, they would decline this offer as we had picked this pub and it might have been full of politically motivated anarchists. OK then, we suggested we go to the nearby shopping centre and ask folk. Oh dear, the producers and directors worried as we headed for the complex, where do we ask permission? Do we need to inform the police? 'Fucksake, we're anarfuckinchistsman, we don't ask permission, we don't ask the police!' we exploded. Anyway, the nice producer calmed, 'We were only talking to people.' I think they thought we would wander up to the odd individual charging past and whisper, 'Psst – are ye working-class?' That's not the way we seen it. The place was mobbed with shoppers, hustling about their way, laden down with shopping, armies of kids in tow, arm-in-arm, or gangs of youngsters marching about in the throng. As they set the cameras up, we jumped on a low wall.

'Hello, Hey, Huw!' we shouted like stallholders about to set up an auction; we waved everybody forward, and soon a big crowd was gathering round.

'Whet's up, lads?' the dear old Glasgow pensioners asked.

We announced with shouting voices, 'We've got the BBC here, and wa deyin a programme on class, this is Lord Rowallan.'

They crowd strained forward and picked children up to look and folk peered their heads this way and that, exclaiming 'Oh, is that a Lord, is it?' as if he was an exhibit at Madame Tussauds. Johnny looked decidedly uncomfortable as the crowd swelled and folk laughed and shouted.

'His Lordship disnea think there is such a thing as the working class!' my mate called out, hardly suppressing his laughter.

'Let's have a vote!' I shout. 'Who is working-class?'

Every hand went up.

Johnny raised his eyebrows, and asked 'How many people here are proud to be working-class?'

A cheer and a forest of hands shot up.

'No, no!' Johnny protested. 'You, sir, what's your job?'

'Well Ah'm no working see, Ah just got oot o jail, av no foond a job yet.'

'Ha!' says the Laird proudly, 'he's *not* working-class!'

'Aye, he is!'

'No, he can't be, he isn't working!'

'Ye daft bugger!' we all shout.

'Hands up those who are not working,' he calls to the crowd.

About a quarter puts their hands up. 'You see?' he ripostes in triumph, but the crowd didn't see it that way.

'And what ye gaana dey aboot it?' they start to demand, 'Whit ye deyin to mek sure we can work?'

Suddenly the plug is pulled out and a throng of folk start to accuse the Lord of failing all manner of civic and political duties.

'Ye,' an old women shouts, 'Ma sink doesnae work, av complained for twelve months noo.'

'De'ye knaa, there's rats in the closes?' a young mother demands. He is spluttering how terrible it all is, and he is sure there are things can be done. Then he spots a neatly dressed man in the crowd. 'You, sir, can I ask what you do?'

'Aye,' responds the bloke, 'Ah'm a jeweller.'

'A jeweller? You aren't working-class then, are you?'

'Aye, I is, I worked as a welder in the yerds (shipyards), took a higher City and Guilds in welding, and soldering fine metals in ma ain time, when the yerd closed I started ma ain jewellers shop. Ma customers are working-class, and am working-class.'

'No, no, jewellers aren't working-class,' he insisted.

Eventually the crowd got so large and the debates quite heated with all kinds of hatred and class revenge being called down onto the heads of capitalism, royalty and the whole social system that the police started to mill around and look concerned. We at length jumped back on the wall, and thanking everyone for their attendance at the meeting, and moving a vote of thanks to the Laird for being a good sport, we adjourned the meeting to loud cheers and claps. Johnny Rowallan tried all sorts of political twists and turns but had to admit he was surprised that people did still identify with being working-class, although he still insisted jewellers and the unemployed weren't working-class.

One of the showdowns arranged for us was a clay pigeon shooting match. I used to be a dead shot, but since those days my eyes had gone. Also, foolishly, I was wearing a thin training jacket and the discharge from the modern over-and-under 12-bore was battering hell out of my thinly covered shoulder. The clays were coming over thick and fast and I didn't dey ower weel. Mind, neither did he; we ended up in a dead heat – though he swore I cheated! Said I sneaked an extra cartridge into the match, and just what did I shoot at – pillock? Mind, the biggest exchange and one that rattled cages nationwide came as we sat, guns in hand after the shoot-out. We fell to discussing the monarchy and I said outright that Princess Diana was murdered by the Windsor family. He was shocked. I repeated murdered by the monarchy and 75% of the population believe that to be true. (There had recently been a national *Daily Mirror* survey.) Amazingly, the statement went out to millions of homes unedited and Mr Fayed, owner of Harrods and father of the also murdered Dodi, heard it and later quoted outside the courts that even a miner on nationwide TV the other night knew what had really happened. Mind if he had known what Class War's take on the deaths had been he wouldn't have quoted me. I think myself that the *Class War* edition hailing the deaths as great fun was a fundamental mistake and a monumental loss of subversive opportunity. 'Another Murder For The Crown' or 'Diana Murdered By Royal Family' would have been a screaming headline which would have caught the grief of the nation, sold perhaps millions of copies and introduced a whole country to Class War. The paper would of course have had to explain why the monarchy is a parasitic, undemocratic, fetid and obscene institution, which should now be abolished.

The death of Diana could ironically have been turned into a movement against the monarchy per se; forelock-touching buffoons could have become staunch republicans, particularly since the Palace and Her Royal Selfness had distanced herself from any grief or regret. But we missed the boat; 'Haven't Stopped Laughing Yet' was the headline, which accompanied a leaked photo of the dying princess in the car. It not only missed the propaganda moment – it entirely missed the political point. I wasn't always happy with *Class War* headlines and themes. At times, though, they were aimed with deadly accuracy: 'The Real Queen Mum' was one, which exposed the poor old should-have-been queen, sister of the Queen Mother, who had been banged up in an institution and kept secret from the world, her existence unknown even to her sister. At other times the front was loose, flabby and unfocused, which for an anarchist tabloid, claiming the far-left mantle of the *Sun* in reverse, was fatal. The point was, really, that the team itself was at times politically highly unfocused. It sometimes put us completely on the wrong side of a deep and revolutionary analysis of issues and events.

Still, Class War wasn't claiming to be the brains behind the forthcoming revolution, but we did miss a huge opportunity with Diana's death. She was certainly murdered, of course, and by the state; acting on whose orders we may never know, though the reasons may be more evident. She was due to marry a Muslim Arab and her sons were next in line for the throne. What would this do to Middle East politics, attitudes to Israel, American foreign policy, British complicity in anti-Arab causes and pro-Zionist connections? Enough, it can be concluded, to get rid of the troublesome princess with a growing political interest and progression to unpopular causes. Of course the British royal family, so called, had been bumping each other off and standing behind power struggles across Europe, causing wars and mass murder, for centuries, so in a way, what was new?[377]

IN THE YEAR 2000

13 January. My old marra and inspiration, a veteran of the famous, mining folk singing Elliott family, secular freethinker, radical socialist, poet, songwriter and singer Pete Elliott dies. Although never a miner himself, he was born and lived in the heart and soul of the coal communities. Boy, he was a fighter. I loved that aud bloke. He criticised my *Power To The Imagination* mercilessly, just as me dad would have done, not because of its politics, but because of its 'bad grammar and poor spelling'. He thought the working class had to aspire to the best possible performance in all things, especially in print or on screen. Me Dad had made much the same points about my use of words like 'bliddy' while on TV. Pete's wife Pat phoned to tell me, when I was out, and left me the devastating message of his death. They had been regular visitors to Hatfield and knew the miners from many socials and galas at which they all sang. The funeral on 25 January is a secular one, commemorating his life and accepting his death. His coffin is piped in by Colin Ross, with his Northumbrian pipes, playing 'Rap Her Ti Bank", which the massed ranks of friends and singers from around the country join in with in total harmony, skilled of years of folk club choruses. The whole sendoff is marked by the most wonderful traditional music. I feel 'hyme' among my ain folk as they say.

> *Rap her ti bank me canny lad*
> *Wind her away keep turning*
> *The back shift men are gaan yem*
> *They'll be back in the morning.*

July 2000. Arthur launches a one-man coup against the *Yorkshire Area* of the

NUM. He is now reinstalled in the top desk, acting as chair, although that whole manoeuvre under the 'transfer of engagements' (when the Yorkshire Area fused with the National Union as a constituent body) had been quite a tricky deal in the first place. In preparation for the creation a single national union, it had been agreed at the Durham Conference; areas would fuse, and transfer engagements with the National Union as a body. Foolishly, this had been my resolution, which I had won the Area to and spoke for at Conference. Its effect far from being one of empowering the members and displacing layers of bureaucracy gave Arthur the reigns of power in the Yorkshire Area, and a seat of power from which to dominate the whole Union. He now resolves that our rulebook is out of date and brings forward an entirely new rulebook drafted exclusively by him. Its main plank is to take out features of rank-and-file control and intervention. Not least, it removes the panels, those quasi-official sources of branch alliances and direct rank-and-file control. They were developed at first as unofficial bodies to stop the development of Executive Committee rule over the Union. The branches, officials and committee members and whomever else they invited would meet without any of the area officials present, and without any formal control, to discuss the affairs of the Union, challenge the rules and views of the area and National officials and to hold their executive members to recall and account. The new rulebook united the Council for the first time in total and unanimous rejection of the new rules. We had asked if the members, and the[378] branches, could put forward amendments and suggestions for changes in this new rulebook. 'Of course,' declares Arthur, but only if they are in line with the terms of his new draft. When we fail to agree Arthur takes the issue to the NEC, where he barefacedly declares that the Yorkshire Area 'delegates refused to accept his ruling in respect of the NUM Yorkshire Area standing orders … ' He 'reminded the Committee [the NEC] of his responsibility in accordance with Rule 11a to ensure that the business of the Union is conducted in a proper manner and in accordance with rule.'[379] He points to a set of rules he helped to draft earlier for the National Union: 'In any dispute between an Area and the National Union as to the meaning of any rule the view of the president shall stand.' Well it wasn't even applicable to this case, but they voted in favour; many said they were told that was the rule. Arthur had ruled that all the existing rules were now out of date, and only his new rules could be applicable. 'The President explained that Group Meetings – known as Panel Meetings – no longer had any relevance or standing within the Standing Orders and must be deleted.'[380] The two facts, (a) that the whole Area's representative body felt that panels had so much relevance and standing they were prepared to vote to a man to defy him, and (b) that the only reason panel meetings were not in the new standing orders was that he, Arthur Scargill, had unilaterally written them out, had escaped the great man's understanding. There was not the slightest idea in Arthur's mind that *he* should in fact bow to the will of the whole Yorkshire Area representatives rather than that *they* – Area officials, branch delegates, secretaries from every single branch, representing all the Yorkshire miners – must bow to his will. The new rules also drafted a typical Arthurian tautology: 'The Model Rules must be the rules: any amendment to the rules proposed can only be constitutional if they conform to the model rules.' In other words, you can't in fact change them! This was demonstrated when Kellingley and Maltby and others tried to reinsert the provision for panel meetings into the rulebook. Arthur ruled the proposals out of order as this was an attempt to establish 'unofficial bodies' and in fact the panel meetings had been unofficial bodies ever since 1995: when the Area Executive Committee was abolished, the purpose of the panel (ostensibly to discuss a report from the EC) went also.[381,382] He affixes to the NEC agenda minute 6, Yorkshire Area Standing Orders, that

> a Special (Emergency) Yorkshire Area Council Meeting held on 5 June 2000 refused to accept his [AS's] ruling in respect of the NUM (Yorkshire Area) Standing Orders and therefore it was necessary for him to make a report to the NEC ... A Yorkshire Area representative asked if it would be possible for the Yorkshire Area to amend Standing Orders (Appendix C). The President pointed out that amendments to Standing Orders (Appendix C) would be considered provided they did not conflict with either the Transfer of Engagements instruments or the Union's National Rules[383]

– both of which he himself had drawn up. Any rational organisational body would start to hear alarm bells ringing that in effect the biggest area of the NUM was at issue with just one man, who sat in the National president's chair and at the same time was trying to run the entire Yorkshire Area in unanimous opposition to the views of the elected representatives. Three of the NEC abstained! One voted against, and five voted to support Arthur's view and instruct the Yorkshire Area to follow Arthur's ruling. It was noteworthy that two of the Yorkshire Area's NEC members who were traditionally Arthur loyalists were absent from the meeting, as well as the Yorkshire Area general secretary, probably because the clear view of the area they represented ran against the political and personal loyalties to Arthur and so they, rather than face down the conflict of loyalties, found reasons not to attend. None of the Yorkshire delegation, and there were, despite the absences, three in attendance, voted to support Arthur's view. In June, the Yorkshire Area had 2,300 members; of the representatives from the other Areas on the NEC, Ken Hollingsworth of COSA had 277, Billy Kelly of Lancashire had 3, Ian Lavery of North East had 195, Keith Stanley of Nottingham 199, and Idwal Morgan of the Cokemen 126. Collectively they represented 800 workers against Yorkshire's 2,300. If the NEC itself had been democratic enough to operate a card vote system the Yorkshire Area view would have prevailed.[384] No one seems to have questioned what things were coming to when there was a total rebellion by an area against the solitary view of one man, albeit the National president.

The other totally vexatious part of Arthur's new set of rules was that our standing orders talked about an Area general secretary, as well as they might: the Area had always had an Area secretary. Arthur argued that it no longer had an Area secretary as an official. He argued that somehow by sleight of hand we had agreed that we would no longer have a full-time Area secretary after Ken Homer had gone out redundant. Of course, we had never agreed any such thing and not one person in the Area Union could be found to accept that we had agreed or intended any such thing. We pointed to Frank Cave as the Area general secretary; Arthur with a flourish then ruled:

Since 1994, the NUM (Yorkshire Area) has operated with one full-time official, namely F. W. Cave who is identified in the Standing Orders as *Chairman* of the Area and Secretary to the National Delegate Meeting.[385]

BUT, we all howled, that is only in the draft you have drawn up and not in the standing orders we have been working to. Further, if there have to be new standing orders we want to draft in features of the old standing orders we like and wish to keep, like an Area secretary and panels.

No, rules Arthur, such standing orders wouldn't be in line with the model standing orders *that he had drawn up*.

I am next summoned to Arthur's office where he tells me I will no longer represent the Area at appeals and tribunals and will no longer be paid for any work by the Area Union. It is a bitter blow and one I will struggle to surmount. I had not been on a great income prior to this decision but I could guarantee 2 or 3 days' wages a week from the Area. He tells me I should hand over all the casework to Raleys, who will instead send one of their own solicitors to represent the cases. In fact, no one but myself ever appears at inquests or medical boards and I do this at my own expense. Arthur informs me he has asked Raleys to consider having me represent the tribunals on their behalf rather than Harry Eyre, their top industrial lawyer. It would certainly be more cost-effective and consistent. They decline this offer, I am told for 'political' reasons – although the only politics in their business is the internal struggles within the Union and their impact on the firm.

Meantime a huge bureaucratic manoeuvre is being prepared behind closed doors in the NEC. It is agreed to include limited members' votes in the votes of areas when there are card votes. A number of grave injustices are inbuilt in this decision. First, the limited member is no longer associated with a specific branch, which he used to attend, or the nearest branch, which he can attend. He is a member in name only; he cannot express a view as to which way 'his' vote is cast. Second, the 'limited member' in the vast majority of cases is not actually paying subs at the time his vote is being cast; his payment is deferred until and unless his compensation claim is completed.

This means not only that a man whose case falls is not and never has been a member, because he only pays back money on successful cases; it means a person effectively not a member of the Union is now being allocated a vote. It means that a deceased member who was dead before the claim was submitted or died during the process of its running is also accredited a vote. Limited membership was extended to people not only who were no longer members, but who had never been members and never worked in or at a pit. As if that wasn't bad enough, the actual votes of these limited members were to be cast at the discretion of the Area president; in the case of the biggest area that is Arthur Scargill. Without consultation with any of these 'limited members' it also came to mean that the residue of cases which were being handled at the National Office for want of somewhere else to process them were also cast at the sole discretion of the National president – not allocated to areas on a pro rata basis, but cast by him, in this case also Arthur Scargill. It meant that on contentious and hotly fought issues of democratic principle, where the branches for or against a particular proposal were evenly balanced, the votes were cast in a totally partisan fashion to swing the vote behind the view of their Area or National president – in both cases Arthur Scargill.

It was in simple terms a disgraceful manipulation. If there had been an overwhelming desire to allow limited members to vote, they could have done it, actually, by being allocated to local branches as they had previously been. They could then have come to meetings, heard the arguments, given their own opinions and voted to influence the branch policy and overall vote. Even if this procedure had not been carried out, the branches where members actually voted could have debated and decided on the issue, and the limited members' votes could have been attached to the Area vote AFTER the decision was made – they would not then have been used to influence the internal vote. It would still have been undemocratic, but less so than the travesty which was about to be unleashed.

The manoeuvre was one we vowed to fight to the bloody end. It split the Union, and our past comradeships, more deeply than any other issue.[386]

July 2000. The NUM Conference at Blackpool presents the Yorkshire delegation with an opportunity to try and take back some of its own decision-making. The pre-Conference review of the agenda, where all the last-minute to-ing and fro-ing between areas takes place, sees Arthur absent and instead Kevin Malloy who is pro-Scargill in the chair, but without any block vote, and his branch are represented by a more independent voice.

Kevin was a person perhaps more than any of the others who was used and dispensed with in the scramble for power. Set up as Yorkshire Area president he wasn't even allowed to park in the Area Offices and spent ages searching the surrounding streets for a place to park, before he could open the Area meetings. Since he was the Area president, who can have made such a decision?

The North East Area has a resolution in, calling for the restoration of Annual Conferences. As stated earlier we had never actually agreed as an area to Biennial Conferences. A number of branches such as Hatfield who didn't happen to have officials on the NEC weren't represented. The Yorkshire Area as such had always been against Biennial Conferences and so the delegation decided to support the resolution, indeed that I should second it on behalf of the Area. When Arthur found out later that night, he went ballistic and set off round the hotel bars to find the culprits. He found me and we had a blazing row. He told me delegations couldn't change Area policy. I argued that was true, Area policy had been against Biennial Conferences and no NEC subgroup could change that position. He said the Area had endorsed it and 'nobody, and that means you too,' opposed that. I vowed that was untrue and that I would oppose Biennial Conferences with my last breath. I would never have let it go. He then sends off for his secretary to pull up the minutes of the meeting of this Area Council, which, it seems, was on the cusp of the Christmas break. 'The Special Delegate Conference' decision had indeed been endorsed. But who by? I doubted that I had ever been at such a Council and I doubted that most other delegates had either, unless it was one of those slipped through with a stack of other business and taken as endorsed 'on the nod', as was becoming increasingly the case. When it came to the floor of Conference, our delegates got up to support the North East resolution, while Kevin Malloy cast the Area's vote against![387] Under the NEC report on Affiliations, I get up to denounce the ongoing farce of the IEMO and our £20,000 per year affiliation costs. Arthur in his summing up of the Conference announced that I had been 'the only discordant voice' at an otherwise harmonious Conference. I was sure however that I hadn't been the only rain on his parade, though this Conference was another of those for which the verbatim report has not been circulated and I am reliant on my own notes and memory.[388]

October 2000. Scargill discovers the internet and our website (*www.minersadvice.co.uk*).[389] From now on he goes into overdrive to shut us down:

> I note with deep concern that you are also reporting on National Union of Mineworkers internal matters and meetings of the NUM … clearly in breach of rule and an act detrimental to the interests of the Union.

This is the language of expulsion; it is the kind of homing-in focus he has used on other occasions with other people. His whole endeavour of late has been to drive me out of the Union, stop my influence and opposition to his egocentric, bureaucratic schemes. He wants the Advice Centre closing and is livid we are actually producing this website, which was at that time discussing the battle raging at Rossington Colliery and the less than firm support from the Barnsley office. We were exposing what was going on with the rulebook and the attack upon members' control of the Union. I had also commented on the withdrawal of wages and loss of earnings which had befallen me. To this, Arthur responds in a disgraceful low-blow attack: 'You are not employed, having taken voluntary redundancy from the industry.'

Voluntary redundancy? We had fought to an utterly exhausted standstill and still I had tried to rally a last-ditch stand. The pit had closed, there had been no transfers, I had been made redundant. I would never have chosen it, and damn well he knew that, but knew, too, what a slur it was to be accused of having 'sold your job'. All the men working at Hatfield and Rossington and at pits all over the country on 'lease and licence' were on exactly the same basis as myself. We had all been made redundant and were all full and active members of the Union in the now privatised industry.[390]

'Your actions clearly violate Rule 18.D (vi) and (vii) of the unions rules and it is my intention to submit a report to both the National Executive Committee and the Yorkshire Area Council.'[391] I replied to Arthur and warned that after more than 30 years as an active and loyal member of the Union I wasn't going to make it easy for him if he was going to go down this road, and it would become very bitter:

> I do not consider any of the redundancies at Hatfield voluntary. The

British Coal Corporation closed the mine, we had done everything bar shoot the bastards to keep it open but they ploughed ahead. You know the impact of the short term enhanced redundancies; it caused men to take what they could and not go through the review procedure. I wished this had not been the case, I and others tried to get the men to reject the offers but they did not feel able to, and I will not condemn them for that, they had been fought to a standstill and they gave everything flesh and blood could muster, nobody could have asked for more. In my own case I was actually getting to the point of no return with VWF seriously, I could no longer use vibration tools on a daily never mind hourly basis and had been confined to general dog's body on the 5 p.m. shift. My chances of transfer or re-employment with contractors given the state of my hands from vibration damage were nil. However, there were no transfers all bar two – one man from Selby who was a crane driver and the medical room attendant; no others were offered. There would be no transfer fees, no transport, and at that time I didn't drive. So even if I had been offered a transfer, and as I say nobody was, I couldn't have taken it. I do not consider any of the above to be VOLUNTARY by anyone's use of the term. My circumstances in this regard are little different than any other man at Hatfield or Rossington and what this actually has to do with my being employed or not I do not see.[392]

This is followed up by the circulation of the following statement:

NEC DECISION

THE NATIONAL EXECUTIVE COMMITTEE AT ITS MEETING ON 9TH NOVEMBER HAVE UNANIMOUSLY AGREED THAT DAVID DOUGLASS AS A NUM BRANCH OFFICIAL AND UNION MEMBER SHOULD BE INSTRUCTED THAT ALL AND ANY CORRESPONDENCE/DOCUMENTS CONCERNING THE NUM –WHICH IS OBTAINED FROM EITHER ATTENDANCE AT NUM MEETINGS OR REPORTS FROM NUM MEETINGS-MUST BE DELETED IMMEDIATELY FROM HIS WEB SITE.

THE NATIONAL EXECUTIVE COMMITTEE ALSO UNANIMOUSLY AGREE THAT IN FUTURE IF DAVID DOUGLASS REPRODUCES ON HIS WEB SITE OR ANY OTHER WEBSITE MATERIAL, LETTERS, DOCUMENTS, OR INFORMATION OBTAINED OR ARISING FROM NUM BRANCH MEETINGS, AREA COUNCIL MEETINGS, NATIONAL EXECUTIVE COMMITTEE MEETINGS OR ANY OTHER SOURCE WITHIN THE UNION, THEN THE NEC WILL IMMEDIATELY TAKE ACTION AGAINST HIM IN ACCORDANCE WITH RULE.

WE AS A FOUR-MAN SUB COMMITTEE WILL RECOMMEND THAT DAVE DOUGLASS CLOSES 'THE MINING COMMUNITY ADVICE CENTRE' AND IN FUTURE ANY ADVICE MUST EMANATE FROM THE HATFIELD MAIN BRANCH AND BE IN LINE WITH NUM POLICY.[393]

The full report of the issue actually states:

The Committee also made clear that this website should be closed down particularly as it carried advice to members and non-members alike that they should contact the Advice Centre ...[394]

The suggestion was that the Advice Centre was operating instead of the NUM and against the NUM. Arthur knew damn well it wasn't, but knew it operated ex officio to the Branch as well as in the service of the Branch. It was the worst kind of creature in his eyes: it was totally outside his control. The NEC hadn't it seems been made aware of the full-screen adverts to join the NUM, the contact details of all NUM branches and areas and the NUM-approved solicitors and services and the clear advice, then as well as now, that claimants should seek the support of the NUM. Truth was, most of them didn't know how to read the website or draw down its information. That was hardly the point as far as Arthur was concerned: we were discussing policy, debating issues, distributing facts and information that the members could read without caveats and controls – that was the real cause of disagreement.

November 2000. I am hauled before a disciplinary committee of the NEC. I have resisted all pressure to shut down the website. I do not believe even Arthur Scargill and the NEC of the NUM are powerful enough to shut down the internet, or stop the rank and file using it. I am sitting stewing in the waiting area outside the big presidential office upstairs in Arthur's Castle, while the wise and strong of the NEC deliberate. Then, in my head, I hear the refrains of Jock Purdon, at first distant:

Don't let the bastards grind you down boys.
Don't let the bastards grind you down.

And it came to me:

When you're fighting the fat cats,
Yes, all the union bureaucrats.
No don't let the buggers grind you down.

And I stood up and started to sing:

Don't let the bastards grind you down boys,
Don't let the bastards grind you down.
When you're standing for what's right
Stand your ground, keep up the fight.
No, don't let the bastards grind you down.

And I started to pace up and down singing, me heart filling with confidence and strength. By the time they opened the door, I swung in there like the Red Army entering Berlin.

Thanks, Jock.

First bloke to say owt was aud Billy Kelly from the Lancashire Area. 'I want you to know, Dave,' he says, 'that I am proud to be associated with you lad, proud of the things you have stood for over the years and proud of the way you stick to your principles.' Well, that was quite a revelation, and others joined in with similar thoughts, while I thought Arthur looked rather taken aback. Mr Morgan from the Cokemen assured me, 'There is nothing sinister here Dave, we are a committee to find out about the website and this Advice Centre of yours – we are not here to punish you or nothing like that.' Then we got down to it, as Arthur let loose his reams of complaints. He had had his 'executive officer' run off copies from the website. 'There's nothing here about the NUM, David, this is an independent operation.'

'That's just the front page, Arthur, see all those squares down the side, you have to click on them and they open up all those sections, they show NUM services across the country, they give NUM information and contact addresses, it advertises the NUM lawyers. If you're going to hang me for a website at least understand how to read the bliddy thing.'

His EO gets sent off to run more of the pages from the site off, while I explain the work of the Community Advice Centre. It is voluntary, it is funded by donations, it is used by the NUM but not controlled by them. When the pages come back, he homes in on the entry about the death of Terry French. When Arthur doesn't like something, he always has secret and hidden reasons why he knows things and you don't. In hushed tones, he tells us Terry's murder is still being investigated. There might be more to it and I shouldn't just blast it out on the pages of the website.

At this point, I cry out: 'Had on a minute, dinnet try and use Terry against me. Terry was my mate and comrade, if he was in this room he'd be sitting alongside me, not with you buggers. The piece on Terry is an act of solidarity to inform all his comrades of the tragedy, it's not a secret, it's been in the national press anyway.'

But things get worse. Since Arthur had decreed I was no longer employed and could not receive loss of earnings any more, I had nonetheless continued to attend inquests and medical boards. The death certificates and PM reports for our fallen comrades were essential in processing claims for posthumous awards for the miner's widow and family. I had sent the bill in to the Finance Office, usually £2 a certificate. Arthur then instructed the Finance Office NOT to pay for the death certificates or PM reports. I wrote in utter disbelief:

> ... I am told you will not pay for the PM reports I have ordered. If this is correct, can you explain why? Every day seems to carry a new restriction on the work I do for coal communities. I am at a loss to understand your motivation.[395]

Arthur replies:

> If you do any work, which is not authorised by the NUM Area or the NEC, then the responsibility must lie with the Hatfield Branch or you personally.
>
> I trust that you now understand the situation and that you will cease sending any letters which are in complete conflict with your undertaking to carry out Union instructions.[396]

From now on, in I pay for the PM and death certificates myself. I think this is the lowest ebb in my relations with Arthur. I do not enjoy conflict, despite my life; I do not enjoy adversity and hostility, I am by nature a conciliator; that I should be at war with Arthur Scargill of all people sickens me. But we stand in different corners of a political arena of the left; this is about ideology and principle. It would not be the first time people of Arthur's political persuasion and my own have clashed, and over similar points of principle, albeit on much bigger political canvasses.

November 30. I take my Second Dan and achieve a first-class pass. A FIRST CLASS PASS from Alan Rushby is quite an achievement and one of which I am duly proud.

THE BORTH O THE BAIRN

Emma gives birth, in Doncaster Royal Infirmary, to Caitlin Angel Rodgers. Both are well. Paul is as happy as I have ever seen him, as are his folks, Maureen, and me. Words fail me, I could just cry from relief and happiness that both are fit, well, and beautiful. I am to be given the greatest job of my life: Emma and Paul would like me to look after the baby 2 days a week until she starts school. The part-time work for the Union and the Advice Centre brings in just enough money to live on, but affords me 2 days per week free now that Arthur has stopped the work I previously did for the Area. It is the best possible use I could ever have for my time. Our bonds and love grow deep and strong. She will over the coming years be a constant companion, as we play and swim, skate, read and travel. I have loved that girl since the first moment I seen her in her Mam's arms. I love her joy, her sheer bliss at being alive.

YORKSHIRE AREA COUNCIL MEETING, 22 JANUARY 2001

Arthur has agenda'd 'David Douglass Hatfield NUM Website'. He is still trying to stop our discussion of the political and democratic struggles within the Union and industry, but he has dropped a bollock this time. As the meeting opens, I raise a point of order on behalf of the Hatfield Main Branch. Frank Cave is in the chair and asks what my point of order is. Hatfield Main NUM Branch does not have a website, never has had a website and has no intention of developing one. We cannot discuss something that doesn't exist. Arthur chips in: 'Well it's somebody's website.' 'Sorry, Arthur,' I responded, 'It isn't agenda'd "Somebody's Website", it's out of order,' and Frank, laughing, is forced to agree.

The steam is rising out of Arthur's ears as he insists the matter isn't over yet. Further on the agenda we come to another item under Correspondence: 'Attendances at Conferences and Council Meetings – D. Douglass'. Arthur formally had ruled that since I am not employed I cannot have a loss of earnings and therefore I will no longer be able to claim my day's wage for attending any NUM Council or Conference meetings. I am already on the breadline. Again I raise a point of order: 'This letter instructing them that I will no longer be able to afford to attend wasn't written to the Council, doesn't come from a branch, had no branch stamp, isn't a resolution, and has no constitutional place on this agenda.'

Arthur insists that if the Hatfield Branch does not attend we are breaking the rules; I respond that our president Mr Nixon when he can get time off work from Hatfield Coal Company will attend; I will be confining myself to the duties of secretary. I have already decided that if any further attempt is made to close the Advice Centre or discipline me I will resign from my position and the Union if necessary, affiliate the Advice Centre to the IWW as such and run it as an IWW advice centre on the same financial basis as I was doing. We had already discussed it as a Branch and the minutes show we were on the verge of disaffiliation as a Branch. We considered affiliating the Hatfield Miners to the IWW if push comes to shove. I had all of that in my back pocket and had already warned Frank that I was on the verge of breaking free from the restrictions, which were everywhere now, trying to stop me doing my job and following my vocation. The NUM was not more important than the miners and the task of representing them and the community.

Heated exchanges followed, with resolutions from the floor that the Area should formally employ me and that those branches should use me as a tribunal rep, and Arthur insisting it wasn't necessary – Raleys solicitors would handle anything I did. Jeff Stubbs, the long-suffering left executive and leading member of our unformalised 'democratic alliance', warned that if David Douglass resigns from his position as Branch secretary at Hatfield then, quicker than you can think, Hatfield Main Branch will fold. 'David Douglass is the administration and inspiration for all Union activity at Hatfield and if anybody at that top table had ever been out there during the time they have been fighting for unionisation and recognition they would know that.' The matter was allowed to pass, for now. The disputes were to get worse.

March. The fiery leader of the Yorkshire region of COSA (Colliery Officials and Staffs Association, the 'professional and white collar section' of the NUM) now falls into the cross-hairs of the National president. David Murdoch is to be disciplined for his involvement with the Yorkshire Compensation Recovery Scheme. This had been a private operation set up in consultation with and with some funding from the Doncaster MBC. It was also operating in full view of the NUM and had staged joint workshops with us. The aim was to make sure miners didn't miss common-law damages and benefits for hand and arm vibration syndrome and chest diseases. A huge vacuum had existed because Arthur was reluctant to fund a strong battle for the claims, for fear they fell flat. Into the vacuum had come YCRS. I had been the only other person offering advice and representation in Doncaster and guiding people to the NUM. David shared an office space with YCRS but he dealt with the NUM members and the non- and ex-members were directed to YCRS. To be right, it was run by Davie's daughter. Only when the full extent of the claims started to emerge, and solicitors and general legal oddjobmen started jumping on the bandwagon, was it clear these claims were a licence to print money. Then, and only then, the NUM officially claimed hegemony over all miners and former miners and anybody else for that matter. This brought the official Union into conflict with YCRS and Dave as a serving official of the Union into conflict over his involvement with them. Dave was referred to the National Disciplinary Committee, suspended from his position and generally became persona non grata. He was heading for expulsion.[397]

THE SCREW TIGHTENS

July 2001. I turn up with all my tax and National Insurance details, statements from the Inland Revenue and copies of the minutes employing me as the Hatfield Main Branch secretary, and welfare rights worker for the Advice Centre. Arthur is able to bamboozle the meeting that this isn't the same as being 'employed' by the mining companies and therefore doesn't count. Life has suddenly got infinitely harder. The Branch decides it cannot afford for one of the days it pays me to be spent at Barnsley, as that isn't the priority for them. I stop attending Council meetings and for months Hatfield is unrepresented. I am the only delegate from a working mine anywhere in the country who cannot claim loss of earnings for attending the meetings of the Union. The Council is evenly split between, on one side, our democratic opposition forces and, on the other, the Scargill sycophants, most of whom have their eyes on Union positions and see Arthur's patronage as a step up that ladder.

At length Maltby Branch very loyally agree to pay my shift attending the Council meetings and also pay me for representing their members at appeals and tribunals, which saves the day somewhat but greatly increases the antagonism between their officials and the Area officials. There are concerted efforts to bring Maltby back into the loyalist camp and out of the ranks of the dissidents.

Rossington Colliery votes for all-out strike action. At the end of 8 weeks the law allows the employer to sack the entire workforce. Cleverly, the Branch ballots again while still on strike and again wins a further spell of all-out strike action without loss of legal immunity. After 3 months on strike, Rossington is still standing alone, failing to win the sort of support it expected from the Area. They go back to work without settlement, utterly pissed off with the Union. For a time the Rossington officials fight an internal sniping war with the Yorkshire officials and they join the growing ranks of our dissidents.

EQUAL VALUE

The Union concludes its long-running equal-value claims on behalf of the canteen women. We had first submitted these in 1977. The UDM had tried to embarrass the NUM by signing a deal on behalf of the canteen women who it said it represented, although the claim predated the UDM's existence by a decade and more. They settled for £1,000 each across the board regardless of service. British Coal assumed that all the women on hold with the NUM claim would now start battering our doors down to settle for the same amount. It didn't happen; the women on advice from the Union stuck to their guns and wouldn't budge. By 9 2001 April British Coal had conceded a minimum of £3,000 lump sum to any person, part-time or full-time, regardless of years worked. That was the bottom line; the rate was paid at £1,000 per year of service, with top payments of £40,000 and the average of £10,000. All the 'UDM' women had now to do was transfer their claim and their membership to the NUM at no cost to them. This was quite some coup for the Union and it wasn't long before Peter Hain acting for the government agreed 'ex-gratia' to give the UDM cases the same settlement as the NUM despite the fact that they had agreed a fraction of the compensation on their behalf.

But the coup de grâce was when the government agreed to pay all the NUM's legal costs and lost back-subs that the women would otherwise have been due to pay from their compensation. More than £1.7 million in contributions, and £600,000 in legal costs, came back from the government coffers and into NUM funds. It was probably the best piece of negotiation Arthur presided over in his whole career, although the chief legal negotiator had been the hard-working Danny O'Conner, a man of monk-like quiet endeavour.

It was work well done, but across the coalfields there was hell on. Thousands of former canteen workers were not included in the settlement. How they had fallen from the case I have never been able to establish. It had something to do with the claim changing its basis from 'sex discrimination', to 'equal value', with a test number of cases and comparators and God knows what else. Eventually a load of women, who had worked side-by-side with the ones being awarded the money, had ended up with nothing. Arthur had gained an informal agreement from Hain that these women too would be made an 'ex-gratia' payment – one would have thought for common justice with the one granted unprompted to the 'UDM' cases. It never came. The women were outraged and staged noisy demonstrations in all the miners' regions. It must be said that quite a number of these women were never in the Union, although most had been.

Arthur tried all kinds of guile and charm to get Hain to concede on moral grounds the case of the others who had been legalistically excluded. He pointed out that the massive boost in compensation given to the UDM claimants had no legal basis whatsoever – it had been a moral judgement. Arthur asked for the same moral judgement to be extended to the other women, but it has never been forthcoming. It was and is a shame, which put the damper on an outstanding victory. Worse still, unprincipled Labour MPs in some of the coalfields, in order to save government blushes and doubtless their own seats, tried to blame the NUM for the debacle. They claimed we had taken our eye off the ball and not transferred all the claims from one legal premise to the other. Actually if my memory serves me right we had been told at every stage that the cases we were running were purely sample, test-case comparators and that when we won for them all the other cases would be conceded by legal precedent. Some change in the law, and the passage of time, however, had invalidated that guarantee, and what with a civil war raging in our backyard, the sequestration of our funds, a state-led character assassination of our National leaders, and the virtual wiping out of our Union and industry, yes, it is possible someone in our war-torn offices didn't notice that the ground had shifted.

Arthur strongly denied that the NUM was mistaken in any of this; the fact that these same 'Labour' MPs were telling the women the NUM ought to pay their compensation doubtless forced him to. There is no doubt in my mind that the UDM cases were conceded without legal obligation, while the unregistered NUM cases were not, because the Blair government did not want to hand the NUM a moral and political victory over the Tory scab yellow-dog union of the

UDM. They were happy to tip the scales back in the direction of the UDM in order to weaken the authority of the NUM in a policy continued without the slightest variance since Thatcher's day, and government civil servants still carried the same unchanged brief in this regard.

That was the reason why the government would not concede to the NUM (who represented the vast bulk of miners and even more retired and ex-miners), a claims-handling agreement to allow the Union to legally process and financially benefit from the hundreds of thousands of HAVS and chest disease claims, while the UDM with a fraction of the workforce and even less retired and former miners *was* conceded that status. It had damned the NUM cases to third-party legal action through the proxy of outside legal firms, while the UDM by contrast had established a legal business which trawled the country picking up thousands of unsuspecting miners' claims. It had netted them a multi-million-pound fortune and in the process made for the officials of the UDM, Thatcher's grand strikebreaking lieutenants, fortunes beyond the dreams of working men.

Under New Labour, the UDM HQ in Mansfield had been given a £200,000 fund from the DTI to improve its buildings for official government medical testing for all claimants in Nottingham.[398] At the same time, the huge Barnsley NUM HQ was denied the right to become the official medical centre even without any grants from the government. This injustice had continued without the slightest blip on Thatcher's instructions through all the years of the Blair government with their full knowledge and approval. John Battle, the New Labour coal minister, refused (in 1997) to even discuss such a claims-handling agreement with the NUM, but had allowed the DTI to conclude an agreement with 'The Solicitors Group', who represented nobody but themselves, and then with the UDM themselves and their legal persona Vendside. It wasn't until all but the lamest and oldest horses had bolted, the fortunes had been made and the UDM copper-bottomed with compensation revenues that the NEC in January of 2001 was able to report that Helen Liddell had agreed to discuss the matter. Following her, Peter Hain, the next minister with responsibility for the coal industry, had expressed total surprise at this bias; apparently Helen hadn't taken the complaint too far, though it was all now too late to do us any good or them (the UDM) any harm.[399]

April. Arthur and the NUM decide to run a CAC (the Central Arbitration Committee, the independent body adjudicating on applications relating to the recognition and derecognition of trade unions) case on Union recognition at Hatfield. It is a shock straight out of the blue. Neither the Branch nor I was consulted. We had at this stage only 30% of the workforce represented and we knew that if we failed we should be debarred from bringing another claim for years, no matter how many members we had in the meantime. It was tactically stupid. Arthur phones me up 2 days before the tribunal to ask if I want to attend. At that notice I can't. The other officials are working, and its being an anti-union pit they aren't going to get time off work. The CAC rules that it will NOT allow a ballot at the pit for Union recognition as the Union hadn't demonstrated that the workers were dissatisfied with the existing arrangements. [400]

May 2001. Arthur runs for the Socialist Labour Party against Peter Mandelson to be MP for Hartlepool. It is a battle between Old and New Labour, for roots working-class socialism and Blair's brand of Labour Conservatism. Given the constituency and the foul smell around Mandelson I would have thought Scargill would have romped home. However, there is bad blood between steelmaking and mining, a legacy of 12 months of scabbing, with justification for it sought through a continuous attack upon Arthur and the NUM by the media, the politicians and the steel union. Some of that old shit still sticks. Arthur loses; a monkey is also challenging the position and it secures a healthy vote, but it is Blair's monkey who wins.

ORGREAVE REVISITED

June. We restage the Battle of Orgreave. An amazing project by the art company Artangel director and producer Jeremy Deller to restage that historic event. He wanted me to do the political and historic commentary and overview, although I also do some on-site instruction and guidance and can't resist getting stuck into the ranks of riot-shielded re-enactors. Most of these are usually Vikings, Romans or Cromwellian troops, but we have a crowd of about 100 miners and one or two former cops from the period. The miners are continually warned and reminded that the guys in the uniforms are not real cops and too much force is being used against them. We are each paid £100 per day for restaging the battle; as one of the Barnsley lads commented in the thick of the battle, 'When we did this forst time it were for £1 per day and bag of sandwiches.' We were warned early on in the day that anyone using excessive force would be escorted from the scene and not paid his fee. As the line of long-shield units come marching toward us, banging their shields with their truncheons, and the old memory swept to the fore, the blood begins to boil and the hair stands on your neck in preparation for letting go. A former miner shouts 'Fuck their £100, lads, let's have these bastards!' and into the thick we dive.

19 November 2001. The first premier screening of *The Battle Of Orgreave*. It is at the Odeon, Leicester Square. Some of the lads have got dressed up and brought their wives. It is a big celebrity do with Tony Benn and lots of 'stars' of the left theatre, TV and politics in the audience. I am there with Emma, chuffed to wee bits. I think it was a terrific undertaking. The Yorkshire preview will be in Sheffield for those who can't afford to get down to London (they aren't paying any overnights).

9/11 – DAY OF JUDGMENT

I was flying from I think Thailand, but was anyway on a long-haul flight and waiting in the departure lounge bar, when on every channel we see repeatedly this image of planes flying into the Twin Towers in New York. It is like a recurring advert or trailer for some product, over and over again. I can't make out the sound coverage so it is hard to understand what has been done to whom by whom. Then the truth bit by bit is revealed – at least the truth they have allowed to be revealed, because there are very worrying loose ends which the US state has simply ignored.

Michael Moore did an excellent exposé of these: worrying connections between the agents of the bombers and the American state and its secret service; the perpetrators of the attack having been let loose and given their heads; their political and religious gurus having been allowed to leave every situation in which they could have been captured; and their nearest and dearest having been the only foreigners – certainly the only Arabs – allowed to fly out of the country even while every airport in the land was closed down tight as a box. The al-Qaeda attack had been sponsored and supported by rich Saudis. Fundamentalists from Pakistan and Afghanistan, the shock troops of political Islamism, had initially been trained, armed and financed through the CIA and the US state directly in their war against Afghan socialism and its Soviet military defenders. They had been covertly armed and financed through Oliver North in his shady deals with the mullahs of Iran and contras in Nicaragua. All of this had been done in an effort to use the political distortions of medievalist religion against anything that smacked of 'socialism' or genuine people's democracy.

Now the beast had turned, and struck without the slightest compassion for innocent Americans. There are legitimate violent responses to American imperialism and its enforcement of global poverty and reaction, but this wasn't a progressive attack, and to Al Qaeda there are no innocent Americans, indeed there are few innocent anybodies anywhere – Christian, Jew, atheist or Muslim. The attacks were timed to kill the maximum number of ordinary American people in the early morning rush hours. For the hapless occupants of the aeroplanes, the families with their little children by their sides being taken to their deaths in the cruellest and most heartless fashion, the period of execution must have been agonising and heartbreaking.

Did the US state know who had attacked them? Did they choose to retaliate against the reactionary political ideology they had helped to develop? No, they took the opportunity to start another war, a war without limit against Iraq, a state and a people who had nothing whatever to do with the attack. They simply played on the general political ignorance of the greater part of the US population who know not one end of the Middle East from the Midwest, and declared that Saddam had been responsible, and that Saddam was somehow hooked up with Bin Laden, his avowed enemy.

The more one looks at the horror of 9/11, its size and impact, the more one gets a tiny glimpse of what the start of our 'preemptive Soviet nuclear strike' would have looked like. We always said that the US masses would realise at once that US imperialism was responsible for the attack and would understand, imagining the chaos, the deaths, the destruction magnified a hundred and a thousand fold. I think we were probably deluding ourselves. But were we? As time has gone on, those recurring images, those symmetrically collapsing monoliths of corporate America and the masses of people within them and around them have posed many questions, disturbing questions. Not a single building expert or demolition expert in the world can explain how two aircraft flying into them could fell the massive Twin Towers so perfectly and symmetrically. In fact, the image is one of a classically controlled and expertly exercised demolition with planted charges, not an outside impact. They fell just where they stood, they came down in perfect detonated sequence, floor by floor.

One has only to look again at the way each building crumbles, in exactly the style of the civil demolition of chimneys, power station cooling towers and old high-rise structures. Are the explosive charges, which precipitate the start of the collapsing 'domino' sequence, heard by TV crews and recorded forever on tape, and taking place some time after the planes have done their worst? Or did someone make that up? If there were internal explosive charges already set, before the planes hit the building, when and why were they placed there? Was this a covert civil engineering contingency to allow the massive building to be demolished without damage to nearby premises, nothing to do with the subsequent highjacking and murder? If it was no one has owned up to it, and yet, it does look like a controlled civil engineering demolition, no matter how far-fetched that sounds.

The so-called commission on 9/11 didn't look at one piece of forensic evidence to ascertain how materially the damage and impact matched the attributed cause; it was simply taken as read, unlike any other MVA or crime scene. Satellite evidence now demonstrates that residual hotspots remained at 'ground zero' for over 5 days after the attacks; this is attributed to molten metal residues radiating through the collapse. The impact of a crashing airliner could not we are told by metallurgy experts generate enough heat to melt metal, but explosives and blast could. Dr David Griffins in his unstinting and highly dangerous work into this subject establishes if not what did happen, then without doubt what did not happen. Simply put, it would take more than these suicide bombers to do the damage done to the Twin Towers or the Pentagon.

Some now point the finger at Vice President Cheney and the so-called 'neo-cons' in the Pentagon, and the wish to bring about another Pearl Harbor, to outrage American opinion so deeply they would countenance what was to become a total war on the third world and the Middle East in particular, the creation of a new enemy to take the place of the old 'Evil Empire' which was communism and the USSR.

In another counter-twist to the story, though, and in order to rubbish the doubters of the official line, a group of nutcases have now taken over and developed the doubts into a well-publicised and much-maligned 'conspiracy theory' which claims there were no planes used on that day, that the planes were not flown into the buildings, that the helpless souls aboard the planes did not in fact get hijacked or die. The state-controlled press and media people around the world have leaked this 'theory' everywhere into the debate and superglued it to the original skeptical observations.

Needless to say, the presence of the planes, the hijacking and the deaths of the passengers are not seriously in question. But it seems that the plan to commit *an* act involving planes and hijacking was known about, and allowed to happen, and that the damage from the planes' impacts could not, unassisted, have achieved the mass destruction it is alleged to have done. In a sentence, there was high-level state indulgence with the attack. Does that mean they knew every detail, or foresaw the extent of the death and destruction? No, that degree of involvement would amount to greater complicity than I for one am suggesting.

What is certain from our side, from the side of armed revolutionary struggle, is that armed acts of 'terrorism' carried out by fundamentalist, political, Islamist jihadist on innocent men, women and children across the globe have certainly taken bombing off the armed-struggle agenda for the vast majority of revolutionary organisations. Our cause could never be furthered by being confused with *their* cause and most armed groups have concluded that the press and the media can't be relied upon to explain the difference in motives and targets. Al-Qaeda in the depth of its mad sincerity wishes to bomb us out of degeneracy, and into an Islamic non-pluralist world dedicated to the words of the prophet and the worship of Allah.

It is a medievalist tribal vision based upon total subservience of women as a sex, and the rejection of all forms of pluralist or communist ideology. The word of God as interpreted from the Qur'an is the only law and vision which will be allowed.

It goes without saying that this team stand in contradistinction to all progressive people. One needs only look at the heroic resistance forces in Iraq fighting night and day at terrific cost to the US occupation. 90% of all armed resistance is by them. The other 10%, of bombs and assassinations, are by al-Qaeda forces in the heart of the resistance communities and *against* the resistance fighters. In straight military terms, they play the role of imperialism, and in objective political terms, too, they stand in the camp of capitalism, a very backward and deformed version of it, perhaps in a mirror image of the crusades and the excesses of colonial expansion, but of the same genre without a doubt. It is also clear, although not with specific detail, that there is a conspiracy of opposites and outright manipulation by the US state and its own mad religious and political fundamentalists working in concert to control the actions of the medievalists. It's probably true that without assistance and manipulation by CIA and Pentagon Special Forces they would not pose anything like the threat they do.

ADIEU SCARGILL, ADIEU SCARGILL, ADIEU

During the heady days of May '68 a million workers marched past the French presidential palace, singing 'Adieu de Gaulle, Adieu de Gaulle, Adieu!' He looked from his window and asked, 'But where are they all going?' It was inconceivable that *he* and not *they* would be going.

Many looked forward to at least the prospect of Arthur reaching his 65th birthday, when of course the rules (and the law) would ensure he retired and the longsuffering membership could at last submit nominations as to who it would like as the new president. Maybe, even, there would be more than one candidate, and we could actually have an election in which the members would vote. Surely he wouldn't try to rule from the constitutional grave, would he?

A letter to Yorkshire branches on 5 December 1991 from the president informed us of a Special Meeting of Yorkshire NUM Council (the assembly of branch representatives) on 11 December. There was no agenda.

When the meeting was convened, the first point of business Arthur imposed was to remove Nigel Pearse, the Area vice chairman, from the chair; he would assume the chair himself. Next, instead of the rule necessitating that only one representative per branch (the delegate) could vote, branch secretaries and trustees who were present could vote. The Maltby delegate objected to this, insisting we should stick to the rule of one vote per branch, and also that we should be informed of what it was we were going to be voting on.

Mr Scargill began by saying that owing to serious illness Frank Cave would need to retire very quickly. There were only two options open: one, an election to replace him, or option 2. Option 2 was given verbally without any documentation. Frank, National vice president (and, we had always assumed, the Yorkshire Area secretary – but Arthur had ruled earlier we didn't in fact have an Area secretary) would retire. The president – Arthur – would leave full-time employment on 31 June 2002 and then become 'honorary president' until 31 December 2011.

He would also continue to preside over the IEMO (International Energy and Mineworkers Organisation) to that date. From within the NEC of the NUM, the NEC elects a lay chair, who chairs all meetings, the Appeals Committee and the General Policy Committee of the IEMO, the IEMO Central Bureau and the International Executive. A lay vice chair is to be elected from NEC every 2 years.

As I've mentioned already, I had taken to describing the IEMO as 'an officers' club totally unaccountable to the members in any country and functioning as a well-heeled version of Saga Holidays for full-time officials or lay officials being patronised.' That it was almost exclusively controlled by Arthur is witnessed by the fact that under these proposals, ostensibly to do with the NUM, he would stay as president of the IEMO while the treasurer of that organisation, we were told, was one of the clerks in the Barnsley offices, and now the chairs of the IEMO and most of its committees would be filled by whoever the NUM's NEC chose to vote into them. Obviously the tens of millions of miners and energy workers worldwide, who we are told look to the IEMO for leadership, aren't invited to nominate or vote on who will be its representatives. Actually, I doubt whether the multitudes even knew of its existence.

Mr Scargill will be paid only £12,000 p.a. from the Yorkshire Area fund to pay for ongoing work.

The proposal was a bombshell, riddled with injustice. Not least, it meant one of these National positions could be filled only by a Yorkshire candidate and not anyone selected from the other affiliated coalfields. A Scottish NEC member later described the proposals as being for a Yorkshire Union of Mineworkers. What is also remarkable is that this proposal came solely from Arthur himself, nobody else. He put the proposal to the NEC the following day.[401]

Nigel Pearse, the Area vice chair, spoke passionately against these proposals saying: 'When your time is up you go, you leave it to the Union membership to decide who follows you.' Oddly, one delegate spoke passionately in favour of the proposals and in detail, illustrating that they at least knew what proposals were coming up and which way they would be voting. (In fact many of the Yorkshire

NEC members had earlier been called in to one of Arthur's cosy fireside chats in which he takes you into his esteemed confidence and 'relies on you' to support the line.)

At this point Jeff Stubbs, the Maltby delegate, raised a point of order in that this meeting contravened the rules – specifically rule 29a, which states that these matters should first be circulated to branches, and therefore the members, before any such meeting could be convened.

When put to the vote the proposals were carried by 5 votes to 3 (Maltby, Gascoigne Wood, and Stillingfleet opposing). (The lack of my vote on behalf of Hatfield here is surprising; I can only assume I was absent when the vote was taken, or it wasn't counted.)

At the following Ordinary Council meeting of the Yorkshire Area, on 17 December 2001, Arthur begins the meeting by saying Maltby had written in objecting to the decisions of the last meeting. He would allow the delegate to speak briefly in support of that objection and then rule against it! The Maltby delegate flatly refused to go down this road because the minutes of the 11th had not been circulated to branches, and were not on this agenda.

The first time the branches as such got to see these devastating proposals was via a branch circular of 19 December. This circular informed the branches that these proposals had in fact already been put before the NEC on 12 December and been approved for circulation. Only on 7 January 2002 were minutes of the special Area Council and subsequent meeting circulated. These minutes announced that the Yorkshire Area had already agreed to the proposals by 5 votes to 3! Before any of the branches, to say nothing of the rank-and-file members, had seen a sight of them! At Hatfield, the proposals produced outrage, and news began to filter out to the press, which is where most members got to hear about it. The whole thing was supposed to be 'confidential'. I came in for some vicious criticism for having spoken to the press about the proposals, and in reality having given the game away.

A further Special Council Meeting and Special National Delegate Conference were convened to finalise the proposals.

The Yorkshire meeting again seen challenges to the minutes and the legality of the earlier decisions; these failed by 4 votes to 5 and the meat of the proposals was debated.

Delegates variously made the point that we were depriving the members of the Union of the right to decide who their National officials would be, including the right to dismiss and re-elect them. Representatives were representatives, not rulers. The other affiliated sections, like Wales, Scotland and the North East, were having a Yorkshire appointee imposed on them from the Yorkshire Area alone. Arthur was insisting the position of honorary president was just that, it was just a title. Nigel Pearse asked why he needed a title; he was Arthur Scargill! People would still know who he was without any title. I asked, if it was just a title then why were we abolishing the position of National president? Why, if we were having two employees in Yorkshire, couldn't we have the Yorkshire Area secretary and president back, which Arthur had fought so long to get rid of? Why was it a package? You could only have all and not some of the proposals; why couldn't we put forward alternative proposals, and why was it all being rushed through now? The questions kept coming, but supporters of the move weren't interested.

Halfway through the debate Arthur announces that the legal advice he has been given by the TUC is that more than 50% of the proposals are illegal and cannot be implemented. So will the proposals now be amended to fall in line with the requirements of TU legislation (to say nothing of members' rights)? No they will not; the package will despite its impracticality still be put as it is, and this will also be the case at the forthcoming National Conference.

The vote would be crucial. If Arthur had lost here he would lose at Conference and he couldn't afford to do that. Those against: Maltby, Hatfield, Kellingley, Gascoigne Wood, and Stillingfleet. Those for: Yorkshire Winders, Prince of Wales (widely rumoured not to have consulted the members on the decision), Wistow, Riccall and most surprising of all Rossington, previously regarded as a dissident branch. Arthur then called for a card vote, which, on the face of it, the oppositionists ought to have won given the actual sizes of the branches. He would not, as per usual, use December 2001 membership figures but instead used January 2002. Where these figures came from we are not sure, but it resulted in a vote of 1,207 for and 1,128 against. A number of people expressed great surprise at what seemed to be inflated membership numbers for some approving pits. One colliery for example was commonly believed to have 220 members but was given a card vote equal to 275 workers. Just the margin of difference needed for Arthur to win the vote. Truth is we didn't know for certain but there was great mistrust.

In Yorkshire, two Area agents are to be taken on at a fixed annual salary paid from Yorkshire Area funds in a joint election in January 2002 (now February). Agent number one (the one with the highest vote in Yorkshire) will be responsible for delegate meetings, staffing and finance of the Yorkshire Area and the NUM nationally, with agent number two in charge of industrial relations matters in the Yorkshire coalfield. Branches can only nominate one candidate for both positions, and so cannot select the most suitable candidate for each post.

Also, the Yorkshire Area must agree to continue the affiliation fee of the whole Union to the IEMO at least until 2011.

All of this was put to the NEC and a National Conference convened to approve it.

This was all bad enough. When it gets to the floor of the National Conference however it gets worse. Arthur, despite calls for an impartial chair, decided to chair the Conference himself, contrary to all past practice and natural justice. He starts to make out the case as to why it's no big deal if he stays on beyond age 65: 'Why no question marks about the retirement age of judges at 75? Why not one single question or one single comment or observation about the appointment on Monday of a new Archbishop in Scotland at the age of 67?'[402]

Jeff Stubbs, the Area agent from Maltby, made heroic efforts to raise crucial points of order. These were centred on rule 26b, a rule inserted by Arthur himself, which protects his employment until his 65th birthday when he must retire. This rule itself had built-in protection to ensure that it could never be changed by any

Conference, ever. Arthur's new set of proposals run into his old rule. Despite protests from the floor, Arthur ruled that this rule didn't apply at this Conference! Davie Guy for the North East spoke in his quiet and remorselessly logical voice, pointing to the injustices contained in the 'package' of proposals:

> What I prefer to see, it is my opinion, I think it is the right way to go on, if you are going to maintain unity in the union you have got to ensure that everybody gets a chance, fair debate and fair discussion on these issues. What ought to have happened here – we have got plenty of time, the President can stop here till next year, we have got plenty of time to alter these rules – these should have been done at the National Conference. Each rule should have been dealt with individually to allow areas to decide which of them they wished to support and which of them they wished to reject. That is the way to conduct the democracy of the union, not packaging. Packaging gets through things, which on a different day if it had been dealt with differently would probably not have been agreed to. It is a bad way, in my opinion, for the NEC to approach the rule amendments in a package.[403]

The North East Area was later to raise the strange connection between affiliations to the IEMO for 10 years in conjunction with Arthur as honorary president for the same ten years. Some very dodgy interplay seemed afoot. Also, almost unnoticed, Arthur would likewise retain the position of chairman of the trustees of the NUM's Full Time Officials and Staff Superannuation Scheme, again for ten years.

> The question 'Why?' hangs about like a ghost at a wedding but no one seems to suggest how these apparently separate anomalies hang together. The North East Area motion to the (now, since the rule change) Biennial Conference called for 'The annulling of the NEC decision to allow the National President, Mr A. Scargill, to remain in the position of Chairman of the Trustees of The Full Time Officials and Staff Superannuation Scheme as National President.' It was excluded from the agenda.[404]

The North East's objections in particular were centred on the Special Delegate Conference and the proceeding NEC meeting. Anticipating some sharp moves, they had sent in a letter requesting that the issue of strengths of Area card votes be discussed by the NEC. This letter was not discussed. When it came to the vote, like the earlier vote in Yorkshire some area strengths seemed way above their actual membership, and the National Office vote of 822 wiped out the combined voting strength of South Wales, North East and Scotland. These National Office votes posed serious questions: Who says the figure is 822? Were any of these 822 consulted as to the vote or asked their opinion? (Of course they were not.)

We were given assurances from Arthur that given the legal advice, the 'chair' of the NEC and (we think) the 'secretary' will now have to come up for nomination from branches and, where more than one candidate is standing, face a national ballot of the membership. However, in order to stand, candidates must have nominations of at least 30% of the electorate; this again militates almost impossibly against non-Yorkshire nominations. In any case, he refused to rewrite the proposal or refer it back to areas for amendment in the light of the legal advice and insisted that the vote would be taken on his package as it stood. This was utter nonsense and had most of the Conference shaking their heads in utter disbelief.

Arthur ruled that there would be area card votes. The card vote would be those men working in the industry plus limited members.

Limited members were mainly ex-members who were having their industrial compensation cases handled by any of the NUM constituent bodies. A portion of the limited members' fees was payable to National Office.

This means areas such as South Wales, Scotland and the North East, who process such claims themselves through 'retired membership' schemes paid only to those areas, will not have those members counted in the vote. The effect is that 'dead areas' with no working mines or miners will easily outvote three areas in which miners still labour. Only 4,000 working miners belong to the NUM, but a collective card vote of 11,623 was recorded in favour of the proposals. Among this figure was a vote of 822 for 'the National Office'! Obviously 822 people do not work in the National Office, so one assumes these are people who are having claims handled by the National Office.[405] NONE of these limited members, and especially not those of the National Office, have ever been asked to vote on the issue or even consulted on it. Arthur's National Office vote outvotes the whole working mine membership of two areas, the North East and Scotland. At the end of the Conference we come to the voting. It is a 'done deal', we already know; it was put now and not at the normal Conference in order to ensure the balance of power within the Yorkshire Area swung the whole Area's vote behind the proposals. Even then it couldn't have been done without the unmandated use of 'Area Office' votes to swing it. Now on the floor of Conference one area after another votes, and then Arthur casts *his* own personal 'National Office' vote of 822 members.[406]

So the vote goes through. The whole thing is literally scandalous; it cost us dear in disillusioned membership, in reputation and in our ability as a Union to do the things we are supposed to be there for: to fight for the miners. The press had recently broadcast loud and clear that another, terminal assault is due on the already minute mining industry. The miners' website www.minersadvice.co.uk years before warned that 'long-term' strategies for the remainder of deep-mined coal did not extend beyond 5 years, even at the biggest collieries. *The Independent* on 27 November 2001 had announced: 'UK Coal may close its 13 deep mines threatening more than 6,300 jobs it revealed yesterday.' Nothing has been done to build a strategy to meet this final threat to our existence. Prince of Wales will close in September 2002 and a number of others will go down like dominoes. And all the while we have this grotesque sideshow, which simply robs us of our reputation for being able to fight and our members' actual ability to do so.

Some will find it hard to believe that a man so respected, indeed loved, by the-rank-and-file members during our great struggle of '84/85 should have come to this kind of level.

Nigel Pearse had begged Arthur to withdraw these silly proposals, for the sake of his, Arthur's, reputation and that of the Union. He refused, and that in our view was the worst mistake made by Arthur in his whole career. History will tend to remember all this rubbish rather than the fine upstanding man he was in '84/85 and that is truly sad. Although perhaps the reverse is true: as the left makes Arthur into some immaculate conception, they will not know or care about the struggles within the Union for workers' democracy and rank-and-file control. Although evidence of all this period is very rarely in the public domain, it does exist and those wanting to re-read the blow-by-blow scandal of this Conference can find it in the report of the Special Delegate Conference, as already referenced in a footnote above. I have placed copies of the reports in the Doncaster Library Archive Service, and since they are my personal copies, I trust nobody will be able to suppress them or confiscate them.

HATFIELD MAIN DIES AGAIN

Hatfield Coal Company, the private outfit started by the colliery manager Jeff Ainley, which has been viciously anti-union, goes bankrupt owing to some financial panic in Japan and withdrawal of investment funding. We start a nationwide campaign to save the colliery, and again have to go cap-in-hand to find some nice capitalist to buy it. Ideas of a workers' buyout are damned by the knowledge that the men this time round are not receiving any redundancy handouts. We have to file to the industrial tribunals for the basic 90-day consultation payments. We briefly fall out again with Barnsley and Raleys over their handling of the closure and statutory compensation questions. The struggle to maintain the Branch while we fight to survive as a pit is also very bitter, with pressure for us to wind up now the pit had closed. At length Mr Richard John Budge, once of RJB fame, buys the colliery. It was our campaign and the pressure we were able to exert through MPs and ministers not to fill the shafts that allowed him to do so. He at once refuses to recognise the Branch and we set off on a 100% campaign once more.

I notice in the Report of Finance and General Purposes Committee that Glencraig, Lawrence Daly's house provided by the Union, has been sold. Few people other than myself knew whose house this had been. I enquire why it's being sold and I am told Mrs Daly is moving back to Scotland. This turned out to be incorrect – she actually stayed in the area. I assumed Lawrence had died, and nobody contradicted me. Actually, the National leadership knew he was still alive, and obviously his family who were devoted to the man still cared for him and were in regular contact with him. I and most rank-and-filers knew nothing of this or Lawrence's illness, which had taken him from the public scene.

January 2002. Frank Cave, the National Union and Yorkshire Area General Secretary, dies at 59. He had struggled hard with his illness and fought to stay on his feet. I liked Frank – big, brash, Yorkshire as Ilkley Moor, a bull in a china shop and a man who could rattle the biggest table with his fist and make the strongest man quake. We had been great comrades during the strike and in the years following. Then there had been an intermediate period when he ruled as Yorkshire secretary but with Arthur increasingly breathing down his neck; he watched my back, though he was forced to put more and more restrictions upon my activities. At length a full-scale civil war was raging again in Yorkshire and across the Union. Frank nailed his colours to Arthur's mast, became National secretary of his SLP, and would stand no criticism of him, formal or otherwise. It pained me to have to clash with Frank, to face each other down, though usually we defused it with some mutual amusing insults, curses, and laughter, agreeing to disagree: 'Ah'd say tha had mad cow disease but tha's a vegetarian.'

BANNER THEATRE

Banner Theatre launch perhaps the crowning glory of their entire career in the shape of the multimedia *Burning Issues*. It marks the twentieth anniversary of the miners' strike of '84/85, and will tell that story in legs-astride, arms-akimbo, angry and forceful guitar and poignant words. It will have a backdrop of live and moving film of the times, it will hear the overriding voices of men women and children, it will be an assault on all senses and be live and living on the floor of the room. I am proud that they asked me to play such a leading part in presenting overviews and commentary throughout the show. I think it is the best of any media presentation of those historic events. My fear is that when they go it will go; it should have been filmed as they presented it, audiences and all, and kept forever.

BEHOLD YOUR FUTURE EXECUTIONER!

9 June 2002, 8-30 a.m. Wood Street: medical to check for pneumoconiosis. Made a devastating shock discovery: I do have pneumoconiosis, I'm devastated, shocked to me roots. I am referred to my own Dr Weeks. I look with him at the X-rays of my lungs and the clouds and specs peppering the organs, I think 'Behold your future executioner.' I suppose I thought it would never affect me. Subsequent investigation into the bronchitis element proves worse. The spirograph (an instrument that provides a continuous tracing of the movements of the lungs during respiration) produced only 89% of the expected FEV (the forced expiratory volume – the air which can be breathed out in a second) for a person of my age and size. I had always concluded that what with karate and aerobics and exercise I was fitter and physically younger than most. This lung test proves my lungs are equivalent to a person 67 years old. I have lost 10 years of respiratory value, 10 years of lung capacity, I can't put it back, I can't undo the damage. It strikes me down with depression and all the happy slants you want to make of it don't make matters any better. The doctor says of my general fitness that perhaps I use what lung capacity I have more efficiently and energetically than other people with more lung capacity; it cheers me up for a while, then I think I don't know how that can make sense. Mind, the lads at the pit say I got it from singing about it, as I didn't spend enough time underground to catch it there … pillocking bastards.

ON THE BREADLINE

Attempts by Arthur to squeeze me out of any involvement with the Union are starting to strangle me. I am reliant on the shift or two which Hatfield Branch pays me, and that is because of donations from the claims I win for the former miners in the community and the lads at the pit. The Advice Centre relies on voluntary funding from any work I can be paid for. In June 2002, I circulate all the areas appealing for funds to continue the work I do in the Area. Wayne Thomas, the South Wales Area secretary, replies with a kindly letter, though their own financial pressures at branch level prevented him including any kindly cheque. Their executive is most complimentary about the well-known work I do for the pit communities and expresses their amazement that the Yorkshire Area doesn't support my efforts. He suggests instead, then, that I should approach the NEC.[407] My response to this suggestion sums up just where we were in this battle:

> No I didn't write to the NEC for obvious reasons; really, Mr. Scargill has twice made it clear that the Advice Centre ought to be closed, that I should not operate it. We should run only the NUM office, deal only with NUM members and Ltd members, and advise no one else. Add to that, that he has instructed me only to deal with NUM members of the Hatfield Main Branch, and not make any enquiries on anyone else's behalf, even members, to Raleys Solicitors, nor to represent anyone at Tribunals or Appeals as Raleys must do these, and not to ask for assistance in attending inquests for families of the Doncaster miners who have died of lung diseases, not even to be able to claim the £2.50p for the PM reports from the Finance Office, despite the fact that nobody else attends these. All expenses for work done on delegations, conferences, meetings, enquiries, committees and bodies I have been elected to have been stopped, I cannot claim loss of earning for anything …

By the AGM of Yorkshire Area on 17 June, the strangulation of any opposition to Arthur's hold on the Area is squeezing the pips from common sense and democracy. We had been given permission (by the NEC) to replace our two full-time Area agents at the end of April 2002. Since the decline in membership and cutback in funding, the practice had been for the full-time officials, the president and general secretary, to be selected from the Area agents. In this case, only two Area agents would then remain. It had been agreed that the one with the biggest number of votes would be elected 'de facto' general secretary, and take on that role (Arthur insisting no such *actual* position existed), and the runner up de facto the president. This was to be consolidated in the forthcoming amended standing orders (standing orders 7a and 17, printed June 2002). There was no problem with this, and it had fitted Arthur's plan to have two of his right-hand men elected Area agents, those being Steve Kemp (secretary) and Ken Rowley (president) – just to back himself all ways. The vote did not however go Arthur's way. First, it was discovered that Rowley had been caught in one of Arthur's obstructive rule changes and that he was too old to stand. There were, ultimately, five candidates – Nigel Pearse, running in tandem with Jeff Stubbs as part of our democratic opposition; Chris Skidmore (who had previously along with his Rossington Branch been at war with Arthur and his top table); and, running in tandem now with Steve Kemp, Kevin Malloy, from Selby. Chris tells me of the decision of his branch, Rossington, to run him against Nigel: 'I did not willingly "put up" against Nigel who has been a pal of mine since 1983; Rossington wanted a "say" or recognition for Donny Area and any position would do!' Nigel had not distanced himself from the Scargill-negotiated pay deal of 1999, which made poor relations of the Lease License miners at Rossington and Ellington, so the Rossington miners wanted him off. Nigel, who was the Area vice president, had at every turn been prevented from taking on the role of acting chair and frequently was berated and undermined by Arthur when he did so. The result of the ballot was given first to Nigel – we think this was a mistake and he wasn't suppose to have seen it – who assumed the chair at the next meeting. It announced that Jeff was first and Steve second. The folder with the result in was held for Arthur to see, since he was away. On his return and at the next meeting, on 20 May, Arthur declared that Steve was the first winner, and pronounced what the votes had been. Jeff couldn't accept this at first and was deeply suspicious, calling for an inquiry into the way in which the Electoral Reform Society had counted the single transferable votes – in particular, how the count was stopped before all the second and third preferences had been counted. The society, on their own behalf, claimed they had been instructed to stop the count at the first outright victor. It was to get worse: after announcing the vote result Arthur then goes on to accept nominations for Area president, refusing to acknowledge that Jeff, as full-time Area agent, and even as a runner-up, is a full-time Area official and therefore is the president.

We are outvoted by Arthur's caucus, and then Kevin Malloy from Selby is voted in as Area president. When Maltby and other branches challenged this, Arthur, as was his wont, pulled forward examples of Yorkshire Area chairmen who had not been Area officials and were voted into position. True – but only as short-standing acting chairs, not as Area presidents. Next, Nigel is removed from his position of vice chair, and Chris elected in his stead.

Arthur is always able to confirm the authority for his actions by referring to long-gone past meetings and decisions, past rule changes, past minutes – all taken at a different time in a different context but all remarkably able to give authority to his decisions miles down the road. Forward planning or clever retrospective construction? None of us has ever been able to make out.

> The President [Arthur Scargill] said that the two Area Agents elected on 29 April 2002 had been elected as Area Agents and not as Area Officials … The President said Jeff Stubbs, the second Area Agent, was not an Area Official and had not been elected as an Area Official. The President said that Area Agents like the Area representatives on the NEC had always attended Area Council meetings but were not Delegates and nor were they Area Officials.[408]

So here we had Jeff, possibly first or at least runner-up in a ballot vote of the membership, not an Area official, not a delegate and actually not a member of Council. He is subsequently advised that he may only speak on special permission from the chair, which as time goes on and the struggle gets more bitter, becomes more and more restricted. We weren't always right in our interpretations of the rules; Arthur who had drawn them up was frequently legalistically correct, but what was certain was that the rules, and the non-rules, compliance and non-compliance were all aimed at securing his hold on power and policy. Where he could block us through skilful manoeuvring within the spirit of rules he did, where he had to ignore his own rules and bureaucratically blast us aside and trample over democracy he did also. As was the way of these meetings, which were a cacophony of debate and argument, resolutions and political quick-stepping, all resolutions were vetted by all sides for beartraps.

Not withstanding that, it was unanimously agreed we can take the Area banner and an official Area delegation to greet Mark Barnsley at the gates of Whitemoor prison when he is released on 25 June, after 8 years in prison following a miscarriage of justice. Jeff, Nigel and I are delegated to attend.[409]

NEC Meeting 28 June 2002. It is reported that Ian Lavery is elected National chairman, unopposed, and Steve Kemp the National secretary. I couldn't have been more pleased that Ian took the position. I had actually swung the Yorkshire Area to accepting a non-Yorkshire candidate. Ian was a passionate Northumbrian whom I greatly respected. I had high hopes Ian would strike an independent course. However, Ian's vision of the Union both internally and externally wasn't the same as mine. It was to bring me, inevitably, into conflict and confrontation with him. I was to wish, as I had with Arthur, that I could be falling out and having rows with someone I actually didn't like. Despite our disagreements we remained friends, and he has done me the honour of appearing at numerous events and conferences I have organised, and not least has spoken at the launch of my book *Strike, Not The End Of The Story*, at the National Coal Mining Museum for England.[410]

SCARGILL'S LAST NUM CONFERENCE

When Arthur Scargill's last NUM Conference finished in Blackpool in 2002, I feel a certain ambivalence. I am both angry and sad; I wish he had finished in the late '80s when the sun still shone out of his backside and he passed his time walking on water. He would have gone with an intact reputation and a Union in which most officials and the bulk of members still held him as a friend and comrade. Instead, to the end we were riven by controversy and the bureaucratic manoeuvres. The scandalous wheeling out of the limited members' votes to outvote the working miners. The brass-neck argument that we had somehow extended 'rights' to our retired members to vote in the affairs of the Union. Instead some bloke in an office will cast these votes, and thousands of others, in any direction he feels suits the purposes of his office, like some rich gambler moving stacks of chips at a roulette game. The impact of Arthur's last revision of the rulebook was still rebounding round the Conference and fundamental questions of democracy and rank-and-file control of the Union were as unresolved as ever.

For some the fight was over long ago; after they had had the stuffing kicked out them, 'What's the point?' took over from any idea of ever winning back the Union to democratic control of any kind, never mind control by the rank and file. Nigel Pearse, a former member of Militant, who oozed enthusiasm and vision, sat at this Conference like a punctured balloon – his enthusiasm gone, hopelessness in its place. That anyone could deflate Nigel shows the impact of the constant bureaucratic attacks and impositions. Yet I confessed to a certain feeling of profound regret that this was Arthur's last Conference, despite the fact that he stayed on as 'honorary' president, and president of the the International Energy and Mineworkers' Organisation.

I am still sad at the passing of this epoch; he has been after all part of my life in one form or another for these last 35 years or so, as a comrade and fellow miner, as a fellow fighter against the system, a fellow picket and revolutionary, also in latter years as a demagogic opponent and entrenched bureaucrat, determined it seemed to knock himself off the esteemed perch on which I and many others had placed him. So I too stood in standing ovation as he closed his final Conference. It would have given too mean and too inaccurate an impression not to have done so; his life and contribution cannot be characterised or diminished by these last 10 years of egocentric Stalinist degeneration.

A further 50% of the remaining coalfield could be closed by Christmas, with UK Coal's stampede to close the Selby coalfield, the winding up of Prince of Wales Colliery, and the death of the last deep mine in Scotland, Longannet. Despite courageous resolutions calling for action on parity of wages, and a host of other terms and conditions, nothing is seriously being offered that will halt the downward spiral as the last of the coalfields bleed to death. The recent energy debate in the Commons foretells a nuclear future, something we had long predicted.

Just prior to Conference, at the end of May, *The Guardian* ran a most bizarre feature article. In banner headlines, Roy Greenslade proclaimed 'Sorry, Arthur'. Accompanied by photos of Arthur and Roger Windsor, the NUM executive officer and *Daily Mirror* informant, shots from the strike and other key players, the article promised to be a revelation. Now, I have successfully proposed that every miner in Britain be sent a copy of this article by the Union. After all, the allegations themselves were screamed from TV screens and tabloids for days and weeks; if someone is now saying they got it all wrong, the miners and the folk of the pit communities need to be informed.

Arthur will no more preside directly over NUM Conferences or what are now Biennial Conferences. His talents will be directed to the IEMO, a body in which he will have no problems of democratic demands, factions, rulebooks or any other restraints; it having been built in his image and likeness, all such flippancies and irrelevancies having been dispensed with. Arthur's last Conference was graced by Alain Simon, CGT leader of the French miners and co-founder of the IEMO. It was likewise regaled by area leaders from Northumberland and Yorkshire who had been on IEMO conferences dealing with the Middle East and Cuba. The French miners' support for the '84/85 strike is never in question, neither is our solidarity with the Palestinian cause or struggle for independence and justice by the Cuban people; these are not, however, as implied, dependent upon the existence of the IEMO or our affiliation and funding of it. This is not and never has been a workers' organisation; it is a bureaucrats' club, and the memberships of affiliated bodies have not the slightest control over its actions, its statements, its finance or its political direction. That people enjoy trips around the world and have a canny crack over otherwise important issues is not the point. One thing this Conference, like the special one before it, had in superabundance was such red herrings.

The Conference wound up a day early, so delegates could watch the final game in the World Cup; for us however the ball had long ago been dispensed with in order to get on with the game.

THEY SEEK IT HERE, THEY SEEK IT THERE, THAT DAMNED ELUSIVE AREA OFFICE BRANCH

At the end of March, I draw up a statement of 'Concerns Regarding The Alleged "Area Office Branch" and Related Issue of Limited Members Voting Rights And Consultation For That Purpose'. The statement is meant to clear through any fog or misdirection likely to be thrown up over the issue, and set straight just what the forthcoming battle is going to be about, because from past experience I knew the issue would be misrepresented and obscured.

I first set out my own credentials in the Union, the length of membership and the positions I held. I then go on:

During all this time I have never heard of 'The Area Office Branch' of the NUM.[411] The first I have heard of it was today at the AGM 24/3/2003. During all of these years, I never heard this 'Branch' submit a resolution or rule change or amendment, nor second any resolution or rule change or amendment, nor cast any vote for or against any resolution or rule change. I have never known it submit candidates to any position within the Union. Branch votes have been cast throughout the whole period of my membership and their votes recorded as 'card votes' on a variety of issues, including resolutions to Conference, resolutions to Council etc. This record of voting will illustrate that never once has this 'Area Office Branch' voted. Delegates to Council cannot abstain and must cast a vote. In crucial votes such as the decision whether or not to call off the 1984/85 strike for example, the issue was decided on a narrow difference of card votes. No vote for 'The Area Office Branch' was recorded. Indeed, it is more fundamental than that, the roll of branches in attendances always precedes the business of the meeting; 'Area Office Branch' has never attended.

The names and address of Area Branches was traditionally listed in the Yorkshire Area annual diary, names and addresses of branches have annually been distributed to branches in The Area Branch Directory, in neither of these or any other publication does an 'Area Office Branch' appear.

The rulebook lays down conditions that all branches must operate to: the election of officials, the election of a Branch Committee, their subjection to re-election, the submission of Branch Registers containing lists of full members, limited and retired members. The Branch Accounts/Returns must be submitted to Area Finance Office and show income, expenditure etc. 'The Area Office Branch' does not have any branch officials subject to rule, does not hold regular branch meetings, and does not have income and expenditure or accounts. Branches must hold regular meetings at which branch members can attend, vote, and express their views on the direction of the branch or the Area. This Area Office Branch has never done so. Branches have their branch meeting venues listed and the occasion of fortnightly branch meetings and branch committee meetings recorded. 'Area Office Branch' has never done so. All branches must have minutes of branch meetings, and keep these minutes in specially supplied branch minute books. These are the property of the Area, most branches' minute books going back to their inception, for very many decades. I predict there is no such collection of Area Office Branch minute books, because there have been no branch meetings to minute.

None of the above has ever taken place. We can only conclude there is no 'Area Office Branch'. There never has been an 'Area Office Branch.'

b) Area Office Members
There have been members of the NUM based at Area Office, sometimes where it has been inappropriate for such members to belong to a branch (because there wasn't enough members to constitute one, or the branch had closed down for example or because the person works at the Area Office on staff or as an official), they have been associated with the Area Office. The Area Agent or Officials have taken over looking after their interests. Likewise retired members with no branches to go to, or for reasons of ease, might take their claims, problems, and enquiries to the Area Office direct, where they would be looked after by staff, agents or officials. In times of national ballots, or area ballots, the full members of the Yorkshire Area of the NUM based in the Area Office have cast their votes. However, none of this was ever done through the auspices of 'A Branch'.

I then go on to outline the history of limited members and retired members and their voting and representation rights – most of which I have already covered earlier.

'Votes' have been cast to swing decisions on rule changes and elections within the union. This has been done by officials of the Union simply casting thousands of votes 'on behalf of the limited members' (although without their consent or knowledge) to swing the vote in any direction behind any resolution or against any resolution, in favour of any rule change or against any rule change, they happen to support. The effect of this is to have an individual or a tiny group of individuals having the capacity to outvote the vast bulk of the working, full members of the Union on any issue.

Because of the outrage, this caused at last year's Conference we believe there is an attempt to avoid this by invention of 'An Area Office Branch', which will have both full members and all the limited members of the Area will be linked to it. The overall vote of this 'Branch' will then be sufficient to outvote any number of working branches in the Area, with the same undemocratic and we think unlawful effect. It should be noted that although this alleged 'Area Office Branch' did try to cover itself by posting a notice of a 'Branch Meeting' it was only the inhabitants of the Area Office itself who could get to see it. Full members from Flax Colliery or those from the previous Barnsley Main Road Transport Branch now looked after by the Area Office were not informed and neither were hundreds, perhaps thousands of limited members whose votes are intended to be used, without their knowledge or authority.

The Parliamentary Reform Act of 1832 and the issues of the 'Rotten Boroughs' would seem to have direct parallel in these events.

We call upon all those who will advise on this issue to recognize the grave injustice and breach of natural justice here as well as issues of breach of rules and Ultra Vires.

We would suggest – either all area limited members should be again linked to the nearest geographical working branches, which will pose the opportunity for them to vote on issues at branch meetings. Or else they are returned to the Area Branches already established with opportunities to discuss the issues and vote where entitled on the direction their wishes taken them. On no account however should block votes of limited members be cast solely at the discretion of Area or National officials, or a bogus 'Area Office Branch'.[412]

I write on behalf of the Branch seeking assurances from Steve Kemp that only working branches will be voting at the forthcoming AGM, that no dead members' or widows' or limited members' votes will be cast by anyone to outvote the working branches and members. I also raise the question as to why our limited retired members are not associated with their branches as 'limited members', as per the usual rule. Mr Kemp the Area secretary responds that he is 'astonished' I could suggest that past members' and retired member's branches could exercise such votes. The larger question of our disappearing limited members isn't taken up. The two are of course linked. When the retired and limited members were associated with working branches, their numbers were linked to the voting strength of the branch, which would through meetings and face-to-face consultation gain the views and mandates of the members. When area retired members' branches were established by Arthur, all that voting strength was lost from branches. All of the retired members' branches, which were now often bigger than any working branch, were run by ex-officials firmly in the Arthur Scargill camp and sometimes in his political party. I had had visions of a sudden conversion of 'democracy' whereby these branches would be given the power to vote and thus swing the results of elections and votes across the board. That though was not my concern; these branches would have to exercise basic branch democracy and allow for meetings, debates and internal voting. I had considered that such a feature would be *too* democratic for those trying to manipulate limited members' votes, and, as such, that option would be laid aside in favour of something for more secure and reliable. So I respond:

Dear Steve

What a remarkably familiar terminology and style you have, if it wasn't for your signature I would have sworn Arthur wrote the letter ...

One of the features so similar to Arthur's style contained in your letter is the ability to entirely miss the point and pick up instead on an irrelevant feature. Read my letter again, I am not expressing concern at retired members' branches casting votes, but a non-existent 'Area Office Branch' casting the votes of Limited Members, who in a number of cases are dead, in all others don't know anything about it, and in some cases have never ever had any connection with the mining industry. This matter has still not been clarified so you are being 'astonished' for the wrong reason. That being the case we have reason enough to remain fearful at Hatfield that full members risk being constitutionally castrated.[413]

What had happened here was a coup against the members by the leaders. It had been laid out gradually and in such a way that few would see what was coming. Prior to the Annual Conference of June 2000, Arthur had introduced to the preceding NEC meeting 'Voting Procedure at Conference'. Quite correctly, it asked for endorsement of limited members' votes being counted in the area card votes, and set out the justification for this. It also sought exemption for those classed as 'limited members' who wouldn't in fact have paid any subs until their claims had run their course and this was agreed.[414] There was of course no problem at that time with this, since the vast majority of limited members were represented in working branches with full rights to speak and vote. The problem only arose when, following instructions and changes of rule introduced by the president, limited members were taken away from branches and located amorphously at Area and National Office. The NEC had actually no authority to make such a far-reaching and undemocratic change, particularly one without rule changes or formal resolution to Conference. Instead, it sailed through almost unnoticed in the ratification of the NEC report. I had actually risen to challenge the suggestion that 'National Office' could cast votes of limited members and outlined a nightmare scenario in which Arthur could outvote the whole Conference on his tod. I was actually making a far-fetched joke to warn of the dangers. Arthur assured from the chair that National Office held very few limited members, that most resided in area offices controlled by the branches, and that my fears would not be realised. We were none of us aware that an idea we thought of as actually extending democracy would in fact take the votes away from the limited members and then use them to neutralise those of working miners. Had we seen through it at the time we would have made strong objections. Nobody else got up to voice any fears or seek any assurances.

On 24 March in response to branches flooding the Area Office with complaints and challenging the existence of the Area Office Branch, the matter had been referred to Harry Eyre, Raleys' industrial relations legal expert, and he had suggested advice be taken from legal counsel and the certification officer, 'and in particular clarify if Limited Members can vote in forthcoming elections of chairman and vice chairman of the area.'[415] We were none too happy with the wording of the minute; the issue wasn't whether limited members should vote, but how such a vote could be exercised. Presented in that way, a QC or the certification officer could simply say 'yes', without addressing the issue of the vote having being used without the knowledge or consent of the member in question. All elections were now suspended pending the result of the advice received from the QC and certification officer.

In our naivety, we were pleased with this course of action. The issue was out in the open and we were certain any independent review by almost anyone, ner mind a qualified, highly rated lawyer, would bring the issue back to earth and restore democracy. We weren't sneaky enough; we didn't see the licence this decision would give the officials to stall elections indefinitely and end up with the result they wanted anyway.

The whole purpose of the limited member debacle was to influence the result of the Area elections and who would occupy the positions of power in the Yorkshire Area and therefore within the Union as a whole. Jeff Stubbs was seen as the main challenge to the status quo; on the face of it, counting up the number of branches he had behind him and whose members had already endorsed him as their candidate, he would win. To prevent this the votes of hundreds of limited members would have to be deployed by the existing officials to outvote the branches. With the indeterminate suspension of the election, however, a) the status quo could continue and b) what we didn't realise was that the longer the suspension went on the more the balance of power within the branch vote itself was changing. Pits were closing and with them branches; it was no secret that most of those coming up in the firing line were the pits that supported Jeff.

Inside some of the pro-Stubbs branches, serious challenges to the existing branch officials were being promoted by his opponents at Area, while in the anti-Stubbs branches all attempts to displace sitting officials were being stuffed by bogus use of rules, and appeals to the Area officials. In at least one branch, officials told men turning up to vote at a branch meeting for whoever they wished to select that *they* didn't have that right and only the branch officials could pick who the branch voted for. The longer the delays went on, the more the balance of power was shifting against the opposition.

Membership in Yorkshire was 1,905; nationally, including Yorkshire, the figure was 3,042 (2003).[416]

'PUSHED?'

5 April 2003. The last couple of months I have the distinct impression that I am being 'nudged', or somehow helped from who-knows-where. My long-buried *History of the Liverpool Waterfront, 1850–1890*, had been painstakingly rewritten and was off at AK Press, and with Roger down at Keele checking it over. I have a couple more references to check out, not least Taplin, who got to publish his *Liverpool Dockers and Seamen* years ago, though I actually researched the bugger years before he discovered this time and place was of special interest. Ney bother, though, I am nearly at the happy stage of looking for illustrations when oot the

blue, at a car boot sale in Donnie, I come across four prints of the Liverpool Docks in 1889! Uncanny, and as far as I can tell these are not some mass-produced piece of nostalgic tat but paintings which were contemporary before their images became prints, even then not widely distributed. Coincidence.

Then today, doon in the smoke for a Labour Research Department conference on 'Racialism in the Workplace', I land at Kings Cross nearly an hour early and decide to have a walk around to Housman's Peace Bookshop, always a place of pilgrimage when in London, not least, he vainly admits, because they sometimes have copies of my out-of-print books, which I can buy for visiting students and friends. In a stack of books marked 'All books 50p' I find two Left Book Club editions (which I collect). Left Book Club for 50p a hoy? What a coup. Then suddenly I can't believe it – *A Man's Life*, by Jack Lawson. A book of immense impact when researching my Durham books way back at Ruskin in the 1970s. Lawson tells the story of my neighbouring village, Boldon, and shatters a few illusions about Geordie miners standing for a millennium as a distinct people. Here he tells of Boldon as a frontier town in the coal rush, the transitory miners from Lancashire, Staffordshire, Yorkshire and the mining races of the whole island brought together like gold rush prospectors, nowt in common but horny hands and humpty backs. The book is a treasure despite Lawson's capitulation to the right-wing trajectory of so many Labour politicians. To get one at all is a prize – but to find one for 50p!

'The poowa' wasn't finished yet. Here was a tribute to the Morden Tower poets; my heart leapt. Morden bliddy Toower. Founded by my anarchist marras Tom Pickard and 'their lass' Connie, a smoky candle-lit, sit-on-the-floor, bring-together-the-dissident-young-poets squat. The working-class writers together with the art students, the writers, the wild left-wing intellectuals, working-class hooligans and young delinquents. Morden Tower, a centre of intellectual Pan-Geordie/American beat-attitudes. The book was a tribute by the modern poets who came to read and some of the homegrown Northumbrian variety, many of them my contemporaries. But there was more than this, apart from the hand-written inscription from one of the contributors to someone unknown. Here was a message from Jackson. Tony Jackson had impacted on my young life and train of thought like a signalboxman throwing the points. Like many of my early comrades I was happy in the thought he was still out there somewhere, still in his beard, still being a Sooth Shields Ginsberg, still breaking images and idols, still writing beautifully and with his knack of the collective recognition and shared encounter. Pickard had told me at his wedding that Tony had suffered years of some paralysing disease and had died the year before. Shite – I never got to speak to him again. Never got the chance in these latter years to stand back and tell him how much I appreciated his friendship and verbal clips roond the ear. He had been buried in a cardboard box, which is aboot reet. Jackson's piece, written I suppose in the middle 1990s, was to be the last thing I would ever have from him, for it seemed to speak from the page, to me. It was aboot Morden, but it was aboot all of our formative years and the happy way in which it had shaped us all. These were things too weird and personal to be sheer coincidence surely?

Jackson writes:

Between 1964 when I was just a brief boy of only 19 when Tom and
Connie first opened the doors for Ginsberg, Nuttall, Hollo, Corso, Bly et
al. and today this year quarter of a century later

We all; threw up/YUK got old high got sad lost youth fell in love
many times got addicted to various stuff cleaned-up even stops smoking
but as divine Stein would have said had she been around poetry under
any other name is equal junk or even ice cream

While some shot-up other injected Black Mountain and to od. on
either had much the same effect we're told.

And now years later with a number gone and some dead others not
even able to walk or climb the stone stairs up into the tower

We all still remember days of open explore and tremble excitement
that is how it was those days before many of us still remember.

Tony is right. I think my whole life has been lived with reference back to those
early days, like I am on leave from them, abroad on holiday, while they continue,
and I will surely return to them. I am promised to ease out of Yorkshire and all
this, and back onto Tyneside and the Toon. I suppose stupidly I expect to pick
up where I left off in 1966, to call back in doon the Bridge and everyone will still
be sitting there, guitars strumming, singing in chorus. Arguing the toss about the
world. Something like the scene from *Titanic* when the old lady is reborn into
her youth and the ship in its youth and is welcomed at last to the rest of the
passengers who have been there so long before her. Was it just our youth, or the
age of our youth? It's had my heart in a tight grip for the rest of my life.

As for being nudged from some place beyond, I have come to the realisation
that even in strict materialist terms, there is no definitive answer as to what
'reality' is. Only assumptions, based upon what seems to actually make sense and
seems real. Scientifically, however, reality is not like that at all. In quantum
analysis for example reality such as we perceive it, is upside down, inside out, and
here and there at the same time, *really*. Time and space are not at all like starting
at one end and journeying to the other, but circular and multi-dimensional, with
simultaneous and parallel options. Scientific and quantum reality is nothing like
our common-sense perceptions of it.

DEATH OF ME MAM

Saturday 3 May 2003. In the middle of in-depth interview for an anniversary
documentary on the strike, Veronica phones to say me Mam has died. She was
with her, stroking her head, when she died. It has been long and bitter for me
Mam, so that she died peacefully is a blessing. She had prayed to be allowed to
die, for at least a year and maybe longer. The quality of her life had gone, she was
in constant pain and, worse, frustration from incapacity and dependency on folk
she thought indifferent to her. She complained of being beaten, starved and
roughly handled, often hungry and neglected. We comforted ourselves that this
was the result of her medication, and the constant bruises and eventually
fractured leg to do with her frailty. We couldn't stand to think her complaints

were well founded. They were often investigated, with the resultant hostility from staff, which made them fearful of personal encounters, and so reluctant to be too close too often. That was real enough. She was trapped, she begged 'to go home'; she dreamed that she still had a home, often believed she was waiting for the taxi to take her. It was heartbreaking. Still, she bucked up and twinkled every time we came, and that was at least once a fortnight. She had the blessing of meeting her great granddaughter, talking with her, loving her, and it was mutual. Caitlin could see through the strange physiognomy and circumstances and ravages of time and pain, and confided, quite out of the blue: 'I love Dave's Mam.' She had said it after reflection. She charged off to bring her a drink; she wanted to do it – her cup was like hers, she needed a drink.

I am bitterly sad, though not like when Da died. This is expected, for me Ma welcome even. I feel strangely alone. Only me and Veronica are left now, of that group of people all that time ago who were The Douglasses of Wardley Colliery. Soon everything we were, and what we all were, and the things we did, and why we were here, and what it was all for, will all be gone too. I suppose I recognise the queue is getting shorter and I am moving up. I am the last of my line – no more Douglasses after me. Tomorrow I will go and see Veronica up hyme and we will work out all the things we have to do, about the funeral, and every sad thing that goes with this business. Closing down a person's life. My Ma's life. God, how did so much love happiness, pride and care come down to a lifeless old body in a bed? It doesn't seem fair. From my Ma's beliefs will she be with me Da, perhaps in their youth, back in the London of their courtship? Will she be back with her Ma and Dada, back in the green fields of the unspoilt Kells of her girlhood?

Or does it compact into a synthesis of the whole encounter with life and lives? She will be doubtless giving God a piece of her mind, deyin her Irish wag of temper, tapping her foot with her hand on her hip, and demanding why he kept her hanging on so long and she a good woman. Me Ma was buried with my sister Marina, on 9 May. Me Da's ashes are spread on the top. Heworth cemetery now holds another guest that holds me telling the tale as I revisit the cemetery. I was shocked by the Catholic service down at St Albans new church, no longer now a wooden construction, still less hosted in the local Grand cinema. The ceremony and service is now bereft of the magic of the Latin high mass and looks for all the world like a Protestant service. Women now serve on the altar, people pick up the host and they even give out communion wine! Revisionists!

AUDIT ... THE MINUTE BOOKS!

There is a demand from Steve Kemp the Area general secretary for 'an audit' of minute books. I for one had never heard of an audit of minute books; in my view, it is simply a device to delve deep into discussions and debates and policy matters decided upon at branches, to know what we are discussing in private. It is an attempt to find something to hang us for, some misdemeanour or breach of rule. We object strongly, though everything in our minute book is just as it occurs and as we relay it to Council; but it does make us resolve to be very careful the way we minute things in future, given that outside eyes will now be reading 'over our shoulders'.[417]

We submit the book 'under grave protest' although other branches' objections take the form of not submitting theirs. Council meetings become a monthly battleground of resolutions, one after another being ruled out of order and denied explanation or debate. Challenge after challenge is made to the chair, though rarely successful. A strangulating grip is being held on debate and discussion; following the battle over resolutions moved out of order we move into the second field of endless conflict: minutes – what's in them, what's not in them, and the way they are worded. There are certainly two sides in the Area and two sides in the Council. It is a struggle about democracy, about control, about elections and about principle, it is a far more embittered conflict than any of the preceding decades of battles between the 'left and the right' or the 'moderates against the militants'. Our opposition can be slandered as neither moderate nor right-wing; the ground being occupied by the other side is in my view solely in defence of bureaucracy.

By the second week of July we are locked into a wrestling match with the newly enthroned Area officials. We have tabled a request to have the financial report of the Union agenda'd for discussion at the next Area Council meeting. The report was rotten with ambiguity and mystery; and this was especially so since it was the first test of how finances would work under the new 'lay' positions of Arthur's new rulebook. It was a straightforward enough request; the members were asking what items on the report meant and I couldn't tell them. Steve responds: 'The financial report will not be included for the next meeting of the Area Council to be held on 21 July 2003.' He then goes on to berate me for not complying with rule in either signing the letter or having it stamped with the branch stamp as per rule.

> Quite frankly I am surprised that you have asked for this to be put on the agenda for the Council meeting when of course if you wish to raise questions resulting from the Financial Report you could ask either by letter or arrange a meeting with me at Barnsley and I would answer them to the best of my knowledge. Furthermore why have you waited until now to put forward this proposal when the above named correspondence was sent on the 8th July 2003.

Well, the last point was absurd, of course. Branch meetings were held fortnightly, just 2 weeks since receiving the correspondence it had been discussed at a Branch meeting and matters arising returned. It couldn't be done any faster; items for discussion could only come from a Branch meeting. But why wasn't it allowed to be discussed at a meeting out in the open, together, and not as some private matter behind closed doors and without the debate of the other delegates? I didn't know whether I had signed the letter or not, but Steve knew damn well it had come from me, on behalf of the Branch. I went on:

> The ink pad fell into obscurity and the stamp without it of course doesn't work, neither do we have a candle wax seal and ring to drip on the back of the envelope, the quill pen broke sometime around the middle ages.

Steve comrade this is the age of the Personal Computer, not inkpads. The important question is what is raised in the correspondence, what are the issues, not 'does the item contain a branch stamp?' To focus on the latter while ignoring the former, is once more simply a device to dodge the issues being raised. … I will try and buy a new ink pad when I go to buy my hose and pointy Shakespearean shoes.[418]

The charges and counter-charges do get very barbed, though. In August comes a renewed charge from the Area secretary that I am not employed by anyone and therefore I can't claim loss of earnings, as I have no earnings. This is particularly cutting, having had this argument out with the preceding two chairs, one of them Arthur himself. I have already submitted my P60s, my statements and those of the Branch to the Inland Revenue and had statements issued by them confirming my contributions and employment status. Despite this it keeps getting thrown back into the swill and on 3 August I make a formal complaint to the new National chair, Ian Lavery. But Ian was in political alliance with Steve, who he also regarded as a close mate and comrade. Wherever possible we tried to resolve the more contentious issues between four walls and between the three of us. At the end of July relations between the Area officials and the Hatfield Branch hit the skids in a big way. We discover that the National president and the National/Area secretary have held talks with Budge, the new owner at Hatfield, about Union recognition at the pit, but they didn't invite me or the Branch president to these talks. Worse, they wouldn't give us information on the matters discussed or what progress what been made. I accuse 'sections' of the Union of behaving in the same way to the Hatfield Branch as the coalowners do.

Steve Kemp insisted that he would report to the NEC first, and they would notify me if the need arose. We were outraged.[419]

After clashing innumerable times with the chair and secretary of the Area, over items the Branch wanted on the Yorkshire Area agenda but were ruled out of order, I find that two letters sent in to the secretary appear on the agenda! This time I object to letters appearing on the agenda, 'without a branch stamp, and not from a branch meeting, and not a proposal' – three of the grounds usually used to rule resolutions out. The chair rules however they can stand. I challenge the chair and lose.[420] How come Arthur, the honorary president, whose job we were told was purely titular, is representing on our (that is the NUM's) behalf a member of UCATT? This is a great excuse to bring Arthur to the meeting, who argues that the NUM can recruit and represent anyone it wants, not just workers in the coal industry or ancillary trades. This is a revelation, but since Arthur wrote the rules, who can argue? He also tells me it is quite wrong that the position of honorary president is purely that of a title – he never said so, and he would conclude all work with the Union when his current cases were concluded. The rules (the rules which he had written and introduced and to great measure voted in) stated 'The Honorary President [would] … continue to deal with all the cases he was currently dealing with, and any other matter which the NEC or the National Officials instructed him to deal with.'[421] Arthur and the National officials interpreted this rule as meaning any time they wanted Arthur to do virtually anything on behalf of the whole Union he could do so without the knowledge or approval of the NEC because the minute had said 'or' and not 'and'. Such sleights-of-hand are never an accident or an oversight. We can be quite sure they are carefully planned to introduce measures the Union and the NEC will insist were not the intention, but too late, too late – 'The rule clearly states … ' or 'The minute states … ', '… and you voted for it.' This was why in subsequent meetings the Yorkshire Area became such a battleground over the wording of minutes and the meaning of decisions – the branches wanted every *i* dotted and every *t* crossed.

Things went into a different gear, though, when Ian asked *me* to explain issues I had raised about his salary. First off, the confusion came from a formal financial report, which, we were later told, had wrongly and inexplicably mixed Area salary with National officials' titles and roles. Both National officials were, under the new Scargill rules, 'lay' members and therefore unpaid. The second point was that the level of the salary was double what had previously been allocated to an Area official. It looked, and it was down in black in white, as if a new inflated salary was now being paid, and from where we didn't ken, to the 'lay' officials, unless their respective areas had suddenly decided to double their salaries without actually any increase in income.

Well, questions had to be asked; unfortunately those questions, posed as basically as that, had been sent in a personal letter to Jeff Stubbs the Area agent. It never occurred to me that Jeff's post was being opened and read on a regular basis. Ian was quoting my private letter to Jeff back to me, and asking for an explanation of its content. He had also picked up on my suggestion that I was minded to call a conference of Class War Colliers, possibly a Democratic Miners Conference, to discuss out in the open the grossly undemocratic nature of the Union at this time and the chronic manipulation of the rules against the membership. Ian asks for explanations about this forthcoming conference. Steve Kemp the Area general secretary then asks me in a formal letter if it is my intention to organise a conference of a Democratic Miners Organisation or *Class War Colliers*. If it wasn't so daft it would be laughable.[422] Ian tells me years later he had no idea the draft he had was from a private letter and assumed it was a circular.

26 Sept 2003

Dear Steve

This starts to feel like a witch-hunt. I gather there isn't anything in the minute book you can get me for so are you searching for additional information? There is no such organization as *The Miners Democratic Organisation*, not as far as I know anyway, so since it doesn't exist I don't know how it can have a conference.

Class War Colliers are the miners who read *Class War*, its not an organization no matter how loosely one uses the terms and in any case its business is entirely its own, do you want to know who reads *Class War* now? and what they talk about if ever they meet? Do the same enquiries apply for the Socialist Labour Party; they obviously operate a caucus within the NUM and are surprisingly well briefed on a number of issues and confidential matters they ought to know nothing about.

If what you are driving at is, do I believe the people who believe in democratic change in the union should organize to fight for it, yes I do. But that as of yet is just a belief, I take it my thoughts are now subject to rule restrictions as well?

Frankly, Steve this begins to sound very sinister, if you're trying to set me up for disciplinary action, as others have done before, it can only be because I am fighting to restore democracy and transparency in this union. I can assure you I will not be silent, shut up or stay with my head under the desk no matter what you or anyone else tries to do to me …[423]

I respond to Ian:

… The quotes you make come from a private letter I wrote to Jeff Stubbs, where I expressed *some* thoughts on how *I* (that's me) thought a movement within the NUM which wanted to fight for democratic change ought to go for first base. It doesn't exist, it is not an organization it is an aspiration, but fortunately for those who oppose it, as yet unorganized. I believe that aspiration *ought* to be organized. In the same way that the SLP is clearly organised at local, area and national level within the NUM; except that a movement for democratic change would have to be by definition open. Those are my *thoughts* Ian …

I have never made secret my views on the wrong direction I think this union has gone in, on the matter of the IEMO and its rules, democracy etc.

I intend to fight and keep on fighting to change that direction. In so far as I can do that within the very rules I oppose which are designed to prevent change I will do so. Where that becomes impossible, other avenues *in my opinion* will inevitably be found.[424]

15 December 2003. The Hatfield Main Branch makes an attempt to burst through the wall of silence and stifling of democracy within the Yorkshire Area of the NUM. The officials have sat on all complaints and have doctored every agenda, ruling out any contentious issue, refusing to read our correspondence, ignoring what didn't suit while answering at branch level that which could be kept there. Debate was not allowed, information and questions not allowed. Worst of all, outside of the few dissident branches, the members at large were totally unaware of what was going on. Indeed, history would never know what was going on because minutes, even supposing you could ever get to read them and you were clever enough to decipher them, would never record the contentious issues or what was happening. If you had a point of order or matter arising from the minutes or the agenda you had to submit it in writing, obviously to forewarn the officials and brief their supporters in the loyalist branches, and to decide whether to take it on, ignore it or rule it out of order.

'DEMOCRACY' IN THE NUM IN THE CLOSING DAYS OF 2003

We decided to submit our 'Complaint On Agenda Business' in writing all right, and submit it to Steve Kemp the general secretary, but also produce enough copies of it for every delegate prior to the meeting, and in the hope it would be reproduced and circulated among the members so they could understand what was happening. This action would be considered 'unconstitutional' – actually, it was letting the cat out of the bag and also ensuring some evidence would remain for posterity.

Missing Resolutions From Hatfield

Nine months ago elections were due for the position of Chair, Vice Chair and half of the NEC.

These elections have not been held.

This is in breach of the rules and constitution of the Yorkshire Area and is therefore also unlawful.

The reason for the delay is the introduction by the Area Officials of an entirely bogus 'Area Office Branch' the accumulated votes of which *are* capable of deciding the result of any election, and outvoting the views and wishes of the working membership at pits.

It was resolved last March to put the question of the existence or otherwise of that 'Branch' to the view of John Hendy QC *and then take the matter to the Certification Officer*. The views of the QC are now known to the Area Officials, but have been withheld from the Area delegates, branches and membership. It is well rumoured that the QC ruled against there being any such Area Office Branch or right of Area Officials to cast block votes and influence elections in that way.

The matter was not referred back to the Yorkshire Area whose query it was and decision it was to refer the matter to a QC, but instead was referred to the NEC, who then referred the matter to another QC for a second opinion. The views of that second QC have not been given to the Yorkshire Area. Have not been seen by the NEC, although it is thought they are in the possession of the Area Officials. It is believed by many that the second QC Mr. Langstaff supports the view of Mr. Hendy, that there is no Area Office Branch or votes.

The Hatfield Branch has put forward a resolution that this Area Council now discusses the matter with a view to seeking some timetable to having it resolved.

The Chair who actually lost his mandate for that position *nine months ago* and sits without any authority whatever, has ruled the resolution out of order. That a non elected Chairman can rule out of order a resolution calling for implementation of the *rules on his own election* is also unlawful in our view (Ultra Vires and against all terms of Natural Justice).

As things stand this could go on indefinitely without resolution.

For these reasons, we will challenge the chair in order that we can simply discuss what we are going to do and discover what is the timetable for progress.

We will call for the implementation of the decision of last March, namely that the question be now put to the Certification Officer.

We are resolutely against any notion that 'The NEC' as some self governing body can decide this issue without the members of that Committee first discuss the matter with their Areas and take their views from their Areas. That means the Yorkshire Area must discuss the matter first, then mandate its NEC members before the NEC as such reach any decisions.[425]

DEDUCTIONS FROM COMPENSATION

I have long clashed with Arthur and then the subsequent Area leaders over the charging of unlimited membership fees and high-percentage administration fees. This is a levy on ex-members, people who have left the industry and let their membership lapse. Full members, of course, and retired members have no such levies. But the majority of claimants are now ex-miners and ex-members. I think a flat fee or even a percentage is OK within reason; people using the Union's services who have dropped out of membership should expect to pay something, but the current rate is open-ended. It is possible to end up owing the Union money and recover not a penny piece according to the current formula. Arthur argues that they wouldn't allow that to happen. Well, big deal: we won't take all the former miner's compensation even though he has signed an agreement saying we can – we will allow him to keep some! The formula allows limited membership subs to be paid while the claim is running.

Truth is, most of them aren't 'running' anywhere; there is such a colossal backlog and log-jam the bulk of the claims haven't even been looked at and sit in bundles in offices all over the country while the clock is ticking on their fees. Claims can run for years upon years and the bills tot up each week, on top of which the Union will take a further 5% 'administration fee'. Small settlements, which the bulk of the chest cases are, end up with potential fees to the Union of 50% or more. I am outraged and continue to campaign against this injustice in spite of Arthur and Frank's approval of the scheme. It is one of the differences that sour my relationship with the two former comrades, and their league of sycophantic supporters on the EC and Council.[426]

Our ongoing protests against the deduction of these charges and fees were now sidestepped by passing all such correspondence on to Dave Barber at Raleys. Dave had nothing whatever to do with the decision to make the deductions and Raleys passed them on to the NUM, but they were charged with not paying out any cheques until the member had done so. The Branch continues to object to disproportionate deductions from members' compensation; I start an ongoing campaign to scrap or modify the amounts of money we deduct from our limited members for handling their common-law claims. It has been a bitter bone of contention since Arthur introduced it. During this whole time despite the efforts of myself and our *opposition* branches the Area leadership set its face firmly against any modification or refunds. I had reluctantly suggested a compromise of a total of 5% inclusive of the 'admin' charge and back subs. Arthur argued, as he does at such times, his 'Chicken Little' case: the sky would fall, the Union would go bankrupt, past claimants would sue us, etc. Since complaints are being directed to Raley's and Dave Barber I write:-

Dear Dave

I do not think you are the person I should be addressing these comments to, since the current unsatisfactory situation is clearly not your fault and I do not hold you responsible for any of it.

Mr. Lee when he signed the mandate was agreeing to a 3% deduction from his compensation for the services of the Union in making his claim. This he considers reasonable. He was not however signing a blank cheque to the Union to deduct unlimited amounts from his compensation by way of back subs and ongoing subs.

Mr. Lee I believe had 10% deducted from his compensation while more recent cases have had more than 12%. Actually there is nothing to stop The Union taking 50% or more from his compensation. This is unreasonable and Mr. Lee had no intention of allowing such huge deductions from his compensation. The length of time the claim has run has no relationship whatever to the amount of work being done on his claim and is purely to do with administrative back logs on behalf of the other side and the sheer volume of work. That being the case the amount deducted is purely arbitrary and unfair.

I have a number of men in the office complaining about these deductions and most expressing the view that they were misdirected by us, because had they known they could have their claims run entirely without any deductions by solicitors on the High Street, they would have done so. This dissatisfaction is also due I believe to recent widespread publicity put out by the government and some local MPs alerting claimants that solicitors shouldn't be deducting money from their compensation.

While I do see the distinction between Raleys actions and firms deducting money for themselves, many of our claimants do not.

I have raised these matters with Steve Kemp on numerous occasions and tried through the decision-making bodies of the NUM to challenge them but have been ruled out of order on every occasion …[427]

As the number of our complaints and examples build up, 'the rule' is simply wheeled out to show the Area is within its rights to deduct the large percentages from the compensation; at the same time press and government publicity is adding to the unrest among former members who now believe they have been misled. Another of our old lads came into my office, showing that he had had over £400 taken from him from a total compensation of just over £3,000. It was deeply upsetting to look into those wizened faces; still in disciplined honesty, they say: 'Look lad, if the Union says I have to pay it, I will pay it, but it doesn't seem right, that's all.' It wasn't right, not morally. It sours the good work done by the Union and obscures the fact that we are recovering far higher levels of compensation than most of the hick fly-by-night firms on the High Street. It has to be said, mind, that there were people who took an even more strident view than Arthur and Frank on the question of ex-miners who had dropped out of membership. Somehow, these men had become mixed up in the high tide of antagonism against the contractors, and anyone regardless of circumstances who had accepted redundancy. Some branches really wanted nothing to do with them, or to make life so difficult for them they would have nothing to do with us. Back in February '97 Kellingley and Maltby demanded that ex-members pay their back subs to the date they left the industry and *then* start paying their limited membership fees for the duration of the claim. Had that resolution been carried then it would have meant no ex-member placing his claim with the NUM.

On 22 December 2003, we write formally as a Branch to dissociate ourselves from the actions of the Area and we pin copies of our letters of protest and disassociation on the Advice Centre noticeboard, something we wouldn't normally have done had we been able to exercise some democratic review of the problem.

The Durham Area by contrast had charged a one-off 7.5% membership fee, which was a maximum and covered the lapsed member for all future representation in DSS Tribunals and appeals as well as all common-law cases; this seemed a far more reasonable deduction.[428]

During 2008/09 a press furore and a campaign by some MPs against private solicitors 'double charging' the old, sick and disabled miners, led to a number of firms being taken before the Law Society and even the courts, where some leading lawyers were struck off or suspended. Beresfords, were most newsworthy because of the rags-to-riches success of the firm. Vendside and UDM came under the spotlight, but Raleys itself was next in line. Although they hadn't actually as a firm benefited from this sorry scheme, at least two of their best lawyers were suspended from practice. It is true to say, though, the press missed the real point of the whole story. That is, that it was the Tory and then New Labour governments' refusal to allow the NUM a Claims Handling Agreement to process the claims that led to the explosion of cowboy firms and the gravy train of the NUM and ex-members having to use third-party legal representation in the first place. A government-endorsed scheme with the NUM would have allowed the Union to cover its extra costs and re-engage its former miners but would have controlled dispersements and stopped 'double fees' being paid (basically the practice was to take the government's dispersement payments but then the charge the claimant for the same expenses.) Nobody, including the NUM, came out of this business smelling of roses, though some of us had fought hard to stop the exploitation of our former members.

2004

In January we are circulated with a notice (BS Circular 03/2004) which tells us essentially that we are not allowed to put forward rule changes that seek to change rules. The internal Union civil war rages as the last of our industry sweeps down the whirlpool of virtual decimation.

I am invited to be an adviser in the making of the TV drama *The Key*. I also get to play in the picket crowd scene and battle with the cops. I think it is an excellent film, written and produced by Donna Franceschild, but it is savaged by the critics as a ripoff. Can't see that myself; it is right on the ball of current issues as well as in historical continuity with older struggles, of Glasgow working-class families and the womenfolk in particular.

16 February. After months of bitter battles to break the 'rotten borough' power of the limited membership scam and all that it involved in area and national bureaucracies wielding massive personal votes to influence elections and the direction of the Union, justice could no longer be obstructed. The legal opinions, which the National officials had sat on, were finally reported to the NEC. Brian Langstaff QC and John Hendy QC both stated that limited members do not have any vote directly or indirectly in the matters and affairs of the Union. Surprisingly, though, they declared that the previous decisions made using those illegitimate votes should be allowed to stand.[429] We had won, and it wasn't so long before the Area leaders headed by Steve Kemp conceded that there was no Area Office Branch, though he declared that there had once been one, but it would no longer be casting votes to determine the outcome of elections and policy. My immediate response was that we should be magnanimous in our victory, that we should now let bygones be bygones, get on and work together. I was, on reflection, too hasty; we had won the issue, but the announcement of that judgement had allowed the balance of power within the Area to swing behind the sitting leadership and direction. We had been outflanked after all, although the moral victory was ours.

My Last NUM Conference

This is the year of my last NUM Conference. It's at Blackpool, which I have always loved coming to. I bring Emma and Paul and Caitlin with me to enjoy staying in the hotel and going out after the Conference sessions. The energy minister (Timms) is the guest at the Conference. He sits on the stage, 5 feet from me, as I deliver a blast on government energy policy and apathy on the coal industry. I talk of the plight of Hatfield, the untapped reserves, the potential for clean-burn technology and the fact that New Labour will stand aside and let it all turn to dust rather than make any initiatives of its own. Why should Britain's coal reserves be in the hands of a few rich individuals and the whims of the bankers? He didn't answer me or any of the other delegates who streamed out lists of demands and injustices, as he sat taking notes. Within months he had been moved, as had so many other energy ministers before him. This is the last Conference for a number of other delegates too; we are given a hearty round of applause, but none of the surviving delegates truly believes they will be here in 2 years time themselves.

14 June 2004. I am speaking at Don Valley School. It's the twentieth anniversary of the strike and I talk to the whole school in two big hall-filling lectures against the backdrop of the Hatfield banner, which looks amazing suspended from the basketball hoop in the massive sports hall. The kids all sit in

rapt attention and genuine interest; mostly it's their granddads, from Brodsworth Colliery just along the road, or Bentley, who were part of the struggle – they already know lots from their own families. The questions, though, are twofold: 'What do you do if you want a poo down the pit?' (the response to which drew a collective 'urrrg' across the room), and 'What was it like fighting the cops?' I have taken them a large piece of coal; amazingly, these kids from the heart of the former South Yorkshire coalfield have never ever seen or touched coal.

In October 2004, the NUM, on the verge of bleeding to death following the closure of the vast Selby coalfield, with the closure of its five Selby branches, and the impending closure of its Hatfield Branch, which had stubbornly clung on in the hope of the mine being developed, published what might be seen as its final shot of the war.

In a moderate and conciliatory language, it titled its submission *For A Balanced, Diverse, Secure Energy Policy Based on Indigenous Fuels.*

That the NUM had lowered its demand and its vision, which it had fixed on going back to the *Plan For Coal* and becoming the nation's primary energy supplier, and now accepted almost any role at all, was itself a mark of the times. The paper was the NUM's submission to the DTI consultation on 'A Carbon Abatement Technologies Strategy for Fossil Fuel Power Generation.' The Union's submission stated:

> Instead of pursuing the logic of painfully learned lessons from the days of oil shock, the Thatcher and Major Conservative Governments virtually threw away the bulk of the UK deep-mined industry, and at enormous costs, within sight of the definitive run down of UK oil and gas reserves. The cost amounts to around £30 billion in today's money in redundancy and pit closures, in written off investment for closed mines and in the wider economic costs of closing coal – with some major costs still persisting to this day, along with enormous suffering in the mining communities. The total figure amounts to nearly half of total government oil revenues since 1985. Furthermore, the marketisation of the energy sector in the UK from the mid-1980's onwards, with the disastrous consequences of electricity privatisation, has left the country, in effect, without an energy policy. The present government has not moved very far from the 'new' market logic in energy and unsurprisingly is finding itself with a mounting and potentially severe energy crisis, set for post 2010 Britain. It is unlikely that its stated aims of energy conservation, efficiency and investment in renewable energy will be achieved – aims supported for several decades by the NUM – unless it tempers this exclusive market logic.[430]

The coal industry that remains continues its decline toward probable total extinction. Membership of the NUM in the context of this chapter stands at 2,000 nationwide and falling, following the closure of the Selby complex in November 2004. While the miners who remain are proud and still defiant, still, even at this late hour, fighting to improve hours of work and safety standards, few would expect to be in the industry by 2010 despite plentiful rich seams of coal already accessible to working collieries.

Nowhere is the stark abandonment more clear than at Selby, the vast coal complex comprising five interlinked mines – Wistow, Riccall, Whitemoor, Stillingfleet and North Selby – all the coal coming to bank through a massive drift at Gascoigne Wood. It was the largest deep mine project ever undertaken anywhere in the world. It covered 110 square miles in the Vale of York. It had involved sinking ten shafts and driving 124 miles of tunnels. These, the super pits, the most modern and productive in Europe, turning 11.4 million tonnes per year, and to which miners from across Britain had retreated in the promise of long-term employment, closed after scarce 27 years in production. During its 27 years, the Selby complex turned in excess of 110 million tonnes. At the time of closure, coal was coming to bank at roughly half the costs of heavily subsidised imported coal. Reliable estimates put the untapped reserves in the Barnsley seam at 600 million tonnes – maybe *120 years* of production. The overall opinion of the National Union of Mineworkers was that the potential for surface land development, and building in the highly desirable areas in which the mines were sunk, posed quicker returns in the land portfolio of the company than its mining licences.

13 November. I am making an exhibition of myself at the Tate Gallery in London. My mate Jeremy Deller, who made *The Battle of Orgreave* reconstruction TV documentary, has produced an exhibition for the Tate Britain art competition. Jeremy is a sort of 'happening' agent, a coordinator of circumstances and things, which he brings together in artistic form, rather than as a painter or sculptor. This exhibition is a collage of influences, a résumé of folk art across Britain including the miners' gala. In that regard I have loaned them the Yorkshire Area NUM banner and copies of pictures, posters and books on miners litter the exhibition table, although some people seem to think they are free handouts and nick them. I too am on display, as an influence in Jeremy's life. I am free to talk about miners and banners and galas. On other occasions, he has had Quakers and cyclists likewise standing about, ready to talk about God and life or pedal power. The exhibition bumf explains that these live parts of the exhibition are available to talk to you if you wish. The thronging metropolis art visitor doesn't always seem to get this, and we have a Monty Pythonesque situation where folk will sidle up to me and look at me like I am a statue, then ask, 'OK, what you want to talk about?' It reminded me of the sketch where people paid for a conversation in the manner of ordering a meal from a menu. I explained that I wasn't there just to talk to order or at random, but about the banner and the gala or stuff relevant to the exhibition. More than once I was asked what selection of topics I could talk on, particularly by Americans, who were observing that the exhibition was 'rather too political don't you think?' (It had some eerie scenes from Waco and interviews with local townspeople as well as extraordinary flights of bats, which blacked out the evening sky like something from an old horror movie.)

I was chuffed to wee bits when Jeremy won the competition. The exhibition minus me went on tour, with the Hatfield banner doing its curtain call in galleries and art centres across the land.

Wednesday 17 November 2004. *The Doncaster Star* leads with the headline 'Poverty Streets', followed by 'Former pit village has the worst illness, deprivation and social problems'.

They were not telling the occupants of those former pit villages anything they didn't know, of course. But what was perhaps shocking was that this report came at the end of an intense period of government initiatives and widely publicised programmes aimed at lifting the pit communities from poverty, offering regeneration with well-paid jobs and revamped services. The programmes were always considered all smoke and mirrors.

The report undertaken by health officials, focused on Denaby Main, concluded that it was 'the most deprived community in Doncaster'. Doncaster itself, of course, an apex of 12 or 13 recently closed mines and a number which had closed in earlier years, was nationally among the most deprived in Britain. 88 communities had been investigated and researched using the 2001 Census reviewing health, employment, education and housing. Denaby Main scored 43.8 % in the index. The other black spots were:

Clay Lane	42.6 %
Highfields	42.6
Stainforth	41.4
Carcroft	40.6
Askern	40.1
Hyde Park	39.4
New Rossington	38.5
Toll Bar and Almholme	38.4
Woodlands	37.9
Mexborough	37.1

Of those, only Hyde Park and Clay Lane could be said to be other than former pit communities, although of course pits like Brodsworth and Bentley had drawn on the town at large for workers. The report went on to disclose child poverty rates: highest in Askern, Balby, Bentley, Carcroft, Denaby Main, Dunscroft, Edlington, Highfields, Hyde Park, Intake Lower, Wheatley, Mexborough, New Rossington, Stainforth, Thorne, Toll Bar, Almholme, Woodlands and Wheatley Park. Of these only Balby, Hyde Park and Intake could be deemed not specifically mining communities. Long-term illness was around 40% higher and early death rates were likewise centralised around the same string of former pit villages.[431]

In January of 2010, the pit town of Edlington becomes famous. Two little lads of 10 and 11 torture and brutalise two other boys of 9 and 10. The press and TV home in like vultures and we are told in vivid terms of the squalor and deprivation of the area. Cameron calls it a symptom of 'broken Britain'. Nobody mentions who broke it, or that Edlington had fought 12 hard months to keep the mine and soul of this community alive, and had it beaten out of them. Jobs went and traditions and community values and comradeship followed. Benefit dependency, followed by hopelessness and drug addiction. Visions of social solidarity, of standing together were ripped out of Doncaster. The two lads in question had come from Intake, which is cited in the above report. They had been raised into a family of indifference and hard knocks. Then dropped into a community with whom they had nothing in common, with a carer out of their depth. It is a symptom of the state of 'anomie' I have tried to describe in this book. Thatcher, Major and the New Labour governments created this situation, by killing our communities, and their values, based on hard work and solidarity, trade unionism and socialism. The two lads and their alienated parents know nothing of those things anymore. However, it was not the fault of communities like Edlington, and Doncaster as a whole, who fought and still fight to hold tight to those visions.

These are the last days of the miners, if not the last days of coal, which will remain untapped and sterilised in abandoned mines throughout Britain. It is unlikely in the extreme that, once filled in and abandoned, the pits would ever be recovered. Costs of sinking new shafts would be beyond the commercial constraints of a private mining industry, which would be unlikely to tie up massive investments for long-term returns, but, more crucially, once the tradition of mining is lost, and this generation of miners who are mostly middle-aged are forced into early retirement or new careers – where they can be found – who will then go down?

Certainly, the era of men working laying flat in 18-inch (45cm) seams such as started my early career and ended with the closure of Emley Moor in West Yorkshire after the '84/85 strike will never be resurrected. Mining is a tradition, very often a family industry; once the connection is severed, it is unlikely to be reconstructed on any scale.

Countervailing forces in the former pit communities do however exist. Turnout to the Durham Miners' Gala, for example, 11 years since the last Durham colliery closed, goes from strength to strength and witnesses both pride and anger as the banners retake the streets carrying their old message of class and socialism, of mining history, of the culture of pit folk. 50,000 turned out in July (2004), despite monsoon downpours of rain and heavy overcast skies. The Durham Area in particular has a massive project of resurrecting banners, old and more recent, involving the whole community in research and local history and the organising of events to bring long-gone banners, and long forgotten communities, back into life and self-identity. By 2009, 90,000 people cheer the banners through the streets, including those of all the coalfield areas and the few working pits we have left.

Everywhere the twentieth anniversary of the '84/85 strike has been the cause of important community gatherings, of the staging of plays, of school inquiry and research, and of multiple TV documentaries from television producers both here and around the world, probing the pit communities, testing memories and temper and conviction. People in the pit communities have now had time to pause and reflect not simply on the strike and its defeat but the aftermath: 'Where we have been'; what all of that about class and culture and community really meant, and 'Where are we now?' Does it still mean something, and how can we retain what is left? The antisocial spread of emptiness consumes everything around it and one needs real determination not to succumb to it.

Some welfares such as that at Rossington, based upon what was the second-last working mine in Doncaster, have built on their role as the centre of the village, and now host permanent outreach centres of Northern and Doncaster Colleges, offering ongoing computer courses and retraining schemes. At the same time, they offer an advice facility for mining pensioners and claimants of all varieties.

June, I propose the Yorkshire Miners' Gala is revived to commemorate the 20th anniversary of the strike.

It will be the last time the NUM formally takes its banners, bands and communities onto the streets of Yorkshire.[432]

At the end of November, I am invited to address a joint university seminar on the culture of the coalfields, hosted at Caphouse Colliery in Wakefield. It is a most prestigious invitation for me, to be lecturing here, among all the academics, but its more important to me that the miners who act as guides at the pit request to sit in at my lecture in particular.

17 November 2004. After a yearlong campaign to win over 50% of the workforce to the NUM Branch at Hatfield Colliery, I finally succeed; though Budge the owner writes into the Area Office to ask for talks to concede recognition at the pit. I am determined that the Branch itself shall be a central part of these talks, as we are suspicious that the recognition for mutual benefit of Barnsley and Budge might not recognise me as secretary or give me access to the colliery. We shall never know; weeks later Coal Power goes into liquidation with dozens of debtors and unpaid miners banging on the door. I recall a series of mass meetings again, and in a real test of loyalty the receivers canvass the workforce for who their representative will be; unanimously, members and non-members nominate myself. This is Hatfield's third closure in 10 years!

Budge for the first time ever has to be present with me in formal meetings over monies owed to the men and the fate of the pit. At this crucial time, the officials start banging on about when the sacked men will start paying their full dues again. I contend that the pit is still alive, it is still operational, we are fighting to save the colliery, the men have been compulsorily dismissed; this is a dispute situation and we don't have to pay subs. In fact, this very issue had been covered at the NEC on 8 July 1993 under rule 5a (vii):

> All members whose employment has been terminated by the employer,
> either by enforced redundancy or where the Union considers a member
> has been victimized by being wrongfully dismissed … shall be entitled to
> remain full members of the union.

This was subsequently ratified by the whole NEC on the understanding that men who voluntarily took redundancy would not be covered, but those who had the pit shut underneath them would. There should have been no argument in Hatfield's case.

The officials however argue that the pit is closed, the men no longer work there, if they don't pay full subs they aren't members. If we don't have members we can't have a branch, and if there is no branch there is no me in their hair.

Of course they didn't say that last bit out loud but that's the strong conclusion I draw. Whereas we are now searching the world and lobbying Doncaster Metropolitan Borough Council and the government to save the pit, they appear to me to be trying to close the Branch and create a sufficient gap to shake me and the members free from the NUM in the hope that if the pit does reopen it will be under their control and not ours.

The miners are united along with all former NACODS members in the same NUM Branch. I meet the leaders of the council and MPs. We march, we lobby Parliament, we have a forceful meeting with Timms the Energy Minister, we plan an occupation, senior overmen refuse to turn off the pumps and power. By March 2004, all the men have been made redundant. We succeed in saving the shafts but we lose our argument to exempt the men during this period from payment of full subs, although I carry on paying mine.

Hatfield Main Branch closes, for the first time in nearly 100 years. My role here is now finished.

With the pit finally closed the soul of these villages, Stainforth, Dunscroft, Hatfield, Thorne and Moorends dies. Corrosive antisocial crime, poverty, hopelessness and fear start to eat the heart out of shared values and common culture.[433]

Norman Cornish, *The Pit Road*, Oil

9

THE HARP THAT ONCE BETRAYED US ALL

THE PROVISIONAL SURRENDER

On 1 April 2005 the Irish anarchist Grassroots movement invited me over to their weekend Dublin conference on community resistance and organisation. I would be thrilled to be their major speaker on their Friday opening night. I had asked for a podium from which to place my fairly extensive notes, since I was speaking on the strike and the period since, and been warned that few in the audience would either have been alive during '84 or anyway have any memory or knowledge of it. Also of course I was talking about politics and characters in a different country, although Arthur Scargill had been in Dublin just 2 weeks prior addressing a public meeting as a guest of the Irish TUC, among whom he was greatly admired and respected. He spoke to a crowd of some 3,000 and with his presentation of acting, mimicry and passion he had earned from a spellbound audience a standing ovation.

My own intervention would be somewhat more modest, although for Grassroots it was regarded as quite a coup. The hall was a centre for local events, a crèche, welfare rights and community lobby groups. It reminded me a little of a big Dutch squat, although the hall was only hired. They had a meal being prepared in the big kitchen and many of the Irish anarcho groups had stalls round the hall. The Anarchist Communists, a split from the British ACF, with their paper *Organise*, had in fact developed a far more secure understanding than their British cousins with whom I had locked horns on occasion, but in honesty were also changing under pressure from their contact with rank-and-file workers. A number of them were down from up north, and I had a canny crack with them about the 70s and politics back then.

The Solidarity Campaign is the Irish anarcho-syndicalist movement, who I had come across on a number of occasions; they were streets ahead of their English equivalents in the Solidarity Federation. There were claimants' groups, and tenants' groups, IndyMedia, and the local radio network which seemed to be run by a matrix of them all.

Of course, who else should sidle up with their demob suits and American accents, but two Sparts? It marked quite a change for them, since they had previously given Ireland a big detour for fear of being shot for their terrible position on Ireland and the resistance. Apparently they had changed their line to be more accommodating to the struggle, but by then the struggle had become rather less charged than previously. They came up and engaged me in debate, and actually bought copies of everything I had – *Class War*, *Imagination* and *Strike, Not the End of the Story*. Later they got up to make their usual points about the Soviet Union, Solidarity in Poland, the need for a Trotskyist party, Labourism etc. I spelt out the differences between our position and theirs in as comradely a fashion as I could, given their record with regard to me, only to find when I actually got to read their damn paper they had an attack upon me on the back page. Never mentioned it to my face or raised it in the hall. It was the same old myth about the 'racialist' march to the scab wharfs. Actually, it had been a demonstration in support of the South African NUM's call for solidarity blacking of South African coal, which of course was coming in at the scab wharfs – where else?

Veronica had told the cousins I would be over, and I spotted them at once as they came in, although I had never seen them since we were 12 or so. Tom and his wife Christine, and Mary. He actually got up to make a point, but also say proudly 'that's my cousin up there', which felt great. We scarcely got a minute, though, as the radio wished to talk to me and the groups and I was staying with Aileen, one of the organisers. They brought me a copy of Christine's book (in her maiden name, Broe), *Solas So'las*. The Irish '*solas*' means light; with the accents it means consolation, and together they communicate an ancient universal concept of silence. Her book, which I read going back on the plane, was largely about taking care of her mother as she died slowly, suffering worsening Alzheimer's. I had time for a rabid flurry of words, and to pass out copies of *Strike*, before they left and I was whisked round the room and out the door with the blind radio producer to find us an off-licence. Actually there were a couple of drop-dead gorgeous nurses who were on strike at the time, who had come and sat in the front row, and we had started to talk animatedly to each other. With one tall, striking girl in particular there was a promise that more could come of this, but I kept getting taken off to meet intense young, and some not so young, Irish political activists, and though I had kept saying to her, 'I'm coming back – don't go away!' it ended up with just a hug at the end of the night and a lift home elsewhere. Hm. It turns out there was another member of the family in the audience, the son of my cousin Madge, who now lives in Dublin; he reported back that the night had been fascinating but he couldn't catch up with me or the other cousins for a crack.

I had spoke for an hour and a quarter, without a break or interruption, and it went down well with laughter and cheers and a flurry of applause at the end, and was followed by some tub-thumping stuff from the people in the audience about life and work and struggle in Dublin.

What was absent? Sinn Féin was absent. I had made a point to talk about the recent accusations on the missing millions and the similarity with the setup of the miners and our leaders vis-à-vis the Libyan money and the Soviet gold. I talked about the state's black propaganda campaign against the miners and Sinn Féin, hoping to strike a resonance with the Irish struggle, but there was none. Sinn Féin had clearly changed its composition since the battling days of the '70s when it emerged. It was now an establishment, mainstream political party; it no longer was down in the street with the protesters and campaigners. It wasn't regarded, at least among this crowd, as a party of the resistance anymore.

It was quite painful to be told time and time again how ordinary people seen it as corrupt, bankrupt and bourgeois, to be told that in its record and that of its councillors and representatives on schools, hospitals and general cuts and attacks upon welfare it was like every other Irish political party. It was odd, too, that I was arguing in support of an organisation to which I no longer belonged, and with which I had had no real contact for probably over a decade.

The peace process had clearly changed the organisation, as well as the reverse. I could start to see, albeit from a distance, how tensions between the armed wing and this process would be having an effect. It would require that I took some time when up north to talk to republicans on the ground and see how they see it. On deeper reflection and on closer inspection, I already knew this process was afoot. Indeed I and the comrades in the British Sinn Féin cumainn had been the first victims of it, when the decision was made to close all non-Ireland cumainn. The bold Marxist resolutions coming in thick and fast to the Ard Fheis from over the water, the revolutionary socialist alliance, which objectively was developing between the Ulster cumainn in the thick of the armed struggle and the left-leaning 'British' industry-based cumainn, had set alarm bells ringing a lang time syne. The struggle within the organisation, for the revolutionary socialist republican political and armed campaign to be the organisation as a whole, was never achieved. At first we thought the struggle was with the right wing, the old green Tories, the plain and simple Irish nationalists, the traditional church-dominated Irish folk myth faction, against the armed young workers and their political representatives who felt root and branch part of the world revolutionary socialist struggle. Of course not all the armed sections had been Che Guevara with a red and green star; there were some of the old guard with old-guard perspectives within the IRA too – this often demonstrated itself in the choice and care with targets. It now seemed that this process of struggle had gone up a peg or two since the ceasefire and peace agreement, and Good Friday, and power-sharing. The left had been pushed hard off the stage, as had the armed struggle itself, and even the quest for a 32-county Irish republic, ner mind a soviet socialist one based on the small farmers and workers. The quest to become a respectable establishment party seemed to have taken its place. I am forced to sit down and make a serious assessment of where we have been and where we have arrived, though this is not likely to be the last we see of this struggle.

Meantime I begin a painful examination of where the Provos have gone and how?

HOW AND WHEN DID WE GET HERE?

Disagreement with the current strategy has nothing to do with the presence or absence of armed struggle. Whether an organisation is armed or unarmed does not determine of itself whether the organisation is more or less principled or progressive. At all times we, that is those of my particular political orientation, have regarded violence, revolutionary class violence, to be a tactic, not a principle. A phase of struggle which is not one characterised by armed struggle doesn't mean the organisation in that phase is therefore less principled or 'macho'. The assessment of the current situation and the detection of massive retreats in the programme and principles of Sinn Féin and the IRA is not some kind of sulk about them having given up the armed rebellion. (Comrade Kilburn had mocked, in an earlier phase, that somehow you can only be a real grown up revolutionary if you have a beard, gun and steely countenance.) Much of this process had been going on behind the scenes, while we still called for 'Victory To the IRA'. While we still hailed Sinn Féin, and seen Gerry as a very astute leader of 'our' organisation in Ireland, we believed, throughout, that the agenda for a 32-county socialist Ireland, run owned and controlled by the working class and small farmers, was firmly in place. And that all of the tactical positioning, the ceasefires, the peace talks, the intervention into conventional political forums, were clever footwork to disarm and outmanoeuvre the British state by playing them at their own game. We did not know, and I suspect most of the rank and file of the movement did not know, that it was we who were outmanoeuvred and outflanked, and the game was on us.

What has developed here is the symptom of something deep and, by July 2005, terminal.

The signing of the Good Friday Agreement in 1998 marked the end of an almost subliminal and in many respects remarkable process. It marked the disintegration of the raison d'être for the Provisional movement, at least as an armed insurgency. However, even at that late stage of the surrender process it was being sold as a highly conditional agreement which demanded as much from the other side, the British state and loyalism, as the republicans had conceded. Over the following 6 years as these representatives of 'the other side' backed away from their obligations, they demanded that more and more of the figleaves hiding republican impotence were stripped away, so that the once virile and thrusting young movement could now be seen, in the words of Trotsky, to be 'dangling its impotence before the eyes of the world'. The process on the republican side continued at a quicker pace; it was clear this agreement was highly one-sided and unconditional, at least in the terms in which the original aims and aspirations of that movement would have viewed them.

The British state had restated its claim to the 'north' as a body that was politically and separately distinct from the 'south'. It continued to postulate that the 6 counties of the north constituted a separate ethnic, political entity from the other 26 counties of Ireland. In so doing it rejigged the electoral process that determined the 'majority' wish of the people, by splitting off the minority from the opposing majority population, then declaring this now distinct minority to be a separate majority opinion. It thus turned a stomping majority vote and expression for an independent Ireland into a vote against that wish by allowing the 20% minority to veto the majority vote and stifle any fulfilment of that decision. It was inherently undemocratic and fraudulent when it was devised in 1921, and had been the rationale for all IRA upsurges since the signing of the sellout treaty along those lines by Free State traitors. The Provisionals at their inception had pledged never to accept such an undemocratic and unprincipled formulation. The Good Friday Agreement accepted this undemocratic formulation and the loyalist veto, so long as the majority within the minority remained a majority within the minority. The Provisionals had by this action kicked away the platform upon which they had stood, and for which hundreds had died. The situation was somewhat worse than 1921 in so far as the Dublin government had now under British pressure amended its constitution, deleting points two and three that laid claim to whole island of Ireland, to accept that the northern six counties were outwith the geopolitical land mass of 'Ireland'. Britain refused to project any future point at which it would not occupy and administer the six counties as part of 'Britain', unless the Loyalists agreed. This would seem to further rule out a withdrawal from the six counties, even if a majority within the six counties agreed it, i.e. if the nationalist community birthrate expanded to the point where they could outvote the loyalist population. Only if the majority of loyalists agreed to the withdrawal would the British state agree, even if there was now no longer a majority for this among the six counties. This agreement, at a stroke, grants the loyalists a veto for perpetuity regardless of any normal or even rigged electoral process. While it is true the Provisional IRA was not defeated militarily, one would struggle to find any description of this, in republican terms, other than an utter sellout and de facto defeat of the movements aims. It is incalculably worse than the offer on the table during the time of the earlier Sunningdale Agreement, which the Provos had helped to bring down. But by May 1998 they had agreed to take part in the new Stormont parliament and help administer the province. By the time of this agreement, the pass had already been sold, opposition crushed, isolated, sickened and disillusioned. How had the leadership taken us down this road? How could they have gotten away with it? Looking at where we were, at those fine aspirations, at that courage and conviction, how have we got here to such a dire and miserable abandonment of those aims? It has been a slow but relentless process, one taken in measured increments, each portion of the retreat covered by a rationale of 'defiance and continuation of the struggle by other means', using 'dynamic' tactics. Perhaps the scale of the project wasn't visible, even while it was being constructed all around us. I suppose self-deception – an utter suspension of belief that such an act of wanton betrayal was possible – must have played the major part in not allowing us to see the elephant in the living room.

'Change' is not and never has been the issue for me; pragmatism and a flexible approach to tactics are essential ingredients for any movement which is serious in its objectives. And it was with arguments of pragmatism that the tactics and areas of 'manoeuvrability' were sold to the membership. Good Friday, it had been guaranteed, wasn't a 'settlement'. It was repositioning to make progress. However, this 'repositioning' was linked unshakably with disarmament and the ending of the armed struggle. That feature was mis-sold, as part of an 'overall' disarmament process; in fact it was always a unilateral one. The Orange ultras and loyalist military never gave the slightest intimation that they would join this process to any degree at all. In 1995 the IRA and the political wing were swearing to the high heavens that such a development was not on the cards. Wall slogans and murals, saluting the peace process, at the same time hailed the armed struggle and swore that there would be no surrender of the armed capacity of the IRA. It is unclear how far the Sinn Féin leadership endorsed this line, as within five years it had started a process of decommissioning, in fact dissolution of the arms and explosives, and a de facto winding-down of the volunteers.

This was sold as 'a new phase of the struggle' and, with other such 'historic' and 'courageous' descriptions, took on the nature of Orwell's *1984* 'doublespeak', and the sellout pigs of *Animal Farm*. The political qualitative change marked here by these events is cataclysmic. Socialism had been all but abandoned along the way; many of the socialists were dropped or isolated before that, and now republicanism itself was being dumped in place of standard 'constitutional nationalism', of the kind last seen in the pre-rebellion Irish Home Rule Party. From now on in, Sinn Féin would be tied to a logic and glowingly overt political programme aimed at recognising and consolidating both Dublin and Stormont as constitutionally legitimate arenas of operation. Sinn Féin may be an awkward bedfellow and a restless sleeper, but there is no mistake who it is in bed with, and whose bed it actually is. A number of my old comrades over the water believe that today's Sinn Féin shares the same proximity to Irish republicanism as Blair's New Labour project did to socialism. Actually there is something disturbingly familiar also in the style, personalities and PR aura of both Blair and Adams, like they were cut from the same cloth. A question both raise is: how did they manage to get away with it, and while we were watching, too? It seems impossible to have a definitive answer to this question, though we can perhaps start to chart its emergence; a clear revisionist programme and leadership is much harder to identify.

The retreat from all non-Ireland-based branches of Sinn Féin had multiple effects. It cut the movement in Ireland off from the Irish in Britain in organic terms. It severed the input from a sector of the Irish and British–Irish population which was heavily proletarian, trade unionist and revolutionary socialist and communistic. This in turn organically cut the Irish republican movement from its interconnection with the British trade union/labour and far left movements. Sinn Féin's socialist and Marxist trajectory would be halted and cut off from its active daily input. This shifted the balance of political influence within the organisation.[434] How did they get away with this, with such a politically mature section of the movement? Good question – I suggest it was because of an intrinsic belief and trust in the leadership. That we, a section, may be a victim of some political conservatism, and sectarianism here, but the broad strides of the republican movement under its current leadership were correct and trustworthy. The same process had happened in other times in many other places.

Around the same time there emerges a clear though faceless rejection of Marxism and revolutionary socialism within the Ireland-based cumainn, and the movement at large. Up to this point serious political education, schools, debate and papers were all under the sway of Marxism and far-left political evaluations. Connolly was seen as the founding father of the movement and the inspiration for its current direction, towards a workers' and small farmers' socialist republic owned and controlled by the working people, as part of the global struggle of the workers of the world. *Questions of History* was written and produced by the H-block prisoners. Its authority was boundless, its mission the Irish republican socialist revolution in the context of a critique and polemic with more conservative and nationalist visions of Irish history and struggle. The 2,000 copies of the book, meant to be our shop window of principle and perspective to the world, an external address, were suppressed and remained largely a purely internal document. Even then it was much mauled, often by 'comrades' who one would have thought understood its significance, not least around and within *An Phoblacht/Republican News*. The even more significant second volume never seen the light of day, and I believe exists only in manuscript, or pre-print form.

Within the organisation, for the first time in print, two clear political lines started to emerge. On the one hand was a policy position paper presented by those whose statement, *Questions of History*, overtly reflected and supported the same point of view. The head of Sinn Féin's Political Education Commission was also the former head (OC) of the prisoners at Portlaoise (the prisoners as a whole stood on the far left and Marxist left of the organisation, reflecting the political vision of both the armed wing and the youth of the organisation overall). The paper was complex in so far as it was addressing subjects and areas of polemic unknown to most party members, who had no real notion of the political power struggles behind the scenes and throughout the organisation. It argued that no overall 32-county-wide, class-based struggle existed, and that instead the struggle in the north was being effectively isolated and left in limbo, while a social-democratic, reformist, accommodationist strategy was being pursued in the south.

Identifying the 'bucket of water' tendency on the other side – how it emerged, from where, who it was, how it thought, what was its rationale, and how the hell/why the hell was it ever in the Provisionals in the first place? – has been like ghost-hunting. As time has gone on and this inquiry has continued the ghosts have started to come out of their cupboards and out from under the floorboards. Intriguingly, the alternative paper had been put forward by Tom Hartley, a man I had not come across personally or politically but who had risen to become a general secretary of Sinn Féin. To all intents and purposes Hartley carried the line of the old 'Stickies' within the Provos. Philip Ferguson, a fellow former Sinn Féiner, writing in *Weekly Worker* (5 May 2005; 'Behind the Betrayal'), tells us:

> Hartley, whose politics seem quite influenced by the nationalist wing of the pro-Moscow Communist Party of Ireland (CPI), argued in favour of a pan-nationalist front. This would be formed by working for unity with Fianna Fáil, the SDLP – and even Fine Gael! – to advance an Irish national agenda. This paper was extraordinary considering Irish history. It basically turned its back on every significant struggle and leader since Wolfe Tone by rejecting a struggle for national liberation based upon the people of no property – a concept at the very heart of Irish republicanism – and advocating class collaboration with the very sections of Irish society which had always sold out the struggles and which were clearly working with the Brits to maintain the status quo.

It was odd, but here was re-emerging the very political road from which the Provisionals had made such a decisive political break and from which they had marched with such determination.

The retreat from armed struggle as a major instrument of victory, and even as a balance in the 'Armalite and ballot box' strategy – with no clear policy direction change to accompany it, and no open policy debate reassessing the role for armed struggle and possible new policy directions – robbed the hitherto dynamic movement of direction and perspective. The IRA as a central component of the organisation was becoming sidelined and ignored. Their intrinsic faith in the political leadership allayed any fear of treachery, and step by step forestalled any rebellion. At this time, the Soviet Union, whatever its original nature may or may not have been, was withdrawing from its world role as counterbalancing superpower to US imperialism. As a result national liberation movements the world over were suddenly friendless, moneyless, and without military backing. In country after country, armed liberation movements were being defeated, changing tack, suing for peace on almost any terms and giving up visions of socialism and anti-imperialist crusades. 'The World Revolution' which had been stalking the world, and of which the young Provies felt a part, was slowing and going into counterspin.

The ANC and the PLO had changed tack, had entered the world of 'acceptable politics', were shifting ground to find acceptable compromises. For those undeclared and faceless leaders of the new direction in the background of the republican movement such changes were inspirational and evidence that this was the time for change. The upfront representatives of the new direction Adams and McGuinness were less than candid about where they were actually leading the movement. Such changes would not be sold as abandonment of the struggle, but shifting the emphasis, changing the ground to fight on, while holding fast to the cause. Loyalist politicians' demands for transparent disarmament and declarations of a permanent end to the armed struggle were still being met by ridicule and resolve. This was meant to be a peace process affecting all sides; it was emphatically not surrender on behalf of the Provos.

A CASE OF THE KETTLE CALLING THE FRYING PAN

Standing on its head the reality of what was going on, it was the revolutionary and leftist current which was secretly being lined up for accusations of abandoning the armed struggle. It was said that these Marxists were turning away from the guerrilla war and toward some workerist mass movement alternative. Those in the mainstream of the movement, and even within the party, tended to be less clued up than their comrades to the left and right. 'Carry on regardless' could cynically be described as their position, or perhaps more kindly, a philosophy which asked 'Why change a winning formula?' The winning formula would seek to maintain the armed potential and combativity of the army wing, while making advances in politicising the whole of Ireland and challenging the political structures north and south. This perfectly sensible position was flawed by the fact that they linked it to support for and accepting the version of reality put on it by the centre/ nationalist leadership. This leadership was, in the words of Philip Ferguson, involved in a

> whispering campaign ... that the people behind the Connolly paper were
> hostile to the armed struggle and wanted it called off. It was more or less

implied that a vote for that paper was a vote to end the armed struggle. Also, various people were removed from the leadership in both the party and the army without any transparency in the process at all. Supporters of the nationalist position would sometimes go so far as to throw a tantrum, shrieking and carrying on as if voting for the Connolly position was a betrayal of the nationalist population of the north.[435]

In fact it was the leadership of Adams and those in his coterie who had been working on far-reaching revisionist plans which would mark the end of the Provisionals as a force for revolutionary socialist and anti-imperialist struggle. What they were working on was little short of a full revival of the late-lamented Sunningdale Agreement of 1973, the defeat of which had so marked off the Provisionals from the Stickies in outlook and direction. The slow inoculation of the whole movement with these plans is a wonder of deception. They were floated as 'just supposing', as 'ideas not policies' and 'trying new approaches'. That they were proffered by men highly trusted and creditworthy, transparently honest and likable, was all the more disarming for that. Soon these 'ideas', without official sanction or open debate, without any internal debate and exposure of where they were going and what stood behind them, were appearing in print and in public as 'Official' documents, in more ways than one, subsumed into the body of Sinn Féin.

It emerges at the end of December 2005 that a key British agent has been working as Gerry's right-hand man, his backroom adviser and his voice in the ear. He has doubtless been a leading architect of the whole recent trajectory. It is Denis Donaldson, who is 'outed' by a process of events and comes clean in the press: 'I was a spy,' he admits in a headline of the *Irish Times* (18 December). Donaldson now decides to spill the beans – more than likely to forestall and derail any deeper, more searching inquiry into how far this penetration has gone. It allows the Sinn Féin leadership to feign ignorance and claim a clean sheet once again. Donaldson admits to having been a plant for the last twenty years. He was working directly for the British state, not to discover plots and strategies, not to direct the line of fire against our insurgents – although some of that clearly comes into it – but to redirect the whole republican movement off message and onto another political route entirely. He had been a leading member of Sinn Féin, and one of its key strategists of this last two decades; only Adams himself was his senior in developing the movement and struggle away from its earlier directional stance and to where it now stands. Donaldson had been with Adams, concocting this brew, since the late '70s. However, despite his lofty influence it is clear that to move such a monumental movement away from traditional values and founding principles could only have been achieved with a great deal of help from others also well placed as spies and agents.

It really raises fundamental questions about who was running the Provisional movement in the last few years.

Was it the British? Was it the Adams leadership? Or was it the Adams leadership and the British together, both working to a common goal?[436]

Certainly Donaldson, by the early 1990s, was advocating a winding down of the role of the IRA and seeing the armed struggle as an obstacle to Irish unity. That this was the same hymnsheet that Adams and McGuinness were singing from does beg the question as to whether the whole kit and caboodle of the leadership wasn't simply the Irish shop window of the British state's advanced counterinsurgency strategy. Dirtier and more despicable yet is the evidence that key opponents of the Adams/ McGuinness surrender strategy were lined up for assassination by the British army and its special forces. The *Sunday Independent* states that a senior Sinn Féin British agent passed on information to Garda Special Branch officers, which was shared with the RUC. This set the IRA up for its most severe assault on May 1987, when seven members of the East Tyrone unit were ambushed in Loughgall. The unit was led by Jim Lynagh, a dissident. Other information on IRA operations was passed on, leading to further assassinations of several key IRA dissidents.

As with a number of great movements and revolutionary betrayals before and since, one is left dumbstruck asking how such men and women, such giants, could have been so won over to something previously so totally alien?

Adams, like Blair, did not get elected then turn bad. They actually sought office with the clear intention of taking control and then direction of their respective movements away from the routes they had been going down hitherto. (That is not to suggest for one moment that the 'old' Labour Party and PLP were somehow on a socialist road before Blair, it clearly wasn't. It had been sort of vaguely left of centre in actual fact, but millions still seen it as a vehicle for radical change and endeavour.) Adams had behind the scenes been preparing a political coup before his election as president in 1983. This might not have been widely known within the organisation and many perhaps seen the charisma and form rather than its quite determined content. Adams almost from the beginning started to talk the 'common-sense', 'practical' view which should always start alarm bells ringing in any organisation of radical intent. James Connolly had earlier sarcastically declared: 'Our demands most moderate are, we only want … The earth!' Truth was, our demands were not moderate at all, though Adams was now preaching the gospel of 'moderation' and 'caution', warning of the dangers of being seen as too radical, and voicing the need to not put off more moderate and 'ordinary' people who were more restrained. Almost upon election he struck his colours to the mast of a faction battle with the 'ultra-left' within the party and movement. It was Adams's 'Enemy Within' speech:

> We must be mindful of the dangers of ultra-leftism and remember at all times that, while our struggle has a major social and economic content, the securing of Irish independence is the prerequisite for the advance to a socialist republican society. Therefore … republicans have a duty to beware of any tendencies which would narrow our demands and our base. This is true not only of forces outside our movement, but also of tendencies within our party.[437]

With Martin McGuinness we see perhaps a different process, clearly a man who started out putting his life on the line for the cause, by what route we do not know; he was converted to selling short the movement and seeking more tangible, more pragmatic goals.

Here we see the inextricable goals of republican socialism suddenly separated to two stages, the first to achieve independence, before the second stage of achieving a socialist society can be achieved. Such a perspective would open up a whole new agenda of winning forces across the board to the first mission while allowing the second part to drop from view. Then as the struggle for socialism is seen as an obstacle to the achievement of an independent republic, the display of left-wing positions and a class identity are seen as against the goals of the movement. How could non-socialists be won to the cause of an independent Ireland, if the movement identified itself as republican socialist? Such an identity was militating against the fundamental aim of the movement – independence. New alliances with nationalist politicians, and organisations in the mainstream, couldn't be courted and allied with, so long as the socialist republican policy remained in place. It was an obstruction to the newfound direction of the movement.

Interviewed in the *Irish Times* (10 December 1986) Adams declared that socialism wasn't on the agenda; the movement could only grow with support of non-left, conservative forces to the right and centre.

Movement and 'progress' became objects for their own sake; first socialism could be abandoned and best forgotten and then republicanism itself became the obstacle.

How could we win the new alliances, the new platforms, and open up progress if our stark and radical republicanism put off those who were nationalist, but not republican? Principles started to be abandoned as the crew of a falling hot-air balloon throws out ballast in order to maintain altitude. The hard-won 'woman's right to choose' on the question of abortion, won in the teeth of traditionalist Catholic opposition in principled fights since the inception of the movement, was abandoned without principle in 1986. This was argued for not because of a change of heart or in the value of the principle, but purely as an electoral and PR device to make their passage into the southern political scene more acceptable. From the 1980s onward, the aims of opening a dialogue, of creating broad alliances, of establishing new platforms, of achieving 'movement', determine that everything, literally everything and anything, can be abandoned to set the party centrally on this new stage.

It would not be long before the elephant in Gerry's new living room was armed struggle, and the existence of the IRA itself. The whole perspective now at the centre of the movement is political manoeuvring, electoral positioning, making friends and influencing people whoever they may be. New legislation demanded that all councillors renounced armed struggle and any method of struggle other than the constitutional 'bourgeois democratic' variety and that this be attested to in an oath of office. In 1989, the Ard Fheis agreed that this should be undertaken. The Armalite was now being abandoned alongside republicanism and socialism, in favour of just the ballot box, but then what of the principles remaining in the pursuit of that ballot box strategy?

The principled Provisional position at first had been abstentionist; we recognised neither the 26-county Dáil, nor the 6-county Stormont, nor the writ of the British parliament to govern Ireland. Sinn Féin would not stand in elections, or, if they did, they would, as was the position of our early British communists, not take their seats. After the success of Bobby Sands, one of the political prisoners dying in the H-blocks, in running for the Westminster Parliament, the propaganda value of using the electoral process to expose the process became clear. We could contest parliamentary elections as a protest, as a focus but not take up seats. Next it was agreed that standing in and contesting council elections 32-county-wide would be a good propaganda and functional exercise in putting across a radical and revolutionary alternative. Using the state electoral machine was a tactic in overthrowing the states, north and south, as part of an overall combined political and military perspective. With the emerging new Sinn Féin position, protest gave way to reform. Governing the province, fighting for grants, jobs, new rights, educational facilities, recreational facilities, schools, hospitals, parks. Sinn Féin councillors were taking seats on committees and boards, fighting for tangible improvements and working within the system to make the system work and accommodate their communities. This didn't look like fighting for a thoroughgoing alternative to the state; more than that, the IRA could hardly continue its bombing campaign in cities and against institutions while its political representatives were working to bring the benefits of those bodies to the Catholic community. Sinn Féin was, remarkably, though it seemed to loyalism and many in the British media, being absorbed into the system, and without too much fundamental change to the system. By 1992, Sinn Féin had ten seats on Belfast City Council; it was helping run the city, and administer it. They sat on committees with all the other political constitutionalists and nobody could tell, from what they did, any difference. The first Sinn Féin lord mayor of Belfast was Alex Maskey, for the year 2002–3. He poses in his grand chair, in his chain of office, in front a large Union Jack. He is not a rogue from his movement's principles, he is actually embodying them. As Liam O Ruairc observed in one of his series of *Weekly Worker* articles,

> The problem is that, once legitimacy of the Dublin government is recognised, there cannot be two legitimate governments and two legitimate armies; one has to recognise that the official Irish army is the only legitimate army and that an illegal army is therefore illegitimate. The republican objective is to bring down Leinster House, not enter it. However, in 1986, in order to grow electorally in the south the Provisionals dropped abstentionism and recognised its legitimacy.[438]

Hitherto the IRA had not recognised Leinster House, as this was the seat of the partitionists, treatyists and their descendants. Only the IRA was the legitimate representative of the 'The Irish Republic' and the government of that Irish republic as first declared by the 1916 rebellion and declaration of Dáil Éireann.

By 1992 we had the de facto emergence of new Sinn Féin in the stamp and colour of New Labour and, on reflection, by something of a very similar process with some notable exceptions. Blair had for a time stood on the left of his party, advocated socialism, though never been an old-style Labour anti-capitalist or even a Fabian anti-capitalist. He had declared in his maiden speech to the Commons his commitment to socialism. His position in support of CND and good left causes, his alleged admiration for the miners and pledges to seek justice for those victimised men and their families, suggested a man of the left. He may not have built the revisionist bandwagon which was wheeled out as the answer to successive electoral defeats, but was quick to jump on board when Neil Kinnock and his razzmatazz machine rolled by. By slick PR messages, and behind-the-scenes administrative and political coups, by cronying, by patronage, by deception and all sorts of well-heeled professional gamesmanship he was able to win over the whole party apparatus and alter its political culture and rationale. This ensured that the new MP cadre and new members to the party came increasingly from the ranks of professionals, and graduates, carried the New Labour passport and not the old raggy arsed cloth cap, or manual working-class tradition and language of Keir Hardie. Adams, I am almost certain, had explained to me in the '70s, that he was a Marxist – 'an Irish Marxist' was the expression he used I seem to recall. Certainly he had read with interest and some support our political pamphlets and stood in the camp of the revolutionary left. He stood on the firm ground of the military north, Irish Republican, left-wing, internationalist, Ulster. Gerry had appeared in print with pamphlets explaining the logic and justice of republican socialism. When the transformation occurred the books and pamphlets were purged from existence; the line had changed, 'old' Gerry had gone, lost without trace. It put me in mind of the YCL/CP book-burning which occurred in the back garden of the People's Bookshop in Newcastle. Radical and 'ultra-left' books and early party positions found in the Left Book Club editions were being purged from the shelves and were cravenly burnt. (It was my juvenile attempts to rescue some of these old books that started my lifelong hobby of collecting them.) Philip Ferguson tells us:

> Each edition of Adams's first book, *The Politics of Irish Freedom*, was re-edited several times to remove certain criticisms of the SDLP and Fianna Fáil and any other views of his subsequently deemed to have been 'ultra-left'.[439]

Like the process in the Labour Party, old adherents of the old-time religion left in disgust; others became bitterly disillusioned. Those unwilling to go were given the cold shoulder or the big heave-ho on one pretence or another. At the same time as the line changed and the transformation started to take on a different political and social persona, it attracted a different kind of member, and more of the new model leadership.

'Four Legs Good Two Legs Better,' as 'the pigs' had changed the slogans of the revolution to mean their opposite:

> The exercise of self-determination is a matter for agreement between the people of Ireland. It is a search for that agreement and the means of achieving it on which we will be concentrating.[440]

'Self-determination' hitherto had been a matter of principle set in stone, 'the people of Ireland' as a whole and directly were the only body in justice who could determine the future of the island of Ireland as a whole. Speaking here for the first time of 'agreement between the people of Ireland' said one thing. It said that the different communities would exercise that right independently, separated, and not 'as a whole' together as one people. It was a profound shift, further than any republican or even British political force had ever gone, because it was actually referring to agreement with 'loyalism'. It was essentially saying that only if the Loyalists conceded an agreement to a 32-county political constitution, and ipso facto ceased by that action to be loyalists, could a 'united Ireland' or 32-county Ireland be achieved.

Previous betrayals and fudges and gerrymandering had granted to the loyalist a veto. So long as they, the minority, didn't agree to an all-island Ireland, the British state and its army would protect them and that view. The old-style doublespeak had, through the creation of new political entity, the 6-county 'Ulster', declared that so long as 'a majority' (within the minority artificial statelet) wished to be part of the UK, Britain would defend them and remain in occupation. This 'majority' was based on loyalism being the dominant political force numerically within the 6 counties. This was the yardstick which all British governments since its creation in 1921 had declared and set their clocks by. Far-sighted legalists had long posed the doomsday scenario to loyalism that the day might come when they were no longer actually the majority even within the 6 counties. That day was, with or without the Provos, coming ever closer, as the Catholic/republican birthrate was slowly achieving an equalisation with the loyalist population whose birthrate was falling. Even without the Provisionals or any republican force, by the British state's own expandable yardstick and twisted version of 'democracy', the day was coming when British presence could be constitutionally voted out of 'Ulster' with or without the approval of loyalism.

Some equally farsighted person or department had foreseen that this clock was ticking, and sought some means by which 'democracy' could be suspended indefinitely regardless of numbers of respective populations. Who in their wildest imagining could have envisaged that the instrument for such a thoroughgoing permanent loyalist veto would be the so-called 'republican' Provisional movement? The statement is clearly talking in terms of agreement with 'loyalism', regardless of what percentage of the population north or south that term actually represents. This was the creation of a new super veto. Those who see talk of 'accommodation with loyalism' as applying only so long as it represents the majority of the minority, are only in fact claiming a less thoroughgoing surrender to the loyalist veto. Either position is a total abandonment of Republicanism, and a surrender of the raison d'être for the Provisionals' existence. Liam O Ruairc observed:

> In seeking an alliance with parties that accept the unionist veto as the foundation of any political settlement, the Adams leadership was implicitly acknowledging that any future political arrangement would be predominately internal one, leaving the constitutional status of the Six Counties unaltered.[441]

Gerry's much-vaunted struggle for 'inclusionism' of the republican community was again Orwellian exclusionism of republicanism as a political force per se. McGuinness spelt it out among all the bluster of the Bodenstown commemoration, which had once been such a proud and principled event. For those that were still listening, this was a strange commemorative speech (1993). For now he was talking of short-term arrangements, with no actual aim for the armed wing anymore. There was no longer any immediate imperative to drive the British state out of Ireland. This was now a far-off, long-term objective, effectively on the back burner. Adams too was talking of transitional arrangements, transitional demands, long-term far-off objectives and short-term aims and goals within the existing structure of occupation and partition.

AUGUST 1994: THE PROVISIONAL IRA's 'CESSATION OF MILITARY OPERATIONS'

Recognising the potential of the current situation and in order to enhance the democratic peace process and underline our definitive commitment to its success, the leadership of Óglaigh na hÉireann have decided that as of midnight, Wednesday August 31st, there will be a complete cessation of military operations. All our units have been instructed accordingly ... We believe that an opportunity to create a just and lasting solution will only be found as a result of inclusive negotiations ... It is our desire to significantly contribute to the creation of a climate which will encourage this. (IRA statement)

The IRA wanted now to wind up but to appear not to surrender. It wished to walk back to work with its banners flying, as the miners had done. But unlike the miners the fate of its operational ability after it had done so was very dubious. As it turned out, Paisley and the other ultra-loyalists wanted the IRA to come and publicly surrender, to have photos of weapons being destroyed or handed in. They wanted a humiliating defeat, as if the end wasn't humiliating enough. This caused the IRA to take the terms off the table in 1996, but it was little more than bluff with little left to stake up on the table. The organisation had already been politically gutted by then. Still the danger of a split and a regroupment around some unreconstituted IRA militia was an opportunity or a danger depending how you looked at it.

After a round of re-elections of all the parties involved in Britain and the 26 counties and an enlargement of the Sinn Féin popular mandate, all the parties came back round the table again and the IRA reannounced its long-term, open-ended end of engagements (July 1997). It was the final prelude to the utter abandonment of a fine, heroic and once principled organisation. The IRA had not actually been defeated; it had given up. Through a long process, described in short above, it had been in my sincere view utterly betrayed and the republican population led up the garden path. A direction they had already marched some distance at great costs away from. That this wasn't some accidental 'drift', or war weariness, or 'fresh thinking', or any of the positive spin, diehard supporters of Sinn Féin, like the three wise monkeys, try to put on it. This was clear counter-revolutionary subversion of the most revolutionary armed people's movement in Europe. A clever and careful long-term strategy of political stealth, PR, spin, black propaganda and plain murder. But all done so cleverly and with such sleight of hand that 'the movement' to a large extent still thinks it was all their own idea, and the movement is still the movement. Sadly, or maybe thankfully, it actually isn't. We must be prepared to accept that actually Gerry and Martin could well be long-time, deeply planted British counter-revolutionary agents themselves; or else were converted on the road to Damascus. The facts speak much louder than innuendo and coincidence, though it brings me no joy to have to say so. We have been screwed once again, as we were back in the '20s and late '60s. The yawning gap in this line of analysis of course is, what of the masses? The Good Friday Agreement was massively voted in favour of, by people who had fought for decades and resisted everything that assassination, terrorism and occupation could throw at them.

Why did they accept the new turn? In part, it was their absolute intrinsic faith in the leadership and faithfulness of Provisional Sinn Féin, a party and a movement they had embraced with all their hearts and soul. That they demanded a new phase, a new strategy is undeniable, that they believed this new turn, this new agreement would nonetheless continue their political aspirations to a republican socialist Ireland is also beyond doubt.

So am I any closer to understanding what happened? How it happened, yes, but why? What is it, in the midst of huge pushes forward, in organisations and rebellions and revolutions, that makes a certain group, usually of high-placed individuals decide to pull the plug on the whole endeavour and sell the pass? At what point do these people actually lose sight not only of where we are going but why?[442]

Are they from the beginning always trying to find a suitable opportunity to sell us out, are they corrupt and spineless from the beginning, are they agents of the enemy, or are they turned by leadership, power, money, prestige or what? It is a question which can be posed time and time over, from the Soviet revolution to China, from the British Labour Party to Sinn Féin, from Mexico to Spain, from the TUC to countless strikes and unions and movements around the world. Are they traitors from the beginning, is a traitor and misleader bred into the woodwork of every organisation and movement we construct? Those questions I am no closer to answering.

10

GHOST DANCERS

Over a period of 200 years, the native inhabitants (the 'Indians') of the United States of America fought a heroic war of resistance to hold onto their way of life and their freedom. To steal their land, the newly emerged American state resorted to an increasingly genocidal programme of mass extermination. The government fought ruthlessly to bring the native peoples to heel, to break their resistance, to desecrate their gods, wipe out their culture and their way of life.

They were a threat to the vision of the new America, to no-holds-barred-capitalism and wringing dry the Earth and its resources. Despite attempts at treaties, recourse to the new state laws, and appeals for justice, the massacre continued. At length, united and determined resistance halted the onslaught for a minute period; then the US state reacted with fury, breaking the back of the Native American resistance crippling their culture. They aimed to take their faith from them, to rob them of their souls so they would henceforth have no past, no memory, only dependence on the new social order.

But the native people would not let this memory and vision pass. There arose a new religion, central to which was the Ghost Dance. The tribes all dressed in traditional costume and the old music, the drums and the rhythms of a millennium rang out again with the cries of the medicine men and voices of the wise elders and women. The tribe would dance in huge numbers, doing the Ghost Dance. The Ghost Dance promised that if we danced in enough numbers, if with enough belief we kept banging those drums, then the white man would lose his strength, the buffalo would return to the prairie, and the fish to the streams and birds to the sky. The power and magic of the tribes would be restored and the old ways would come back.

One eyewitness account of the Ghost Dance said:

Before dancing, the ritual participants would enter a sweat lodge for purification. Then the worshippers, painted with sacred red pigment, would adorn themselves in a special costume that was believed to be a gift from the Father. The hallowed clothing was usually made of white cotton muslin cloth embellished with feathers and painted symbols seen in the wearers' visions, as well as a prominent eagle figure. While many tribes of Plains Indians wore the ghost shirts and partook of the dance, only the Lakota believed that the clothing would protect them from the bullets of the white man.

One of the songs sung at the ceremonies celebrated this:

Verily, I have given you my strength,
Says the Father, says the Father.
The shirt will cause you to live,
Says the Father, says the Father.[443]

The actual dance was performed by all members joining hands to create a circle. In the centre of the formation was a sacred tree, or symbol of a tree,

decorated with religious offerings. Looking toward the sun, the dancers would do a shuffling, counter-clockwise side step, chanting songs of resurrection. Gradually the tempo would be increased to a great beat of arousal. Some dances would continue for days until the participants 'died,' falling to the ground, rolling around and experiencing visions of a new land of hope and freedom from white people that was promised by the messiah. The dance often produced mass hypnosis in its transfixed participants, and thus, it became known as the Ghost Dance. Curious onlookers were prohibited, furthering the sense of mystery about the ritual and elevating the tension between the dancers, settlers and soldiers.[444]

A Lakota Sioux described the Ghost Dance:

> The visions ... ended the same way, like a chorus describing a great encampment of all the Lakotas who had ever died, where ... there was no sorrow but only joy, where relatives thronged out with happy laughter.

The movement was spreading, the culture would not die, they would dance, and sing and remain; thousands were joining.

The authorities hated it – it scared them. Here was defiance beyond reason. The era of the red man had gone – why wouldn't they disappear with it?

On 29 December 1890, the US Army surrounds the demonstration and shoot down the dancers. They wish to wipe out the memory and the spirit of the Indians, not just the Indians themselves.

In 1984, the government came to tame the miners, wipe out communities, close the mines, kill a vision, kill an industry and a Union that supported that vision, of society and community and the value of labour. The miners and their families fought and lost; more than half of them were eliminated from the industrial landscape. But the miners fought on, regained their position, rekindled the flame and retook the biggest share of the energy market on the Union's terms. So the government came back, between 1992 and 1994, with a final solution to the problem of these miners, and closed all but a handful of the remaining mines.

Smashed the communities, suppressed the spirit of rebellion and vision of commonwealth and common worth. But the miners' communities and spirit refused to die. At Durham, they kept on marching, kept on beating the drum, playing the martial tunes, flying the flags of triumph and history, class and vision. They were Ghost Dancers, subliminally dreaming that if you keep flying those banners carrying our past and our hopes, keep singing the songs of ancient culture and hearing the voices for change and justice, then the mines will reopen, the NUM will regain its position of strength and respect and the bosses and state will disappear from the prairies. Arthur will walk on water again. Keeping the faith that if we don't surrender our souls, our inner sense of who we are, these magnificent bandsmen and women, and our storm troops lang since confined to barracks will be ready for the turn of the wind, which will see us march back to social power and position, repossessing our disposed souls.

Year by year the marchers got stronger, the numbers of banners being found and remade increased, the communities began to rally, more bands were formed, of young people – in the crowds now among the old flat caps and wizened faces were the faces of youth and strength.

In 1994 not a single Durham mine remained, yet 50,000 marched. It was the twentieth anniversary of the great strike, and the banners marked that epic struggle and the ruthlessness of the police and state.

Amid the crowds of families and dancing miners and their children, the riot police suddenly appeared – tooled up: shields, clubs and helmets with visors. They demanded the bands stop marching, and the crowd disperse. The bandsmen and women didn't miss a note and blasted out their martial defiance. As women swept up children and old men took to the sidelines, masses of the young men, and the older fighters from 20 years earlier, swept down toward the ranks of police, carrying bottles and bricks. We were planning to mark the strike and make a last stand now, like our sisters and brothers at Wounded Knee.

But unlike at Wounded Knee the forces of the state were outmatched and it was they who withdrew, before they got the hiding of their lives in front of the tens of thousands of miners and their families, a battery of cameras and crowds of tourists. They withdrew to thunderous cheers and the bands boomed out their big drums, flags streaming through the afternoon breeze. The march resumed its path through the closed-off city, as every march had done since 1860. On the 25th anniversary, 5 years later, 90,000 marched and assembled, ignoring and defying the squads of robocops pushing their arrogance through the families. They Seethe. But 'The Ghost Dance' continues.

GENOCIDE ON LEBANON[445]

In the second week of July 2006, the Israelis launch a blitz on Lebanon. They bomb Beirut with their F111s; they bombard the coastal towns with naval guns and missiles. Within 2 weeks 300 are dead, nearly half of whom are little kids, thousands are wounded, hundreds died later and half a million people are displaced and homeless. The country's power supply, sanitation and water are bombed out of existence. Bridges and roads, transport and military bases, such as they are, are destroyed. They have moved in to wipe Lebanon off the map. Another Zionist 'final solution'.

The excuse is the capture of two Israeli soldiers during a daring attack by Hezbollah, and the random firing of Katyusha rockets into northern Israeli cities. Hezbollah succeed in destroying an army outpost and capturing a couple of soldiers. The Israelis will countenance no opposition to their domination of the Middle East; the result is the destruction of Lebanon, a collective punishment of the whole population and incidentally tens of thousands of tourists and students from all over Europe for whom Lebanon had become a place of residence or wonder. The European Union tries to draft a resolution instructing Israel to stop the massacre and declare a ceasefire; Blair vetoes it and despite the total imbalance between the relative forces and the disproportionate number of deaths on the Arab side condemns Hezbollah for causing the war. For the first time in a long time, I feel like dropping everything and picking up a rocket launcher and going off to fight Israel and the Zionist conquistadors.

With US approval, Israel next threatens to take the war to Syria. Iran is already on the US/British hit list as the source of all 'terrorism' in the region. Iran, no lover of anything Syrian, declares that if Syria is attacked Iran will consider this the prelude to an attack upon them. You wouldn't have to be a genius to work that one out. In the middle of this late but necessary common front against Zionist expansionism and racism, al-Qaeda continues its internecine war of terror in a bloodbath against everyone in the Iraqi resistance, bombing civilians of all descriptions and wreaking havoc among all the forces trying to form a liberation front. Objectively and quite literally, al-Qaeda is in a common front with imperialism and Zionism, whatever its fanatical rhetoric.

Daily war crimes are visited on southern Lebanon in scale and brutality of those in Vietnam and the Nazis in Europe. Villages are ordered to evacuate by occupying Israeli forces, with whole families, impoverished and terrified, packed into trucks and farm vehicles, clinging to a few possessions, their traumatised children clinging to folks and grandfolks. Then as they leave the army calls up air support who deliberately strafe the vehicles and kill the families. Leaflets are dropped onto villages ordering all civilians to leave as an aerial bombardment is going to commence. As the families stream from the safety of their shelters, up the roads out of the towns and villages, helicopter gunships mow them down. The world looks on. Blair and Bush veto all calls from around the world for an immediate cessation of violence, announcing that nothing has been achieved yet. This means they support the continued killing, knowing that over a third of those being butchered are children and more than another third are totally innocent families. This is a self-declared 'Christian', the sanctimonious critic of the 'terrorists' – as if the London bus bomb and tube bombs are any different at all in terms of victims and purpose from the victims of Lebanon.

The attempts of the invading Israelis to bomb, destroy and kill until they have wiped out Hezbollah actually destroyed Lebanon as a functioning Arab state. Only after the position of utter devastation and defeat of that people will they then stop. Blair and Bush support the war; they are allies in the same campaign of heartless murder. The contempt for world opinion is such that a UN observation post, manned by international unarmed soldiers, is shelled and bombed for hours until it is totally destroyed despite pleas from the UN Security forces to stop; ten direct phone calls are ignored and rescuers are bombed and shelled as the UN compound is blasted. The eyes and ears of the world will not witness or record this massacre in any serious fashion; that is what this Israeli action is all about. It also shows clearly that it will brook no interference from the so-called United Nations. With the US and Britain in the triple alliance of murder, who is going to stop them?

Day 15, and 400 Lebanese are dead, mostly civilians, mostly children. Half a million are displaced and homeless, starving and dying of hunger and thirst. The population of Lebanon is 4 million, it has no air force and no navy, it has a weak, uncoordinated, ill-equipped army. It depends upon diplomacy and 'world pressure' for its survival and it is not surviving. Previously the Lebanese had been persuaded to force the self-declared protectors of the country, the Syrian army, to leave; Lebanon was now a democratic part of the world family of civilised nations again and it needed no armed Arab ally to protect it; so the Syrian military left, leaving only the raggylad troops of Hezbollah to continue their war in the south against Israeli occupation and in solidarity with the Palestinian people's ongoing war of liberation. Impotent, the world looks on as F111s and guided missiles pound anything that looks like the infrastructure of civilisation. Ambulances and Red Cross stations, clearly marked, are bombed regardless, indeed one ambulance has been hit by a airborne bomb directly in the centre of the red cross – clearly no accident but a cynical indication of their regard for basic humanity.

Hezbollah is the only defence now, is the only means of retaliation and courageously they are taking on the Israeli forces, killing at least 15 soldiers and destroying armoured vehicles in one afternoon ambush in what the Israeli thought was another easy civilian town. Hezbollah is far from diminished – they are now universally hailed as heroes as were the IRA after Bloody Sunday in Derry.

This war, along with that fought in Vietnam at the very awakening of my political involvement, is the worst I have ever lived through, though of course not experienced, not yet. For the first time in my lifetime the beast of imperialism, with its Zionist assassin off the leash, has no superpower counterbalance of any description to call it into check. The rich and powerful nations have passed the control of the world to the US state. But resistance, no matter how crude, revenge, no matter how unfair, will inevitably result. Does anyone think Britain and America's populations will be allowed to go unpunished for the crimes of their leaders? I doubt it. My own blood boils daily and I am wretched that I cannot have not taken up armed resistance to this injustice; in truth if such a force was being raised I feel certain I would lay everything else down and join it. I say that in the clear love of my family and everything they mean to me. I doubt that I will get the chance to prove it. Why didn't I form such a force myself? Not possible of course without an already existing international armed and equipped organisation. The left in Europe long ago stopped trying to develop these; those few brave cadres who had tried were hunted down and shot, killed in gun battles or murdered in their cells as the high tide of red revolution retreated and left them exposed and isolated. Thousands, perhaps tens of thousands, of Muslim young men just might; though they may misjudge their enemy and mistake their target, should that happen it will be nonetheless perfectly predictable and understandable. It has to be said that, on a world scale, Blair has been far worse than Thatcher or any preceding British prime minister of any party since the end of World War Two, maybe longer.

By May 2007, the Lebanese army is at war with a section of the Palestinian resistance. The huge Palestinian camp at Sidon is surrounded with mass artillery and shelled without mercy; helpless women and children are killed wholesale as buildings are demolished and bodies and carnage litters the streets, against a tiny Islamist faction, Fatah Islam. The Palestinians are being giving the treatment the Israelis gave the Lebanon as a whole. There is even less of an outcry, but HYPOCRISY screams from the corpses of those endlessly beleaguered people. If I were a Palestinian child I would grow up hating the world and vowing vengeance upon it, wouldn't you? To simply retaliate against the ones who directly oppressed them would be a lifetime's work, ner mind those who stood silently by and said nowt. At precisely the same time, Israel starts to bomb the Gaza Strip, the hapless civilians are murdered by gunships, and rockets they say are aimed at Hamas. On the streets, Palestinian fights Palestinian as the secular forces attempt to control the spreading military influence of Islamist Hamas.

ET TU, BRUTE

This month and November, the miners receive an unexpected kick in the teeth from our former comrades in the 'green movement', with the Climate Camp and an amalgam of hippie-type environmental anarchos attacking coal-fired power stations. In Didcot, they occupy the plant. At Ferrybridge, they host a Greenham-style camp and invite everyone to close the plant, attacking the perimeter in an effort to stop the conveyor belts. Where were their photos of Maggie Thatcher and John Major? After all, these two had done more to close down coal-fired power stations than any raggy-arsed environmentalist had.

Did the Green guerrillas have any programme for the miners and their families? Did they have any suggestions as to what will become of our already impoverished communities? Clean coal stations? Not a mention – coal in every shape and form is the enemy. This could be the pro-nuclear lobby in drag. All attacks on coal generation are de facto arguments for nuclear generation. Windmills and tidal generation are not going to replace coal; they are not seriously proposed as an alternative by anyone – closing down the coal generators is an argument for building new nuclear stations. Nuclear experts tell us this very week that 70 new nuclear power stations are planned around the world. Tony Blair must be delighted; his spokesmen were quick to come on TV and explain that yes, the protesters are right, the coal stations will close or 'be phased out', as they put it. He said nothing about windmills replacing them.

The fact was that the anti-coal protesters had fallen completely for the whole scam. The low-sulphur pits had been closed in Britain, and the option to fit desulphurisation filters to all coal power stations, which at a stroke would have reduced emissions by 50%, was rejected by Blair. Low-sulphur coal would be imported to Britain; transporting it will almost restore the pollution it saved. At the same time, Blair launched a major roadbuilding programme and gave the green light for development on the green belts all over Britain, easily smothering any savings in coal pollution with transport pollution. In fact the Energy Commission Report of 1990 on the 'greenhouse effect' had found that, globally, coal-fired-generated electricity was responsible for 7% of the Earth greenhouse CO_2. Coal burning in the UK constituted 37% of the overall national total, in global terms 0.5%.[446]

THE WALLS CLOSE IN

I am up at the caravan at Berwick and visiting Alnwick and roond Toon. The walls of post offices, libraries, backs of buses and public places are plastered with a grim warning: 'ILLEGAL BONFIRES WILL BE REMOVED'. So the collective village or estate bonfire, so much a feature of my childhood and my parents' early years too, is now deemed antisocial, and 'illegal'. The cheek of working folk – thinking they can plan social activity and community events for themselves without approval from some corporate bigwig or police officer, and without asking approval of some person who now runs every aspect of our lives![447] It goes along with the big iron gates and fence now straddling the pier at South Shields, for example, and announcing that you cannot now walk along the pier without you apply for special permission and a special person with a special key letting you walk along to the end, or fish, in case it's stormy. It follows on the banning of conkers in the schoolyard in case of allergies, or making slidies in the snow, or climbing trees. This year pantomimes will ban throwing sweets out to the kids in the audience in case of allergies or them hitting someone.

Carmarthenshire council discusses draining its public park paddling pools because they are warned they must employ 'Baywatch style lifeguards' at each one rather than the local park attendant; the pools are less than 2 feet deep.[448] Pick-your-own strawberry farms are put

out of business because insurance companies responding to Health and Safety Executive instructions refuse to give cover without the mass installation of fences and guide rails. The 'danger' of falling in a ditch, or on uneven ground, into bushes, or being pricked requires a labyrinth of restraining walkways, fences and rails, making the whole operation quite unpractical and financially inoperable.[449]

Across the entire island, children are forbidden from playing outside on the streets, being out of sight of their parents, or moving more than 50 yards from their own house, by parents driven mad with fear by the tabloid press. The belief that it 'is too dangerous' and that every man is a potential child-killer or kidnapper is now entrenched in the overwhelming part of the population, but among mothers in particular.[450] Theatre groups, community halls, playgroups et al. who have in their possession plastic swords and plastic guns are subject to 'firearms controls' and are forced to appoint a firearms officer and secure holding area to store the 'firearms'.

Police curfews are now imposed at 9 p.m. throughout the country to ban youngsters playing out in their own streets, backyards or fields, just in case parents haven't already done so. Schools start to ban the playing of tuggy or linking arms in collective games. Susan Tuck, head teacher at Bracebridge Heath Primary, Lincolnshire, declares touching between children 'inappropriate'.[451] Numbers of children 'abusing' other children and facing conviction and prosecution start to rise alarmingly as any childish sexual activity is deemed 'rape' and 'sexual assault'. In Rotherham toddler–parent playgroup schemes ban toast-and-tea breakfast sessions as 'too dangerous'.[452] In Somerset, a 5-year-old receives a formal interview and reprimand from police officers who attend at his home because he chalked a hopscotch pitch on the pavement outside his own house. Elsewhere three young teenage girls were arrested for chalking moons and fairies outside their grandmother's house.[453] Shannon Smith aged ten is arrested, fingerprinted and threatened with an Anti-Social Behaviour Order, but instead is issued with a fixed-penalty notice for 'Criminal Damage': she had drawn a 3-inch letter 'S' in crayon on a wall.[454] Elsewhere a child is arrested for throwing a piece of cucumber at another child, while four uniformed officers formally caution a primary-school student for calling another student 'gay'.[455] Officers had called to arrest Aaron for scrawling 'Harry Is Gay' on a wall, but discovering he was seven confined themselves to giving him a hefty telling-off.[456] In Crawley, a *20-month-old baby* eating Quavers in her pushchair drops two of them from the bag as her grandmother, Barbara Judd, pushes her along. A sharp-sighted police officer with a community warden in tow issued Barbara – in lieu of the baby – an £80 fixed-penalty fine.[457]

A 16-year-old boy is given an £80 fixed-penalty notice for 'letting go of a balloon'; on objecting to payment his parents are told their property will be seized to pay the bill, plus collection tariffs, if it isn't paid.[458] A Down's Syndrome boy with a mental age of 5 in a special-needs school is charged with 'racially aggravated assault' for pushing away another student who came too close to his dinner. She was Asian; although the boy had no recognition of race or what crime he is supposed to have committed, two uniformed police officers insist on going through all the witness statements and placing an advert for witnesses to the 'racially aggravated assault' in local papers as well as charging the terrified boy.[459] A Blackpool photographer is cautioned that taking photos of people in the street is unlawful.[460] Copeland Council, after imposing a curfew on bins, making it an offence to put a bin out before 7 a.m. in the morning, then have Gareth Corkhill arrested for not having his bin lid shut properly; this results in £210 fine, with the threat of impounding his car and sending bailiffs into his home to seize furniture to meet the costs, followed by a prison sentence should he further fail to meet the fine.[461]

THEY REALLY ARE WATCHING YOU

Meanwhile surveillance cameras now number one for every 14 people in the whole country. Medical records are now held centrally without our approval and are accessible by numerous state bodies without our knowledge or approval. New passports will contain detailed records on your life, criminal record and God knows what else. In June 2007, it was revealed that the DNA of hundreds of children under the age of 10 (the government's age of 'criminal responsibility') had been stored on the Police National Database. 883,888 records of children and young adults between 10 and 17 were stored, along with, incidentally, those of 46 people over the age of 90. More shockingly, a great number of these profiled people had never been convicted or even cautioned for any offence. Three-quarters of 'the young black male population' would be soon on the database.[462] The total number of records stored without the consent and knowledge of the subjects or their parents together with those actually convicted with an offence is at this time four times higher than across Europe and something like 500% higher than those held per capita in the USA.[463] By August of 2007, DNA records are being filed at the rate of one every 45 seconds without their owner's knowledge or consent or any offence having been committed. The net is closing tighter and tighter. New Labour has up to this month introduced 22 NEW Criminal Justice Acts, not just new laws, but whole rafts of laws in each Act. By the last month of Blair's government, they had enacted an average of one new law every 3 hours of a decade of government. The jails are bursting at the seams and Britain rates as one of the top five jailing countries per capita across the whole world, although top of the charts is still the USA, the world's jail capital.

In May 2008, the government rejects the report of the specialist committee it set up to look at legislation related to marijuana. It rejects the conclusion of the committee that the drug should remain category C and instead should be upgraded, with all that means in terms of arrest and jail terms, to category B. The science is rejected in favour of the opinions of the editorial positions of the tabloid press. The tabloids have driven the Blair government quite mad and regularly formally advise the home secretary on what laws to introduce and what sentences to pass on them. The *Sun* and *News of the World* are seriously the new legal and social advisers for the Home Office. Since Blair, the position of attorney general has been a blatantly political appointment, which interferes with sentencing by the courts largely under the influence of the tabloids. The government has waged a determined campaign to wipe out judges' discretion in sentencing based upon circumstances, and impose instead across-the-board draconian prison terms regardless of the circumstances of the offence, usually in response to howling tabloid press headlines.

Much of the population believes it is under siege; young adults are treated as children and children as babes in arms, or else unaccompanied kids are at once regarded as criminals and hoodlums. Meantime childhood is to be legally extended with the withdrawal of liberty from young adults under the age of 18 and their compulsory detention in educational faculties against their will and consent. Something like 250,000 teenagers will lose their right to leave school and make their own way in the world as they have done hitherto in every preceding generation.

At the stroke of a pen, the age at which young workers and students who smoke can legally buy cigarettes or be given cigarettes is raised by 2 years to 18. Supermarkets start announcing that if you don't look 30 and haven't got ID they will not serve you with alcohol, despite the law actually stating you can legally drink at 18.[464] Nobody sees the civil liberties implication of this change or the dangerous precedent it sets in terms of wiping out people's traditional liberties to take risks with their own lives if they so wish. It is a further step in attempting to juvenile young adults and take control of more and more of people's daily lives and choices.

The state propaganda industry runs the daily gossip and feeds the paranoia and fears of the mass of the population. 'News' is really part of the entertainment industry now, with a sweep of the country or Europe or America in search of daily doses of 'outrage'. Quite minor misdemeanours or utterly personal breakdowns and private tragedies are thrown up on the national stage for the 'good' citizens to shake their heads at, or to feel the warm glow of not being in the limelight themselves. A pregnant 13-year-old in some hitherto unimportant part of the country will suddenly find herself the front-page scandal of every puerile tabloid reader, while even the once staid BBC News will dredge up tiny little cameos of moral digression and throw them into the world spotlight as viewing for millions upon millions of people without the slightest significance to their lives.

We witness a form of public hanging, the public birching, the naked destruction of individual and families' lives daily across forests of newsprint and hourly TV broadcasts. 'Documentary' is now more often than not hijacked by government propagandists giving the official line on drugs, Arabs, drinking, teenage sex and crime. Twice, thrice *Crimewatch* or *Police Action* propaganda films present the work of the police, forgive the excesses of the police, film from the side and stance of the police. The crowd in the scene being battered are always the working-class scum, the body on the floor in the blood and the handcuffs always the thug, the cop always the long-suffering person under pressure. It is the modern Roman circus – be grateful you are one in the stand and not in the sand of the ring; the louder you cheer the destruction of the state's victim, the more you hope not to join them. Many will not, for they have decided long ago not to rock any boats and do exactly what their rulers tell them, whatever it is. Of course, there are bad bastards, and bad and cruel things happen, but why make a nationwide focus of such minor and broadly socially irrelevant events? Simply to create the climate of the wolves at the door and fear of the neighbourhood and the city. You get to the point where you only trust the leaders, the politicians and the police – who else will protect you against this raging mob? But looked at objectively, or even out of the window, there's nothing there, really!

1926

On 12 November, we mark the 80th anniversary of the end of the great 1926 miners' lockout. Whereas the start of the movement and the General Strike was marked in Doncaster, this one I have organised in Newcastle. It says something of the quality of the NUM that in both cases the chairman of the NUM Area chairs our seminars and conferences. In this case it is Davie Guy, who adds his own detailed backdrop to the dispute in the North East. Most unions would run a mile from appearing on the programme sponsored by the IWW, Class War and the CPGB (*Weekly Worker*) but notwithstanding Steve Kemp's disassociation from us, the NUM is happy to play a full part with former branch officials, miners and their families turning out together with the usual anarcho purists arguing the council communist nonsense.

'POETIE ARMSTRONG'

December. In one of those out-of-the-blue experiences that happen periodically and convince me that there is indeed some supernatural winged person looking after me, I am invited to help make a BBC documentary on Tommy Armstrong, the great poet and sangster of the coalfields in the years before his death in 1920. He was the forerunner of folk like Bobby Thompson and Billy Connolly – a satirist and comic who pilloried the coalowners and their agents and wrote passionate songs of the miners and their struggles and tragedies. I am to trawl through the places of Tommy's life in Tanfield Lee and Stanley and interview his surviving relatives the historians and folk artists who have made him their passion. That they call on me to present the programme and do the interviews is rather like that privilege I received when asked to write the introduction to the official *Durham Miners' Gala Book*.

It turns out to be a wonderful magical day, which I thoroughly enjoy. A touch of sadness is added when I discover that Pat Elliott, one of the surviving Elliotts of Birtley family, has died. I knew she was suffering greatly and was dying, I regret not having been able to go to her funeral. She and the family had become great friends of the Doncaster miners and the Hatfield folk in particular; they were regular performers at our socials and galas.

HANG SADDAM

After Xmas they hang Saddam. He is led into a bearpit of jeering Shiite militants who chant the names of his enemies and curse him to hell. The gang that bring him in are masked and disguised. The spectacle is being filmed onto mobile phones and circulated to jubilation across the internet. He is quiet and dignified and asks them if this is what men have become. It is simply a vindictive act, little better than a summary execution. The American occupying forces having stage-managed the trial. It is a farce from the start, with defence lawyers assassinated or dismissed, and even the judge replaced as too sympathetic. That Saddam has committed crimes is beyond question; that those trying him have done far more and on a far bigger scale is patently beyond question too. That Iraq is infinitely worse off under them than under him is witnessed every bloody and desperate day. Even the nationalities and religious factions he suppressed have never had it quite so desperately fatal as they do now – with the possible exception of the autonomous Kurdish region, which was already effectively free of him before the second invasion started. They have no shame, so it is pointless to be shocked, but the British gutter media reprint all the photos. A little earlier, they have cried to high heaven over breaches of the Geneva Convention when Iraqis show photos of captured British soldiers. Saddam is after all a prisoner of war, handed over to a mob. He is indeed guilty of killing innocent Iraqi civilians, but Bush and Blair have killed a great many more and in addition have wrecked the lives of millions upon millions in Iraq, something Saddam would never have done.

OLD COMRADE OLD FOES

Jim Shipley, my old marra and comrade, gets in touch. I am chuffed to bits. He was at times so close to me and has shared a lot of my pit life. I have been after him to seek his approval for the bits on him on this work. I at length write to his Dad, who remarkably is still alive and still toodling aboot in his three-wheeler with their lass and causing a great deal of political agitation, bless him. (Jim's life story would put my own in the shade so I am only including the sections, which intersect mine!)

The first week of the New Year David Irvine dies, of cancer, a natural death given his armed struggle involvements and the dangerous paths he had walked. Dave had been a member of the UVF's ruling Army Council. Then a lengthy prison sentence and contact with 'the other side' committed him to a root-and-branch study of the history of Ireland's working class, north and south, Catholic and Protestant; he began to see what the cause of socialism was all about and started to move mountains of prejudice in his own mind and that of his comrades. Dave was one of the men we had looked to in the mid '70s to 'come across' to some sort of vision of a 32-county workers' republic with guarantees for the former loyalist community. As it turned out, he was to meet the Provisionals coming across from the other direction.

Leaving prison, David helped found the Progressive Unionist Party (PUP), an organisation that effectively was the voice of the working-class militia. Increasingly this party was moving toward some concept of socialism and some vision of a united working class, no matter how contradictory that seemed to many on the left and not least those previous victims of their sectarian murder campaigns. David and his group wholeheartedly threw themselves into the Good Friday Agreement, and seen in it the conditions under which a united Ulster working class could regroup for the struggle for socialism. It seems an impossible contradiction that this man, a fighter for imperialism and British loyalism, could start to painfully draw the fog from his own eyes and start to see at least the outlines of reality. He began a dialogue with the British left, was featured in a number of Marxist papers, and addressed revolutionary groups. He was surprisingly nice, an amiable comic and intelligent man. Despite this he was not murdered by 'his own side' though God knows how many plans had been developed in the early years for him to go far earlier than he did.

REDISCOVERING TYNESIDE

Here and there as I rediscover Tyneside, I come across surviving pockets of the Sixties, jungle clearings among the modernist identikit buildings and lifestyles. In Eldon Square, where we use to hang out in our youth and beatattitudes, bright Saturday morns see flocks of Goths, black and masqueraded, studded and booted. They swarm as we used to swarm, lang hair and garish; they look, in the half-light of Saturday afternoon shoppers, as we looked. They dance, and snog, and pose, strut their stuff, watch out for the new chick on the block, and listen for cool parties. Around the Square, stern-faced cops eye them with disapproval, as they eyed us, before finally banning us altogether.

Doon in the Bridge toilet, I am forced to head for the cubicle for a crap – a bit embarrassing really and not something, one discusses with strangers – when I encounter two likely lads having a piss. As I head for the cubicle door one cries out: 'Ya not having a shite are ye?' And the other adds: 'Ah hate people having a shite while I'm having a piss,' and his mate, 'Me anarl.' 'What for, like?' I stammer. 'Whey, man, it's just unhygienic.' It is indescribably a Geordie thing to say, which non-locals perhaps winnet ken. I am down at Newcastle quayside market on a Sunday morning, strolling among the throngs and the stalls. On one is a huge painting of a striking young woman, naked and nubile. From the young girls standing behind me, a voice complains: 'Ah wish they'd stop using that picture of me, ye knaa?'

Down at South Shields the communistic traditions of trade unionism and community ensure that the quiz night is an odd affair; they all tell each other the answers to the questions – helping each other out, like.

ANARCHISM RULES. OK?

In March at the Davie Jones memorial rally and lecture, Arthur teases 'Davie Douglass, the only anarchist I know to defend the rule book.' I laugh, 'I only support the rules which defend the members against you, Arthur.' I note the intrigue and internecine war still rages with the dying embers of our Union. Steve Kemp the general secretary is now up for election. You need a third of the potential voters' reps to vote for you to appear on the ballot paper; Steve now doesn't have a pit. His challenger is Chris Kitchen, secretary at Kellingley. Ironically it was Steve and his bureaucratic caucus which had won Chris Kitchen and the Kellingley Branch from Jeff Stubbs voting alliance over to them with the offer of the vice presidency, and it had switched the balance of power and wrecked our election strategy. Now only three pits, and as far as I could see two branches, remained, Maltby and Kellingley. I didn't know, but after the riot-torn relations with Maltby I couldn't see them putting Steve on the ballot paper and they didn't. He loses, but the NEC allows him to stay on some extra months.

Chris now theoretically has the levers of power, but finds increasingly a number of levers don't work and power still seems to reside elsewhere. The intrigue continues. Here and there are complaints that the Union's massive treasure chest is battened down and can't be released for use to fund our pending court cases on miners' damaged knees. Some say it is already earmarked for the legendary IEMO, should the last pit fall at last, but that of course is speculation I couldn't possibly repeat. Within a year or so, Arthur has latched onto justifiable discontent at Maltby, and a legal challenge is submitted against Chris and his stewardship.[465]

By the end of March, Rachel Horne had sent me her completed theses and DVD on the coal communities. It made me weep as her deeply moving work always has. On this occasion I wept wretchedly at my loss, our loss, the loss of something I had that was precious and I will never have again, we will never have again. Oh, not the job, working in the pit – though that too, that physical challenge, which tests you against the earth, the equation that ensures your surface self is determined by your underground worth; the tasks of industry but also comradeship and joint toil and achievement. The loss of that meaning, the self and social worth, something that bonded us like an enormous family across counties and countries, through time and history. The way in which that work, my physical and mental commitment to it, who I am and was, becomes part of the essence of *me*, loved and respected by my family and friends. The Dave they see was that man underground, setting off in the eerie wee hours of the morn or the dead of night. Bold, healthy, strong and prosperous, heartily acknowledged, socially part. Like a footballer losing his legs, something that was so deeply me has been taken from me, from us, and is crippling beyond description.

Rachel has a way of reflecting this in a way only a daughter and granddaughter of a miner could. It is a lang, lang time to grieve, but I feel the loss of so much – those communities, Dunscroft and Doncaster, and the shoulder-to-shoulder, invisible solidarity of generations of miners in living witness to struggle and vision and hope and strength. No, it is not romantic – proud, yes, but not romantic. Somehow the loss is linked with guilt, guilt now the colliery is back in operation with a couple of hundred men toiling back in the seams and rocks of Hatfield, going down deeper to the Barnsley seam. Guilt because the work is well underway and I am not with them. Even suppose the adamantly anti-union firm would employ me, I genuinely suffer from the incurable effects of HAVS and my days of forcing the big drill into stubborn unyielding rock, or machine-gunning the top with the windy pick, are over. I have never been a big humper and lumper and my ability to carry heavy girders and materials was never my strong point. I can still shovel, aye; put practically what good is that without the skills of pick and drill? I am aware, too, of the dust already in my lungs and now clearly observable on X-ray. Research suggests that from the earliest detectable form of the disease, 52 men in 1,000 would develop the deadly PMF in a period between 10 and 20 years;[466] another stint of years underground will inevitably increase the dust I breathe and shorten my life as a consequence. Does my body deserve more punishment? Do I take it back into almost certain death, painful and lingering as the dust seals off my airways? Or perhaps I toss the coin of fate one time too many and this time end my days cut up in some vicious machine, crushed in a fall of ground or by a runaway mine car. I could go back and push myself to the limits of a shortened life; force my hands and arms to crippled twisted stumps – but 'Why?', Emma and Caitlin both ask.

Next year I can draw my NCB pension. I have to stop work sometime. Fate or rather politics and the class war did me a good turn in getting me out a little earlier than would otherwise have been the case, and more or less intact and still able to enjoy the rest of my life. Should I be so ungrateful as to turn in the good hand and deal again? Is there something at the back of my mind or rooted in my soul that says my life has no validation unless I remain a coalminer – I believe there is, although my sane mind tells me how absurd that is. Coalmining does become a sort of obsession, an addiction which leaves you few ways out and when you get out you feel somehow cheapened. Truer perhaps is the nostalgia for hard honest toil and earning a wage, and having a loving family in the context of a community and a social class, and an international vision for justice, for achieving something and living for something incontestable. If that sounds romantic let me tell you my feet were never more assuredly on the ground than when I was living that life. But it wasn't just the pitwork, it was having a companion, a child, marras, comrades. I could get the pit work back and a shadow of the other perhaps ... for as long as I lived. Forbye.

MORE WEIRD EVENTS

A little later, I am demobbed after an anti-NF mobilisation in Newcastle city centre and wandering along the now sorely-depleted stalls of the Quayside Sunday market. I come across a second-hand book and record stall, which as usual I can't pass without a browse. There, looking inviting is a big pile of Commando comics. Ee, the Commando comics coloured my vision of the world as a little lad. Well, they taught me German for a start: 'Kamarad, Britischer, Gottinhimmel, Donnerundblitzen,' and inspired wa war games of British and Germans. They had set my imagination ablaze with visions of battles at sea and breaking through the waves in fast wee MTBs. I suppose they were part of the fuel that nearly took me to the Royal Navy. I picked up, bought a couple of the little books to relive my memories, and wandered down the quay. As I turned over one of the books, I observed ... my own initials written in pen on the back in my own childish handwriting! Now gaan on, tell me that's not bliddy weird!

Meantime ... Surprise, surprise! I am invited formally by the NUM to be the guest speaker at its October weekend school at Scarborough. Regime changes, and the dust having settled, I am seen now as an elder statesman of the Union rather than one of its factions. It's quite an honour, and I will of course accept.

The end of June 2007. Blair finally resigns but hands over to Brown. Around the same, time *The Guardian* reports: 'The real jobless totals in cities such as Liverpool and Glasgow and former mining regions could be as high as 10%.' The paper reveals what folk in the pit communities and cities formerly based in mining and steel and manufacture have been saying – that the true figure for the unemployed is three times higher than officially declared. The map they reproduce showing levels up to 10% could be a map of the British coalfields. The report is based upon Sheffield Hallam University research showing more than 1.7 million unemployed had been excluded from official figures. 1 million of the 2.7 million on incapacity benefit were actually just the unemployed, many of them miners persuaded to claim that benefit rather than be 'jobseekers' or be declared looking for work. Professor Fothergill, who led the study, said: 'This does not mean that one million incapacity claims are fraudulent, but these men and women would almost certainly have been in work in a genuinely fully employed economy.'[467]

At the break of 2008, I host my birthday party. I had thought to maybe not tell anyone how old I actually was. Why – am I that conceited? No, I have never liked being defined by an age, as if in abstract knowing how old someone is tells you who and what they are. I resisted it when I was 16 and hate it as much now. Actually, it's my 60th and I have planned a BIG party, although it being the day after New Year and a working day for most people it will be a struggle to get there. All my old friends and comrades have been invited and some terrific leaflets designed by Simon from the Tyneside Anarchists and the IWW.

Tom declines, though; he is off camping over Christmas and New Year with his dog on his own:

Newcastle these days I find depressing: I prefer the memories of a busy and agreeably squalid Quayside to the empty sterility of the modern one. The last time I was up there, I remember great swirling shoals of Idiot people and their gruntlings. There must have been thousands of the brutes all baying at the moon or slipping in their vomit. I find it difficult to retain any optimism in the company of Homo Stupidiensis ...[468]

New Year's eve morning, I feel a sudden and deep fear and anxiety. I rationalise it is the looming chasm of my 60th birthday. I feel the closeness of a huge expanse of silent, empty death. It is far from exhilarating. I check my body parts and find they are all in good working order. I am without aches, pains or missing organs. My daughter, granddaughter and son-in-law will join me later today for a night cruise down the Tyne and arrive back under the bonny lights of the Tyne's bridges in time for the birth of 2008. My party will bring comrades and friends from the all over the island and things seem set for a great night. Actually, it is the day when the Earth is closer to the Sun than any other time of the year; didn't feel very warm to me. But still the empty feeling in the pit of me belly, like standing looking into a vast and pitch-black, empty void. The cure on reflection would be for some bright young nubile thing to jump on me bones and snog me to oblivion, but I'm awake now and the cold light of day suggests that I have more chance of a seat in heaven than that happening. The cruise was a wonderful idea, that historic route of centuries of keelmen through the once barren then industrial landscape of the Tyne banks.

I was shocked by the amount of yuppy occupation spreading off down the Newcastle side of the riverbanks, the owners keen to gaze on the river's murky depths now there is no work to do and nothing industrial to spoil their view. But it doesn't eclipse the triumph of that trip. The return up the river, as the clock struck midnight and Rabbie's *Auld Lang Syne* rang out, with fireworks exploding over the city and the bridges illuminated in multicoloured lights, was a profound experience.

Ee, I had some belly-churning hours on the morning of the second, that awesome birthday – almost half of my life over already, as Woody Allen once said. But the party itself was everything I could have hoped for, all the aud Tyneside anarchists from this story returned to be there: Wallace, the Arrowsmiths, Renwick, Les Howard, Tom Pickard, Brian and Irene Hume, folk from far and wide, Schlacke up from London, Romano from the Karate club, sentinels from my past. Corcoran and his band belted out the fiddle tunes, and Dave Rodgers from Banner Theatre strutted his stuff on stage. Keith Armstrong read a great poem dedicated to William Wallace's right arm, which he discovered had been hacked off during the mutilation of the body down in London and sent up for display on the old Tyne Bridge as warning to any as might similarly resist. The rest of the body was likewise hacked to pieces and spread to the cities of Britain. It is something of comment that we got the right arm. Star of the show was Pickard, though. His 'Fuck' poem was sensational and I resolved that if he outlives me I want that read at my funeral. It is something of a verbal volley over the coffin, although if anyone still knows what a gun is by then I'll have that too.

COPS AND NUKES AND TEENAGE DETENTION

Second week of January 2008. Parliament approves a massive expansion of nuclear power and a programme of nuclear power station building! Well, in this case, it's not nice to be proved right, but this was always the long-term plan from the time the miners were first put in the Thatcherite crosshairs and the Myron Plan dusted off. At the end of January, the North East Area of the NUM ceases to be 'a trade union'. Someone discovers that since there are no mines left in Northumberland and Durham there are no employers and workers – so, under the current employment law, the North East Area NUM can't be a trade union. The Durham Area becomes the Durham Miners Association again, the name adopted at its inception 139 years ago but never fully relinquished. On the 23rd, 20,000 cops march though London demanding 'their rights', back money and talking of strike action. In the front row at the head of the march is Richard Barnbrook, the BNP candidate for Lord Mayor of London, but also marching not far behind is Tony Benn, wearing the 'Fair Play For The Police' cap – the uniform today for the guardians of our laws. They are booed by Class War and various ex-miners and printers, who apart from telling them to 'Get a job!' and

'Get your hair cut!' and 'Go back to Russia!' remind them what they did to us when we fought for our rights. Pity we couldn't lay about them with riot sticks and dogs and horses like they did to us. Meantime the Association of Chief Police Officers demands a permanent police presence in working-class schools, with daily searches of young people coming in (mainly just to see what they can find and boost their instant 'crime-detection' and 'clear up' figures). Doubtless it goes along with the 16–18 forced detention for all teenagers in the government's 'Education Bill'.

In October they announce plans to draft former SAS and commandos fresh from the war zones in as 'teaching assistants' and offer free education packages to former squaddies to retrain as teachers. They demand fingerprinting and DNA samples from every man, woman and child in Britain.

The walls are getting higher, and the encirclement of freedoms tighter and tighter. There are, in October of 2008, 6,000 speed cameras, 4.2 million CCTV cameras. 3,000 covert probes are launched into financial and mobile phone records, 'trawling' – in other words looking for trouble.[469] 'Some times I think this whole world is one big prison yard, most of us are on the inside while the rest they are the guards.'[470] In March 2008, one in every 500 people on the island of Britain is in jail or penal detention.[471] In October, in the teeth of universal opposition, the Brown government brings in the first tranch of its £5 billion ID cards scheme, this one for non-European immigrants. Meantime a £21 billion programme to routinely tap all emails and phone calls is revealed. It will be the biggest surveillance system ever undertaken: the 'Interception Modernisation Programme'. The degree of surveillance is staggering: 57 billion text messages, or *1,800 every second.*[472]

At the end of December 2008, it is announced that infant and primary schools have been fitted with CCTV cameras and microphones to watch and listen in to children from 4 years old. Classwatch Ltd,[473] which sells and fits the equipment, admits their purpose is to 'compile evidence'. In a weak defence of the covert operation, the company says the equipment is to protect teachers from groundless accusations of 'child abuse or inappropriate behaviour'. Put another way, it is an attempt to find evidence of 'child abuse or inappropriate behaviour' and is in any case universally condemned by the teachers' unions. But the lie is further demonstrated when it is revealed that the cameras and microphones are aimed equally at areas where there are no teachers, like the dinner rooms, the play, changing, and toilet areas. The aim is, clearly, to record what the children themselves are saying and doing. Stockwell Park High School in South London installs 96 security cameras at a cost of £60,000 for classrooms and corridors; the expenditure stops the refurbishment of the school baths, which are then closed.[474]

All this is in fact yet another feature of the Blair–Brown government's perverse obsession with children's behaviour – in this case, trawling through the casual conversation of 4-year-olds upwards in the hope of discovering some evidence of 'crimes' and 'inappropriate behaviour' among the kids themselves. It is also linked to the plans of the Department for Children, Schools and Families to enforce 'sex and relationship' proscriptions upon infants and junior schools.

By December 2009, council child protection officers acting on the new government instructions and quoting 'Safeguarding Children Legislation'[475] are holding seminars and briefings with teachers and schools staff on how to spot 'inappropriate behaviour', also counselling in what is inappropriate behaviour. Among these are the following:

– Breast-feeding your baby beyond what someone (we don't know who has drawn up these notions certainly not science or common sense) believes to be 'too long'. This of course is an entirely personal or cultural matter and nothing whatever to do with 'inappropriate behaviour'.

– Bathing or undressing your own child! (Examples given are your 9-year-old in the bath, or your 'muddy 11-year-old boy'.) It is even inappropriate to be in the bathroom with your 9-year-old (for example) child. Allowing your sick or distressed child to share your bed.

– Children of 4 and 6 playing infantile games of sexual discovery.

Coming across any of these 'should set alarm bells ringing', staff are instructed. A subject suggested for group discussion is, 'At what age you should have stopped cuddling your child', the expected answer given the context presumably being 'sooner rather than later', and most certainly not 'never'. The alarm bells which should be ringing are for whichever sad, lonely and alienated person drew up such a dehumanised list of proscriptions. One would certainly think it gives a strong indication of psychopathic tendencies in the author, and that they are hugely out of touch with normal, healthy relationships among families and between children.

Commenting on the surveillance equipment, the Department declared that it doesn't prescribe what schools do 'to tackle security' – nor the rights of little children either, it seems.

19 January. Social Services announce that they confiscated almost *700 children* in December, taken from parents, brothers, sisters, and friends – an 86% increase on June of 2008. A hysterical reaction verging on the criminal. Almost 60,000 children come under the control of 'Social Services' in 2009, with new codes of practice announced in July that will succeed in taking far more children 'into care'.[476] The press-led fury over the brutal neglect and death of a toddler (Baby P) and the finger of guilt pointed at the local social services who had been monitoring the child, and 'let it slip through the net', sent the whole child abuse industry in hyperdrive. In this case, social workers charged with the discretion of assisting families cope at home, or determine on the validity of information, simply refer all cases for confiscation from the family and thereby cover their own backs, regardless of the massive damage done to the child whisked away into an institution, or among clinical and strict strangers. It is in fact institutional and legal child abuse on a grand scale, and almost entirely driven by the media and moral witch-hunters off on a crusade.

This is not to suggest there are not real and ongoing cases of wilful child neglect, torture and death. In part this is linked to the collapse of extended families and working-class communities and the rise of selfishness and loss of empathy and compassion engendered by the whole Thatcher project. These kids obviously need real social care in the community and among friends and family, not de facto isolation and detention among strangers and crown officers.[477] It is also a fact that the vast majority of social workers are middle-class and come from backgrounds and values that are totally alien to the mass working-class populations of housing estates and inner cities that they are sent to police. Things they deem 'abuse', or circumstances where kids are found 'in need of protection', are to many working-class folk simply normal situations of social hardship, and people making the best of the circumstances and environments they find themselves in. The social services do not understand the extended family and community interaction of neighbours and friends in family relationships, or the relative freedom of children in these communities to make choices, and friendships outside the insular nuclear family of the middle-class model.

In June of 2009, we have a prime not to say despicable case in point. In Nottingham, a first-time mother identified only as Rachel has her baby taken from her at birth, and is allowed subsequently to see her only 90 minutes a month, under the strict and restrictive supervision of social workers – a sort of jail visit for the mother and child. Rachel is 24 years old; she has committed no offence, has done no harm of any kind to her baby or any other baby, or anyone else for that matter. Nottingham Social Services, after the report from one bright spark of a middle-class social worker, decided that working-class Rachel wasn't intelligent enough to have a child and it should be taken from her. Her child was born 13 weeks prematurely with severe medical complications. The child is in hospital for 6 months at the end of which, against the impassioned pleas and desperation of her mother, social services seize the child and put her into foster care. Rachel is a rational, normal, balanced person, no greater or lesser in the brains department than the average person in the street. A solitary social worker decides to bring in an IQ test for the having of babies. The department employs a psychiatrist, paid by them, who ratifies that Rachel is of low intelligence.

The whole fascistic process gets worse, as the child is put up for adoption against her mother's demands, after which she will be allowed no further contact with her child. The council bans Rachel making a medical challenge to its judgement or the view of their house psychiatrist. She has been told she will never be allowed to inform her child she is her mother, never allowed to use the terms 'daughter' or 'mother' in relation to her. The whole case demonstrates the inherent injustice of the system and the brutal powers social services departments are able to bring to bear on hapless families.[478]

In March, Ian Paisley retires as 'first minister' for the newly 'self-governing' British statelet of Northern Ireland and leader of his Democratic Unionist Party. He is in his 80s and widely interviewed; they point out that his apparent iron determination that Ulster Says No to all things Irish has rusted somewhat. He points out to them that he has not conceded one inch on his resolve and it is Sinn Féin and the republicans who have wilted in their mettle not him. Any political metallurgist would doubtless agree with him.

FALLEN COMRADES

Emma and Caitlin come with me to the annual memorial to Joe Green and Davie Jones, the two lads killed in the '84 strike, Arthur comes straight over and gives Emma a big embrace and kiss on the cheek, while Caitlin gets her first ever hug and kiss from a world-renowned union leader. The ceremony is as usual deeply moving. Emma shed a few tears, not least for the sight of Mark Jones, Dave's Dad, standing with his wreath and an ocean of emptiness in his heart that was once filled by his lad, now gone to our cause. There but for the grace of God could any of us have gone, and I reflect too, that it could be Emma and Caitlin standing with their wreaths for me.

Arthur writes to tell me he can't make my retirement do, but in the process says some very comradely and kind words of appreciation, while noting 'there have been occasions when we have not always seen eye to eye' – true, but then I don't suppose I know anybody to whom that wouldn't apply. Serious disagreements aside, and I've given as little quarter as Arthur during those disputes, he is still a man I hold in immense respect. The entire Yorkshire Area NUM leadership along with the National secretary however sign up to attend.

HATFIELD MAIN NUM BRANCH REBORN

Hatfield pit votes by nearly 80% in a workplace ballot to demand Union recognition in an overwhelming turnout of more than two-thirds of the workforce. The Union is forced to go to a CAC and have the recognition imposed on the colliery since the management still will not accept the view of the miners, or in this case, the law.

10 May. '1968 and All That' – an amazing commemoration of that glorious year, held in Conway Hall, London. Guest speakers are Astrid Proll, the now freed member of the Red Army Fraction; Eamonn McCann, my aud sparring partner from the Troops Out days; Alain Krivine from the French Trotskyist movement which played such a big part in launching the French May Days; Sheila Rowbottom, a cornerstone of progressive women's liberation; Ian Bone and myself! Mind, Ian and me didn't share the big stage and had smaller rooms, but it was still a huge privilege to be among the wise and good of those heady days. Also Astrid's meeting was peppered here and there with undercover policemen asking what they thought were subtle questions. Basked in the event, smoked dope, drank, argued, sang – and that was just in the pub afterwards.

'LEAVE IT IN THE GROUND?'

Green protesters blockade a coal train going to Drax and dump the contents of the wagons onto the tracks. They unfurl a banner saying 'Leave It In The Ground'. Yes, and the miners and their families on the scrap heap. A bouncy young middle-class girl announced to the TV: 'Coal has no place in Britain's energy supply.' So there. Were we consulted? Do the views of the workers matter? Self-declared green rulers will impose their view on the rest of us. I'm bliddy fuming, but the state of the NUM these days means I cannot mobilise any counter force or even get a miner on TV to rebuff the propaganda. It gets worse, with a mass attack on the first 'clean coal' power station, at Kingsnorth in Kent.[479] The climate camp has declared 'coal' as the number one enemy, along with the miners of course, but we aren't mentioned by name. I fume with indignation. I try to organise a contingent of trade unionists and IWW members to mount a counter-demo calling for clean coal and workers' control of the mining and energy industry. Now *they* are furious and a huge polemic rips through the movement, including the IWW. Tyne and Wear Branch accepts the motion with one comrade calling the rest racialists, and then another, over the net, speaking in support of total pit closures regardless of job losses or communities, the Earth being more important than the miners, thus spectacularly missing the point.

I agree to go down to the climate camp and speak directly to them. Fool – it'll end in tears. Plus I'm camping in a soggy field and travelling on the train, at my own expense; why don't I just keep my big gob shut? Tyne and Wear Branch of Amicus, who give me £200 to get a bed and breakfast for the four days, save me from the soggy field, however. With a little added cash, Emma books me into a luxury hotel so I at least will not be rolling about in the mud and shitting in a hedgerow. The final coup comes when I ask Arthur to come and address the eco-warrior hordes with me, and he agrees! This is no mean commitment for a man of his age and standing in the movement, and shows how seriously we as a Union and a people take the question of coalmining and the environment.

Now You Are Sixty!

My retirement cruise down the Sprotborough Canal on 20 June was a unique event in many ways. Where else would miners, Union officials, former members of our armed insurgency and karate masters get to mingle with the children in their party frocks and nice shirts? They are joined by my family and many friends. I am most honoured indeed, that the general secretary of the NUM, Chris Kitchen, the president of the Yorkshire Area, Chris Skidmore, and the vice president, Ken Hartshorne, all attend, together with my fellow TGWU organisers, the former communist president of Hatfield Main NUM, Brian Robson, and long-time Branch activist Mick Mulligan. Emma has persuaded me that this time it will not be a folky, free-versey, politico evening, but instead an R&B disco, drinky, dancy evening. That's what it was. The TGWU gave me a classic watch and chain for me waistcoat and Romano, my Fifth Dan Italian karate comrade, sparring partner, railwayman and friend, gave me a wonderful tribute, which risking accusations of a swollen head I'll quote:

> Congratulations on your retirement after 60 years of battling against the injustice.
>
> Its time to hang your gloves up.
>
> You fought all over the world just like Giuseppe Garibaldi and his Geordie friends to
>
> Liberate all countries from the oppressors.
>
> You were always on the front line during the miners strike holding no fear.
>
> You are a legend.

Carry on doing karate. It will keep you young. And don't forget to chase those lovely sexy women.

I'm sure there is one out there who will love to spend the rest of your life with you.

God Bless You

Romano

STUART CHRISTIE

25 Monday June. Stuart Christie my old comrade takes over the task to get the whole of this massive work published. It means I have to pay to get it printed etc., but at least it will be out and be professional, and who knows may recover some of the costs over the years, if I don't get jailed for it. We agree it will come out in three volumes, and follow the natural periods of the book. It'll take a huge £18,000–£20,000 chunk out of my pension, but what do I want? I want it out.

Suppose just six people read it, it will be a monument to all those wonderful events and people who have passed through it, this is my life, this is my tale, and I think it worth telling.

11 July. I gain my Yellow Belt in Aikido, the first grade but I'm very proud to do so. Aikido is the most cerebral of all the martial arts – magic, and like all magic very difficult to follow and get a grasp on. At the time of writing I'm an Orange Belt, though still land like a sack of spuds when I hit the deck.

The author with granddaughter Caitlin

ANOTHER FIGHT IN ANOTHER FIELD FOR THE MINERS

In August, Arthur Scargill and me enter another big field to fight the corner for the miners and coal our industry and cause. Last time it was that field at Orgreave. This time it's the climate camp at Kingsnorth Power Station and instead of thousands of cops there's thousands of eco-warriors who now believe coal is killing the planet and want to stop all new coal stations. If truth were known, they want to close down all coal stations per se. This time there is only Arthur and me; we have no squads of pickets, no marching bands and no flying banners. It is in many respects just as daunting a prospect, but it shows the quality of this man. Our differences aside, he came into the teeth of opposition with an unpopular and untrendy message, among people who are hardly receptive to his old-school brand of Marxist-Leninist socialism, but prepared to debate for a long time why the NUM and clean coal technology are allies in the struggle for a socialist ecology and a just world.

Arthur is now 70 and I am 60. I think we present a figure of two rather battered and scarred alley cats come for a peace conference with the league of dogs. Actually, I thought later, we were rather like two old Hell's Angels come to preach the benefits of sex and drugs and rock and roll to a Salvation Army convention. This is a sad and confusing conjunction of forces. I have never in my life experienced a situation where the miners and what we do is the unpopular foe except among the ruling class and Tories. Outside of the Young Conservatives, I have never known young people regard mining and pitheads as their enemy.

What is worse is that these are my traditional constituency; they have the aura of the hippies, they aspire to the freedoms and love of life which our '60s/'70s generation did. I come across the Newcastle and Scottish camp, and know many of the activists from the Toon scene and demonstrations. Previously we have always held each other in a silent mutual respect; now there is a mutual distance, coolness, a sort of mutual 'Et tu, Brute?'

However, I see here also the mortified conviction of my own anti-nuclear youth. My conviction that myself and the whole world were on the brink of extinction. The certainty that if we delay we are all doomed to a wretched and painful end. Now it is climate change, and the gathering speed with which the Earth is crashing toward climatic obliteration – ironically for all carbon-based creatures including the vegetable kingdom, as we know it. A change that will cleanse us all from the surface for eternity.

They camp like some latter-day Woodstock; they are a commonwealth, locked in debate and dedication, little communities with kids romping through the fields. Long-haired, dreadlocked, singing and dancing. It is deeply wounding to be the enemy. This is an Anti-Durham Gala; everywhere are workshops on the dreaded mining, on resistance around the world to mining of all descriptions. Pictures of headgear and opencast, industry and miners, and the campaigns against them. It is like a Durham Miner's Gala on bad acid. Instead of everywhere a celebration of the miners, our work, our communities, everywhere there are protests for our end.

I am shocked that many of the left groups are now groupies to the eco-movement and have abandoned all attempts at class analysis. Arthur's worst critic is the local secretary of the Socialist Party (as Militant have become), who tells him the NUM and miners' struggle was yesterday's cause; this was where the struggle was now. That Eon and the big generators, to facilitate their profits, are using us. I argue the opposite – that every attack on coal feeds the nuclear agenda, sets the agenda for government policy. I remind them too that *they* are enthusiastic supporters of the power companies when it comes to ramming wind turbines down the throats of protesting locals resolved not to have them. Around the tent are dotted trade union members of the SWP; are they now ready to bury him having once been full of his praise?

For a month, the *Weekly Worker* has carried uncritical adverts for the camp while the *Morning Star* warned me I was underestimating the forthcoming climate holocaust and declined my article criticising the camp. I have the honour to have written the official NUM bulletin, *The Miners and The Climate Camp*, which *The Miner's* editor Ken Capstick has managed to reduce from eight sides to four with a bit of clever editing. I've humped 2,000 of them in a huge bag from

Doncaster and have spent the morning spreading them round the field, where they are received with less than enthusiasm. About 150 climate campers sit in the tent, from 1,500 in the field. The bottom-line argument is we shouldn't be generating so much power anyway, it should be cut by 50% and we need to get used to not having electricity. There is sympathy for the miners, generally accepted as the most exploited people in Britain over the last century, but there have to be losers if we are to save the planet, and we have been chosen to be them. Few people believe that CO^2 capture works, and anyway will not be ready 'in time' to stop the climate going into free fall. Right across the left and green movement, more and more people are coming over to the government programme for nuclear power, and an end to coal mining and coal burning in Britain. I am asked to give a workshop on the relevance and importance of the great '84/85 coal strike; nine people come. The relevance clearly isn't too well established. 'The Earth' becomes an abstraction; humanity is some sort of foreign and alien invader and the storm troops, this time not of the TUC but of tidal waves, poverty and death, are the miners. Of course, Arthur's arguments are not mine; he talks of 'dirty foreign coal' and unfair competition, slave labour and child labour – these are not my arguments. Import controls are not a progressive answer, but I am for a level playing field of subsidies; and a 'fair trade' standard of terms, conditions and union rights would be for the millions of coalminers abroad as much as for us.

The cops are arseholes. As usual, I am stopped and searched – two, sometimes three times a day, against my consent and often with force. Indeed, I am almost arrested, which would have been proved interesting in court. They could hardly argue they had reasonable grounds for suspecting I was going to sabotage the power station when I had gone down two-thirds of the country with half a tonne of literature in its defence.

But the intervention breeds a backlash. IndyMedia, the standing channel for the bulk of the climate campers, is soon awash with vitriolic attacks on Arthur, the NUM and unions and me in general. Some of it is just poison, and goes to demonstrate that calling yourself an anarchist in no way guarantees reason, argument or even being a particularly nice person. It comes from a fusion of the anti-union and anti-industry anarchists, a cocktail once mixed which is sure to produce anti-working-class invective in one form or another. Ner mind. I plough on, resolving not to read the daily traffic on this channel for fear of driving myself mad chasing my own tail round in an email game of verbal ping-pong on the net. I recognise from my earlier encounter with this team, reflected in *All Power to the Imagination*, that although vociferous they are usually rarely more than a handful of people untouched by the world of the working class.

As round two, and with the support of the Tyne and Wear Branch of the IWW, I organise a dynamic 'Labour Movement Conference on Class, Climate Change and Clean Coal'. Held at the Bridge, the conference is star-studded, with Arthur, the regional RMT secretary, Ian Lavery, the National president of the NUM and all the regional and area leaders of both. The NUM couldn't have cooperated more if this had been their own specific conference; they threw themselves into supporting it. On the other side, Greenpeace, Green Anarchism, all enthusiastic blockaders of Drax and the coal trains also jump at the chance of debating these crucial and phlegm-flecked issues. By the middle of September, with the conference organised for 1 November, I'm starting to worry about the success of the conference – not lack of support but oversubscription and mass attendance. The upstairs room at the Bridge stripped of its tables will hold 100, no more. As it turned out, we had about 120. Bob Crow couldn't come, having fractured his leg in a friendly football match against the managers' team, and he didn't mean under the table either. It is a heavy diet of facts, figures, fears, pride, memories and hopes. There are fractious moments. Ian is accused of being too threatening and telling the greens to bollocks. Davie Hopper, who has taken up the chair in the second half, resolved to cut down on lengthy stage presentations from the guest speakers in order to free up the time for floor debate, is then accused of putting his own biased oar into the debate too often. He resigns the chair and storms off downstairs. I can feel his indignation at having been assailed by two comrades from different sides of the room and told to 'chair the meeting', while Kev Bland, from the Green Anarchists, sitting alongside Dave on the stage waiting to speak, joins in and tells him he's biased and he's only cutting down on the greens' speaking time. Dave is not used to this and will not swallow it. It is an excuse for most of the Yorkshire NUM delegation to follow him down into the bar, where they punish themselves with drink and tales.

This is not though a debate we can walk away from. Arthur hadn't helped on this occasion. I was chuffed he came, but then he spoke double his allocated time, leaving at the end of his presentation with streams of facts and figures hanging in the air, to be challenged and shot down after he'd gone. It is stormy throughout, contentious but vital. We each at least now clearly see where the other is coming from. It is said we are not too far apart, but only really on the question of opencast coal, and even on that I'm not sure I agree with the nonsense that is rattled out about it. If we believe the greens, this book will have scarce 10 years in existence before it is floating on the tide of universal floodwaters along with the bodies of starved humanity and the last of the animals, the result of global warming having reached its tipping point and throwing us unavoidably into certain doom. Am I sceptical, or is it wishful thinking?

January 2010. Britain experiences its coldest winter in 30 years. Germany has temperatures of 30 degrees below zero, Norway 40 below. Europe, Russia and Scandinavia face arctic temperatures.

GEORDIES, WA MENTAL

11 September. Three big boxes of advanced copies of the first part of this work arrive. *Geordies* is back in toon. It looks wonderful, feels wonderful. I sit down to reread it, through the eyes of a total stranger who hadn't seen it before. Invariably there are *still* mistakes in it despite having proof-read the words off the print. Some of them are new ones, caused by the computer doing the scanning not speaking Geordie and 'correcting' the word to English even though it didn't really

make sense anymore. Ain becomes am, mainly because it looks like am. Damn machines. The review copies gaan out far and wide with the promise of some national media reviews and two local radio station interviews for Newcastle and Sheffield. Stuart who has managed this project assures me the book *must* cover its costs because he doesn't get paid until it has, that's the deal, so he has more than his fingers crossed.[480]

My karate sensei Alan, the fittest man I know, is struck down with some paralysing mysterious condition, which renders him unable to move. He is rushed to Sheffield hospital after being trapped for 36 hours in his house completely immobile. The suspicion is some form of paralysing cancer, but we live in hope, as test after test, CAT and MIR scans turn up blank.

Mid October. Have a great programme with the Rony Robinson Show on Radio Sheffield, broadcasting at prime time 2–3 p.m. to nearly 200,000 in Sheffield and Derbyshire, about my book. I do almost an hour off the cuff – cut and thrust of memories, events, histories, controversies. Rony of course knows me these past 25 years, and we have crossed paths through my own radio programme on Radio Sheffield in '83, and his outside broadcast coverage of the coalfield's most tumultuous years. It's a great programme though I say so myself; we scarce catch a breath and my old comrades and workmates phone in to the station after I've gone and extend their regards.

AN ANARCHIST SWANSONG

The Anarchist Bookfair this year is something of a swansong for me. I have the launch of *Geordies*, though to be right not many came to that apart from the Newcastle anarchists. There is a rapidly arranged debate with me and one of the founders of the climate camp, Jim Paton. It is a rip-roaring debate, and the big lecture theatre is packed to capacity. Jim though isn't one of the loonies, or primitivists; he actually has lost patience with the camp, and didn't go this year because of the 'liberalism' and middle-class agenda that the camp has. It's a highly constructive debate with Jim setting out the case as to why the world needs coal and what we couldn't have without it, including their wind turbines, bikes, plastics, medicines etc. BUT, he argues, actually as the old colliers used to do, that coal is too precious to burn. The aud lads used to argue that the day would come when the real worth of coal was found and they would be selling it in glass bottles in the chemist's shop.

This year we also co-join the anarchists with the national shop stewards network, who host a packed session on the work of the network. It is well attended by anarchist and syndicalist workers, shop stewards and some branch officials. Class struggle anarchism is clearly the dominant wing of this Bookfair and it's nice to see so many feet on the ground. Mind there are of course the usual freaks and weirdoes that make this movement so novel. A transgender bloke was wearing a plastic miniskirt, bare legs and knee-high boots, which first made me think 'Daft bastard!', but then I thought 'So what? If that's his thing, why am I bothered?' A bookstall outside with posters denouncing the unions, another crying a pox on Marx and the Marxists; the blood boils, then I think, 'What, am I one of those fundamentalists whose belief is so slender it can be insulted by a challenge?' I smile sweetly as I pass them back and forth and resist the temptation to cry 'Get fucked off, you stupid bastards!'

The Freedom Bookshop party is a delight; it's the first time, I'm sure, I've ever been there – down that tiny back lane off the main drag, up that winding ancient staircase like Raph's Spitalfields house. Crowds of anarchos, drinking, smoking dope, laughing, debating, dancing, and my latest failed chat-up introducing line: 'Em, what is your ethnicity?' She was a Filipino, and devastatingly beautiful, articulate, and weel spoken-for, I guess (sigh for the days as they used to be).

End of October. The madness of Big George (Brown) continues. Ancient rights to freely gather fallen wood and dead trees from forests are abolished; from now on, it will be yet another offence. The relentless war on all forms of free, unregulated behaviour continues. Soon nothing will remain which is truly free and doesn't require the consent and approval of the government and law. One predicts gathering nuts, berries and conkers must be next.

A BLACK PRESIDENT

3 November. Wake up to the election of America's first 'black' (mixed race) president, Barack Obama. Seems ridiculous does not it, to actually mention the colour of someone's skin, as significant in a political election, but in the USA it's become a central factor. Decades of ruthless race discrimination, prejudice, murder, slavery and injustice had put America's black population largely at the bottom of the social pile, and at times in revolutionary insurgency against the largely white-faced corporate bosses and the US state. Deep-seated race hate and mortal fear of the non-white man has coloured American politics since the time of the War of Independence through to the Civil War, world wars and the civil rights movement and the rise of the black revolutionary insurgency.

So the vote is a milestone in race relations, in people of both colours taking off their colour lenses and voting for the man in spite of his pigmentation, but it also represents a determination of people of colour to stand together and vote for Obama as a symbol of their resolve to be second-class citizens no more. He is for them something of the black gloved fist raised at the Olympic Games 40 years before. Not that this is some working-class man of the people. Nobody of that ilk could get near the presidential election. It requires boatloads of money to get the publicity machine rolling and the corporate bodies behind you and your own small fortune to get on the ballot paper let alone run a nationwide campaign. This one was the most expensive in US history and will end up costing many millions of dollars.

But now what? Does Obama actually stand for anything politically different from the Bush regime? In essence, no he doesn't. He advocates liberal capitalism and some constraints on the market, some state intervention, some local and native protectionism. But on a global and domestic scale, this is still the old wine albeit in a dramatic new bottle. Imperialism will still be given its head, Israel will still be the US pit bull in the Middle East, belligerence to Cuba and dissident South American states will remain unchanged. Life for the US workers and their families will be very much business or, increasingly, no business as usual. The issues of global warming and clean coal technology have started moving very slowly; public over private transport has been mentioned, petrol consumption gets now a mention. However, vicious anti-union laws and maverick union-busting operations look likely to continue untouched. Social justice in health care and education, housing and lifestyles though now on the nursery slopes of existence have faced the most vicious fight by the private corporations to stop them being launched. Overall, once the party dies down and life returns to normal, in a few years' time it's going to be obvious nothing much if anything has changed. Perhaps by then American workers will realise the whole damn system, and especially one which robs them of democratic control of their own lives by electing a ruler not a representative every once in a while, isn't a good recipe for justice.

Meantime no one can deny what this moment means to black America, to the old American progressive movement. At the inauguration on 20 January 2009 a crowd of a million people besiege the Capitol steps while Pete Seeger, his old face beaming, sings out 'This land is your land, this land is my land.' A million people joined in: 'As I was rambling, I saw above me a sign that said "Private Property" but on the other side, it didn't say nothing, *that* side was made for you and me.' It made me cry; cry because this was real America, progressive America, the heart of America really. Will the disillusionment with Obama take it from them – that and the concerted efforts by the super-rich to block his every move, plus his failure to actually stand at the head of a social and political movement strong enough to impose its authority on the American state and confront reaction? We don't know, but right now it's a milestone of sorts, though it didn't take long for the privileged sections of American society to regroup and launch a multi-million pound TV and hoarding campaign against Obama, who is portrayed as Hitler, and his reforms aimed at bringing healthcare to the poor.

AMANG THE CLARTS OF HATFIELD PIT TIP

Mid November. I am back at Hatfield pit, tramping round the moonscape of the muddy surface heap with a TV crew from Holland as part of their forthcoming 25th anniversary of the strike programme. The pit is now cut to its basic buildings. The old Victorian offices have gone, the big baths and canteen are gone. The grassed-over tip, which once linked the toil and sweat of industry to the grazing community of young 'uns on their sledges, and blokes walking their dogs, has now gone, flattened and cleared in preparation for the long expected clean-coal power station and green energy park.

Tonight we will meet up with Harry Harle,[481] Pat and Maggie Bennet and some of the local characters from the pit, at the Broadway, in the thick of the Saturday night bash. It sounds like an unlikely scheme, but the night coincides with a charity do for a teenage boy with cancer, setting off on the long isolated road to treatment and hospitals. It is noisy, packed to the doors, and everyone is out in their finery, drinking and boogying on down, especially Pat. Billy Gallagher, now in his 70s, is here with his new wife. He was one of our most experienced flying pickets and an ace road navigator, a man deeply committed to the NUM and this community, a strong, outspoken, coalface chargeman and father of combative coalminer sons. He is hearty and loud and happy. They look and act just like teenagers, quite to the dismay of the real teenagers. I had been unsure what reception I will get, but as it turns out I am hailed as the long-lost neighbour and workmate I am truly am. I donate a copy of my book to be a raffle prize, and lo and behold – one of the Malees, the militant Donnie/Irish Union and republican families from Stainie, win it. I couldn't be more pleased. Here and there are the odd now ageing hippies of my first '70s encounter with them. Here too I recognise the faces of kids that played round the doors, but are now grown up and teenage, taking their place in the community. I am struck by how mature and well-behaved the teenage boys are. They joke about the swearing in the book. The camera crew just blend into the evening and film the dancers, the debates and laughter at the tables. I don't know quite what they hope to capture here but can't escape the warmth of that crowd. The atmosphere is so positive I make a mental note of having book number two launched here.

YET MORE LAW

The Blair–Brown government introduces a new law to make sex with prostitutes illegal if they work for a pimp, suffer from drink or drugs problems or have been brought here from another country to work. Then in the typical get-into-jail-free style that has marked this government's jurisprudence, they add that no defence can be admitted that the girl declared she wasn't any of those things. How would anyone know she was lying? Not our problem, declares the home secretary.

End of November. Have a long spot on George Galloway's Press TV promoting the book; though most of our animated conversation dealt with the '84/85 strike and the state's attempt to use our families as punishment shootings through the denial of their welfare entitlements, and the low-life actions of the occupying police forces. We also, though, dealt with questions of climate change and coal's contribution to it – in terms of production worldwide – and the prospects of the revival of our UK coal industry and the rebirth of the once mighty NUM. That is not on the cards to that degree of course, even by the most optimistic of visions. But it's interesting crack and is clearly a useful publicity device.

I am full of admiration for George's broadcasting presentation and his command of the role. It's an Iranian worldwide channel so will reach into the homes of millions across the globe. It opens up the chance of a follow-up as the rest of the book comes out. Incidentally, I am followed on by Tony Blair's sister-in-law, a pro-Palestinian and socialist whose book on her brother-in-law is scathing, and was being reviewed by George. She tells me my picture of the solidarity and grit of the pit families had her in tears.[482]

Ee, it's strange the way things come round again. Received unexpectedly an email from Rob Davies. Rob man, you'll recall from the old YCL days, explained to me the sense of free-verse poetry and put the first subversive copy of the Trotskyist paper *Red Flag* in my trembling 15-year-old hands (mind, it was too late; anarchism had already interfered with me by then). He writes poignantly to remind me of our first encounter, as if I'd forgotten him:

> At the time, I was working on a farm at Hexham and then I got a job on the Quayside. I got kicked out of the YCL for being a Trotskyist and joined up with Gerry Healy for a time. When I got married, I moved down south in Somerset to work in the car component industry. I was senior shop steward for a while, until I lost my sight in the late '70s. After that I started to do youth work for the YMCA. We moved up to Alnwick 18 months ago. It is great being back.[483]

SCARY STUFF

In an episode indicative of the control-freakery of the Blair –Brown project, the police raid Parliament. An MP (Damien Green, Tory opposition spokesperson on immigration) is arrested, his parliamentary office is occupied, searched and photographed and his computer and personal files and records seized. This is the first time ever police have raided Parliament, and they do so without approval of the DPP, or a search warrant, brushing aside all objections. It is a fearsome political development, carried out under the catchall heading of 'anti-terrorism'. It is aimed at stifling the criticisms made by Mr Green of the government's chaotic immigration policy. In particular, there is the news that 5,000 *illegal* immigrants were cleared for work in security and government departments.

Mr Green's information comes from concerned civil servants, and police objectives appear to be to stop him making political propaganda, discover who the civil servants are and suppress any new information coming out. It is a tiny coup, and a dangerous precedent in terms of democracy. There are muffled cries from MPs but nothing like what one would have demanded or expected from them, who, one would have thought, would recognise the road to hell being embarked on here. It is illustrative that the police accuse Mr Green of 'grooming' the civil servants. In July of 2009, it is revealed that the *News of the World* (right now the government's favourite newspaper, bloodhound and witch-hunt panic starter) has bugged the mobile phones of thousands of famous people, and has posed as various institutions and official bodies in order to gain contact details and private information. Among the items bugged and recorded is the private life of John Prescott, the former deputy prime minister. What is more scandalous is that the police have full knowledge of the illegal operation and neither take action on it or inform anyone, including the deputy prime minister, that it's still going on.

Meantime the Blair–Brown project to make us all do what they decide is best for us moves on again, with the passing of laws to close down the last remaining tobacco shops in Britain. From now on, it will be against the law for any shop to display tobacco products to the public: no shop displays, no glass trays. For newsagents and corner shops it's a kick in the balls, for the tobacco shops specialising solely in pipe tobacco and cigars etc. it's the end. For civil liberties and the right to decide what to do with our own lives it's another blow in the long line of draconian legislation aimed at forcing the government's will down the throats of the population. The same day they trail news that they will ban, i.e. make illegal, hot-food shops and takeaway shops anywhere within a 400-yard radius of a school, a library, a park or a community centre. The ban will extend to new takeaway food shops anywhere where there already are some. This time it isn't smoking: it's eating the food the government doesn't think we should be eating, so they will actually ban shops from the key areas where there are 'vulnerable' people, i.e. anyone who goes to a school, a library or a park, to stop them being tempted from straying from the government's chosen path of righteous behaviour and food consumption. On the other side of the 'Do What You're Told' operation, Plane Stupid occupy part of Stansted Airport and stop all flights, grounding thousands of passengers, mainly families with their kids going on holidays. This isn't action against 'The Government'. This is action to physically stop people using the planes, because Plane Stupid have decided 'we' shouldn't be doing it. Like the government, this crowd have decided they will impose their self-declared salvation upon us like it or not.

Just before Christmas, we book a log cabin in Centre Parcs up in Cumberland for an activities extended weekend. As is the wont of those who rule us and dispense their paranoid and perverse instruction, poor Santa is no longer allowed to sit the children on his knee and hear their requests for Christmas. They must now sit on a stool in front of him; likewise, the photo with the kids is now posed with Santa's arms directly down by his sides, he being now unable to hug them. The perfectly normal, natural and wholly appropriate is now deemed inappropriate along with much else. Still, the weekend spent with loads of kids and parents swimming, bowling, tennising, cycling and running in the middle of dense woodland is unspoiled, and I lose 3 pounds while I'm away.

Saturday 20 December. Adrian Mitchell dies of a heart attack. Though who'd believe such a heart would give out? Our lives crossed many times since the old heady days of Tony Jackson, Tom Pickard and the Morden Tower poets. Though he was already a famous 'beat poet' of the Liverpool Scene, half a generation older than me, we appeared in underground mags and the beat scene platforms from time to time together. He was one of the fearless voices of our movement; I had met up with him again just this May, at the commemoration at Conway Hall of May '68, where again he recited, this time in honour of Astrid Proll, his poem 'Tell Me Lies About Vietnam'. The stars that once lit the heavens of our constellation are now slowly dying, and the skies are becoming dark again.

ANOTHER BLOODY PAGE

The day after Boxing Day Israel pens another bloody page in its holocaust against the Palestinian people. Within 2 days over 300 people are dead, 1,000 injured, 800 seriously, among them many babies and children, as F111s supplied to them by the USA swoop in and mercilessly bomb the captive Gaza Strip. Gaza has already been starved for months by a blockade of the enclave, which has stopped medicine, water and food reaching the crowded impoverished and totally helpless population. In a rerun of the massacre in Lebanon, the world looks on, does nowt, and virtually says nowt. The retiring US president, George Bush, true to form, blames the Palestinians and calls on *them* to stop their attacks. The UN, more or less the mouthpiece of US foreign policy, has to say something, so condemns *both* sides and in so doing repeats the stupid justification offered by Israel for the genocide. That being that the home-made rockets and pipe bombs which Hamas militants launch into their occupied territories are equivalent to the war of terror being waged against the Palestinian people. In 8 years, these crude pipe bombs have killed 20 Israelis; in 2 days, more than 300 Palestinians are dead and the bombing continues to push up the score. The Palestinians have no defence whatever against the mighty ultra-modern technical military wizardry of the Zionists; they must stand and bleed and die at the whim of Israel. My blood boils and I feel utterly futile. Demonstrators in London attack the Israeli Embassy and I wish I was with them. The TV and press blatantly spread the lies of 'retaliation' or treat the massacre as 'a war' of equal sides and horrors.

DEATH OF MY SENSEI
On the eve of New Year's Eve, Romano phones and tells me that Alan, my long-time friend and karate sensei, is dead. He had been through a hell of operations and tests lately, and the worry was it was Hodgkin's lymphoma. We trained with him less than a week ago – we had all been confident he would struggle through it. Young Alan, his son, had found him dead at the top of his stairs. The family is devastated, as am I. He was a giant presence in my life, a rough diamond right enough, but a man of deep wisdom that he hid behind his granite outer layer.

WAR CRIMES
Saturday 3 January 2009. I speak from a platform on Grey's Monument in Newcastle on the Israeli holocaust against Gaza. There are 1,000 people, many of them Palestinian and Arab, and maybe 50% Muslim. It is 4 degrees below, freezing. There are angry Arab voices, many appeals to God; the platform is united only on its opposition to Israeli mass murder. For a time, there is some angry pushing and shouting between Fatah and Hamas supporters. The mullahs remind the factions we are there about the kids and families and this must be everyone's priority. This calms the pushing, although rival secular and Islamic chants still end every speech.

I speak in a hard and clear voice, but in the cold and confusion of some mixed emotions, I just ad-lib and don't use the notes I made on an envelope. As a result, I don't say what I want to say, I lose much of the class and political distinction I am trying to make. The speech is OK; it's well received, but it should have been a good one, not an OK one. I hate the state of Israel; I hate its genocidal ethnic cleansing, super-colonialism, apartheid, fascistic strategy and ethos. But I hate the politics of Iran, the politics of Hamas, I hate the jihadists too. This crowd is bigger than the one of hundreds that flocked round the Haymarket in the prelude to the mass Grosvenor Square demonstration of 1968. But then we called for victory to the Vietcong. Hamas isn't the Vietcong – we do not want to see their politics gain power over the more secular but inept and now discredited Fatah. I hate the references to God, I hate the widespread participation of the mullahs and Islam and the cries for another theocracy.

But the point is, Palestine belongs to the Palestinians, their choice of who represents them is theirs, the choice of which social system they want is theirs, and I support their right to self-determination whatever that might be, but I refuse to not have a view and a preference or to campaign for them. In the crowd are the Elliotts from Birtley, and Sean and his missus, the Wobs, and many other familiar faces. I am proud to have been on stage and speaking in the name of the NUM and adding also some comments in a personal capacity to do with rocket launchers and a single democratic secular socialist Palestine of Jews and Muslims, Christians and atheists and a united Jewish and Arab working class on the basis of socialism across the Middle East.

Within 10 days of the invasion 758 Palestinians were dead, overwhelmingly non-combatants, almost half children. Many are ordered into buildings, which are then blown up. UN refugee centres are bombed after the UN gave the Israeli army the coordinates to protect the women and children and old men. UN drivers and Red Cross drivers displaying their flags and neutral humanitarian designation are shot and shelled.

War crimes abound. Miliband the British foreign secretary and the Brown government talk of 'deaths on both sides'. So far 13 Israelis have died and 758 Palestinians, with thousands of Palestinians seriously wounded and dying. An attempt to call a 'ceasefire' is doomed, (a) because the Americans abstain and therefore give the green light to Israel to continue its holocaust – Israel's allies in America and Britain do not want it to stop – and (b) if Hamas agreed to 'stop smuggling weapons into the Gaza Strip and firing at Israel' this would be a de facto recognition, first, that the legal and democratically elected government of the region has no right to defend itself or arm itself, and, second, that they would allow the illegal occupation and expansion of Israeli settlements and ethnic cleansing of Palestinians from the region to continue without opposition. The lies and double standards are the worse I have ever witnessed, with international relief and welfare agencies from all sources declaring Israel in breach of the Geneva Convention and all the accepted norms of decency and humanity. Hamas rockets are denounced across the media; nobody mentions the disproportion of Israel's F111s, nuclear weapons, heavy tanks and battleships. In the 3 weeks of murder 1,000 Palestinians are dead, almost 200,000 homeless and helpless, thousands seriously injured. The files of war crimes accumulate as cold-blooded murder is wrought upon the helpless women and children and old men and unarmed civilians. Red Cross and UN flags and buildings are wilfully blown up, indeed targeted. People are told to leave the buildings, but are then shot down on the streets. It is clear Israel's agenda is terrorism and inflicting the maximum amount of death and destruction on the Palestinian people as a whole for their support for Hamas. Of the 13 Israelis killed the majority are soldiers.

Among the Palestinians 1,000 are mostly noncombatants and nearly half children. In London 100,000 demonstrate to the Israeli Embassy. True to form, the cops attack the crowd for the very idea they can protest against 'our side'. There is no doubt that Brown, like Blair, supports the Israeli state and everything it does. I don't know how the average Palestinian feels in terms of the wish for revenge. I know I've never supported cruise missiles like I do at present and wish to God Fatah had a couple with which to retaliate. I don't want revenge on ordinary Israelis; I do want the tanks and planes blasted out of existence and their government and state smashed. That's me – what will the orphans in the ruins of Gaza up to their knees in their relatives blood think? What would you think?

SAMURAI

13 January. The funeral and cremation takes place of my sensei Alan Rushby. I have been asked, by the members of the karate club to say the eulogy, an honour tinged with so much sadness.

The ceremony is a mass gathering, karate men and women from near and far, past and present. Alan started teaching 40 years ago and has an accumulated army of students, many of them high grades. A huge wedge of the Donnie pub scene accompanies his family, deeply upset and stricken by their loss. Alan was the centre of the crack and was a well-known character round town where he held forth on every subject and issue but never without a comic angle and insightful thought. All his mates from the market pubs turned out too. Annette, his former wife and a karate sensei herself, spoke a poem in perfect Japanese, 'The Death of a Samurai'. His daughter Catherine got up to share some comic and moving memories, then me:

'Alan's embodiment of karate wasn't just some physical expertise, although he had that in large measure. It was about feeling good about yourself, about enjoying the life flowing through your veins, about taking life in both hands and enjoying it. That was what Alan's karate revealed to you.

'You only had to look at the way Alan lived his own life to know what this was all about. Al loved life to the limit, and in keeping with that 1960s generation he was part of, tested every boundary, tested every frontier in his long varied and colourful life. Alan's life is a kaleidoscope of experiences, of all descriptions. Those of us who have had the privilege of listening to those tales will know what I am talking about.

'Alan loved the crack, loved the cut and trust of working-class humour and culture, he was a great raconteur, a sort of fusion of Sid James, Del Boy, and Richard Prior, shot through with Zen but framed in his own unique character. The centre of any crowd, the life and soul of any party, was Alan telling the tale.

'Alan had no time for God, he believed too much in justice and fairness for that. But Alan was a cipher for the spirit of joy in the world. I don't think I ever seen him sad, can't think of a single time when he didn't have a comic response to whatever life flung at him. This wasn't as well as his karate – this was part of his karate.

'Alan's karate wasn't and isn't a sport. You don't leave this karate in the dojo.

It was with him every minute in the whole way he perceived the world and the people in it.

'I mentioned Zen. Anyone who ever took what Alan said on face value missed a great deal of the point. That point often took days, sometimes weeks, to sink in, and when it did, you realised he was talking of a far deeper perception than you had realised. Alan would challenge all wisdoms, all philosophies all beliefs. Challenge all your deeply held convictions, all your sensitivities. Nothing was inappropriate to Al; if you had a view, if you had a belief you'd better get ready to defend it as vigorously in the tap room as you would do an attack in the dojo. I think everyone in here knows me and Al went many rounds downstairs in the bar, as he refused to accept a damn thing I said about my carefully worked out philosophies and doctrines. Likely as not dismissed in an instant as bullshit. If you were vulnerable in any way shape or form Alan would test you on it, probe you on it, provoke you to screaming point on it ... until you learned to absorb the impact, to accept the challenge, to roll with the force, to fear nothing that words or insecurities which would otherwise be used to disarm discredit or weaken you mentally and physically before you even got to the physical attack. Alan understood well that self-belief and self-confidence were the strong mental stance that had to accompany the strong physical stance. Alan's Zen wisdom came in the form of pillock, piss-taking; outsiders didn't understand it. Many of the things Alan said were more about seeing how you yourself responded to them than anything he believed himself. Alan kept his wisdom and powers of instruction in some rough and ready forms, but that they were totally effective is beyond doubt. Like Zen, sometimes the point was that there wasn't a point. Or as the man said, when sitting just sit, when walking just walk,

'Alan's skills as a teacher cannot be underestimated. I teach you the techniques he would say, you have to provide the conviction, but truth is Alan's conviction gave us conviction.

'All of us who trained with Alan, and many people here trained much longer with him than my fifteen years, know what sort of a teacher he was. He would take you from absolutely nothing, from a quivering mass of indecision and immobility in my own case, and give you two things, one the technique, which he would relentlessly pursue you on, painstakingly, hour on hour. Perfection of the technique – he would never ever allow anything just to do, never pass anything which wasn't right, never ever accept the easy road, and you would stand exactly where you were and not move on till you had it right. Alan went through no motions; you did it right, or what was the point? Second, he would give you confidence in yourself and your technique. When Alan criticised you he took the skin off your back ... but when he praised you, it was like being awarded a much-prized medal. Alan's esteem and Alan's praise were like gold nuggets. When Alan awarded me my First Dan in 1999 it was one of the most important and gratifying awards anyone in any field of my whole life has ever bestowed upon me, and I am entirely grateful for having had the huge privilege of training with this man, being one of Alan's students in the community of his students, a more unique collection of people and a loyaller set of mates you will find nowhere in the world. What we are, the characters that we are, the human beings that we are, in strong measure come down to you Alan – sensei.'

Everyone was pleased with the words. Truth was, if I'd had all day it wouldn't have been enough time to exhaust the memories of Alan and his life and adventures and the things he left us with. We will be talking about those things for the rest of our lives.

VIETNAM

So, almost at the end of the book, we come almost full circle and back to Vietnam. Vietnam had been the grist to the mill of my generation around the world. Their courage had inspired us. Their oppression had forced us to rethink notions of pacifism and non-violence. Their victory had shown the vulnerability of imperialism. The struggle against the US state's war effort and support for the resistance and for social revolution in the USA had radicalised and politicised the generation who sought and craved freedom and justice with an undying

The author, Kenhga River, North Vietnam, 2009

passion.[484] Ideas of alternative systems, lifestyles, freedom permeated our souls for a lifetime.

I had promised myself all my life that if time and money permitted I'd travel to Vietnam, as a pilgrimage, as a search and enquiry to see how it had all worked out. At the end of January 2009, I left for an extended tour of Vietnam. That tour touched my soul; it was for me a most deeply appreciated encounter. I was surprised that it was the spirituality of Vietnam that affected me more than the politics, perhaps because the politics as we collectively had perceived they would evolve didn't, not in the way we thought. I was going to say 'But that was their choice and that was one of the goals they were fighting for.' Actually, it was our choice, our actions in the USA and Europe and the failure of *our* revolutionary movement, our revolution that left *them* with no choice. I've heard self-styled purer-than-pure British revolutionaries declare their contempt for the Vietnamese state – that they *failed*, that they now have capitalism and multinational exploitation. Ahem! We failed, and failed those people who fought harder than anyone in the whole world for our common goal. We left them isolated and alone, and in the words of a young communist when I challenged him on where they were now, asked 'What were we supposed to do, where were we supposed to go?'

The above two paragraphs were once the start of a whole very large chapter. Nevertheless, this book is too huge, too diverse to fit all of my experience in Vietnam in here. I have with great reluctance taken the rest of the chapter out, and it will sit with thousands of photos waiting the funds to bring out a separate book exclusively on my Vietnam experience, with hopefully masses of the most wonderful (I think) photos. If any reader by the way wants to publish this book, or pay for my fine ChristieBooks publishers to do so I'd snatch ya arm off or dance at ya wedding or wake, whichever you'd deem appropriate. I'll end by saying this: Vietnam is without doubt the noisiest country in the world. But yet I found an inner peace I have found nowhere else; it joins the inspiration which took me aye and the bulk of a generation to fight for 'two, three, many Vietnams' as our comrade Che once put it.

The author in the mountains of North Vietnam, 2009

So Where Are We Now? And Had Me Jaw

While I'm away, on my long tour of Vietnam, the world keeps turning. I've also incidentally read me way through a host of books including Raph Samuel's wonderful *The Lost World of British Communism*. He made me reflect upon things that frankly I had never ever considered. For the first time in my life, he made me reflect on the reified way we talk of 'the class'. As if the class were a living, animate, thinking creature. We talked of it as having demands, aspirations, morality, principles, a past, a present and future. I had never thought of how seriously crazy this must sound to non-leftist politicos. 'And the word was made flesh' came to mind, as a simple collective expression of social classes took on the living, breathing identity of a sentient being, almost more than life. I had forgotten how deeply insightful Raph could be. He talks of 'the Communist faith' as an alternative religion and the community of communists as an alternative 'England' with alternative 'English'. This was our country, with all the patriotisms and imperatives to defend and promote, with leaders, laws conventions and a complete alternative history with heroes and meanings quite distinct from the formal 'country'. Readers of this autobiography will recognise at once how perceptive Raph was. I could hear his rich, cultured, kindly voice right through the book, as if he was speaking each sentence. I could see his physical gestures, the toss of the mane of hair, his stare into the collective eyes of his audience, his deep and searching reflections into his memory and link into timeless movements of history.

Will the Real IRA Please Stand Up?
The 'Real IRA' launches a carefully targeted assault on a British army barracks in occupied Ulster. It kills three British soldiers. A little later 'Continuity IRA' kills a policeman. Obviously, not to lose out to the Realies. They've both learned from the disaster of Omagh, but they still lack any popular mandate to restart the armed struggle. They come over as sore losers to the Provos' new constitutional road, with no programme to get us from the doldrums in which we all sit becalmed and back into the trade winds, which were booling along before Adams and his team disarmed us politically and militarily. Although the target is well chosen, it has no impetus – it has no specific reason right at this juncture. It is simply a demonstration to say they are still here. Mind, I have to say again that the British state has never had any right in Ireland, has no right now and never will have any.[485] That being the case, even a small minority of Irish workers has the right to resist the occupation, be it ever so limited and atomised from any mass movement of the people.

Just when I thought Arthur and me were comrades again (following our joint intervention at the climate camp and the mass Newcastle 'Climate and Class' meeting), I am asked to present evidence and support for the NUM *against*

Arthur Scargill. True, true. There is an 'A. Scargill v. NUM Certification Officer Hearing, 18–20 May 2009, in London, Commissioners Court.' You could not make it up. Readers might recall we, that us on the left of Arthur in the democratic faction of the NUM, had fought a protracted struggle against his rulebook, and the imposition of its terms against the unanimous objection of the Yorkshire Area, and then against the subsequent National rulebook which he had drawn up and imposed on the Union nationally.

He had only succeeded in doing this by the most blatant abuse of the votes of limited members in his mythical 'Area Office Branch'. Then the invention on the hoof of a 'National Office Branch'. These have been discussed in detail earlier. It was a fiddle, of course, but we drew back from using the 'Tory courts' and anti-union legislation and with both arms tied behind our backs slogged it out internally with much acrimony and bitterness until, two secret QC legal decisions later (each decision given in confidence and without the knowledge of our team, let alone the members), they, the Area officials, declare that they accept the limited members' votes will not be used like this; they still believe the mythical branch had existed but conceded it had never worked correctly and would be suspended, for some future consideration. There the matter lay.

Of course the war continued. Jeff Stubbs, our most senior advocate, was sacked. But then more branches closed and the balance of power swung back to us. It allowed us to win a victory, successfully seeing Chris Kitchen elected Area secretary and general secretary of the National Union; it meant Steve Kemp, the previous secretary with whom we had clashed so bitterly, lost his position. Chris Skidmore, Area president, had increasingly found himself at war with Arthur, who still insisted on inhabiting the building, deploying staff and speaking in the name of the Union. There was *still* a position of dual power, no matter what the members had voted for. So just as the dust was beginning to settle, and we thought normalised relations might return to the Area there came a change of leadership in the Maltby Branch. The new officials at Maltby then found themselves at war with the current Area officials, on fundamental questions of democracy, and Arthur was able to link these unconnected issues to his own agenda and thus gain a beachhead from which to launch a counterattack upon the Area officials. The election aspirations of Steve Mace from Maltby now ran headlong into the obstructive rules, which Arthur had brought in to control and restrict us in general, and me in particular. *Arthur* now complains to the Certification Officer that these rules are unfair, because they block a member's right to stand for NEC positions.[486] He insists that an Area Office Branch ought to be re-formed. He goes further, and alleges that the general secretary Chris Kitchen is inefficient and negligent.

Arthur alleges that an Area Office Branch, had there been one in existence, could have nominated the Maltby candidate; and that, if they had, he could have appeared on the ballot paper. And, had that happened, he might have been elected to the NEC. And, had that happened, he may well have been selected as National secretary by the NEC. Not much speculation there, then.

We have our day in court, and Arthur, now playing his favourite role of lawyer, 'put it to you Mr Douglass' that I surely could remember the existence of an Area Office Branch. I remind him that the day previously he can't recall casting over 800 votes on behalf of a National Office Branch. (Apart from the fact that at a National Conference, only areas are represented, not branches.) I agree with him that the rules are exclusionary and that he drafted them and excluded me twice from running for the NEC. Remarkably, he responds: 'Two wrongs don't make a right, and the Commissioner is here to decide on whether the rule is fair, not who drafted it.'

So what is it all about really? Well I don't have a crystal ball, but here's my view of where Arthur sees all this going.

Arthur has his sights set on the re-formation, or more correctly the *formation* since it has never existed before, of an Area Office Branch. He will be in the Area Office Branch and expects he will be automatically its chairman. He argues that anyone not attached to a pit branch or section and who is a member of the NUM would belong to the Area Office Branch. He argues further that the rules mean *anyone* in any profession or trade or job, with no connection whatever to mining, can belong to the NUM. This would mean that while the working branches declined in numbers with the ongoing contraction of the coal industry, the Area Office Branch, doubtless with him in control, would be expanding. The size of the branch would grow; the number of card votes would grow. The power would return to him, in terms of nomination of candidates' votes for positions, resolutions and direction of the Union and, lastly and most importantly, control of funds. You don't have to be a genius of strategy to see that the entire Socialist Labour Party membership in Yorkshire and Humberside, Lancashire and Nottingham would gain membership of the NUM and be co-joined to this Area Office Branch. None of this had anything to do with Steve's Mace case, which was entirely legitimate and was upheld by the Commissioner. Arthur strenuously denies that this is his intention and the Area Office Branch in fact would be a very small branch.

But why any of this now? Arthur is 72. Comrade Kitchen told him the contract will not be renewed. This in my view is an attempted coup by Arthur to take back the power, influence and money of the NUM to exercise for his own visions and likeness.

The outcome of the learned judges' decision on the NUM arrives. They rule:

– That no Area Office Branch existed, especially during the time in question.

– That its creation was a matter for the Area, given the noted problem of the balance between working and non-working members.

– That the member at Maltby had suffered discrimination by the 30% rule, given that only 3 working pits existed in Yorkshire, and that had prevented him standing for the NEC.

The NEC elections would therefore have to be re-run. It meant of course Chris Kitchen, the National and Yorkshire Area secretary, was no longer now a member of the NEC.

The decision is right of course; the 20% and 30% rule *was* intended to exclude people from having the chance to stand; it had successfully excluded me, and

Chris Skidmore in an earlier period. We have no fear of democracy; the decision always should be down to the members providing they get the chance to actually consider the options.

The NEC election when it was restaged was the most bitter and slanderous I ever recall. We call for a vote for Kitchen and Dave Hatfield the acting NUM secretary at Hatfield. The members vote for Kitchen and Mace, which was a balanced and mature response.

THE DEATH OF LAWRENCE DALY

Eeh – my aud mate, my aud drinking partner, folk singer comrade and then left bureaucrat turned foe, finally dies in his 80s. I had thought he had died years before, but just a few years ago had discovered he was still living. Lawrence had become seriously ill, and was confined to a home. He was allowed to slip into obscurity. I longed to meet up with him again. He had ended up living the last 10 years of his life in a nursing home in Luton, although with his family still in regular caring contact.

Lawrence had been among his great many other accolades a member of the prestigious International War Crimes Tribunal investigating America's war on Vietnam. It had been established by the great veteran peace campaigner Bertrand Russell and included internationally famous philosophers, lawyers, parliamentarians, historians, writers and scientists. Lawrence's voice was there, not only as a representative of the British working class, but also in an internationalist historian and intellectual capacity, equally with Sartre, de Beauvoir, Deutscher and the others. He visited Vietnam as the bombs fell, defied all caution and went to see for himself whether or not the USA were devastating civilian towns. The authors of the new, comprehensive though flawed book on the 1984/85 strike, *Marching to the Fault Line*,[487] report that:

> One of the authors treasures the memory of standing with Daly on Euston station at midnight, some time in the early '70s, after long sessions in the pub, and reciting the whole of Act 1, Scene 2 of Julius Caesar. First Daly played Brutus, then they changed parts and he played Cassius.[488]

I never succeed in tracking him down again and on 23 May 2009 he died.

What can we say of Lawrence in conclusion? A pitman of the old school, a Marxist and communist steeped in the old-time religion of communist organisation and history. A brilliant Union orator and negotiator. An intellectual, font of music, song and poetry. A comic and storyteller.

DIP YA BREAD IN

In June 2009. Parliament and the country are racked by revelations of across-the-board corruption in the 'mother of parliaments'. MPs from all parties, Cabinet members and backbenchers compete to outdo each other in claiming 'expenses'. Thousands, tens of thousands are paid out in totally bogus scams, claiming for non-existent houses, non-existent mortgages, and all the normal living expenditure which us poor mortals would pay from our wages and salaries. The MPs, almost without exception, treat their salaries as savings and all other expenditure as 'expenses'. It produces a massive fury at the ballot box both in mass abstentions of Labour voters, and in switching to non-sullied usually far-right parties like the BNP. The left do pathetically in the Euro elections, gaining no more than 2.5% nationally, while the BNP gain two MEPs, one of whom is in Yorkshire. They gain a council seat in Barnsley, while Doncaster elects a far-right racist Tory as town mayor, running under the flag of the so-called 'English Democrats Party'.

Even as the government crumbles daily before scandal and the ongoing economic crisis and government debts, they draft a new set of repressive laws. This time they bring forward a bill to fine and jail parents of 'children' who misbehave at school, or don't go to school or don't join in the sports which they have decided are now compulsory. Given that the 'children' are the young adults who would last year have left school and now are forced to stay on until they are 18, non-compliance is hardly surprising. Now the faceless powers redesigning our lives start a huge propaganda campaign against drinking, against the working-class night out. The campaigners crow that they have made tobacco and smoking antisocial and potentially criminal, and they can do the same with alcohol. It is now typical that compulsion and punishment marks everything this tyrannical government forces upon us. Whoever wins the next election it is a trend unlikely to stop until the masses of working people demand that the state gets off our back, and we take back the freedom to run our own lives as we see fit.

Wind Turbine Estates

In July of 2009 the environment secretary Miliband announces a firm commitment to making 33% of all energy generation come from 'renewables'; it means mainly wind turbines. They are hopelessly inefficient and non-cost-effective. He warns us electricity bills will have to rise by third or half over the next decade to pay for them. Expect power cuts and power shortages, we are warned. 'The government is forecasting that by 2017 there will be power cuts of around 3,000 megawatt hours per year – the equivalent of the whole of Nottingham being without electricity for a day.'[489] The prediction is that 16 million will be without power on winter evenings. Clean coal? Not if it means British miners. To impose the windmill programme he placed a green paper before parliament removing the rights of appeal and veto from the public and regional and local councils. The government is consciously designing an energy policy that is utterly inadequate and will result in death, injury and discomfort, all on the back of a dogma.

This history is now so up to date and contemporary it's getting creepy. You'll be reading this on the bus as I will be sitting next to you writing it … time then to call a halt.

SO HAD ME JAW THEN

It is time to draw this book to a conclusion – well short, I hope, of the actual conclusion of my life. I still have adventure ahead. I have studied Aikido under Sixth Dan instruction of Master Jon Stokoe and hope to carry on with that. I hoped maybe to travel to China and train with the Shao Lin, and study Chinese, Kung Fu and Buddhism, but have to be realistic about the truly gruelling regime which this involves and the fact that I may not now be able to take such Olympian-quality punishment (that's the hard-core Kung Fu, of course not the Chinese or Buddhist instruction). I had also underestimated not only the range of tuition and basic levels of welfare and hygiene while training, from something roughly equivalent to a hard-core French Foreign Legion and train till you drop or die, to little cosmetic sorties into Wushu and just going through the motions. I have also realised that all of these schools are 'authentic' in the way that King Edwin's original battleaxe, having been reshafted twelve times and had new heads fitted ten times, is authentic – it's a direct continuation of something that was there and was passed on, but isn't the same one that started out. Not least, I have underestimated how difficult it is to actually get there and how costly that whole process can be.

I have instead lashed out on my long-awaited, long-time journey through Vietnam, a sort of pilgrimage and act of contrition for the west's rape of that gentle land. I had thought I would take on only one major financial project at a time, but have now been force to accept that I must pay up myself to get this work into material existence and oot amang the greet populace. This last book, if you're reading it, means I've thrown everything I've got into its production. The book may sell in sufficient quantities to retrieve some of my money and poor Stuart Christie to actually get paid something, but, it being very much a DIY enterprise, without the assistance and support of charities and grants, or high commercial publicity, that might be a wish too far.

I thought of a move into my Berwick caravan and sending my massive library of books and posters and pictures off to libraries and archives, and give up most of the possessions I have accumulated in my long and varied life; a prospect which reduces my daughter to tears at fear her Dad will end up a bag person sleeping in a doorway with nothing to show for my life.

I have now at the end of the book stopped working and taken early retirement and will live on my miner's pension, going to conferences, rallies, demos and festivals, and dossing round the country as I did before the work imposed the tyranny of the clock upon me.

There is time yet to return to Holland and the sacred Amsterdam before all that it was is changed and sanitised. India, too, long has lived in my soul and deserves the elongated visit, which remarkably has thus far escaped me. I intend that I shall never now rest from physical challenges of the gym, the dojo, the mountain track – although I intend where possible to have no more teeth welded together or reconstructed, or skin sewn back into place or face full contact again. Although the deadly 'karate circle' and sparring will still infuse fear and a challenge into me belly. Financially I will have a declining pool of resources and this will all too soon inhibit the options of my remaining life. Forbye, after leaving school all them years ago, facing a lifetime of adventure and travel and experience, I did so with no reserve at all and a minute income. The prospect didn't bother me then, and I'd be foolish to let it do so now.

Conclusions

Are there any conclusions? I leave the world not a lot more unstable than when I first intervened into it at 14, to challenge every injustice and clear every danger from the planet. Although by the age of 15 I fully expected to be blown to kingdom come in the impending nuclear conflagration, I regret to leave to my granddaughter and her children a world plagued with uncertainty and impending disasters at every hand. Global capitalism is perhaps more unrestrained and fierce than it has been since its early imperial inception. Prospects for the simple but profound vision of socialism, justice for the working people of the world, a global common treasury for all, are now further away than when I first stuck on my first socialist badge and picked up the red and black flags of syndicalism and communism. On almost every front on which we drove forward in the '60s, the reactionaries, the repressors, the exploiters have driven us back beyond our starting point.

I have come to the reluctant conclusion that mankind is only half-way through its colonisation of the planet and intends to dominate it intensely to the almost complete elimination of all other species and their habitats. We were naively optimistic to think we would stop half way and leave some of the globe untouched and wild, an evidence of the time before us. The next generation has a strong likelihood of witnessing the end of all forests and wildernesses and free animal species. They may witness the complete emptying of the oceans and seas of all fish and mammals. Our stamp on the planet will be total and absolute. Everything will be man-made. There will be room only for us, and then frequently only some of us. That is unless there is a massive worldwide movement that revives 'The Internationale' again and takes back the planet from our rulers. However, a future world commonwealth will surely be built with industry providing the abundance of wealth we need, and not against industry. We cannot reject the creative capacity created by capitalism, only its unchecked and unregulated chaos. There is no golden age of agriculture; there will be no return to the tiny village hamlet as a unit of production. We must seize the potential of science and industry and put it to the benefit of the world's peoples while preserving and expanding natural unspoiled areas of forests and wilderness.

The bricks in the wall continue to get higher and higher. Yet this is no time to despair. We have come a long way still. We have stumbled back down a difficult hill. But the only way is up. We have no choice but to take back the planet, to continue to fight for global change but at the same time not to let the state dictate the way we live right now. Living your life by your own values unfettered and unrestrained by the state's is a dangerous road but for people with freedom in their hearts it is the only way we can live. Everywhere and in every phase of life now the state intervenes to restrict what we do, how we should think, which value

473

judgements are permissible and which are not. They have neither the moral nor the philosophical right to do so and we must hold fast to the moral courage not to seek the easy life by allowing them to.

For me, I have had an incredibly lucky, sexy and happy life. I have most assuredly had a guardian angel looking down on me and have survived the most daunting of potential fatal disasters and looked death in the face on several occasions. By rights I have been on borrowed time for some considerable time and I am profoundly grateful for the chance I have had time to share my time with my daughter and granddaughter and sister. On the political front too, somewhere in an office of the MI6 or MI5 or the Special Branch, is some bloke I owe a great vote of thanks for, one of those old Oxford or Cambridge communist spies perhaps. I have been dragged by the collar out of a number of possible life sentences, when all ahead looked grim iron bars. Time might come when I could yet find the bullet or the jail sentence that has chased me about all my life.

I remain combatant until I die, as certain today that the glorious and happy doctrine of love and revolution, which we preached in the Sixties, is as relevant and necessary as it ever was. Perhaps the Beatles were right after all – for all you need *is* love, and we are all *Stardust*, as Joni Mitchell once observed. But although love in your heart is necessary, it isn't *all* you need – a box of AKs and rocket launchers will also be necessary to fight for justice across the world and let everyone experience the stardust that we all are. I would not suggest violence is the only road to progress and I have loved and admired those who have taken paths of non-violence, but never dodged resistance and confrontation albeit without the use of physical force. My differences with this philosophy as will be seen by this work are differences of degree, although these are for me tactical and not moral considerations. It is not enough to shout 'Down with all oppressors, down with all oppression!' – it is necessary to actually knock them down with the greatest mass support possible, or when necessary by any means possible and with the numbers available that time and the presence of the moment of history allows. But as Che once said, 'At the risk of sounding ridiculous, the true Revolutionary is motivated by Love.'

> *Farewell to you, my chicks, soon you must fly alone.*
> *Flesh of my flesh, my future life, bone of my bone,*
> *May your wings be strong, may your days be long, safe be your journey.*
> *Each of you bears inside of you the gift of love –*
> *May it bring you light and warmth and the pleasure of giving,*
> *Eagerly savour each new day and the taste of its mouth –*
> *Never lose sight of the thrill and joy of living.*[490]

The Young Redundant Miner
(tune California)

And its goodbye Jeffery Ainley
You can no longer detain me
and the union won't persuade me to
 work here anymore
I've had me fill of striking, fighting
 and excitement
I'm finally delighted to give up this
 bloody war

Its goodbye to that pit head
That nearly had me stone dead
from cutter blades and rock falls and
 explosions in the mine
No more those early mornings
and me face split wide with yawnings
no more those bloody night shifts
that scramble me insides.

Oh, the truth is Jeffrey Ainley
you have finally convinced me
that this mining game is over
so I'm off tomorrow morn
Just give me my Redundie
I'll have a life of Sundays
I can protest in the sunshine
and sleep me days away.

I've worked me shift while laid flat
when the rock falls filled the chock track
When the top was hold and broken
and the rocks were flushing in
But to do so without wages
is entirely outrageous
Get me cards out Ainley
Coz I'm bliddy jacking in

Oh goodbye to the brass band
and pack me up me wigwam
me caftan and me headband
It's the open road for me
I'll become a hippy biker
In the fresh air at me leisure
I'll have a life of please
and I'll never graft again

Chorus

So tek your job and stuff it
Take your pit and shut it
I never liked the bastard
and I hate the bugger now
The job is not worth having
when you cannot earn a living
So goodbye Jeffery Ainley
and your bliddy stinking mine

(I was inspired to write this song based upon the Hatfield management, but actually about young 'Beetham's' miners from Markham and Brodsworth, who given the situation choose to become 'heavy rock' miners rather than continue as hard rock miners.)

1: Faces tended to have the initial of the seam they were in, and the number of the coalface. Thus B30 meant Barnsley seam, face no. 30.

2: See NUM Annual Report, 1979, pp. 144–50.

3: The Doonbeat, as we called it, was an old warehouse at the back of Worswick Street bus station in Newcastle – a beat scene, blues and R&B nightclub that was open all night, with blues and jazz that was real blues and jazz and a clientele so cool and right-on it has never been matched. For a 15-year-old trainee beatnik like me it was the start of an undying love-affair with weird and dangerous.

4: A 'heavy-metal' rock band, m'lud.

5: These would be the selfsame MPs and union officials who would sing the hallowed praises of the sanctity of the ballot, and its precious importance – having themselves demonstrated their own utter contempt for the votes and demands of their members and constituents.

6: The politics of Zionism, rooted as they are in a mystical belief in their selection by God as his chosen people, are at once a denial of secularism. The literal truth of the bible and the Torah, and a great many nasty political skeletons in the cupboard, has meant they operate an almost manic suppression of debate of their 'ideology'. In part, this is due, too, to the impossibility of debating any fundamentalist view based upon the absolute certainty that God has chosen you. In part due too, to their considerable sympathy amongst Jews and Gentiles at large; being able to hide their political sectionalism under a cloak of 'Jewishness' on the one hand, and present their political opponents as 'anti-Jewish' and 'anti-Semitic'. Amazingly, people who one Palestinian Jew described as 'Gentiles who speak Hebrew' often accuse the Palestinian people, who are Semitic, of being anti-Semitic. Largely these people are Americans with a taste for genealogy 'discovering' their Jewishness, who in the process become more 'Jewish' than the original native Palestinian Jews are. This invisibility cloak is very good at getting the Zionists out of trouble and avoiding having to face up to the nonsense and nastiness of their politics – they just slip on the cloak and are at once covered by an anti-racialist force field which is virtually impenetrable. For the British Anti-Zionist Organisation, breaking through this cloak of deception was vital. The libel action taken against the Sunday Mail by BAZO-PS was just such a breakthrough. The paper had labelled the organisation 'Anti-Jewish'. This was in response to a campaign BAZO had been spearheading demonstrating the mass of evidence of Zionist–Nazi collaboration during World War Two and under the regime of Nazi Germany. Of course, not all Jews were Zionists, and the anti-Zionist Jews were Jews of all descriptions, but mainly communists and revolutionary socialists of one sort of another; so the Zionists and Nazis had had mutual enemies. If one had to choose which Jews were to be slaughtered, and which saved, well then let the reds go to the camps and the ovens. While the communist Jews argued that German Jews were German and Jewish, Hitler argued that they were not German. The Zionists agreed: Jews needed 'their own' homeland. The publication of these allegations whipped the Zionists and their supporters in the raw and the newspaper accused the organisation of being 'anti-Jewish'. BAZO reacted with fury, citing its many Jewish members, brought to the court religious and non-religious anti-Zionist Jews, who at length explained the clear difference. The paper was forced to concede its error and published a front-page retraction. However, the struggle within the National Union of Students was not so clear-cut. David Aaronovitch, with whom I had already clashed over the thorny issue of a Scottish Union of Students, was the secretary of the NUS. He would tolerate no argument, no debate, and while he had a grip on the NEC and the student paper The National Student, he would allow no adverts for BAZO or its activities, or debates on its politics.

7: The Arab nation predates capitalism in the west, or the wars and class struggle, which divided the Arab peoples into different countries. Britain and France divided the Middle East between themselves, creating Syria, Lebanon, Palestine, Transjordan, Iraq and then Kuwait, dividing and dispersing Kurdistan in the process. The dream of pan-Arab unity has long been a progressive demand among the Arab masses. Egypt's President Nasser was probably the most serious contender for bringing about Arab unity and socialism as he saw it. His nationalisation of the Suez Canal and radical agricultural reform programme, together with positive promotion of secularism and crushing of Islamist fundamentalism, set alarm bells ringing in the west. Egypt was invaded by Israel, Britain and France in 1956. With the help of an unexpected veto from the USA in the UN, Nasser forced down the foreign armies. On the back of widespread popularity, he preached that the immense wealth of the region should benefit all the Arab people rather than the super wealthy. The rich, self-interested sheikdoms and oil-soaked corrupt regimes of the region made no secret of their dislike and hatred for Nasser. Along with parochial capitalist and bureaucratic interests, they were to damn attempts to create a single Arab state in the region with the UAR (United Arab Republic). Pan-Arabism remained an unfulfilled aspiration, which for a time was taken on by the Ba'athists, with the mantle being picked up increasingly by Saddam. (Not, I should note in the case of Nasser or Saddam, with any vision of popular direct working class control by the people themselves; though Nasser was probably nearer to British social-democratic ideas of socialism than Saddam, who would never have countenanced democracy of any sort.)

8: Minutes of Ministers Committee on Economic Strategy 23 October 1979; leaked to and published in the Financial Times.

9: National Union of Mineworkers, *The Miners and The Battle for Britain* (London, 1979).

10: Ibid.

11: NUM Annual Conference Report, July 1981, Address by NCB Chairman Sir Derek Ezra MBE, p. 449.

12: See the excellent photographic history, Peter Arkell and Ray Rising, *Unfinished Business: The Miners' Strike for Jobs 1984–85* (London: Lupus Books, 2009), p. 11.

13: NUM Annual Conference Report, 6 July 1981, pp. 212–34.

14: I had always claimed that I would rather be a branch official of the NUM than a national official of any other union, and I sincerely meant it.

15: NUM Annual Conference Report, 6 July 1981.

16: There is a photo and report in Arab Review, 1982.

17: NUM Yorkshire Area, Annual Reports, 1982, General Secretary's Report by Owen Briscoe, p. 66.

18: Ibid., p. 67.

19: NUM Annual Conference Report, 1983, Report of the NEC meeting, May 1983: Industrial Relations, p. 33

20: 'Interview with Dave Douglass: Preparing For Power – The Next Step'. South *Yorks Industrial Bulletin*, RCP, no. 3, March(?) 1983.

21: Peruvian Peace Proposal, 5 May 1982: Draft Interim Agreement on the Falkland/Malvinas Islands: (1) An immediate ceasefire, concurrent with: (2) Mutual withdrawal and non-reintroduction of forces, according to a schedule to be established by the Contact Group; (3) The immediate introduction of a Contact Group composed of Brazil, Peru, the Federal Republic of Germany and the United States into the Falkland Islands, on a temporary basis, pending agreement on a definitive settlement. The Contact Group will assume responsibility for (A) Verification of the withdrawal; (B) Ensuring that no actions are taken in the Islands, by the local administration, which would contravene this interim agreement; and (C) Ensuring that all other provisions of the agreement are respected. (4) Britain and Argentina acknowledge the existence of differing and conflicting views regarding the status of the Falkland Islands; (5) The two Governments acknowledge that the aspirations and interests of the Islanders will be included in the definitive settlement of the status of the Islands;(6) The Contact Group will have responsibility for ensuring that the two Governments reach a definitive agreement. Source: R. Reginald and Jeffrey M. Elliot Tempest in a Teapot: The Falkland Islands War (San Bernardino, Calif.: Borgo Press) 1983.

22: NUM Yorkshire Area, Annual Reports, 1981, Presidential Address by Arthur Scargill, p. 6.

23: NUM Annual Conference, July 1982, Preliminary Agenda,.

24: Doncaster Royal Infirmary.

25: Rachael was my girlfriend. Modern eyebrows may rise, but Maureen and me operated a free relationship although to be right not usually so free as to allow an ongoing other relationship; however we were undergoing a sort of trial transition at this time and our complicated social relationships were more fluid than usual.

26: Harry Murray of the LAW, quoted in *The Cause of Ireland*, Platform Films Production. Directed by Chris Reeves 1983 (16mm/VHS, 104 minutes).

27: *The Miners' Campaign Tapes* were a priceless initiative from Chris and Platform Films. There were six separate films dealing with a major aspect of the strike, and presented by the strikers and the women themselves. They put forward the facts and film, which the national media was refusing to air. We ensured every branch had at least one copy of each film and they were put on in every pub and miners clubs across the coalfield where the striking miners congregated for a pint, or a kitchen, or a union meeting. Our fundraisers sometimes took them abroad and occasionally they found themselves and the film on mainstream European

TV. People in Europe were often far more aware of the facts of our case than many British people, for that reason. They are currently available on DVD from the BFI, 020 7815 1350, www.bfi.org.uk/filmstore

28: For a defence of their attack and timing see Alex Mitchell, *News Line*, 17 September 1983, p. 2.

29: Arkell and Ray, *Unfinished Business*, p. 9.

30: Brian Crozier, of Shield, in *The Big Picture*, BBC Look North, Nick Wood, 1993.

31: Francis Beckett and David Hencke, *Marching To The Fault Line: The 1984 Miners Strike And The Death of Industrial Britain* (London: Constable, 2009) p. 33.

32: Arthur Scargill, *Miners in the Eighties* (Barnsley: National Union of Mineworkers, Yorkshire Area, 1981).

33: Beckett and Hencke, *Marching to the Fault Line*, p. 30.

34: Quoted also in Geoffrey Goodman, *The Miners' Strike* (London: Pluto 1985).

35: In 1925 in response to a mass strike and threatened solidarity action, the government forced the owners to withdraw the wage reduction and lengthening of hours by giving a subsidy. They weren't ready either, and simply bought time while their emergency powers were being put in place. When they were, the subsidy was withdrawn and the cuts re-enacted.

36: *Marching to the Faultline*, p. 35.

37: Scargill, *Miners in the Eighties*.

38: *The Changing Coalfield Consensus*; p. 26.

39: *Business Magazine*, part owned by the Financial Times. Story quoted from *The Miner*, March 1986, p. 4.

40: Beckett and Hencke, *Marching to the Fault Line*, p. 47 (although actually the book wrongly says 1 March 1985).

41: In July 1984, a secret review of the five named colliery closures, which sparked the strike in Yorkshire, Scotland, Durham and Wales by mining engineers, and sent to Ned Smith, NCB director, highlighted the fact that Cortonwood should never have been included on the hit list. (National Archives (Coal) 26/1410.) But it didn't have to have been Cortonwood to spark the action anyway.

42: This is the standing monthly Council of all NUM branches in Yorkshire. It features a delegate from every branch, the members of the Yorkshire Area Executive Committee, and the Area NUM officials. Branches vote initially on a show of hands unless a card vote is called for, in which case branches will be allocated numbers of votes in accordance with the number of members they have.

43: An excellent description of this meeting and a history of the Hatfield pit villages can be found in David Douglass (ed.), *A Year of Our Lives: Hatfield Main, A Colliery Community in the Great Coal Strike of 1984/85*, composed by the activist women, children and men of the communities, published by Hooligan Press, Hatfield, 1986. It is now extremely rare despite the fact that every member of the Branch and women's support groups was given copies at the end of the strike. The booklet stands in need of republication if anyone out there is listening.

44: A full description of this process of events can be found in my earlier booklet

Pit Sense Versus the State: A History of Militant Miners in the Doncaster Area (London: Phoenix Press, 1994). I am told copies still come up on ebay. It should also be available on the inter library loan service.

45: Beckett and Hencke, *Marching to the Fault Line*, p. 117.

46: BBC *Inside Out North*, February 2009. Copy in the author's possession.

47: *Strike Log Book*, 1984, Doncaster Area, NUM Yorkshire Area, p. 12. This book should have been deposited in the NUM Offices at Barnsley at the end of the strike but given that a great deal of strike material has disappeared or has never been made available, I have deposited it with the Doncaster Library Service Archive at Balby.

48: David Jones collapsed from an injury he had received on the picket line and died later in Mansfield Infirmary. Dr John Jones, a Home Office pathologist, said that in his opinion, David died from a haemorrhage and the cause of the bleeding could have been a collision with a post or a vehicle. Many think it was more likely to have been a crush injury caused by mass police pressure, but that the Home Office didn't want to blame the police for the death. There was a second inquest paid for by the NUM to test the view of this first one.

49: *Workers Power*, 20 June 1984, p. 1. At a time when the whole of MacGregor's strategy was to break the Nottingham and Midlands miners away from the NUM, expelling them lock, stock and barrel would do the job for him, of course. The idea that we hadn't already spoken to mass meetings of Notts men, and tried, for the four months up to this paper coming out, to speak to them on gates and round their estates, apart from the work the striking Notts men were doing all the time, is another folly.

50: Beckett and Hencke, *Marching to the Fault Line*, p. 33.

51: President of the Northumbrian Miners, comic, colourful, and brimming with humanity and with pride in Northumbrian ethnicity.

52: Beckett and Hencke, *Marching to the Fault Line*, p. 44.

53: Maurice Jones, 'Monumental Misjudgement', *The Guardian*, 17 March 2009.

54: Maurice Jones, editor of *The Miner*, 'Foreword', in *Against All Odds*, a collection of strikers' poems (Barnsley: National Union of Mineworkers, September 1984).

55: Frank Ledger, CEGB director of operations 1981–86. Quoted in the BBC2 documentary, *Who Kept the Lights On?: Managing The Power Supply*.

56: Quoting from BBC2, *Who Kept the Lights On?*, itself heavily based upon Frank Ledger and Howard Sallis, *Crisis Management in the Power Industry: An Inside Story* (London: Routledge, 1995).

57: David Douglass, *Strike Not the End of the Story: Reflections on the Major Coal Mining Strikes in Britain* (Overton, Wakefield: National Coal Mining Museum for England) p. 38 (still available in the NCMM shop). The book quotes, inter alia, Ian MacGregor with Rodney Tyler, *The Enemies Within: The Story of the Miners' Strike, 1984–5* (London: Collins, 1986) p. 281.

58: Beckett and Hencke, *Marching to the Fault Line*, p. 56.

59: Ibid., p. 57.

60: Ibid., p. 88–9.

61: Ibid., p. 58.

62: Ibid., p. 72.

63: R.W. Buckton, General Secretary, ASLEF. ASLEF correspondence and Report no. 68/1984, 30 March. Document in my '84/85 strike collection in Doncaster Library Service Archives at Balby, Doncaster. It is also mentioned in Bill Ronksley's, '20th Anniversary of the NUM Strike, Diary of Events and ASLEF, NUR and the NUM Strike', kindly given to me by Bill and in my possession.

64: Ibid.

65: Picket Log Book (book 1), NUM Yorkshire Area, Doncaster HQ, end of April 1984

66: Strike Coordination Committee, NUM Yorkshire Area, Minutes, 11 May 1984, p. 3.

67: Slater was the last of the Tyneside and in particular South Shields mining/seafarers tradition which had dominated the area since the early and mid nineteenth century; while he went to sea, his brother became a branch official at Westoe pit in Shields. In the old days, crews and miners were interchangeable, coal and seafaring being somewhat seasonal.

68: Beckett and Hencke, *Marching to the Fault Line*, p. 65

69: Ibid.

70: Internal Home Office documents.

71: Strike Coordinating Committee, Minutes, 3 April 1984.

72: Ibid., 16 April 1984

73: Bruce Wilson, *Yorkshire's Flying Pickets in the 1984–85 Miners' Strike* (Barnsley: Wharncliffe, 2004).

74: Strike Coordinating Committee report, 8 May, quoted in Douglass, *Pit Sense Versus the State*.

75: Picket Log Book (book 1), p. 41.

76: See a reference to this in Picket Log Book (book 1), p. 25.

77: It also means I am directly responsible for paying the petrol costs of those cars – on average, depending on the target, £10 per car, £1,680 per day – in cash, all of which I pick up from the Barnsley offices, every week, with restricted amounts for weekend pickets. I carry £9,000 in a poly bag, often on public transport and nobody is the wiser. Not that anyone would have dared touch the Union's money, which I had to account for penny by penny. I have names of drivers, registration numbers of cars, and names of pickets. I deliver these week by week to Barnsley. As the picketing ranges further afield, and pickets stay long term in working coalfields, I am forced to travel with the money, deep into enemy country, and then additionally pay out food expenses too. It is quite a task and responsibility. I don't think for one minute of the extreme danger I could be in in strike-torn, poverty-stricken areas from criminal and rogue elements. I carry the cash like the Word of God – the Union's money cannot be violated.

78: Owen Briscoe, the Area general secretary.

79: Catweasel – alias Frank Cooper – was named after a medieval wizard on a children's time-travelling saga who spoke Saxon and looked like the longed-haired, wispy-bearded hippie Frank was. He was a Hatfield collier, and one of the Beetham's Miners Bikers' chapter. Frank was famous for assembling, stripping down and testing powerful bikes in his bedroom, and near the end of the story he becomes a self-learned computer expert. As pit deployment and managerial functions move toward computer systems, Frank is frequently allowed out of the pit to restore crashed systems. Oddly they always crashed on a Friday when he was on night shift and had to be called back to the pit, paid overtime and given the Friday night off work in lieu. He always knew when they would crash.

80: I suppose up until this point I hadn't mentioned Class War, the dynamic punko London and urban youth anarchist group. I first made contact with them at what I thought was their first founding conference; well actually, I think they had had four papers out previously, by the time they invited me to speak. Actually, it was their second conference; the organisation was finding its feet, elaborating its politics, sharpening the edge of inner city class hatred. Ian Bone, one of the group's founders, drew a line in the sand between themselves and 'anarchists' in general. 'We had bigger plans to create a revolutionary movement that would sweep all these fucking wankers away for good,' said Ian. 'There might be casualties along the way (but if you boxed clever) not too many. There was nothing more anarchists liked than Defence Campaigns that would give them something to do for a year or so in their otherwise clueless approach to politics. We didn't want to waste time on traditional anarchist defence campaigns. We wanted offensive campaigns – as fucking offensive as fucking possible.

'They were real rough and ready but, God love them, they knew where their bread was buttered. They were overwhelmingly working class, totally bloody eccentric, cool, right on, whatever you wanted to call it. The most significant discussions – and the most heated – came up under the 'sexual politics' debate. The main thrust of their politics was: (1) Everyone was bisexual. (2) Coupledom and monogamy was shit. (3) Prostitution was a way forward for working class and CW women. (4) All social workers should be shot. (5) Middle class feminism was wank and sisterhood was a middle class illusion. (6) Everyone should go to Stonehenge and not Glastonbury. (7) Pornography was a good thing. Fuck knows what Dave Douglass was thinking. It all smacked of some anarcho Maoist collective discussion in the early 70's interlinked with a Brian Rix farce. Meanwhile there was a miners' strike raging while we contemplated our belly buttons and below…The discussion dribbled away at the frayed edges in the late afternoon sunshine. I can't remember what happened the following day – I can't recall being bi-sexualised by anyone. '

Actually I got the impression everyone in the room just wanted to make it clear they weren't going to give up anything they indulged in for some politically correct party line; all the things the middle class lefties and anarcho talkers wanted to restrict in the name of some new morality, they were having none of. They had street cred oozing out of their ears, the political line in analytic Marxist terms left much to be desired but point them in the right direction and they'd mow down anything their path. They were viciously hostile to middle class lefties, pacifists, the mealy mouthed social workers of the petit bourgeois liberal 'Marxist Leninist

Trotskyist politically correct' tendency – which was most of the left. They admired only the struggle of the workers themselves. The conference was packed with leather jackets, bovver boots, Mohicans, skinheads, and heavy-rock type lang-haired freaks. (That was just the women.) I addressed the conference 'Comrades and Fellow Hooligans', and stomping boots and banging tables announced I had hit the spot. From that point on, I think they won my heart, the world of renewed class war on the streets and in industry was shouting in my lughole that I needed to reassess my politics, and look at this whole anarchist, anarcho syndicalist bit again.

81: NUM National Conference, Craig Memorial Hall, Sheffield, 19 April 1984.

82: There is a record of the votes each respective area resolution achieved at this Conference in Douglass, *Strike Not the End of the Story*.

83: I say only Notts ignored it. Leicester made no such call to join the strike and all bar 31 men in the entire coalfield scabbed, with the official and formal collusion of their area union.

84: George Spencer, one of the leaders of the Nottingham miners in 1926, broke the miners' united stand against the coalowners' impositions and led the Nottingham miners back to work. He then went on, with the active assistance of the coalowners and government, to form Nottingham and District Miners Industrial Union. The breakaway was encouraged by the owners to spread into the Miners Federation areas and divide the workforce. They were for decades a damper on union organisation in Nottingham and South Derbyshire, and the owners conceded special agreements and rights to their members while administering isolation and victimisation to Union miners. Spencer's vision was one of seeing in the 'district agreements' that the owners were imposing, the opportunity for Nottingham miners to advance their own interests, against those of the coalfields as a whole. The National Union of Mineworkers was formed in 1944, and Spencer and his breakaway absorbed into the national structure, with – on Spencer's insistence – substantial areas of ongoing autonomy for the district associations and areas.

85: See Douglass, *Pit Sense Versus the State*,

86: David Hart, adviser, in *The Big Picture*, BBC North. Nick Wood.

87: Ned Smith, former head of the NCB's Industrial Relations Department, *The Big Picture*.

88: Ian MacGregor, Ibid.

89: Strike Coordinating Committee, Minutes, 27 April 1984.

90: Lynk had argued it was a clear majority of 10,000 out of a total membership figure of just under 200,000. He said if we couldn't get 110,000 out of 200,000 we didn't actually have the backing of the men for an all-out strike. (Conference Report, 19 April 1984, p. 111.)

91: NUM National Conference, Craig Memorial Hall, Sheffield, 19 April 1984, p. 111.

92: All of this section's facts and quotes associated with it come from NUM National Conference, Craig Memorial Hall, Sheffield, 19 April 1984.. Documents in the author's possession and at most remaining NUM area offices.

93: NUM Annual Conference, 2 July 1994, Presidential Address by Arthur Scargill, p. 5.

94: Beckett and Hencke, *Marching to the Fault Line*.

95: Ibid., p. 107

96: Ibid., p. 106

97: Ibid., p. 108.

98: There had been 'plans for coal', and very elaborate ones, since nationalisation in 1947, but the formal agreement and commitment to developing the coal reserves, giving specific assurances on the ongoing development of the coal industry, was struck in 1974 by the incoming Labour Government elected on the back of the miners' strike of that year.

99: 'Pupils Riot in Support of Miners', Alison Kille, incomplete scrapbook cutting, probably from *Doncaster Post*, 28 March 1984.

100: Ibid.

101: Steve was another of the lang-haired, heavy-metal Beetham's miners, also a champion chess-player.

102: Picket Log Book (book 1), p. 65.

103: And a legend in his own lifetime around the Hatfield pit villages, Dick 'had sat at the feet of the master', namely the great Northumbrian revolutionary pitman George Harvey, who also happened to be the lodge secretary and area EC member of the Durham miners during my Dad and Granda's day at Wardley. All that opens up fields of new histories and new stories far too numerous to retell here. Dick was a great socialist of the old school. He had recently, on his very late retirement from Parliament, made a programme with Radio Sheffield. He was the longest serving miners' MP in Parliament, and had hung on to ensure a replacement of his own political stamp. He had actually asked me if I was on the 'miners list', as he wanted me to succeed him. I wasn't, and had no aspiration to enter that place, though it was a great compliment. He told the radio people: When Ah was young ye knaa, the movement was debating the tactic of the ballot box or the bullet; in my youth I took the side of the bullet. After a lifetime in Parliament, with no lasting achievement by any of us, I think I was right the first time.'

104: Quoted in *Socialist Action*, May 1984

105: Before the strike, the very notion of homosexuality among either sex in the pit community would have produced revulsion. Any poor unfortunate miner discovered to be 'queer' would be badly treated, often beaten and driven from his work, and the community at large. This strike, and the brave solidarity of the gay and lesbian community, particularly those from London, in making a stand with us, despite some of us, in the teeth of hostility, opened some eyes and many more hearts. To be a southerner was a hurdle enough, to be cockney and queer was quite some barrier to see over. People dared to think unthinkable things, to embrace impossible ideas, to overcome the most entrenched of stereotypical notions and cautions. At the end of the strike, the Hatfield Main banner took part in the Gay Pride march in London. The proposal had produced howls of laughter and pisstaking when it was raised at the mass branch meeting. But they voted that we go, and we went. Such would have been quite impossible before the start of the strike, so too the acceptance that some men, aye, even coal miners, could be gay and not really very much queer at all. One lad in particular, an activist from Goldthorpe Colliery, had fought for and won that right, and in so doing the respect of every Doncaster picket.

106: Arkell and Ray, *Unfinished Business*, p. 22.

107: Ibid.

108: See Douglass, *Pit Sense Versus the State*.

109: (Alan Robe.) So called because, following the slaying of a WPC in London outside the Libyan Embassy, Alan would wind the window of the Transit down and air machine gun the ranks of police, making the word 'Gaddafi-Gaddafi-Gaddafi' spell out the noise of a machine-gun rattle. The Libyans seem to spell it Khadfi by the way, and they should know.

110: 'Home coal' was the fuel miners – working and retired, as well as their widows – received as a concessionary part of their wages. The miners had, however, to ensure the delivery of this fuel themselves (in the Yorkshire Area anyway), and had set up 'home coal garages', which employed men on behalf of the miners, and for which they paid each week from their wages. It was run by a Home Coal Committee, and these purchased and ran fleets of home coal lorries.

111: I hadn't seen him for years, though he had phoned me once to see if I was in the market for a huge printing press. Then with the launch of the second part of this trilogy, *The Wheel's Still in Spin*, he turned up, weatherbeaten, fit and with his ancient aud socialist Labour Party firebrand dad Leagay, and his two big grown up lads.

112: Strike Coordinating Committee, Minutes, 13 June 1984. Doncaster Library Service Archives, Balby, Doncaster.

113: M. A. McCarthy, *Picketing in Nottinghamshire: Active Pickets in the Notts Coalfield*, (Notts Rank and File Strike Committee).

114: Notts Working Miners Committee publication.

115: Strike Coordinating Committee, Minutes file.

116: Strike Coordinating Committee, Minutes, 8 June 84.

117: Ibid.

118: Ibid., 11 June.

119: Strike Coordinating Committee, Minutes, 20 June 1984.

120: Ronksley, '20th Anniversary of the NUM Strike'.

121: Picket Log Book (book 1), 24 May 1984.

122: Sirs had at first seemed straight. However in the confusion of the Orgreave situation and what looked like ISTC's unilateral declaration of war upon us, other incriminating features started to emerge. Apart from the state itself, there were a number of ad-hoc bodies working on behalf of the state. One of these, the Industrial Research and Information Service, seems to have been one of those cold-war CIA bodies which had been planted within the European labour movement, this particular one in Britain to contain the activities of reds, militants and subversives. Apart from whatever money and resources the CIA put into it, it also drew heavily from major capitalist firms: Allied Lloyds, United Biscuits,

Hanson Trusts, ICI, Boots and P&O. It also drew funding from the British intelligence servicing budget. One of its directors was indeed Bill Sirs. This looked to us like a strategic position. The role of the steel industry and more particularly ISTC was crucial in breaking solidarity action in support of the miners, not just in their own field – with Orgreave being the most spectacular – but also breaking first the railway workers' blockade and then crucially the dockers' solidarity action. Along with the native scab operation and saturation policing, Sirs's steel scabs were the deepest stab in the back of all. What none us knew was where and why this front had opened up against us. We assumed it was a state action plain and simple. Another director of this team was Ken Cure of the then AEU, the engineering workers' union. Needless to say at a time when we cried out for solidarity action from our comrades in the foundries and heavy engineering factories, their leaders, like those of the steelworkers, were playing for the other side. Truth was though, it was a monumental failure of strategy on behalf of our own NEC, which allowed this particular gulf to open up. None of this exonerates any of the workers in steel and engineering who scabbed; you didn't need leaders to tell you what to do or to tell you that taking the bread from another worker's mouth was morally repugnant.

123: Strike Coordinating Committee reports, quoted in Douglass, *Pit Sense Versus the State*.

124: Much of this was covered in the Channel Four Dispatches documentary, *Spy In The Camp*, Autumn 1994. Also Seumas Milne, *The Enemy Within: Thatcher's Secret War Against the Miners* (London: Verso, 2004) and is reported in NUM Annual Conference Report, 1995, pp. AR 86–7.

125: Yorkshire Strike Coordinating Committee, Minutes, 13 June 1984.

126: Ibid., 14 June 1984.

127: Ibid., 21 June 1984.

128: Ronksley, '20th Anniversary of the NUM Strike'.

129: Resolution of ISTC Conference, 21 June 1984.

130: BSC letter 'To All Red Card Managers, NUM Dispute', 23 May 1984. It goes on to say that urgent appeals to the NUM for sufficient coke to keep two furnaces on low blast have been unsuccessful.

131: Ibid.

132: Arkell and Ray, *Unfinished Business*, p. 23.

133: The workers' occupation at Upper Clyde Shipbuilders, 1971.

134: *Workers Newsletter*, June 1984.

135: MacGregor, quoted in Beckett and Hencke, *Marching to the Fault Line*, p. 91.

136: Area Council Meeting, 16 July 1984, quoted in Douglass, *Pit Sense Versus the State*, p. 56.

137: See David Douglass, *All Power To The Imagination* (London: Class War Federation, 1999).

138: Beckett and Hencke, *Marching to the Fault Line*, p. 107.

139: Figures based on Yorkshire Strike Coordinating Committee documents in the author's possession. And possibly still around at Barnsley NUM HQ.

140: Strike Coordinating Committee, Minutes, 11 June 1984

141: *Workers Power*, 20 June 1984.

142: Strike Coordinating Committee, Minutes, 29 May 1984.

143: Yorkshire Strike Co-ordinating Committee, Minutes, 4 June 1984. Incidentally, the people making these decisions were Ken Homer, Frank Cave, Johnny Walsh, Frank Clark, Alan Gosling, myself, and T. Barroclough. Ken Homer rarely ever attended these meeting and never vetoed its decisions. Targets were selected by popular rank-and-file consensus, expressed through pithead 'grumble meetings' to the panels and so to the panels' elected representatives on the committee. The committee decided when and how to attack the targets. I say this because another left myth is that the committee and its strategy were unrepresentative of rank-and-file opinion.

144: Ronksley, '20th Anniversary of the NUM Strike'.

145: Strike Coordinating Committee, Minutes, 11 June 1984. Which later makes us consider why they just didn't land coke directly at the Flixborough Wharf, which belonged to BSC, and had its own private line to the steelworks. Britain wasn't the sole manufacturer of coke any more than it was the sole producer of coal. It reinforced the growing notion that the whole performance was a distraction tactic. It may be that the track was in disuse, but the point here is that its repair would have been a minor difficulty compared with the armoured operation of running a police-convoyed army of trucks through the most militant coalfields in Britain twice a day. Unless of course it killed two birds with one stone by keeping us out of Notts and the key strategic arterial points in this conflict.

146: Douglass, *Strike Not the End of the Story*, p. 36.

147: Ronksley, '20th Anniversary of the NUM Strike'.

148: Beckett and Hencke, *Marching to the Fault Line*, pp. 112–13.

149: Ronksley, '20th Anniversary of the NUM Strike'.

150: Strike Coordinating Committee, Minutes, 4 April 1984.

151: Beckett and Hencke, *Marching to the Fault Line*, p. 109

152: Arkell and Ray, *Unfinished Business*, p. 27.

153: Strike Co-ordinating Committee, Minutes, Minutes, 25 June 1984.

154: Ibid.

155: Strike Coordinating Committee, Minutes, 27 June 1984.

156: 'Close Down Coal House Plan', document in the author's possession.

157: Strike Coordinating Committee, Minutes, 28 June 1984. *Leeds Other Paper*, 6 July, centre pages.

158: Ian MacGregor, NCB Chairman, June 1984.

159: See Douglass, *Pit Sense Versus the State* for a full description of the debates within the NUM Yorkshire Council throughout the strike.

160: I formally moved it as a resolution from Hatfield, with the support of all the Doncaster branches, at the 17 September Area Council meeting. It aimed at flooding into London alongside the Stop The City demonstration on 27 September. It succeeded in gaining only the votes of 15 branches – that was, Doncaster's 12, plus 3 others including Maltby, with Ted Millward, their dynamic delegate, speaking in support.

161: It should also be noted there was an 'anti-union' anarchist wing – *Wildcat*, *International Communist Current* and others who not surprisingly found themselves on the wrong side of this fight. Determined though they were not to support 'the union', they found it impossible to support 'the miners' without doing so, and ended up in one form or another against the strike and its conduct and organisation. Their role was, and remains, utterly anti-working-class and reactionary. A full discussion on the nature of this anti-union 'left' can be found in my polemics 'Charge of The Left Brigade', published in Class War's *Heavy Stuff* no. 5, in *Refracted Perspective: The Left, Working Class Trade Unionism and the Miners* (London: 121 Bookshop, Brixton, 1991), and in more detail in my All Power to The Imagination (op. cit.). In a sense it is a debate with no one. This current, annoying and offbeat though they are, in reality are the tiniest of fractions at the margins of the far left political milieu. They never actually do anything other than write in IndyMedia and condemn the actions of the working class. Class War needless to say threw themselves body and soul into the strike and were heartily received by the miners and the coal communities. The memory of their intervention was to remain deep and longlasting. Their papers are still around in pit communities and many regional offices of the NUM, especially the anti-Thatcher, anti-MacGregor ones pinned on walls with pride.

162: Strike Coordinating Committee, Minutes, 18 June 1984.

163: Ibid.

164: There are references to this in the Doncaster Picket Log Book.

165: You will find a brief description on the withdrawal of all benefits to strikers their families and redundant miners in the NUM Annual Report, 1985, pp. 66, 67.

166: See Doncaster NUM Panel minute book, which I managed to salvage; the rest, if they are still in existence, will presumably be at Barnsley in some dark corner. I'm depositing this minute book in the Doncaster Library Service Archive at Balby so it's at least accessible.

167: Thatcher, *The Downing Street Years*, p. 372

168: One answer perhaps would have been to let the word stand, but then introduce a clause clarifying what it could not be assumed to mean, thus removing the dangerous ambiguity we had in mind. They, of course, may have insisted on that word precisely because it was ambiguous.

169: Arthur.

170: Beckett and Hencke, *Marching to the Fault Line*, p. 114.

171: Ibid.

172: Ibid., p. 118.

173: Ibid., p. 119.

174: Ibid.

175: Ibid.

176: Beckett and Hencke, *Marching to the Fault Line,* p. 126.

177: Beckett and Hencke, *Marching to the Fault Line*, p. 127.

178: In fact, under Arthur's leadership the area allowed us to extract and use old steel arches from abandoned roadways to keep the mines operating. Some of us fiercely opposed this; I had condemned it as tantamount to us producing our own steel.

179: Margaret Thatcher, *The Downing Street Years* (London: HarperCollins, 1993).

180: Arthur Scargill, *The Miner*, 1994.

181: Thatcher, *The Downing Street Years*.

182: In researching and writing this book I approached NACODS, and sent a letter to Peter McNestry c/o them, to ask for an interview and input into these events. I received a reply from neither.

183: NUM Annual Conference Report, 1985, p. 57.

184: The National Reporting Centre was a body invented by the Association of Chief Police Officers. It wasn't accountable to Parliament or any local police authorities, and there are no records as to its terms of reference or how it was financed. Every police force in the country came under its control and was directed from a national centre, with every police car and van given an NRC number. From this point in, the NRC would issue instructions as to how police were to act. They made up laws and rules as they occurred to them, and acted as though common law, in which they had no actual jurisdiction, were the statutory laws of the land; especially where they favoured the NCB employers' or the government's policy toward the miners strike. Common law has throughout history been hostile to the very existence of trade unions and their actions; only legislation forced through by the actions of unions and their parliamentary supporters had intervened to grant indemnities and exemptions. The Tories had started a programme of removing these protections and, where they hadn't achieved it, the police acted as though they had, enforcing common-law restrictions on the unions and their members, and enforcing common-law rights of employers and their customers. They were in effect a national political police force. See NUM Yorkshire Area, Report of the Area Officials, March 1985, p. 6.

185: I list some of these in *Tell Us Lies About the Miners: The Role of the Media in the Great Coal Strike of 1984/1985)* (Doncaster: DAM/Canary Press, 1985).

186: We had the devil's own job to keep our pickets on these sites for 8 hours per shift. They used to complain 'Nothing's happening,' and take off. Of course, we didn't want anything to happen – we wanted the pickets in position to keep anything from happening. The strike log included ongoing complaints from railworkers who were having to imagine pickets who weren't there. The following entries in the Doncaster Picket Log Book (book 2) are typical: '11th May 9 45 am. J Church phoned from Barnsley. Sent one car to Drax Power Station. When they arrived no pickets were on the gates. There is a lot of movement with oil trains, there seems to be more trains on the move. He recommends Drax should be manned 24 hours a day.' ... '10 10 am Brodsworth HQ phoned Askern and asked why they did not send cars to Drax. The reply was they "did not want to picket Drax they wanted to go to Nottingham."' ... '14 May 10 50 am J Parry Brodsworth. "Only 1 car at Drax and oil getting in. Not enough men to cover 3 gates. No cars from Armthorpe concentrated on Nottingham. No cars from Askern. Will put rota up and get someone there."'

187: EMC was the Embryonic Military Caucus, our prelude to a workers' militia. If not us, then who?

188: She goes on to star in a TV drama with John Hurt.

189: A slight understatement, given that 2,500 men worked in Leicester and only 31 were on strike. The team had called itself 'The Dirty Thirty'; they didn't know there was one more striker until the last day. Their story can be found in David Bell, *The Dirty Thirty: Heroes of the Miners Strike* (Nottingham: Five Leaves, with the assistance of the Arts Council, 2009).

190: The previous book (the second) in this trilogy, *The Wheel's Still In Spin*, speculates how far Ted was set up by the secret state as a fall guy in order to clear the way for the election of the hard-right Thatcher government. Geoffrey Goodman, the Mirror's industrial editor, had discovered that Thatcher and Joseph had both voted against Heath in the 'Who Governs Britain?' election of 1974. See Geoffrey Goodman, *From Bevan to Blair: Fifty Years' Reporting from the Political Front Line* (London: Pluto, 2003).

191: Barbara Bloomfield, Guy Boanas and Raphael Samuel (eds), *The Enemy Within: Pit Villages and the Miners' Strike of 1984–5* (London: Routledge, 1986).

192: Thatcher, *The Downing Street Years*, p. 375.

193: Beckett and Hencke, *Marching to the Fault Line*, p. 188

194: Letter to the author from Alison Aiken, 18 January 2009

195: As already noted, there are descriptions of the internal NUM debates and resolutions in Douglass, *Pit Sense Versus the State*; this particular one is found on pp. 62–3.

196: Area Consultative Committee Minutes, Tuesday 15 January 1985.

197: There are strong suggestions that Howells, a close confidant of Neil Kinnock, had worked out the strategy for retreat with him.

198: This item is discussed in Douglass, *Pit Sense Versus the State*, p. 65.

199: Ibid., p. 66.

200: All of these facts and figures are from Area EC and Area Council reports, quoted in Douglass, *Pit Sense Versus the State*, pp. 67–9

201: See Douglass, *Pit Sense Versus the State* for a detailed consideration of all these decisions and debates.

202: Ian Lavery, *The Miner*, April 1994, pp. 4 , 5.

203: Thatcher, *The Downing Street Years*, p. 377–8.

204: Bloomfield et al. (eds), *The Enemy Within*.

205: Quoted in *Who Kept the Lights On?*

206: Ibid.

207: The years in prelude to the 1926 miners lockout and then the General Strike found the British state torn by two conflicts at once: one, the Irish uprising led by the IRA, and two, the mounting revolutionary potential gathering behind defence of the miners. To fight on two fronts, with the influence of one spreading over into the other, revolutionary armed violence and insurrection, together with ideas of anarcho-syndicalism and Bolshevism fused with republicanism, was too explosive and imminent a mixture. The result was to damp down and derail one, through the signing of the infamous 'Treaty' by Collins, which took the rebellion off Britain's back and allowed the mass-withdrawal of troops from Ireland and their deployment in 1921 to the coalfields and major British cities. On this occasion the war with the current generation of the IRA was still very much alive. Although few organic links existed between the striking miners and the Provos, (we were working on it) the danger of cross-fertilisation of arms and ideas, even some organic unity between the more politicised communities and branches, was a real possibility. Thatcher doubtless knew of the dangers of this strategy.

208: All the quotations and facts of this piece come from the BBC documentary programme *Who Kept the Lights On?*; and documentary or contemporary sources in the field; and personal knowledge of pickets and community responses.

209: What had started as a promising career with the Boomtown Rats, and the takeoff of the band in the USA, crashed severely with *I Don't Like Mondays*, written about a 16-year-old girl's shooting spree in San Diego, California, which killed two adults and injured eight children and one police officer. Across America came a violent backlash, as 'the public', fed and incensed by the media, suggested Geldof and his band were taking the piss out of a national tragedy. Every radio station in the USA banned the record; some mobs had bonfires of the Rats' records in public outrage. The Rats went boom for real and were finished. Geldof went into bankruptcy, and was living off his wife Paula Yates's earnings until her TV programme (*Sex with Paula*) also hit the skids after she said 'fuck' too often on live TV, and her show was cancelled. They were reduced to living off friends in a house borrowed from Elton John. So when the 'anti-establishment' Bob was asked by Maggie Thatcher if he would head up the famine relief campaign for her, he jumped at the chance, and she killed two birds with one stone: detracting from the miners and their financial appeals and earning herself Brownie points for her humanitarianism. Bob later got given his own TV company (Planet 24 Productions). He then went on to be given a knighthood, which as an Irish citizen he constitutionally wasn't entitled to, even suppose we supported such things.

210: NUM Biennial Conference, Blackpool, 2004, National Chairman's Address by Ian Lavery.

211: Deserters from the NCB, not from the Union, I might add. They would rather stay 'in the field' living on their wits than go back and face defeat.

212: NUM Annual Report, 1985, p. 4 quoting NCB Reports/accounts, pp. 31, 29, November 1984.

213: Beckett and Hencke, *Marching to the Fault Line*, pp. 213–4

214: It is true, of course, that having engaged in secret financial transactions, the legal repayments would of necessity confirm their existence, and expose all parties to possible legal actions as a consequence. That, however, while it was a consideration for those we owed money to, did not remove our obligation to repay the debts by any means, legal or covert.

215: At the time, the UDM had only 1,332 members, not all of them miners. Clare Walker, who headed up Vendside for the UDM, was earning £260,000 p.a. She was a former head of the Department of Trade and Industry (DTI) claims department. She worked a 20-hour week. Vendside/UDM took a unique handling agreement, which excluded the use of outside solicitors, and pocketed

£19 million in fees from the government. Additionally they 'farmed out' 10,000 other claims to outside firms and earned a further £25 million referral fees. Not content with that, they then levied an additional fee on the claimants themselves, gaining them another £2 million. (For the full story see *The Times*, 28 June 2005, front and inside pages.) The NUM and NACODS were denied the right to have any claims handling agreement, and were forced to pursue their members' claims through outside private solicitors. Scargill writes ' ... at least one year before this agreement was reached I asked on behalf of the NUM and was denied a similar type of agreement. I point out in my letter dated 30 June to H. Liddell that it is obvious the DTI has deliberately discriminated against the NUM to the financial advantage of the UDM ... ' (Area Circular no. 28/nm. 5 July 2000). The claims handling agreement between the UDM and the DTI was finalised on 17 November 1999.

216: Ibid., p. 219.

217: Ibid., p. 225.

218: It could be added that Sharp, the Rossington 'super scab' and sole member of the UDM in the Doncaster coalfield, was killed in suspicious circumstances after the strike at Thorne Colliery where they had dumped him as a 'security man', but maybe it was just an accident, as the police concluded. A lad on a scramble bike landed on top of him while he lay, inexplicably, on the ground

219: Froggy (Keith Frogson), a Notts striker, by then 62, in his local, had been watching the ITV documentary *Real Life*, about the struggle of a mother in a nearby mining community to save her son from the epidemic of heroin addiction which was sweeping the now abandoned communities. He gave the people in the pub, many of whom scabbed, a particular vocal airing to his view that they had caused all this hardship by their actions. An embittered scab goes home, gets a samurai sword, seeks Froggy out and inflicts massive head injuries leaving him laid dead on the pavement before trying to murder Keith's family too by setting fire to their house.

220: The carnage hasn't finished. At the time I write this its ongoing costs, including those following the Major closures, plus the continuing deprivation, the soaring energy prices, the fuel imports, the further destruction of manufacture etc., together have approached £30 billion and show no sign of ending. The figure for the unnecessary depletion of gas and oil reserves displacing coal, the new plan for the mass expansion of nuclear energy, as well as the blank cheques for the forests of inefficient and environmentally damaging wind turbine estates has yet to be calculated.

221: David Douglass, *Tell Us Lies About The Miners: The Role of the Media in the Great Coal Strike of 1984/1985* (Doncaster: DAM–IWA, 1985). Douglass, David, *Come And Wet This Truncheon: The Role of the Police in the Coal Strike of 1984/1985* (Doncaster: DAM–IWA, 1986).

222: Communist Party of Great Britain. It would eventually formally dissolve itself, the Leninist Faction then reconstituting itself as the CPGB Provisional Committee. (Until it could become a real Communist Party again, when it would drop the 'Provisional Committee' label.)

223: Actually I overestimated the strength of the CPGB during 1926. It comprised only a few thousand members.

224: Letter from the Spartacist League, 27 March 1985; E. McDonald to D.D.

225: Jonathan and Ruth Winterton, in a subsequent research project, pointed out that, in so far as it is possible to generalise, the more typical strikebreaker was 'unlikely to be a youngster or a face worker, more likely than not to have joined the industry in the previous ten years and come from an alien family, and almost certain to live outside a mining community and to be non-political or Conservative. Superscabs were newcomers to the industry at 36% of pits and old hands at 23%, but both were involved at 41% of collieries. The pre-Christmas strikebreakers were mostly newcomers at 46% of pits, old hands at 23% and both at 30%. The deserters (post-Christmas strike breakers) were predominantly newcomers at 34% of the collieries and old hands at 25%, but 41% of pits regarded them as drawn evenly from both groups.'

226: NUM, Doncaster Panel, Special Panel Meeting, 17 April 1985, Doncaster Panel Minute Book.

227: NUM Yorkshire Area: Special Rule Revision Conference, 19 April 1985; Ordinary Council Meeting 20 May 1985; Special Rule Revision Conference and Council Meeting, 17 June 1985.

228: Raphael Samuel, *The Lost World of British Communism* (London: Verso, 2006). It also contains a wonderfully insightful preface by his wife and comrade Alison Light. In the book Raph, almost uniquely in his long literary career, lets fly with scathing negative comparisons on the then current state of CPGB ideology and social leanings, against his vivid memories of the CPGB of his past.

229: Emma Douglass, in Douglass, *A Year Of Our Lives*.

230: NUM Special Delegate Conference Report, 2 April 1985.

231: Doncaster NUM Panel, Minutes, 8 May 1985 (final minute book).

232: Ibid., 18 September 1985.

233: Ibid. Most precious of the areas of job control, and most hated universally by management, was the 'priority system', which gave the NUM exclusive control of who operated faces and headings.

234: British Coal statistics, 14 May 1986; all of these documents I intend to place in the Doncaster Library Archive Service at Balby, Doncaster.

235: Prison letters 29 April, 12 May, 3 June, 23 June 1987, in author's possession.

236: NUM Special Rules Revision Conference Report, 1985, p. 689.

237: NUM Annual Conference Agenda, 1985, p. 6.

238: Ibid., pp. 10, 14.

239: Ibid., pp. 20, 22.

240: NUM Special Rules Revision Conference Report, 1985, p. 709.

241: NUM Annual Report, 1986, Other Industrial Relations Matters, p. 58

242: Doncaster NUM Panel, Special Meeting, Minutes, 28 August 1985 (final minute book).

243: Branch Secretary's Circular 98/85.

244: A puffler is an underground chargehand who takes command of a situation.

245: I have reflected on the true motive and nature of this 'Soviet State', after the first 4 or 5 years of genuine workers' power and what replaced it, and the nearest I get to a simile is something of the Southern Confederate states raggy lad armies after the formal defeat of their side. They continued to wear the uniforms, sometimes even fly the flag, raid the Federal states banks, railroads and enterprises. This time they did it for themselves, but still with political and social hatred for the Federal States of America. Round their campfires, they still sang rebel songs; and among the population, support for the rebs was rife and deep-rooted, regardless of the fact that the cause had actually died. They had become actually criminals, but criminals with a political past and a vendetta. Perhaps something of this nature pervaded the Kremlin long after actual socialism had been destroyed.

246: Extract from report to A.S., November 1985.

247: An exception is Martin Walker, *A Turn Of The Screw* (London: Canary Press, 1985). Martin's ability to reconstruct the climate of the pit after the return, particularly the new management regime, is priceless.

248: NUM Yorkshire Area, Annual Council Meeting, March 1986, Presidential Address by Jack Taylor, sheet 5.

249: Letter to the author, AS/DJS/N.O.01, 10 February 1986.

250: It was a tough decision, tactically and principally – what to do with blackleg union members having lost the dispute? In the heat of the fray, and literally fighting tooth and nail to keep the scabs outside the gates, we would seriously have injured or killed them, while their police protectors were battering us down and had no compunction about killing us if necessary. Against this background, among the Durham Mechanics section, anyone found scabbing was at once expelled from the Union. As the number of scabs increased throughout the course of the year, the number of now non-union mechanics increased. These in turn, of their own volition, formed the first breakaway 'scab' union, the Colliery and Allied Trade Association, and applied to the certification officer for recognition. There was now a formal opposition to the NUM with the potential for widespread growth as the striking miners failed and returned to work. The 'back to work' campaign, under the direction of the counter-insurgency consultant David Hart, homed in on the development, and the Nottingham and Derbyshire scabs applied for affiliation to CATA. In August 1985 the CATA balloted its members for permission to form a new union, the Union of Democratic Miners, which was overwhelmingly agreed. Offices, funds, banners and records were forced by the courts to be handed over to them in the areas where they were the majority. Control of pensions, welfare and a hundred other features of mining life and community were also handed over to them, along with the right to negotiate terms and conditions in the whole of the mining industry. This position was later consolidated by the Blair government, who granted them legal executive status to negotiate compensation for mining diseases and massively build up their dwindling funds and organisation. The same terms were denied to the NUM. Billy Etherington, the larger-than-life president of the Durham Mechanics, was often called (jokingly) 'the founder of the UDM', after his policy of automatic expulsion. In Yorkshire the leadership was long-sighted, insisting that the scabs, even while they crossed our lines, stayed members of the Union, and when we went back that we had an obligation to represent them.

251: NUM Annual Conference Report, 1997, Presidential Address, pp. 18–19.

252: Some of this was leaked in the *Financial Times*, 30 December, by John Lloyd.

253: Terry French, prison letters, 27 January 1987; document in author's possession.

254: Brian Mentz, *Doncaster Evening Post*, Monday 6 July 1987.

255: Incidentally, a new coalfield three or four times the size of the Selby field sits undeveloped and unknown to all but the miners to the north of Selby and York and in what is now called Cleveland, and into south Durham. Likewise a massive coalfield sits beneath the dreaming spires of Oxford. This is not counting the numerous thick and profitable seams left in Selby itself, perhaps 80 to 150 million tonnes. South Derbyshire retains massive untouched reserves. Large pockets remain in all the old traditional fields and under the coasts. In South Wales, in a comprehensive report on known reserves back in 1946, the South Welsh coalfield was put at 7.6 billion tonnes recoverable. In 1992, Moses, the NCB Chairman, informed the South Wales NUM that only 18% of that reserve had been extracted. (NUM Annual Conference Report, 1992, p. a-c 132). The Coal Task Force set up in response to the Heseltine closure plan reported: 'UK coal resources are substantial. The technically recoverable reserves total 45 billion tonnes, with recoverable reserves from existing mines and new mine projects currently assessed at between 3 and 5 billion tonnes. There are also substantial reserves of coal in thick seams between 1200-2000 metres deep, both in mainland UK and under the North Sea. (Coal Task Force report, p. 3, quoted in NUM Annual Report of the NEC, 1992-93, p. AR 20.) We, i.e. NUM activists with an interest in geology (and that's almost all of us), estimate Britain has more coal reserves remaining than the sum total of all the coal we have mined since pre-industrial days.

256: At first shotfirers and deputies were in the miners' lodges. Many shotfirers, before taking the deputies' tickets, remained in the NUM at conventional coalface mines even after nationalisation. However, under pressure from the architects of the new NCB, a middle layer of 'supervisors and lower managers' were given exclusive rights to organise within NACODS. In the last two years before Hatfield's third closure, NACODS grades, including senior overmen, joined the NUM in an effort to secure a single union presence.

257: NUM Annual Conference Report, 1987, p. 437.

258: NUM Annual Conference Report, 1988, p. 467.

259: NUM Annual Conference Report 1987, p. 20.

260: Ibid., p. 22.

261: Ibid., p. 470–2.

262: Chairman of British Coal, the renamed NCB, 1986–90.

263: NUM Annual Conference Report, 1987, pp. 475–6.

264: NUM Annual Conference Report, 1987, p. 389.

265: Inland Consumption of Solid Fuels 1970–2003. Figures supplied by Kevin Hughes MP; document in Doncaster Archives collection.

266: The Term 'wildcat' had come from the Wobblies – the IWW (the Industrial Workers of the World) and its informal, on-site organisation and rapid-fire action. The symbol of the IWW was the Wildcat leaping, tail bolt, claws drawn, into the air, hence wildcat strike action. Of course the Wobs could have adopted the cat because of the pre-existence of the term wildcat action. Whatever its origin, it was hated by bosses and well-heeled union leaders alike.

267: 'The men' generally refers to the face men and heading men. Fitters and electricians are usually ex-officio to the team and, although of the same sex (male), not usually referred to as 'the men' in this context.

268: Incredibly, from time to time I come across other far-left groups, namely Socialist Organiser and the tiny and twisted International Communist Party, who allege that I had been a member of the Sparts. I don't know who would be most insulted, me or them, but on one thing me and they will agree, that was never the case or ever likely to be. It should be also patently obvious to anyone on the planet that I would die in defence of a picket line rather than cross one.

269: I confess to relaying this story and drawing much from sacred images of my memories. I am apt to write in the manner I would talk in, sat round a pub table and having a crack rather than standing at the podium giving a formal lecture. I am apt also to forget that you don't know these characters famous to me and the South Yorkshire and Doncaster coal communities. Morris, in brief, was a Cornish tin miner who migrated to Yorkshire during one of the many recessions in price of that mineral. The Cornishmen are miners generation on generation as much as Northumbrians; they brought hard rock mining skills to the world. Morris picked up the slack in that trade by working on a fairground circuit, as a bare-knuckle fighter, and any punter who could go two rounds with Morris got £5. Few ever could, and £5 for such an ordeal was cheap in anyone's book. The Morris fist is a daunting enough prospect to look at, ner mind feel in anger. He re-found mining and community, mates, and action he could excel in among the Hatfield miners of Doncaster, among whom he is now a legend. Morris could knock you dead with a punch. He believed in the Union with a faith that is deeper than that of any religious devotee. At the time of writing, Morris is still an NUM member and still working in the pits, and can still knock you dead with one punch.

270: NUM Special Delegate Conference Report, Thursday 11 October 1990, p. w21.

271: Ibid., p. w20.

272: Which although it sounded fiery actually denoted the colour code of the shift and not its political complexion.

273: NUM Annual Report, 1988, p. 19.

274: South Yorkshire Coal (British Coal), Annual Report 1988/89, 'Director's Statement'.

275: Ibid., 'Employee Relations'.

276: Or, rather, near-verbatim report, since the long-suffering transcriber needed the skills of a multilinguist to decipher the diverse dialects of the coalfields and didn't always succeed. See Conference Report 10 November 1989. Previous practice had ensured that every delegate would receive a copy of all the Conference reports, but in the midst of the internal struggles, who said what when became highly controversial, and numbers of copies in circulation become very much restricted. Most area NUM offices should have at least one copy, though.

277: One of Arthur's powerful arguments to the members to take action over salaries was the number of people already in the industry on salaries, and to use the refrain; 'If it's good enough for the managers and the directors and Arthur Scargill then it's good enough for the coal miners.' In this speech, the managers and Arthur Scargill etc. turn the theme to say we didn't want to take strike action over something which we wanted, and was being offered and was likewise enjoyed ...

278: NUM Conference Report, 10 November 1989, pp. 31–3 and 48.

279: Ibid.

280: NUM Yorkshire Area, Report of the Area Officials 1990; Safety Report for the South Yorkshire Group for the Period January to December 1990 (C. R. Brabbins. Senior Mining Engineer), p. 15.

281: The meeting is at once adjourned pending the second stage meeting, with the Area NUM agent, the Area industrial relations officer, together with the local management and all the IR dept from St George's HQ. When we reconvene, their side line up behind the long tables like a court-martial and look grim, on our side are me and the Area agent; there is no Tony – he's late. Then I hear Tony's motorbike roaring down the pit lane; I glance out the window and see the magnificent sight of his long hair flying out behind his unhelmeted head, and a bloody great samurai sword slung over his shoulder. As he walks into the room, I manage to seize the sword in its scabbard and lay it ceremoniously on the table before the startled ranks of NCB management and industrial relations. 'I don't know how you do it at other pits, Mr White, but at Hatfield we lay our weapons on the table to demonstrate our good faith.' At first there was silence, then the room erupted in laughter – even George's. 'You fuckers take the biscuit, you really do!' voiced George, laughing. 'And you know I like you fuckers, you've got bottle,' he added genuinely. At length, after the return of seriousness, the cards were on the table along with the sword. Mr White, an Area director, says: 'The message is Dave, there's going to be change, we need change to make this pit pay once in its life or we none of us are going to be here.' To this, in my summary, I concluded: 'And our bottom line is, get off our backs and let us dey the job, or your deed reet, there won't be a bliddy pit to work in.' Tony was given a final warning on his conduct and set free. He never changed. The sword, by the way, he seen in a second-hand shop en route to the meeting and he thought now was a good a time to buy one. It long being his wish to own one, it never dawned on him coming to the meeting with it would demonstrate the undermanager's allegations. Edson was later transferred to Armthorpe pit next door, where he was somewhat of a sensation among our fellow militants there – they took to him like a duck to water and deemed him the best undermanager they had ever had. I last saw George campaigning with the men against the closure of the pit in 1993/94, standing on picket lines and marching with his family in torrential rain with 'his men' all over the country.

282: This is an expression carried from the taproom game of dominoes. A player who cannot come up with the required numbers to play when it is their turn knocks (taps) the table with one of their dominoes. A man 'knocking' at work or whatever is missing.

283: 'The Babes in the Wood Meet the Bull in the China Shop: Cooper & Lybrand Meet the Hatfield Miners', LIFO Strength Management Strength Development, Lifeskills Now, 1988/1989; now in the Doncaster Archive collection, probably under my name or Hatfield Colliery. See also 'Indiscipline and Rebellion in the 18th 19th and 20th Century Coalfields', All Power To the Imagination, p. 108.

284: NUM National Conference Report, 8 July 1991, Presidential Address by Arthur Scargill.

285: High Court of Justice, Queen's Bench Division, Mr Justice Otton, 1990 BCC and NUM (Hatfield Main Branch).

286: See David Douglass Files, mining collection 1990, The Last Days of Coal, Doncaster Archive and Library Service, Balby.

287: The Workers Revolutionary Party, when it imploded in 1986, produced a handful of sections, all at war with each other and everyone else, some of the battles quite caustic. The majority split from their International Committee of the Fourth International. Those who continued to support it formed what was initially known as the Workers Revolutionary Party (Internationalist); they soon became the International Communist Party, based in Sheffield. They stood in several elections before renaming themselves the Socialist Equality Party (still a Trotskyist group). Still part of the International Committee of the Fourth International, which publishes the World Socialist Web Site.

288: Letter to author, from ICP, Rotherham. Document in 'The Trotskyist Left and the Miners' File at Doncaster Library Archive Service, Balby.

289: In Northumbria it is a custom at weddings to fling handfuls of coins from the window of the wedding cars as they leave the bride's house, en-route to the wedding, then after the wedding, then finally as the couple leave for their honeymoon. The kids from miles around will stand and chant 'Hoy oot! Hoy oot!' (literally 'Throw out!, Throw out!').

290: NUM Annual Conference Decisions, 1990, Alterations to Rule, pp. 4–7.

291: NUM Annual Conference Report, 1990, p. a-c 37.

292: Ibid., p. a-c 51–2.

293: It was reported at the NEC meeting of 9 April 1992 that discussions toward a merger had terminated. NUM, NEC, 9 April 1992, p. 483. Many thought this was because Arthur had been led to believe he would get an automatic national position within the merged union. Deputy General Secretary had been mooted, but then the TGWU had refused to guarantee it.

294: NUM Annual Conference Report, 1990, pp. 26 and 38.

295: Ibid., p. a-c 137.

296: *Doncaster Star*, 23 July 1990, p. 1.

297: Lightman Inquiry, response by Arthur Scargill.

298: NUM Special Delegate Conference, 10 October 1990, p. L-15.

299: NUM Special Delegate Conference, 10 October 1990.

300: Ibid., p. L-21.

301: Ibid., p. L-17.

302: It should be said as a final footnote that the state in Britain has got down and dirty on more occasions than this. Crazy bastards in MI5 and the CIA were convinced Wilson was a secret Bolshevik ready to open the bases to the Russians. They believed Wilson had had Gaitskell murdered because of his support for the USA, NATO and the Bomb, so systematically they set about sabotaging his government and at one point in 1966/67 were well down the road of an armed coup. In the '20s, they had invented the Zinoviev Letter, to turn out the first Labour government and spread the word that the Bolsheviks controlled the Labour Party. It worked. In 1926 we had the same Russian Gold story and slanders of miners' leaders with their 'fingers in the pie' being spread by the press barons. In 1914, a right-wing army rebellion turned against the Liberal government and its plans for Irish Home Rule. Sir Roger Casement, a Protestant Irish republican was engaging in public campaigns to support the Home Rule Bill and warn of loyalist military machinations in the state and armed forces. MI6's predecessor attached a number of high-placed agents on his case and in particular fed lurid stories to the press and public of his homosexuality, as means of discrediting his political principles.

303: NUM Annual Conference, 1991, Agenda, resolutions 10 and 38. Blackpool, 8 July 1991.

304: David Douglass, 'No Coal Turned in Yorkshire', in *Coal, Culture and Community*, proceedings of the conference at Sheffield Hallam University, November 1993 (Sheffield: PAVIC, Sheffield Hallam University, 1994).

305: Ibid., p. 167.

306: Peter Prowse and Michael Clapham, 'Strategic Responses to Flexibility – A Case Study In Coal', in *Coal, Culture and Community*, p. 150.

307: *Yorkshire Miner*, August 1992, p. 1.

308: Bare drafts of the work and complementary materials can be found in Doncaster Archive and Library Service, archives at Balby Doncaster. Filed under David Douglass, The Last Days of Coal.

309: NUM NEC, 14 May 1992, Minutes, p. 156. TUC Women's Conference Blackpool, Report, p. 499.

310: NUM Annual Conference, 1992, Report, p. AR-115.

311: The Molly Maguires were a violent direct action movement of Irish miners in the American mines, who if they couldn't get justice through strikes would assassinate mine-owners or the agents or blow up their mines. They reached their peak in the 1870s. See Louise Adamic, *Dynamite* (Edinburgh: AK Press, 2008).

312: NUM Annual Conference, 1992, Report, p. AC-94.

313: Ibid., p. AC-120.

314: Although the nuclear industry did.

315: NUM Annual Conference, 1992, Report, p. AC-128.

316: Thatcher, *The Downing Street Years*, p. 370.

317: Ibid.

318: NUM Special Delegate Conference, 15 October 1992, Report, p. SC-9.

319: NUM Special Delegate Conference, 15 October 1992, Report.

320: Jeremy Clarkson, 'Last of the Line', *BBC Top Gear Magazine*, April 1994, pp. 124–9.

321: Jonathan Foster, Senior Lecturer in Journalism at Sheffield University, quoted in Jeremy Deller, *The English Civil War Part 2: Personal Accounts of the 1984-85 Miners' Strike* (London: Artangel, 2001, following the event The Battle Of Orgreave on 17 June 2001).

322: See NUM Yorkshire Area Ordinary Council, 16 November 1992, Resolutions 7 and 8.

323: 9 December. In among the confusion and the effort to raise this standard of resistance once again, Mick Renwick phoned to say his Ma was dead. A dynamo of a woman, lifelong pitman's wife, mother of three at times warring, dissident sons. Had chased me with a pair of scissors to cut my long flowing hair when I was 15. Had walked in on wor crowded teenage sex sessions, had seized our booze. A terror of the anarchists. His old pitman Dad, a veteran thin seam hewer from the Wallsend Rising Sun Colliery, with whom she had shared her life, is devastated.

324: *Daily Worker*, 12 December 1992, Dave Douglass Column.

325: Because of the already huge size of this book I've had to cut out vast tracts of holiday and incidental anecdotes of me and Emma's adventures travelling round the world.

326: Sorry to say, by the time of publication, the Hoggatat and Mouseshit, as well as much else of the old Kracken Dam, are gone.

327: Yorkshire pit twang for a water canteen, like the round cowboy variety.

328: Brenda Nixon, 'Our Anger Has Never Diminished', in *No Wonder We Were Rebels: The Kane Story* (Doncaster: Armthorpe Branch, NUM, 1994).

329: Nixon, 'Our Anger Has Never Diminished'.

330: Revolutionary Communist Tendency.

331: I.e.,take it on.

332: British Coal, letter to employees, 26 April 1993.

333: Ibid.

334: Men on the face and in tunnel drivages get paid the bonus for those particular jobs, men outbye, or on the surface, on other work draw a composite 'pit bonus' of percentages of the aggregate of those bonuses, from 100% to 40%. With the one day of strike action, Selby was being docked one day's bonus, at the face, or in the drivages, and one day's pit bonus for everyone else. In Doncaster the face and heading workers get four-fifths of the weeks bonus while those on pit bonus receive no bonus for the whole week.

335: *News Line*, 13 May 1993.

336: Ibid.

337: Ibid.

338: Letter from me Da, 30 March 1993.

339: NUM Annual Conference, 1993 Report, p. AC 114.

340: Ibid., pp. AC 120–2.

341: The statement doesn't say so, but it is referring to the national ballot for industrial action against the John Major closure programme, and the massive Hatfield 'yes' vote in favour.

342: *Doncaster Star*, 4 December 1993, p. 5.

343: There was a long-standing opinion among lower-paid, surface and outbye workers that the Union as well as the management were only interested in the face workers, that the NUM was a 'face workers' union'. It was also true that the face workers were more impulsive and militant, that many strikes revolved around and were led by them. Lower-paid workers often resented this and tended in their culture to be more moderate, though in truth almost all were heart and soul Union men, albeit with a permanent grumble.

344: Me and Jeff had known each other all of our industrial careers, had face trained together at Rossington Colliery, had been at turning points in the underground life and trials of Hatfield Colliery, and many of its administrative manoeuvres from opposite sides of the desk, though often with the same mining mission. I could never understand his born-again opposition to the Union as he had increasingly taken over the reins of colliery power.

345: *Yorkshire Miner*, March 1994, pp. 2, 3.

346: *Doncaster Courier*, 2 April 1993.

347: NUM Biennial Conference, Blackpool, 2004, National Chairman's Address by Ian Lavery's.

348: Royce Turner, *Coal Was Our Life : An Essay on Life in a Yorkshire Former Pit Town* (Sheffield: Sheffield Hallam University Press, 2000).

349: Ibid.

350: Ibid.

351: Ibid.

352: NUM Annual Conference, 1995, *Report*, p. AR-83.

353: NUM NEC, 4 May 1994, pp. 221–2.

354: Quoted in *South Tyneside Herald and Post*, 26 March 2007, p. 7.

355: Ibid.

356: *NUM Yorkshire Area Annual Reports, Report of the General Secretary, Owen Briscoe*, p. 55.

357: At the risk of sounding ridiculous, in honesty I have to say that I have always liked Jeff Ainley as a bloke. I admired him as a mining engineer; he was confident and skilled and inspired trust and commitment. As man manager he was a different animal – hated the Union, hated our input, resented us to the point of pure fury and obsession.

358: NUM Annual Conference, 1995, Agenda.

359: See regular features in CPGB's *Weekly Worker* of the period, tracing its rise and fall contemporaneously. Also in my All Power To The Imagination, and features on www.minersadvice.co.uk the miners' website.

360: A folksy little ditty popular at that time was If God Had A Name; mine was a parody of the words and sentiment.

361: NUM NEC, 9 January 1997, Appendix A-B and 1-2-3.

362: NUM Biennial Conference, 2004, Business 26 June.

363: NUM Biennial Conference, 2004, Decisions D-10; note that there is a mistake on this record since it says that Resolution 7 on IEMO became Composite A, which was on pneumoconiosis; actually it is wrongly numbered in that there are two Resolution 7s. In fact the resolution should read Resolution 10 and not 7.

364: Letter to the author FC/JR 26 February 1997. In Walking with Barnsleybores collection.

365: Letter to the author SK/JLT 8th October 2002. In Walking with Barnsleybores collection.

366: NUM NEC, Economic Sub Committee Report 1996–7, p. 9.

367: Special Council Meeting, 18 August 1997.

368: NUM Special Delegate Conference, 8 January 1998, Report.

369: NUM Special Delegate Conference, 27 November 1998, Report.

370: NUM Biennial Conference, 1998–2000, NEC Report, Joint Negotiating Committee. p. 13.

371: Ibid.

372: NUM Annual Conference, 1998, Agenda, p. A-8.

373: NUM NEC,10 September 1998, Minutes, p. 92, item 8.

374: The Union had agreed to the development of a massive new office block just beside the City Hall at Sheffield, with promises of an NUM Library, conference centre and much else. It had been awarded grants from Sheffield City Council, and the investment of lots of Union money. We were between closure waves, struggling to our feet following Thatcher, about to be mown down by Major. The office became a huge white elephant for the Union, which is still stuck with it at the time of writing. The National Union took up residence in the offices of the Yorkshire Area, something that the Area Office has often regretted agreeing to.

375: NUM Special Delegate Conference, 12 November 1998, Report.

376: NUM Special Delegate Conference, 1 July 1999, Report.

377: A high-profile coroner's court in April 2008 with a majority jury verdict ruled that Diana was 'unlawfully killed'. This was after the French pathologist refused to give evidence and face cross-examination in support of his extraordinary findings on the alcohol and CO^2 levels present in the body of the driver Henri Paul. The levels of intoxicants and CO^2 would suggest Mr. Paul would have been dead long before the car collided with the mystery Fiat or the lethal concrete pillars and therefore been quite unable to drive. One of these features had to have been false. I am not convinced that the royal family itself was involved in these events, but I am certain however that sections of British Special Forces and the secret state were.

378: Letter AS/JR from Arthur Scargill, 24 May 2000.

379: NUM NEC, 20 July 2000, Minutes, p. 300.

380: Ibid., p. 301. There is a more or less accurate minute of this contentious meeting in Special (Emergency) Council Meeting, 5 June 2000, Minutes. Minutes are filed in the Annual Conference folder for 2000 in the Doncaster

Archives.

381: Letter AS/JR from Arthur Scargill to the Kellingley Branch, 11 May 2000.

382: NEC report of 20 July 2000, reported to National Delegate Conference, Monday 20 October 2000, Miners' Offices, Barnsley.

383: NUM NEC, 20 July 2000, Minutes, pp. 300–1.

384: NUM Safety and Health Subcommittee, 17 August 2000, Minutes, p. 324.

385: NUM NEC, 20 July 2000, Minutes, p. 301.

386: NUM NEC, 30 June 2000, Minutes, p. 295.

387: NUM Biennial Conference, 2000, Decisions, p. D-5.

388: This is not to suggest such a report wasn't printed or isn't in existence at the Area Offices. Only that they were not distributed to every delegate as had been the custom and practice since the founding of the Union.

389: See *www.minersadvice.co.uk* – this was an extremely advanced website, far outclassing most of the professional sites of the period, and for which we had Adrian Covell to thank. Adrian, a former pitman, had taught himself the inside-outs of computers and all sorts of technical wizardry. Later he would also launch the Stainforth Online site. He remained our senior technical manager throughout this story, as well as being an accomplished review writer.

390: Letter AS/nm from Arthur Scargill, 23 October 2000.

391: Ibid.

392: Letter AS/NM from David Douglass to Arthur Scargill, 25 October 2000.

393: NUM NEC, 9 November 2000, Policy Document. (Capitals and italics as in original.)

394: Ibid., p. 337.

395: Letter from David Douglass to Arthur Scargill, 20 November 2000.

396: Letter AS/JR from Arthur Scargill to David Douglass, 27 November 2000.

397: NUM NEC, 8 March 2001, Minutes, p. 370.

398: NUM NEC, 11 March 1999, Minutes, p. 142.

399: NUM NEC, 11 January 2001, Minutes, p. 353.

400: NUM NEC, Biennial Report 2000–2, p. 18.

401: NUM Special NEC, 12 December 2001 (in NUM NEC Minutes), p. 526.

402: NUM Special Delegate Conference, 17 January 2002, Report, p. SC-10.

403: Ibid., p. SC-22.

404: NUM Biennial Conference, 19 March 2002, Preliminary Agenda, last unnumbered page.

405: Actually, the DTI had just settled over 800 canteen women's long-running equal pay claims. They agreed to pay the back subs of all the women involved. This meant 800 or so canteen women were members of 'the Union' but were not associated with branches or areas. Arthur simply claimed these votes as individual card votes and cast them at his own discretion. Bad though that was, the so-called 'National Office Branch' he had invented on the spot would have to have been an area, not a branch, to cast such a vote at Conference.

406: Ibid., p. SC-40.

407: Letter WT/DAL/CAJ, from South Wales Area to David Douglass, 25 June 2002.

408: Annual Council Meeting, 17 June 2002, Minutes.

409: Ibid.

410: I was also later to be the subject of an entirely scurrilous criminal accusation by a mentally unstable individual (nothing to do with the NUM, I hasten to add). The accusation though utterly unfounded was nonetheless very damaging; Ian and my old adversary Steve Kemp didn't flinch in their absolute loyalty to me and belief in my total innocence, which was firmly and rapidly proven.

411: Arthur was later (in a case he brought against the Union to the commissioner) to make much of this statement. Of course, the term 'Area Office Branch' had been used before March 2003, and of course I had heard it. What I was saying was that it was simply a term, a shorthand description of the services offered to workers without an actual branch. Nobody had ever previously suggested it was an actual NUM branch as such.

412: Hatfield Circular 24/3/2003. In Walking with Barnsleybores collection, Doncaster Archive Service Collection

413: Letter SK SK/JLT from Hatfield Branch to Area Secretary, 25 March 2003, AGM Yorkshire Area Voting.

414: NUM NEC, 30 June 2000, Minutes, Voting Procedure at Conference. p. 146.

415: NUM Yorkshire Area Council Meeting, 24 March 2003, Minutes, item 3.

416: NUM NEC, Biennial Report 2002–3, p. AR 70.

417: Letter SK/JR to Hatfield Branch, 31 July 2003.

418: Letter SK/JLT to David Douglass, 18 July 2003; BS Circular No. 72/03. Also my response, same date.

419: A whole wedge of correspondence covers these matters, including SK/JLT 22 July 2003, my response 22/ 25 July and my letter to the national secretary 23 July 2003. Found in Walking with Barnsleybores collection, Doncaster Archives.

420: My letters to SK. Found at ibid.

421: NUM Yorkshire Area Council Meeting, 15 September 2003, Minutes.

422: SK/MR 26 September 2003.

423: Letter from David Douglass to the general secretary, 26 September 2003. Walking with Barnsleybores collection, Doncaster Archives.

424: Letter to Ian Lavery, 11 October 2003.

425: Complaint on Agenda Business – Hatfield Main Branch to Area Council, 15 December 2003.

426: Letter AS/MF/no.01 from Arthur Scargill to the author, 3 November 1999. In Walking with Barnsleybores collection, Doncaster Archive Service.

427: Letter DB/AW/KAH/L16321/1/LEE. 20 from Hatfield Main Branch to Raleys Solicitors December 2003; re: Unreasonable deductions from compensation: Mr Lee and others.

428: In November 2006 the deduction became a voluntary contribution paid toward the Union's ongoing legal fighting fund, and in June 2007 they agreed to pay back the deduction to any member who felt they shouldn't have paid any deduction. It must be said though that this latter decision was in the face of a spurious press campaign and the local Blairite Kevin Jones MP misrepresenting the lapsed members' fees as some sort of fraud. See also *Newcastle Evening Chronicle*, 15 June 2008, p. 2.

429: NUM NEC, 16 February 2004, Minutes, p. 267.

430: 'For A Balanced, Diverse, Secure Energy Policy Based on Indigenous Fuels.' NUM, submission to the DTI Consultation on 'A Carbon Abatement Technologies Strategy for Fossil Fuel Power Generation', pp. 3, 4. Andrew Glyn, Fellow and economics tutor at Corpus Christi College, Oxford, pointed out the spiralling cost of closures with a report early in January 1985, noting that there wasn't a single pit closure in the country that would actually save the government money. He demonstrated that for example keeping Cortonwood Colliery in production even with its outdated infrastructure and lack of investment would cost the government £75 per worker; the costs of letting it close in lost revenue and payments to all sources amounted to £295 per worker per week. But you would achieve the priceless government aim of actually getting rid of the miner and the influence of his Union.

431: By July 2007 an official report by the Joseph Rowntree Foundation on 'the north' showed the massive imbalance of wealth and income north to south, but also pockets of wealth within areas of gross mean poverty, which skewed the picture to be less unequal than it actually is. Middlesbrough, suffering the loss of heavy engineering, shipyards and steel mills, recorded 49.4% of the population living on solely the fundamentals of life; Tyne Bridge West (Newcastle) 48.5%; South Hylton, Sunderland 45.2%. The report showed a dramatic widening of the gap between rich and poor compared with the previous Census results for 1991/1981/1971. This was a direct result of 'the changing nature of industry in the region over the period', that is, the ongoing knock-on effects of the Thatcher closures, then the Major closures, plus all the ancillary closures that which attend them, together with the policy of deindustrialisation of the major proletarian centres. 'In the 1980s the UK economy switched from being a manufacturing one to a service and financial one.' Well actually, the authors are being rather coy – they didn't 'switch', did they? 'In the past the coal and steel-based economies were plugged into the areas where the coal came from, such as the North East and South Yorkshire. Now companies want to be where the financial centre is, which is London ...' London and the south generally were said in the report to be 'booming'. Vera Bard, MP for Redcar, Teesside (also the solicitor general): 'Across Teesside there are around 46,000 people on incapacity benefit. Many of these people worked in manual jobs in heavy industries in the 1980s and suffered as a consequence from the nature of their work.' The report demonstrated in a large table which I haven't reproduced here that the number of people living below the base line of poverty leapt by 20% in Middlesbrough East; the same figure applied for Tyne Bridge West, which includes Benwell, Elswick and Scotswood. In South Hylton it leapt by 17.6 %. For the complete table and a fuller review of the report see the *Sunday Sun* (Newcastle upon Tyne), 22 July 2007, pp. 10–11. By June 11 2008, local northern papers were still reporting the ongoing poverty and deprivation. *The Journal* (Newcastle upon Tyne): 'Children across the North East are the most likely in the UK to live in poverty ... 'Around 160,000 children in the region live in households below the government's minimum standards, with nearly a third of all homes at risk.' The number of pensioners below the base poverty line was now 12%. In the two years between 2005 and 2007, 28% of North East children were living in families surviving on less than 60% of the national average weekly wage. Alan Beith MP (Berwick) is reported in the same issue as saying: 'More than one in four children in the North East are at risk of living in poverty and that figure rises to one in three when housing costs are taken into account.' (www.journallive.co.uk/north-east-news/todays-news/2008/06/11) In March 2009 the *Financial Times* reported: 'The number of adults claiming incapacity benefit in the English and Welsh coalfields was a staggering 336,000 in 2007, and since the financial crash in September 2008, the number of unemployed men claiming benefit has risen between 75–100% depending on the area.' These regions are 'ill-equipped to weather the recession', the report said. The stability of these former thriving communities in the coalfields, including those in Notts, it would be fair to say, has been destroyed, with some turned into wastelands. See Arkell and Rising, *Unfinished Business*.

432: Letter SK/JLT from Steve Kemp, Secretary, Yorkshire Miners, to David Douglass, 19 June 2004.

433: There is a clinical account of the chronology in *NUM NEC, Biennial Report*, 2002–4, p. AR 23.

434: Obviously, this is not to suggest in any way that there wasn't a healthy 'native' Irish republican socialism at home, only that that socialist wing had always been infused by the experiences and internationalism of that tendency and political tradition abroad. There had been a great interaction between Irish republicans and the rest of the English-speaking world in Britain, America, Australia etc. as well as strong interventions into international struggles across the globe. Conservative nationalist forces boxed shy of this tradition, and hailed the Gaelic windswept bogs, myths and legends of the 'pure' and Catholic Celt. Even during the explosive outbreak of the Provisional movement they had tried to warn against 'foreign' Marxist doctrines and influences, had seized upon the risen youth's tendency to revolutionary socialism and tried to claim the notion of a socialist Ireland as an ancient creed bred in the bones of saints and shamrock of the island.

435: Philip Ferguson, 'Behind the Betrayal', *Weekly Worker*, 5 May 2005, p. 11.

436: *Ed Moloney, A Secret History of the IRA*, quoted by Angelique Chrisafis, *The Guardian*, 20 December 2005; also quoted in Liam O Ruairc, 'Tip of the Iceberg', *Weekly Worker*, 5 January 2006, p. 9.

437: Gerry Adams, 'President's Address', *An Phoblacht/Republican News*, 17 November 1983, pp. 8–9; also quoted in Liam O Ruairc, 'Going Respectable', *Weekly Worker*, 21 April 2005.

438: *Weekly Worker*, 21 April 2005.

439: Ibid.

440: Hume–Adams statement, 23 April 1993.

441: Liam O Ruairc, 'Ideologically Wrong, Tactically Stupid', *Weekly Worker*, 19 May 2005, p. 8.

442: In November 2009, the INLA declares its armed struggle over and disbands to pursue a political strategy within the Irish Republican Socialist Party. The INLA trajectory to this same point took a radically different route, though to some extent they had already had their options sharply curtailed by the decimation of their ranks, and the changed political situation on the ground. They had not however accepted any of the new logic of Sinn Féin's accommodation with the British system.

443: Richard E. Jensen, R. Eli Paul and John E. Carter, *Eyewitness at Wounded Knee* (Lincoln, NE and London: University of Nebraska Press, 1991). See also Alvin M. Josephy, Jr., *500 Nations: An Illustrated History of North American Indians* (New York: Alfred A. Knopf, 1994).

444: www.bgsu.edu

445: I have removed a whole chapter dealing with the wave of Islamic Fundamentalist/Political Jihad from this section. It dealt with 'Islamic terrorism' in London, New York, Bali, Madrid, and round the world and sought to analyse the Arab and Afghan and other Islamic political and religio-political movements. It was simply too big and I had been too self-indulgent. I hope to put this piece in the 'Your View' section of the miners' website www.minersadvice.co.uk

446: Quoted in NUM Annual Conference, 1990, *Report*, p. AR 28.

447: Also incidentally illustrates the Blair–Brown government's obsession with self-righteous imposition and compulsion, and the extent to which it will give words and 'crimes' new meanings to fit its new proscriptions. An example is charging those who build a bonfire with 'littering'. In November 2009, a young mother is likewise charged with 'littering' for letting her baby throw bread to the ducks in the local park.

448: *Metro News*, 6 January 2009, p. 14.

449: *Daily Mail*, 4 June 2009, p. 25.

450: Telford Town Park, Shropshire for example employs wardens to ask lone adults why they are in the park where there are children! The council told objecting adults that a 'duty of care' existed for children using the park and lone adults had not had Criminal Records Bureau checks to allow them to walk round the park. *Daily Mirror*, 10 September 2008, p. 31.

451: *Daily Mirror*, 10 February 2007, p. 31.

452: Stephen White, ibid., p. 31.

453: GMTV, Breakfast, 15 May 2007.

454: *Daily Express*, 29 September 2007, p. 29.

455: GMTV, Breakfast, 15 May 2007.

456: *Daily Express*, 29 September 2007, p. 29.

457: *Daily Express*, 17 May 2007, p. 37.

458: BBC, Look North, 29 May 2008.

459: BBC, Breakfast News, 18 April 2008; *Daily Mail*, 19 April 2008, pp. 16, 19.

460: Breakfast News, 18 April 2008.

461: *Daily Mail*, 22 April 2008, p. 1.

462: *The Times*, 15 June 2007, p. 3.

463: Ibid.

464: Tesco began this practice in April 2008, 'gazumping' the previous '21' rule their competitors had brought in to demonstrate how good and law-abiding they were.

465: The legitimate complaints of the Maltby Branch and their delegate Steve Mace, over exclusion from the right to stand in an NEC election, are joined with Arthur's attempts to reinvent the fictional Area Office Branch, retake power in the Union and in the process sack Chris Kitchen. Steve finds himself in an alliance and linked to issues he is not actually concerned with. Arthur launches a legal appeal against the injustice of the current rulebook that is the rulebook he imposed upon us.

466: NUM Yorkshire Area, Annual Reports 1980, p. 33. (PMF – progressive massive fibrosis – is the highest and deadliest form of pneumoconiosis, which has reached a point of self-degeneracy and without any further input of dust will continue to spread and seal off the airways.)

467: *The Guardian*, 13 June 2007, p. 29.

468: Letter to DD, 1 December 2007.

469: *Daily Express*, 6 October 2008, p. 4.

470: Bob Dylan, 'George Jackson'.

471: The situation has become something of a joke, with the DJs at the South Shields discos and bowling alleys announcing at 10 minutes to 9 that 'All those on curfews, ASBOs and tagging ought to leave now.' This not only produces a laugh but often a number of teenagers getting up to leave displaying their tags, along with one toothlessly smiling granny with a tag visible round her ankle, under her fashionably cut-down culotte combat pants.

472: *Daily Express*, 6 October 2008, p. 4.

473: See *Mail On Sunday* 28 December 2008, p. 4 for information on Classwatch Ltd and the firm's chairman, Tim Loughton, the Tory shadow minister for children (no change there then).

474: *Daily Mail*, 22 July 2009, p. 30.

475: Children Act 1986 and 2004, Education Act 1996 and 2002.

476: *Daily Mail*, 22 July 2009, p. 20.

477: *The Times*, 19 January 2009.

478: *Daily Mail*, 4 June 2009, pp. 42–43. At time of writing Rachel is trying to take a case to the European Court of Human Rights, as well she might.

479: Actually at present it is simply 'clean-coal-technology-ready' and at the time of the protest was operationally just the same as any other coal-powered station. What drove the anti-coal lobby mad was that this was the first new coal power station in decades.

480: As we approach publication day for this last book in the histrilogy *Stardust and Coaldust*, March 2010, *Geordies* is still about £700 from break-even point, *The Wheel* still £5,500. The major problem for works like this is actually getting them before the eyes of the reading public without the benefit of the commercial well-heeled well-connected mass distribution network.

481: Harry had become NUM Branch treasurer at Hatfield soon after the strike, in which he played a starring role as a flying picket. A colliery electrician, he stood over six feet tall, a handsome bachelor and darling of the ladies far and near. Harry was also the most comic and zany of men, given to acts of spontaneous humour, which left you helpless with laughter. There are too many of these to recount here, but one which sticks in my mind was a furious lobby of the Branch Office by irate heading men screaming at each other and us about tactics and direction. In the thick of this Harry grabs my little finger with his little finger and starts to sing (and I joined in with) 'C'mon you people now, smile on your brothers, everybody get together try and love one another right now' and doing a joyful hippie dance with waving arms, repeated over and over till the crowd collapsed in laughter and muddy and grimy they all joined in. On another occasion, I am sitting exhausted after a gruelling pit inspection in the office supping tea with me boots and socks off, when he seizes my foot and bites my big toe. I scream and chase him down the corridor in fury, and am then reported to the colliery manager for swearing. I am saved by the fact the manager also thinks biting my big toe is great piece of comedy.

482: PressTV – programmes – *Real Deal*, George Galloway, and 21 November 2008 if you care to look it up on the net.

483: Email from Rob Davies to the author, 23 November 2008.

484: I am asked the poignant question, if it's undying where is it living now? Good question and I wished I knew the answer, because if I did I would go and live there. For many activists of course the cause did die and in turn, that killed the movement. On a world scale although we won many battles, the war for social change and free communism was lost. Our outposts in the end were starved, subverted and defeated by the socially superior productive capacity of western capitalism. Many were murdered, across the world by the million, and at home, one by one. Remnants of that movement survive and we still preach and try to live the old-time religion of freedom and revolution. On a world scale, the new movement is marked by the hugely progressive Third World revolutions, particularly in Latin America. While the anti-globalisation and environmental movement has something of us about it, it is deeply flawed on questions of class, industry, and alienation from what remains of the working-class movement in Europe and America.

485: Leaning as I do to anarchism, I don't think the British state has a right in Britain either, but in democratic terms it has less of a right in Ireland. There are different qualities of struggle on which one must take a stand now, and not wait until the final settlement of accounts when all questions, all oppressions, are resolved worldwide; nor until the revolutionary upsurge meets our checklist for 'pure' workers' revolution. Not to do so would be to simply make a principle of abstention from the struggles in which peoples and the working class are actually engaged in, short of all-out world anarchist-communist revolution. Imperialism and wars of national liberation are just such a contest. I favour a socialist independence as part of a global struggle, but that is not a prerequisite to supporting liberation struggles against imperialism. This throws the whole question of 'support' and 'defence' to less than 'pure' class struggles back into the mix again. (See the earlier considerations of this feature, in this book and the previous *Wheel Still In Spin*.)

486: Steve Mace, a Maltby Branch official, is unable to get on the ballot paper for the NEC because the rule says you must get nominations from branches equivalent to 30% of the area membership. The effect at this time is to exclude anyone other than nominations from the much bigger Kellingley Branch. The rule is patently unfair, but it is the rule Arthur invented to keep me from running when the situation was reversed and his team were in office and we were the opposition.

487: Beckett and Hencke, *Marching to the Fault Line*.

488: Ibid., pp. 20–1.

489: *Daily Mail*, 1 September 2009, p. 30.

490: 'The Joy Of Living', written by Ewan MacColl in 1986 after failing to get up Suilven mountain when he was 72 and he realised, at first desolately, that his days of shinning up mountains were over. 'My desolation lasted for several days and then my grief and sense of loss gave way to nostalgia and I wrote "The Joy Of Living". In an odd way it helped me to come to terms with my old age.' *The Essential Ewan MacColl Songbook: 60 Years of Songmaking. Compiled and annotated by Peggy Seeger* (New York and London: Oak Publications, 2001) .